CHILD GROWTH AND DEVELOPMENT 95/96

W9-AEC-897

Second Edition

Editor

Ellen N. Junn
California State University, Fullerton

Ellen Junn is an associate professor of Child Development and Director of Educational Equity at California State University, Fullerton. She received a B.S. in experimental psychology from the University of Michigan and an M.A. and Ph.D. in cognitive and developmental psychology from Princeton University. In addition to her work on educational equity issues, Dr. Junn's research and publications focus on developments in children's conceptions regarding adult social relationships and on college teaching effectiveness.

Editor

Chris J. Boyatzis
California State University, Fullerton

Chris Boyatzis is an assistant professor of Child Development at California State University, Fullerton. He received a B.A. in psychology from Boston University and an M.A. and Ph.D. in developmental psychology from Brandeis University. Many of his research interests lie at the intersection of social and cognitive development in early childhood. Dr. Boyatzis has published research on children's nonverbal behavior and social status, symbolic development, and play and art. He has also written on the use of literature and film to teach developmental psychology.

Annual Editions
A Library of Information from the Public Press

Cover illustration by Mike Eagle

The Dushkin Publishing Group, Inc.
Sluice Dock, Guilford, Connecticut 06437

The Annual Editions Series

Annual Editions is a series of over 60 volumes designed to provide the reader with convenient, low-cost access to a wide range of current, carefully selected articles from some of the most important magazines, newspapers, and journals published today. Annual Editions are updated on an annual basis through a continuous monitoring of over 300 periodical sources. All Annual Editions have a number of features designed to make them particularly useful, including topic guides, annotated tables of contents, unit overviews, and indexes. For the teacher using Annual Editions in the classroom, an Instructor's Resource Guide with test questions is available for each volume.

VOLUMES AVAILABLE

Africa
Aging
American Foreign Policy
American Government
American History, Pre-Civil War
American History, Post-Civil War
Anthropology
Archaeology
Biology
Biopsychology
Business Ethics
Canadian Politics
Child Growth and Development
China
Comparative Politics
Computers in Education
Computers in Business
Computers in Society
Criminal Justice
Drugs, Society, and Behavior
Dying, Death, and Bereavement
Early Childhood Education
Economics
Educating Exceptional Children
Education
Educational Psychology
Environment
Geography
Global Issues
Health
Human Development
Human Resources
Human Sexuality
India and South Asia
International Business

Japan and the Pacific Rim
Latin America
Life Management
Macroeconomics
Management
Marketing
Marriage and Family
Mass Media
Microeconomics
Middle East and the Islamic World
Money and Banking
Multicultural Education
Nutrition
Personal Growth and Behavior
Physical Anthropology
Psychology
Public Administration
Race and Ethnic Relations
Russia, the Eurasian Republics, and
  Central/Eastern Europe
Social Problems
Sociology
State and Local Government
Third World
Urban Society
Violence and Terrorism
Western Civilization,
  Pre-Reformation
Western Civilization,
  Post-Reformation
Western Europe
World History, Pre-Modern
World History, Modern
World Politics

Cataloging in Publication Data
Main entry under title: Annual Editions: Child growth and development. 1995/96.
    1. Child psychology—Periodicals. I. Junn, Ellen N., *comp.* II. Boyatzis, Chris J., *comp.* III.
Title: Child growth and development.
ISBN 1-56134-337-4   155.4'.05

Second Edition

Manufactured in the United States of America

Printed on Recycled Paper

Editors/ Advisory Board

EDITORS

Ellen N. Junn
California State University, Fullerton

Chris J. Boyatzis
California State University, Fullerton

ADVISORY BOARD

Mary Belcher
Orange Coast College

Mary Ellen Dallman
University of Wisconsin
Stevens Point

Gene Elliott
Rowan College of New Jersey

JoAnn M. Farver
University of Southern California

Kathy Fite
Southwest Texas State University

Trisha Folds-Bennett
College of Charleston

Charles D. Hoffman
California State University
San Bernardino

Richard Ida
American River College

Marcia Lasswell
California State Polytechnic
University

Nancy G. McCarley
Mississippi State University

Joann Montepare
Tufts University

Kelly R. Morton
California State University
San Bernardino

Derek Price
Wheaton College

Jone Sloman
Wheelock College

Connie Steele
University of Tennessee
Knoxville

Faye Steuer
The College of Charleston

Harold Strang
University of Virginia

STAFF

To the Reader

In publishing ANNUAL EDITIONS we recognize the enormous role played by the magazines, newspapers, and journals of the *public press* in providing current, first-rate educational information in a broad spectrum of interest areas. Within the articles, the best scientists, practitioners, researchers, and commentators draw issues into new perspective as accepted theories and viewpoints are called into account by new events, recent discoveries change old facts, and fresh debate breaks out over important controversies.

Many of the articles resulting from this enormous editorial effort are appropriate for students, researchers, and professionals seeking accurate, current material to help bridge the gap between principles and theories and the real world. These articles, however, become more useful for study when those of lasting value are carefully *collected, organized, indexed,* and *reproduced* in a *low-cost format*, which provides easy and permanent access when the material is needed. That is the role played by *Annual Editions.* Under the direction of each volume's *Editor,* who is an expert in the subject area, and with the guidance of an *Advisory Board,* we seek each year to provide in each ANNUAL EDITION a current, well-balanced, carefully selected collection of the best of the public press for your study and enjoyment. We think you'll find this volume useful, and we hope you'll take a moment to let us know what you think.

We are delighted to welcome you to this second volume of *Annual Editions: Child Growth and Development 95/96.* Almost anyone who has reflected on the amazing sequence of events that lead up to the birth of a newborn baby will tell you that the process of prenatal development and childbirth is an awesome achievement. Perhaps more intriguing is the question of what the future may hold for this newly arrived, squalling creature—for instance, will this child become a doctor, a lawyer, an artist, beggar, or thief? Although philosophers and prominent thinkers such as Darwin and Freud have long speculated about the importance of infancy on subsequent development, not until the 1960s did the scientific study of infants and young children flourish. Since then, research and theory in infancy and childhood have exploded, resulting in a wealth of new knowledge about child development. Past popular accounts of infants and young children as passive, homogeneous organisms have been replaced with investigations aimed at studying infants and young children at a "micro-level," as active individuals with many inborn competencies, who are capable of shaping their own environment, as well as at a "macro-level" by considering the larger context surrounding the child. In short, children are not "blank slates" and development does not take place in a vacuum; children arrive with many skills and grow up in a complex web of social, historical, political, economic, and cultural spheres.

As was the case for our previous edition, we hope to achieve at least four major goals with this volume. First, we hope to present you with the latest research and thinking to help you better appreciate the complex interactions that characterize human development in infancy and childhood. Second, in light of the feedback we received on our previous edition, we placed greater emphasis on important contemporary issues and challenges, exploring topics such as recovered memories of childhood abuse and understanding development in the context of ethnic and cultural differences. Third, attention is given to articles that also discuss effective, practical applications. Finally, we hope that this anthology will serve as a catalyst to help students become more effective future professionals and parents.

To achieve these objectives, we carefully selected articles, including a few classics, from a variety of sources, including scholarly research journals and texts as well as semiprofessional journals and popular lay publications. Every selection was scrutinized for readability, interest level, relevance, and currency. In addition, we listened to the valuable input and advice from members of our advisory board, consisting of faculty from a range of institutions of higher education, including community and liberal arts colleges as well as research and teaching universities. We are most grateful to the advisory board as well as to excellent editorial staff of The Dushkin Publishing Group.

Annual Editions: Child Growth and Development 95/96 is organized into five major units. Unit 1 focuses on conception, prenatal development, and childbirth. Unit 2 presents information regarding developments in cognition, language, and learning. Unit 3 focuses on social and emotional development. Unit 4 is devoted to parenting and family issues such as working parents, marital transitions, siblings, and discipline. Finally, unit 5 focuses on larger cultural and societal influences (e.g., poverty, homelessness, television) and on special challenges (e.g., sexual abuse, attention deficits, children with AIDS).

Instructors for large lecture courses may wish to adopt this anthology as a supplement to a basic text, whereas instructors for smaller sections might also find the readings effective for promoting student presentations or for stimulating discussions and applications. Whatever format is utilized, it is our hope that the instructor and the students will find the readings interesting, illuminating, and provocative.

As the original title indicates, *Annual Editions* is by definition a volume that undergoes continual review and revision. Thus, it is in this spirit that we welcome and encourage your comments and suggestions for future editions of this volume. Simply fill out and return the comment card found at the end of this book. Best wishes and we look forward to hearing from you!

Ellen N. Junn

Chris J. Boyatzis
Editors

Contents

Unit 1

Conception to Birth

Seven articles discuss the development of the child from the prenatal stage to birth.

The concepts in bold italics are developed in the article. For further expansion please refer to the Topic Guide and the Index.

Unit 2

Cognition, Language, and Learning

Nine selections consider the growth of a child's cognitive and language abilities and their experiences in the learning process in school.

The concepts in bold italics are developed in the article. For further expansion please refer to the Topic Guide and the Index.

Unit 3

Social and Emotional Development

Eight articles follow a child's emotional development
into the larger social world.

Unit 4

Parenting and Family Issues

Eight articles assess the latest implications of child development with regard to attachment, working parents, day care, discipline, and neglect.

The concepts in bold italics are developed in the article. For further expansion please refer to the Topic Guide and the Index.

Unit 5

Cultural and Societal Influences

Eight selections examine how society and culture impact on the development of the child.

The concepts in bold italics are developed in the article. For further expansion please refer to the Topic Guide and the Index.

The concepts in bold italics are developed in the article. For further expansion please refer to the Topic Guide and the Index.

Topic Guide

This topic guide suggests how the selections in this book relate to topics of traditional concern to students and professionals involved with the study of infant and child development. It is useful for locating articles that relate to each other for reading and research. The guide is arranged alphabetically according to topic. Articles may, of course, treat topics that do not appear in the topic guide. In turn, entries in the topic guide do not necessarily constitute a comprehensive listing of all the contents of each selection.

TOPIC AREA	TREATED IN:	TOPIC AREA	TREATED IN:
Aggression/ Violence	1. Eugenics Revisited 21. Children without Friends 31. Why Spanking Takes the Spunk Out of Kids 35. Why Leave Children with Bad Parents? 36. Screen Violence and America's Children 38. How to Recognize and Prevent Child Sexual Abuse	Discipline	24. The Good, the Bad, and the Difference 31. Why Spanking Takes the Spunk Out of Kids 32. Tarnished Trophies
		Divorce and Stepparents	28. Marital Transitions 33. America's Children
		Drug Abuse	6. When a Pregnant Woman Drinks 35. Why Leave Children with Bad Parents?
Attachment	8. Amazing Minds of Infants 17. Young Children's Understanding of Everyday Emotions 18. Understanding and Accepting Separation Feelings 26. Working Mothers and Their Families	Emotional Development	17. Young Children's Understanding of Everyday Emotions 18. Understanding and Accepting Separation Feelings 19. Development of Self-Concept 21. Children without Friends 22. Guns and Dolls 24. The Good, the Bad, and the Difference 26. Working Mothers and Their Families 29. Secret World of Siblings 30. Sibling Connections 31. Why Spanking Takes the Spunk Out of Kids
Birth and Birth Defects/Teratogens	3. Making Babies 5. Prenatal Purgatory 6. When a Pregnant Woman Drinks 7. Fantastic Voyage of Tanner Roberts		
Child Abuse	6. When a Pregnant Woman Drinks 11. Civilizing of Genie 31. Why Spanking Takes the Spunk Out of Kids 35. Why Leave Children with Bad Parents? 37. Memories Lost and Found 38. How to Recognize and Prevent Child Sexual Abuse	Family/Parenting	17. Young Children's Understanding of Everyday Emotions 18. Understanding and Accepting Separation Feelings 19. Development of Self-Concept 22. Guns and Dolls 24. The Good, the Bad, and the Difference 25. Little Big People 26. Working Mothers and Their Families 27. Putting Children First 28. Marital Transitions 29. Secret World of Siblings 30. Sibling Connections 31. Why Spanking Takes the Spunk Out of Kids 32. Tarnished Trophies 33. America's Children 35. Why Leave Children with Bad Parents? 37. Memories Lost and Found 38. How to Recognize and Prevent Child Sexual Abuse
Cognitive Development	4. Do You Hear What I Hear? 8. Amazing Minds of Infants 9. Infants to Toddlers 10. Where Pelicans Kiss Seals 11. Civilizing of Genie 12. Child Development and Differential School Performance 13. Understanding Bilingual/Bicultural Young Children 15. How Asian Teachers Polish Each Lesson to Perfection 16. How Kids Learn 24. The Good, the Bad, and the Difference 39. Young Children with Attention Deficits		
Creativity	10. Where Pelicans Kill Seals 32. Tarnished Trophies	Fertilization/ Reproductive Technology	3. Making Babies 5. Prenatal Purgatory
Cultural Influences	13. Understanding Bilingual/Bicultural Young Children 15. How Asian Teachers Polish Each Lesson to Perfection	High-Risk Infants/ Children	5. Prenatal Purgatory 6. When a Pregnant Woman Drinks 21. Children without Friends 27. Putting Children First 33. America's Children 34. Homeless Families 35. Why Leave Children with Bad Parents? 37. Memories Lost and Found 38. How to Recognize and Prevent Child Sexual Abuse 39. Young Children with Attention Deficits 40. Children with AIDS
Day Care	18. Understanding and Accepting Separation Feelings 26. Working Mothers and Their Families		
Developmental Disabilities and Challenges	39. Young Children with Attention Deficits		
		Homeless Children	34. Homeless Families

TOPIC AREA	TREATED IN:	TOPIC AREA	TREATED IN:
Hyperactivity	39. Young Children with Attention Deficits	**Preschoolers/ Toddlers**	10. Where Pelicans Kiss Seals 13. Understanding Bilingual/Bicultural Young Children 14. Equitable Treatment of Girls and Boys in the Classroom 17. Young Children's Understanding of Everyday Emotions 18. Understanding and Accepting Separation Feelings 19. Development of Self-Concept 21. Children without Friends 22. Guns and Dolls 23. Girls and Boys Together . . . But Mostly Apart 24. The Good, the Bad, and the Difference 29. Secret World of Siblings 31. Why Spanking Takes the Spunk Out of Kids
Infant Development	4. Do You Hear What I Hear? 8. Amazing Minds of Infants 9. Infants to Toddlers 18. Understanding and Accepting Separation Feelings 19. Development of Self-Concept 26. Working Mothers and Their Families		
Language Development	11. Civilizing of Genie 13. Understanding Bilingual/Bicultural Young Children 16. How Kids Learn		
Learning/Literacy	12. Child Development and Differential School Performance 15. How Asian Teachers Polish Each Lesson to Perfection 16. How Kids Learn 32. Tarnished Trophies 39. Young Children with Attention Deficits	**Schooling**	12. Child Development and Differential School Performance 13. Understanding Bilingual/Bicultural Young Children 14. Equitable Treatment of Girls and Boys in the Classroom 15. How Asian Teachers Polish Each Lesson to Perfection 16. How Kids Learn 19. Development of Self-Concept 22. Guns and Dolls 23. Girls and Boys Together . . . But Mostly Apart 24. The Good, the Bad, and the Difference 32. Tarnished Trophies 39. Young Children with Attention Deficits 40. Children with AIDS
Memory	8. Amazing Minds of Infants 16. How Kids Learn 37. Memories Lost and Found		
Nature/Nurture Issue	1. Eugenics Revisited 2. Nature or Nurture? 6. When a Pregnant Woman Drinks 8. Amazing Minds of Infants 11. Civilizing of Genie 22. Guns and Dolls		
Peers/Social Skills	17. Young Children's Understanding of Everyday Emotions 19. Development of Self-Concept 21. Children without Friends 22. Guns and Dolls 23. Girls and Boys Together . . . But Mostly Apart 29. Secret World of Siblings	**Self-Esteem/Self-Control**	17. Young Children's Understanding of Everyday Emotions 19. Development of Self-Concept 20. All about Me 21. Children without Friends 24. The Good, the Bad, and the Difference 32. Tarnished Trophies
Personality Development	17. Young Children's Understanding of Everyday Emotions 19. Development of Self-Concept 21. Children without Friends 22. Guns and Dolls 25. Little Big People 28. Marital Transitions 29. Secret World of Siblings	**Sex Differences/ Roles/Behaviors/ Characteristics**	2. Nature or Nurture? 14. Equitable Treatment of Girls and Boys in the Classroom 22. Guns and Dolls 23. Girls and Boys Together . . . But Mostly Apart
Play	21. Children without Friends 22. Guns and Dolls 23. Girls and Boys Together . . . But Mostly Apart	**Socialization**	14. Equitable Treatment of Girls and Boys in the Classroom 15. How Asian Teachers Polish Each Lesson to Perfection 17. Young Children's Understanding of Everyday Emotions 21. Children without Friends 22. Guns and Dolls 23. Girls and Boys Together . . . But Mostly Apart 24. The Good, the Bad, and the Difference 25. Little Big People 27. Putting Children First 29. Secret World of Siblings
Prenatal Development and Diagnoses	3. Making Babies 4. Do You Hear What I Hear? 5. Prenatal Purgatory 6. When a Pregnant Woman Drinks		
		Television	36. Screen Violence and America's Children

Conception to Birth

Our understanding of prenatal development is not what it used to be. Although the first nine months of life are still the most dramatic in terms of change and growth, scientists now understand more about prenatal development than before. As a result, the fetus is known to be more skilled and able than previously realized. The article "Do You Hear What I Hear?" discusses the newly recognized abilities that arise during prenatal development.

There are also dramatic changes in available reproductive technology. Advances in this new "prenatal science" include fertility treatments for couples who have difficulty conceiving and a host of prenatal diagnostic tests, such as amniocentesis and alpha-fetoprotein testing, which assess the well-being of the fetus as well as detect genetic or chromosomal problems. These technological developments are discussed in the articles "Making Babies" and "Prenatal Purgatory."

Perhaps the oldest debate in the study of human development is the "nature versus nurture" question. Scientists have moved beyond thinking of development as due to genetics *or* environment, now recognizing that nature *and* nurture interact to shape us. Each human is a biological organism, and each is surrounded, from the moment of conception, by environmental forces. Hence, there is no escaping nature or nurture. "Eugenics Revisited" and "Nature or Nurture? Old Chestnut, New Thoughts" help us consider the nature and nurture of our IQ, mental health, sexual orientation, and other aspects of who we are. "Eugenics Revisited" is especially valuable because it helps the reader appreciate several crucial facts about the nature/nurture debate. First, although both genes and experience are crucial in shaping us, many scientists have recently emphasized the power of genes. However, research evidence shows that there are fewer certainties about genetic influence than some scientists might let on. Second, findings from the nature/nurture debate can

always be interpreted from more than one perspective to support more than one view. Finally, whether we embrace genes or environment as the primary factor in determining development, there may be ethical, political, legal, and societal consequences of taking that particular stance.

Students of child development should realize that the classic "nature/nurture" controversy applies as much to prenatal development as to any other stage of childhood. While prenatal development is largely the result of the unfolding of an individual's genetic blueprint, the fetus is also in an environment within the mother's womb. Hence, within the womb the fetus is vulnerable to teratogens, hazards from the environment that interfere with normal prenatal development. One potential teratogen is alcohol. Thousands of babies are born every year with fetal alcohol syndrome, a constellation of permanent physical, behavioral, and neurological defects that result from the mother consuming alcohol while pregnant. We are learning more about potential harm to the developing fetus due to increasing rates of maternal drug use. As a consequence, pregnant women are being held to more stringent legal standards culminating in legal battles that pit the rights of pregnant women against the rights of their fetuses. "When a Pregnant Woman Drinks" addresses some of these troubling and controversial issues.

Our notions of childbirth have themselves evolved throughout history. Although in earlier decades many women gave birth to their babies at home or in comfortable, natural settings, the vast majority of births in Western societies now occur in a hospital. Some critics claim that childbirth is seen by the medical community not as a natural life event but as a "disease" treated in many ways like surgery; women are often treated during childbirth as passive, immobilized patients subject to many specialized tools and surgical techniques. For example, to be prepped for labor, a pregnant woman is often administered labor-inducing drugs, an episiotomy is performed, and anesthesia is administered. Other evidence for the surgical nature of childbirth includes the fact that more than one in five births in the United States is now a cesarean section, making it one of the most common surgical procedures in this country. A more personal account of the birth process of one baby is given in "The Fantastic Voyage of Tanner Roberts," which details, in a contraction-by-contraction analysis, the emotional as well as technical aspects of childbirth.

Looking Ahead: Challenge Questions

Where do you stand on the nature/nurture issue? Does it comfort you—or unsettle you—to know that the genes you inherited influence your intelligence, mental health, susceptibility to some diseases, and so on? How would you respond to someone who claimed that a person's IQ or sexual orientation is "determined" by nature?

In light of the vast array of prenatal diagnostics and medical procedures now used, does technology play too great a role in determining who can have children? How would you balance the personal wish for a child and the expense and ethical complications of available reproductive technology? Assuming new procedures continue to be developed, what options might be available to parents in the future?

If the fetus possesses many sensory and perceptual skills and is capable of basic forms of learning, should parents try to "teach" their fetus? What might be the advantages and disadvantages of this "early schooling"?

Should society pit the rights of a pregnant woman against those of her fetus? Rather than determining how pregnant women should be punished for alcohol and drug abuse, should there be more emphasis on prevention of such abuses that can cause birth defects?

EUGENICS REVISITED

Scientists are linking genes to a host of complex human disorders and traits, but just how valid—and useful—are these findings?

John Horgan, *senior writer*

"How to Tell If Your Child's a Serial Killer!" That was the sound bite with which the television show *Donahue* sought to entice listeners February 25. On the program, a psychiatrist from the Rochester, N.Y., area noted that some men are born with not one Y chromosome but two. Double-Y men, the psychiatrist said, are "at special risk for antisocial, violent behavior." In fact, the psychiatrist had recently studied such a man. Although he had grown up in a "Norman Rockwell" setting, as an adult he had strangled at least 11 women and two children.

"It is not hysterical or overstating it," Phil Donahue told his horrified audience, "to say that we are moving toward the time when, quite literally, just as we can anticipate . . . genetic predispositions toward various physical diseases, we will also be able to pinpoint mental disorders which include aggression, antisocial behavior and the possibility of very serious criminal activity later on."

Eugenics is back in fashion. The message that genetics can explain, predict and even modify human behavior for the betterment of society is promulgated not just on sensationalistic talk shows but by our most prominent scientists. James D. Watson, co-discoverer of the double-helix structure of DNA and former head of the Human Genome Project, the massive effort to map our entire genetic endowment, said recently, "We used to think that our fate was in our stars. Now we know, in large part, that our fate is in our genes."

Daniel E. Koshland, Jr., a biologist at the University of California at Berkeley and editor of *Science*, the most influential peer-reviewed journal in the U.S., has declared in an editorial that the nature/nurture debate is "basically over," since scientists have shown that genes influence many aspects of human behavior. He has also contended that genetic research may help eliminate society's most intractable problems, including drug abuse, homelessness and, yes, violent crime.

Some studies cited to back this claim are remarkably similar to those conducted over a century ago by scientists such as Francis Galton, known as the father of eugenics. Just as the British polymath studied identical twins in order to show that "nature prevails enormously over nurture," so do modern researchers. But the primary reason behind the revival of eugenics is the astonishing successes of biologists in mapping and manipulating the human genome. Over the past decade, investigators have identified genes underlying such crippling diseases as cystic fibrosis, muscular dystrophy and, this past spring, Huntington's disease. Given these advances, researchers say, it is only a matter of time before they can lay bare the genetic foundation of much more complex traits and disorders.

The political base for eugenics has also become considerably broader in recent years. Spokespersons for the mentally ill believe demonstrating the genetic basis of disorders such as schizophrenia and manic depression—and even alcoholism and drug addiction—will lead not only to better diagnoses and

treatments but also to more compassion toward sufferers and their families. Some homosexuals believe society will become more tolerant toward them if it can be shown that sexual orientation is an innate, biological condition and not a matter of choice.

But critics contend that no good can come of bad science. Far from moving inexorably closer to its goals, they point out, the field of behavioral genetics is mired in the same problems that have always plagued it. Behavioral traits are extraordinarily difficult to define, and practically every claim of a genetic basis can also be explained as an environmental effect. "This has been a huge enterprise, and for the most part the work has been done shoddily. Even careful people get sucked into misinterpreting data," says Jonathan Beckwith, a geneticist at Harvard University. He adds, "There are social consequences to this."

The skeptics also accuse the media of having created an unrealistically optimistic view of the field. Richard C. Lewontin, a biologist at Harvard and a prominent critic of behavioral genetics, contends that the media generally give much more prominent coverage to dramatic reports—such as the discovery of an "alcoholism gene"—than to contradictory results or retractions. "Skepticism doesn't make the news," Lewontin says. "It only makes the news when you find a gene." The result is that spurious findings often become accepted by the public and even by so-called experts.

The claim that men with an extra Y chromosome are predisposed toward violence is a case in point. It stems from a survey in the 1960s that found more extra-Y men in prison than in the general population. Some researchers hypothesized that since the Y chromo-

From *Scientific American*, June 1993, pp. 122-128, 130-131. © 1993 by Scientific American, Inc. All rights reserved. Reprinted by permission.

some confers male attributes, men with an extra Y become hyperaggressive "supermales." Follow-up studies indicated that while extra-Y men tend to be taller than other men and score slightly lower on intelligence tests, they are otherwise normal. The National Academy of Sciences concluded in a report published this year that there is no evidence to support the link between the extra Y chromosome and violent behavior.

Minnesota Twins

No research in behavioral genetics has been more eagerly embraced by the press than the identical-twin studies done at the University of Minnesota. Thomas J. Bouchard, Jr., a psychologist, initiated them in the late 1970s, and since then they have been featured in the *Washington Post, Newsweek,* the *New York Times* and other publications worldwide as well as on television. *Science* has favorably described the Minnesota team's work in several news stories and in 1990 published a major article by the group.

The workers have studied more than 50 pairs of identical twins who were separated shortly after birth and raised in different households. The assump-

tion is that any differences between identical twins, who share all each other's genes, are caused by the environment; similarities are attributed to their shared genes. The group estimates the relative contribution of genes to a given trait in a term called "heritability." A trait that stems entirely from genes, such as eye color, is defined as 100 percent heritable. Height is 90 percent heritable; that is, 90 percent of the variation in height is accounted for by genetic variation, and the other 10 percent is accounted for by diet and other environmental factors.

The Minnesota group has reported finding a strong genetic contribution to practically all the traits it has examined. Whereas most previous studies have estimated the heritability of intelligence (as defined by performance on intelligence tests) as roughly 50 percent, Bouchard and his colleagues arrived at a figure of 70 percent. They have also found a genetic component underlying such culturally defined traits as religiosity, political orientation (conservative versus liberal), job satisfaction, leisure-time interests and proneness to divorce. In fact, the group concluded in *Science*, "On multiple measures of personality and temperament...monozy-

gotic twins reared apart are about as similar as are monozygotic twins reared together." (Identical twins are called monozygotic because they stem from a single fertilized egg, or zygote.)

The researchers have buttressed their statistical findings with anecdotes about "eerie," "bewitching" and "remarkable" parallels between reunited twins. One case involved Oskar, who was raised as a Nazi in Czechoslovakia, and Jack, who was raised as a Jew in Trinidad. Both were reportedly wearing shirts with epaulets when they were reunited by the Minnesota group in 1979. They also both flushed the toilet before as well as after using it and enjoyed deliberately sneezing to startle people in elevators.

Some other celebrated cases involved two British women who wore seven rings and named their firstborn sons Richard Andrew and Andrew Richard; two men who both had been named Jim, named their pet dogs Toy, married women named Linda, divorced them and remarried women named Betty; and two men who had become firefighters and drank Budweiser beer.

Other twin researchers say the significance of these coincidences has been greatly exaggerated. Richard J. Rose of Indiana University, who is collaborating on a study of 16,000 pairs of twins in Finland, points out that "if you bring together strangers who were born on the same day in the same country and ask them to find similarities between them, you may find a lot of seemingly astounding coincidences."

Rose's collaborator, Jaakko Kaprio of the University of Helsinki, notes that the Minnesota twin studies may also be biased by their selection method. Whereas he and Rose gather data by combing birth registries and sending questionnaires to those identified as twins, the Minnesota group relies heavily on media coverage to recruit new twins. The twins then come to Minnesota for a week of study—and, often, further publicity. Twins who are "interested in publicity and willing to support it," Kaprio says, may be atypical. This self-selection effect, he adds, may explain why the Bouchard group's estimates of heritability tend to be higher than those of other studies.

One of the most outspoken critics of

the Minnesota twin studies—and indeed all twin studies indicating high heritability of behavioral traits—is Leon J. Kamin, a psychologist at Northeastern University. In the 1970s Kamin helped to expose inconsistencies and possible fraud in studies of separated identical twins conducted by the British psychologist Cyril Burt during the previous two decades. Burt's conclusion that intelligence was mostly inherited had inspired various observers, notably Arthur R. Jensen, a psychologist at the University of California at Berkeley, to argue that socioeconomic stratification in the U.S. is largely a genetic phenomenon.

In his investigations of other twin studies, Kamin has shown that identical twins supposedly raised apart are often raised by members of their family or by unrelated families in the same neighborhood; some twins had extensive contact with each other while growing up. Kamin suspects the same may be true of some Minnesota twins. He notes, for example, that some news accounts suggested Oskar and Jack (the Nazi and the Jew) and the two British women wearing seven rings were reunited for the first time when they arrived in Minnesota to be studied by Bouchard. Actually, both pairs of twins had met previously. Kamin has repeatedly asked the Minnesota group for detailed case histories of its twins to determine whether it has underestimated contact and similarities in upbringing. "They've never responded," he says.

Kamin proposes that the Minnesota twins have particularly strong motives to downplay previous contacts and to exaggerate their similarities. They might want to please researchers, to attract more attention from the media or even to make money. In fact, some twins acquired agents and were paid for appearances on television. Jack and Oskar recently sold their life story to a film producer in Los Angeles (who says Robert Duvall is interested in the roles).

Even the Minnesota researchers caution against overinterpretation of their work. They agree with their critics that high heritability should not be equated with inevitability, since the environment can still drastically affect the expression of a gene. For example, the genetic disease phenylketonuria, which causes profound retardation, has a heritability of 100 percent. Yet eliminating the amino acid phenylalanine from the diet of affected persons prevents retardation from occurring.

Such warnings tend to be minimized in media coverage, however. Writers often make the same inference that Koshland did in an editorial in *Science:* "Bet-

ter schools, a better environment, better counseling and better rehabilitation will help some individuals but not all." The prime minister of Singapore apparently reached the same conclusion. A decade ago he cited popular accounts of the Minnesota research in defending policies that encouraged middle-class Singaporeans to bear children and discouraged childbearing by the poor.

Smart Genes

Twin studies, of course, do not indicate which specific genes contribute to a trait. Early in the 1980s scientists began developing powerful ways to unearth that information. The techniques stem from the fact that certain stretches of human DNA, called polymorphisms, vary in a predictable way. If a polymorphism is consistently inherited together with a given trait—blue eyes, for example—then geneticists assume it either lies near a gene for that trait or actually is the gene. A polymorphism that merely lies near a gene is known as a marker.

In so-called linkage studies, investigators search for polymorphisms co-inherited with a trait in families unusually prone to the trait. In 1983 researchers used this method to find a marker linked to Huntington's disease, a crippling neurological disorder that usually strikes carriers in middle age and kills them within 10 years. Since then, the same technique has pinpointed genes for cystic fibrosis, muscular dystrophy and other diseases. In association studies, researchers compare the relative frequency of polymorphisms in two unrelated populations, one with the trait and one lacking it.

Workers are already using both methods to search for polymorphisms associated with intelligence, defined as the ability to score well on standardized intelligence tests. In 1991 Shelley D. Smith of the Boys Town National Institute for Communication Disorders in Children, in Omaha, and David W. Fulker of the University of Colorado identified polymorphisms associated with dyslexia in a linkage study of 19 families exhibiting high incidence of the reading disorder.

Behavioral Genetics: A Lack-of-Progress Report

CRIME: Family, twin and adoption studies have suggested a heritability of 0 to more than 50 percent for predisposition to crime. (Heritability represents the degree to which a trait stems from genetic factors.) In the 1960s researchers reported an association between an extra Y chromosome and violent crime in males. Follow-up studies found that association to be spurious.

MANIC DEPRESSION: Twin and family studies indicate heritability of 60 to 80 percent for susceptibility to manic depression. In 1987 two groups reported locating different genes linked to manic depression, one in Amish families and the other in Israeli families. Both reports have been retracted.

SCHIZOPHRENIA: Twin studies show heritability of 40 to 90 percent. In 1988 a group reported finding a gene linked to schizophrenia in British and Icelandic families. Other studies documented no linkage, and the initial claim has now been retracted.

ALCOHOLISM: Twin and adoption studies suggest heritability ranging from 0 to 60 percent. In 1990 a group claimed to link a gene—one that produces a receptor for the neurotransmitter dopamine—with alcoholism. A recent review of the evidence concluded it does not support a link.

INTELLIGENCE: Twin and adoption studies show a heritability of performance on intelligence tests of 20 to 80 percent. One group recently unveiled preliminary evidence for genetic markers for high intelligence (an IQ of 130 or higher). The study is unpublished.

HOMOSEXUALITY: In 1991 a researcher cited anatomic differences between the brains of heterosexual and homosexual males. Two recent twin studies have found a heritability of roughly 50 percent for predisposition to male or female homosexuality. These reports have been disputed. Another group claims to have preliminary evidence of genes linked to male homosexuality. The data have not been published.

Two years ago Robert Plomin, a psychologist at Pennsylvania State University who has long been active in behavioral genetics, received a $600,000 grant from the National Institute of Child Health and Human Development to search for genes linked to high intelligence. Plomin is using the association method, which he says is more suited than the linkage technique to identifying genes whose contribution to a trait is relatively small. Plomin is studying a group of 64 schoolchildren 12 to 13 years old who fall into three groups: those who score approximately 130, 100 and 80 on intelligence tests.

Plomin has examined some 25 polymorphisms in each of these three groups, trying to determine whether any occur with greater frequency in the "bright" children. The polymorphisms have been linked to genes thought to have neurological effects. He has uncovered several markers that seem to occur more often in the highest-scoring children. He is now seeking to replicate his results in another group of 60 children; half score above 142 on intelligence tests, and half score less than 74 (yet have no obvious organic deficiencies). Plomin presented his preliminary findings at a meeting, titled "Origins and Development of High Ability," held in London in January.

At the same meeting, however, other workers offered evidence that intelligence tests are actually poor predictors of success in business, the arts or even advanced academic programs. Indeed, even Plomin seems ambivalent about the value of his research. He suggests that someday genetic information on the cognitive abilities of children might help teachers design lessons that are more suited to students' innate strengths and weaknesses.

But he also calls his approach "a fishing expedition," given that a large number of genes may contribute to intelligence. He thinks the heritability of intelligence is not 70 percent, as the Minnesota twin researchers have claimed, but 50 percent, which is the average finding of other studies, and at best he can only find a gene that accounts for a tiny part of variance in intelligence. "If you wanted to select on the basis of this, it would be of no use whatsoever," he remarks. These cautions did not prevent the *Sunday Telegraph,* a London newspaper, from announcing that Plomin had found "evidence that geniuses are born not made."

Evan S. Balaban, a biologist at Harvard, thinks Plomin's fishing expedition is doomed to fail. He grants that there may well be a significant genetic component to intelligence (while insisting that studies by Bouchard and others have not demonstrated one). But he doubts whether investigators will ever uncover any specific genes related to high intelligence or "genius." "It is very rare to find genes that have a specific effect," he says. "For evolutionary reasons, this just doesn't happen very often."

The history of the search for markers associated with mental illness supports Balaban's view. Over the past few decades, studies of twins, families and adoptees have convinced most investigators that schizophrenia and manic depression are not caused by psychosocial factors—such as the notorious "schizophrenogenic mother" postulated by some Freudian psychiatrists—but by biological and genetic factors. After observing the dramatic success of linkage studies in the early 1980s, researchers immediately began using the technique to isolate polymorphic markers for mental illness. The potential value of such research was enormous, given that schizophrenia and manic depression each affect roughly one percent of the global population.

They seemed to have achieved their first great success in 1987. A group led by Janice A. Egeland of the University of Miami School of Medicine claimed it had linked a genetic marker on chromosome 11 to manic depression in an Amish population. That same year another team, led by Miron Baron of Columbia University, linked a marker on the X chromosome to manic depression in three Israeli families.

The media hailed these announcements as major breakthroughs. Far less attention was paid to the retractions that followed. A more extensive analysis of the Amish in 1989 by a group from the National Institute of Mental Health turned up no link between chromosome 11 and manic depression. This year Baron's team retracted its claim of linkage with the X chromosome after doing a new study of its Israeli families with more sophisticated markers and more extensive diagnoses.

Schizophrenic Results

Studies of schizophrenia have followed a remarkably similar course. In 1988 a group headed by Hugh M. D. Gurling of the University College, London, Medical School announced in *Nature* that it had found linkage in Icelandic and British families between genetic markers on chromosome 5 and schizophrenia. In the same issue, however, researchers led by Kenneth K. Kidd of Yale University reported seeing no such linkage in a Swedish family. Although Gurling defended his result as legitimate for several years, additional research has convinced him that it was probably a false positive. "The new families showed no linkage at all," he says.

These disappointments have highlighted the problems involved in using linkage to study mental illness. Neil Risch, a geneticist at Yale, points out that linkage analysis is ideal for studying diseases, such as Huntington's, that have distinct symptoms and are caused by a single dominant gene. Some researchers had hoped that at least certain subtypes of schizophrenia or manic depression might be single-gene disorders. Single-gene mutations are thought to cause variants of breast cancer and of Alzheimer's disease that run in families and are manifested much earlier than usual. But such diseases are rare, Risch says, because natural selection quickly winnows them out of the population, and no evidence exists for distinct subtypes of manic depression or schizophrenia.

Indeed, all the available evidence suggests that schizophrenia and manic depression are caused by at least several genes—each of which may exert only a tiny influence—acting in concert with environmental influences. Finding such genes with linkage analysis may not be impossible, Risch says, but it will be considerably more difficult than identifying genes that have a one-to-one correspondence to a trait. The difficulty is compounded by the fact that the diagnosis of mental illness is often subjective—all the more so when researchers are relying on family records or recollections.

Some experts now question whether genes play a significant role in mental illness. "Personally, I think we have overestimated the genetic component of schizophrenia," says E. Fuller Torrey, a psychiatrist at St. Elizabeth's Hospital in Washington, D.C. He argues that the evidence supporting genetic models can be explained by other biological factors, such as a virus that strikes in utero. The pattern of incidence of schizophrenia in families often resembles that of other viral diseases, such as polio. "Genes may just create a susceptibility to the virus," Torrey explains.

The Drink Link

Even Kidd, the Yale geneticist who has devoted his career to searching for genes linked to mental illness, acknowledges that "in a rigorous, technical, scientific sense, there is very little proof that schizophrenia, manic depression"

1. CONCEPTION TO BIRTH

and other psychiatric disorders have a genetic origin. "Virtually all the evidence supports a genetic explanation, but there are always other explanations, even if they are convoluted."

The evidence for a genetic basis for alcoholism is even more tentative than that for manic depression and schizophrenia. Although some studies discern a genetic component, especially in males, others have reached the opposite conclusion. Gurling, the University College investigator, found a decade ago that identical twins were slightly *more* likely to be discordant for alcoholism than fraternal twins. The drinking habits of some identical twins were strikingly different. "In some cases, one drank a few bottles a day, and the other didn't drink at all," Gurling says.

Nevertheless, in 1990 a group led by Kenneth Blum of the University of Texas Health Science Center at San Antonio announced it had discovered a genetic marker for alcoholism in an association study comparing 35 alcoholics with a control group of 35 nonalcoholics. A page-one story in the *New York Times* portrayed the research as a potential watershed in the diagnosis and treatment of alcoholism without mentioning the considerable skepticism aroused among other researchers.

The Blum group claimed that its marker, called the A1 allele, was associated with a gene, called the D2 gene, that codes for a receptor for the neurotransmitter dopamine. Skeptics noted that the A1 allele was actually some 10,000 base pairs from the dopamine-receptor gene and was not linked to any detectable variation in its expression.

Since the initial announcement by Blum, three papers, including an additional one by Blum's group, have presented more evidence of an association between the A1 allele and alcoholism. Six groups have found no such evidence (and received virtually no mention in the popular media).

In April, Risch and Joel Gelernter of Yale and David Goldman of the National Institute on Alcohol Abuse and Alcoholism analyzed all these studies on the A1 allele in a paper in the *Journal of the American Medical Association.* They noted that if Blum's two studies are cast aside, the balance of the results shows

BRAIN OF SCHIZOPHRENIC (*right*) appears different from the brain of his identical twin in these magnetic resonance images. Such findings suggest that factors that are biological but not genetic—such as viruses—may play a significant role in mental illness.

The Huntington's Disease Saga: A Cautionary Tale

The identification of the gene for Huntington's disease, which was announced in March, was hailed as one of the great success stories of modern genetics. Yet it provides some rather sobering lessons for researchers seeking genes linked to more complex human disorders and traits.

The story begins in the late 1970s, when workers developed novel techniques for identifying polymorphisms, sections of the human genome that come in two or more forms. Investigators realized that by finding polymorphisms linked—always and exclusively—to diseases, they could determine which chromosome the gene resides in. Researchers decided to test the polymorphism technique on Huntington's disease, a devastating neurological disorder that affects roughly one in 10,000 people. Scientists had known for more than a century that Huntington's was caused by a mutant, dominant gene. If one parent has the disease, his or her offspring have a 50 percent chance of inheriting it.

One of the leaders of the Huntington's effort was Nancy Wexler, a neuropsychologist at Columbia University whose mother had died of the disease and who therefore has a 50 percent chance of developing it herself. She and other researchers focused on a poor Venezuelan village whose inhabitants had an unusually high incidence of the disease. In 1983, through what has now become a legendary stroke of good fortune, they found a linkage with one of the first polymorphisms they tested. The linkage indicated that the gene for Huntington's disease was somewhere on chromosome 4.

The finding led quickly to a test for determining whether offspring of carriers—either in utero or already born—have inherited the gene itself. The test requires an analysis of blood samples from several members of a family known to carry the disease. Wexler herself has declined to say whether she has taken the test.

Researchers assumed that they would quickly identify the actual gene in chromosome 4 that causes Huntington's disease. Yet it took 10 years for six teams of workers from 10 institutions to find the gene. It is a so-called expanding gene, which for unknown reasons gains base pairs (the chemical "rungs" binding two strands of DNA) every time it is transmitted. The greater the expansion of the gene, researchers say, the earlier the onset of the disease. The search was complicated by the fact that workers had no physical clues about the course of the disease to guide them. Indeed, Wexler and others emphasize that they still have no idea how the gene actually causes the disease; treatments or cures may be years or decades away.

The most immediate impact of the new discovery will be the development of a better test for Huntington's, one that requires blood only from the person at risk

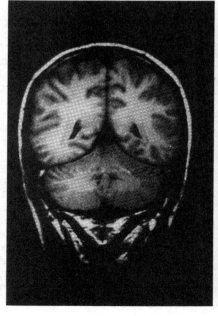 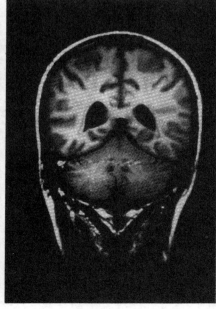

10

NANCY WEXLER helped to find the gene responsible for Huntington's disease by studying a population in Venezuela that has been ravaged by the disorder.

and not other family members. By measuring the length of the mutant gene, the test might also predict more accurately when carriers will show symptoms.

As difficult as it was to pinpoint the gene for Huntington's, it will be almost infinitely harder to discover genes for behavioral disorders, says Evan S. Balaban, a biologist at Harvard University. Unlike Huntington's disease, he notes, disorders such as schizophrenia and alcoholism cannot be unambiguously diagnosed. Furthermore, they stem not from a single dominant gene but from many genes acting in concert with environmental effects. If researchers do find a statistical association between certain genes and a trait, Balaban says, that knowledge may never be translated into useful therapies or tests. "What does it mean to have a 10 percent increased risk of alcoholism?" he asks.

no association between the D2 receptor and alcoholism, either in the disorder's milder or most severe forms. "We therefore conclude that no physiologically significant association" between the A1 allele and alcoholism has been proved, the group stated. "It's a dead issue," Risch says.

Gelernter and his colleagues point out that association studies are prone to spurious results if not properly controlled. They suggest that the positive findings of Blum and his colleagues may have derived from a failure to control for ethnic variation. The limited surveys done so far have shown that the incidence of the A1 allele varies wildly in different ethnic groups, ranging from 10 percent in certain Jewish groups to about 50 percent in Japanese.

Blum insists that the ethnic data, far from undermining his case, support it,

since those groups with the highest prevalence of the A1 allele also exhibit the highest rates of "addictive behavior." He contends that the only reason the Japanese do not display higher rates of alcoholism is that many also carry a gene that prevents them from metabolizing alcohol. "They're pretty compulsive," explains Blum, who recently obtained a patent for a genetic test for alcoholism.

These arguments have been rejected even by Irving I. Gottesman of the University of Virginia, who is a strong defender of genetic models of human behavior. He considers the papers cited by Blum to support his case to be ambiguous and even contradictory. Some see an association only with alcoholism that leads to medical complications or even death; others discern no association with alcoholism but only with "polysubstance abuse," including cigarette smoking. "I think it is by and large

garbage," Gottesman says of the alleged A1-alcoholism link.

By far the most controversial area of behavioral genetics is research on crime. Last fall complaints by civil-rights leaders and others led the National Institutes of Health to withdraw its funding from a meeting entitled "Genetic Factors in Crime: Findings, Uses and Implications." The conference brochure had noted the "apparent failure of environmental approaches to crime" and suggested that genetic research might yield methods for identifying and treating potists, notably Richard J. Herrnstein, a psychologist at Harvard, have made this assertion. Others reject this view but insist biological research on attributes linked to violent crime, such as aggression, may still have some value. "People who are unwilling to address genetic and biochemical factors are just putting their heads in the sand," says Goldman, the alcoholism expert. "It is not fair to say that just because there have been geneticists who have had a very narrow view of this in the past, we shouldn't explore this now."

In fact, investigations of the biology of violent crime continue, albeit quietly. Workers at City of Hope Hospital in Duarte, Calif., claim to have found an association between the A1 allele—the alleged alcoholism marker—and "criminal aggression." Last year a group led by Markus J. P. Kruesi of the University of Illinois at Chicago presented evidence of an association between low levels of the neurotransmitter serotonin and disruptive-behavior disorders in children. Kruesi concedes there is no way to determine whether the serotonin levels are genetically influenced. In fact, the serotonin levels might be an effect—a reaction to an environmental trauma—rather than a cause. "This might be a scar marker," he says.

One reason such research persists is that studies of families, twins and adoptees have suggested a genetic component to crime. Glenn D. Walters, a psychologist at the Federal Correctional Institution in Schuylkill, Pa., recently reviewed 38 of these studies, conducted from the 1930s to the present, in the journal *Criminology*. His meta-analysis turned up a small genetic effect, "but nothing to get excited about." He observes that "a lot of the research has not been very good" and that the more recent, better-designed studies tended to turn up less evidence. "I don't think we will find any biological markers for crime," he says. "We should put our resources elsewhere."

"Better Breeding"

Fairly or not, modern genetics research is still haunted by the history of eugenics. "It offers a lot of cautionary lessons," says Daniel J. Kevles, a historian at the California Institute of Technology, who wrote the 1985 book *In the Name of Eugenics*. The British scientist Francis Galton, cousin to Charles Darwin, first proposed that human society could be improved "through better breeding" in 1865 in an article entitled "Hereditary Talent and Character." He coined the term "eugenics," from the Greek for "good birth," in 1883.

Galton's proposal had broad appeal. The American sexual libertarian John Humphrey Noyes bent eugenics into an ingenious argument for polygamy. "While the good man will be limited by his conscience to what the law allows," Noyes said, "the bad man, free from moral check, will distribute his seed beyond the legal limit."

A more serious advocate was the biologist Charles B. Davenport, founder of Cold Spring Harbor Laboratory and of the Eugenics Record Office, which gathered information on thousands of American families for genetic research. After demonstrating the heritability of eye, skin and hair color, Davenport went on to "prove" the heritability of traits such as "pauperism," criminality and "feeble-mindedness." In one monograph, published in 1919, he asserted that the ability to be a naval officer is an inherited trait, composed of subtraits for thalassophilia, or love of the sea, and hyperkineticism, or wanderlust. Noting the paucity of female naval officers, Davenport concluded that the trait is unique to males.

Beginning in the 1920s the American Eugenics Society, founded by Davenport and others, sponsored "Fitter Families Contests" at state fairs around the U.S. Just as cows and sheep were appraised by judges at the fairs, so were human entrants (such as the family shown above at the 1925 Texas State Fair). Less amusingly, eugenicists helped to persuade more than 20 U.S. states to authorize sterilization of men and women in prisons and mental hospitals, and they urged the federal government to restrict the immigration of "undesirable" races.

No nation, of course, practiced eugenics as enthusiastically as Nazi Germany, whose program culminated in "euthanasia" ("good death") of the mentally and physically disabled as well as Jews, Gypsies, Catholics and others. As revelations of these atrocities spread after World War II, popular support for eugenics programs waned in the U.S. and elsewhere.

Gay Genes

The ostensible purpose of investigations of mental illness, alcoholism and even crime is to reduce their incidence. Scientists studying homosexuality have a different goal: simply to test whether homosexuality is innate, as many homosexuals have long professed. That claim was advanced by a report in *Science* in 1991 by Simon LeVay of the Salk Institute for Biological Studies in San Diego. LeVay has acknowledged both that he is gay and that he believes evidence of

biological differences between homosexuals and heterosexuals will encourage tolerance toward gays.

LeVay, who recently left the Salk Institute to found the Institute of Gay and Lesbian Education, focused on a tiny neural structure in the hypothalamus, a region of the brain known to control sexual response. He measured this structure, called the interstitial nucleus, in autopsies of the brains of 19 homosexual males, 16 heterosexual males and six heterosexual women. LeVay found that the interstitial nucleus was almost twice as large in the heterosexual males as in the homosexual males or in the women. He postulated that the interstitial nucleus "is large in individuals oriented toward women"— whether male or female.

Of course, LeVay's finding only addresses anatomic differences, not necessarily genetic ones. Various other researchers have tried to establish that homosexuality is not just biological in its origin—caused, perhaps, by hormonal influences in utero—but also genetic. Some have sought evidence in experiments with rats and other animals. A group headed by Angela Pattatucci of the National Cancer Institute is studying a strain of male fruit flies—which wags have dubbed either "fruity" or "fruitless"—that court other males.

In December 1991 J. Michael Bailey of Northwestern University and Richard C. Pillard of Boston University announced they had uncovered evidence of a genetic basis for male homosexuality in humans. They studied 161 gay men, each of whom had at least one identical or fraternal twin or adopted brother. The researchers determined that 52 percent of the identical twins were both homosexual, as compared with 22 percent of the fraternal twins and 11 percent of the adopted brothers.

Bailey and Pillard derived similar results in a study of lesbians published this year in the *Archives of General Psychiatry*. They compared 147 gay women with identical or fraternal twins or adopted sisters: 48 percent of the identical twins were both gay, versus 16 percent of the fraternal twins (who share only half each other's genes) and 6 percent of the adopted sisters. "Both male and female sexual orientation appeared to be influenced by genetic factors," Bailey and Pillard concluded.

This conclusion has disturbed some of Bailey and Pillard's own subjects. "I have major questions about the validity of some of the assumptions they are making," says Nina Sossen, a gay woman living in Madison, Wis., whose identical twin is heterosexual. Her doubts are shared by William Byne, a psychiatrist at Columbia University. He notes that in their study of male homosexuality Bailey and Pillard found more concordance between unrelated, adopted brothers than related (but non-twin) brothers. The high concordance of the male and female identical twins, moreover, may stem from the fact that such twins are often dressed alike and treated alike—indeed, they are often mistaken for each other—by family members as well as by others.

"The increased concordance for homosexuality among the identical twins could be entirely accounted for by the increased similarity of their developmental experiences," Byne says. "In my opinion, the major finding of that study is that 48 percent of identical twins who were reared together were discordant for sexual orientation."

Byne also criticizes LeVay's conclusion that homosexuality must be biological—although not necessarily genetic—because the brains of male homosexuals resemble the brains of women. That assumption, Byne points out, rests on still another assumption, that there are significant anatomic differences between heterosexual male and female brains. But to date, there have been no replicable studies showing such sexual dimorphism.

Byne notes that he has been suspected of having an antigay motive. Two reviewers of an article he recently wrote criticizing homosexuality research accused him of having a "right-wing agenda," he says. He has also been contacted by conservative groups hoping he will speak out against the admittance of homosexuals to the military. He emphasizes that he supports gay rights and thinks homosexuality, whatever its cause, is not a "choice." He adds that genetic models of behavior are just as likely to foment bigotry as to quell it.

"Hierarchy of Worthlessness"

Despite the skepticism of Byne and others, at least one group, led by Dean Hamer of the National Cancer Institute, is searching not merely for anatomic or biochemical differences in homosexuals but for genetic markers. Hamer has done a linkage study of numerous small families, each of which has at least two gay brothers. He says his study has turned up some tentative findings, and he plans to submit his results soon. Hamer's colleague Pattatucci is planning a similar study of lesbians.

What purpose will be served by pinpointing genes linked to homosexuality? In an information sheet for prospective participants in his study, Hamer expresses the hope that his research may "improve understanding between people with different sexual orientations." He adds, "This study is not aimed at developing methods to alter either heterosexual or homosexual orientation, and the results of the study will not allow sexual orientation to be determined by a blood test or amniocentesis."

Yet even Pillard, who is gay and applauds Hamer's work, admits to some concern over the potential uses of a genetic marker for homosexuality. He notes that some parents might choose to abort embryos carrying such a marker. Male and female homosexuals might then retaliate, he says, by conceiving children and aborting fetuses that lacked such a gene.

Balaban, the Harvard biologist, thinks the possible dangers of such research—assuming it is successful—outweigh any benefits. Indeed, he sees behavioral genetics as a "hierarchy of worthlessness," with twin studies at the bottom and linkage studies of mental illness at the top. The best researchers can hope for is to find, say, a gene associated with a slightly elevated risk of schizophrenia. Such information is more likely to lead

to discrimination by insurance companies and employers than to therapeutic benefits, Balaban warns.

His colleague Lewontin agrees. In the 1970s, he recalls, insurance companies began requiring black customers to take tests for sickle cell anemia, a genetic disease that primarily affects blacks. Those who refused to take the test or who tested positive were denied coverage. "I feel that this research is a substitute for what is really hard—finding out how to change social conditions," Lewontin remarks. "I think it's the wrong direction for research, given that we have a finite amount of resources."

Paul R. Billings, a geneticist at the California Pacific Medical Center, shares some of these concerns. He agrees that twin studies seem to be inherently ambiguous, and he urges researchers seeking markers for homosexuality to consider what a conservative government—led by Patrick Buchanan, for example—might allow to be done with such information. But he believes some aspects of behavioral genetics, particularly searches for genes underlying mental illness, are worth pursuing.

In an article published in the British journal *Social Science and Medicine* last year, Billings and two other scientists offered some constructive criticism for the field. Researchers engaged in association and linkage studies should establish "strict criteria as to what would constitute meaningful data." Both scientists and the press should emphasize the limitations of such studies, "especially when the mechanism of how a gene acts on a behavior is not known." Billings and his colleagues strive to end their article on a positive note. "Despite the shortcomings of other studies," they say, "there is relatively good evidence for a site on the X chromosome which is associated with [manic depression] in some families." This finding was retracted earlier this year.

NATURE OR NURTURE?

■

Old chestnut, new thoughts

Few questions of human behaviour are more controversial than this: are people programmed by their genes, or by their upbringing? There is no simple answer, but the academic world is starting to hear a lot more from the genes brigade—on both sides of the political spectrum

ARE criminals born or made? Is homosexuality a preference or a predisposition? Do IQ tests measure innate abilities or acquired skills?

For the past 50 years, respectable academic opinion, whenever it has deigned to deal with such layman's questions, has come down firmly for nurture over nature. Nazism discredited even the mildest attempts to produce genetic explanations of human affairs. And economic growth after the second world war encouraged most western governments to imagine that they could eliminate social problems by a mixture of enlightened planning and generous spending—that, in effect, they could steer (even change) human nature.

In this atmosphere, the social sciences flourished as never before. Sociologists made lucrative careers producing "nurture" explanations of everything from school failure to schizophrenia. Geneticists stuck to safe subjects such as fruit flies and honey bees, rather than risk being accused of a fondness for jackboots and martial music.

The fashion is beginning to change. The failure of liberal reforms to deliver the Great Society has cast doubt on the proposition that better nurture can deliver better nature. The failure of sociologists to find even a few of the purported (Freudian or social) causes of schizophrenia, homosexuality, sex differences in criminal tendencies and the like has undermined their credibility. And a better understanding of how genes work has made it possible for liberals who still believe in the perfectibility of man to accept genetic explanations. In at least one case—homosexuality—it is now the liberals who espouse nature and their opponents who point to nurture.

The pro-nature people are still a minority in universities. But they are a productive and increasingly vocal minority—and one which is beginning to increase its influence in the media. Open the American newspapers and you can read left-inclined pundits like Micky Kaus arguing that income inequality is partly the result of genetic differences. Turn on the television and you can see intelligent, unbigoted people claiming that male homosexuals have a different brain structure from heterosexual men.

This is only the beginning. Richard Herrnstein, a professor of psychology at Harvard University, and Charles Murray, a controversial critic of the welfare state, are collaborating on a study of the implications of biological differences for public policy. The book will highlight the tension between America's egalitarian philosophy and the unequal distribution of innate abilities.

The reaction of orthodox opinion has been scathing. America's National Institutes of Health provoked such an angry response to its decision to finance a conference on genetics and crime that it decided to withdraw the money. Mr Murray lost the patronage of the Manhattan Institute, a New York-based think-tank, when he decided to study individual differences and social policy.

Even in these days of politically correct fetishes, on no other subject is the gulf between academics and ordinary people so wide. Even the most hopeful of parents know that the sentiment "all men are created equal" is a pious dream rather than a statement of fact. They know full well that, say, one of their sons is brighter, or more musical or more athletic than another; they see, despite their best attentions, that girls turn every toy into a doll and boys turn every toy into a weapon; they rarely persist in believing that each and all of these differences is the result of early encouragement or training. They know that even if full equality of opportunity could be guaranteed, equality of outcome could not. Ability is not evenly distributed.

But parents' opinions are unscientific. Not until 1979 did a few academics begin to catch up. In that year the Minnesota Centre for Twin and Adoption Research began to contact more than 100 sets of twins and triplets who had been separated at birth and reared apart, mostly in the United States and Britain.

The centre subjected each pair to thorough psychological and physiological tests. If two twins are identical (or "monozygotic"), any differences between them are due to the environment they were reared in; so a measure of heritability can be attached to various mental features. The study concluded that about 70% of the variance in IQ was explained by genetic factors. It also found that on a large number of measures of personality and temperament—notably personal interests and social attitudes—identical twins reared apart are about as similar as identical twins reared together.

The Minnesota study represents the respectable end of an academic spectrum that stretches all the way through to outright racists. If IQ is 70% inherited, then perhaps much of the IQ difference between

From *The Economist*, December 26, 1992–January 8, 1993, pp. 33-34, 36. © 1993 by The Economist, Ltd. Distributed by The New York Times Special Features.

races is also inherited. The logic does not necessarily follow, since the differences could all lie in the 30% that is nurture; but still it is a hypothesis worth testing—at least for those prepared to risk being called politically incorrect.

Unfortunately, because there are no black-white pairs of identical twins, nobody has yet found a way to test whether racial differences in IQ are genetic. It would require getting 100 pairs of black parents and 100 pairs of white parents to rear their children on identical incomes in an identical suburb and send the children of 50 of each to the same good school and 50 of each to a bad one. Impossible.

This means that racial differences in IQ tend to attract scientists with dubious motives and methods. With increasing enthusiasm over the past decade, some psychologists have disinterred a technique already consigned to the attic by their Victorian predecessors: using physiological data to measure intellectual skill.

Arthur Jensen, a professor of educational psychology at the University of California, Berkeley, has assembled a large body of results purportedly demonstrating that IQ is closely correlated with speed of reaction, a theory abandoned around 1900. He claims that intelligence is correlated with the rate at which glucose is consumed in the brain, the speed of neural transmission and a large number of anatomical variables such as height, brain size and even head size.

Jean Philippe Rushton, a professor of psychology at the University of Western Ontario, Canada, has revived craniometry, the Victorian attempt to correlate head size with brain power. (In "The Adventure of the Blue Carbuncle", one of Arthur Conan Doyle's most ingenious Christmas stories, Sherlock Holmes deduces that a man is an intellectual from the size of his hat: "It is a question of cubic capacity . . . a man with so large a brain must have something in it.")

Mr Rushton has studied data on the head sizes of thousands of American servicemen, gathered to make sure that army helmets fit. Adjusting the raw data for variables such as body size, he argues that men have bigger craniums than women, that the well-educated have bigger craniums than the less educated, and that orientals have bigger craniums than whites, who have bigger craniums than blacks.

Mr Rushton has done wonders for the protest industry. David Peterson, a former premier of Ontario, called for his dismissal. Protesters likened him to the Nazis and the Ku Klux Klan. The Ontario Provincial police even launched an investigation into his work. An embarrassed university establishment required Mr Rushton to give his lectures on videotape.

Even if you could conclude that blacks have lower IQs than whites after the same education, it is not clear what the policy prescription would be. Presumably, it would only add weight to the argument for positive discrimination in favour of blacks, so as to redress an innate inferiority with a better education. The "entitlement liberalism" that prevails in American social policy and finds its expression in employment quotas and affirmative-action programmes already assumes that blacks need preferential rather than equal treatment. Indeed, to this way of thinking, merit is less important than eliminating group differences and promoting social integration.

The gene of Cain

Compared with the study of racial differences, the study of the genetics of criminality is only slightly more respectable. Harvard's Mr Herrnstein teamed up in the early 1980s with James Wilson, a political scientist, to teach a class on crime. The result was "Crime and Human Nature" (1985), a bulky book which argues that the best explanation for a lot of predatory criminal behaviour—particularly assault and arson—may be biological rather than sociological.

Certainly, a Danish study of the children of criminals adopted into normal households lends some support to the idea that a recidivist criminal's son is more likely to be a criminal than other sons brought up in the same household. But Mr Herrnstein and Mr Wilson then spoil their case with another Victorian throwback to "criminal types"—people with low verbal intelligence and "mesomorphic" (short and muscular) bodies who, they believe, are more likely to be criminal.

One reason such work strikes horror into sociologists is that it suggests an obvious remedy: selective breeding. Mr Herrnstein has suggested that the greater fertility of stupid people means that the wrong kind of selective breeding is already at work and may be responsible for falling academic standards. "We ought to bear in mind", Mr Herrnstein ruminates gloomily about America, "that in not too many generations differential fertility could swamp the effects of anything else we may do about our economic standing in the world." Luckily for Mr Herrnstein, studies reveal that, despite teenage parents in the inner cities, people of high social status are still outbreeding those of low social status. Rich men have more surviving children—not least because they tend to have more wives—than poor men.

In one sense, it is plain that criminality is innate: men resort to it far more than women. Martin Daly and Margo Wilson, of McMaster University in Canada, have compared the homicide statistics of England and Wales with those of Chicago. In both cases, the graphs are identical in shape, with young men 30 times as likely as women of all ages to commit homicide. It is perverse to deny the connection between testosterone and innate male aggressiveness. But it is equally perverse to ignore the fact that the scales of the two graphs are utterly different: young men in Chicago are 30 times as likely to kill as young men in England and Wales—which has nothing to do with nature and much to do with nurture. The sexual difference is nature; the national difference is nurture.

The most successful assault on the nurturist orthodoxy, however, has come not over race, or intelligence, or crime, but over sex. In the 1970s the nurturists vigorously repulsed an attack on their cherished beliefs by the then fledgling discipline of sociobiology. Sociobiology is the study of how animal behaviour evolves to fit function in the same way that anatomy does.

When sociobiologists started to apply the same ideas to human beings, principally through Edward Wilson of Harvard University, a furore broke out. Most of them retreated, as geneticists had done, to study animals again. Anthropologists insisted that their subject, mankind, was basically different from animals because it was not born with its behaviour but learnt it.

In the past few years, however, a new assault from scientists calling themselves Darwinian psychologists has largely refuted that argument. Through a series of experiments and analyses, they have asserted that (a) much sophisticated behaviour is not taught, but develops autonomously; and (b) learning is not the opposite of instinct, but is itself a highly directed instinct.

The best example of this is language. In 1957 Noam Chomsky of the Massachusetts Institute of Technology (MIT) argued that all human languages bear a striking underlying similarity. He called this "deep structure", and argued it was innate and not learnt. In recent years Steven Pinker of MIT and Paul Bloom of the University of Arizona have taken this idea further. They argue that human beings have a "language organ", specially designed for learning grammatical language. It includes a series of highly specific inbuilt assumptions that enable them to learn grammar from examples, without ever being taught it.

Hence the tendency to learn grammatical language is human nature. But a child reared in isolation does not start to speak Hebrew unaided. Vocabulary, and accent, are obviously 100% nurture. In this combination of nature and nurture, argue the Darwinian psychologists, language is typical of most human traits. Learning is not the opposite of instinct; people have innate instincts to learn certain things and not others.

This is heresy to sociologists and anthropologists, who have been reared since Emile Durkheim to believe the human mind is a *tabula rasa*—a blank slate upon which any culture can be written. To this, John Tooby and Leda Cosmides of the University of California at Santa Barbara, two leading thinkers on the subject, have replied: "The assertion that 'culture' explains human variation will be taken seriously when there are reports of women war parties raiding villages to capture men as husbands."

Nor will the Darwinian psychologists concede that to believe in nature is to be a Hobbesian fatalist and that to believe in nurture is to be a Rousseau-ist believer in the perfectibility of man. Many totalitarians are actually nurturists: they believe that rearing people to worship Stalin works. History suggests otherwise.

The making of macho

Physiologists have also begun to add weight to the nature side of the scale with their discovery of how the brain develops. The brain of a fetus is altered by the child's genes, by its and its mother's hormones and, after birth, by its learning. Many of the changes are permanent; so as far as the adult is concerned, they are all "nature", though many are not genetic. For example, the human brain is feminine unless acted upon by male hormones during two bursts—one in the womb and another at puberty. The hormone is nurture, in the sense that it can be altered by injections or drugs taken by the mother. But it is nature in the sense that it is a product of the body's biology.

This discovery has gradually altered the views of many psychologists about sex and education. An increasing number recognise that the competitiveness, roughness, mathematical ability and spatial skills of boys are the product of their biology (genes and hormones) not their family, and that the character-reading, verbal, linguistic and emotional interest and skills of girls are also biological. Hence girls get a better early education when kept away from boys. This conclusion, anathema to most practising educational psychologists, is increasingly common among those who actually do research on it.

Indeed, radical feminism is increasingly having to recognize the biological theme that underlies its claims. Feminists demand equality of opportunity, but they also routinely argue that women bring different qualities to the world: consensus-seeking, uncompetitive, caring, gentle qualities that inherently domineering men lack. Women, they argue, should be in Parliament or Congress in representative numbers to "represent the woman's point of view", which assumes that men cannot.

Many homosexuals have already crossed the bridge to nature. When sociobiologists first suggested that homosexuality might be biological, they were called Nazis and worse. But in the past few years things have turned around completely. The discovery that the identical twin of a homosexual man has an odds-on chance of being homosexual too, whereas a non-identical twin has only a one-in-five chance, implies that there are some influential genes involved. And the discovery that those parts of the brain that are measurably different in women and men are also different in heterosexuals and homosexuals adds further weight to the idea that homosexuality is as natural as left-handedness. That is anathema to pro-family-value conservatives, who believe that homosexuality is a (misguided) personal choice.

Assuming that the new hereditarians are right and that many human features can be related to genes (or, more likely, groups of genes), it might one day be possible to equip each member of the species with a compact disc telling him which version of each of the 50,000-100,000 human genes he has. He might then read whether he was likely to have a weight problem, or be any good at music, whether there was a risk of schizophrenia or a chance of genius, whether he might go manic-depressive or be devoutly religious. But he could never be sure. For beside every gene would be an asterisk referring to a footnote that read thus: "This prediction is only valid if you are brought up by two Protestant, middle-class, white parents in Peoria, Illinois."

Making Babies

*The Boom in the Infertility Business Is Raising Hopes,
and Increasing Criticism*

[handwritten: not right word?]

Nancy Wartik

Nancy Wartik, who lives in Brooklyn, N. Y., is a contributing editor for American Health *magazine.*

In his spotless embryology lab at the Center for Reproductive Medicine at Century City Hospital, David Hill is peering into the viewer of a formidable-looking microscope, trying to make a baby. On a monitor next to the scope is the vastly magnified image of a woman's egg—smaller, in reality, than a tiny speck of dust—and of the microscopic suction rod holding it in place. Right now, Hill's attention is on the semen sample next to the egg. With his right hand, he's manipulating controls that send a needle far finer than a hair chasing after what looks to be a batch of teeny, wriggling long-tailed polliwogs.

"The best sperm tend to go off to the edge and go around and around the drop like little race cars," Hill says as he hunts down a pack of them. "It's very fortuitous for embryologists."

When he's zeroed in on the sperm he wants, Hill draws them up into the needle by sucking on a rubber mouthpiece that's connected to a slender hose and clenched between his teeth—an oddly low-tech note in this whole sophisticated operation. After he's drawn some 50 sperm into the needle, he moves it over to the egg and presses down against its translucent outer shell (the *zona pellucida*). Under the pressure of the needle, the egg squashes in on itself alarmingly, like a beach ball poked with a stick. But as soon as Hill punctures the *zona pellucida,* deposits a fraction of the sperm and retracts the needle, the egg springs back into shape. Beneath its cloudy shell, the sperm buzz madly about like trapped insects.

The procedure he's just completed is a subzonal insertion, usually known by its friendly acronym, SUZI. Eggs and sperm that Hill manipulate in this way can't, for one reason or another, achieve fertilization on their own. So he's helping them bypass the arduous trek to conception. The sperm-injected eggs (usually a total of seven or eight for each couple) go into an incubator and are maintained at body temperature for 14 to 18 hours. Depending on the number that make the leap to embryo status, about four of the best quality will be loaded into a catheter and inserted into the woman's womb.

"I can't wait to come into the lab, open up the incubator and see whether any of our efforts have resulted in decent embryos," says Hill. "It's just like opening a little Christmas present. I never get tired of it."

In Hill's sterilized lab, surrounded by the tools of his trade, it's easy to lose sight of what's actually happening. For couples who come to Century City, as to a fast-growing number of similar clinics around the country, these procedures represent a last chance to achieve a desire as old as human history: that of giving birth to a child. On behalf of these couples, Hill is waging a daily battle of technology against nature. And despite a swelling arsenal of controversial new techniques and procedures, nature usually wins.

Three years ago, John Taylor [this name and those of the other patients have been changed] got the call from his doctor, just before a weekend business trip to New Orleans. After months of trying unsuccessfully to conceive, John and his wife, Leslie, had sought medical help. Now they were awaiting results of his sperm test. The voice at the other end of the line had bad news. "The doctor told me I had absolutely no sperm," recalls Taylor, 36, a television lighting designer.

"The two of us stood in the kitchen and bawled our eyes out. I was destroyed. I felt emasculated. I come from a large family, and the fact that I'd never be able to have my own children—never, there wasn't a hope in hell—was devastating."

From *Los Angeles Times Magazine,* March 6, 1994, pp. 18-21, 42-46. © 1994 by Nancy Wartik. Reprinted by permission of the author.

At the end of his weekend trip, in a bizarre twist of events, Taylor returned to hear that there had been a mix-up at the lab, and he did have a sperm count. But it was low, the doctor warned him; pregnancy would still be problematic. "If the guy had been standing there, I'd have decked him for putting me through all that," he says. "But I was also pleased. At least he'd given us back some hope."

Today, $20,000 poorer and their insurance coverage for infertility exhausted, the Taylors wonder whether there was much point in those hopes being raised. Both partners have undergone surgery to correct reproductive-tract problems; each has tried fertility drugs. They've tried timed insemination, with John's sperm inserted directly into Leslie's uterus when ultrasound scanning showed she was ovulating. Twice they've attempted, and failed at, "test tube" conception at Century City. To cut costs on the pricey medication a woman takes during such attempts, they've journeyed to Tijuana to purchase their drugs at cut-rate prices.

Running the gantlet of these treatments has "put an incredible strain on our marriage," says Taylor. "Frankly, I'm surprised we're still together. In many respects, our lives have been on hold with this thing for three years."

In a few months, the Taylors will return to Century City to try a new procedure developed in Belgium that Hill has recently begun working on. The ultimate refinement of existing sperm-injection methods, it involves shooting a single sperm directly into the heart of an egg and seems to produce higher fertilization rates than multiple-sperm procedures such as SUZI; the Belgian clinic that first used it is now claiming pregnancy rates of more than 30%.

This could be the Taylors' winning ticket in the baby lottery. But Leslie, 38, a small, jeans-clad TV director who sits curled on the sofa in their North Hollywood home, is tiring of the demands of the pregnancy chase. "I only want to try direct injection once," says Leslie. "John wants to try it twice. I'm emotionally and physically beyond it. I've been on hormone injections for three solid months; I feel fat and bloated and like I could cry at the drop of a hat. Why is it that we cannot conceive a child? Why?"

"It can make you feel guilty," says John. "You look back over your life, you say: 'I've always tried to be a decent person. Did I do something wrong? Is God trying to punish me? Was it my lifestyle?'"

He's not willing to give up, however, and his determination is carrying both of them. "All through this, we've had a willingness to fight, not to take the first defeat and say, 'OK, it's over,'" he says. "When you start something like this, you've got to finish. Otherwise you spend the rest of your life wondering 'What if?' I'm still not convinced we're finished."

To Leslie, he adds, "I won't ask for more than two tries. But you go in every time thinking, this is the time it's going to work."

More often than not, however, you'll be wrong.

Inside the administrative offices at the Century City reproductive clinic, which occupies part of a floor in this small private hospital, are homey touches: stuffed animals nesting on file cabinets, a sign that reads "Never give up!" On the outer walls hang photos of children conceived as a result of treatment here and letters from their grateful parents. There is praise for the "incredible staff" at Century City, and the word *miracle* shows up often.

Each year, more than 300 couples come here seeking children. For many, it's a court of last appeal, after months or years of lower-tech efforts such as drugs or surgery have failed. In general, those who choose high-tech conception follow a similar regimen. A woman begins with daily injections of powerful hormone-regulating drugs to stimulate her ovaries to mature more eggs than the single one that normally matures each month. If the therapy succeeds, the crop of eggs—about 10 on average but in some cases more than 30—is "harvested." While a patient is under local or general anesthesia, a doctor inserts a needle either vaginally or through an incision in the stomach to suck the eggs from her ovaries.

In regular in-vitro fertilization (IVF), eggs are then combined in a petri dish with the sperm sample, fresh or frozen, that a man has dutifully provided. In gamete intra-Fallopian transfer (GIFT), developed as a slightly more "natural" alternative to IVF—eggs and sperm don't unite in glassware, but are inserted together into the Fallopian tubes. The resulting embryos are transferred into the uterus, the Fallopian tubes or, sometimes, both. At many IVF centers, extra embryos now can be frozen, meaning a woman doesn't have to go through the stressful process of an egg retrieval at each attempt.

Louise Brown, the first baby conceived through IVF, was born in Britain in 1978. Three years later, the first American high-tech baby was born at a Norfolk, Va., clinic. Since then, the infertility business in the United States has mushroomed into a $2-billion-a-year enterprise, much of its expansion spurred by the development of assisted reproductive technologies, including IVF and the many different methods it has spawned for manipulating eggs and sperm outside the body. It is, at best, an imperfect science—expensive, unregulated and relatively untested, especially in the area of long-term effects.

But the market for reproductive technologies is sizable. According to the National Center for Health Statistics, about 2.3 million married American couples are infertile (meaning they haven't been able to conceive after a year or more of trying). For up to 15% of them, according to the American Fertility Society, high-tech approaches are considered the only hope. With the U.S. government disinclined to allocate research dollars to a politically touchy area such as reproductive technology, this country has lagged behind Australia and parts of Europe—but not too far. There are now about 350 U.S. infertility clinics, including at least two multi-state chains; at least 45 reproductive clinics that perform IVF and other assisted technologies are crowded into California alone. More than 33,000 assisted-reproductive-technology procedures were initiated in 1991, the last year for which figures are available, up 30% from 1990.

Originally used only to treat blocked tubes, assisted reproductive technologies are now applied to a range of female infertility problems, including endometriosis, ovulatory disorders and the catch-all condition of "unexplained infertility." More recently, researchers have zeroed in on male infertility. Women had long been accorded the lion's share of the blame when a marriage was barren, but when reproductive specialists peered closely into their petri dishes, they discovered that the man was wholly or partly responsible for a couple's problem 40% to 60% of the time.

For some men, approaches that range from eschewing hot tubs to undergoing corrective surgery will do the trick. But others have sperm that are so few in number, sluggish, malformed or otherwise defective that doctors could do nothing but point them toward the nearest sperm bank—until recently. In the late 1980s, embryologists found it was possible to aid recalcitrant sperm in fertilization by opening the egg's outer shell to give the sperm easier access. This type of "micromanipulation," known as partial zona dissection, was followed by SUZI. Then, in 1992, came the Belgians' encouraging announcement of intracytoplasmic sperm injection, or ICSI (pronounced ICK-see by those in the field), the no-nonsense technique in which a single sperm is propelled to the egg's center.

"It's actually somewhat surprising the technique works," admits Jacques Cohen, scientific director of assisted reproduction at New York City's Cornell Medical Center and a pioneer in the development of micromanipulation. "We used to think there was a certain sequence of processes that was absolutely necessary before the sperm was able to fertilize the egg. Now we know that's not true; those processes can be completely surpassed."

As these dazzling technologies establish themselves as the wave of the future, troubling issues surround their use. Most conspicuous are the ethical dilemmas that seem to grab headlines weekly. There is much outrage at the idea of 60-year-old women becoming mothers and apprehension that scientists might soon start using eggs from aborted fetuses to produce babies—meaning that a child could have a biological mother who was never born. And last fall, two U.S. scientists "cloned" a human embryo, making an exact genetic copy of the original and raising the specter of an assembly-line baby-manufacturing industry.

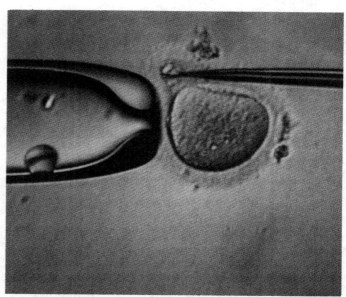

The needle on the right contains a semen sample to be inserted into the egg, center.

But at the moment, these issues don't apply in clinical practice—or apply to only a tiny handful of those who visit programs. (Realistically, not many 60-year-old women crave new motherhood.) For most infertile couples, the considerations are more mundane: In 1991, only 15% of individual attempts at test-tube conception produced what's known in the field as a "take-home baby"—with figures higher or lower depending on the procedure and the patient involved.

'The door never completely closes on the infertile couple,' says David Hill. 'They can end up childless and financially depleted.'

If success rates are low, however, prices are not. A completed attempt (some women drop out early because they don't respond to initial hormone therapy) ranges from $8,000 to $13,000 or more. Lumped into the category of "luxury" treatments such as tummy-tucks or orthodontia, assisted reproductive technologies in many cases are not covered, or only minimally covered, by insurance. And there's no money-back guarantee.

In worst-case scenarios, patients run up huge tabs in repeated futile efforts to have a baby. "The door never, ever completely closes on an infertile couple," acknowledges Hill. "There's always the latest snazzy technique to rekindle hope. They can end up at the end of the line childless and financially depleted."

Contemplating this scenario, a small but vocal number of critics, several of them on Capitol Hill, have raised their voices in a growing chorus of complaint.

Too often, they say, the assisted-reproductive-technology field is battening on emotional desperation. "The technology doesn't work," says Ann Pappert, who's working on a book to be titled "Cruel Promises: Inside the Reproductive Industry," and one of a group of experts who attended a 1990 World Health Organization policy conference on IVF. "A lot of couples go into it thinking: 'All right, I know the reality but I'm going to be the exception.' I've heard that over and over and over again. The whole technology is presented in a manner that encourages them to think that way. A lot of clinics, the way they talk to the patients sort of pumps them up to keep going back. It's a business, and like any business, you have to keep your clients coming.

"How many people would go to an IVF clinic if they read that 85% of couples go home without a baby?" she asks. "It's not that I think clinics should only emphasize the negative, but there isn't a balanced picture presented. If you go to your OB-GYN, does he have a wall of baby pictures? It's a form of emotional manipulation."

Advocates of reproductive technology see things differently. Diane Aronson, executive director of the Somerville, Mass.-based national infertility consumer group RESOLVE, came to the organization years ago with her own problems. "These couples may be in a vulnerable position, but that doesn't mean they're not thinking, rational folks," she says. "Plenty of people decide, 'IVF is not for me.' That's their option. But everyone should have the right to become informed about IVF, to assess the risk and evaluate it for themselves." The question, though, is whether couples have a chance to make a truly informed decision. Does the data exist to help them weigh whether the short- and long-term risks are worth the potential benefit? Many in the field admit that the answer is no.

In 1989, the Canadian government assembled a royal commission to come up with guidelines and funding recommendations for the country's use of reproductive technology. The commissioners reviewed hundreds of studies from international research on the use of reproductive technologies for infertility problems. Last year, they concluded that only one procedure—standard IVF for treatment of blocked tubes—had been proven in studies to give women a better chance of birth—about 10% per attempt—than no treatment at all. It recommended that no other form of the procedure get health-care coverage.

The commission didn't say whether IVF works for other types of infertility, or that procedures such as GIFT or micromanipulation are not effective. But, says Dr. Patricia Baird of the University of British Columbia in Vancouver, the pediatrician and geneticist who headed the inquiry, "we were really rather disturbed by the quality of the studies out there. Many of them have methodological weaknesses or small sample sizes. There's a real hodgepodge of women being treated, so you can't judge what the success rate is for different categories of diagnosis. There may be categories for which it's really not doing any good, and we need to sort that out, because IVF is invasive and expensive, and there are risks involved."

She adds: "It seems to us that everything except IVF for blocked tubes should be offered in the context of research trials, in which women are told these aren't proven treatments. They shouldn't have to pay, and they should have full information and informed consent."

The World Health Organization also has criticized the profit-driven proliferation of reproductive technology in countries around the globe and called for more clinical trials. Ask Dr. Maria Bustillo, current president of the Society for Assisted Reproductive Technology, if the United States should begin offering these in the context of clinical trials, and she laughs.

"I'd love it," says Bustillo, who is the director of reproductive endocrinology at Mt. Sinai Medical Center in New York. "I'd love to be able to go back and do some really basic studies. It would be wonderful if people didn't have to pay these high costs, when we don't yet have the data to give them answers. But we can't even get money for doing basic research on endometriosis. Where would we get the dollars to do this?

"A lot of things in medicine related to women's health get started and adopted without sufficient study; the purse strings have not been controlled by women.

But without the data that clinical trials would provide, reproductive centers are operating in a questionably gray area. For example, programs typically tell couples that their odds of giving birth stay the same for each IVF attempt, up through the fourth try (after which birth rates are known to dip precipitously). That may, in fact, not be so. A 1992 study by a Yale University professor, frustrated at his own and his wife's failure with multiple attempts, suggests that the chance of pregnancy drops even before the fourth try. Of 571 women who started treatment at Yale, 13% got pregnant on the first attempt, 10.7% succeeded on the second go-round, 6.9% on the third and 4.3% on the fourth. Edward H. Kaplan, professor of management sciences and of medicine at Yale, who authored the study, is cautious about applying his results to other clinics, but he believes that "you could end up spending a whole lot of money trying to get pregnant when the chance is really very small."

Roberta Geist, 43 and a real estate agent, *has* spent a whole lot of money—more than $30,000—trying to get pregnant. She's tried GIFT once and IVF once. At the moment, she's lying in a Century City recovery room after her third egg retrieval; she's preparing to try IVF again. Geist's chances of pregnancy, she's been told, are 10% to 14%. "While you have your period, you can still have a child," she says hopefully. "This should work."

Married at 38, Geist discovered after a year of trying

to conceive that her tubes were blocked, her hormonal levels not optimal. "My husband won't let me adopt," Geist says. But she very much wants a baby. "I have that maternal instinct now," she says. "I want to be a mother. I'd love for this to work. If it doesn't, I don't know, I'll deal with it, but. . . ." A nurse standing nearby gives Geist a hug. "This is going to work," she says.

It doesn't. In fact, a month later, after her fourth failed attempt, Geist gave up on the idea of genetic motherhood and was going to try again with a donor egg.

Further complicating the picture for patients confronting the assisted-reproductive technology labyrinth is the dramatic fluctuation in take home baby rates from clinic to clinic. Rates can vary from less than 5% at some programs to a high of more than 30% at others, according to Dr. David Meldrum, director of the Center for Advanced Reproductive Care at South Bay Hospital in Redondo Beach. "These are very complex procedures, with many different variables," Meldrum says. "The research hasn't been done yet that will show you, you must do this particular thing at this particular time to get the best results. Without that knowledge, each program varies in the small details that make the difference between success and lack of it."

He adds: "I've visited programs having great difficulty. They have individuals trying extremely hard to have a good outcome, they're very well trained, they're in agony, and yet it's difficult to put your finger on exactly where the problem is."

Couples can improve their odds by using groups like RESOLVE or the resources of the American Fertility Society to get success rate data on clinics that register with the society (most do). But checking on a particular clinic's rates in that manner still won't reveal how many of those who signed on at the clinic actually took a baby home, because the group presents such rates in terms of how many births a program has had, per egg retrieval, rather than in terms of births per started attempt.

"About 15% of women don't get to egg retrieval, but those failures are discounted as if they never happened," notes Michael Katz, a supervisory investigative specialist with the Division of Service Industry Practices at the Federal Trade Commission. "The [American Fertility Society] position is that the whole process doesn't start until the egg is recovered. Our position is that the process starts when the consumer begins kicking over dollars; those drugs cost quite a bit of money."

In recent years, the FTC, virtually the only agency to watchdog these clinics, has chastised several for representing their success rates in a misleading way, exacting promises from each to practice truth-in-advertising. But that's virtually as much outside regulation as the industry has been subject to. Although a voluntary lab accreditation program was recently initiated by the Society for Assisted Reproductive Technology, nothing currently mandates that IVF labs be licensed or prove their competency in any way.

That could change. In 1992, Congress approved a bill scheduled to go into effect at the end of this year that gives each state the option to require that its IVF programs be licensed according to a national standard. It also demands that such clinics annually report success rates—including numbers of started attempts as well as of egg retrievals—to the government. Still, Rep. Ron Wyden (D-Ore.), who sponsored the initial bill, refers to it as "baby steps," and some complain that because clinic licensing won't be federally administered, the law has no teeth in it.

Such minimal scrutiny, combined with a technology evolving at warp speed, and stiff competition (billboards, radio spots, ads in upscale magazines designed to win business) to attract the minority of infertile couples who can afford assisted reproductive techniques, leaves a margin for abuse.

The new ICSI procedure could be a case in point. In Britain, embryologists who want to use it must prove their competence, then apply for a treatment license. In the United States, any lab that wants to offer the technique can do so. Last fall, the procedure won its 15 minutes of fame here, touted in headlines and on "Donahue" and "Eye to Eye With Connie Chung," as the panacea for male infertility. "In big urban centers, people will call around to clinics asking, 'Do you offer it?'" notes Barry Behr, director of the human embryology and andrology lab at Stanford University. "If you say no, they'll call elsewhere. It's a rat race; you almost have to stay one-up on the program down the road to get business."

As the hype flew, embryologists from around the country took off to Brussels to do a workshop at the clinic where ICSI had been developed. They returned to the United States with certificates to hang on their walls, stating that they'd taken the course. Yet, says micromanipulation pioneer Jacques Cohen of Cornell, "I'm afraid it is going to be used quite wrongly by most programs. It's one of the most difficult technologies I've ever been involved with. A lot of people think you can just take a needle, put a sperm in it and stick it in the egg. But you need the expertise to apply the procedure correctly."

Century City's David Hill, who spent several days studying the procedure at Reproductive Biology Associates in Atlanta, where the first U.S. ICSI baby was born last fall, readily admits that he's still straddling a learning curve. The fertilization rates he's getting aren't better yet than those with SUZI. "It is more challenging than other micromanipulation procedures," says Hill, "but we won't charge extra for it until I've gotten three pregnancies. As I feel more comfortable with it, we may slowly, slowly start using it in lieu of SUZI."

Not all clinics may be that circumspect. Behr also fears that some programs will move straight to prescribing this more high-tech, and pricey, treatment for infertile couples when lower-tech solutions might do instead. That sort of practice, he adds, is relatively common. "It's one of the big controversies in the field today: At what point do you resort to these aggressive, invasive procedures?" he asks. "Some labs claim success using these aggressive treatments, while others can have success without them. In my mind, it's when you don't have to resort to pulling out every stop that you're doing a good job."

Today is a good day at Century City; there have been two positive pregnancy tests. Although the chance of a miscarriage during assisted-reproductive-technology pregnancies is 25% (slightly higher than the percentage in the general population), positive tests are still cause for rejoicing. "I have a whistle I blow when someone gets pregnant," embryologist David Hill says. "I used to take Polaroids of myself doing handstands, but I stopped because of my back."

Hill's concern for the patients he works with is evident. Why aren't they getting pregnant? he says of the Taylors. I wish I knew. If I could bleed a pint of my own blood to get them pregnant, I would do it. In this business, that's not an infrequent feeling."

Now sitting behind his desk, Hill is contemplating another troubling subject. Early last year, a collaborative study by epidemiologists from around the country suggested that the hormones used to stimulate women's ovaries to release extra eggs might raise their risk for ovarian cancer. Let's assume for the sake of argument that there is an inherent risk," says Hill. "Now I happen not to believe it. I think no study yet clearly shows that association. But let's say there was an association. This may still be something patients are willing to undertake, as long as they have a realistic estimate of the ratio of risk to benefit."

The problem is, the information doesn't exist to help patients make that assessment. Moreover, Robert Spirtas, chief of the contraceptive and reproductive evaluation branch at the National Institutes of Health, disagrees that this particular study should be discounted. He admits that the research had methodological flaws because the author had limited data. Still, he says, "the study raises an issue that we had really better look at" and notes that the institute plans to fund its own study on ovarian cancer and fertility drugs, which millions of American women have now taken.

To date, the potential risks of reproductive technologies have gone virtually unexplored. In 1990, the World Health Organization sharply criticized the infertility community for doing more research on "new and expanded uses for the technology" than its effects on women using it, or on their children.

"This is one vast clinical trial, and no one is monitoring it," says author Ann Pappert. "No one has a clue about what the long-term effects of these technologies will be on the babies or on women, and nobody's doing much to try to find out. The whole history of reproductive medicine is filled with these breakthroughs that, 10 or 20 years down the road, fill hospitals with patients having breast implants or IUDs removed, or DES problems [related to the drug given to pregnant women in the '50s that caused cancer in some of their daughters]. The truth is that instead of waking up after the fact, we should stop now and see if we're creating another problem."

With 23,000 high-tech babies born in this country, the American Fertility Society puts the birth defect rate in these children at less than 3%, a figure equivalent to that in the general population. Preliminary data from Australia, however, suggests that the rate of certain defects may be elevated in high-tech babies. Moreover, about one in three assisted reproductive-technology babies is a multiple birth—twins, triplets or, rarely, a higher number—a result of transferring several embryos at once into a woman's reproductive tract. Children of multiple births are significantly likelier to suffer a range of health and developmental problems that can be a consequence, as pediatrician and geneticist Patricia Baird puts it, "of being born too soon and too small."

And the advent of micromanipulation has raised an entirely new series of concerns. For some years, scientists have subscribed to a theory of natural selection to explain why 200 million or more sperm are in the average ejaculate when only one is needed to fertilize the egg. The thinking has been that it's the hardiest sperm that helps create a human being. But when an embryologist assumes godlike stature by arbitrarily selecting that single sperm from a marginal batch, it stands the concept of natural selection on its head. Critics fear that the children of ICSI could be the products of a conception not "meant" to occur.

IVF practitioners disagree. "Natural selection is baloney," scoffs Michael Tucker, scientific director of Reproductive Biology Associates. "The female reproductive tract is not an assault course, OK? It's not simply that Sparky Sperm, the biggest, meanest, toughest one, runs the marathon and gets to the top of the egg first. Other than the simple fact that sperm move toward the egg, the fertility event is close to being random."

Still, Tucker concedes it would have been preferable if direct injection could have been tested in animals before being used in people. Earlier forms of micromanipulation were evaluated on non-human subjects, but ICSI is tricky to perform with animal sperm and eggs. In Belgium, where efforts are under way to track

ICSI babies into young adulthood, rates of genetic defects seem to be no higher than in the general population. And for the most part, geneticists agree that a sperm can be malformed or sluggish without those attributes affecting its chromosomal content. Still, they point out that the generation of male children produced by micromanipulation is likely to endure its own infertility problems.

Patricia Olds-Clark, a Temple University medical school geneticist who is studying a mouse model of infertility, says: "Their sperm are carrying genes that won't allow the sperm of their sons to fertilize in a normal way. And what's true in mice is going to be true in humans."

Moreover, Cornell's Jacques Cohen admits that there may be "problem groups" for whom micromanipulation is riskier. "Patients with unexplained fertilization failure who come to micromanipulation because regular IVF didn't work may have an increased incidence of congenital malformations," he notes. "But those patients are rare, and they are counseled accordingly." At least, they are at Cornell. Whether other clinics tell similar patients of this risk is not clear.

The Society for Assisted Reproductive Technology's Maria Bustillo has heard it all before. She knows that when the negative side of the assisted-reproductive-technology balance sheet is totaled up, it smacks of a conspiracy being perpetrated by avaricious doctors on hapless couples. But she doesn't buy that point of view.

'You can tell a patient till your face is blue that her chances are less than 2%,' says Maria Bustillo. 'Then she goes through with it.'

"We make a mistake if we just blame the providers of this technology," she insists. "A lot of this is patient-driven. You have a couple in front of you, she's 43 with a borderline FSH level (a hormonal measure) and you tell her till your face is blue that her chances of having a baby are less than 2% with IVF. And she goes through with it and gets an embryo or two, then wants to do it all again. Do I withhold that, as a doctor? If I do, they may go and get worse treatment somewhere else."

In fact, infertile couples themselves remain among the most ardent defenders of their right to persevere in the face of slender odds or possible risks. Between 1990

and 1992, Maria DiPaulo, 40, of Queens, N.Y., and her husband, Stan, 41, tried IVF seven times, thanks to insurance that paid all but $4,000 of their $70,000 in medical bills. The two knew their chances would plummet after attempt No. 4. But, says Maria, "I wouldn't have cared if it was just a 1% chance." She was also aware, since she repeatedly mainlined hormones, that "there could be repercussions in the years to come from all the drugs I took. But I guess I think about today; I don't worry about that far down the road. You get so set on doing whatever you can to make this pregnancy happen that risk isn't an obvious factor anymore."

The DiPaulos, who recently adopted a little girl, say that as frustrating as their experience was, it was ultimately a positive one. "I think we never could have adopted if we hadn't gone through all this," Tony says. "It meant a lot to say we did everything we could."

Then there's Terry Matthews [her real name], 33, a New Hampshire travel agent who was born with only one ovary and lost the other to a cyst at age 24. Matthews, who tried to adopt but couldn't find an available birth mother, was told that, using a donor egg, she had a 30% to 35% likelihood of success—a decent gamble. But she says slimmer odds wouldn't have deterred her. "When you make these decisions, they're not based on facts and figures; it's pure emotion," she says. "I don't know how low they would have had to have gone for me to say forget it—10%, 5%? I don't know. This was the only chance I had to have a child." In November, 1992, on a second IVF attempt, she gave birth to a boy, from her sister's donor egg.

Ultimately, not even the sternest critics believe the IVF industry should grind to a halt. "I'm not calling for a moratorium," says author Pappert. "I just think there needs to be a hell of a lot more work done on determining the safety margin and on deciding who really needs it. And there needs to be more supervision."

As for the Taylors, their determination to try ICSI hasn't wavered, but their focus is shifting slightly. As they prepare to return to Century City, they're also beginning the paperwork for adoption proceedings. "You grow up, as a woman, envisioning yourself going through the process of giving birth to a child that is biologically yours and your husband's," says Leslie. "I think that physical void will probably always exist, but from what I understand, when they put a baby in your arms, it's yours."

Adds John: "It's difficult. We're definitely going to give it another shot. But time keeps passing. We want an end to this. And I think this year we'll see that. One way or another. I think by the end of the year, we'll have a child."

Do You Hear
What I Hear?

SHARON BEGLEY

She slides into the world with eyes alert, the tiny ridges of her ears living antennae scanning the conversation frequencies in the room. She finds her mother's voice with her ears, and then her eyes. Her cheek feels the sweaty chest, she hears the calming heartbeat that has been her Muzak for nine months, she turns her face, and sucks. Surely the infant could not have learned to recognize her mother's voice, resonate to her heartbeat, and find food in the few short minutes since birth?

Surely not. Once scientists discovered over the last 25 years that newborns can learn and understand, remember and recognize, it was only a short leap to asking when and how those talents bloomed in utero. Life in the womb represents the next frontier for studies of human development, and the early explorations of that frontier—through ultrasound, fiber-optic cameras, miniature microphones—have yielded startling discoveries. Scientists have found hints of consciousness in 7-month-old fetuses and measured brain-wave patterns like those during dreaming in 8-month-olds. They have pushed sentience back to the end of the second trimester and shown that fetuses can learn. Some research has been sensationalized and used to support prenatal "universities" that purport to teach fetuses words, numbers and letters. That is doubly unfortunate, for with no hype at all the fetus can rightly be called a marvel of cognition, consciousness and sentience.

After 28 weeks in utero, the fetus can hear—the rumbling of the mother's intestines and stomach, the whoosh of blood through her arteries. Walls of fat and muscle between fetus and outside world cut the volume by about 30 decibels, says Dr. Denis Querleu of the Hospital of Roubaix, France, who placed a tiny microphone in the uterus. Bass sounds penetrate better than treble, with the result that "it sounds like Lauren Bacall talking from behind a heavy curtain," says psychologist Anthony J. DeCasper of the University of North Carolina. "But the melody of language is still conveyed almost intact." By

> **With no hype at all, the fetus can rightly be called a marvel of cognition, consciousness and sentience**
> ———

the third trimester, the fetus can respond to sound. Car horns can make a fetus jump and its heartbeat, pulsing since the fourth week, quicken. Pregnant women have had to flee fortissimi concerts to calm their kicking, punching passengers. "But if we repeat the loud noise many times, there is less cardiac reaction," finds Querleu.

That lack of response, called habituation, is primitive learning. Sea slugs are quite adept at it. Still, it shows that a fetus is retaining the memory of experience and altering its behavior as a result. Some memories inscribed in the brain can even be retrieved after birth. When Peter Hepper of Queen's University in Belfast repeatedly played to 30-week-old fetuses the theme song from a popular soap opera, they relaxed. After birth the babies became "quite alert" when they heard the tune, says Hepper. Nor is hearing limited to music. When DeCasper and associate William Fifer rigged up a nipple and a two-track tape recorder so that one pattern of sucking played the mother's voice while another rhythm produced a stranger's, eight out of 10 newborns sucked to hear Mom.

Voices sound so different in the womb that the baby is almost surely remembering not pitch or intonation but rhythm. When DeCasper and associate Melanie Spence had 16 pregnant women read aloud "The Cat in the Hat" to their abdomens twice a day for the last six and a half weeks of pregnancy, the babies later modified their sucking patterns to make the tape machine play the Dr. Seuss tale, not a verse with a different meter. Says DeCasper, "It's the first direct demonstration that human speech has a discernible effect on the fetus."

Such findings are music to the ears of companies selling "prelearning" tapes and prenatal "universities." In a typical program, expectant parents intone numbers, letters, words and colors like mantras. Although anecdotal reports from delighted parents tell of 1-year-olds who play piano and 14-year-olds with IQs above 235, researchers are skeptical. Says DeCasper, "The promises of extra prenatal stimulation are simply guesses stemming from the unwarranted gen-

A fetus remembers some experiences and may alter its behavior as a result

eralization of selected findings, ill-conceived theories of human development, faulty logic, anecdotal information and a dose of hubris."

Even in its cramped chamber, the fetus can perform like an acrobat. It begins to move spontaneously at seven weeks, to open and close its mouth by the 11th week, to grasp its hands at 12 weeks, to frown and squint and grimace and suck its thumb by the fourth or fifth month. It moves in response "to touch, sound and light, and is becoming more attuned to the world," says psychologist Darwin W. Muir of Queen's University in Ontario. At 12 to 16 weeks, if its foot or hand grazes its body, it responds by jerking back in an uncoordinated way; by 24 weeks, as its nervous system becomes connected, it moves only what was touched. Whether the fetus is tranquil or restless may correlate with its future personality: anecdotal evidence hints that extremely active fetuses will be unusually anxious children. Whatever makes them respond to sound or motion with violent somersaulting rather than a gentle kick may also shape them into shy, fretful children, withdrawn from a world of unwanted stimuli.

By six weeks, the brain is visible and electrically active; by eight, it has the convoluted folds and shape of an adult brain. About 100,000 nerve cells sprout every minute until, by birth, there are 1 billion. Mother's movements stimulate the fetus's balance and motion detectors. Babies deprived of this movement, as when a high-risk woman is confined to bed, may lag behind in sensory-motor development. "Neural pathways that the child will use to think and remember are being laid down in the womb," says Dr. Mortimer Rosen of Columbia University College of Physicians and Surgeons. By the start of the last trimester the brain's neural circuits are as advanced as a newborn's, capable of paying attention and discriminating new from old. When a loudspeaker directs speech syllables at a mother-to-be's abdomen, the fetus's heart slows, a sign of attentiveness. The heartbeat speeds up as the fetus gets bored with the sounds, then slows again if new ones flow into the womb.

Light penetrates the womb, but dimly: the brightest is toned down to a diffuse orange glow. A midterm fetus will try to shield its closed eyes from the shining of a probe. The eyes open at about the 26th week, and from then on will open and close as the fetus sleeps and wakens. After 32 weeks, the fetus spends half its time in REM sleep, the brain state associated with dreaming. If the fetus feels a contraction of the uterus, or any other stimulus, it can be disturbed from REM and enter a period of quiet sleep, its brain activity dampened. In this way, says Dr. Peter Nathanielsz of Cornell University, "these constantly changing features of the fetal environment may play an important role in brain development."

Perhaps the strongest means of communication between mother and fetus is hormonal. Stress hormones cross the placenta and "may affect fetal development, the level of excitability and brain development," says Nathanielsz. They could even be responsible for effects that mothers, and researchers, attribute to sound: if Mom hears a jackhammer, her adrenaline levels may surge. That will be transmitted to the fetus, whose somersaults can then be blamed not on the noise but on the chemical. Because the fetal brain is immature, little short of starvation or exposure to toxic substances is likely to leave an indelible mark.

After nine months, the fetus speaks back. Research on sheep suggests that "the fetus plays a major role in controlling the onset of labor," says Nathanielsz. In response to signals from its brain, the fetus's pituitary gland pumps out the hormone ACTH, which stimulates its adrenal cortex to grow and secrete a hormone which, after several steps, stimulates the uterus to contract. Labor begins. The fetus is about to move from its twilit antechamber into the glare of the outside world.

With TESSA NAMUTH *in New York and bureau reports*

See How They Grow

At eight weeks
the embryo, about 1.5 inches long, has all its organs in place and is now called a fetus. Its heart has been beating for a month; limbs, hands and feet have taken shape. A week before, neural cells in the brain began to connect. The fetus moves.

By four months
the fetus frowns, moves its lips, turns its head. Its hands grasp, its feet kick. The first signs of hair have appeared. In a female fetus, all 5 million ova have formed.

In the seventh month
the fetus has a chance for survival if it is born prematurely. Its eyes have opened and can perceive light. It processes and responds to sound. In a month, its brain will have as many cells as it will have at birth.

In the ninth month
the cerebral cortex is well defined. Brain waves have developed patterns like those seen when a newborn sleeps, wakes and dreams.

Prenatal Purgatory

Today's prenatal tests are a giant step toward healthier babies, but playing the waiting game for results often leaves couples in emotional limbo. Here's a know-everything guide to keeping your confidence up until you get the lowdown.

Donna Haupt

Donna Haupt is a freelance writer specializing in health and medical issues, and the mother of a 2-year-old boy.

Two years ago, when I was four months pregnant with my first child, a prenatal blood test came back abnormally low, indicating the baby I carried might have Down Syndrome, a chromosomal abnormality that causes mental retardation. Terrified but desperate for reassurance, my husband and I decided to verify the findings with an amniocentesis, an invasive and slightly risky procedure that conclusively checks for some 200 birth defects.

Although we decided we'd abort the fetus if the test proved positive, our decision didn't quiet our fears—or our tears—in the two agonizing weeks we waited for the results. As it turned out, our child did not have Down Syndrome. But we'd paid a hefty price in anxiety to receive this news.

In the United States today, about 95 percent of all children are born with no significant birth defects, according to the American College of Obstetricians and Gynecologists (ACOG). But while prenatal technology has largely brought hope and comfort into parents' lives, the testing process itself, with its waiting periods, can put couples in a kind of limbo, afraid to invest themselves emotionally in the pregnancy until the results confirm their baby's well-being. Even for couples who wouldn't consider abortion, the waiting period can feel hellish. The anxiety may be heightened if an expectant couple

doesn't understand the risks involved in each of the tests and the odds against having a baby with a particular defect.

"The perfect prenatal test would be safe, painless, and precise, but unfortunately none meet all three criteria," says Timothy R. B. Johnson, M.D., director of the division of maternal-fetal medicine at Johns Hopkins Hospital and University School of Medicine in Baltimore. "That's why it's important for every woman to weigh the benefits and potential risks before consenting to any test."

Should a test reveal bad news, the decision to abort or continue the pregnancy is strictly a personal one. But not every defect is a tragic one: in some cases, it's possible to treat the infant in the womb. Knowing what to expect can allow physicians to arrange for the best care to be available at birth and allow parents to prepare themselves emotionally for baby's arrival.

Knowledge also carries you from one test check point to another, easing the stress of waiting for results. To prepare yourself for the big tests, here's an advanced look at everything you'll need to know.

Ultrasound

The test Available today in almost every major hospital and in some doctor's offices, ultrasound can be performed at about six weeks of gestation and can be used at various points throughout pregnancy to allow a doctor to "see," by way of high-frequency sound waves, the fetus inside the womb. By mid-pregnancy, the doctor can inspect the fetal heart, skull and spine, accurately date the baby and determine whether there are

twins, make sure the fetus is growing properly, and, under ideal conditions, detect most anatomical malformations.

Risks The test itself is painless and safe: You lie on your back while the doctor moves a microphonelike device called a transducer across your abdomen. As the sound waves reflect off fetal tissue and organs, a computer translates them instantly into images on a black-and-white TV screen. A newer technique called transvaginal ultrasound delivers waves from a probe inserted into the vagina, allowing doctors to more closely view fetal placement and growth.

If a congenital heart defect is suspected because of family history, lupus, diabetes, or exposure to certain medications such as lithium, an exam called fetal echocardiography can be done on the four chambers of the heart. Best performed after the 18th week of gestation, when structures are large enough to be viewed clearly, ultrasound can still detect lethal heart defects early enough for a woman to consider having an abortion. And it can also serve to warn doctors of problems that may need immediate medical care at birth.

Candidates ACOG does not recommend the routine use of ultrasound during pregnancy, although the 28 reasons it cites warranting the test are so wide-ranging that some physicians suggest the test for virtually all pregnant women. Its cost can be a concern: A basic scan can run anywhere between $75 and $350, and most insurance companies require a medical reason for the test before reimbursement is considered.

Alpha-Fetoprotein

The test Performed at 16 weeks, this test

screens a sample of your blood for Down Syndrome and neural tube defects (NTDs), such as spina bifida, in which the vertebrae that normally protect the spinal cord fail to form properly. A hole is left in the backbone where nerves are pushed out and damaged. NTDs afflict 1 to 2 babies in 1,000.

Risks Although an alpha-fetoprotein (AFP) screening is virtually risk-free to perform, the test is notorious for its high "false-positive" rate, indicating problems with the fetus when none exist. The AFP test measures a protein manufactured mainly in the liver of the fetus. When the level is abnormally low, it can mean the baby has Down Syndrome or trisomy 13, a chromosomal defect that also causes mental retardation. When AFP levels are too high, it may indicate that the baby carries an NTD.

Candidates These days AFP screening is routinely offered to all pregnant women primarily because a full 90 percent of mothers who deliver a child with a NTD have no family history of the defect that would have flagged them as high-risk. And the majority of Down Syndrome babies—a full 80 percent—are born to women under age 35. After that point, however, the likelihood of giving birth to an infant with a chromosomal abnormality increases with age: from 1 in 192 at age 35, to 1 in 21 at age 45.

AFP screening successfully detects about 80 percent of these abnormalities but the rate of misdiagnosis is not insignificant: Only 2 to 4 percent of women with elevated levels of the protein actually have an abnormal fetus, and studies show a low AFP is even less predictive in identifying problems. "Very often, these false-positive results are skewed by twins or a pregnancy that is further along than originally believed," says John Larsen, M.D., professor of obstetrics, gynecology, and genetics at George Washington University in Washington, DC. "It's important that women see AFP only as a screening tool to determine whether further tests like ultrasound and amniocentesis are warranted." No state requires AFP screening, although California doctors are mandated to offer it to their patients. The test usually costs no more than $35.

Amniocentesis

The test Used as the definitive indicator of NTDs as well as more than 100 genetic diseases, amniocentesis has the added benefit

The Test	At What Point During Pregnancy	The Waiting Period
The Waiting Is the Hardest Part		
Ultrasound	Usually 6-8 weeks	None
Chorionic Villi Sampling (CVS)	9-12 weeks	7-10 days
Amniocentesis	15-18 weeks	2-3 weeks
Alpha-Fetoprotein (AFP)	16 weeks	7-10 days

of telling you the sex of your child. Performed between 15 and 18 weeks, usually on an outpatient basis in a hospital or doctor's office, the procedure first uses ultrasound to identify the position of the fetus and placenta. Once a pocket of amniotic fluid is found, the doctor inserts a long, thin needle through the abdomen and extracts about one ounce of fluid for testing. A local anesthetic is used so you needn't expect any pain, and only slight pressure is felt when the needle goes in.

Risks The procedure itself carries a .5 to 1 percent risk of miscarriage and an equally small chance the lab tests will fail and the test will need to be repeated. But it can take as long as two weeks for the results to come back, putting you late into the second trimester when labor must be induced should you choose to terminate the pregnancy. For Mary and Peter Wendel* of Ann Arbor, Michigan, both computer systems analysts, the wait for test results during Mary's first pregnancy was a distressing necessity. Earlier genetic blood tests had revealed Peter to be a carrier of a rare chromosomal disorder, known as translocation, that leads to heart problems and mental retardation. "I have a brother who is severely retarded and I knew having a child with the disorder would be too devastating for us," Peter says. "The wait for the amnio results was the most trying period in our married life, but it was worth it to know our baby was healthy."

Candidates "Amniocentesis is the flagship of prenatal tests," says Sharon L. Dooley, M.D., associate professor in the department of obstetrics and gynecology at the maternal-fetal medicine division of Northwestern University Medical School in Chicago. "It's accurate, precise, and can offer you valuable information about the genetic

health of a fetus." Although amnio may not be necessary for all women, the test is considered an important, informative tool. Some centers are beginning to offer amnio as early as 12 weeks' gestation, but because precise AFP screening can't be performed at this stage, serum screening for defects is still recommended at 16 weeks. Most insurance companies cover the cost of amnio, which ranges from $600 to $1,000, but there usually needs to be a medical reason.

Chorionic Villi Sampling

The test Chorionic villi sampling (CVS) is a relatively new procedure that can give couples news on the genetic well-being of their baby as early as nine weeks' gestation. Some 80 specialized medical centers around the country now offer the procedure, which involves taking a sample of chorionic villi, the tiny, hairlike projections that cover the gestational sac. The tissue is then sent to a lab for testing, with results usually back within seven to 10 days, depending on how overburdened the lab is.

Two types of CVS can be performed, both using ultrasound to identify the placement of the fetus and placenta within the womb. For a standard CVS, a thin plastic tube is inserted through the cervix and the villi is suctioned into a syringe for examination. If uterine fibroids block access to the chorionic membrane surrounding the fetus, a transabdominal CVS can be performed, in which a needle is inserted through the abdomen to remove sample villi. Both procedures take mere minutes to perform and are usually described as only minimally uncomfortable. Afterward, a woman may find that a small amount of cramping and bleeding occurs, although these reactions are usually no cause for concern.

"The minute I heard CVS could give me

reassurance earlier than amniocentesis, I decided to do it," says Katherine Stern, a 39-year-old advertising executive in Croton-on-Hudson, New York. She admits she would have aborted the fetus if serious problems had been discovered. "I was frightened by all the high-risk factors I faced at my age and CVS simply enabled me to enjoy my pregnancy sooner."

Risks Following another CVS in her second pregnancy, Stern suffered a ripped placenta and two weeks of bleeding from the procedure. In her case, the trauma didn't harm the fetus. But CVS does carry risks: The National Institutes of Health in Bethesda, Maryland, reports a 1.5 percent chance of miscarriage from the procedure, and some centers report rates as high as 10 percent when they begin doing CVS. What's more, because the test cannot detect NTDs, women are usually advised to have a follow-up AFP screening later in pregnancy.

"The caveat for CVS is to have the procedure performed at an experienced medical center," says Mark Evans, M.D., director of the division of reproductive genetics at Hutzel Hospital in the Detroit Medical Center. "You want to know their rates of miscarriage and failure to get specimens. But in experienced hands, the risks of CVS are no greater than amniocentesis."

Candidates CVS is for any woman whose pregnancy is considered high-risk or who simply wants to know the genetic status of her baby at the earliest point possible in her pregnancy—usually about six weeks before the amnio is performed. While CVS is no longer considered an experimental procedure by ACOG, many insurance companies still consider it "investigational" and refuse to pick up the cost: usually ranging between $600 to $1,000.

A Sneak Peek at Tomorrow's Tests

In the not-too-distant future, a simple and safe blood test may be all a woman needs

> ## A Prenatal Test to Give Your Doctor
>
> YOUR PHYSICIAN WILL guide you in deciding which prenatal tests are necessary, based on your medical and family histories. But there are other considerations. Before you gear up for the big exams, do your homework. Ask your doctor:
>
> 1. What are the dangers of the test? Does it involve a trivial or nonexistent risk, like that involved in taking blood or urine, or could it cause physical harm to you or your baby? How much does the procedure cost, and does your insurance cover it? Is it regularly performed in your area, or do you have to search for an experienced clinic? Would the test ever have to be performed twice?
> 2. What information does the test provide? How long does it take for the results to come back, and will another test center give a quicker reading? Is the information reliable? Are there frequent false positive (the test says something is abnormal when it's not) or false negative (the test is read as normal when there's actually a problem) results?
> 3. Would the test results alter treatment? Does the information gained enable doctors to save your child in utero, or help them arrange for prompt treatment at birth?
> 4. If you and your partner would choose to terminate a problem pregnancy, would knowing sooner be important? If abortion isn't a consideration, would diagnosing a defect early on still offer an emotional benefit, allowing you and your partner to prepare for the baby's arrival?

to learn if her baby is healthy. Since the 1970s, doctors have known that fetal cells leak into the mother's bloodstream after the eighth to 10th week of pregnancy. But until recently, it has been nearly impossible to distinguish them from those still circulating from past pregnancies. And the technology needed to separate them from the mother's blood ended up altering the fetal cells so that they could not be used in genetic tests.

But in 1989, in a development that could open up an entirely new approach to prenatal testing, scientists in England were able to isolate fetal cells from the blood of expecting women, multiply and analyze the genes within them, and finally determine the sex of the babies.

Pressing ahead still further, University of Tennessee researchers are using newly evolved DNA techniques to track down chromosomal abnormalities in fetal cells circulating in maternal blood. With cautious optimism, Sherman Elias, M.D., one of the researchers, predicts: "In five years, we could have a diagnostic blood test for genetic defects that doesn't endanger a pregnancy in any way."

WHEN A PREGNANT WOMAN DRINKS

ELISABETH ROSENTHAL

Elisabeth Rosenthal is an emergency-room physician in New York City.

At the human and behavior genetics Laboratory at Emory University, in Atlanta, a videotape recording shows a smiling 8-year-old girl peering from behind thick glasses at two clear plastic boxes topped by red bows, each containing a chocolate-chip cookie. The game, a psychologist explains, is to open both boxes and remove the cookies—and no eating until both cookies are out. The girl's 35-year-old mother observes.

The child seems to understand and, with the eagerness of a race horse at the gate, lunges at the boxes. For an endless few minutes, she pulls intently at the ribbons and tugs doggedly at the bows, clearly not up to this most elementary task. Fi-

nally, the mother comes to the rescue by untying one box and, with the second still sealed, the grinning child pops a cookie in her mouth.

"Ugh. This is too painful to watch," exclaims Dr. Claire D. Coles, the center's director of Clinical and Developmental Research, as she puts the tape on pause. "Look at that nice little girl. Her face is dysmorphic. She's too small for her age. And her fine motor coordination is awful.

"What's worse, look at the mother. She's also mildly dysmorphic. She spent her childhood in special-ed classes. The whole family suffers from prenatal alcohol exposure. All three kids, the mother, her brother."

In the last decade it has become unquestionably clear that alcohol is a potent teratogen,

which can cause irreversible damage to the body and brain of the developing fetus. Experts like Dr. Coles now believe that women who are pregnant or contemplating pregnancy should not drink—at all.

Fetal alcohol syndrome and its more subtle variant, fetal alcohol effect, are umbrella terms used to describe the condition affecting the scarred offspring of drinking mothers. Victims with the full-blown syndrome, whose mothers generally drank heavily throughout pregnancy, often suffer physical malformations and mental retardation. Even those less fully affected, sometimes the progeny of women who drank only intermittently, may end up with lifelong learning disabilities and behavioral problems.

No one knows exactly how many individuals are afflicted

with fetal alcohol damage, but the estimates are staggering. The Centers for Disease Control estimate that more than 8,000 alcohol-damaged babies are born each year, or 2.7 babies for every 1,000 live births. Others feel that these figures are low. On some Indian reservations, 25 percent of all children are reportedly afflicted.

Although the syndrome was first described in 1973, the broad impact of alcohol-related fetal injury has only recently become apparent to scientists. "The Broken Cord," Michael Dorris's moving memoir about raising a severely alcohol-affected child, brought the syndrome to wider public attention when it was published last summer.

Some experts believe fetal-alcohol exposure is the most

common-known cause of mental retardation in this country. Dr. Robert J. Sokol, dean of the School of Medicine at Wayne State University in Detroit and director of Wayne State's Alcohol Research Center, estimates that 1 out of 10 retarded adults in residential care has fetal alcohol syndrome.

Experts in birth defects see the survivors of drinking pregnancies everywhere. When Dr. Coles recently lectured at a reform school, she recalls, she thought, "My God, half these kids look alcohol affected." And as the syndrome becomes better known, others are beginning to recognize it as well.

"I get a lot of calls saying, 'I've just figured out what's wrong with our 18-year-old adopted son. He's dropped out of school; he's always had learning problems; he's never fit in,' " says Dr. Ann Streissguth of the University of Washington, who has followed a group of children with alcohol-related disabilities for 14 years.

Still, as Dr. Coles says, "the vast majority of kids like this have never been identified or followed. People probably just assumed they were a little stupid or a little funny looking."

As she speaks, I stare sheepishly at the faces of the Atlanta girl and her mother still frozen on the screen: their eyes just slightly too far apart, their thin upper lips, their smallish heads. Although I received my medical training within the last 10 years, without Dr. Cole's coaching I would have missed this diagnosis.

IN SCREENING FOR ALCOhol-related injuries, an expert in birth defects, or dysmorphologist, examines the suspect child for the unusual facial characteristics, small head and body size, poor mental capabilities and abnormal behavior patterns that typify alcohol-related birth defects. In infancy, the evaluation is usually prompted by knowledge of a mother's drinking, or because a newborn develops the shakes or seizures typical of alcohol withdrawal. But at this stage the symptoms are easily overlooked. Only 20 percent of those with the full

syndrome have marked facial abnormalities, and those with the effect look fine.

"Except when a child is grossly dysmorphic," the syndrome is not diagnosed, says Dr. Sterling K. Claren, Aldrich Professor of Pediatrics at the University of Washington School of Medicine in Seattle. As for fetal alcohol effect, he adds, it "really cannot be diagnosed in newborns."

Many children with the full syndrome come to expert attention only after they fail to gain weight and meet developmental landmarks. Sometimes a physician notices an abundance of physical complaints—crossed eyes, heart murmurs or recurrent ear infections—that suggest congenital malformation. Some are not recognized until years later, when they begin having trouble at school. Some are not recognized at all. Dr. José F. Cordero of the Center for Disease Control's Division of Birth Defects and Developmental Disabilities believes that as many as two-thirds of cases of the full syndrome remain undiagnosed, with the figure for those less severely affected even higher.

Dr. Coles and her staff, as part of their study, crisscross Atlanta, turning their trained eyes on the progeny of alcoholic pregnancies to look for signs of damage. On a day in November, she visited a ramshackle housing project to examine a one-month-old boy whose mother is an alcohol and cocaine abuser. She put the baby through a series of tests: shaking rattles near his ear, tweaking a toe with a rubber band, recording his cry.

The boy has no physical signs of fetal alcohol syndrome, she later explains, but his behavior is worrisome. "He is too irritable, too distractable," she said. "Kids at 30 days should be calm and able to focus on a rattle." But, she added, "If you weren't trained you might not recognize this as a substance-abuse baby."

Anne Cutcliffe's adopted daughter had seen various doctors before she was referred to Dr. Coles for an evaluation at age 2. "I guess I recall when I got her at 9 months, she was not

an attractive child," said Mrs. Cutcliffe, who lives in Atlanta and has five older children. "She only weighed 10½ pounds and her eyes were crossed. All she could do was turn from her stomach to her back. I guess it proves love is blind, because I never did see all those things that other people saw." The girl's biological mother was an alcoholic.

AS MANY AS 86 PERCENT of women drink at least once during pregnancy, according to the Public Health Service, and experts estimate that between 20 and 35 percent of pregnant women drink regularly. In a 1989 study of 2,278 highly educated women (39 percent had postgraduate degrees), 30 percent consumed more than one drink a week during pregnancy; only 11 percent smoked.

Alcohol freely crosses the placenta, and the fetus's blood-alcohol level will equal that of the mother's. A recent study in The New England Journal of Medicine showed that women have lower levels than men of the stomach enzyme that neutralizes alcohol, leaving them particularly vulnerable to high levels of alcohol in the bloodstream. The mother's blood alcohol must reach a certain level—the toxic threshold—before the fetus is at risk. Binge drinking seems to be particularly risky. While a drink each night might never push a mother's blood level above the danger threshold, a night of drinking in honor of a birthday might well raise the level enough to endanger the fetus.

The type of damage produced by drinking depends on the fetus's stage of development. The first trimester of pregnancy is devoted to the organization of the fetus's bones and organs, while the second and third trimesters center on growth and maturation. The brain develops throughout the nine-month period. "So we'd predict physical malformations from heavy drinking in the first trimester and growth retardation from drinking in the third," says Dr. Claren. "But brain damage can occur at any time." In addition, the toxic

threshold for brain damage seems to be much lower than for damage to other organs.

There is a rough correlation between the amount a mother imbibes during pregnancy and the severity of the baby's defects, but scientists are struggling to understand the many other factors that come into play. One major mystery is why so many drinking women frequently have apparently normal babies. Even in hopeless alcoholics, the chance of having a baby with the full-blown syndrome is only 35 percent.

The fetus may be more vulnerable on certain days of pregnancy. "Two drinks may be above the threshold on day 33 and on day 39, below," Dr. Claren said.

Women may also differ in their genetic susceptibility to having children with the syndrome, a tendency which some believe may follow ethnic and racial lines. Dr. Sokol has found that black women are seven times more likely to have fetal-alcohol affected children than white women with similar drinking habits. (Pregnant or not, studies have found that black and Hispanic women are more likely to be abstinent than white women. And a woman's alcohol consumption tends to rise with her level of education and income.) The Centers for Disease Control data show that the syndrome is 30 times more commonly reported in Native Americans than it is in whites, and six times more common in blacks.

Dr. Coles believes these figures may be "partly an artifact of reporting. Researchers don't go into nice private hospitals and start looking for alcohol-damaged babies." At least one study found that women of lower socio-economic status are diagnosed correctly more often.

Although experts stress that there is no evidence in human beings that a rare single drink does damage, most say that with so much still unknown the only prudent course for the pregnant mother is abstinence. "Pregnancy is a time when women should be conservative with their bodies," says Dr. Claren. "Women think three or four times before they take an aspirin. They quit smoking. Then they turn around and have a drink? Some obstetricians advise women not to drink. Many others make up some dose of liquor which they think is O.K. To me that's crazy." Experts recommend that women who are breast-feeding also abstain, because brain maturation continues after birth.

The good news is that those who stop drinking at any time during pregnancy can increase their chances of having a healthy child. In a study conducted by the Boston University Fetal Alcohol Education Program, 85 women who drank heavily stayed with the program until they gave birth. Thirty-three of the women gave up or reduced their drinking before the seventh month of pregnancy; among these women, there was not one baby born with a growth abnormality, according to Dr. Barbara A. Morse, the program's director. Of the 52 women who continued to drink heavily, 21 gave birth to babies with growth retardation, and 5 of these babies had identifiable fetal alcohol syndrome. Moderate drinkers during early pregnancy are advised to quit while they're ahead: "If a woman comes to me three months pregnant and says 'I'm a regular drinker,'" says Dr. Claren, 'I say, 'Whatever you did is probably safe but stop now.'"

The Boston University group has led the way in calling for better counseling and improved drug-treatment opportunities for pregnant women. "Pregnancy is a time of incredible motivation for women," says Dr. Morse, noting that of those heavy-drinking women in the program who received counseling two-thirds were able to cut down considerably or stop altogether. Unfortunately, many in-patient alcohol rehabilitation programs exclude pregnant women, she said. Massachusetts recently opened four residential programs (or 35 beds) to treat pregnant alcoholics and

other substance abusers, making that state the leader nationwide.

RESEARCHERS ARE NOW focusing on moderate drinking during pregnancy in the hopes of learning more about alcohol's most subtle effects. Dr. Nancy Day of the University of Pittsburgh has studied the offspring of close to 700 women since 1988, most of whom reported consuming less than one drink a day during pregnancy. There were no babies with the full syndrome in the group, but there was a correlation between mothers who drank prenatally and the size of the child's head. Many also had an unusual number of "minor physical anomalies"—like crooked toes and funny ears. Most worrisome, the newborns had unusual brainwave patterns, of EEG's, potentially indicative of immature development of the brain.

Animal studies suggest that relatively low-level drinking can lead to damage. Dr. Claren's group at the University of Washington gave monkeys binges of alcohol once a week during pregnancy. The babies were unusually irritable, impulsive and distractable—a familiar triad of symptoms. "The good news is that the mothers had to get enough alcohol to get intoxicated to produce the defects," says Dr. Claren. "The bad news is that even if they only binged during the first three weeks of pregnancy"—equivalent to the first four to six weeks of the human term—"the babies still ended up with behavioral abnormalities."

There were physiological abnormalities as well. Though their brains were the right size and CT scans were totally normal, examination of their brain cells showed abnormal levels of dopamine, an important neurotransmitter. Dr.

Claren sees these findings as a strong physiological correlate of fetal alcohol effect. He hopes PET scans, which can sense chemical abnormalities in the brain, may be helpful in nailing down the often elusive diagnosis.

TWO RESEARCH groups, Dr. Coles's in Atlanta and Dr. Streissguth's in Seattle, have followed alcohol-affected children for 6 and 14 years respectively. They find that some of the traits that are only hinted at in newborns blossom in early childhood, creating potentially disastrous school experiences. In Dr. Coles's group, children at age 6 showed poorer memory, shorter attention spans, lower I.Q.'s, diminished achievement levels and other learning disabilities when compared to normal children. Dr. Streissguth's group also reported attention deficits and other behavior problems at this age.

These shortcomings may add up to a limited ability to learn and to learn from experience. These kids "have a unique flavor among the learning disabled," observes Dr. Claren. "They seem to be really untrainable." Anne Cutcliffe remembers her daughter, at 6, making such slow progress in reading that her teachers decided she should repeat the first grade. When she started first grade a second time, after the four-month summer vacation, she had lost even the small progress she'd made the year before and had to start again at the most basic level.

Most children with the full syndrome will be found, with formal psychological testing, to be "developmentally delayed" and will qualify for special education. But some will limp along in regular classes. Even those who qualify for special education are often

put into classes that don't meet their needs.

Most treatment programs for the mildly mentally handicapped were designed for patients like those with Down's syndrome, who are quiet, good workers and enjoy repetitive tasks. Parents and health professionals describe the alcohol-affected in very different terms: impulsive, unable to learn from mistakes, undisciplined, showing poor judgment, distractable, uninhibited. "We have to shift gears" to meet the needs of alcohol-affected kids, says Dr. Streissguth. He has applied for Federal funding to develop special therapeutic programs designed for them.

The flip side of the alcohol-affected personality is a winning one: outgoing, loving, physical, trusting. But together they lead to trouble. "She'll walk up to anyone on the street and stare at them and make conversation," says Anne Cutcliffe of her daughter. "Immediately she's buddies. It doesn't matter who." And Dr. Streissguth agrees that as young adults those with the syndrome often take sociability and physicality to unwelcome extremes: "They talk too loud and they stand too close. They seem not to pick up on normal social cues."

Paradoxically, researchers in the field say, alcohol-affected children who perform best on standardized tests end up with the toughest existence. Those who are obviously dysmorphic and mentally retarded receive social-service assistance and often end up in group homes. The others "fall into a pit," says Dr. Coles. Many drop out of school in frustration and their disabilities consign them to the margins of society, sometimes involved in prostitution and petty crime. "These are outgoing, trusting, fun-loving people, who are not able to evaluate the risks out there," said Dr. Streissguth.

The Fantastic Voyage of Tanner Roberts

Pamela Warrick

Times Staff Writer

At 10:04 a.m. on Jan. 30 Tanner Max Roberts ended a remarkable journey.

On that sunny Thursday in a suite at St. Joseph Medical Center in Burbank, Tanner was born. As births go, this one was uneventful. But being born—the original voyage from darkness into light—is by its very nature a most extraordinary experience. It has been variously described as euphoric, traumatic, even catastrophic for the baby.

Many of the mysteries surrounding the process, including questions as basic as how labor begins, remain unsolved. Yet over the last decade, ultrasound and other diagnostic devices have opened a window into the womb. Today, it is scientifically possible to, at the very least, imagine what it is like to be born. Here, according to medical texts, published research and expert interviews, is the story of how it might have been for one baby.

Day 266

On the afternoon of the 266th day of Cindy Roberts' pregnancy, the onetime champion freestyle swimmer lowers her swollen body into a warm bath. Submerged, she feels almost weightless.

All morning, she had been out walking around shopping malls, hoping to hurry the start of labor. She is tired of being pregnant, tired of being big. This pregnancy, she sighs, has gone on long enough.

Inside her belly, another beautiful swimmer floats in his own watery world. On other afternoons, he would stretch and tumble in his amino bubble. Now, there is no room for acrobatics.

Even with arms and knees pulled in tight in classic fetal position, his body fills the entire uterine envelope. The womb has stretched to almost 60 times its normal size, but its occupant's world is shrinking. . . .

Why labor begins when it does is a mystery. The pressure of the fetus on the pelvic floor might have something to do with it. The fetus might trigger it by excreting certain chemicals that signal a level of anxiety about the increasingly cramped surroundings.

The placenta, once spongy with nourishing blood vessels, is growing tough and fibrous in anticipation of its impending functional failure. Just as the fetus's days *in utero* are numbered, the placenta too has a finite life span.

At nearly nine pounds—three pounds more than he weighed just a month ago—Tanner is physiologically ready to be born. Cartilage nicely shapes his ears, hair decorates his head and the soles of his feet are sufficiently creased to give him an identifiable footprint.

His head is big and heavy—25% of his body weight. So it is gravity, as much as biological destiny, that pulls him head down into the pelvic basin.

The Pain Begins

That night in the frozen-food aisle at Lucky, Cindy Roberts stops short. A sharp pain, starting in the small of her back and reaching around her middle like fingers of flame, causes her to gasp.

She grabs her contracted belly; from rib cage to pelvis, she is as hard as a basketball.

For weeks, painless Braxton Hicks spasms (named from the gynecologist who discovered them) have been flexing her uterine muscles. But these practice contractions, which stretch the uterus and pump it up for the rigors of labor, have prepared neither Tanner nor his mother for the ordeal to come.

After 20 minutes in the checkout line and only one more serious contraction, Cindy loads a week's worth of groceries into the trunk of her gray Suzuki and heads home, smiling. It hurts but at least something is happening.

After six hours of mild and irregular spasms, the uterus settles into a predictable rhythm, contracting every 10 to 15 minutes, each contraction lasting 10 to 15 seconds. By now Tanner 'knows'—if only by the flood of anxiety-producing proteins in his system—that something is happening.

Prostaglandins, the hormones that have kept Cindy Roberts' cervix intact and the uterine contents secure, have stopped circulating. Suddenly

From *Los Angeles Times*, March 1, 1992, pp. E1, E12, E13. © 1992 by the Los Angeles Times. Reprinted by permission.

released from these chemical inhibitors, the uterine muscles begin the natural process of expelling the foreign body the uterus has hosted for the last 9 months and 7 days.

The walls of the uterus begin to randomly contract—and with them, the very walls of Tanner's home. Even without a fully developed nervous system, the fetus at term is capable of experiencing pressure, confinement, restraint. And that might well be what Tanner is feeling.

After six hours of mild and irregular spasms, the uterus settles into a predictable rhythm, contracting every 10 to 15 minutes, each contraction lasting 10 to 15 seconds.

By now, Tanner "knows"—if only by the flood of anxiety-producing proteins in his system—that something is happening.

3 O'Clock Wake-Up Call

At 3 a.m., Cindy and Tom Roberts are wide awake. With son Kevin, 3, asleep in another room, they time Cindy's contractions with a stopwatch. Six to eight minutes apart. Tom rubs Cindy's back during each spasm. The contractions are growing more frequent and more intense. Time to call the hospital.

Cindy goes to the kitchen and downs two glasses of Gatorade and two Carnation Instant Breakfast bars for energy. When the time between contractions has narrowed to five minutes, Tom calls a friend to stay with Kevin.

Until now, the pre-dawn hours have been Tanner's favorite time for "dreaming." Being suspended in body-temperature amino fluid is not unlike being adrift in a sensory deprivation tank.

Before the onset of labor, the fetus also takes advantage of these quiet hours to "breathe." Even though his lungs are still collapsed and full of fluid, Tanner heaves his tiny chest and abdomen up and down, simulating the inhaling and exhaling that will sustain him outside the womb.

Each breathing episode is marked by a flurry of rapid eye movements of the sort measured in REM sleep— the stage when most dreaming is known to occur. (By seven months, a fetus is neurologically equipped to dream.)

But now, with the first real breath just hours ahead, breathing practice is over and dreams are put away. Tanner's activity is reduced to internal functions and basic reflexive responses.

Even Cindy's ingestion of glucose-heavy Gatorade—a predictable fetal stimulant—provoked only slight reaction. And the ride to the hospital does not seem to startle this small passenger.

The Pain Begins II

"How soon can I get an epidural?" Cindy Roberts wants to know.

It is 5 a.m. and her cervix is dilated 2 centimeters. It must open to 10 centimeters (about 4 inches) for the baby's head to push through. Each contraction thins and widens the cervical ring, but only slightly and awfully slowly. Or so it seems to Cindy.

In the meantime, she wants an anesthetic.

Tanner is stressed. Every time the uterus contracts, it flattens the placenta, which does his breathing for him. It also compresses the umbilical cord, which delivers the oxygen and removes carbon dioxide.

At the height of each contraction, Tanner is cut off. He can't get oxygen and he can't get rid of the toxic gases. With every spasm, he grows hypoxic (oxygen deprived): a life-threatening condition in an older child or in an adult, but the fetus is equipped to respond. Peppering the outside of his aorta are reddish-brown nodules—factories for making the hormones that will sustain him through labor and disappear during childhood.

In a distinctly fetal version of the "fight or flight" response, the stress hormone noradrenaline surges through Tanner's system. Instead of rushing blood to the skeletal muscles for "flight" (unnecessary for a fetus with nowhere to go), this specialized protein directs fresh blood to the heart and brain—the two organs most vulnerable to permanent damage from lack of oxygen.

In the Labor Room

When Cindy arrived at St. Joseph Medical Center, her contractions were 4 to 5 minutes apart. Now they have slowed to every 7 minutes. "I hate this," she says. "I hate this."

"When babies see the hospital door, they say 'Forget it!'" jokes nurse Rita Yates, who has seen this happen before.

Cindy is not laughing.

In Labor-Delivery Suite 2, a hotel-like room with furniture that converts from Danish modern to OR traditional, Yates pulls a webbed belt and fetal monitor around Cindy's middle to measure the labor.

She rubs petroleum jelly over the mother's taut abdomen to form a seal around the monitor microphone to enhance transmission. As the monitor begins to pick up the fetal heartbeat, a pen on the nearby console inscribes the rate on a long strip of graph paper.

Above the jagged line that is Tanner's changing heart rate, a second pen charts the variations in uterine muscle tone, drawing a picture of each contraction.

The nurse turns up the volume as the monitor picks up the sound of Tanner's heartbeat. From inside the mother's body, it ker-thumps and whooshes, ker-thumps and whooshes.

"There's that washing machine," says Tom Roberts. "Doesn't he sound great? It's supposed to be a boy. That's what they said."

Tanner's world is not a silent one. The most familiar sounds are a muffled version of his mother's voice and the sounds inside her body—the gurgling, rumbling and slurping noises of her internal organs and vessels as they pump, vibrate, murmur and digest.

Because fluid is a great conductor of sound, Tanner's fully developed hearing registers noise from outside his mother as well. Tanner is especially attuned to—and easily stimulated by—his father's distinctive baritone and the sweet, little-boy voice of brother Kevin.

Now, a new sound booms through his world: The echo of his own heartbeat. As broadcast by the sensitive fetal monitor, it is an imposing sound.

With each contraction of the uterine wall, Tanner's heartbeat jumps from its resting rate of about 140 beats per minute to its "stressed" rate of 160 to 170.

When the cervix is dilated to more than 4 centimeters, or almost half open, Tanner's mother is given her first medication. As Demerol begins to drip into her vein, Cindy relaxes.

Tanner, heart rate dipping to 130, then 120, begins to fall asleep.

'Breathe, Cindy!'

"Breathe through it, Cindy. Breathe! The baby needs you to BREATHE. . . ."

Contractions are coming every 3 to 4 minutes, each one lasting 25 seconds. The Demerol does not stop the pain, Cindy growls. She hugs her husband's old blue bathrobe tight against her chest as nurse Cindy Cox urges her to "relax those muscles. Breathe deep. Relax. You're almost done, almost done. . . . Done.

"Pretty soon," Cox announces, "you'll have him in your arms."

"He'd better be," snaps the exhausted Cindy.

Tanner's nap is over. With each contraction, his heart rate soars to 160, 170, 180 beats per minute.

Blood cells rich in oxygen-loving hemoglobin supply the oxygen-heavy blood Tanner needs to cope. Without these specialized cells, interruptions in the fetal oxygen supply would be damaging indeed.

While each contraction cuts off Tanner's only source of oxygen, the minutes of rest between each contraction resupply the deprived placenta and umbilical cord. The mother's deep breathing during contractions helps rush the fresh blood to the fetal heart and brain.

During a lull between two particularly intense contractions, a new sound is heard: metal instruments being lined up on a sterile-clothed bedside table.

Clank, clank. Tanner's heart rate leaps for a moment and then returns to its normal pace.

The Doctor Arrives

At 8 a.m., the Verdugo Mountains behind the hospital are still pink from the sunrise. Cindy Roberts' obstetrician, Dr. Wayne Furr, arrives and determines her cervix is almost completely dilated. But the "bag of waters" still has not ruptured.

Using a tool made for the purpose, the doctor reaches into the birth canal and tears the diaphanous membranes of the amino sac. About half a liter of clear fluid spills out.

Before he leaves the room, the doctor tells Cindy her labor is progressing well and she can have that epidural anesthetic now. Between contractions, Cindy sighs, "Thank you."

Tanner is startled by the rush of the escaping fluid. And, with the next contraction, he is startled again by the impact of the loss. No longer are the contractions diffused across a watery bed. Now Tanner's head, knees and shoulders are pressed hard against the muscular uterine wall.

Because the spinal anesthetic acts only on the mother's spinal nerves, the 8 cubic centimeters of Marcain have no direct effect on the fetus. But for the next 30 minutes, the drug eases the frequency and intensity of contractions. It also reduced the mother's blood pressure and slows her breathing.

After 30 minutes, contractions resume with as much or greater force. They are coming every 2 minutes now. Each one lasts a full minute. Between spasms, the mother sleeps. But not Tanner.

For him, this is the start of the most stressful part of his journey.

Head First

By 9 a.m., Cindy's cervix is fully dilated and her labor suite has been transformed into a delivery room. The upholstered rocker and blond wood furniture have been covered with sterile blue drapes. A chest in the corner has become a high-tech warming table. And doctor, nurse and father are gloved, capped and gowned for the imminent birth.

As Tanner is pushed farther and farther down the birth canal, his body stretches out, like toothpaste being squeezed from the tube. Each expulsive push by the uterus impels his head against the pelvic girdle.

His feet kick out behind him, jabbing his mother's rib cage. The pressure on his skull is enormous from all sides as it makes its way through the narrow passage. (The skull of an adult could not easily withstand such pressure.)

But the flexible fetal skull is designed for this very event. Instead of a single fused bone, Tanner's head consists for four bony plates. As his skull is compressed, the plates slide over one another to allow the head to pass through.

The stress of contractions is formidable indeed. Skull compression, coupled with Tanner's increasing lack of oxygen, causes stress hormones to explode through his system. In an adult, this level of stress would mean that a stroke or a heart attack is occurring. But once more the fetal constitution is prepared.

As in earlier episodes of stress, blood rushes to the heart and head. But this time the stress is so strong, it causes more of Tanner's system to shut down. Like sea mammals during lengthy underwater stays, Tanner's body instinctively reacts to save itself. The heartbeat slows to a frightening 100, 90, 80 beats per minute and then leaps again to 180.

His body is compressed by his mother's contractions and her pushes. And as he nears his entrance to the world, the compressions help press the fluid from his lungs in preparation for the first breath.

Tanner's body, now wedged between his mother's sacral bone in back and pubic bone in front, suddenly turns slightly to fit through.

The Final Countdown

"1 - 2 - 3 - 4 - 5 - 6 - 7 - 8 - 9 - 10! 1 - 2 - 3 - 4 - 5 - 6 - 7 - 8 - 9 - 10! 1-2-3-4-5-6-7-8-9-10-11-12!"

Tom Roberts, who as Thomas Kane makes his living as the voice for such companies as Lincoln Mercury and Exxon, booms out the numbers as Cindy bears down, down, down to push out the baby.

"Here we go. Go, go, go, go, go, go, go!" cheers nurse Yates.

"Oh!" pants Cindy as the top of the baby's head emerges.

Tanner is squeezed tight in the birth canal as his head "crowns." The doctor gently touches the top of his wet, curly haired head. Over the next few seconds, Tanner's head, face down, emerges. As his chin clears the mother's body, his head spontaneously turns left.

His face is puffy and scrunched. Although squinting fiercely against the sudden light, Tanner's dark blue eyes are open. His lips are fluttering and he is making tiny bubbles with the clear mucus around his mouth.

Before any more of the body emerges, the doctor cradles Tanner's head and suctions his nose and mouth. Tanner takes his first breath—actually a large gasp, followed by whimpering, and then a lusty cry.

The tiny air sacs in his lungs suddenly inflate and he is ready for the next gasp. After a few minutes, the big gasp will settle into routine inhalations and exhalations.

Tanner's left shoulder is delivered, immediately (although gently) followed by the right shoulder. The rest of Tanner slides out easily.

His trunk and head are luminescent pink; his limbs are still gray-blue from lack of oxygen. His fingers and toes are gray. Tanner's body is wet, but only slightly bloody as the doctor lifts him onto his mother's abdomen.

It's a Boy

"Hello, baby, Hello, baby," whispers Cindy to the dazed but alert infant balanced on her belly.

"He's beautiful, just beautiful," reports nurse Yates.

"Very healthy. A real solid guy," adds the doctor.

"Isn't he just great!" announces the father.

Tanner seems to be able to focus slightly on objects about 8 inches from his face—the distance to his mother's face as she cradles him in her arms. Wrapped in a white flannel blanket, Tanner, drawn by his mother's voice, seems to gaze into her eyes. Unquestionably, he knows her.

The umbilical cord, still connecting baby and mother, slows and then stops pulsing. The obstetrician clamps the cord at both ends and hands the father a pair of surgical shears. Tom severs Tanner's final connection to the interior world.

Now Tanner's blood flows not to his mother for nourishment, but to his own lungs, intestines and other organs. The fetal path of blood through the heart is abandoned and blood is rerouted to Tanner's newly inflated lungs.

The baby is laid on a table next to the mother's bed to be dried and warmed. He cries loudly as eye-drops are put in. Meanwhile, the placenta is delivered from the mother.

Tanner can see very little, mostly shadows, mostly black and white. He seems to be able to focus slightly on objects about 8 inches from his face—the distance to his mother's face as she cradles him in her arms.

Wrapped in a white flannel blanket, Tanner, drawn by his mother's voice, seems to gaze into her eyes. Unquestionably, he knows her.

The room is quiet now, but everything about his new environment is intense to Tanner. The baby is overwhelmed from the avalanche of stimuli—first sounds, first sights, first touches. His mother lightly strokes his cheek. "Everything's going to be fine," she tells him. "Just fine."

☐

Today, Tanner is 4½ weeks old and weighs 11 pounds. His eyes are still blue, but his hair is growing blond like his mother's.

His pediatrician, Dr. Gary Smithson of Glendale, reports that despite a brief bout of non-threatening jaundice, Tanner has been healthy since the day he was born. "He did have some of the longest fingernails I've seen on a baby," says Smithson, who gave Tanner his first manicure two hours after birth.

He sleeps up to three hours at a time and is a good eater. He still responds vigorously to the sound of his father's and his big brother's voices. On his third day home from the hospital, his mother awakened from a nap to find Tanner's chubby hands clutching her cheeks.

"Our eyes met for an instant," says Cindy, "and it was like he was looking right into my heart. . . ."

Cognition, Language, and Learning

- **Early Cognitive and Language Development (Articles 8–11)**
- **Learning in School (Articles 12–16)**

We have come a long way from the days when the popular characterization of cognition among infants and young children included phrases like "tabula rasa" and "booming, buzzing, confusion." Infants and young children are no longer viewed by researchers as empty-headed vessels passively waiting to be "filled up" with knowledge. Today, experts in child development are calling for a reformulation of assumptions about children's cognitive abilities, as well as calling for reforms in the ways we teach children in our schools.

Hence, the articles in the first subsection highlight some of the new knowledge on the cognitive abilities of infants and preschoolers. Recent research indicates that babies have wonderfully active minds. In "The Amazing Minds of Infants," Lisa Grunwald notes that by employing ingenious experimental techniques, scientists are discovering that infants possess many heretofore unrealized skills.

The period beginning with a child's first words marks an important transition, signaling a farewell to infancy and the entrance into the speaking world of the community. The article "The Civilizing of Genie" addresses early language acquisition among infants and young children. The tragic case of Genie, an abused child who was prevented from engaging in any normal interaction, offers critical insights into the importance of the environment for sustaining normal language development.

Without question, the writings of Jean Piaget have dominated and reshaped researchers' views about the active nature of children's thinking abilities. This notion of the inherently active and cognitively competent child has clear and important implications for maximizing learning among children. Hence, the articles "Where Pelicans Kiss Seals" and "How Kids Learn" join Piaget in stressing the importance of creative, imaginative play, and active hands-on experiences as effective vehicles for promoting cognitive growth and learning in preschoolers and school-age children. Thus, play and art become valuable "windows" into a child's cognitive growth.

As Erik Erikson noted, from about age 6 to 12 years, children enter the period of "industry versus inferiority" and become preoccupied with learning the tools of their culture. In our culture, these tools are the "three R's"—learning to read, write, and do arithmetic in school. Thus, the second subsection of this unit addresses developments and influences on cognition in school-age children. "Child Development and Differential School Performance: A Challenge for Teachers in School Development Program Schools" presents important information on the development of literacy skills and how to facilitate these skills among children.

Researchers now recognize that children's learning in school, as well as educational philosophies and practices, is affected deeply by cultural and societal norms. For example, "Equitable Treatment of Girls and Boys in the Classroom" raises our consciousness about how cultural assumptions translate into actual practices that ultimately affect children's learning. Consider, for instance, the possibility that differences between girls' and boys' school achievement may be due to the fact that boys receive significantly more class time and attention from teachers than girls do. Likewise, "How Asian Teachers Polish Each Lesson to Perfection" shows that Asian children academically outperform American children due in part to differences in teaching strategies, the educational system, and parental expectations.

Finally, as our nation's population continues to diversify and grow both in numbers and in the range of ethnicities and cultures, educators are finding it increasingly necessary to become multiculturally knowledgeable and sensitive. The article "Understanding Bilingual/Bicultural Young Children" addresses some common misconceptions regarding bilingual children and offers successful educational approaches for professionals working with bilingual children. For many, learning has never been a simple or easy endeavor, but as our knowledge of factors that influence cognitive development expands, we may find ways to offer greater learning opportunities to future generations of young learners.

Looking Ahead: Challenge Questions

Given that infants are more cognitively competent than once thought, what do you think about accelerated, formalized efforts to speed up young infants' cognitive skills? What advantages or disadvantages do you envision for infants who are exposed to teaching and drilling at early ages?

Why might pretend play or imaginative art activities be useful in promoting children's cognitive development and intelligence? How might you educate classroom teachers to utilize more creative forms of artwork or imaginative play as a regular part of their classroom instructional practices?

People naturally suffer from "cultural ethnocentrism," or the idea that the beliefs and practices of one's own culture are more desirable and even superior to those of other cultures. Remaining cognizant of this bias, how would you give advice on child development to people from different cultures who engage in different child practices?

Given the increasingly diverse demographic changes now sweeping much of our country, how might you better understand and respect children from different cultural backgrounds and experiences while optimizing learning for all children in the classroom?

In spite of recent gains that women have made in this country, why do you think research shows that gender bias continues to exist in classrooms today? What effects do these biases have on future generations of children? As a future professional, how could you redress this persistent though often subtle bias?

What lessons can we learn about education in Asian countries that might help improve children's mathematics learning in the United States? Why is it important that U.S. children should excel in math and science?

How would you rate American schools in terms of their ability to help children learn? What things would you change about our educational system. Why?

The Amazing Minds of Infants

Looking here, looking there, babies are like little scientists, constantly exploring the world around them, with innate abilities we're just beginning to understand.

Text by **Lisa Grunwald**
Reporting by **Jeff Goldberg**

Additional reporting: **Stacey Bernstein, Anne Hollister**

A light comes on. Shapes and colors appear. Some of the colors and shapes start moving. Some of the colors and shapes make noise. Some of the noises are voices. One is a mother's. Sometimes she sings. Sometimes she says things. Sometimes she leaves. What can an infant make of the world? In the blur of perception and chaos of feeling, what does a baby know?

Most parents, observing infancy, are like travelers searching for famous sites: first tooth, first step, first word, first illness, first shoes, first full night of sleep. Most subtle, and most profound of all, is the first time the clouds of infancy part to reveal the little light of a human intelligence.

For many parents, that revelation may be the moment when they see their baby's first smile. For others, it may be the moment when they watch their child show an actual

---

At three months, babies can learn—and remember for weeks—visual sequences and simple mechanical tasks.

---

preference—for a lullaby, perhaps, or a stuffed animal. But new evidence is emerging to show that even before those moments, babies already have wonderfully active minds.

Of course, they're not exactly chatty in their first year of life, so what—and how—babies truly think may always remain a mystery. But using a variety of ingenious techniques that interpret how infants watch and move, students of child development are discovering a host of unsuspected skills. From a rudimentary understanding of math to a

sense of the past and the future, from precocious language ability to an innate understanding of physical laws, children one year and younger know a lot more than they're saying.

MEMORY

Does an infant remember anything? Penelope Leach, that slightly scolding doyenne of the child development field, warns in *Babyhood* that a six- to eight-month-old "cannot hold in his mind a picture of his mother, nor of where she is." And traditionally psychologists have assumed that infants cannot store memories until, like adults, they have the language skills needed to form and retrieve them. But new research suggests that babies as young as three months may be taking quite accurate mental notes.

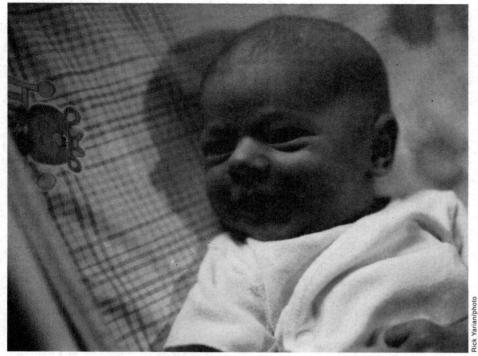

Babies show an unexpected ability to remember surprisingly intricate details.

Rick Yarian/photo

In his lab at the University of Denver, psychologist Marshall Haith has spent much of the past four years putting infants into large black boxes where they lie and look up at TV screens. The program they see is a Haith invention: a sequence of colorful objects appearing on different sides of the monitor. Using an infrared camera linked to a computer, Haith follows the babies' eye movements and has found that after only five tries the babies can anticipate where the next object will appear. With a little more practice, they can foresee a four-step sequence. And up to two weeks later, most can still predict it. Says Haith: "The babies are not just looking. They're analyzing, creating little hypotheses."

Similar findings by Carolyn Rovee-Collier, a psychologist at Rutgers University, suggest that infants can remember surprisingly intricate details. In a typical experiment, she places a baby in a crib beneath an elaborate mobile, ties

one of the baby's ankles to it with a satin ribbon, then observes as the baby kicks and—often gleefully—makes it move. When, weeks later, the baby's feet are left untied and the mobile is returned to the crib, the baby will try to kick again, presumably recalling the palmy days of kicking the last time. But if the mobile's elements are changed even slightly, the baby will remain unmoved—and unmoving. "When we change things," explains Rovee-Collier, "it wipes out the memory. But as soon as we bring back what had become familiar and expected, the memory comes right back. What we've learned from this is that even at two and a half months, an infant's memory is very developed, very specific and incredibly detailed."

Rachel Clifton, a psychologist at the University of Massachusetts, says that an infant's experience at six months can be remembered a full two years later. Clifton stumbled upon her findings while researching motor and hearing

skills. Three years ago she placed 16 six-month-olds in a pitch-dark room with objects that made different sounds. Using infrared cameras like Haith's, she observed how and when the infants reached for the objects. Later, realizing she had created a unique situation that couldn't have been duplicated in real life, she wondered if the babies would remember their experience. Two years after the original experiment, collaborating with psychologist Nancy Myers, she brought the same 16 children back to the lab, along with a control group of 16 other two-and-a-half-year-olds. Amazingly, the experimental group showed the behavior they had at six months, reaching for objects and showing no fear. Fewer control-group toddlers reached for the objects, and many of them cried.

Says Myers: "For so long, we didn't think that infants could rep-

---

At five months, babies have the raw ability to add.

---

resent in their memories the events that were going on around them, but put them back in a similar situation, as we did, and you can make the memory accessible."

MATH

At least a few parental eyebrows—and undoubtedly some expectations—were raised by this recent headline in *The New York Times:* "Study Finds Babies at 5 Months Grasp Simple Mathematics." The story, which reported on the findings of Karen Wynn, a psychologist at the University of Arizona, explained that infants as young as five months had been found to exhibit "a rudimentary ability to add and subtract."

Wynn, who published her research in the renowned scientific journal *Nature,* had based her experiments on a widely observed phenomenon: Infants look longer at things that are unexpected to them, thereby revealing what they do expect, or know. Wynn enacted addition and subtraction equations for babies using Mickey Mouse dolls. In a typical example, she had the babies watch as she placed a doll on a puppet stage, hid it behind a screen, then placed a second doll behind the screen (to represent one plus one). When she removed the screen to reveal three, not two, Mickey Mouse dolls, the infants stared longer at such incorrect outcomes than they had at correct ones. Wynn believes that babies' numerical understanding is "an innate mechanism, somehow built into the biological structure."

Her findings have been met with enthusiasm in the field—not least from Mark Strauss at the University of Pittsburgh, who a decade ago found that somewhat older babies could distinguish at a glance the difference between one, two, three and four balls—nearly as many objects as adults can decipher without counting. Says Strauss: "Five-month-olds are clearly thinking about quantities and applying numerical concepts to their world."

Wynn's conclusions have also inspired skepticism among some researchers who believe her results may reflect infants' ability to perceive things but not necessarily an ability to know what they're perceiving. Wynn herself warns parents not to leap to any conclu-

sions, and certainly not to start tossing algebra texts into their children's cribs. Still, she insists: "A lot more is happening in infants' minds than we've tended to give them credit for."

LANGUAGE

In an old stand-up routine, Robin Williams used to describe his son's dawning ability as a mimic of words—particularly those of the deeply embarrassing four-letter variety. Most parents decide they can no longer speak with complete freedom when their children start talking. Yet current research on language might prompt some to start censoring themselves even earlier.

At six months, babies recognize their native tongue.

At Seattle's University of Washington, psychologist Patricia Kuhl has shown that long before infants actually begin to learn words, they can sort through a jumble of spoken sounds in search of the ones that have meaning. From birth to four months, according to Kuhl, babies are "universal linguists" capable of distinguishing each of the 150 sounds that make up all human speech. But by just six months, they have begun the metamorphosis into specialists who recognize the speech sounds of their native tongue.

In Kuhl's experiment babies listened as a tape-recorded voice repeated vowel and consonant combinations. Each time the sounds changed—from "ah" to "oooh," for example—a toy bear in a box

was lit up and danced. The babies quickly learned to look at the bear when they heard sounds that were new to them. Studying Swedish and American six-month-olds, Kuhl found they ignored subtle variations in pronunciation of their own language's sounds—for instance, the different ways two people might pronounce "ee"—but they heard similar variations in a foreign language as separate sounds. The implication? Six-month-olds can already discern the sounds they will later need for speech. Says Kuhl: "There's nothing external in these six-month-olds that would provide you with a clue that something like this is going on."

By eight to nine months, comprehension is more visible, with babies looking at a ball when their mothers say "ball," for example. According to psychologist Donna Thal at the University of California, San Diego, it is still impossible to gauge just how many words babies understand at this point, but her recent studies of slightly older children indicate that comprehension may exceed expression by a factor as high as a hundred to one. Thal's studies show that although some babies are slow in starting to talk, comprehension appears to be equal between the late talkers and early ones.

PHYSICS

No, no one is claiming that an eight-month-old can compute the trajectory of a moon around a planet. But at Cornell University, psychologist Elizabeth Spelke is finding that babies as young as four months have a rudimentary knowledge of the way the world works—or should work.

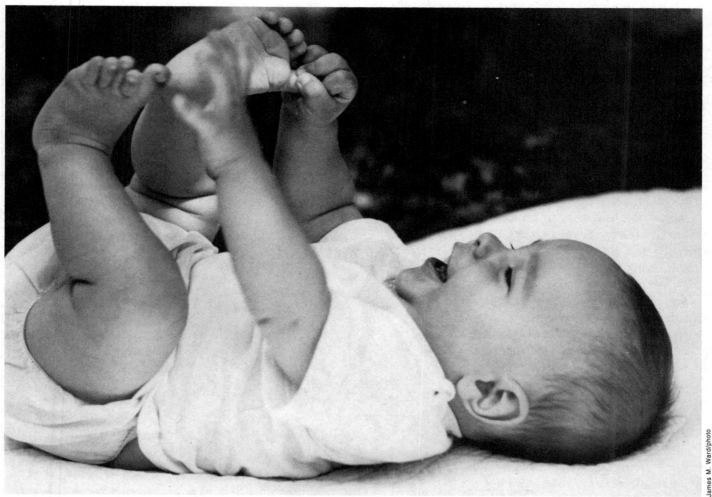

Babies learn how physical objects behave by moving their body parts.

Babies have a built-in sense of how objects behave.

Spelke sets her young subjects up before a puppet stage, where she shows them a series of unexpected actions: a ball seems to roll through a solid barrier, another seems to leap between two platforms, a third seems to hang in midair. Like Karen Wynn with her math experiments, Spelke measures the babies' looking time and has recorded longer intervals for unexpected actions than for expected ones. Again like Wynn, Spelke believes that babies must have some "core" knowledge—in this case, about the way physical objects behave. Says Spelke: "At an age when infants are not able to talk about objects, move around objects, reach for and manipulate objects, or even see objects with high resolution, they appear to recognize where a moving object is when it has left their view and make inferences about where it should be when it comes into sight again."

The notion of an infant's possessing any innate mechanism—other than reflexes like sucking that fade with time—would have shocked the shoes off the pioneers of child development research, who believed, as some still do, that what we know can be learned only through experience. But the belief in biologically programmed core knowledge lies at the heart of the current research—not only with math and physics but with other cognitive skills as well. Indeed, Carnegie Mellon's Mark Johnson believes that the ability of infants to recognize the human face is not learned, as previously thought, but is present at birth. Studying infants, some only 10 minutes old, Johnson has observed a marked preference for pictures of faces to pictures of blank ovals or faces with scrambled features. He believes that we are born with a "template" of the human face that aids our survival by helping us recognize our meal ticket.

James M. Ward/photo

EMOTIONS: THE SHY AND THE LIVELY

A growing number of researchers believe early temperament may indicate later troubles.

One thing that infants are *not* good at is hiding what they feel. Fear, glee, rage, affection: Long before babies start talking, emotions tumble out of them in gestures, tears and belly laughs. But measuring infant temperament—finding a way to quantify its traits—has always been harder than measuring skills.

Around the country, researchers are now combining questionnaires filled in by parents, home visits by trained observers, and newly devised lab tests to explore the mystery of temperamenat. Concentrating on babies older than eight months (the age at which the full range of infant emotions has emerged), investigators have designed more than 50 experimental situations to provoke emotions from fear to sadness, from interest to pleasure. Most children's reactions fall within an average range on such tests. But there are babies on either extreme, and psychologist Nathan Fox at the University of Maryland has begun to explore their responses. Putting his babies in electroencephalogram (EEG) helmets, he has found that particularly inhibited babies show a distinctive brain-wave pattern, which others believe may predict later emotional problems, including depression. Although some scientists agree that early behavior can predict later temperament, other researchers argue that enduring character traits are the exception, not the rule. For psychiatrist Stanley Greenspan of Bethesda, Md., the ability of infants to change is an article of faith. Specializing in babies as young as three months, Greenspan says he can treat what he calls the garden-variety problems of sleep disorders, tan-

Long before babies begin talking, emotions are graphically expressed in their gestures and facial expressions.

WHO/photo

trums and anger in a few sessions. (Don't imagine tiny couches for infant patients; although the babies are closely observed, it's the parents who often get treatment.) For more severe problems, such as suspected learning disorders, he recommends more intensive early intervention—often involving a team of therapists—and has found that this can make a huge difference: "Babies who were very scared, shy and inhibited can completely change and become very assertive, outgoing and confident over a number of months."

The University of Washington's Mary Rothbart has compared infants in Japan, the Netherlands and the U.S. and notes that northern European mothers are most prone to ignore their babies' fussiness with

a stiff-upper-lip approach. When tested at one year by having their mothers leave a room, the Dutch babies are the most distressed and ignore their mothers upon their return. Psychologists call this response an "insecure attachment relationship," and some regard it as an early warning of later anxiety disorders. Says Rothbart: "In the process of soothing a baby, you're helping to teach it to shift its attention away from negative sensations. Adults with anxiety disorders may never have learned to do this." Tellingly, when Dutch mothers were instructed to soothe and play with their fussy babies, the follow-up sessions showed positive results. "With intervention," concludes Rothbart, "you can turn things around."

TAKING INFANTS SERIOUSLY

The ultimate question becomes, should education begin at three months?

One question that might leap to the minds of parents newly informed of their infants' skills is a simple one: So what? What does it mean if children really have these unexpected abilities?

Pointing to the findings on memory that she has published with partner Rachel Clifton, Nancy Myers suggests that if memories of the babies' experience allowed them to be unafraid in the pitch-black room, then exposing children to a wide variety of events and places may make them more accepting of similar situations later on. "I don't want to say that mothers should make an extreme effort to stimulate their babies," Myers says, "but taking a baby to different places, allowing him to see and smell different things, is an important means of establishing familiarity. It will allow the baby to feel freer in the future."

But what about other kinds of skills: Should infants' innate abilities with language or math be consciously nurtured and pushed along?

In Philadelphia, instructors at the Institutes for the Achievement of Human Potential have been coaching parents since 1963 to teach their babies to read from birth. Touting "genetic potential," their program recommends that parents write out on cards everything from "nose" to "kiss" to "Mommy." The new findings about infants' skills have hardly gone unnoticed at the Institutes, where director Janet Doman says: "For the past thirty years, we've been saying that children can learn at very early ages. It's nice to know that science is finally validating what we've known all along."

Yet many of the scientists performing the experiments question the value of such intensive efforts. Says Rutgers's Carolyn Rovee-Collier: "Most of us agree that an infant could be taught to recognize letters and numbers. But the problem is that parents who do these kinds of programs start investing a lot in their infants and become very bound up in their success. It puts great strain on the infants and the parents."

University of Denver psychologist Marshall Haith agrees: "Babies are born prepared to take on the world. We've got to get away from the feeling that we've got this wonderful brain sitting there and we've got to keep pumping information into it. Nature wouldn't have done anything so stupid."

To most researchers, the moral of the story seems to be: Respect your baby, but don't go nuts. "Don't waste your child's fun months," says Karen Wynn, who says her findings about math "should be viewed as no more than a new insight for parents who have young children." Says the University of Pittsburgh's Mark Strauss: "Ideally, we can tell parents a lot more about subtle things they can watch happening in their infants, and that will make watching and getting involved more fun."

Infants to Toddlers:
Qualities of Effective Transitions

Jerlean E. Daniel

Jerlean Daniel, Ph.D., is an assistant professor at the program in child development and child care in the School of Social Work, University of Pittsburgh. She is the former director of the University Child Development Center and has had 18 years of experience directing child care programs.

For some time scholars have acknowledged that young children in group care and education programs thrive emotionally, socially, and cognitively in environments where there are trained, consistently available, nurturing adults in sufficient numbers to promote time for interaction between adult and child (Phillips & Howes, 1987). Although this is readily recognized within the context of a given group of children, the same factors are important when a child is assigned to a new group. The qualities of an effective transition between groups must be given the same attention for the child to have a positive transition experience.

The following discussion of effective qualities of an infant-to-toddler transition is based on relevant child-development literature as well as the author's 18 years of experience as a child care center director. In particular, the eight years as director at the University of Pittsburgh Child Development Center (UCDC) provided the experiences drawn upon for this article. (UCDC was accredited by the National Academy of Early Childhood Programs in 1992.) Consider the following scenario.

At a late-fall planning meeting, the infant-group staff discussion turns to a question of who will be the next children to make the transition to the toddler group. The infant-group staff believes that three children will be ready to move to the older group in March. Louise is the primary caregiver for two of the three infants. The third infant, Billy, knows Louise well. Louise has worked the early shift for the past six weeks that Billy has been coming to the center at 6:30 A.M., since his mother's shift changed. Billy still takes a morning nap because he has to get up so early. He is progressing well in all areas of development.

Aeisha, who was two months premature at birth, is walking fairly well but is not yet as sure-footed as she will need to be to go for walks with the toddler group. Aeisha will be 18 months old in early February. A month's delay to March, before moving permanently to the toddler group, should give her enough time to develop more physically. Her verbal skills are slightly ahead of what is normal for her age. She really enjoys the company of "Sam," short for Samantha. Having children who know each other go through transition together is helpful.

Sam is a robust, take-charge child with two older brothers. When a toddler occasionally visits the infant room, Sam is quite skillful at engaging the toddler in activities of her choosing. The infant-group staff believes that, by March, all three can make an effective transition to the toddler group.

Billy's primary caregiver, Sue, will talk with Billy's mother to determine if she has relevant information about her work-shift rotation over the next several months. They will also discuss ways that each of them can make sure that Billy gets the rest he needs to enable him to enjoy the active morning schedule as well as the afternoon naps in the toddler group.

Louise will talk with the other two families about the transition to the toddler group. She particularly wants to encourage Aeisha's parents to observe in the toddler room. Louise wants to know if the parents share her concern about Aeisha's walking or have any other concerns that Louise might not be aware of. Thus begins the gradual evolution of the transition from infants to toddlers.

At UCDC an infant group consists of 12 children between the ages of 6 weeks and 18 months. Children have their own schedules in the infant group. The staff–child ratio is one caregiver to four infants. Each child is assigned a primary caregiver; thus each infant has a consistent person with whom to bond. In addition, the caregivers have the opportunity to provide more personalized, quality care for each child.

UCDC parents also frequently bond with the primary caregiver. Special friendships often develop between caregivers and parents in the form of an ad hoc extended family.

Toddler groups at UCDC consist of 15 children and 3 staff. The age range is 18 months to 3 years. In the toddler group, primary caregivers are not assigned, but children choose their own primary person over time. In the toddler group, children have their first center experiences with glue, scissors, wooden blocks, puzzles, and a regularly scheduled group time with stories and songs. Toddlers also have a different daily routine and more complex social demands from peers.

UCDC's philosophy provides ample opportunity for the children to select their own activities from a developmentally appropriate environment prepared in advance by the teaching staff. The staff facilitates the children's exploration of the room by taking their cues from children about timing the introduction of new activities or needing to allow enough time for the children to revisit cherished enjoyable endeavors.

Although UCDC's infant groupings range in age from 6 weeks to 18 months, standard practice in child care centers throughout the country is to divide children in this age range into at least two different age groupings. The UCDC practice of maintaining this range as an intact group takes a lot of effort to keep everyone safe and constructively engaged in a group that includes walkers, crawlers, and those who are not yet turning over. As the staff plan for the day, they use to advantage the children's different rhythms of sleeping, eating, and awaking times. They also must get down on the floor, using their bodies as barriers or perches or as part of an obstacle course for investigative children.

The theoretical basis for a single infant cohort for children between 6 weeks and 18 months is found in the work of Margaret Mahler (1968) and Erik Erikson (1963). According to Mahler, children from birth through 18 months undergo a complex psychophysical process that includes building the original necessary symbiotic ties with the mother through the gradual separation into the child's own self (individuation). As the child matures physically and is able to move away from the mother, the child continually needs to elicit psychological feedback in the form of protection and reassurance from her. The stability of this parent–child relationship is crucial to the *self* that the child will become.

Erik Erikson's conceptualizations of the child's psychosocial growth from birth through 18 months—the development of trust through autonomy (1963)—correspond with Mahler's separation and individuation phases. Parental responses to the child's physical

need for comfort are the building blocks for the child's contiguous psychosocial growth. Physical maturation in the 6-week to 18-month age range offers repeated, increasingly complex opportunities for the child to practice psychological separateness, or autonomy.

Although the child's attachment to the substitute caregiver in a child care situation is not the same as her attachment to the parent, the attachment is important nonetheless (Mahler, 1968, pp. 49–50; Dittmann, 1981, p. 134). On a daily basis in the program (center or family day care home), the child relies upon this substitute caregiver for the psychosocial supports to face challenges, retreat for refueling nurturance, seek protection, and gain approval for continued positive growth. UCDC views the 6-week to 18-month infant groupings as a developmentally appropriate response to the physical and simultaneous psychosocial needs of the child.

Transition as mountain climbing

Let us consider further the perilous nature of transitions, particularly at 18 months. Gil Foley, formerly of Albright College in Reading, Pennsylvania, offered one of the best descriptions of Mahler's separation and individuation process (personal communication, UCDC Parent Meeting, 1988). Foley likened this developmental sequencing to learning to mountain-climb. He asked parents to imagine that they were the learners. Initially, the expert climber is right there, showing the novice which foot and hand to put where. The beginner's movements are tenuous and faltering at first. There are missteps and slips; it is scary. The presence of the expert, the person who has experience and knowledge, is comforting. The expert encourages the novice, alters her directives to fit the circumstances, and generally facilitates the halting movement up the mountain.

Climbing the mountain becomes easier with practice. Without realizing, the novice moves up ahead of the teacher. Perhaps, just wanting to share a triumphant moment with the nurturant expert, the novice looks back, beaming, only to discover that the expert is not there and the learner is alone on the mountain. In terror and completely vulnerable, the novice stiffens, shaken, until the expert, on whom the beginner has grown to depend, comes to the rescue. Once comforted properly, the novice can then return to the task, reassured by the expert's close proximity.

The first approach at the foot of Mount Olympus

The actual UCDC transition from the infant group to the toddler group takes approximately four to six weeks. Throughout this period the child's day begins as it customarily does between parent and child. The parent takes the child to the infant room and says goodbye. During the first week, after breakfast, the child goes with the primary caregiver from the infant room for short visits to the toddler room.

The toddler-group staff, naturally, greet the infant-room visitors warmly. These new adults are not total strangers. Throughout the child's stay at the center, he or she comes into contact weekly with center adults other than the primary caregiver. The infant-group caregiver and the child stay only about a half hour the first couple of visits. Usually as the visits lengthen, the infant-group caregiver stays for about an hour. She and the child explore the new environment together. Many items in the toddler room are not available in the infant room, for example, paste, scissors, pets, and different people.

During the first few days, the infant-group staff person serves as the infant's primary guide to the new surroundings. Toddler-group staff do not consciously seek interactions with the young visitors until late in the first week, when the infant has had an opportunity to look them over from afar, note the friendly cordiality between the infant-group and toddler-group adults, or perhaps have contact that occurred naturally out of the infant's close proximity to the new adult. Toward the end of that first week, the toddler-group staff begin to interact more consciously with the visiting child. Toddler-group staff, for example, invite the visitor to join a particular activity. The infant-group caregiver remains nearby or in view, according to the needs of the child. Sowing the seeds of the subtle shift in expertise from one trustworthy adult to another has begun.

The backward glance

During the second week the child gradually stays two-and-a-half to three hours (until just before lunch). The toddler-group staff now share the role of nurturant expert with the infant-group caregiver, who makes sure before leaving the toddler room that (1) the child knows that the caregiver is leaving but will return to take the child back to the infant room for lunch; (2) the child is engaged in an activity; and (3) the toddler-group staff know that the infant-group caregiver is leaving and has let the child know that the toddler-group staff will be there as needed to support him or her.

By now the child has at least one favorite new activity and might seek out a particular child or be sought out by one of these older children. As expected, Foley's described slippage in the midst of all of the new and exciting experiences and accomplishments brings fear and uncertainty. Perhaps the riding toy that the child wants is already occupied by someone who has no intention of sharing. If the

incident occurs when the infant-group caregiver is not in the room, a toddler-group caregiver moves in to comfort, reassure, and redirect. If the young visitor is not yet ready to rely on the new adult or is too upset to be comforted by the new adult, then the infant-group caregiver is called to return to the toddler room for a while and eventually take the child back to the infant room. The transition continues the next day.

During week three, the child stays in the toddler room for lunch. By now the toddler-group staff have indeed supplanted the infant-group staff as the people with the expertise regarding this "toddler mountain." The toddler room represents a wide plateau full of challenges that suit the curiosity of the young, visiting, new toddler (Dittmann, 1981, p. 136). The toddler-group staff know much more about the nuances of the "plateau" than do the infant-group staff. The toddler-group staff know and gladly share the secrets of the complex social mores of taking turns and sharing. They know just what to substitute when there are not enough riding toys for everybody.

Parent involvement

Keeping a steady flow of communication with parents from the beginning to the end of the transition is important. Most of the initial communication with the infant-group staff is verbal. Both toddler- and infant-group staff encourage parents to visit the new room—preferably before the transition begins.

At the midway point (the third week) in the infant-to-toddler transition process, the children know, upon entering the building, which direction to go to get to each of the rooms. Children often pull the parent toward the new toddler room. Staff urge parents not to give in to this but to keep the original routine. Staff explain that a parent leaving a child in the new room before the transition is complete interjects into the process the potential emotional turmoil of having to separate from a parent in a strange situation. Separating from a staff person with whom the child is only secondarily attached and from whom the child expects new adventures routinely is far less anxiety provoking for the child. If the parent places him- or herself physically into the transition process, all of the dynamics change. The transition is no longer a gradual build-up over time of exhilarated exploration of the mountain but rather an additional source of distress, much like the feeling of abandonment.

Parents are often excited about the transition process, particularly when all indications are that it is going well. Some parents find resisting the pull of the child to the new room difficult. Others try to rush the process. Such parents are greeted warmly in the toddler room but sent back to the infant room to start the day. A typical staff response is, "Hi, it's good to see you this morning. Billy is really enjoying the toddler room. We are going out again today to collect leaves. Billy needs to go to tell Louise 'Good morning' and have his breakfast so that he is ready to come back to stay for a while."

UCDC staff experience has been that not until about 20 months does the normal psychosocial vulnerability of the 18th month begin between parent and child. This outside-the-family activity (the transition process from infants to toddlers) may so expand the concrete experiential base of the child that it delays the typical, psychologically developmental vulnerability of the approximately 18-month-old child. By 20 months the parent knows that the new room is not bringing about these changes; rather, they are the result of the natural phenomenon that occurs between parent and child during rapprochement (Mahler, 1968). The toddler-group staff are adept at helping parents as they process this normal psychosocial growth spurt. Parents have grown in their trust of the toddler-group staff over these first couple of months such that they are able to accept and use the insights of the toddler-group caregivers. Whether or not this "clinginess" of child to parent, delayed to about 20 months, is of a different intensity is worth investigating.

Almost there

Usually during the fourth week in the infant-to-toddler transition, the child begins taking naps in the new room. This gives the transitioning infant plenty of time to get to know the new surroundings, new adults, and new children before having to sleep among them. After naptime the child goes back to the infant room. UCDC staff strive not to tax a child to the point that she or he wants to leave the new room. Keeping a child excited about the new adventure is easier if she or he leaves the situation before wanting to do so. This practice lessens the emotional pressure on the child in a new situation.

"Mommy, this is my new room"

By the fifth or sixth week, the new toddler has completed transition—successfully reached the top of the mountain. At this time the new drop-off routine begins. Parent and child go to the toddler room together and say their goodbyes for the day. Staff strive to keep this morning separation an upbeat affair. Children are encouraged to show their parents the new room, some item that the child likes to play with, or a display that the child helped create. Toddler-group staff make quite a fuss over the fact that the child is now a toddler, and they indicate how glad they are to have the child as a part of the toddler room.

Trouble spots and adjustments

Certain interruptions in the transition process either make continuing impossible or protract the process into several additional, usually traumatic, weeks; thus, as a general UCDC rule, if the family is changing residences, is going on vacation, is expecting a new baby, knows that a parent will be traveling more than usual, or will be experiencing some other potentially stressful event during the scheduled transition time, staff and parents plan the transition to either occur earlier or be delayed, as deemed necessary.

Although the typical infant-to-toddler transition facilitation schedule occurs in the morning after breakfast, it is altered when necessary to suit the needs of the child (Dittmann, 1981, p. 134). Jennifer, for example, had difficulty getting used to the new room after breakfast, when all of the children were there and the room was full of activity. She clung to the infant-group caregiver for dear life. Jennifer typically arrived at the center at 6:30 A.M. The infant-group staff person was thus able to take her to the new room earlier so that she could get adjusted and gradually move into the toddler experience before the room filled to its enrollment capacity.

During the first two weeks of transitions, the staff members involved in the original room alter their schedules to accommodate the child's new routine. Part-time staff fill in for infant-group staff involved in the transition process.

Conclusion

This has been an account of how one child care center staff puts theory into infant-to-toddler transition practice. The first principle of conduct is to protect and nourish each child's psychosocial development. Toward that end, transitions between infants and toddlers occur over a period of several weeks, involving parent–staff consultation and continual adult support. Children are given the time they need to manage the transition in small, incremental steps. The result is a smooth transition that allows the child both the independence and the support needed to make a positive growth step. Moreover, the effective transition enables the child to move from one quality environment to another. Similarly, within the program, the transition from the toddler group to preschool must take into consideration the needs of the young three-year-old. Children face multiple transitions in life. Appropriate adult intervention can help them build positive coping skills.

References

Dittmann, L.L. (1981). Where have all the mothers gone, and what difference does it make? In B. Weissbourd & J.S. Musick (Eds.),

Infants: Their social environments (pp. 129–145). Washington, DC: NAEYC.

Erikson, E. (1963). *Childhood and society* (2nd ed.). New York: W.W. Norton.

Mahler, M. (1968). *On human symbiosis and the vicissitudes of individuation: Vol. I. Infantile psychosis* (3rd ed.). New York: International Universities Press.

Phillips, D., & Howes, C. (1987). Indicators of quality child care: Review of research. In D. Philips (Ed.), *Quality in child care: What does research tell us?* (pp. 1–20). Washington, DC: NAEYC.

For further reading

Balaban, N. (1992). The role of the child care professional in caring for infants, toddlers, and their families. *Young Children, 47*(5), 66–71.

Bredekamp, S., & Rosegrant, T. (Eds.). (1992). *Reaching potentials: Appropriate curriculum and assessment for young children: Vol. 1.* Washington, DC: NAEYC.

Buzzelli, C.A. (1992). Research in review. Young children's moral understanding: Learning about right and wrong. *Young Children, 47*(6), 47–53.

Cawlfield, M.E. (1992). Velcro time: The language connection. *Young Children, 47*(4), 26–30.

Coleman, M. (1991). Planning for the changing nature of family life in schools for young children. *Young Children, 46*(4), 15–20.

Dittmann, L.L. (Ed.). (1984). *The infants we care for.* Washington, DC: NAEYC.

Gonzalez-Mena, J. (1986). Toddlers: What to expect. *Young Children, 42*(1), 47–51.

Gonzalez-Mena, J. (1992). Taking a culturally sensitive approach in infant-toddler programs. *Young Children, 47*(2), 4–9.

Gottschall, S. (1989). Understanding and accepting separation feelings. *Young Children, 44*(6), 11–16.

Greenberg, P. (1991). *Character development: Encouraging self-esteem & self-discipline in infants, toddlers, & two-year-olds.* Washington, DC: NAEYC.

Greenberg, P. (1991). Do you take care of toddlers? [Photostory]. *Young Children, 46*(2), 52–53.

Greenberg, P. (1992). Promoting positive peer relations. [Photostory]. *Young Children, 47*(4), 51–55.

Hignett, W.F. (1988). Food for thought. Infant/toddler day care, yes; *BUT* we'd better make it good. *Young Children, 44*(1), 32–33.

Honig, A.S. (1985). High quality infant/toddler care: Issues and dilemmas. *Young Children, 40*(5), 40–46.

Honig, A.S. (1986). Research in review. Stress and coping in children *(Part 1). Young Children, 41*(4), 50–63.

Honig, A.S. (1986). Research in review. Stress and coping in children *(Part 2). Young Children, 41*(5), 47–59.

Honig, A.S. (1989). Quality infant/toddler caregiving: Are there magic recipes? *Young Children, 44*(4), 4–10.

Honig, A.S. (1993). Mental health for babies: What do theory and research teach us? *Young Children, 48*(3), 69–76.

Howes, C. (1989). Research in review. Infant child care. *Young Children, 44*(6), 24–28.

Jervis, K. (Ed.). (1984). *Separation.* Washington, DC: NAEYC.

Karnes, M.B., Johnson, L.J., & Beauchamp, K.D.F. (1988). Enhancing essential relationships: Developing a nurturing affective environment for young children. *Young Children, 44*(1), 58–65.

McCracken, J.B. (1986). *Reducing stress in young children's lives.* Washington, DC: NAEYC.

Meyerhoff, M.K. (1992). Viewpoint. Infant/toddler day care versus reality. *Young Children, 47*(6), 44–45.

Pizzo, P.D. (1990). Family-centered Head Start for infants and toddlers: A renewed direction for Project Head Start. *Young Children, 45*(6), 30–35.

Ross, H.W. (1992). Integrating infants with disabilities? Can "ordinary" caregivers do it? *Young Children, 47*(3), 65–71.

San Fernando Valley Child Care Consortium. (1988). *Setting up for infant care: Guidelines for centers and family day care homes.* Washington, DC: NAEYC.

Warren, R.M. (1977). *Caring: Supporting children's growth.* Washington, DC: NAEYC.

Weissbourd, B., & Musick, J.S. (Eds.). (1981). *Infants: Their social environments.* Washington, DC: NAEYC.

Whitebook, M., & Granger, R.C. (1989). "Mommy, who's going to be my teacher today?" Assessing teacher turnover. *Young Children, 44*(4), 11–14.

Where Pelicans Kiss Seals

IN THE SURPRISING WORLD OF CHILDREN'S ART, DELIGHTFUL IMAGES AND ORIGINAL RULES ARE CREATED TO REPRESENT THE WORLD.

ELLEN WINNER

Ellen Winner is a psychologist at Boston College and at Project Zero of Harvard University.

The story of how children learn to draw seems at first glance to be a simple one: At a very early age they begin by scribbling with any available marker on any available surface. At first the children's drawings are simple, clumsy and unrealistic; gradually they become more technically skilled and realistic.

But the development of drawing is not quite so simple and straightforward. In fact, the story turns out to be quite complex. Watch a 2-year-old scribbling. The child moves the marker vigorously across the page, leaving a tangled web of circular and zig zag lines. It looks as if the marks themselves are an accident—the unintended result of the child's arm movements. But if you replace the child's marker with one that leaves no trace, the child will stop scribbling, as psychologist James Gibson and Patricia Yonas, then a graduate student, showed in 1968. Even though very young children enjoy moving their arms vigorously, they are also interested in making marks on a surface.

If we do not watch a scribble in the making, but only see the final product, it may look like a meaningless tangle of lines. And this is how scribbles have traditionally been viewed—as nonsymbolic designs. But 1- and 2-year-olds are rapidly mastering the concept that words, objects and gestures stand for things. So why shouldn't they also grasp that marks on a page can stand

for things? Some of the more recent studies of children as they scribble suggest that these early scrawls are actually experiments in representa-

TO A 2-YEAR-OLD, SCRIBBLES AREN'T JUST SCRIBBLES, THEY'RE A PLANE FLYING ACROSS THE SKY.

tion—although not purely pictorial representation.

Psychologist Dennie Wolf, preschool teacher Carolee Fucigna and psychologist Howard Gardner of Project Zero at Harvard University studied how the drawing of nine children developed from age 1 to 7. The researchers took detailed notes on the process of scribbling, and their investigations show us that children have surprising representational abilities long before they spontaneously produce a recognizable form.

At first the representation is almost entirely gestural, not pictorial. Wolf observed a 1½-year-old who took the marker and hopped it around on the page, leaving a mark with each imprint and explaining as she drew, "Rabbit goes hop-hop" (Figure 1). This child was symbolizing the rabbit's motion, not its size, shape or color. The meaning was carried primarily by the marker itself, which stood for the rab-

bit, and by the process of marking. Someone who saw only the dots left on the page would not see a rabbit. Nonetheless, in the process of marking, the child was representing a rabbit's movement. Moreover, the dots themselves stood for the rabbit's footprints. Here in the child's earliest scribbles we already see glimmerings of the idea that marks on a page can stand for things in the world.

Two-year-olds rarely spontaneously create recognizable forms in their scribbles, but they have the latent ability to do so. When Wolf or Fucigna dictated to 2-year-olds a list of features (head, tummy, arms, legs), these children plotted the features systematically on the page, placing them in correct relative positions (Figure 2). But they lacked the notion that a line stands for the edge of an object and had no way to represent parts of features, since each feature was either a point or a patch. The children clearly understood, however, that marks on a surface can be used to stand for features "out there," off the page, and that they can be used to show the relative spatial locations of features.

Typically at age 3, but sometimes as early as age 2, children's spontaneous scribbles become explicitly pictorial. They often begin by making gestural scribbles but then, noticing that they have drawn a recognizable shape, label and further elaborate it. For example, one 3½-year-old studied by Wolf, Gardner and Fucigna looked at his scribble and called it "a pelican kissing a seal." He then went on to add eyes and freckles so that the drawing would look even more like a pelican and a seal (Figure 3). Another child, on the eve of his second birthday, made some seemingly unreadable marks, looked at his picture and said with confidence, "Chicken pie and noodies" (his

Reprinted with permission from *Psychology Today*, August 1986, pp. 25-26, 30, 32-35. © 1986 by Sussex Publishers, Inc.

word for noodles). Clearly he saw the similarity between the lines on the page and noodles on a plate.

Sometimes children between 2 and 3 will use both gestural and pictorial modes at different times. A 2-year-old studied by art educator John Matthews of Goldsmiths College in London drew a cross-like shape, then looked at it and called it "an airplane." One month later, this same child moved his brush all around in a rotating motion while announcing, "This is an airplane." The label was the same, but the processes and products were different. In the first case, the drawing was an airplane because it looked like one. In the second case, it was an airplane because the marker moved like one, leaving a record of the airplane's path.

With pictorially based representations, the child begins to draw enclosed shapes such as circular forms and discovers that a line can be used to represent an object's edge. This major milestone marks the child's invention of a basic rule of graphic symbolization. This invention cannot be attributed to closer observation of nature, since objects don't have lines around them. Nor can it be attributed to the influence of seeing line drawings. As shown by psychologist John Kennedy at the University of Toronto, congenitally blind children and adults, when asked to make drawings (using special equipment), also use lines to stand for an object's boundaries.

Sometime around 3 to 4 years of age, children create their first image of a human—the universal "tadpole"—consisting of a circle and two lines for legs. Figure 4 shows a typical tadpole, with a circle standing for either the head alone, or, more probably, head and trunk fused; it has two legs but no arms. It was drawn by a 3-year-old; by 4, children begin to distinguish the head from the trunk and often add arms to their figures.

The tadpole is indisputably a purely graphic (rather than gestural) representation of a human. But why would children universally invent such an odd image to stand for a person? Many people believe that children draw humans in this queer fashion because this is the best they can do; the tadpole is simply a failed attempt at realistic representation. According to some investigators, including psychol-

Figure 1: While hopping a marker around the page, a 1½-year-old said, "Rabbit goes hop, hop, hop" and made these marks.

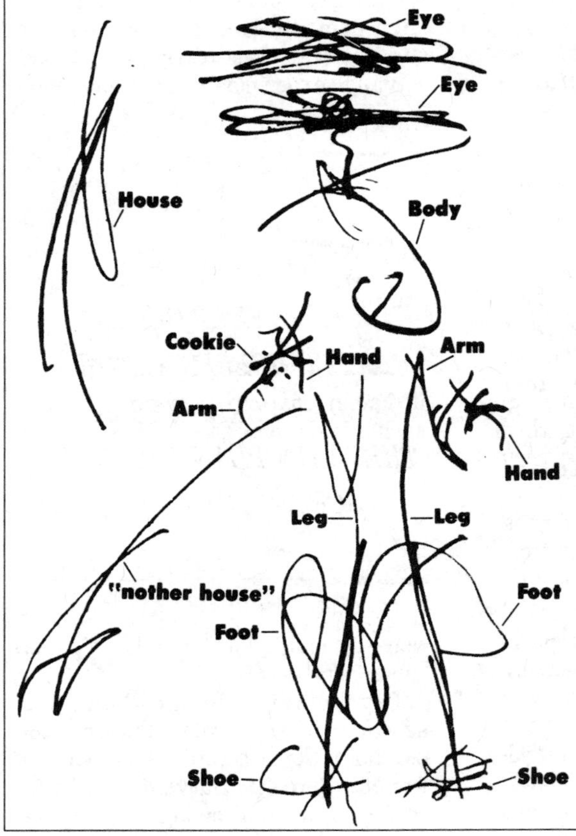

Figure 2: When someone dictates a list of body parts, even 2-year-olds can show them in their correct positions.

ogist Jean Piaget, children's drawings are intended to be realistic, but children draw what they know rather than what they see. Hence, the tadpole, with its odd omissions of trunk and arms, must indicate children's lack of knowledge about the parts of the human body and how they are organized.

Psychologist Norman Freeman of the University of Bristol has a different way of accounting for the typical omissions. He notes that children draw a person from top to bottom, in sequence. We know from verbal-memory tasks that people are subject to "primacy" and "recency" effects—that is,

after hearing a sequence of words, they recall best the words they heard first and last and tend to forget those that came in between. The child, Freeman argues, is showing such effects in drawing, recalling the head (drawn first) and legs (drawn last) and forgetting the parts in the middle. As Freeman sees it, tadpoles result from deficient recall, not deficient concepts.

But other research suggests that we should look on the tadpole more positively. Psychologist Claire Golomb of the University of Massachusetts in Boston suggests that children know more about the human body than

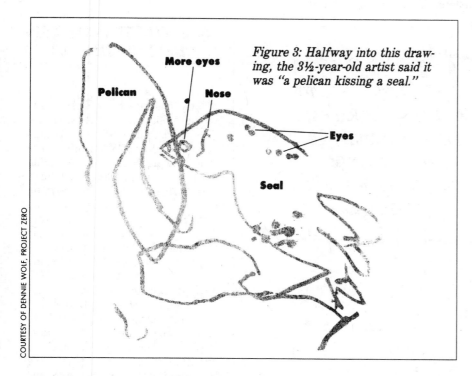

COURTESY OF DENNIE WOLF, PROJECT ZERO

More eyes

Pelican

Nose

Eyes

Seal

Figure 3: Halfway into this drawing, the 3½-year-old artist said it was "a pelican kissing a seal."

about how to draw it, and their body-part omissions are not due to forgetting. She found that when 3-year-olds were asked to name body parts, they almost always mentioned arms, although they typically omitted them from their tadpoles. She also discovered that such children were less likely to create tadpoles when they made Play-Doh people or when they were given a two-dimensional assemble-the-parts task. Even on a drawing task, when Golomb gave children a drawing

WHY DO 3-YEAR-OLDS FIRST DRAW A PERSON AS AN ODD ARMLESS 'TADPOLE'— A CIRCLE WITH TWO LINES?

of a head with features to complete, 3- and 4-year-olds (who ordinarily drew tadpoles) typically differentiated a head and a trunk. Finally, if children were asked to draw someone playing ball—a task implicitly requiring that

they draw arms—they were likely to include them (Figure 5).

One 3-year-old drew a tadpole but described it in full detail as she drew it, naming parts that were not there, such as feet, cheeks and chin. Clearly, this child was not trying to show all of these parts, because she made no special marks for them. Instead, her simple figure stood for an entire human in all its complexity.

Although adults make drawings that are far more complex, they, too, do not (and cannot) draw all that they see. Young children are more selective than adults, no doubt because drawing is difficult for them, but also because they have not yet been fired up by the peculiarly Western pictorial ideal of realism.

Psychologist Rudolf Arnheim, formerly of the University of Michigan, argues that children try to create the simplest form that can still be "read" as a human. Because they have a limited repertoire of forms, they reduce them to simple geometric shapes. In the case of the tadpole, they usually reduce the human body to a circle and two straight lines.

Adult artists often deliberately select a limited repertoire of forms and, like children, reduce natural forms to a few simple geometric shapes. They recognize that realism is but one ideal among many and may choose not to be realistic. Young children, however,

seem to draw simple geometric shapes in part because realism does not spark their interest. Once they do catch the desire for realism, Golomb says, that desire begins to overcome their natural tendency to simplicity, leading them toward more complex, graphically differentiated drawing.

By late childhood or early adolescence, children in our culture begin to master linear perspective, the Western system for creating the illusion of three-dimensional depth on a two-dimensional surface, invented and perfected during the Renaissance.

Many people believe that the ability to use perspective is taught, either explicitly in art class or tacitly through exposure to pictures showing such perspective. But something far more creative on the part of children may be happening, says psychologist John Willats, formerly of the North East London Polytechnic.

Willats seated groups of children of different ages in front of a table with objects on it and asked them to draw what they saw (Figure 6a). The children, 108 in all, who were from 5 to 17 years old, used six different systems of perspective; these, Willats found, formed a developmental sequence:

The 5- and 6-year-olds were entirely unable to represent depth. They simply drew a rectangular box for the tabletop and let the objects float above it (stage 1: Figure 6b). Seven- and 8-year-olds drew the tabletop as a straight line or thin surface and placed the objects on that line (stage 2: Figure 6c). Again, their pictures contained no recognizable strategy for representing depth.

At about age 9, children made their first readable attempts to depict the third dimension. They drew the tabletop as a rectangle and placed the objects inside or on top of the rectangle (stage 3: Figure 6d). These children had invented a system for representing depth: To depict near objects, draw them on the bottom of the page; to depict far objects, draw them on the top of the page. In other words, transform near or far in the world into down or up on paper. No one teaches a child to draw this way. Moreover, no child actually sees a tabletop as a rectangle (unless looking at it from a bird's-eye view). Hence, this strategy is a genuine invention.

Younger adolescents drew the tabletop as a parallelogram rather than as a rectangle (stage 4: Figure 6e). As in the previous stage, they incorrectly drew the lines parallel, not converging, but they now correctly used oblique lines to represent edges receding in space. Again, such a system for representing depth is neither taught nor based on visual experience, since using parallel lines is not optically correct.

In the last two stages, older adolescents drew in perspective, making the lines of the tabletop converge. Some made the lines converge only slightly (naïve perspective—stage 5: Figure 6f); others achieved geometrically correct perspective (stage 6: Figure 6g).

This sequence cannot be explained simply by a growing desire and ability to draw objects as they really appear, because as children develop, their drawings actually get less realistic before they get more realistic. A tabletop, viewed from eye level, might be seen as an edge (stage 2), or from a bird's-eye view it might be seen as a rectangle (stage 3). But no one ever sees a tabletop as a parallelogram (stage 4) or with incorrectly converging edges (stage 5).

Willats believes this sequence does not result from copying pictures in perspective. After all, he argues, in our culture drawings with perspective rarely depict a rectangular surface as either a rectangle (stage 3) or a parallelogram (stage 4).

But I believe these two stages may indeed be attempts to copy the perspective seen in pictures. A tabletop drawn in perspective shows its surface (and stage 3 is an advance over stage 2 because it shows the surface), and its lines are at nonright angles (and stage 4 is an advance over stage 3 because the angles are oblique). But if children are trying to copy perspective drawings, they are doing it at their own developmental level. For example, in stage-4 drawings, children reduce what should be a trapezoid to a simpler, more regular parallelogram.

One way to test the effect of exposure to pictorial perspective is to ask children to copy such pictures. Freeman did just this, finding that although children could not copy the model's perspective system accurately, they could adopt a system more advanced than the one they used spontaneously. Freeman showed children

PICASSO: I USED TO DRAW LIKE RAPHAEL, BUT IT HAS TAKEN ME A WHOLE LIFETIME TO LEARN TO DRAW LIKE CHILDREN.

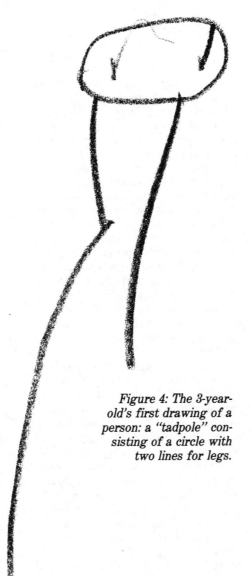

Figure 4: The 3-year-old's first drawing of a person: a "tadpole" consisting of a circle with two lines for legs.

ARE SMARTER CHILDREN BETTER ARTISTS?

Some children show more drawing ability than others and produce elaborate, realistic drawings at an early age. When others are still drawing tadpoles, these children are drawing human figures with differentiated body parts in correct proportion and are even putting depth cues into their drawings. People often assume that these advanced artists are brighter than those who lag behind and produce primitive, undifferentiated, unrealistic drawings.

Indeed, psychologists have developed intelligence tests based, in part, on the assumption that drawing level reflects cognitive level, IQ or both. For instance, as part of the Stanford-Binet Intelligence Scale, children are asked to copy shapes, and the Goodenough-Harris Draw-a-Man test uses drawing as a measure of IQ, with more parts and details yielding higher scores.

But studies of both normal and abnormal people show that drawing ability is independent of ability in other areas. The most dramatic evidence comes from studies of idiot savants who, despite severe retardation, autism or both, draw at an astonishingly sophisticated level.

The best-known case, studied by psychologist Lorna Selfe, formerly of the University of Nottingham, is that of Nadia, an autistic child who, as early as age 3½, drew in an optically realistic style reminiscent of Leonardo da Vinci. In addition to her studies of Nadia, Selfe compared retarded autistic children who were gifted in drawing with normal children of the same mental age. She found that the retarded children were better able to depict proportion, depth and the overlap of objects in space.

In a similar vein, psychologists Neil O'Connor and Beate Hermelin of the Medical Research Council Developmental Psychology Project in London studied five young-adult idiot savants who had special drawing ability but very low verbal and performance IQ scores and com-

ARE SMARTER CHILDREN BETTER ARTISTS? (continued)

Top: Nadia, 5½, extremely autistic and artistic, made the drawing (left) that resembles a Leonardo da Vinci sketch (right). Below: An early elementary school child drew in perspective, revealing unusual ability.

pared them with other equally mentally retarded people who had no special drawing ability. They gave these two groups a battery of tests, including the Draw-a-Man test. On this test the retarded artists performed at a much higher level than the equally retarded nonartists; their performance was also much higher than their IQ scores would have predicted. The retarded artists particularly excelled in their ability to depict body proportion, rather than in depicting specific features, providing details or in their levels of motor control and coordination.

If gifted artists—both retarded and nonretarded—aren't necessarily more intelligent, what skills enable them to draw better than other people? To address this question, O'Connor and Hermelin used a battery of other tests, all of which assessed visual memory. When retarded artists were compared with retarded nonartists, the artists outperformed the nonartists on all tests.

Visual-memory skill, independent of IQ, also seems to help normal children to excel at drawing. Recently, Hermelin and O'Connor compared artistically gifted normal children with nongifted children matched in IQ. They found that the artists had superior memory for two-dimensional designs and were more skilled at identifying incomplete pictures.

With psychologist Elizabeth Rosenblatt at Harvard's Project Zero, I recently completed a study along the same lines. We compared preadolescent children, selected by their art teachers as gifted in drawing, with other children selected as average in drawing ability. We showed the youngsters pairs of pictures and asked them to indicate their preferences. Later we showed them the paired pictures again, but one member of each pair had been slightly altered (in line quality, color, form, composition or content). We asked the children to identify which member of each pair had been changed and to say what was different about it.

The artistically gifted students performed significantly better than the nonartists on both aspects of this task, even though, when they first saw the pictures, they did not know that they would be asked later to recall them. Apparently, children with drawing talent simply cannot forget the patterns they see around them, just as musicians often report being unable to get melodies out of their minds.

Figure 5: A young child, asked to draw people playing ball, includes arms.

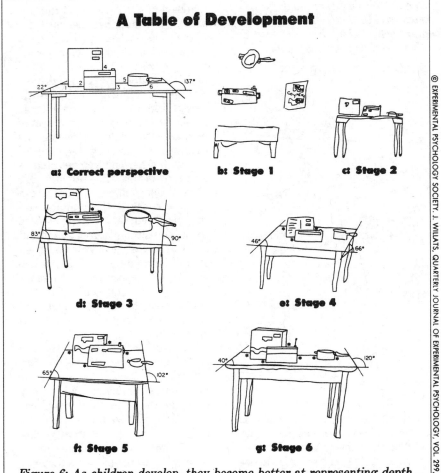

Figure 6: As children develop, they become better at representing depth. The first table (a), drawn in correct perspective, shows what the children were trying to copy.

© EXPERIMENTAL PSYCHOLOGY SOCIETY. J. WILLATS, QUARTERLY JOURNAL OF EXPERIMENTAL PSYCHOLOGY, VOL. 299, 1977, P. 162.

ages 5 to 8 a drawing of a table in oblique perspective (stage 4) and asked them to copy it. About half of the children produced stage-3 drawings. What is significant is that, in their attempts at imitation, half of these children—who were at the age when they would be expected to make stage-1 or stage-2 drawings—actually drew at stage 3.

Thus, children do not acquire perspective by directly copying pictures drawn in perspective. But exposure to such pictures does stimulate them to try a perspective system at least one step more advanced than they might otherwise use.

Children as well as adults are in conflict when drawing in perspective because this way of drawing does not match what we know about objects. For example, a table drawn in perspective does not show the top surface as a rectangle, yet we know the tabletop is rectangular. Although we would like to show things as we see them, we also want to show them as we know they are. Perhaps this is why, as shown by psychologist Margaret Hagen and Harry Elliot, then a graduate student at Boston University, adults prefer drawings with stage-4 perspective to those with stage-6 perspective; stage-6 drawings make objects look too distorted.

Knowing that a good pictorial likeness is not necessarily an exact copy of a scene as it actually appears, artists often deliberately break the rules of perspective. For example, to correct for the size distortion called for by the rules of perspective, they may draw a distant mountain larger than it would appear in a photograph. Perhaps for similar reasons, children may not at first draw objects with optical realism; they are interested in showing things in the most informative way rather than showing exactly how things look.

Do children improve further as they get older? If realism is the standard, the answer is clearly yes. For example, their figures become more complex, and they can represent depth through linear perspective. But I believe, on esthetic grounds, that children's drawings actually get worse with age.

Because preschool children are unconcerned with realism, their drawings are free, fanciful and inventive. Suns may be green, cars may

float in the sky and complex, irregular forms in nature are reduced to a few regular geometric shapes. They produce simple, strong pictures that evoke the abstractions found in folk, "primitive" and contemporary art (Figure 7).

The older child's drawing may be more realistic, neat and precise, but, in my opinion, it is also less imaginative and less striking (Figure 8). Suns are now appropriately yellow and placed carefully in the corner of the picture, and cars now rest firmly on the ground.

This development is inextricably tied up with acquiring the technical skills essential for adult artistic activity. Nonetheless, once such skills are mastered, artists often turn back to young children's drawings for inspiration and may work hard to do consciously and deliberately what they once did effortlessly and because they had no choice. "I used to draw like Raphael," Picasso is quoted as saying, "but it has taken me a whole lifetime to learn to draw like children."

Figures 7 and 8: This 6-year-old's drawing (top) is free, fanciful and inventive. An 11-year-old's drawing (bottom) is neater and more realistic but also less inventive.

THE CIVILIZING OF GENIE

"In 1970, a wild child was found in California. Genie, now 24, has stirred up new questions about language and intelligence."

Maya Pines

Maya Pines writes regularly about behavior and is a contributing editor of Psychology Today. *Her 1973 book,* The Brain Changers: Scientists and the New Mind Control *(Harcourt Brace Jovanovich), won the National Media Award of the American Psychological Foundation.*

Only a few cases are recorded of human beings who have grown up without any real contact with other humans. So rare is the phenomenon that when a 12-year-old "wild boy" was found in the forest of Aveyron in 18th-century France, the government ordered him brought to Paris to be examined by doctors in an institution for deaf-mutes. There he came under the care of the physician Jean Itard, who also acted as the boy's tutor. Itard left detailed records of his experience, which was later dramatized in the 1970 movie *The Wild Child.* Although the boy was not deaf, and despite Itard's work, the child never learned to speak.

In 1970, a wild child was found in California: a girl of 13 who had been isolated in a small room and had not been spoken to by her parents since infancy. "Genie," as she was later dubbed to protect her privacy by the psycholinguists who tested her, could not stand erect. At the time, she was unable to speak; she could only whimper.

The case came to light when Genie's 50-year-old mother ran away from her 70-year-old husband after a violent quarrel and took the child along. The mother was partially blind and applied for public assistance. The social worker in the welfare office took one look at Genie and called her supervisor, who called the police. Genie was sent to the Los Angeles Children's Hospital for tests. Charges of willful abuse were filed against both her parents, according to the *Los Angeles Times.* On the day he was due to appear in court, however, Genie's father shot himself to death. He left a note in which he wrote, "The world will never understand."

The discovery of Genie aroused intense curiosity among psychologists, linguists, neurologists, and others who study brain development. They were eager to know what Genie's mental level was at the time she was found and whether she would be capable of developing her faculties. "It's a terribly important case," says Harlan Lane, a psycholinguist at Northeastern University who wrote *The Wild Boy of Aveyron.* "Since our morality doesn't allow us to conduct deprivation experiments with human beings, these unfortunate people are all we have to go on."

Genie is now 24 years old. Through years of rehabilitation and special training, she has been observed and repeatedly tested. Hundreds of videotapes record her progress. She has been the subject of several journal articles and a book. Since the book was published in 1977, additional studies have brought into focus some of the issues raised by Genie's case. Far from settling any scientific controversies, she has provided fresh ammunition for arguments on both sides of a major issue: is there a "critical period" in a child's development during which, if language acquisition is not stimulated or encouraged, it may be impaired later on or not emerge at all? She has inspired a California researcher who worked with her, Susan Curtiss, to develop a controversial hypothesis about how language learning affects the two hemispheres of the brain. Genie has also stirred up debate about the relationship between language and other mental abilities. As a result, new research is now in progress on the surprising language ability of some mentally retarded children.

As described in Curtiss's book, *Genie: A Psycholinguistic Study of a Modern-Day "Wild Child"* (Academic Press), Genie is living proof of human resilience. It is surprising that she survived at all. Her father apparently hated children and tried to strangle Genie's mother while she was pregnant with her first child. According to Curtiss's book, when an earlier baby girl was born, he put the child in the garage because he couldn't stand her crying; the baby died of pneumonia at two-and-a-half months. A second child, a boy, died two days after birth, allegedly from choking on his own mucus. A third child was rescued and cared for by his grandmother when he was three years old and is still alive. Genie, the fourth child,

From *Psychology Today,* September 1981, pp. 28-32. © 1981 by Maya Pines. Reprinted by permission.

was denied such help, however, because shortly after she was born, her grandmother was hit by a truck and killed.

From the age of 20 months, when her family moved into her grandmother's house, until she was 13 and a half, Genie lived in nearly total isolation. Curtiss's book, and newspaper reports, describe Genie's life at the time: naked and restrained by a harness that her father had fashioned, she was left to sit on her potty seat day after day. She could only move her hands and feet. She had nothing to do. At night, when she was not forgotten, she was put into a sort of straitjacket and caged in a crib that had wire-mesh sides and an overhead cover. She was often hungry.

If she made any noise, her father beat her. "He never spoke to her," wrote Curtiss. "He made barking sounds [and] he growled at her. . . . Her mother was terrified of him—and besides, she was too blind to take much care of Genie. The task fell largely on Genie's brother, who, following his father's instructions, did not speak to Genie either. He fed her hurriedly and in silence, mostly milk and baby foods. There was little for Genie to listen to. Her mother and brother spoke in low voices for fear of her father.

When Genie arrived in Children's Hospital in November 1970, she was a pitiful, malformed, incontinent, un-socialized, and severely malnourished creature. Although she was beginning to show signs of pubescence, she weighed only 59 pounds. She could not straighten her arms or legs. She did not know how to chew. She salivated a great deal and spent much of her time spitting. And she was eerily silent.

Various physicians, psychologists and therapists were brought in to examine her during those first months. Shortly after Genie was admitted as a patient, she was given the Vineland Social Maturity Scale and the Pre-school Attainment Record, on which she scored as low as normal one-year-olds. At first, she seemed to recognize only her own name and the word *sorry*. After a while, she began to say two phrases that she used as if they were single words, in a ritualized way: *stopit* and *nomore*.

Psychologists at the hospital did not really know how much she understood. Nor did they know how to evaluate whatever language she had: to what degree did it deviate from the standard pattern? They eventually asked Victoria A. Fromkin, a UCLA psycholinguist, to study Genie's language abilities. Fromkin brought along a graduate student, Susan Curtiss (now an assistant professor of linguistics at UCLA), who became so fascinated by Genie that she devoted much of the next seven years of her life to researching the girl's linguistic development.

Working with Genie was not an easy task. Although she had learned to walk with a jerky motion and became more or less toilet trained during her first seven months at Children's Hospital, Genie still had many disconcerting habits. She salivated and spat constantly, so much so that her body and clothing were filled with spit and "reeked of a foul odor," as Curtiss recounts. When

excited or agitated, she urinated, leaving her companion to deal with the results. And she masturbated excessively.

Nevertheless, Genie was decidedly human, and her delight at discovering the world—as well as her obvious progress—made the struggle worthwhile. When Curtiss started working with Genie, she began by simply spending time with her or taking her to visit places, in order to establish a relationship. She took Genie to the super-market, where Genie walked around the store and examined the meats and the plastic containers with some curiosity. Every house seemed exciting to Genie, who had spent so much of her life cooped up in one room: on walks she would often go up to the front doors of houses, hoping that someone would open the door and let her in.

During her first seven months of freedom, Genie had learned to recognize many new words—probably hundreds by the time Curtiss started investigating her knowledge of language systematically in June 1971. And she had begun to speak. On a visit with Curtiss to the home of one of the therapists, Genie eagerly explored every room, then picked up a decorator pillow; when asked what is was, she replied "pillow." Asked if she wanted to see the family cat, Genie replied, "No. No. Cat," and shook her head vehemently. Most of the time, however, she said nothing.

At first Genie spoke only in one-word utterances, as toddlers do when they start to talk. Then in July of 1971, she began to string two words together on her own, not just while imitating what somebody else had said. She said "big teeth," "little marble," "two hand." A little later she produced some verbs: "Curtiss come," "Want milk." In November of the same year she progressed to occasional three-word strings: "small two cup," "white clear box."

Unlike normal children, however, Genie never asked questions, despite many efforts to train her to do so. Nor did she understand much grammar. And her speech development was abnormally slow. A few weeks after normal children reach the two-word stage, their speech generally develops so rapidly and explosively that it is difficult to keep track of or describe. No such explosion occurred for Genie. Four years after she began to put words together, her speech remained, for the most part, like a somewhat garbled telegram.

While Genie did not speak in a fully developed, normal way, she acquired some language after she was discovered. That contradicted one aspect of the theory that says language can be learned only during a critical period between two years of age and puberty. According to Eric Lenneberg, a Harvard psychologist who put forth the theory in 1967, the brain of a child before the age of two is not sufficiently mature for the acquisition of language, while after puberty, when the brain's organization is complete, it has lost its flexibility and can no longer acquire a first language. Genie proved him wrong in one sense, Fromkin says, since the child "showed that a certain amount of language can be learned after the critical period."

On the other hand, Genie failed to learn the kind of grammatical principles that, according to Noam Chomsky, distinguish the language of human beings from that of animals. For example, she could not grasp the difference between various pronouns, or between active and passive verbs. In that sense, she appeared to suffer from having passed the critical period.

Her language deficiencies could not be attributed to a lack of teachers. Though at first it did not seem possible that she could ever attend any school, within a few months of her arrival at Children's Hospital she began going to nursery classes for normal children. She soon transferred to a special elementary school for handicapped children. Next, she spent several years in a city high school for the mentally retarded. Outside school, a speech therapist worked with her consistently for many years. Meanwhile, one of the therapists and his wife took Genie into their own home to live with their two teenage sons, a teenage daughter, a dog, and a cat. They tried to teach Genie to trace with her fingers the shape of sandpaper letters, to recognize words or work with Play-Doh, as well as deal with the demands of family life. She apparently had no trouble writing her name, and drew a number of pictures based on experiences she had had.

Nor did Genie's deficiencies appear to be inborn. Although many details of her early history are unclear, and Genie's mother had given contradictory accounts of them, Genie seems to have been a normal baby. She suffered from an Rh blood incompatibility, but received an exchange transfusion one day after birth. During her first year of life, before she was isolated from the rest of her family, she may have been on the road to language, since her mother reported that she heard Genie saying words right after she was locked up.

The gift of language has always been viewed as distinctively human, or even as proof of the existence of the soul. Its source has mystified human beings for millennia. In the 13th century, Frederick II, Emperor of the Holy Roman Empire, decided to perform an experiment to find out what kind of speech children would develop if left to their own devices in their early years; he wondered whether it would be Hebrew, Greek, Latin, or the language of their parents. He selected a few newborns and decreed that no one speak to them. The babies were suckled and bathed as usual, but songs and lullabies were strictly forbidden. Frederick II never got his answer, however, for the children all died. The experiment was never repeated.

In the early 19th century, Itard tried desperately to teach Victor, the wild boy of Aveyron, to speak. He began when Victor was about 12 years old—around the time of puberty, as with Genie. However, Victor never spoke more than a few single words, perhaps because of an injury to his throat, where he had a scar.

Chomsky believes that human beings are born with a unique competence for language, built into their brains.

But he adds that the innate mechanisms that underlie this competence must be activated by exposure to language at the proper time, which Chomsky speculates must occur before puberty.

The strongest evidence that certain brain structures require triggering by the environment and that this triggering must occur during certain critical periods comes from research on the brains of cats. The visual centers of cats have very specific "feature detectors," cells that fire only in response to certain lines or angles. If a kitten is kept in a bare room lined only with vertical stripes for the period between its third week and third month of life and is then taken out, it will be able to see chair legs and other vertical objects without trouble but will act as if horizontal surfaces did not exist. By contrast, kittens that are kept in a room with only horizontal stripes during the same period will have no problem jumping from table to floor but will bump into table legs, as if vertical objects did not exist. At the Physiological Laboratory at Cambridge University in England, where this experiment was performed, Colin Blakemore placed electrodes in the bats' brains and discovered that each group of cats lacked a different set of feature detectors. In the visual cortex of cats that had seen only horizontal lines, no cells responded to vertical lines, while in the visual cortex of cats that had been exposed only to vertical lines, no cells responded to horizontal lines. The cells either had somehow failed to become functional or had atrophied from disuse.

Other animals also have critical periods of that sort. Thus, white-crowned sparrow chicks must hear their species' song between their 10th and 50th days of life, according to James L. Gould, a Princeton biology professor. Only during that period can they "tape" and store the parental songs in their brains, an essential step toward reproducing this song later in life. There is some evidence that such songs contain key sounds that automatically trigger the chicks' internal tape recorders to go on—and that those triggers consist of special feature detectors in the birds' brains.

Among human beings, four-week-old babies can recognize the difference between some 40 consonants that are used in human languages, as shown by how their sucking and heartbeats change when different consonant sounds are presented by audiotape. That ability seems to be innate, since babies respond to many more consonants than are used in their parents' language—English for example, has only 24 consonant sounds, yet babies of English-speaking parents react to the consonants present in Japanese. Babies lose that ability as they grow up. By the age of six, when children enter school, their ability to hear the difference between sounds to which they have not been exposed in their own language is severely reduced. Feature detectors responsible for recognizing about a dozen consonant sounds have so far been inferred to exist in the human brain. They need to be triggered by the environment, however: if not, they appear to atrophy.

Had something similar happened to Genie's brain? Curtiss raised that possibility when she reported that Genie, unlike 99 percent of right-handed people, seemed to use the right hemisphere of her brain for language. Since the left hemisphere is predisposed for language in right-handed people, that could account for some of the strange features of Genie's language development.

On tests of "dichotic listening," for example, which involve presenting different sounds to both ears simultaneously and asking the subject to react to them, "Genie's left ear outperformed her right ear on every occasion," Curtiss reports in her book. (Sound from the left ear is linked to the right hemisphere; from the right ear, to the left hemisphere.) Furthermore, "the degree of ear advantage is abnormal: Genie's left ear performed at 100 percent accuracy, while the right ear performed at a level below chance." That indicated Genie was using her right hemisphere as consistently as do people in whom, because of damage or surgery, only the right hemisphere is functioning.

When Genie's brain-wave patterns were examined at the UCLA Brain Research Institute—first as she listened to different sentences, then as she looked at pictures of faces—the data suggested that Genie used her right hemisphere for both language and nonlanguage functions. Genie also proved to be particularly good at tasks involving the right hemisphere, such as recognizing faces. On the Mooney Faces Test, which requires the subject to distinguish real from "false" faces in which features are misplaced and to point out several features on each face, Genie's performance was "the highest reported in the literature for either child or adult," according to Curtis.

From the very beginning, Genie's vocabulary revealed an extraordinary attention to the visual world, which is the special province of the right hemisphere—to color, shape, and size. All of her first two-word phrases were about static objects. While normal children usually start talking about people and actions or about the relations between people and objects, Genie spoke primarily about the attributes of things: "black shoe," "lot bread."

While summarizing the numerous tests made on Genie until 1979, Curtiss noted that Genie's performance had increased consistently over the years. For example, on the Leiter International Performance Scale, which was developed for use with deaf children and does not require verbal instructions, she had an IQ of 38 in 1971, an IQ of 53 in 1972, an IQ of 65 in 1974, and an IQ of 74 in 1977. However, she had made much less progress on tasks governed primarily by the left hemisphere. Even at the age of 20, she still performed at a three-year-old level on tests of auditory memory (a left-hemisphere task): she scored at a 6- to 12-year-old level on tests of visual memory (which tap both hemispheres), and at an adult level on tests of Gestalt perception (a right-hemisphere task).

The theory of language learning recently offered by Curtiss is an attempt to explain Genie's dependence on

her right hemisphere. Possibly, Curtiss wrote in a paper on cognitive linguistics published by UCLA, the acquisition of language is what triggers the normal pattern of hemispheric specialization. Therefore, if language is not acquired at the appropriate time, "the cortical tissue normally committed for language and related abilities may functionally atrophy." Curtiss wrote. That would mean that there are critical periods for the development of the left hemisphere. If such development fails, later learning may be limited to the right hemisphere.

Researchers who have studied deaf children have found similar changes—in reverse—in the brain organization of children who learned sign language in infancy. Two groups of profoundly deaf children were tested at the Salk Institute in La Jolla, California, by Helen Neville. Members of one group could neither speak nor use sign language; when they were shown line drawings of common objects, there was no difference between the brain waves in their left and right hemispheres. The other group had had at least one deaf parent and had learned sign language in early childhood: they showed normal left-hemisphere specialization for language ability (in their case, that meant sign recognition), and their left hemisphere also appeared to be specialized for picture recognition, an ability that is normally confined to the right hemisphere. Based on these and other findings, Neville hypothesized that when any kind of language is acquired in childhood, it is lateralized to the left hemisphere (at least in right-handed people), and that the nature of the language system learned—whether it is auditory or visual—determines, in part, what else goes to the same hemisphere. Together, the two hypotheses present a new view of the development of the brain's hemispheres.

Obviously Genie has many problems besides her lack of syntax or her dependence on the right hemisphere of her brain. During her most formative years—her entire childhood—she was malnourished, abused, unloved, bereft of any toys or companionship. Naturally, she is strange in many ways. Yet her language deficits remain particularly striking since she often found means of explaining what was important to her. She used gestures if necessary (starting in 1974, she received regular lessons in American Sign Language). Once she wanted an egg-shaped container that held panty hose that was made of chrome-colored plastic. She signaled her desire by making the shape of an egg with her hands, and then pointing to many other things with a chromium finish.

In her book, Curtiss describes how Genie occasionally used her limited language to remember her past and to tell about details of her confinement. "Father hit arm. Big wood. Genie cry," she said once. Another time, when Curtiss took her into the city to browse through shops, Genie said, "Genie happy."

In 1978, Genie's mother became her legal guardian. During all the years of Genie's rehabilitation, her mother had also received help. An eye operation restored her sight, and a social worker tried to improve her behavior toward Genie. Genie's mother had never been held legally responsible for the child's inhuman treatment. Charges of child abuse were dismissed in 1970, when her lawyer argued that she "was, herself, a victim of the same psychotic individual"—her husband. There was "nothing to show purposeful or willful cruelty," he said.

Nevertheless, for many years the court assigned a guardian for Genie. Shortly after Genie's mother was named guardian, she astounded the therapists and researchers who had worked with Genie by filing a suit against Curtiss and the Children's Hospital among others—on behalf of herself and her daughter—in which she charged that they had disclosed private and confidential information concerning Genie and her mother for "prestige and profit" and had subjected Genie to "unreasonable and outrageous" testing, not for treatment, but to exploit Genie for personal and economic benefits. According to the *Los Angeles Times*, the lawyer who represents Genie's mother estimated that the actual damages could total $500,000.

The case has not yet come to court, but in the two years since it was filed, Genie has been completely cut off from the professionals at Children's Hospital and UCLA. Since she is too old to be in a foster home, she apparently is living in a board-and-care home for adults who cannot live alone. The *Los Angeles Times* reported that as of 1979 her mother was working as a domestic servant. All research on Genie's language and intellectual development has come to a halt. However, the research Genie stimulated goes on. Much of it concerns the relationship between linguistic ability and cognitive development, a subject to which Genie has made a significant contribution.

Apart from Chomsky and his followers, who believe that fundamental language ability is innate and unrelated to intelligence, most psychologists assume that the development of language is tied to—and emerges from—the development of nonverbal intelligence, as described by Piaget. However, Genie's obvious nonverbal intelligence—her use of tools, her drawings, her knowledge of causality, her mental maps of space—did not lead her to an equivalent competence in the grammar normal children acquire by the age of five.

Puzzled by the discrepancy between Genie's cognitive abilities and her language deficits, Curtiss and Fromkin wondered whether they could find people with the opposite pattern—who have normal language ability despite cognitive deficits. That would be further evidence of the independence of language from certain aspects of cognition.

In recent months, they have found several such persons among the mentally retarded, as well as among victims of Turner's syndrome, a chromosomal defect that produces short stature, cardiac problems, infertility, and specific learning difficulties in females. With help from the National Science Foundation (which had also funded some of Curtiss's research on Genie), Fromkin and Curtiss have identified and started working with some children and adolescents who combine normal grammatical ability with serious defects in logical reasoning, sequential ability, or other areas of thinking.

"You can't explain their unimpaired syntax on the basis of their impaired cognitive development," says Curtiss, who is greatly excited by this new developmental profile. She points out that in the youngsters studied, the purely grammatical aspect of language—which reflects Chomsky's language universals—seems to be isolated from the semantic aspect of language, which is more tied to cognition. "Language no longer looks like a uniform package," she declares. "This is the first experimental data on the subject." Thus the ordeal of an abused child may help us understand some of the most puzzling but important aspects of our humanity.

Child Development and Differential School Performance:

A Challenge for Teachers in School Development Program Schools

Kimberly Kinsler
and
Edward Joyner

KIMBERLY KINSLER, Ph.D., is an associate professor of education at Hunter College, New York, New York

EDWARD JOYNER, Ed.D., is director of the Comer Project for Change in Education at Yale Child Study Center. He is also a middle school principal in the New Haven Public Schools in special assignments.

An understanding of James Comer's six developmental pathways is useful for teachers in responding to varied pre-existing knowledge and behavior of students.

The persistent group and individual differences between students in academic performance have led to the creation of a number of school reform models seeking to alleviate these inequities. Among the most prominent of these models is the School Development Program (SDP) developed by James Comer, M.D., at the Yale Child Study Center. Firmly grounded in learning and child development theory, the SDP model posits a set of basic principles to which all teachers should subscribe in order to understand better the origins and possible solutions to this problem. These principles are:

1) All children are capable of learning;
2) Learning is the product of a complex interaction among six developmental pathways;
3) Children learn best when they form significant relationships with others;
4) *Identification, imitation, and internalization* are major factors in the learning process;
5) Language mediates most learning activities; and
6) All children enter school already possessing *intellectual and social capital* that can and should be used to facilitate the learning process.[1]

While this discussion is not an exhaustive account of factors associated with differential student performance, the information provided herein will do more than advance educators' knowledge of the topic. The intent is to pique their interest to explore further the complexities of children's learning, as well as

From *Educational Horizons*, Vol. 17, No. 4, Summer 1993, pp. 175-180. Reprinted with permission from *Educational Horizons*, quarterly journal, published by Pi Lambda Theta, international honor and professional association in education, Bloomington, IN 47407-6626.

stimulate them to consciously apply these fundamental principles in their classrooms.

All Children Are Capable of Learning

At birth, the child is neither a blank slate nor a being whose traits, attitudes, and abilities have already been genetically predetermined. Although some traits or qualities of an individual are totally determined by genes, such as eye color, others are the exclusive domain of the environment, such as the preference for a particular religion. The vast majority of human traits are the result of complex interactions between the biological features or capabilities of the child and characteristics of the environment to which the child is exposed. For example, if a child has the genetic capability to be six feet tall but is reared in a setting where she or he does not receive adequate amounts of calcium, protein, and other nutrients necessary for optimum physical growth, she or he will not reach this potential, but will be constrained by environmental limitations.

With intelligence, which may be defined as the ability to seek out knowledge in order to understand and adapt to the world around us, genes similarly set a potential range. However, the child's actual intellectual functioning is the result of the environment's ability to elicit, shape, and nurture this potential. Many psychologists believe that, while there may be great variation in the specific manifestations of intelligence, all normal human beings without neurological impairments are innately predisposed to acquire knowledge about their world.[2] A parallel can be drawn using language as an example. All human beings are genetically predisposed to develop language.[3] However, variations in language are largely prescribed by the environment. The environment determines what language is spoken; its dialectical form (e.g., standard vs. non-standard speech); preferred methods of language communication

(e.g., oral, written, or pictorial representations); and the child's relative proficiency within the various forms and modes of language. The linguistic environment to which the child is exposed in his or her formative years is a powerful force in determining how the child uses language.

The interaction between the child and the environment is discussed further in two general ways: first, aspects of the child affected by the environment; and second, the mechanisms by which learning takes place. In interaction, these two systems constitute the "what" and the "how" of child development.

Comer's Six Developmental Pathways

To a teacher, a child presents a unified being greater than the total of any constituent parts. However, behavioral scientists traditionally segment the child into several dimensions for purposes of study. One such system is that of Comer, who has identified six pathways critical to understanding the child's development and functioning.[4]

The Physical Pathway

At the most basic level, the environment must meet the child's basic physical needs in order for that child to grow and to develop optimally. These needs include food, rest, shelter, and release from pain and illness. If these needs are not met, the physical distress that results will cause the child to be disinclined to focus on classroom learning.[5]

The Psycho-Emotional Pathway

Beyond basic physical needs, the environment must nurture a sense of self in the child; that is, an understanding of and positive regard for one's sell, as well as one's ability to contribute productively to society. These attitudes are largely determined by the quality of adult-child interactions. If parents and other significant adults are nurturing, yet foster competent independence, the child will develop a feeling that she or he has value as an individ-

At birth, the child is neither a blank slate nor a being whose traits, attitudes, and abilities have already been genetically predetermined.

ual and can produce works that are esteemed in the world.[6] Conversely, if adults are negligent, overly punitive, or critical of the child's efforts and acts, the child may develop a sense of inferiority and feel unable to make appropriate demands upon or make contributions valued by society. For example, a teacher who is unduly critical of a student's efforts can inhibit the child's school functioning by decreasing his or her motivation to engage in classroom tasks. Over time, the lowered performance that results from decreased motivation erodes the child's self-esteem as it relates to academic pursuits.

The Social-Interactive Pathway

To learn in—and appropriately interact within—a variety of social settings, the child must be able to engage in productive interpersonal relationships. These behaviors are learned through early experiences in the home and in the social network of the community. Later experiences in the school and other social institutions (e.g., the church, synagogue, mosque, or civic and recreational groups) provide the opportunity for the further refinement of social-interactive competence. From the home, and to some extent the community and reference groups, the child derives a notion of belonging.

The early development of a sense of belonging, interpersonal competence, and self-esteem provides the emotional basis to form and engage in the varied instructional relationships that the child will encounter as he or she moves toward full maturation. From the home and the community, the child also acquires knowledge of *interpersonal interaction patterns*, or prescriptions for the appropriate attitudes, verbal responses, and gestures that are viewed as "acceptable" in particular social contexts. For example, many adults correct contextually inappropriate behavior by using the phrase, "This is neither the time nor the place for your conduct." When behaviors learned for one setting (e.g., the home)

are consistent with those appropriate to another setting (e.g., the school), general performance and interpersonal interactions are facilitated.

Comer suggests that when a child's social skills are deemed "appropriate" by the teacher, they elicit positive reactions. A bond develops and the teacher joins other significant adults in supporting the child's development. On the other hand, when the teacher views the child's social behavior as inappropriate, the bond may be fragile or antagonistic. This situation creates a "lose/lose" relationship that renders the teacher ineffective, and that undermines the subcultures supporting the performance of the child.[7]

Speech and Language Pathway

In human development, language has two primary functions: communication and the representation of knowledge. Early in life, the child learns that speech and language can be used as vehicles to convey messages to others, as well as to the self. He or she learns the oral and behavioral cues for imparting messages, and simultaneously learns to interpret the messages of others. These acquired words and symbols also become the categories through which the child reasons with himself or herself.

The origins of these categories reside in culture, or settings in which groups of people communicate, think, and interact with one another and the environment.[8] By determining how the events in the world are explained, cultures not only prescribe conceptual categories, but the manner in which this information will be imparted. Between different subcultural groups and the mainstream culture, differences exist in concepts, gestures, and dialectical patterns, which may hamper successful communication. Children bring the language learned at home and in their respective communities to schools. Many students, particularly in urban and rural schools, speak a dialect of the standard language encountered in the speech and text that predominates most class-

To learn in— and appropriately interact within— a variety of social settings, the child must be able to engage in productive interpersonal relationships.

Crucial to all human interactions is the child's understanding and possession of sound moral and ethical standards, as well as the inclination to act upon these values.

rooms. It is important that teachers not view this difference as synonymous with inferiority. For example, a teacher may misinterpret the circular speech patterns of some African-American children as indicative of retarded communicative development.[9] To facilitate children's language development, teachers must develop strategies to help students learn and appreciate standard language while not rejecting the language used in the home. Teachers need to convey the message so that the pleasures and uses of one are as esteemed and respected as the other.

The Cognitive-Intellectual Pathway

All children are born with the ability to reason and solve problems. This capability allows individuals to override many of their instincts and impulses. As children grow and mature, they apply more and varied thinking strategies, and are able to apply these strategies to increasingly diverse *content* areas. Children also learn that the use of some strategies are appropriate in some contexts and inappropriate in others. For example, the reasoning strategies applied to social studies may be different from those applied in mathematics. The reasoning strategies applied in schools may vary from those applied in the community.

Cognitive scientists study and systematize the reasoning strategies of children, and construct principles to facilitate learning and instruction in varied contexts. Some significant principles useful to the teacher are:

1. All neurologically unimpaired children have the ability to perform the types of reasoning prescribed by the school.[10]
2. A child's relative facility with particular strategies and content may be a function of the extent to which the child is exposed to or is familiar with them.[11]
3. For new information to be understood, it must be embedded in the learner's preexisting knowledge.[12]
4. Instructional tasks must be targeted to the child's nascent ability

and always seek to advance his or her knowledge of processes as well as facts.[13]
5. Teacher expectancy can be a significant determinant of student response.[14]
6. Optimal intellectual development takes place when the teacher incorporates knowledge of the physical, social, psychological, and moral growth needs of children.[15]

The principles cited above can exert a powerful influence on student achievement and overall school performance. It is important that teachers make a conscious attempt to apply them in day-to-day classroom activities.

The Moral-Ethical Pathway

Crucial to all human interactions is the child's understanding and possession of sound moral and ethical standards, as well as the inclination to act upon these values. To a large extent, these qualities are based on socially transmitted principles, which not only delineate the acts for which the individual is held morally responsible, but also prescribe just and fair consequences for moral transgression. Typically, such standards are acquired from the family, church, and school. When these institutions concur in these values, the child's functioning in all these situations is facilitated. However, when one or more of these institutions fails to instill these values or imparts values that are in conflict with other institutions, the child is likely to evidence behaviors that may be viewed by individuals in one context as morally or ethically wrong. For example, the collaborative learning style traditional for many African-Americans, Latinos, and Native Americans may lead to classroom behavior regarded by some teachers as "cheating."

Mechanisms of Learning

The mechanisms vary by which these forms and pathways of knowledge are attained. Some information is acquired in a solitary fashion, through the direct manipulation and observation of objects and events, and the

Teachers must cultivate the behaviors and characteristics that promote holistic child development.

child's subsequent reflection upon these acts. However, the majority of our knowledge is acquired in social interactions with *significant others*.[16] At various points in the child's development, parents, teachers, and peers bear primary responsibility for the transmission of culturally prescribed information. Although the child can learn from almost any individual, those best able to impart concepts and beliefs are individuals with whom the child has significant relationships, for they can dispense those rewards most valued by the child, such as warmth, recognition, and approval.[17]

Identification, Imitation, and Internalization

One such interpersonal mechanism is identification. In this process, the child begins to think, feel, and behave as though the characteristics of another person belonged to him or her. Individuals regarded as powerful, capable, warm, nurturing or in some way similar to the child are likely candidates for identification. The *identificand* is the individual with whom the child identifies from among that field of candidates. Once the identificand is selected, albeit often unconsciously, the child begins to copy his or her behavior and attitudes. These actions and beliefs are subsequently internalized, that is, adopted to such an extent that the child comes to regard them as his or her own. Identification is the primary mechanism for the development of the child's gender identity, notions of appropriate sextyped behavior, moral standards, and sense of self.[18]

Imitation of others' behavior and the internalization of their knowledge need not always involve identification, however. Almost any act the child observes and is capable of copying may be imitated.[19] A more important consideration is what the child will act upon or seek to imitate. Those acts which the child believes will be rewarded or punished by the environment (parents, teachers, and peers) will be respectively imitated or inhibited. Thus, the child can see and learn many undesirable acts from sources such as television and peers, yet still refrain from these behaviors based upon the expected response by significant others, especially someone with whom the child has identified. When behavior is inconsistent with the actions and attitudes of the identificand, these actions will be inhibited, even in the absence of the identificand.

The rejection of significant others is also possible. When the child's identification or attachment to these individuals is weak, what often results is estrangement from, and opposition to, their behaviors and values. Such alienation may be the product of the actual or perceived disapproval of the child by these individuals. The same applies within the school context: The child who has a weak attachment to the school and its teachers, or who

At various points in the child's development, parents, teachers, and peers bear primary responsibility for the transmission of culturally prescribed information.

perceives their rejection of his or her cultural values, may develop an opposition to the knowledge, beliefs, and behaviors with which they are associated.[20]

Language Mediation

As previously indicated, language and speech are important vehicles through which a culture transmits socially sanctioned knowledge and beliefs to its members. According to Vygotsky, most of an individual's knowledge of concepts and processes exists twice, first on the interpersonal level as dialogue between a learner and a more knowledgeable other, and then on the intrapersonal level, as information which has been internalized.[21]

In the classroom, language is the primary medium of knowledge exchange. If instruction is to be successful, interactions between the teacher and the child must involve communications in which each understands the meaning of the other's gestures and concepts, or can readily identify points of disparate knowledge. Con-

versely, if the teacher is unaware of the child's preexisting knowledge, physical needs, and belief systems, efforts at instructional transmission may miss their mark.

Preexisting Knowledge as Intellectual and Social Capital

By the time the child enters school, a wealth of knowledge has already been acquired, including concepts, values, belief systems, reasoning strategies, and interaction patterns. This preexisting knowledge is the child's intellectual and social capital which he or she invests in the school for the purpose of his or her growth and expansion. To achieve these results, teachers must become knowledgeable of this preexisting knowledge for it constitutes the starting point for all meaningful instruction.

As the school system becomes increasingly populated by students from low income and minority backgrounds, teachers find themselves more and more unfamiliar with the knowledge students possess when entering school. As a result, teachers may erroneously conclude that these children have a deficient knowledge base (the cultural deficit hypothesis) or that the child's cognitive "problems" are the result of an inherent inability to learn (the genetic deficit hypothesis). Neither conclusion is true. Preexisting knowledge, whether consistent or inconsistent with that of mainstream students, is always a strength, for it is the *pathway* to the child's understanding. Teachers must not only uncover it, but use it to create meaningful instruction.

Summary

All teachers, but particularly those working in School Development Program schools, must the responsibility for cultivating the behaviors and characteristics that promote holistic child development. They must:

- *demonstrate* warmth, sensitivity and empathy to all students.
- *provide* appropriate instruction, motivation, feedback, reinforcement, and time to learn academic skills.
- *model* the actions and behaviors expected from students.
- *create* a classroom environment that allows students to take risks—and even fail—only to be corrected and encouraged to persist at difficult tasks.
- *create* classrooms where students can learn from one another.
- *create* classroom processes that allow students to identify individual and group needs and develop solutions to them using the democratic process.

Teaching is a reflective activity, and it is paramount that those in the profession be constantly reminded of the personal and professional qualities that promote student learning and overall development. In conclusion, the mission of teaching is the construction of knowledge. Based on the premise that all children can learn, it is the teacher's responsibility to achieve this goal. Differences in children's entering behavior do not prevent learning, but rather necessitate the exploration of new instructional strategies and attitudes appropriate to accomplish

---

Case Study: Child Development and Differential Performance

Directions: Read the following case study and discuss possible responses within your group.

With her fourth grade class, Ms. Brown is reading a chapter on state government. The class is rather diverse, with many children coming from homes which vary in their socioeconomic status, ethnic make-up, and parents' language. In response to her probe questions, Ms. Brown finds great disparities in students' comprehension of the topic. In pondering this state of affairs, Ms. Brown reasons that if everyone in the class is receiving the same input, then the differences in students' understanding must be a function of their differential ability to learn. In the teacher's cafeteria, Ms. Brown relates her theory to a colleague. If you were Ms. Brown's colleague, what would be your response?

this task. Knowledge of Comer's six critical pathways and the mechanisms of learning are valuable tools in this endeavor. Teachers must use these tools to respond more flexibly and creatively to the individual and group differences between children.

---

1. J.S. Coleman, and T. Hoffer, *Public and Private Schools: The Impact of Community* (New York: Harper and Row, 1987).

2. J. Piaget, *The Origins of Intelligence in Children* (York: International Universities Press, 1952) and J. Bruner, *Toward a Theory of Instruction* (New York: Norton and Company, 1966).

3. N. Chomsky, *Aspects of a Theory of Syntax* (Cambridge, Mass.: MIT Press, 1965).

4. J.P. Comer, *School Power* (New York: Free Press, 1982).

5. A.H. Maslow, *Toward a Psychology of Being.* (New York: Van Nostrand Press, 1968).

6. E. Erikson, *Childhood and Society* (New York: Norton Publishers, 1963).

7. J.P. Comer, "Educating Poor Minority Children," *Scientific American*, 259, no.5 (1988), 42-48.

8. R. LeVine, *Culture, Behavior, and Personality* (Chicago: Aldine Publishing Co., 1973).

9. S. Michaels, "Narrative Presentations: An Oral Preparation of Literacy with First Graders," in J. Cook-Gumperz (ed.) *The Social Construction of Literacy* (Cambridge, Mass.: Cambridge University Press, 1986), 94-116.

10. J. Piaget, *The Origins of Intelligence,* and J. Piaget, *The Psychology of the Child* (New York: Basic Books, 1969).

11. Laboratory for Comparative Human Cognition, "Culture and Intelligence," in R. Steinberg (ed.), *The Development of Human Intelligence* (Cambridge, Mass.: Cambridge University Press, 1983), 642-719.

12. J. Piaget, *The Language and Thought of the Child* (Cleveland, Ohio: Meridian Books, 1955).

13. L. Vygotsky, *Thought and Language* (Cambridge, Mass.: NUT Press, 1962).

14. Rosenthal and L. Jacobson, *Pygmalion in the Classroom* (New York: Holt, Rinehart and Winston, 1968).

15. J. P. Comer, "Educating Poor Minority Children."

16. L. Vygotsky, *Thought and Language.*

17. A. Bandura, *Social Learning Theory* (Englewood Cliffs, NJ: Prentice Hall Publishers, 1977).

18. S. Freud, *The Basic Writings of Sigmund Freud,* A.A. Brill, trans., (New York: Random House, 1938).

19. A. Bandura, *Social Learning Theory.*

20. J. Ogbu, and M.E. Matute-Bianchi, "Understanding Sociocultural Factors: Knowledge, Identity and School Adjustment," in *Beyond Language: Social and Cultural Factors in Schooling Language Minority Students* (California State University: Bilingual Education Office, 1986): 94-116.

21. L. Vygotsky, *Thought and Language,* and J. Comer, "Educating Poor Minority Children."

Understanding Bilingual/Bicultural Young Children

Lourdes Diaz Soto

Dr. Lourdes Diaz Soto is Assistant Professor of Early Childhood Education at The Pennsylvania State University. A former preschool teacher, she studies the learning environments of culturally and linguistically diverse young children.

E arly childhood educators have long created exciting and enriching environments for young children but may find an additional challenge when attempting to meet the needs of bilingual/bicultural learners. Teachers currently working with young linguistically and culturally diverse children have asked questions such as: "I feel confident with the art, music and movement activities I have implemented, but how can I best address the needs of speakers of other languages? Are there specific educational strategies that I should incorporate to enhance second language learning? What practical applications can I gain from the research evidence examining second language learning and successful instructional approaches in bilingual early childhood education?"

This review examines:

● demographic and educational trends pointing to the growing numbers of

More and more bilingual/bicultural children are appearing in early childhood classrooms across the country.

bilingual/bicultural young children in America today

● misconceptions about young children learning a second language

● successful educational approaches in early childhood bilingual education

● practical applications of existing research which can be readily implemented by early childhood educators.

Demographic and educational trends

Although the reliability of statistics over the past nine years describing the size and characteristics of the non-English language background (NELB) population has been questioned (Wong Fillmore, in press), it is clear from existing data and projections that language minority students comprise an increasing proportion of our youngest learners. The number of NELB children

aged birth to 4 years old rose steadily from 1.8 million (1976) to a projected 2.6 million in 1990, while the number of children aged 5 to 14 are projected to rise from 3.6 million to 5.1 million in the year 2000 (Oxford, 1984). Additional evidence points to "minority" enrollments, which include culturally diverse learners, ranging from 70 percent to 96 percent in the nation's 15 largest school districts (Hodgkinson, 1985).

Immigrant children from diverse, developing nations such as Haiti, Vietnam, Cambodia, El Salvador, Guatemala, Honduras, and Laos are entering classrooms which are usually unprepared to receive them. La Fontaine (1987) estimates that two-thirds of school-age, language-minority children may not be receiving the language assistance needed to succeed in school. This situation is bound to intensify with the projected increases in total school-age population of language-

From *Young Children*, Vol. 42, No. 2, January 1991, pp. 30-36. © 1991 by The National Association for the Education of Young Children, 1834 Connecticut Avenue, NW, Washington, DC. Reprinted by permission.

minority students, ranging from 35 percent to 40 percent by the year 2000 (Oxford, 1984). Existing demographic data provides evidence that meeting the educational needs of bilingual/bicultural young children is an important mandate for our schools.

The field of Bilingual Early Childhood Education has evolved from two educational domains, contributing to differing philosophies and practices. The elementary domain has, with some exceptions, largely emphasized formal language learning instruction; while the early childhood domain has emphasized a variety of approaches including natural language acquisition. Based upon existing bilingual research and what we know about how young children develop, a supportive, natural, language-rich environment, affording acceptance and meaningful interactions, appears optimal.

Early childhood educators are faced with a recurrent challenge, however, when programs earmarked for speakers of other languages are continually viewed as compensatory, or incorporate deficit philosophies. The practice of many instructional programs has been to develop English proficiency at the expense of the native language. The latter approach is called "subtractive" (Lambert, 1975) because the language learning process substitutes one language for another. This form of "bilingual education" may be a misnomer, since it continues to foster monolingualism (Snow & Hakuta, 1987).

Language learning and cultural enhancement need to be viewed as a resource, and not as a deficiency. Garcia (1986) has suggested that early childhood bilingualism includes the following characteristics:
- the child is able to comprehend and produce linguistic aspects of two languages
- the child is exposed naturally to two systems of language as used in the form of social interaction during early childhood
- both languages are developed at the same time.

Garcia (1983) notes that definitions of early childhood bilingualism must consider linguistic diversity, as well as social and cognitive parameters. Teachers of young children need a broad educational framework because a child's social, mental, and emotional worlds are an integral part of language learning.

Simplistic categorizations of bilingual children are not appropriate, since a variety of dimensions and possibilities exist for individual learners. Both experienced and novice bilingual/bicultural educators have noted differing educational terminology, reflecting the political mood of the nation. The table on page 32 illustrates the variety of terms in use. For example, the term "limited English proficient" (LEP) often cited in the literature points to a child's limitation rather than strength. The definitions proposed by Snow (1987) provide both clarity and recency, and are presented in the table in an attempt to show the range of concepts related to second language education. Casanova (1990) introduced the term "speakers of other languages" (SOL), helping to portray a positive attribute. The addition of the term "speakers of other languages" seems especially useful because there is ample documentation of the existence of both bilingual and multilingual young children in our schools.

Educators need to think in terms of "additive" (Lambert, 1975) bilingualism by incorporating practices which will enhance, enrich, and optimize educational opportunities for second language learners. Minimum standards and compensatory approaches are likely to sustain the existing educational difficulties faced by second language learners, speakers of other languages (SOL), and monolingual (EO) learners currently being deprived of a second language.

Misconceptions about young learners

A variety of misconceptions about second language acquisition and young learners exists (McLaughlin, 1984). **One misconception is that young children acquire language more easily than adults.** This idea was borne of the assumption that children are biologically programmed to acquire languages.

Although we know that early, simultaneous bilingualism will not harm young children's language development, and that they are capable of acquiring a second language without explicit instructions, it is a myth to think that children find the process "painless" (Hakuta, 1986).

Experimental research comparing young children and adults in second language learning has consistently indicated poorer performance by young children, except in pronunciation. Factors leading to the impression that young children acquire languages more easily are that children have fewer inhibitions, and greater frequency of social interactions (McLaughlin, 1984).

A second, related misconception states that the younger the child, the more quickly a second language is acquired. There is no evidence of a critical period for second language learning with the possible exception of accent (Hakuta, 1986). Studies reported by Krashen, Long, and Scarcella (1979), which examine rate of second language acquisition, favor adults. In addition,

---

Table. **Explanation of Terms Used in Second Language Education**

Linguistic minority student	*speaks the language of a minority group, e.g., Vietnamese*
Linguistic majority student	*speaks language of the majority group, i.e., English in the U.S.*
Limited English proficient	*any language background (LEP) student who has limited speaking skills in English as a second language*
Non-English proficient (NEP)	*has no previous experience learning English; speaks only the home language*
English Only (EO)	*is monolingual English speaker*
Fluent English proficient	*speaks both English and another language at home. This student speaks English fluently, e.g., ethnically diverse student born in the U.S., who speaks a second language at home.*

(Adapted from Snow, 1987)

adolescent learners acquire a second language faster than younger learners. Young children who receive natural exposure to a second language, however, are likely to eventually achieve higher levels of second language proficiency than adults.

It may be that "threshold levels" (Cummins, 1977; Skutnabb-Kangas, 1977) of native language proficiency are needed by young language minority learners in order to reap the benefits of

---

It is not true that young children learn a new language more quickly and easily than adults.

---

becoming bilingual. Young children, as a rule, will eventually catch up to, and surpass, most adults, but we need to provide them with a necessary gift of time.

A third misconception is that there is a single path to acquiring a second language in childhood. Wong Fillmore's (1976, 1985, 1986) research emphasizes the complex relationship among individual differences in young second language learners. Wong Fillmore (1985) suggests that three interconnected processes, including the social, linguistic, and cognitive domains, are responsible for variability in language learning. Learner characteristics contribute substantially to differential second language learning in children, but the relationship between learner characteristics and outcomes is not simple. No one characteristic can determine language learning (e.g., gregariousness) because variables such as situations, input, and interactions are also important (Wong Fillmore, 1986).

The research viewing individual differences points to the fact that young learners' second language acquisition abilities vary a great deal and are dependent upon social situations. Teachers of young children need to be cognizant of these variabilities by becoming keen observers of existing knowledge and abilities (Genishi, 1989). The assessment of language is a complex endeavor, and informal observations and teacher documentation can be extremely valuable tools. Readers are referred to Genishi and Dyson (1984) for a practical and sensitive review of how to assess progress in second language acquisition.

The second language learning process cannot be isolated from the young child's cultural learning. Ethnographic studies examining linguistically and culturally diverse children have found that classroom patterns also need to be culturally responsive, since differing approaches may work well with diverse children. For instance, Phillips (1972) found that Native American children were more willing to participate in group speaking activities than non-Native American children. Also, Au and Jordan (1981) found that reading and test scores improved when teachers incorporated narrative speech patterns such as talk story and overlapping speech into classroom routines with native Hawaiian children. Young children need to develop a positive and confident sense of biculturalism.

A great deal of trial and error takes place when a young child acquires a second language (McLaughlin, 1984). Learning to walk may serve as an example of another skill where exploration and experimentation are necessary. Young children progress at their own rate and persist until the skill is mastered. An accepting attitude is necessary during the trial and error phases of language acquisition. Rigid instructional practices emphasizing grammar construction are not appropriate because they can confuse and interfere with the natural developmental progression of second language acquisition (Felix, 1978, Lightbrown, 1977). The developmentally appropriate instructional practices advocated by NAEYC (Bredekamp, 1987) apply to second language learners as well. Young bilingual/bicultural children experience the same developmental progressions, with additional challenges involving second language/cultural learning.

Successful instructional approaches

In the United States, bilingual education is typically defined as an educational program for language minority students, in which instruction is provided in the child's primary language while the child acquires sufficient English skills to function academically. As noted earlier, an *additive* approach focuses on enrichment by the addition of a second language while supporting the native language, and a *subtractive* approach teaches a second language as a replacement, often at the expense of the native language. Programs that offer no aid to students learning a second language are referred to as "sink or swim" or "submersion" efforts (Snow, 1987). While it is beyond the scope of this paper to examine the pervasive "English Only" attitudes in our nation today, it should be noted that bilingual instruction is controversial, and that the sociopolitical climate has often prompted the needs of young bilingual/bicultural children to be overlooked. It is also often the case that programs purporting to include bilingual approaches, in truth, emphasize English only, and a "sink or swim" approach.

Nevertheless, three bilingual education approaches are prevalent for preschoolers and early elementary school students (Ovando & Collier, 1985). The **transitional** approach is widespread and emphasizes the rapid development of English language skills, so the student can participate in the mainstreamed setting as soon as possible. Native language instruction is used initially but the major focus is generally to quickly transfer the learner to the mainstreamed setting. We need to look carefully at these programs in light of Cummins' (1979, 1984, 1985) research, emphasizing the need for learners to obtain optimal levels of native language proficiency.

The **maintenance/developmental** approach emphasizes the development of language skills in the home language, with an additional goal of English mastery. This strategy enhances the child's native language and allows learners to gain concepts in the native language while introducing English as a Second Language (ESL). Children are usually served by additional "pull out" English as a Second Language (ESL) instruction from teachers trained in ESL methods.

The **two-way** bilingual approach serves both the language majority and the language minority, expecting both groups of learners to become bilingual, and to experience academic success. An advantage of the two-way bilingual approach is that children are afforded an opportunity to participate in culturally and linguistically diverse intergroup relations. Recent research points to long-term attitudinal effects from this newly emerging bilingual approach (Collier, 1989).

The role of Head Start in Bilingual Early Childhood Education needs to be acknowledged in light of exemplary service for over 25 years (U.S. Department of Health and Human Services, 1990). Soledad Arenas (1980) describes a bilingual early childhood Head Start effort initiated by Administration for Children, Youth and Families (ACYF). Four contracts were awarded throughout the nation, including: Un Marco Abierto at the High/Scope Center in Ypsilanti, Michigan; Nuevas Fronteras de Aprendizaje at the University of California; Alerta at Columbia University; and Amanecer in San Antonio, Texas. Each program differed considerably, but was based upon an additive philosophy, and serviced Spanish-speaking Head Start children. The evaluation conducted by Juarez and Associates (1980), viewing the impact of the programs over a three-and-a-half year period, found the bilingual preschool curricula to be effective for both Spanish and English preferring young children. In addition, the evaluation concluded that parent and teacher attitudes were favorable, that models can be implemented in differing geographical locations, and that dual language strategies were most related to positive child outcomes.

An important and thorough review of bilingual education research involving 23 different programs found that preschool, elementary, and middle school children who were enrolled in the bilingual programs reviewed, outperformed children on a variety of standardized measures in nonbilingual programs, regardless of the language used for testing (Willig, 1985). Also, research examining bilingualism and cognitive competence favors the attainment of higher levels of bilingual proficiency (Barrik & Swain, 1974; Cummins & Gulutson, 1974; Cummins & Mulcahy, 1976; Duncan & De Avila, 1979; Lessler & Quinn, 1982; Peal & Lambert, 1962; Skutnabb-Kangas, 1977; Hakuta, 1986). Advanced bilingualism has been found to be associated with cognitive flexibility and divergent thinking (Hakuta, 1986). These are powerful findings in an era when the usefulness of bilingual approaches continues to be questioned.

It has been suggested that successful programs progress from native language instruction to initial second language learning, to a stage of enrichment and eventually a return to the native language instruction via the incorporation of literature and social studies, in order to incorporate a healthy sense of biculturalism (Krashen & Biber, 1988). The three components of successful programs serving limited English proficient children reviewed by Krashen and Biber include:

- high-quality subject matter instruction in the native language without concurrent translation
- development of literacy in the native language
- comprehensible input in English

The Carpinteria Preschool Program (Keatinge, 1984; Krashen & Biber, 1988) is particularly interesting because of the emphasis on native language instruction. The children in this program received instruction in Spanish, yet outperformed comparison learners on a test of conversational English (Bilingual Syntax Measure), and exceeded published norms on tests of school readiness (School Readiness Inventory), and academic achievement (California Achievement Test). This particular program supports Cummins' (1984) contention that learners need to obtain a "threshold level" or optimal level of native language proficiency. It appears that native language instruction actually gave students an advantage in their acquisition of a second language.

What can we conclude from this discussion? In an attempt to summarize selected research findings regarding second language acquisition and successful approaches to bilingual education, a list of practical classroom applications is proposed.

Practical applications for teachers of young children

As a caretaker in a decision-making capacity, the early childhood educator plays a critical role in the lives of linguistically and culturally diverse young children. The early childhood setting becomes a home away from home, the first contact with non-family members, the first contact with culturally different people, and the first experience with non-native speakers. A teacher's attitude and knowledge base is crucial in setting the educational goals of acceptance and appreciation of diversity (Ramsey, 1987). The possibilities are endless for teachers of young children who, as role models, are in a unique position to establish the tone, or "classroom climate," through decision making, collaboration, interactions, and activities.

Teachers of young children are currently implementing a variety of educationally sound strategies. In addition, based upon the recent research, and what we know about young children, we can:

1. Accept individual differences with regard to language-learning time frames. It's a myth to think that young children can learn a language quickly and easily. Avoid pressures to "rush" and "push out" children to join the mainstream classrooms. Young children need time to acquire, explore, and experience second language learning.

2. Accept children's attempts to communicate, because trial and error are a part of the second language learning process. Negotiating meaning, and collaboration in conversations, is important. Children should be given opportunities to practice both native and newly established language skills. Adults should not dominate the conversations; rather, children should be listened to. Plan and incorporate opportunities for conversation such as dramatic play, storytime, puppetry, peer interactions, social experiences, field trips, cooking and other enriching activities.

3. Maintain an additive philosophy by recognizing that children need to acquire new language skills instead of replacing existing linguistic skills. Afford young children an opportunity to retain their native language and culture. Allow young learners ample social opportunities.

4. Provide a stimulating, active, diverse linguistic environment with many opportunities for language use in meaningful social interactions. Avoid rigid or didactic grammatical approaches with young children. Children enjoy informal play experiences, dramatizations, puppetry, telephone conversations, participation in children's literature, and social interactions with peers.

5. Incorporate culturally responsive experiences for all children. Valuing each child's home culture and incorporating meaningful/active participation will enhance interpersonal skills, and contribute to academic and social success.

6. Use informal observations to guide the planning of activities, interactions, and conversations for speakers of other languages.

7. Provide an **accepting** classroom climate that values culturally and linguistically diverse young children. We know that young children are part of today's natural resources, capable of contributing to tomorrow's multicultural/multilingual society.

References

Arenas, S. (1980, May/June). Innovations in bilingual/multicultural curriculum development. *Children Today*. Washington, DC: U.S. Government Printing Office No. 80–31161.

Au, K., & Jordan, C. (1981). Teaching reading to Hawaiian children: Finding a culturally appropriate solution. In H. T. Trueba & G. P. Guthrie (Eds.), *Culture and the bilingual classroom: Studies in classroom ethnography*. Cambridge, MA: Newbury House.

Baker, C. (1988). *Key issues in bilingualism and bilingual education*. Clevedon, Avon, England: Multilingual Matters, Ltd.

Barrik, H., & Swain M. (1974). English-French bilingual education in the early grades: The Elgin study. *Modern Language Journal, 58*, 392–403.

Bredekamp, S. (1987). (Ed.). *Developmentally appropriate practice in early childhood programs serving children from birth through age 8*. Washington, DC: NAEYC.

Casanova, U. (1990). *Shifts in bilingual education policy and the knowledge base*. Tuscon, AZ: Research Symposia of the National Association of Bilingual Educators.

Dulay, H., & Burt, M. (1974). Natural sequences in child second language acquisition. *Language Learning, 24*, 37–53.

Duncan, S. E., & DeAvila, E. (1979). Bilingualism and cognition: Some recent findings. *NABE Journal, 4*, 15–50.

Escobedo, T. (1983). *Early childhood bilingual education. A Hispanic perspective*. New York: Teachers College Press, Columbia University.

Felix, S. W. (1978). Some differences between first and second language acquisition. In C. Waterson & C. Snow (Eds.), *The development of communication*. New York: Wiley.

Garcia, E. (1983). *Early childhood bilingualism*. Albuquerque: University of New Mexico.

Garcia, E. (1986). Bilingual development and the education of bilingual children during early childhood. *American Journal of Education, 11*, 96–121.

Collier, V. (1989). Academic achievement, attitudes, and occupation among graduates of two-way bilingual classes. Paper presented at the American Educational Research Association, San Francisco, California.

Contreras, R. (1988). *Bilingual education*. Bloomington, IN: Phi Delta Kappa.

Cook, V. J. (1973). The comparison of language development in native children and foreign adults. *International Review of Applied Linguistics in Language Teaching,* 11, 13–29.

Cummins, J. (1977). Cognitive factors associated with intermediate levels of bilingual skills. *Modern Language Journal, 61*, 3–12.

Cummins, J. (1979). Linguistic interdependence and the educational development of bilingual children. *Review of Educational Research, 49*(2), 222–251.

Cummins, J. (1984). *Bilingualism and special education: Issues in assessment and pedagogy*. Clevedon, Avon, England: Multilingual Matters, Ltd.

Cummins, J. (1985). The construct of language proficiency in bilingual education. In James Alatis & John Staczek (Eds.), *Perspectives on bilingualism and bilingual education* (pp. 209–231). Washington, DC: Georgetown University.

Cummins, J., & Gulutson, M. (1974). Some effects of bilingualism on cognitive functioning. In S. Carey (Ed.), *Bilingualism, biculturalism and education*. Edmonton: University of Alberta.

Cummins, J., & Mulcahy, R. (1978). Orientation to language in Ukrainian-English bilingual children. *Child Development, 49*, 1239–1242.

Genishi, C. (1984). *Language assessment in the early years*. Norwood, NJ: Ablex.

Genishi, C. (1989). Observing the second language learner: An example of teachers' learning. *Language Arts, 66*(5), 509–515.

Hakuta, K. (1986). *Mirror of language. The debate of bilingualism*. New York: Basic.

Hodgkinson, H. (1985). *All one system: Demographics of education, kindergarten through graduate school*. Washington, DC: Institute for Educational Leadership, Inc.

Juarez & Associates (1980). Final report of an evaluation of the Head Start bilingual/bicultural curriculum models. Washington, DC: U.S. Department of Health and Human Services. No. 105–77–1048.

Keatinge, R. H. (1984). An assessment of the pinteria preschool Spanish immersion program. *Teacher Education Quarterly, 11*, 80–94.

Kessler, C., & Quinn, M. (1982). Cognitive development on bilingual environments. In B. Hartford, A. Valdman, & C. Foster (Eds.), *Issues in international bilingual education*. New York: Plenum.

Krashen, S., & Biber, D. (1988). *On course: Bilingual education's success in California*. Sacramento: California Association for Bilingual Education.

La Fontaine, H. (1987). *At-risk children and youth—The extra educational challenges of limited English-proficient students*. Washington, DC: Summer Institute of the Council of Chief State School Officers.

Lightbron, P. (1977). French second language learners: What they're talking about. *Language Learning, 27*, 371–381.

McLaughlin, B. (1984). *Second-language acquisition on childhood: Volume 1: Preschool children*. Hillsdale, NJ: Erlbaum.

Ovando, C., & Collier, V. (1985). *Bilingual and ESL classrooms*. New York: McGraw-Hill.

Oxford, C., et al. (1984). *Demographic projections of non-English background and limited English-proficient persons in the United States in the year 2000*. Rosslyn, VA: InterAmerica Research Associates.

Peal, E., & Lambert, W. (1962). The revelations of bilingualism to intelligence. *Psychological Monographs, 76*(27), 1–23.

Phillips, S. (1972). Participation structures and communicative competence: Warm Springs children in community and classroom. In C. Cazden, V. John, & D. Hymes, (Eds.), *Functions of language in the classroom*. New York: Teachers College, Columbia University.

Ramsey, P. (1987). *Teaching and learning in a diverse world*. New York: Teachers College Press, Columbia University.

Skutnabb-Kangas, T. (1977). *Bilingualism or not: The education of minorities*. Clevedon, Avon, England: Multilingual Matters, Ltd.

Sleeter, C., & Grant, C. (1987). An analysis of multicultural education in the United States. *Harvard Educational Review, 57*(4), 421–444.

Snow, M. (1987). *Common terms in second language education: Center for Language Education and Research*. Los Angeles: University of California.

Snow, C., & Hakuta, K. (1987). *The costs of monolingualism*. Unpublished monograph, Cambridge, MA: Harvard University.

Soto, L. D. (in press). Alternate research paradigms in bilingual education research. In R. Padilla and A. Benavides (Eds.), *Critical perspectives on bilingual education research*. Phoenix: Bilingual Review/Press.

Soto, L. D. (in press). Success stories. In C. Grant (Ed.), *Research directions for multicultural education*. Bristol, PA: Falmer Press.

Swain, M. (1987). Bilingual education: Research and its implications. In M. Long and J. Richards (Eds.), *Methodology in TESOL*. Cambridge, MA: Newbury House.

U.S. Department of Health and Human Services. (1990). Head Start: A child development program. Washington, DC: Office of Human Development Services, Administration for Children, Youth and Families.

Willig, A. (1985). A meta-analysis of selected studies on the effectiveness of bilingual education. *Review of Educational Research, 55*(3), 269–317.

Wong Fillmore, L. (1976). *The second time around: Cognitive and social strategies*. Unpublished doctoral dissertation, Stanford University, Stanford, CA.

Wong Fillmore, L. (1985). *Second language learning in children: A proposed model*. Proceedings of a conference on issues in English language development, Arlington, VA. ERIC Document 273149.

Wong Fillmore, L. (in press). Language and cultural issues in early education. In S. Kagan (Ed.), *The care and education of America's young children: Obstacles and opportunities*. The 90th yearbook of the National Society for the Study of Education.

Wong Fillmore, L., & Valadez, C. (1986). **Teaching bilingual learners. In M. Wittrock (Ed.), *Handbook of research on teaching*. New York: Macmillan.

Equitable Treatment of Girls and Boys in the Classroom

THE MORE THINGS CHANGE . . .

The major federal statute prohibiting sex discrimination in education, Title IX of the Education Amendments of 1972, was signed into law more than 15 years ago. In following years, Congress authorized funding for model sex equity programs through the Women's Educational Equity Act (WEEA, 1974) and required states to work to eliminate sex bias from their vocational education programs (1976).

Women's education advocates anticipated that these programs would encourage both girls and boys to explore nontraditional fields and place a high priority on school performance and career preparation. They foresaw that the range of occupations considered appropriate for both sexes would be broadened and that, as a result, occupational sex segregation would decline and the pay gap between men and women would narrow in the long run.

Although Title IX has increased women's access to education and many excellent model programs have been created under WEEA and the Vocational Education Act, sex differences in educational preparation and occupational choice persist. For example, even though all vocational programs must now be open to both sexes, 70 percent of all girls in vocational high schools study traditionally female fields.[1] And while women made up 53 percent of all college students by 1987, they still received less than 15 percent of all engineering degrees.[2]

The limited impact of the educational equity programs begun in the 1970s has been due largely to inadequate funding and lack of enforcement, particularly after the U.S. Supreme Court's ruling in *Grove City College* v. *Bell* in 1984 limited the application of Title IX to specific programs.[3] But perhaps a major factor in blunting their impact are girls' everyday interactions with teachers and other students in the classroom. Too often, classroom dynamics are laced with unconscious sex stereotyping, as when teachers spend more time with boys in math classes and more time with girls in reading classes. Such subtle but powerful messages have been shown to circumscribe girls' and women's choices regarding academic preparation, achievement, and careers.

In the past two years, AAUW and the AAUW Educational Foundation have launched twin initiatives—*Choices for Tomorrow's Women* and the Eleanor Roosevelt Fund for Women and Girls: Intergenerational Partnerships, respectively—to address the ways women and girls make choices about education, family life, and careers (see "What We Can Do"). This brief, an introductory instrument of those efforts, discusses various theories about the causes of sex differences in academic performance, reviews recent research on sex differences in classroom interaction, and suggests ways to change stubborn patterns of sex discrimination.

GIRLS, BOYS, AND BRAINS

Extensive research shows that girls and boys perform differently on most standardized academic tests. In the U.S. administration of the Second International Science Study test in 1983, for instance, fifth-grade boys scored 6.2 percent higher than the girls. Similarly, in the 1981–82 National Assessment of Educational Progress high-school girls scored higher in reading, but lower in math and science, than boys.[4]

The test results don't tell us why such differences exist; they could be caused by differential ability, preparation, motivation, or expectations about the probability of success. Theories attempting to explain academic performance differences between girls and boys can be divided roughly into two categories: biological and sociological.

Some researchers have suggested that differences in intellectual functioning are caused by inherited, sex-linked genes or by the effect of sex-linked hormones on brain development before birth and at puberty. Although links have been shown between hormones and brain development, no link to intelligence has been proven. Similarly, there is no physical evidence that intelligence genes exist, whether sex-linked or not. Studies claiming to establish such a biological link typically hypothesize cause based on correlation.

For instance, a much-publicized 1980 study by Camilla Benbow and Julian Stanley was widely reported as proving the existence of "male" math genes. During a John Hopkins University study, groups of mathematically gifted junior-high students were administered the math sections of the Scholastic Aptitude Test. The boys in the study consistently outscored the girls and Benbow and Stanley argued that, since all students take the same sequence of math courses from elementary through junior high school, the difference must be due largely to inherited ability.

TEACHERS' CRITICISM OF STUDENTS' WORK

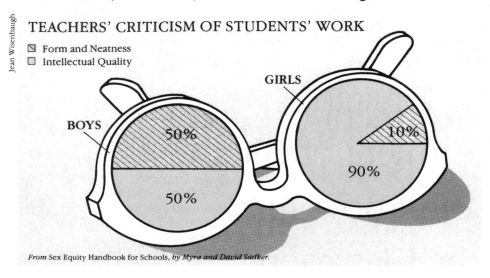

☒ Form and Neatness
☐ Intellectual Quality

BOYS
GIRLS
50%
50%
10%
90%

From Sex Equity Handbook for Schools, *by Myra and David Sadker.*

But critics were quick to point out that Benbow and Stanley had ignored the informal ways boys and girls learn about math, and had assumed that their experiences with math in the classroom were the same. Other researchers in the same study had investigated the students' backgrounds and found that the boys' parents gave them more encouragement and more math- and science-related toys.[5]

A boy took some playdough in a pot to the stove, and announced he was cooking. 'Daddies don't cook,' two little girls told him. He backed away, saying, 'My poppy cooks. . .' and looking uncertain. The teacher then told the two girls that daddies sometimes do cook. The boy immediately returned to the stove and started cooking.[42]

One difficulty with research of this sort is finding a measure that will distinguish learned skills from innate ability. In 1974, psychologists Eleanor Maccoby and Carol Jacklin surveyed this research and concluded that while girls showed slightly more verbal ability, boys had more quantitative and spatial-visualization abilities.[6] But a 1981 study by Janet Hyde pointed out that although those differences were present in the studies reviewed, their magnitude was very small. Sex accounted for less than 5 percent of the differences between boys and girls in verbal, quantitative, and spatial-visualization abilities.[7] In other words, the variation between individuals of either sex is greater than that between the sexes.

Other researchers suggest that gender-role socialization accounts for most of the differences between girls' and boys' academic performance. Gender roles are the range of activities, attitudes, and emotions considered socially appropriate for men and women, and they are learned through interactions with parents, peers, teachers, and other adults, as well as from the print and electronic media. Although children acquire extensive knowledge of gender roles, there are great differences in the extent to which individuals internalize and act out those roles as a part of their identity (masculinity or femininity). One study of math achievement, for instance, found that for students who had enrolled in the same sequence of math courses the difference between girls' and boys' performance on achievement tests was very small; it disappeared altogether when sociocultural factors like parents' attitudes toward the subject and participation in math-related activities—such as building things—were taken into account.[8]

Research suggests that gender-role socialization mediates intellectual achievement in several ways:

• Children learn from parents, teachers, and peers that some activities are inappropriate for their gender, and so they do not consider achievement in those areas possible or desirable. Research shows that parents typically believe that boys do better than girls in advanced math and that they attribute boys' successes in math to talent, but girls' to effort.

• Some of the psychological traits that are differentially acquired during gender-role socialization may be helpful for certain types of learning. In science education, for instance, it is important to explore, to learn by experience, and to take risks—behaviors that are more encouraged in boys than girls.

• Because they are differently socialized,

boys and girls follow a different pattern of intellectual development and develop different learning styles, so they respond differently to the same classroom climate. For example, various studies have shown that girls respond better to a cooperative, rather than a competitive, classroom environment, perhaps because their moral development focuses on what psychologist Carol Gilligan calls the "ethic of care."[9]

• Some researchers suggest that these differences are so deeply entrenched that they amount to different sex-role cultures.[10]

Research has also shown that ideas about appropriate gender roles vary between cultures. A 1987 study revealed that girls scored higher than boys in math achievement tests in Hawaii, for instance. The results were most pronounced for Japanese-American, Filipino-American, and native Hawaiian students, suggesting that math achievement is not seen as inimical to the feminine role in those cultures.[11] Other studies found that Asian-American girls receive more parental encouragement and less negative male peer pressure about preparing for math and science careers.[12]

Different cultures may also produce different learning styles. In Asian-American cultures, for instance, it is typically assumed that everyone can learn if they work hard enough; lack of "natural" ability is not an acceptable excuse for failure. Other researchers have suggested that low-income and minority cultures stress group interaction and cooperation more than white middle-class cultures, which tend to stress individualism and competition.[13] This puts minority girls at a double disadvantage in the classroom.

TEACHING THE HIDDEN CURRICULUM

Research conducted in the past decade has shown that the structure of lessons and the dynamics of classroom interaction all too often create an environment alien, if not hostile, to girls (again, doubly so for girls from certain ethnic groups and social classes). Patterns of differential treatment sometimes are so deeply ingrained that even teachers who strive to be fair and impartial are not aware of all of them. And even when treatment is identical, there may be a negative impact on girls because they may experience it differently than boys.

Schoolrooms Particularly at the preschool and kindergarten level, rooms often are arranged into highly gender-stereotyped play areas, such as a cooking corner for girls and a building-blocks corner for boys. This both reinforces the idea that such activities are incompatible and makes crossing over to "gender-inappropriate" activities more difficult.[14]

Teacher-student interaction The interaction between teachers and students is interladen with subtle messages that affect girls' self-esteem and sense of identity. Research shows that

• minority students of both sexes receive less attention from the teacher, which decreases self-esteem.[15]

• teachers believe that the ideal pupil is orderly, conforming, and dependent, traits that are also identified with the "feminine" gender role. At first glance, this would seem to work to the advantage of female students. In fact, it works against them because teachers tend to give less attention to those they think are ideal pupils. Also, teachers' positive reinforcement of this identification discourages girls from more active, assertive learning styles that tend to get students farther in the long run.[16] (See "Lifelong Lessons" box.)

• boys who do not conform to the ideal

A 1987 study revealed that girls scored higher than boys in math achievement tests in Hawaii. The results were most pronounced for Japanese-American, Filipino-American, and native Hawaiian students, suggesting that math achievement is not seen as inimical to the feminine role in those cultures.[10]

---

pupil role are disciplined, but girls are ignored; this means boys get yet more attention when they misbehave.[17] When both boys and girls are misbehaving, teachers are three times as likely to discipline the boys; this conveys that boys are more important even though the context is negative.[18] This pattern holds true across racial and ethnic lines. (See chart next page)

• teachers initiate 10 percent more communication with boys in the classroom, again strengthening their sense of dominance and importance.[19]

• teachers ask boys more complex, abstract, and open-ended questions, which provide better opportunities for active learning.[20]

• regarding class projects and assignments, teachers are more likely to give detailed instructions to boys and more likely to take over and finish the task for girls, again depriving them of active learning.[21]

• teachers spend more time with girls in reading classes and more time with boys in math classes.[22]

• ninety percent of the praise for boys' schoolwork is directed at the intellectual content and quality of their work, rather

than form or neatness, compared to 80 percent for girls.[23]

• nearly 90 percent of the criticism of girls' schoolwork is directed at the intellectual content and quality of their work, compared to 50 percent for boys.[24] (See chart on preceding page.)

• when teachers criticize boys, they often tell them that their failings are due to lack of effort. Girls are not given this message, the absence of which implies that effort would not improve their results.[25]

Student-student interaction The social relationships between students—patterns of work and play that reflect their understanding of appropriate and desirable behavior—are typically much more gender-stereotyped than teacher-student relationships. Students' social relationships often reinforce the messages that girls are less capable and have fewer career choices than boys. Research shows that

• classroom interaction between boys and girls is highly infrequent from preschool through junior high school; thus, stereotypes about sex-segregated activities are reinforced.[26]

• during high school, girls typically increase their motivation to form relationships and decrease their motivation to achieve academically, which affects crucial education and career choices they make at that time.[27]

• when classes are divided into groups by ability, boys with high math achievement scores are more likely than girls with similar scores to be assigned to the high-ability group.[28]

• within math groups, girls who ask questions of their peers are answered only by other girls; boys who ask questions are answered by both boys and girls.[29]

• when boys and girls work together on science projects, girls spend four times as much time watching and listening, and 25 percent less time manipulating the equipment involved, than boys.[30]

This web of relationships, reflecting unconscious and largely unexamined assumptions about the different capabilities and appropriate roles of men and women, has been called the "hidden curriculum."

LIFELONG LESSONS

The hidden curriculum encourages boys to be more autonomous, to find out things for themselves, and to develop their own abilities and resources. On the other hand, it encourages girls to be more dependent, to wait to hear answers rather than discover them, and to rely on the teacher for guidance. These patterns have far-reaching consequences. (See "Lifelong Lessons" box.)

Self-esteem One result of these pat-

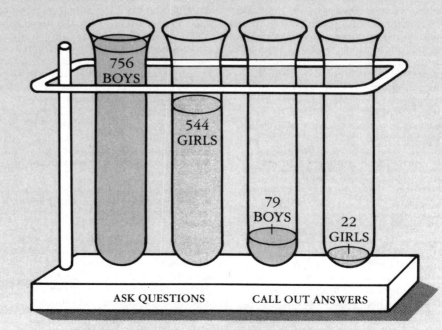

INTERACTIONS IN AN EIGHTH-GRADE SCIENCE CLASS

756 BOYS

544 GIRLS

79 BOYS

22 GIRLS

ASK QUESTIONS   CALL OUT ANSWERS

Jean Wisenbaugh

From "Listening to Adolescents: Gender Differences in Science Classroom Interaction" by Linda Morse and Herbert Handley, in Gender Influences in Classroom Interaction, *Louise Cherry Wilkinson and Cora B. Marrett, eds.*

terns is that girls are much more likely to believe that lack of ability causes inadequacies in their school performance, while boys are more likely to believe lack of effort causes their failures. Whereas effort is something a child can control, ability is seen as immutable. Thus, girls' self-esteem and motivation to succeed are undercut.

Girls are particularly likely to believe that they lack ability in areas stereotyped as more appropriate for boys. Girls tend to attribute failures in math and science tasks to lack of ability, for instance, while attributing failures in language arts to inadequate effort.[31]

Independence Girls do not have as much opportunity to work independently as boys do, and therefore lose the chance to develop habits and skills critical to academic and professional success: taking the initiative, problem-solving, taking risks, persisting despite setbacks, manipulating tools and equipment, and leading groups. These habits and skills are particularly important for science careers.

The children were making paper baskets; the handles had to be stapled in place. The teacher moved around the room, showing the boys how to use the stapler and holding the handle while the boys used the stapler. When the girls asked for assistance, the teacher took the basket and stapled it for them.[43]

Achievement motivation Girls' interest in higher education and nontraditional careers peaks when they are 13 years old. Throughout high school, boys' ambitions steadily increase while girls' decline.[32] Research suggests that the motivation to achieve depends at least partly on an expectation of success. The low self-esteem created when girls believe they are less able than boys, particularly in male-dominated fields, also reduces their motivation to succeed. In addition, girls recognize that lingering sex discrimination in higher education and the workplace means that the cost of success will be higher for them, which further reduces the incentive to try.[33]

Occupational choices Children learn occupational segregation as young as two or three, and these ideas are continuously reinforced by schoolbooks and the media, as well as by teachers' expectations and patterns of interaction at school.[34] By high school, girls' career choices are highly sex-segregated compared with boys'.[35] Because female-dominated occupations are typically paid much less than male-dominated ones, this

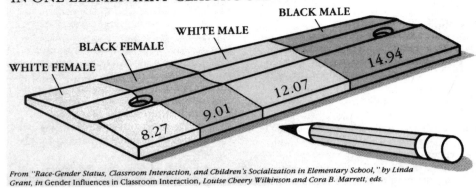

AVERAGE REPRIMANDS RECEIVED BY STUDENTS IN ONE ELEMENTARY CLASSROOM

WHITE FEMALE 8.27
BLACK FEMALE 9.01
WHITE MALE 12.07
BLACK MALE 14.94

From "Race-Gender Status, Classroom Interaction, and Children's Socialization in Elementary School," by Linda Grant, in Gender Influences in Classroom Interaction, *Louise Cheery Wilkinson and Cora B. Marrett, eds.*

Jean Wisenbaugh

pattern of occupational choice contributes to the cycle of poverty for women.

REWRITING THE SCRIPT

Guaranteeing access to education and employment is not enough to end gender stereotyping and provide girls with opportunities for success. The subtle, discouraging messages girls receive everyday about their roles and potential choices must be changed to ones of possibility and achievement. This is especially true for minority and immigrant girls, who will be 29 percent of the new workers in the work force between now and the year 2000.[36]

To foster girls' self-confidence and serious consideration of a range of career choices, parents need to encourage their daughters to be independent, to explore, and to experiment—even if it means they will occasionally get dirty or hurt. Girls need to be provided with toys such as building blocks, erector sets, and chemistry sets, which encourage facility with spatial relationships and mechanics, as well as with traditional girls' toys.

Schools must provide equal access to all resources for girls and boys. This may involve rearranging classrooms, placing, for example, building blocks and cooking toys in the same area. It also means providing a variety of role models in everything from faculty and staff hiring to textbook selection to the designation of speakers at assemblies.

Schools can also provide special programs to help girls make wise choices. The Hispanic Mother-Daughter Program at Arizona State University in Tempe, Arizona, for instance, brings mothers and daughters together for visits to local colleges and universities, classroom exercises in career choices, and presentations by professionals from the community.

Teachers can help by providing opportunities in class lessons and discussions

for girls and boys to learn to identify gender-role stereotypes and how those stereotypes limit their lives. Teachers can also thwart the informal structures of sex segregation by encouraging girls to play with equipment that is *de facto* reserved for boys, and vice versa.

Structuring group projects in ways that ensure girls an equal opportunity to participate is another way teachers can defeat the insidious effects of the hidden curriculum. Although boys typically dominate mixed-sex groups, research has shown that when teachers are trained to set up equitable group projects, girls and boys spend roughly equal amounts of time actively engaged in manipulating the equipment involved.[37]

Researchers have suggested that girls might do better work in classrooms that use cooperative learning techniques, particularly in math.[38] In cooperative learning, students are divided into small groups that work together on a particular subject. Individual students are tested regularly, and groups compete for prizes based on overall group improvement.[39]

Teachers also need to be trained to be sensitive to girls' special needs regarding conflicts between "appropriate" gender roles and wise career choices. Minority and immigrant girls may be struggling with other cultural norms as well. In addition, teachers must learn to praise and criticize the same behaviors by girls and boys consistently, and encourage girls to develop intellectual independence. Such habits and skills can be developed through in-service training such as the Gender-Ethnic Expectations and Student Achievement program initiated in 1984 by the Los Angeles, California, school system. This program trains selected teachers in equity concepts and strategies for overcoming bias in the classroom and sends them back to their school districts as peer trainers for other teachers.

Training in equitable teaching techniques should be included in every teacher education program and required for certification, but many schools of education have dropped sex equity from their agendas. One good resource in this area is the *Sex Equity Handbook for Schools,* a textbook on non-sexist teaching (see "Resources"). The handbook was published under the aegis of the Non-Sexist Teacher Education Project, which was funded under the WEEA in 1978–79 to develop teacher education materials on sex-equitable treatment.

WHAT WE CAN DO

Help to ensure our daughters' futures by joining in these recent AAUW initiatives. **Choices for Tomorrow's Women** aims to empower women and girls to make appropriate life choices. Under *Choices for Tomorrow's Women,* AAUW branches and divisions across the country are working with broad coalitions of allies to break down the institutional barriers that limit the choices of women and girls and provide second chances when inadequate choices were made the first time around.

The AAUW Educational Foundation's **Eleanor Roosevelt Fund for Women and Girls: Intergenerational Partnerships** was established to encourage original research and action to eliminate barriers to girls' and women's participation in education, promote the value of diversity and cross-cultural communication, and gain and disseminate a greater understanding of how women and girls think, learn, work, and play. As its first action project, the fund is sponsoring Teacher Enrichment Sabbaticals that will provide elementary and secondary school teachers the opportunity to improve their effectiveness with at-risk girls and with girls in math and science courses. Within a couple of years, AAUW branches and divisions will be helping to put research conducted under the fund's auspices into practice in schools in their communities.

Within these initiatives you can
• plan a branch program on changing the patterns of differential treatment of girls and boys in the classroom. Invite teachers, administrators, school board members, professors from schools of education, and/or students to participate in the meeting.
• build broad coalitions—including AAUW college/university member institutions that conduct teacher training and/or pedagogical research—in your community around issues of equal access and treatment in education. Use this brief as an initial resource.
• present information on these issues at a Parent-Teacher Association (PTA) meeting. A student-teacher forum on differential treatment in the classroom is one way to approach the subject.
• present information on these issues to the school board, and ask to work with them on strategies for attacking the problem.
• support the Fund for Women and Girls and encourage teachers in your commu-

nity to apply for a Teacher Enrichment Sabbatical (for application information, please contact the Fund for Women and Girls, AAUW Educational Foundation, 1111 Sixteenth Street N.W., Washington, DC 20036; 202/728-7603).
• sponsor a conference or workshop— for teachers, students, or the entire community—presenting research on differential treatment in the classroom, especially that conducted by Fund for Women and Girls sabbatical research awardees. Invite local university and public school faculty as speakers.
• donate materials on gender-role stereotyping and sex bias—including this brief—to the schools for use in curriculum development and the classroom. Provide training materials in sex-equitable teaching techniques to your school system (see "Resources").
• present awards to teachers who use sex-equitable teaching techniques.

During a first-grade testing period, each child was instructed to find the correct page in a seven-page testing booklet and fold the booklet back so only that page showed. When girls who had finished the task saw classmates who were having trouble doing it, they got up, did the task for them, and sat back down. No boys offered to help another child, and no one thanked the girls for their help.[44]

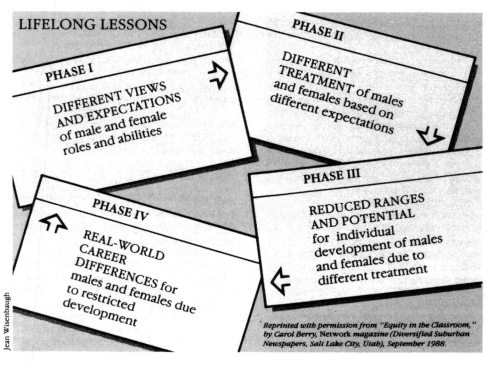

LIFELONG LESSONS

PHASE I
DIFFERENT VIEWS AND EXPECTATIONS of male and female roles and abilities

PHASE II
DIFFERENT TREATMENT of males and females based on different expectations

PHASE III
REDUCED RANGES AND POTENTIAL for individual development of males and females due to different treatment

PHASE IV
REAL-WORLD CAREER DIFFERENCES for males and females due to restricted development

Jean Wisenbaugh

Reprinted with permission from "Equity in the Classroom," by Carol Berry, Network *magazine (Diversified Suburban Newspapers, Salt Lake City, Utah), September 1988.*

• work to have sex-equitable teaching techniques added to the curriculum of your *alma mater* and teacher training institutions in your area and to requirements for teacher certification in your state. Contact your state board of education for information on those requirements and how they may be changed.
• seek support for your efforts by applying for an AAUW Educational Foundation Research & Projects (R&P) Grant. Funding available for 1989–90 includes Issue Focus Grants for projects emphasizing math and science enrichment for girls, mentoring for girls and women, or parenting and family education. For application information, please contact R&P Grants, AAUW Educational Foundation, 1111 Sixteenth Street N.W., Washington DC 20036; 202/728-7609. (Please note that not all of the ideas listed above are necessarily R&P Grant-eligible activities.)
• apply for a WEEA project grant from the U.S. Department of Education. This grants program aims to promote equity for girls and women at all levels of educa-

tion, preschool through adult. The 28 projects funded this year include efforts to develop and evaluate educational materials, establish model programs for educational personnel, perform research and development activities, and provide guidance and counseling services. Contact your state board of education for further information.

• support funding for WEEA, which must be appropriated by the U.S. Congress annually. To keep informed of federal action, subscribe to *Action Alert,* AAUW's legislative newsletter.

In one science class, children were divided into groups to work on constructing an electrical switch. When some of the girls had difficulty assembling their equipment, the teacher repeatedly told them to 'go and ask the boys for help.' [45]

RESOURCES

Classroom Climate Issues Packet, including *The Classroom Climate: A Chilly One for Women?; Selected Activities Using 'The Classroom Climate: A Chilly One for Women?'; Out of the Classroom: A Chilly Campus Climate for Women?* ($7 from the Project on the Status and Education of Women, Association of American Colleges, 1818 R Street, N.W., Washington DC 20009, 202/387-1300), 1982–84.

Learning Her Place—Sex Bias in the Elementary School Classroom ($4 from the Project on Equal Education Rights, 1333 H Street, N.W., 11th Floor, Washington, DC 20005; 202/682-0940), 1985.

Promoting Self-Esteem in Young Women: A Manual for Teachers (single copies free from the University of the State of New York, State Education Department, Division of Civil Rights and Intercultural Relations, Albany, NY), 1988.

Resources for Educational Equity, 1988 (free from the Women's Educational Equity Act Publishing Center, Educational Development Center, 55 Chapel Street, Suite 200, Newton, Massachusetts 02160; 1-800/225-3088, customer service), 1988.

Sex Equity Handbook for Schools, by Myra and David Sadker (New York: Longman, 1982).

Teachers Make the Difference: An Introduction to Education (New York: Harper and Row, 1980). (One of the few teacher training textbooks that deals with sex-equitable treatment in the classroom.)

Title IX: A Practical Guide to Achieving Sex Equity in Education ($3 from the National Coalition for Women and Girls in Education, c/o National Women's Law Center, 1616 P Street, N.W., Washington, DC 20036), 1988.

A DIFFERENT EQUITY

In a pluralistic society such as ours there are many different cultures—defined by intersections of gender, class, ethnicity, location, and other affiliations—which foster different learning styles. Too often, classrooms and teaching techniques are geared to meet the strengths of only one learning style; the learning styles of boys are accommodated over those of girls, just as the intellectual habits of some cultural minorities are catered to more than others by our schools.

Already, 45 percent of our work force is female, including 51 percent of mothers of children under the age of 3.[40] And by 2020, almost 40 percent of our citizens will be minorities.[41] Clearly, the future of the United States will rest largely on our ability to create learning environments that provide equal encouragement, resources, and opportunities to girls and boys from all backgrounds.

FOOTNOTES

1. National Commission on Working Women, "Women, Work and the Future," (Washington, DC: Wider Opportunities for Women, 1989), n.p.
2. National Center for Education Statistics, *1988 Education Indicators* (Washington, DC: Government Printing Office, 1988), p. 122; National Center for Education Statistics, *Digest of Education Statistics 1987* (Washington, DC: Government Printing Office, 1988), p. 176.
3. *The Grove City College* v. *Bell* ruling eventually was vitiated by the U.S. Congress' passage (and override of President Ronald Reagan's veto) of the Civil Rights Restoration Act in

February 1988, and the Department of Justice is once again accepting for review complaints filed under Title IX.
4. National Center for Education Statistics, *Digest of Education Statistics 1988* (Washington, DC: Government Printing Office, 1989), pp. 102–107; Dyanne Tracy, "Toys, Spatial Ability, and Science and Mathematics Achievement," *Sex Roles* 17 (August 1987), p. 132.
5. Camilla Benbow and Julian Stanley, "Sex Differences in Mathematical Abilitiy: Fact or Artifact?" *Science* 210 (1980), pp. 1262–64; Anne Fausto-Sterling, *Myths of Gender* (New York: Basic Books, 1985), Chapter 2.
6. Eleanor Maccoby and Carol Nagy Jacklin, *The Psychology of Sex Differences* (Stanford, CA: Stanford University Press, 1974), Chapter 3.
7. Janet Hyde, "How Large Are Cognitive Gender Differences?" *American Psychologist* 36 (August 1981), p. 894.
8. Elizabeth Fennema and Julia Sherman, "Sex-Related Differences in Mathematics Achievement: Spatial Visualization and Affective Factors," *American Educational Research Journal* 14 (Winter 1977), pp. 65–66.
9. Kirsten Goldberg, "Among Girls, 'Ethic of Caring' May Stifle Classroom Competitiveness, Study Shows," *Education Week,* April 27, 1988, pp. 1, 24.
10. Patrick Lee and Nancy Gropper, "Sex-Role Culture and Educational Practice," *Harvard Educational Review* 44 (August 1974), pp. 370–371.
11. P.R. Brandon, et al. "Children's Mathematics Achievement in Hawaii: Sex Differences Favoring Girls," *American Educational Research Journal* 24 (1987), p. 457.
12. James Campbell and Charlene Connolly, "Deciphering the Effects of Socialization," *Journal of Educational Equity and Leadership* 7 (Fall 1987), pp. 221–222.
13. Dionne Jones, "Cognitive Styles: Sex and Ethnic Differences," paper presented at the Annual Meeting of the American Educational Research Association, Washington, DC, November 13–15, 1986; "Self-Interest and the Common Weal," *Education Week,* April 27, 1988, p. 18.
14. Lee and Gropper, pp. 390–392.
15. Myra and David Sadker, *Sex Equity Handbook for Schools* (New York: Longman, 1982), p. 105.
16. Lee and Gropper, op. cit., p. 389.
17. Ibid, pp. 389–390.
18. Sadker and Sadker, op. cit., p. 103.
19. Jacquelynne Eccles and Phyllis Blumenfeld, "Classroom Experience and Student Gender: Are There Differences and Do They Matter?" in *Gender Influences in Classroom Interaction,* eds. Louise Cherry Wilkinson and Cora B Marret (Orlando: Academic Press, 1985), p. 84.
20. Sadker and Sadker, op. cit., p. 105.
21. Ibid, p. 105.
22. Gaea Leinhardt, Andrea Seewalk, and Mary Engel, "Learning What's Taught: Sex Differences in Instruction," *Journal of Educational Psychology* 71 (1979), p. 437.
23. Sadker and Sadker, op. cit., pp. 108–109.
24. Ibid.
25. Ibid, p. 109.
26. Marlaine Lockheed and Abigaile Harris, "Cross-Sex Collaborative Learning in Elementary Classrooms," *American Educational Research Journal* 221 (Summer 1984), p. 279.
27. Lee and Gropper, op. cit., pp. 383–4.
28. Maureen Hallinen and Aage Sorensen, "Ability Grouping and Sex-Differences in Mathematics Achievement," *Sociology of Education* 60 (1987), p. 67.
29. Lockheed and Harris, op. cit., p. 291.
30. Leonie Rennie and Lesley Parker, "Detecting and Accounting for Gender Differences in Mixed-Sex and Single-Sex Grouping in Science Lessons," *Educational Review* 39 (1987), pp. 67–68.
31. David Ryckman and Percy Peckham, "Gender Differences in Attributions for Success and Failure Situations Across Subject Areas," *Journal of Educational Research* 81 (December 1987), pp. 123–124.
32. Margaret Marini, "Sex Differences in the Determination of Adolescent Aspiration: A Review of Research," *Sex Roles* 4 (October 1978), p. 728.
33. Jacquelynne Eccles, "Gender Roles and Women's Achievement-Related Decisions," *Psychology of Women Quarterly* 11 (1987).
34. Linda Gettys and Arnie Cann, "Children's Perceptions of Occupational Stereotypes," *Sex Roles* 7 (1981), pp. 303–4.
35. Marini, op. cit., p. 729.
36. National Commission on Working Women, op. cit.
37. Rennie and Parker, op. cit., pp. 67–8.
38. Eccles, op. cit. pp. 158–9.
39. Robert Slavin, "Cooperative Learning and the Cooperative School," *Educational Leadership* (November 1987).
40. U.S. Department of Labor, Bureau of Labor Statistics, *Projections 2000* (Washington, DC: Government Printing Office, March 1988); National Commission on Working Women, op. cit.
41. American Council on Education and Education Commission of the States, *One-Third of a Nation: A Report of the Commission on Minority Participation in Education and American Life* (Washington, DC: May 1988), p. 3.
42. Lee and Gropper, op. cit., pp. 402–403.
43. Sadker and Sadker, op. cit., p. 105.
44. Raphaela Best, *We've All Got Scars: What Boys and Girls Learn in Elementary School* (Bloomington: Indiana University Press, 1983), p. 89.
45. Rennie and Parker, op. cit., p. 72.

HOW ASIAN TEACHERS POLISH EACH LESSON TO PERFECTION

JAMES W. STIGLER AND HAROLD W. STEVENSON

James Stigler is associate professor of psychology at the University of Chicago. He was recently awarded the Boyd R. McCandless Young Scientist Award from the American Psychological Association and was awarded a Guggenheim Fellowship last year for his work in the area of culture and mathematics learning. Harold W. Stevenson is professor of psychology and director of the University of Michigan Program in Child Development and Social Policy. He is currently president of the International Society for the Study of Behavioral Development and has spent the past two decades engaged in cross-cultural research.

This article is based on a book by Harold W. Stevenson and James Stigler, entitled The Learning Gap *(1994).*

ALTHOUGH THERE is no overall difference in intelligence, the differences in mathematical achievement of American children and their Asian counterparts are staggering.[1]

Let us look first at the results of a study we conducted in 120 classrooms in three cities: Taipei (Taiwan); Sendai (Japan); and the Minneapolis metropolitan area. First and fifth graders from representative schools in these cities were given a test of mathematics that required compu-

tation and problem solving. Among the one hundred first-graders in the three locations who received the lowest scores, fifty-eight were American children; among the one hundred lowest-scoring fifth graders, sixty-seven were American children. Among the top one hundred first graders in mathematics, there were only fifteen American children. And only one American child appeared among the top one hundred fifth graders. The highest-scoring American classroom obtained an average score lower than that of the lowest-scoring Japanese classroom and of all but one of the twenty classrooms in Taipei. In whatever way we looked at the data, the poor performance of American children was evident.

These data are startling, but no more so than the results of a study that involved 40 first- and 40 fifth-grade classrooms in the metropolitan area of Chicago—a very representative sample of the city and the suburbs of Cook County—and twenty-two classes in each of these grades in metropolitan Beijing (China). In this study, children were given a battery of mathematics tasks that included diverse problems, such as estimating the distance between a tree and a hidden treasure on a map, deciding who won a race on the basis of data in a graph, trying to explain subtraction to visiting Martians, or calculating the sum of nineteen and forty-five. There was no area in which the American children were competitive with those from China. The Chinese children's superiority appeared in complex tasks involving the application of knowledge as well as in the routines of computation. When fifth graders were asked, for example, how many

From *American Educator,* Spring 1991, pp. 12-20, 43-47. Reprinted with permission from *American Educator,* the quarterly journal of the American Federation of Teachers.

members of a stamp club with twenty-four members collected only foreign stamps if five-sixths of the members did so, 59 percent of Beijing children, but only 9 percent of the Chicago children produced the correct answer. On a computation test, only 2.2 percent of the Chinese fifth graders scored at or below the mean for their American counterparts. All of the twenty Chicago area schools had average scores on the fifth-grade geometry test that were below those of the Beijing schools. The results from all these tasks paint a bleak picture of American children's competencies in mathematics.[2]

The poor performance of American students compels us to try to understand the reasons why. We have written extensively elsewhere about the cultural differences in attitudes toward learning and toward the importance of effort vs. innate ability and about the substantially greater amounts of time Japanese and Chinese students devote to academic activities in general and to the study of math in particular.[3] Important as these factors are, they do not tell the whole story. For that we have to take a close look inside the classrooms of Japan, China, and the United States to see how mathematics is actually taught in the three cultures.

LESSONS NOT LECTURES

If we were asked briefly to characterize classes in Japan and China, we would say that they consist of coherent lessons that are presented in a thoughtful, relaxed, and nonauthoritarian manner. Teachers frequently rely on students as sources of information. Lessons are oriented toward problem solving rather than rote mastery of facts and procedures and utilize many different types of representational materials. The role assumed by the teacher is that of knowledgeable guide, rather than that of prime dispenser of information and arbiter of what is correct. There is frequent verbal interaction in the classroom as the teacher attempts to stimulate students to produce, explain, and evaluate solutions to problems. These characteristics contradict stereotypes held by most Westerners about Asian teaching practices. Lessons are not rote; they are not filled with drill. Teachers do not spend large amounts of time lecturing but attempt to lead the children in productive interactions and discussions. And the children are not the passive automata depicted in Western descriptions but active participants in the learning process.

We begin by discussing what we mean by the coherence of a lesson. One way to think of a lesson is by using the analogy of a story. A good story is highly organized; it has a beginning, a middle, and an end; and it follows a protagonist who meets challenges and resolves problems that arise along the way. Above all, a good story engages the reader's interest in a series of interconnected events, which are best understood in the context of the events that precede and follow it.

Such a concept of a lesson guides the organization of instruction in Asia. The curricula are defined in terms of coherent lessons, each carefully designed to fill a forty- to fifty-minute class period with sustained attention to the development of some concept or skill. Like a good story, the lesson has an introduction, a conclusion, and a consistent theme.

We can illustrate what we are talking about with this account of a fifth-grade Japanese mathematics class:

The teacher walks in carrying a large paper bag full of clinking glass. Entering the classroom with a large paper bag is highly unusual, and by the time she has placed the bag on her desk the students are regarding her with rapt attention. What's in the bag? She begins to pull items out of the bag, placing them, one-by-one, on her desk. She removes a pitcher and a vase. A beer bottle evokes laughter and surprise. She soon has six containers lined up on her desk. The children continue to watch intently, glancing back and forth at each other as they seek to understand the purpose of this display.

The teacher, looking thoughtfully at the containers, poses a question: "I wonder which one would hold the most water?" Hands go up, and the teacher calls on different students to give their guesses: "the pitcher," "the beer bottle," "the teapot." The teacher stands aside and ponders: "Some of you said one thing, others said something different. You don't agree with each other. There must be some way we can find out who is correct. How can we know who is correct?" Interest is high, and the discussion continues.

The students soon agree that to find out how much each container holds they will need to fill the containers with something. How about water? The teacher finds some buckets and sends several children out to fill them with water. When they return, the teacher says: "Now what do we do?" Again there is a discussion, and after several minutes the children decide that they will need to use a smaller container to measure how much water fits into each of the larger containers. They decide on a drinking cup, and one of the students warns that they all have to fill each cup to the same level—otherwise the measure won't be the same for all of the groups.

At this point the teacher divides the class into their groups (han) and gives each group one of the containers and a drinking cup. Each group fills its container, counts how many cups of water it holds, and writes the result in a notebook. When all of the groups have completed the task, the teacher calls on the leader of each group to report on the group's findings and notes the results on the blackboard. She has written the names of the containers in a column on the left and a scale from 1 to 6 along the bottom. Pitcher, 4.5 cups; vase, 3 cups; beer bottle, 1.5 cups; and so on. As each group makes its report, the teacher draws a bar representing the amount, in cups, the container holds.

Finally, the teacher returns to the question she posed at the beginning of the lesson: Which container holds the most water? She reviews how they were able to solve the problem and points out that the answer is now contained in the bar graph on the board. She then arranges the containers on the table in order according to how much they hold and writes a rank order on each container, from 1 to 6. She ends the class with a brief review of what they have done. No definitions of ordinate and abscissa, no discussion of how to make a graph preceded the example—these all became obvious in the course of the lesson, and only at the end did the teacher mention the terms that describe the horizontal and vertical axes of the graph they had made.

With one carefully crafted problem, this Japanese teacher has guided her students to discover—and most likely to remember—several important concepts. As this article unfolds, we hope to demonstrate that this example of how well-designed Asian class lessons are is not an isolated one; to the contrary, it is the norm. And as we hope to further demonstrate, excellent class lessons do not come effortlessly or magically. Asian teachers are not born great teachers; they and the lessons they develop require careful nurturing and constant refinement. The practice of teaching in Japan and China is more uniformly perfected than it is in the United States because their systems of education are structured to encourage teaching excellence to develop and flourish. Ours is not. We will take up the question of why and what can be done about this later in the piece. But first, we present a more detailed look at what Asian lessons are like.

COHERENCE BROKEN

Asian lessons almost always begin with a practical problem, such as the example we have just given, or with a word problem written on the blackboard. Asian teachers, to a much greater degree than American teachers, give coherence to their lessons by introducing the lesson with a word problem.

It is not uncommon for the Asian teacher to organize the entire lesson around the solution to this single problem. The teacher leads the children to recognize what is known and what is unknown and directs the students' attention to the critical parts of the problem. Teachers are careful to see that the problem is understood by all of the children, and even mechanics, such as mathematical computation, are presented in the context of solving a problem.

Before ending the lesson, the teacher reviews what has been learned and relates it to the problem she posed at the beginning of the lesson. American teachers are much less likely than Asian teachers to begin and end lessons in this way. For example, we found that fifth-grade teachers in Beijing spent eight times as long at the end of the class period summarizing the lessons as did those in the Chicago metropolitan area.

Now contrast the Japanese math lesson described above with a fifth-grade American mathematics classroom that we recently visited. Immediately after getting the students' attention, the teacher pointed out that today was Tuesday, "band day," and that all students in the band should go to the band room. "Those of you doing the news report today should meet over there in the corner," he continued. He then began the mathematics class with the remaining students by reviewing

It is not uncommon for the Asian teacher to organize the entire lesson around the solution to a single problem.

the solution to a computation problem that had been included in the previous day's homework. After this brief review, the teacher directed the students' attention to the blackboard, where the day's assignment had been written. From this point on, the teacher spent most of the rest of the period walking about the room monitoring the children's work, talking to individual children about questions or errors, and uttering "shushes" whenever the students began talking among themselves.

This example is typical of the American classrooms we have visited, classrooms where students spend more time in transition and less in academic activities, more time working on their own and less being instructed by the teacher; where teachers spend much of their time working with individual students and attending to matters of discipline; and where the shape of a coherent lesson is often hard to discern.

American lessons are often disrupted by irrelevant interruptions. These serve to break the continuity of the lesson and add to children's difficulty in perceiving the lesson as a coherent whole. In our American observations, the teacher interrupted the flow of the lesson with an interlude of irrelevant comments or the class was interrupted by someone else in 20 percent of all first-grade lessons and 47 percent of all fifth-grade lessons. This occurred less than 10 percent of the time at both grade levels in Sendai, Taipei, and Beijing. In fact, no interruptions of either type were recorded during the eighty hours of observation in Beijing fifth-grade classrooms. The mathematics lesson in one of the American classrooms we visited was interrupted every morning by a woman from the cafeteria who polled the children about their lunch plans and collected money from those who planned to eat the hot lunch. Interruptions, as well as inefficient transitions from one activity to another, make it difficult to sustain a coherent lesson throughout the class period.

Coherence is also disrupted when teachers shift frequently from one topic to another. This occurred often in the American classrooms we observed. The teacher might begin with a segment on measurement, then proceed to a segment on simple addition, then to a segment on telling time, and then to a second segment on addition. These segments constitute a math class, but they are hardly a coherent lesson. Such changes in topic were responsible for 21 percent of the changes in segments that we observed in American classrooms but accounted for only 4 percent of the changes in segments in Japanese classrooms.

Teachers frequently capitalize on variety as a means of capturing children's interest. This may explain why American teachers shift topics so frequently within the lesson. Asian teachers also seek variety, but they tend to

No one was leading instruction 9 percent of the time in Taiwan, 26 percent in Japan, and an astonishing 51 percent of the time in the United States.

introduce new activities instead of new topics. Shifts in materials do not necessarily pose a threat to coherence. For example, the coherence of a lesson does not diminish when the teacher shifts from working with numerals to working with concrete objects, if both are used to represent the same subtraction problem. Shifting the topic, on the other hand, introduces variety, but at the risk of destroying the coherence of the lesson.

CLASSROOM ORGANIZATION

Elementary school classrooms are typically organized in one of three ways: the whole class is working as a unit; the class is divided into a number of small groups; or children work individually. In our observations, we noted when the child was receiving instruction or assistance from the teacher and when the student was working on his own. The child was considered to be receiving instruction whenever the teacher was the leader of the activity, whether it involved the whole class, a small group, or only the individual child.

Looking at the classroom in this manner led us to one of our most pronounced findings: Although the number of children in Asian classes is significantly greater than the number in American classes, Asian students received much more instruction from their teachers than American students. In Taiwan, the teacher was the leader of the child's activity 90 percent of the time, as opposed to 74 percent in Japan, and only 46 percent in the United States. No one was leading instruction 9 percent of the time in Taiwan, 26 percent in Japan, and an astonishing 51 percent of the time in the United States (see Figure 1). Even American first graders actually spent more time on their own than they did participating in an activity led by the teacher.

One of the reasons American children received less instruction is that American teachers spent 13 percent of their time in the mathematics classes not working with any students, something that happened only 6 percent of the time in Japan and 9 percent in Taiwan. (As we will see later, American teachers have to steal class time to attend to the multitude of chores involving preparation, assessment, and administration because so little non-teaching time is available for them during the day.)

A much more critical factor in the erosion of instructional time was the amount of time American teachers were involved with individuals or small groups. American children spend 10 percent of their time in small groups and 47 percent of their time working individually. Much of the 87 percent of the time American teachers were working with their students was spent with

these individual students or small groups, rather than with the class as a whole. When teachers provide individual instruction, they must leave the rest of the class unattended, so instructional time for all remaining children is reduced.

Children can learn without a teacher. Nevertheless, it seems likely that they could profit from having their teacher as the leader of their activities more than half of the time they are in the classroom. It is the incredibly large amounts of time that American children are left unassisted and the effect that unattended time has on the coherence of the larger lesson that is the problem.

When children must work alone for long periods of time without guidance or reaction from the teacher, they begin to lose focus on the purpose of their activity. Asian teachers not only assign less seatwork than American teachers, they also use seatwork differently. Chinese and Japanese teachers tend to use short, frequent periods of seatwork, alternating between group discussion of problems and time for children to work problems on their own. Seatwork is thereby embedded into the lesson. After they work individually or in small groups on a problem, Asian students are called upon to present and defend the solutions they came up with. Thus, instruction, practice, and evaluation are tightly interwoven into a coherent whole. In contrast, the average length of seatwork in American fifth-grade classrooms was almost

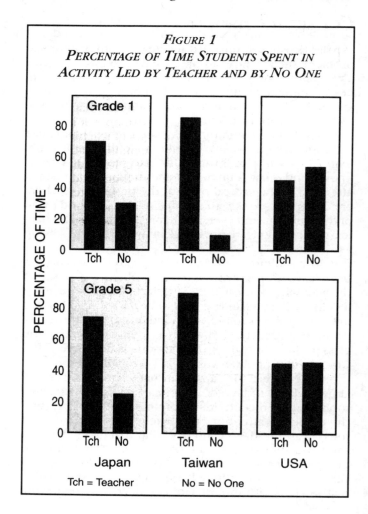

FIGURE 1
PERCENTAGE OF TIME STUDENTS SPENT IN ACTIVITY LED BY TEACHER AND BY NO ONE

twice as long as it was in Asian classrooms. And, instead of embedding seatwork into the ongoing back and forth of the lesson, American teachers tend to relegate it to one long period at the end of the class, where it becomes little more than a time for repetitious practice. In Chicago, 59 percent of all fifth-grade lessons ended with a period of seatwork, compared with 23 percent in Sendai and 14 percent in Taipei. American teachers often do not discuss the work or its connection to the goal of the lesson, or even evaluate its accuracy. Seatwork was never evaluated or discussed in 48 percent of all American fifth-grade classes we observed, compared to less than 3 percent of Japanese classes and 6 percent of Taiwan classes.

Since Asian students spend so much of their time in whole-group work, we need to say a word about that format. Whole-class instruction in the United States has gotten a somewhat bad reputation. It has become associated with too much teacher talk and too many passive, tuned-out students. But as we will see in more detail as we continue our description of Asian classrooms, whole-class instruction in Japan and China is a very lively, engaging enterprise. Asian teachers do not spend large amounts of time lecturing. They present interesting problems; they pose provocative questions; they probe and guide. The students work hard, generating multiple approaches to a solution, explaining the rationale behind their methods, and making good use of wrong answers.

HANDLING DIVERSITY

The organization of American elementary school classrooms is based on the assumption that whole-group instruction cannot accommodate students' diverse abilities and levels of achievement; thus, large amounts of whole-class time are given up so that the teacher can work individually with students. Asian educators are

HOW WE MADE SURE WE WERE LOOKING AT REPRESENTATIVE SCHOOLS

FREQUENT REPORTS on television and in books and newspapers purport to depict what happens inside Japanese and Chinese classrooms. These reports usually are based on impressions gathered during brief visits to classrooms—most likely classrooms that the visitor's contacts in Asia have preselected. As a result, it is difficult to gauge the generality of what was seen and reported. Without observing large, representative samples of schools and teachers, it is impossible to characterize the teaching practices of any culture.

The descriptions that we present are based on two large observational studies of first- and fifth-grade classrooms that we conducted in Japan, Taiwan, China, and the United States. In contrast to informal observations, the strength of formal studies such as ours is that the observations are made according to consistent rules about where, when, and what to observe.

In the first study, our observers were in classrooms for a total of over four thousand hours—over a thousand class periods in 20 first- and fifth-grade classrooms in each of three cities: Sendai, Japan; Taipei, Taiwan; and Minneapolis, Minnesota.[1] Our second study took place in two hundred classrooms, forty each in Sendai and Taipei, plus forty in Beijing, China, and eighty in the Chicago metropolitan area of the United States.[2] Care was taken to choose schools that were representative. Our Chicago metropolitan area sample—the urban and suburban areas that make up Cook County—included schools that are predominantly white, black, Hispanic, and ethnically mixed; schools that draw from upper, middle, and lower socioeconomic groups; schools that are public and private; and schools that are urban and suburban.

Observers visited each classroom four times over a one- to two-week period, yielding a total of eight hundred hours of observations. The observers, who were residents of each city, wrote down as much as they could about what transpired during each mathematics class. Tape recordings made during the classes assisted the observers in filling in any missing information. These detailed narrative accounts of what transpired in the classrooms yielded even richer information than we obtained in the first study, where the observers followed predefined categories for coding behavior during the course of observations.

After the narrative records had been translated into English, we divided each observation into segments, which we defined as beginning each time there was a change in topic, materials, or activity. For example, a segment began when students put away their textbooks and began working on a worksheet or when the teacher stopped lecturing and asked some of the students to write their solutions to a problem on the blackboard.

Both studies focused on mathematics classes rather than on classes in subjects such as reading, where cultural differences in teaching practices may be more strongly determined by the content of what is being taught. For example, it is likely that the processes of teaching and learning about the multiplication of fractions transcend cultural differences, whereas teaching children how to read Chinese characters may require different approaches from those used to teach children to read an alphabetic language.

REFERENCES

[1]Stevenson, H.W., Stigler, J.W., Lucker, G.W., Lee, S.Y., Hsu, C.C., & Kitamura, S. (1987). Classroom behavior and achievement of Japanese, Chinese, and American children. In R. Glaser (Ed.), *Advances in instructional psychology.* Hillsdale NJ: Erlbaum.
[2]Stigler, J.W., & Perry, M. (1990). Mathematics learning in Japanese, Chinese, and American classrooms. In Stigler, J.W., Shweder, R.A., & Herdt, G. (Eds.), *Cultural psychology: Essays on comparative human development.* Cambridge, Cambridge University Press. Pp. 328-356.

more comfortable in the belief that all children, with proper effort, can take advantage of a uniform educational experience, and so they are able to focus on providing the same high-quality experience to all students. Our results suggest that American educators need to question their long-held assumption that an individualized learning experience is inherently a higher-quality, more effective experience than is a whole-class learning experience. Although it may be true that an equal amount of time with a teacher may be more effective in a one-on-one situation than in a large-group situation, we must realize that the result of individualized instruction, given realistic financial constraints, is to drastically reduce the amount of teacher instruction every child receives.

Japanese and Chinese teachers recognize individual differences among students, but they handle that diversity in a very different way. First, as we will see in more detail later, they have much greater amounts of non-teaching time than do American teachers, and part of that time is available for working with individual students. They may spend extra time with slower students or ask faster students to assist them, but they focus their lesson on teaching all children regardless of apparent differences in ability or developmental readiness. Before we discuss how they do that in a whole-group setting, we

---

Tracking does not exist in Asian elementary schools. This egalitarian philosophy carries over to organization within the classroom.

---

need to first address the question of whether American classrooms are more diverse than Asian ones, thus potentially rendering whole-class instruction more difficult.

Whenever we discuss our research on teaching practices, someone in the audience inevitably reminds us that Japan and China are nations with relatively homogeneous populations while the United States is the melting pot of the world. How could we expect that practices used in Asian societies could possibly be relevant for the American context, where diversity is the rule in race, ethnicity, language, and social class?

What impedes teaching is the uneven preparation of children for the academic tasks that must be accomplished. It is diversity in children's educational backgrounds, not in their social and cultural backgrounds, that poses the greatest problems in teaching. Although the United States is culturally more diverse than Japan or China, we have found no more diversity at the classroom level in the educational level of American than of Asian students. The key factor is that, in the United States, educational and cultural diversity are positively related, leading some persons to the inappropriate conclusion that it is ethnic and cultural diversity, rather than educational diversity, that leads to the difficulties faced by American teachers.

It is true, for example, that there is greater variability in mathematics achievement among American than among Japanese children, but this does not mean that the differences are evident in any particular classroom. Variability in the United States exists to a large extent across neighborhoods and schools (rather than within them). Within individual classrooms, the variability in levels of academic achievement differs little between the United States and Japan, Taiwan, or China. It is wrong to argue that diversity within classrooms is an American problem. Teachers everywhere must deal with students who vary in their knowledge and motivation.

Tracking does not exist in Asian elementary schools. Children are never separated into different classrooms according to their presumed levels of intellectual ability. This egalitarian philosophy carries over to organization within the classroom. Children are not separated into reading groups according to their ability; there is no division of the class into groups differentiated by the rate at which they proceed through their mathematics books. No children leave the classroom for special classes, such as those designed for children who have been diagnosed as having learning disabilities.

How do teachers in Asian classrooms handle diversity in students' knowledge and skills? For one thing, they typically use a variety of approaches in their teaching, allowing students who may not understand one approach the opportunity to experience other approaches to presenting the material. Periods of recitation are alternated with periods in which children work for short periods on practice problems. Explanations by the teacher are interspersed with periods in which children work with concrete materials or struggle to come up with their own solutions to problems. There is continuous change from one mode of presentation, one type of representation, and one type of teaching method to another.

Asian teaching practices thrive in the face of diversity, and some practices even depend on diversity for their effectiveness. Asking students to suggest alternative solutions to a problem, for example, works best when students have had experience in generating a variety of solutions. Incorrect solutions, which are typically dismissed by the American teacher, become topics for discussion in Asian classrooms, and all students can learn from this discussion. Thus, while American schools attempt to solve the problems of diversity by segregating children into different groups or different classrooms, and by spending large amounts of regular class time working with individual students, Asian teachers believe that the only way they can cope with the problem is by devising teaching techniques that accommodate the different interests and backgrounds of the children in their classrooms.

Asian teachers also exploit the fact that the same instruction can affect different students in different ways, something that may be overlooked by American teachers. In this sense, Asian teachers subscribe to what would be considered in the West to be a "constructivist" view of learning. According to this view, knowledge is regarded as something that must be constructed by the child rather than as a set of facts and skills that can be imparted by the teacher. Because children are engaged in their own construction of knowledge, some of the major tasks for the teacher are to pose provocative questions, to allow adequate time for reflection, and to vary teaching techniques so that they are responsive to differences in students' prior experience. Through such practices, Asian teachers are able to accommodate individual differences in learning, even though instruction is not tailored to each student.

USE OF REAL-WORLD PROBLEMS AND OBJECTS

Elementary school mathematics is often defined in terms of mathematical symbols and their manipulation; for example, children must learn the place-value system of numeration and the operations for manipulating numerals to add, subtract, multiply, and divide. In addition, children must be able to apply these symbols and operations to solving problems. In order to accomplish these goals, teachers rely primarily on two powerful tools for representing mathematics: language and the manipulation of concrete objects. How effectively teachers use these forms of representation plays a critical role in determining how well children will understand mathematics.

One common function of language is in defining terms and stating rules for performing mathematical operations. A second, broader function is the use of language as a means of connecting mathematical operations to the real world and of integrating what children know about mathematics. We find that American elementary school teachers are more prone to use language to define terms and state rules than are Asian teachers, who, in their efforts to make mathematics meaningful, use language to clarify different aspects of mathematics and to integrate what children know about mathematics with the demands of real-world problems. Here is an example of what we mean by a class in which the teacher defines terms and states rules:

An American teacher announces that the lesson today concerns fractions. Fractions are defined and she names the numerator and denominator. "What do we call this?" she then asks. "And this?" After assuring herself that the children understand the meaning of the terms, she spends the rest of the lesson teaching them to apply the rules for forming fractions.

Asian teachers tend to reverse the procedure. They focus initially on interpreting and relating a real-world problem to the quantification that is necessary for a mathematical solution and then to define terms and state rules. In the following example, a third-grade teacher in Japan was also teaching a lesson that introduced the notation system for fractions.

The lesson began with the teacher posing the question of how many liters of juice (colored water) were contained in a large beaker. "More than one liter," answered one child. "One and a half liters," answered another. After several children had made guesses, the teacher suggested that they pour the juice into some one-liter beakers and see. Horizontal lines on each beaker divided it into thirds. The juice filled one beaker and part of a second. The teacher pointed out that the water came up to the first line on the second beaker—only one of the three parts was full. The procedure was repeated with a second set of beakers to illustrate the concept of one-half. After stating that there had been one and one-out-of-three liters of juice in the first big beaker and one and one-out-of-two liters in the second, the teacher wrote the fractions on the board. He continued the lesson by asking the children how to represent two parts out of three, two parts out of five, and so forth. Near the end of the period he mentioned the term "fraction" for the first time and attached names to the numerator and the denominator.

He ended the lesson by summarizing how fractions can be used to represent the parts of a whole.

In the second example, the concept of fractions emerged from a meaningful experience; in the first, it was introduced initially as an abstract concept. The terms and operations in the second example flowed naturally from the teacher's questions and discussion; in the first, language was used primarily for defining and summarizing rules. Mathematics ultimately requires abstract representation, but young children understand such representation more readily if it is derived from meaningful experience than if it results from learning definitions and rules.

Asian teachers generally are more likely than American teachers to engage their students, even very young ones, in the discussion of mathematical concepts. The kind of verbal discussion we find in American classrooms is more short-answer in nature, oriented, for example, toward clarifying the correct way to implement a computational procedure.

Teachers ask questions for different reasons in the United States and in Japan. In the United States, the purpose of a question is to get an answer. In Japan, teachers pose questions to stimulate thought. A Japanese teacher considers a question to be a poor one if it elicits an immediate answer, for this indicates that students were not challenged to think. One teacher we interviewed told us of discussions she had with her fellow teachers on how to improve teaching practices. "What do you talk about?" we wondered. "A great deal of time," she reported, "is spent talking about questions we can pose to the class—which wordings work best to get students involved in thinking and discussing the material. One good question can keep a whole class going for a long time; a bad one produces little more than a simple answer."

In one memorable example recorded by our observers, a Japanese first-grade teacher began her class by posing the question to one of her students: "Would you explain the difference between what we learned in yesterday's lesson and what you came across in preparing for today's lesson?" The young student thought for a long time, but then answered the question intelligently, a performance that undoubtedly enhanced his understanding of both lessons.

CONCRETE REPRESENTATIONS

Every elementary school student in Sendai possesses a "Math Set," a box of colorful, well-designed materials for teaching mathematical concepts: tiles, clock, ruler, checkerboard, colored triangles, beads, and many other attractive objects.

In Taipei, every classroom is equipped with a similar, but larger, set of such objects. In Beijing, where there is much less money available for purchasing such materials, teachers improvise with colored paper, wax fruit, plates, and other easily obtained objects. In all cases, these concrete objects are considered to be critically important tools for teaching mathematics, for it is through manipulating these objects that children can form important links between real-world problems and abstract mathematical notations.

American teachers are much less likely than Chinese or Japanese teachers to use concrete objects. At fifth grade, for example, Sendai teachers were nearly twice as likely to use concrete objects as the Chicago area teachers, and Taipei teachers were nearly five times as likely. There was also a subtle, but important, difference in the way Asian and American teachers used concrete objects. Japanese teachers, for example, use the items in the Math Set throughout the elementary school years and introduced small tiles in a high percentage of the lessons we observed in the first grade. American teachers seek variety and may use Popsicle sticks in one lesson, and in another, marbles, Cheerios, M&Ms, checkers, poker chips, or plastic animals. The American view is that objects should be varied in order to maintain children's interest. The Asian view is that using a variety of representational materials may confuse children, and thereby make it more difficult for them to use the objects for the representation and solution of mathematics problems. Having learned to add with tiles makes multiplication easier to understand when the same tiles are used.

Through the skillful use of concrete objects, teachers are able to teach elementary school children to understand and solve problems that are not introduced in American curricula until much later. An example occurred in a fourth-grade mathematics lesson we observed in Japan. The problem the teacher posed is a difficult one for fourth graders, and its solution is generally not taught in the United States until much later. This is the problem:

> There are a total of thirty-eight children in Akira's class. There are six more boys than there are girls. How many boys and how many girls are in the class?

This lesson began with a discussion of the problem and with the children proposing ways to solve it. After the discussion, the teacher handed each child two strips of paper, one six units longer than the other, and told the class that the strips would be used to help them think about the problem. One slip represented the number of girls in the class and the other represented the number of boys. By lining the strips next to each other, the children could see that the degree to which the longer one protruded beyond the shorter one represented 6 boys. The procedure for solving the problem then unfolded as the teacher, through skillful questioning, led the children to the solution: The number of girls was found by taking the total of both strips, subtracting 6 to make the strips of equal length, and then dividing by 2. The number of boys could be found, of course, by adding 6 to the number of girls. With this concrete visual representation of the problem and careful guidance from the teacher, even fourth graders were able to understand the problem and its solution.

STUDENTS CONSTRUCT MULTIPLE SOLUTIONS

A common Western stereotype is that the Asian teacher is an authoritarian purveyor of information, one who expects students to listen and memorize correct answers or correct procedures rather than to construct knowledge themselves. This may or may not be an accurate description of Asian high school teachers,[4] but, as we have seen in previous examples, it does not describe the dozens of elementary school teachers that we have observed.

Chinese and Japanese teachers rely on students to generate ideas and evaluate the correctness of the ideas. The possibility that they will be called upon to state their own solution as well as to evaluate what another student has proposed keeps Asian students alert, but this technique has two other important functions. First, it engages students in the lesson, increasing their motivation by making them feel they are participants in a group process. Second, it conveys a more realistic impression of how knowledge is acquired. Mathematics, for example, is a body of knowledge that has evolved gradually through a process of argument and proof. Learning to argue about mathematical ideas is fundamental to understanding mathematics. Chinese and Japanese children begin learning these skills in the first grade; many American elementary school students are never exposed to them.

We can illustrate the way Asian teachers use students' ideas with the following example. A fifth-grade teacher in Taiwan began her mathematics lesson by calling attention to a six-sided figure she had drawn on the blackboard. She asked the students how they might go about finding the area of the shaded region. "I don't want you to tell me what the actual area is, just tell me the approach you would use to solve the problem. Think of as many different ways as you can of ways you could determine the area that I have drawn in yellow chalk." She allowed the students several minutes to work in small groups and then called upon a child from each group to describe the group's solution. After each proposal, many of which were quite complex, the teacher asked members of the other groups whether the procedure described could yield a correct answer. After several different procedures had been suggested, the teacher moved on to a second problem with a different embedded figure and repeated the process. Neither teacher nor students actually carried out a solution to the problem until all of the alternative solutions had been discussed. The lesson ended with the teacher affirming the importance of coming up with multiple solutions. "After all," she said, "we face many problems every day in the real world. We have to remember that there is not only one way we can solve each problem."

American teachers are less likely to give students opportunities to respond at such length. Although a great deal of interaction appears to occur in American classrooms—with teachers and students posing questions and giving answers—American teachers generally pose questions that are answerable with a yes or no or with a short phrase. They seek a correct answer and continue calling on students until one produces it. "Since we can't subtract 8 from 6," says an American teacher, "we have to . . . what?" Hands go up, the teacher calls on a girl who says "Borrow." "Correct," the teacher replies. This kind of interchange does not establish the student as a valid source of information, for the final arbiter of the correctness of the student's opinions is still the teacher. The situation is very different in Asian classrooms, where children are likely to be asked to explain their answers and other children are then called upon to evaluate their correctness.

Clear evidence of these differing beliefs about the roles of students and teachers appears in the observations of how teachers evaluate students' responses. The most frequent form of evaluation used by American teachers was praise, a technique that was rarely used in either Taiwan or Japan. In Japan, evaluation most frequently took the form of a discussion of children's errors.

Praise serves to cut off discussion and to highlight the teacher's role as the authority. It also encourages children to be satisfied with their performance rather than informing them about where they need improvement. Discussing errors, on the other hand, encourages argument and justification and involves students in the exciting quest of assessing the strengths and weaknesses of the various alternative solutions that have been proposed.

Why are American teachers often reluctant to encourage students to participate at greater length during mathematics lessons? One possibility is that they feel insecure about the depth of their own mathematical training. Placing more emphasis on students' explanations necessarily requires teachers to relinquish some control over the direction the lesson will take. This can be a frightening prospect to a teacher who is unprepared to evaluate the validity of novel ideas that students inevitably propose.

USING ERRORS EFFECTIVELY

We have been struck by the different reactions of Asian and American teachers to children's errors. For Americans, errors tend to be interpreted as an indication of failure in learning the lesson. For Chinese and Japanese, they are an index of what still needs to be learned. These divergent interpretations result in very different reactions to the display of errors—embarrassment on the part of the American children, calm acceptance by Asian children. They also result in differences in the manner in which teachers utilize errors as effective means of instruction.

We visited a fifth-grade classroom in Japan the first day the teacher introduced the problem of adding fractions with unequal denominators. The problem was a simple one: adding one-third and one-half. The children were

The most frequent form of evaluation used by American teachers was praise, a technique that was rarely used in either Taiwan or Japan.

told to solve the problem and that the class would then review the different solutions.

After everyone appeared to have completed the task, the teacher called on one of the students to give his answer and to explain his solution. "The answer is two-fifths," he stated. Pointing first to the numerators and then to the denominators, he explained: "One plus one is two; three plus two is five. The answer is two-fifths." Without comment, the teacher asked another boy for his solution. "Two point one plus three point one, when changed into a fraction adds up to two-fifths." The children in the classroom looked puzzled. The teacher, unperturbed, asked a third student for her solution. "The answer is five-sixths." The student went on to explain how she had found the common denominator, changed the fractions so that each had this denominator, and then added them.

The teacher returned to the first solution. "How many of you think this solution is correct?" Most agreed that it was not. She used the opportunity to direct the children's attention to reasons why the solution was incorrect. "Which is larger, two-fifths or one-half?" The class agreed that it was one-half. "It is strange, isn't it, that you could add a number to one-half and get a number that is smaller than one-half?" She went on to explain how the procedure the child used would result in the odd situation where, when one-half was added to one-half, the answer yielded is one-half. In a similarly careful, interactive manner, she discussed how the second boy had confused fractions with decimals to come up with his surprising answer. Rather than ignoring the incorrect solutions and concentrating her attention on the correct solution, the teacher capitalized on the errors the children made in order to dispel two common misperceptions about fractions.

We have not observed American teachers responding to children's errors so inventively. Perhaps because of the strong influence of behavioristic teaching that conditions should be arranged so that the learner avoids errors and makes only a reinforceable response, American teachers place little emphasis on the constructive use of errors as a teaching technique. It seems likely, however, that learning about what is wrong may hasten children's understanding of why the correct procedures are appropriate.

WHY NOT HERE?

Few who have visited urban classrooms in Asia would disagree that the great majority of Chinese and Japanese teachers are highly skilled professionals. Their dedication is legendary; what is often not appreciated is how thoughtfully and adroitly they guide children through the vast amount of material that they must master during the six years of elementary school. We, of course, witnessed examples of excellent lessons in American classrooms. And there are of course individual differences among Asian teachers. But what has impressed us in our personal observations and in the data from our observational studies is how remarkably well most Asian teachers teach. It is the *widespread* excellence of Asian class lessons, the high level of performance of the *average* teacher, that is so stunning.

The techniques used by Chinese and Japanese teachers are not new to the teaching profession—nor are they foreign or exotic. In fact, they are the types of techniques often recommended by American educators. What the Japanese and Chinese examples demonstrate so compellingly is that when widely implemented, such practices can produce extraordinary outcomes.

Unfortunately, these techniques have not been broadly applied in the United States. Why? One reason, as we have discussed, is the Asian belief that the whole-group lesson, if done well, can be made to work for every child. With that assumption, Asian teachers can focus on the perfection of that lesson. However, even if American educators shared that belief, it would be difficult for them to achieve anything near the broad-based high quality that we observed in Asian classrooms. This is not the fault of American teachers. The fault lies with a system that prepares them inadequately and then exhausts them physically, emotionally, and intellectually while denying them the collegial interaction that every profession relies upon for the growth and refinement of its knowledge base.

The first major obstacle to the widespread development and execution of excellent lessons in America is the fact that American teachers are overworked. It is inconceivable that American teachers, by themselves, would be able to organize lively, vivid, coherent lessons under a regimen that requires that they teach hour after hour every day throughout the school year. Preparing lessons that require the discovery of knowledge and the construction of understanding takes time. Teaching them effectively requires energy. Both are in very short supply for most American teachers.

Being an elementary school teacher in the United States at the end of the twentieth century is extraordinarily difficult, and the demands made by American society exhaust even the most energetic among them. "I'm dancing as fast as I can" one teacher summarized her feelings about her job, "but with all the things that I'm supposed to do, I just can't keep up."

The full realization of how little time American teachers have when they are not directly in charge of children became clear to us during a meeting in Beijing. We were discussing the teachers' workday. When we informed the Chinese teachers that American teachers are responsible for their classes all day long, with only an hour or less outside the classroom each day, they looked incredulous. How could any teacher be expected to do a good job when there is no time outside of class to prepare and correct lessons, work with individual children, consult with other teachers, and attend to all of the matters that arise in a typical day at school! Beijing teachers teach no more than three hours a day, unless the teacher is a homeroom teacher, in which case, the total is four hours. During the first three grades, the teaching assignment includes both reading and mathematics; for the upper three grades of elementary school, teachers specialize in one of these subjects. They spend the rest of their day at school carrying out all of their other responsibilities to their students and to the school. The situation is similar in Japan. According to our estimate, Japanese elementary school teachers are in charge of classes only 60 percent of the time they are at school.

The large amounts of nonteaching time at school are available to Asian teachers because of two factors. The first concerns the number of teachers typically assigned to Asian schools. Although class sizes are considerably larger in Asia, the student-to-teacher ratio within a school does not differ greatly from that in the United States. By having more students in each class and the same number of teachers in the school, all teachers can have fewer teaching hours. Time is freed up for teachers to meet and work together on a daily basis, to prepare lessons for the next day, to work with individual children, and to attend staff meetings.

The second factor increasing the time available to Japanese and Chinese teachers at school is that they spend more hours at school each day than do American teachers. In our study, for example, teachers in Sendai and Taipei spent an average of 9.5 and 9.1 hours per day, respectively, compared to only 7.3 hours for the American teachers. Asian teachers arrive at school early and stay late, which gives them time to meet together and to work with children who need extra help. Most American teachers, in contrast, arrive at school shortly before classes begin and leave not long after they end. This does not mean a shorter work week for American teachers. What it does mean is that they must devote their evenings to working alone on the next day's lessons, further increasing their sense of isolation.

LEARNING FROM EACH OTHER

The second reason Asian class lessons are so well crafted is that there is a very systematic effort to pass on the accumulated wisdom of teaching practice to each new generation of teachers and to keep perfecting that practice by providing teachers the opportunities to continually learn from each other.

Americans often act as if good teachers are born, not made. We hear this from both teachers and parents. They seem to believe that good teaching happens if the teacher has a knack with children, gets along well with them, and keeps them reasonably attentive and enthusiastic about learning. It is a commonly accepted truism in many colleges of education that teaching is an art and that students cannot be taught how to teach.

Perhaps because of this belief, students emerge from American colleges of education with little training in how to design and teach effective lessons. It is assumed that teachers will discover this for themselves. Courses in teaching methods are designed to serve a different purpose. On the one hand, they present theories of learning and cognitive development. Although the students are able to quote the major tenets of the theorists currently in vogue, the theories remain as broad generalizations that are difficult to apply to the everyday tasks that they will face as classroom teachers. At the opposite extreme, these methods courses provide education students with lists of specific suggestions for activities and materials that are easy to use and that children should enjoy (for example, pieces of breakfast cereal make handy counters for teaching basic number facts). Teachers are faced, therefore, with information that is either too general to be applied readily or so specific that it has only limited usefulness. Because of this, American teachers complain that most of what they know had to be learned by themselves, alone, on the job.

In Asia, graduates of teacher training programs are still considered to be novices who need the guidance and support of their experienced colleagues. In the United States, training comes to a near halt after the teachers acquire their teaching certificates. American teachers may take additional coursework in the evenings or during summer vacations, or they may attend district or city-wide workshops from time to time. But these opportunities are not considered to be an essential part of the American system of teacher training.

In Japan, the system of teacher training is much like an apprenticeship under the guidance of experienced colleagues. The teacher's first year of employment marks the beginning of a lengthy and elaborate training process. By Japanese law, beginning teachers must receive a minimum of twenty days of inservice training during their first year on the job.[5] Supervising the inservice training are master teachers, selected for their teaching ability and their willingness to assist their young colleagues. During one-year leaves of absence from their own classrooms, they observe the beginner in the classroom and offer suggestions for improvement.

In addition to this early tutelage in teaching techniques, Japanese teachers, beginners as well as seasoned teachers, are required to continually perfect their teaching skills through interaction with other teachers. One mechanism is through meetings organized by the vice principal and head teachers of their own school. These experienced professionals assume responsibility for advising and guiding their young colleagues. The head teachers organize meetings to discuss teaching techniques and to devise lesson plans and handouts. These meetings are supplemented by informal districtwide study groups and courses at municipal or prefectural education centers.[6]

A glimpse at what takes place in these study groups is provided in a conversation we recently had with a Japanese teacher. She and her colleagues spend a good deal of their time together working on lesson plans. After they finish a plan, one teacher from the group teaches the lesson to her students while the other teachers look on. Afterward, the group meets again to criticize the teacher's performance and to make suggestions for how the lesson could be improved. In her school, there is an annual "teaching fair." Teachers from other schools are invited to visit the school and observe the lessons being taught. The visitors rate the lessons, and the teacher with the best lesson is declared the winner.

In addition, national television in Japan presents programs that show how master teachers handle particular lessons or concepts. In Taiwan, such demonstrations are available on sets of videotapes that cover the whole curriculum.

Making use of lessons that have been honed over time does not mean that the Asian teacher simply mimics what she sees. As with great actors or musicians, the substance of the curriculum becomes the script or the score; the goal is to perform the role or piece as effectively and creatively as possible. Rather than executing the curriculum as a mere routine, the skilled teacher strives to perfect the presentation of each lesson. She uses the teaching techniques she has learned and imposes her own interpretation on these techniques in a manner that she thinks will interest and motivate her pupils.

Of course, teachers find it easier to share helpful tips and techniques among themselves when they are all teaching the same lesson at about the same time. The fact that Taiwan, Japan, and China each has a national curriculum that provides a common focus is a significant factor in teacher interaction. Not only do we have no national curriculum in the United States, but the curriculum may not be consistent within a city or even within a single school. American textbooks, with a spiral curriculum that repeats topics year after year and with a profusion of material about each topic, force teachers to omit some of each year's material. Even when teachers use the same textbook, their classes differ according to which topics they choose to skip and in the pace with which they proceed through the text. As a result, American teachers have less incentive than Asian teachers to share experiences with each other or to benefit from the successes and failures that others have had in teaching particular lessons.

Adding further to the sense of isolation is the fact that American teachers, unlike other professionals, do not share a common body of knowledge and experience. The courses offered at different universities and colleges vary, and even among their required courses, there is often little common content from college to college. Student teaching, the only other activity in which all budding teachers participate, is a solitary endeavor shared only with the regular classroom teacher and perhaps a few fellow student teachers.

Opportunities for Asian teachers to learn from each other are influenced, in part, by the physical arrangements of the schools. In Japanese and Chinese schools, a large room in each school is designed as a teachers' room, and each teacher is assigned a desk in this room. It is here that they spend their time away from the classroom preparing lessons, correcting students' papers, and discussing teaching techniques. American teachers, isolated in their own classrooms, find it much harder to discuss their work with colleagues. Their desk and teaching materials are in their own classrooms, and the only common space available to teachers is usually a cramped room that often houses supplies and the school's duplicating facilities, along with a few chairs and a coffee machine. Rarely do teachers have enough time in their visits to this room to engage in serious discussions of educational policy or teaching practices.

* * *

Critics argue that the problems facing the American teacher are unique and that it is futile to consider what Japanese and Chinese teaching are like in seeking solutions to educational problems in the United States. One of the frequent arguments is that the students in the typical Asian classroom share a common language and culture, are well disciplined and attentive, and are not distracted by family crises and their own personal problems, whereas the typical American teacher is often faced with a diverse, burdened, distracted group of students. To be sure, the conditions encountered by teachers differ greatly among these societies. Week after week, American teachers must cope with children who present them with complex, wrenching personal problems. But much of what gives American classrooms their aura of disarray and disorganization may be traced to how schools are organized and teachers are trained as well as to characteristics of the children.

It is easy to blame teachers for the problems confronting American education, and this is something that the American public is prone to do. The accusation is unfair. We cannot blame teachers when we deprive them of adequate training and yet expect that on their own they will become innovative teachers; when we cast them in the roles of surrogate parents, counselors, and psychotherapists and still expect them to be effective teachers; and when we keep them so busy in the classroom that they have little time or opportunity for professional development once they have joined the ranks of the teaching profession.

Surely the most immediate and pressing task in educating young students is to create a new type of school environment, one where great lessons are a commonplace occurrence. In order to do this, we must ask how we can institute reforms that will make it possible for American teachers to practice their profession under conditions that are as favorable for their own professional development and for the education of children as those that exist in Asia.

Note: The research described in this article has been funded by grants from the National Institute of Mental Health, the National Science Foundation, and the W.T. Grant Foundation. The research is the result of collaboration with a large group of colleagues in China, Japan, Taiwan, and the United States who have worked together for the past decade. We are indebted to each of these colleagues and are especially grateful to Shinying Lee of the University of Michigan who has been a major contributor to the research described in this article.

REFERENCES

[1] The superior academic achievement of Chinese and Japanese children sometimes leads to speculation that they are brighter than American children. This possibility has been supported in a few reports that have received attention in the popular press and in several scientific journals. What has not been reported or widely understood is that, without exception, the studies contending that differences in intelligence are responsible for differences in academic performance have failed to meet acceptable standards of scientific inquiry. In fact, studies that have reported differences in I.Q. scores between Asian and American children have been flawed conceptually and methodologically. Their major defects are nonequivalent tests used in the different locations and noncomparable samples of children.

To determine the cognitive abilities of children in the three cultures, we needed tests that were linguistically comparable and culturally unbiased. These requirements preclude reliance on tests translated from one language to another or the evaluation of children in one country on the basis of norms obtained in another country. We assembled a team with members from each of the three cultures, and they developed ten cognitive tasks falling into traditional "verbal" and "performance" categories.

The test results revealed no evidence of overall differences in the cognitive functioning of American, Chinese, and Japanese children. There was no tendency for children from any of the three cultures to achieve significantly higher average scores on all the tasks. Children in each culture had strengths and weaknesses, but by the fifth grade of elementary school, the most notable feature of children's cognitive performance was the similarity in level and variability of their scores. [Stevenson, H.W., Stigler, J.W., Lee, S.Y., Lucker, G.W., Kitamura, S., & Hsu, C.C. (1985). Cognitive performance and academic achievement of Japanese, Chinese, and American children. *Child Development, 56*, 718-734.]

[2] Stevenson, H.W. (1990). Adapting to school: Children in Beijing and Chicago. *Annual Report.* Stanford CA: Center for Advanced Study in the Behavioral Sciences. Stevenson, H.W., Lee, S., Chen, C., Lummis, M., Stigler, J., Fan, L., & Ge, F. (1990). Mathematics achievement of children in China and the United States. *Child Development, 61*, 1053-1066. Stevenson, H.W., Stigler, J.W., & Lee, S.Y. (1986). Mathematics achievement of Chinese, Japanese, and American children. *Science, 231*, 693-699. Stigler, J.W., Lee, S.Y., & Stevenson, H.W. (1990). *Mathematical knowledge.* Reston: VA: National Council of Teachers of Mathematics.

[3] Stevenson, H.W., Lee, S.Y., Chen C., Stigler, J.W., Hsu, C.C., & Kitamura, S. (1990). Contexts of achievement. *Monographs of the Society for Research in Child Development.* Serial No. 221, 55, Nos. 1-2.

[4] Rohlen, T.P. (1983). *Japan's High Schools.* Berkeley: University of California Press.

[5] Dorfman, C.H. (Ed.) (1987). *Japanese Education Today.* Washington, D.C.: U.S. Department of Education.

[6] Ibid.

How Kids Learn

Barbara Kantrowitz & Pat Wingert

Ages 5 through 8 are wonder years. That's when children begin learning to study, to reason, to cooperate. We can put them in desks and drill them all day. Or we can keep them moving, touching, exploring. The experts favor a hands-on approach, but changing the way schools teach isn't easy. The stakes are high and parents can help.

With Howard Manly in Atlanta and bureau reports

It's time for number games in Janet Gill's kindergarten class at the Greenbrook School in South Brunswick, N.J. With hardly any prodding from their teacher, 23 five- and six-year-olds pull out geometric puzzles, playing cards and counting equipment from the shelves lining the room. At one round table, a group of youngsters fits together brightly colored wooden shapes. One little girl forms a hexagon out of triangles. The others, obviously impressed, gather round to count up how many parts are needed to make the whole.

After about half an hour, the children get ready for story time. They pack up their counting equipment and settle in a circle around Gill. She holds up a giant book about a zany character called Mrs. Wishy-washy who insists on giving farm animals a bath. The children recite the whimsical lines along with Gill, obviously enjoying one of their favorite tales. (The hallway is lined with drawings depicting the children's own interpretation of the book; they've taken a few literary liberties, like substituting unicorns and dinosaurs for cows and pigs.) After the first reading, Gill asks for volunteers to act out the various parts in the book. Lots of hands shoot up. Gill picks out four children and

they play their parts enthusiastically. There isn't a bored face in the room.

This isn't reading, writing and arithmetic the way most people remember it. Like a growing number of public- and private-school educators, the principals and teachers in South Brunswick believe that children between the ages of 5 and 8 have to be taught differently from older children. They recognize that young children learn best through active, hands-on teaching methods like games and dramatic play. They know that children in this age group develop at varying rates and schools have to allow for these differences. They also believe that youngsters' social growth is as essential as their academic achievement. Says Joan Warren, a teacher consultant in South Brunswick: "Our programs are designed to fit the child instead of making the child fit the school."

Educators call this kind of teaching "developmentally appropriate practice"—a curriculum based on what scientists know about how young children learn. These ideas have been slowly emerging through research conducted over the last century, particularly in the past 30 years. Some of the tenets have appeared

The Lives and Times of Children

Each youngster proceeds at his own pace, but the learning curve of a child is fairly predictable. Their drive to learn is awesome, and careful adults can nourish it. The biggest mistake is pushing a child too hard, too soon.

● Infants and Toddlers
They're born to learn. The first important lesson is trust, and they learn that from their relationships with their parents or other caring adults. Later, babies will begin to explore the world around them and experiment with independence. As they mature, infants slowly develop gross motor (sitting, crawling, walking) and fine motor (picking up tiny objects) skills. Generally, they remain egocentric and are unable to share or wait their turn. New skills are perfected through repetition, such as the babbling that leads to speaking.

■ 18 months to 3 years
Usually toilet training becomes the prime learning activity. Children tend to concentrate on language development and large-muscle control through activities like climbing on jungle gyms. Attention spans lengthen enough to listen to uncomplicated stories and carry on conversations. Vocabulary expands to about 200 words. They enjoy playing with one other child, or a small group, for short periods, and learn that others have feelings too. They continue to look to parents for encouragement and protection, while beginning to accept limits on their behavior.

▲ 3-year-olds
Generally, they're interested in doing things for themselves and trying to keep up with older children. Their ability to quietly listen to stories and music remains limited. They begin telling stories and jokes. Physical growth slows, but large-muscle development continues as children run, jump and ride tricycles. They begin to deal with cause and effect; it's time to plant seeds and watch them grow.

● 4-year-olds
They develop better small motor skills, such as cutting with scissors, painting, working with puzzles and building things. They can master colors, sizes and shapes. They should be read to and should be encouraged to watch others write; let them scribble on paper but try to keep them away from walls.

■ 5-year-olds
They begin to understand counting as a one-to-one correlation. Improved memories make it easier for them to recognize meaningful words, and with sharper fine motor skills, some children will be able to write their own names.

▲ Both 4s and 5s
Both groups learn best by interacting with people and concrete objects and by trying to solve real problems. They can learn from stories and books, but only in ways that relate to their own experience. Socially, these children are increasingly interested in activities outside their immediate family. They can play in groups for longer periods, learning lessons in cooperation and negotiation. Physically, large-muscle development continues, and skills such as balancing emerge.

● 6-year-olds
Interest in their peers continues to increase, and they become acutely aware of comparisons between themselves and others. It's a taste of adolescence: does the group accept them? Speech is usually well developed, and children are able to joke and tease. They have a strong sense of true and false and are eager for clear rules and definitions. However, they have a difficult time differentiating between minor and major infractions. Generally, children this age are more mature mentally than physically and unable to sit still for long periods. They learn better by firsthand experiences. Learning by doing also encourages children's "disposition" to use the knowledge and skills they're acquiring.

■ 7- to 8-year-olds
During this period, children begin developing the ability to think about and solve problems in their heads, but some will continue to rely on fingers and toes to help them find the right answer. Not until they're 11 are most kids capable of thinking purely symbolically; they still use real objects to give the symbols—such as numbers—meaning. At this stage they listen better and engage in give and take. Generally, physical growth continues to slow, while athletic abilities improve—children are able to hit a softball, skip rope or balance on a beam. Sitting for long periods is still more tiring than running and jumping.

under other names—progressivism in the 1920s, open education in the 1970s. But they've never been the norm. Now, educators say that may be about to change. "The entire early-childhood profession has amassed itself in unison behind these principles," says Yale education professor Sharon Lynn Kagan. In the last few years, many of the major education organizations in the country—including the National Association for the Education of Young Children and the National Association of State Boards of Education—have endorsed remarkably similar plans for revamping kindergarten through third grade.

Bolstered by opinions from the experts, individual states are beginning to take action. Both California and New York have appointed task forces to recommend changes for the earliest grades. And scores of individual school districts like South Brunswick, figuring that young minds are a terrible thing to waste, are pushing ahead on their own.

The evidence gathered from research in child development is so compelling that even groups like the Council for Basic Education, for years a major supporter of the traditional format, have revised their thinking. "The idea of putting small children in front of workbooks and asking them to sit at their desks all day is a nightmare vision," says Patte Barth, associate editor of Basic Education, the council's newsletter.

At this point, there's no way of knowing how soon change will come or how widespread it will be. However, there's a growing recognition of the importance of the early grades. For the past few years, most of the public's attention has focused on older children, especially teenagers. "That's a Band-Aid kind of approach," says Anne Dillman, a member of the New Jersey State Board of Education. "When the product doesn't come out right, you try and fix it at the end. But we really have to start at the beginning." Demographics have contributed to the sense of urgency. The baby boomlet has replaced the baby-bust generation of the 1970s. More kids in elementary school means more parents asking if there's a better way to teach. And researchers say there is a better way. "We've made remarkable breakthroughs in understanding the development of children, the development of learning and the climate that enhances that," says Ernest Boyer of The Carnegie Foundation for the Advancement of Teaching. But, he adds, too often, "what we know in theory and what we're doing in the classroom are very different."

The early grades pose special challenges because that's when children's attitudes toward school and learning are shaped, says Tufts University psychologist David Elkind. As youngsters move from home or preschool into the larger, more competitive world of elementary school, they begin to make judgments about their own abilities. If they feel inadequate, they may give up. Intellectually, they're also in transition, moving from the intensely physical exploration habits of infancy and toddlerhood to more abstract reasoning. Children are born wanting to learn. A baby can spend hours studying his hands; a toddler is fascinated by watching sand pour through a sieve. What looks like play to an adult is actually the work of childhood, developing an understanding of the world. Studies show that the most effective way to teach young kids is to capitalize on their natural inclination to learn through play.

But in the 1980s, many schools have tried to do just the opposite, pressure instead of challenge. The "back to basics" movement meant that teaching methods intended for high school students were imposed on first graders. The lesson of the day was more: more homework, more tests, more discipline. Children should be behind their desks, not roaming around the room. Teachers should be at the head of the classrooms, drilling knowledge into their charges. Much of this was a reaction against the trend toward open education in the '70s. Based on the British system, it allowed children to develop at their own pace within a highly structured classroom. But too many teachers and principals who tried open education thought that it meant simply tearing down classroom walls and letting children do whatever they wanted. The results were often disastrous. "Because it was done wrong, there was a backlash against it," says Sue Bredekamp of the National Association for the Education of Young Children.

At the same time, parents, too, were demanding more from their elementary schools. By the mid-1980s, the majority of 3- and 4-year-olds were attending some form of pre-school. And their parents expected these classroom veterans to be reading by the second semester of kindergarten. But the truth is that many 5-year-olds aren't ready for reading—or most of the other academic tasks that come easily to older children—no matter how many years of school they've completed. "We're confusing the numbers of years children have been in school with brain development," says Martha Denckla, a professor of neurology and pediatrics at Johns Hopkins University. "Just because a child goes to day care at age 3 doesn't mean the human brain mutates into an older brain. A 5-year-old's brain is still a 5-year-old's brain."

As part of the return to basics, parents and districts demanded hard evidence that their children were learning. And some communities took extreme measures. In 1985 Georgia became the first state to require 6-year-olds to pass a standardized test before entering first grade. More than two dozen other states proposed similar legislation. In the beginning Georgia's move was hailed as a "pioneering" effort to get kids off to a good start. Instead, concedes state school superintendent Werner Rogers, "We got off on the wrong foot." Five-year-olds who used to spend their days finger-painting or singing were hunched over ditto sheets, preparing for the big exam. "We would have to spend a month just teaching kids how to take the test," says Beth Hunnings, a kindergarten teacher in suburban Atlanta. This year Georgia altered the tests in favor of a more flexible evaluation; other states have changed their minds as well.

The intense, early pressure has taken an early toll. Kindergartners are struggling with homework. First graders are taking spelling tests before they even understand how to read. Second graders feel like failures. "During this critical period," says David Elkind in his book "Miseducation," "the child's bud-

In Japan, First Grade Isn't a Boot Camp

Japanese students have the highest math and science test scores in the world. More than 90 percent graduate from high school. Illiteracy is virtually nonexistent in Japan. Most Americans attribute this success to a rigid system that sets youngsters on a lock-step march from cradle to college. In fact, the early years of Japanese schooling are anything but a boot camp; the atmosphere is warm and nurturing. From kindergarten through third grade, the goal is not only academic but also social—teaching kids to be part of a group so they can be good citizens as well as good students. "Getting along with others is not just a means for keeping the peace in the classroom but something which is a valued end in itself," says American researcher Merry White, author of "The Japanese Educational Challenge."

Lessons in living and working together grow naturally out of the Japanese culture. Starting in kindergarten, youngsters learn to work in teams, with brighter students often helping slower ones. All children are told they can succeed if they persist and work hard. Japanese teachers are expected to be extremely patient with young children. They go over lessons step by step and repeat instructions as often as necessary. "The key is not to scold [children] for small mistakes," says Yukio Ueda, principal of

Mita Elementary School in Tokyo. Instead, he says, teachers concentrate on praising and encouraging their young charges.

As a result, the classrooms are relaxed and cheerful, even when they're filled with rows of desks. On one recent afternoon a class of second graders at Ueda's school was working on an art project. Their assignment was to build a roof with poles made of rolled-up newspapers. The children worked in small groups, occasionally asking their teacher for help. The room was filled with the sound of eager youngsters chatting about how to get the job done. In another second-grade class, the subject was math. Mariko Inoue, the teacher, suggested a number game to practice multiplication. After a few minutes of playing it, one boy stood up and proposed changing the rules just a bit to make it more fun. Inoue listened carefully and then asked if the other students agreed. They cheered, "Yes, yes," and the game continued according to the new rules.

Academics are far from neglected in the early grades. The Education Ministry sets curriculum standards and goals for each school year. For example, third graders by the end of the year are supposed to be able to read and write 508 characters (out of some 2,000 considered essential to basic literacy). Teachers have time for play and lessons: Japanese chil-

dren attend school for 240 days, compared with about 180 in the United States.

Mothers' role: Not all the teaching goes on in the classroom. Parents, especially mothers, play a key role in education. Although most kindergartens do not teach writing or numbers in any systematic way, more than 80 percent of Japanese children learn to read or write to some extent before they enter school. "It is as if mothers had their own built-in curriculum," says Shigefumi Nagano, a director of the National Institute for Educational Research. "The first game they teach is to count numbers up to 10."

For all their success in the early grades, the Japanese are worried they're not doing well enough. After a recent national curriculum review, officials were alarmed by what Education Minister Takeo Nishioka described as excessive "bullying and misconduct" among children—the result, according to some Japanese, of too much emphasis on material values. So three years from now, first and second graders will no longer be studying social studies and science. Instead, children will spend more time learning how to be good citizens. That's "back to basics"—Japanese style.

BARBARA KANTROWITZ *with* HIDEKO TAKAYAMA *in Tokyo*

ding sense of competence is frequently under attack, not only from inappropriate instructional practices . . . but also from the hundred and one feelings of hurt, frustration and rejection that mark a child's entrance into the world of schooling, competition and peer-group involvement." Adults under similar stress can rationalize setbacks or put them in perspective based on previous experiences; young children have none of these defenses. Schools that demand too much too soon are setting kids off on the road to failure.

It doesn't have to be this way. Most experts on child development and early-childhood education believe that young children learn much more readily if the teaching methods meet their special needs:

Differences in thinking: The most important ingredient of the nontraditional approach is hands-on learning. Research begun by Swiss psychologist Jean Piaget indicates that somewhere between the ages of 6 and 9, children begin to think abstractly instead of concretely. Younger children learn much more by touching and

seeing and smelling and tasting than by just listening. In other words, 6-year-olds can easily understand addition and subtraction if they have actual objects to count instead of a series of numbers written on a blackboard. Lectures don't help. Kids learn to reason and communicate by engaging in conversation. Yet most teachers still talk at, not with, their pupils.

Physical activity: When they get to be 10 or 11, children can sit still for sustained periods. But until they are physically ready for long periods of inactivity, they need to be active in the classroom. "A young child has to make a conscious effort to sit still," says Denckla. "A large chunk of children can't do it for very long. It's a very energy-consuming activity for them." Small children actually get more tired if they have to sit still and listen to a teacher talk than if they're allowed to move around in the classroom. The frontal lobe, the part of the brain that applies the brakes to children's natural energy and curiosity, is still immature in 6- to 9-year-olds, Denckla says. As the lobe develops, so does what Denckla describes as "boredom tolerance." Simply put, learning by doing is much less boring to young children.

Language development: In this age group, experts say language development should not be broken down into isolated skills—reading, writing and speaking. Children first learn to reason and to express themselves by talking. They can dictate stories to a teacher before they actually read or write. Later, their first attempts at composition do not need to be letter perfect; the important thing is that they learn to communicate ideas. But in many classrooms, grammar and spelling have become more important than content. While mastering the technical aspects of writing is essential as a child gets older, educators warn against emphasizing form over content in the early grades. Books should also be interesting to kids—not just words strung together solely for the purpose of pedag-ogy. Psychologist Katherine Nelson of the City University of New York says that her extensive laboratory and observational work indicates that kids can learn language—speaking, writing or reading—only if it is presented in a way that makes sense to them. But many teachers still use texts that are so boring they'd put anybody to sleep.

Socialization: A youngster's social development has a profound effect on his academic progress. Kids who have trouble getting along with their classmates can end up behind academically as well and have a higher incidence of dropping out. In the early grades especially, experts say youngsters should be encouraged to work in groups rather than individually so that teachers can spot children who may be having problems making friends. "When children work on a project," says University of Illinois education professor Lillian Katz, "they learn to work together, to disagree, to speculate,

The early years of a child's education are indeed wonder years. They begin learning to socialize, to study, and to reason. More and more education experts are favoring a hands-on approach to introducing young children to the mysteries of their surroundings.

to take turns and de-escalate tensions. These skills can't be learned through lecture. We all know people who have wonderful technical skills but don't have any social skills. Relationships should be the first 'R'."

Feelings of competence and self-esteem: At this age, children are also learning to judge themselves in relation to others. For most children, school marks the first time that their goals are not set by an internal clock but by the outside world. Just as the 1-year-old struggles to walk, 6-year-olds are struggling to meet adult expectations. Young kids don't know how to distinguish between effort and ability, says Tynette Hills, coordinator of early-childhood education for the state of New Jersey. If they try hard to do something and fail, they may conclude that they will never be able to accomplish a particular task. The effects of obvious methods of comparison, such as posting grades, can be serious. Says Hills: "A child who has had his confidence really damaged needs a rescue operation."

Rates of growth: Between the ages of 5 and 9, there's a wide range of development for children of normal intelligence. "What's appropriate for one child may not be appropriate for another," says Dr. Perry Dyke, a member of the California State Board of Education. "We've got to have the teachers and the staff reach children at whatever level they may be at . . . That takes very sophisticated teaching." A child's pace is almost impossible to predict beforehand. Some kids learn to read on their own by kindergarten; others are still struggling to decode words two or three years later. But by the beginning of the fourth grade, children with very different histories often read on the same level. Sometimes, there's a sudden "spurt" of learning, much like a growth spurt, and a child who has been behind all year will catch up in just a few weeks. Ernest Boyer and others think that multigrade classrooms, where two or three grades are mixed, are a good solution to this problem—and a way to avoid the "tracking" that can hurt a child's self-esteem. In an ungraded classroom, for example, an older child who is having problems in a particular area can practice by tutoring younger kids.

Putting these principles into practice has never been easy. Forty years ago Milwaukee abolished report cards and started sending home ungraded evaluations for kindergarten through third grade. "If anything was developmentally appropriate, those ungraded classes were," says Millie Hoffman, a curriculum specialist with the Milwaukee schools. When the back-to-basics movement geared up nationally in the early 1980s, the city bowed to pressure. Parents started demanding letter grades on report cards. A traditional, direct-teaching approach was introduced into the school system after some students began getting low scores on standardized tests. The school board ordered basal readers with controlled vocabularies and contrived stories. Milwaukee kindergarten teachers were so up-

A Primer for Parents

When visiting a school, trust your eyes. What you see is what your child is going to get.

● Teachers should talk to small groups of children or individual youngsters; they shouldn't just lecture.

■ Children should be working on projects, active experiments and play; they shouldn't be at their desks all day filling in workbooks.

▲ Children should be dictating and writing their own stories or reading real books.

● The classroom layout should have reading and art areas and space for children to work in groups.

■ Children should create freehand artwork, not just color or paste together adult drawings.

▲ Most importantly, watch the children's faces. Are they intellectually engaged, eager and happy? If they look bored or scared, they probably are.

set by these changes that they convinced the board that their students didn't need most of the standardized tests and the workbooks that go along with the readers.

Some schools have been able to keep the progressive format. Olive School in Arlington Heights, Ill., has had a nontraditional curriculum for 22 years. "We've been able to do it because parents are involved, the teachers really care and the children do well," says principal Mary Stitt. "We feel confident that we know what's best for kids." Teachers say they spend a lot of time educating parents about the teaching methods. "Parents always think school should be the way it was for them," says first-grade teacher Cathy Sauer. "As if everything else can change and progress but education is supposed to stay the same. I find that parents want their children to like school, to get along with other children and to be good thinkers. When they see that happening, they become convinced."

Parental involvement is especially important when schools switch from a traditional to a new format. Four years ago, Anne Norford, principal of the Brownsville Elementary School in Albemarle County, Va., began to convert her school. Parents volunteer regularly and that helps. But the transition has not been completely smooth. Several teachers refused to switch over to the more active format. Most of them have since left the school, Norford says. There's no question that some teachers have trouble implementing the developmentally appropriate approach. "Our teachers are not all trained for it," says Yale's Kagan. "It takes a lot of savvy and skill." A successful child-centered classroom seems to function effortlessly as youngsters move from activity to activity. But there's a lot of planning behind it—and that's the responsibility of the individual teacher. "One of the biggest problems," says Norford, "is trying to come up with a program that every teacher can do—not just the cadre of single people who are willing to work 90 hours a week." Teachers also have to participate actively in classroom activities and give up the automatic mantle of authority that comes from standing at the blackboard.

Teachers do better when they're involved in the planning and decision making. When the South Brunswick, N.J., schools decided in the early 1980s to change to a new format, the district spent several years studying a variety of curricula. Teachers participated in that research. A laboratory school was set up in the summer so that teachers could test materials. "We had the support of the teachers because teachers were part of the process," says teacher consultant Joan Warren.

One residue of the back-to-basics movement is the demand for accountability. Children who are taught in nontraditional classrooms can score slightly lower on commonly used standardized tests. That's because most current tests are geared to the old ways. Children are usually quizzed on specific skills, such as vocabulary or addition, not on the concepts behind those skills. "The standardized tests usually call for one-word answers," says Carolyn Topping, principal of Mesa Elementary School in Boulder, Colo. "There may be three words in a row, two of which are misspelled and the child is asked to circle the correctly spelled word. But the tests never ask, 'Does the child know how to write a paragraph?' "

Even if the tests were revised to reflect different kinds of knowledge, there are serious questions about the reliability of tests on young children. The results can vary widely, depending on many factors—a child's mood, his ability to manipulate a pencil (a difficult skill for many kids), his reaction to the person administering the test. "I'm appalled at all the testing we're doing of small children," says Vanderbilt University professor Chester Finn, a former assistant secretary of education under the Reagan administration. He favors regular informal reviews and teacher evaluations to make sure a student understands an idea before moving on to the next level of difficulty.

Tests are the simplest method of judging the effectiveness of a classroom—if not always the most accurate. But there are other ways to tell if children are learning. If youngsters are excited by what they are doing, they're probably laughing and talking to one another and to their teacher. That communication is part of the learning process. "People think that school has to be either free play or all worksheets," says Illinois professor Katz. "The truth is that neither is enough. There has to be a balance between spontaneous play and teacher-directed work." And, she adds, "you have to have the other component. Your class has to have intellectual life."

Katz, author of "Engaging Children's Minds," describes two different elementary-school classes she visited recently. In one, children spent the entire morning making identical pictures of traffic lights. There was no attempt to relate the pictures to anything else the class was doing. In the other class, youngsters were investigating a school bus. They wrote to the district and asked if they could have a bus parked in their lot for a few days. They studied it, figured out what all the parts were for and talked about traffic rules. Then, in the classroom, they built their own bus out of cardboard. They had fun, but they also practiced writing, problem solving, even a little arithmetic. Says Katz: "When the class had their parents' night, the teacher was ready with reports on how each child was doing. But all the parents wanted to see was the bus because their children had been coming home and talking about it for weeks." That's the kind of education kids deserve. Anything less should get an "F."

Social and Emotional Development

- The Child's Feelings: Emotional Development (Articles 17–20)
- Entry into the Social World: Peers, Play, and Popularity (Articles 21–24)

One of the truisms about our species is that we are social animals. From birth, each person's life is a constellation of relationships, from parents at home to friends in the neighborhood and school. This unit addresses how children's social and emotional development is influenced by important relationships with parents, peers, and teachers.

When John Donne wrote in 1623, "No man is an island . . . every man is . . . a part of the main," he implied that all humans are connected to each other and that these connections make us who we are. Early in this century, the prominent sociologist C. H. Cooley highlighted the importance of relationships when he coined the phrase "looking-glass self" to describe how people tend to see themselves as a function of how others perceive them. Personality development theorist Alfred Adler, writing in the early twentieth century, claimed that an individual's personal strength derived from the quality of his or her connectedness to others. The stronger the relationships, the stronger the person. The notion that a person's self-concept arises from relations with others also has roots in developmental psychology. As Jean Piaget once wrote, "there is no such thing as isolated individuals; there are only relations." The articles in this unit respect these traditions by emphasizing the theme that a child's development occurs within the context of relationships.

The unit begins with "Young Children's Understanding of Everyday Emotions," which captures the central role of emotions and socialization of emotions in child development. Children's emotional growth is linked with their cognitive and language growth, their self-awareness, their understanding of others, and their social environment. Thus, children's emotional development influences their own understanding of themselves as well as their relationships with others.

Through interactions with their parents, babies become attached to them. This socioemotional bond develops from warm, sensitive caregiving rather than from mere physical contact. Safety and security needs are fulfilled by the attachment figure, who provides the child with a "secure base" from which to explore the world and to develop a sense of self. However, when the child and the attachment figure must be apart, the child may experience separation anxiety. These issues are discussed in "Understanding and Accepting Separation Feelings."

Not only does self-concept arise through relations with parents, but a child's sense of morality does as well. "The Good, the Bad, and the Difference" explains how the parent-child relationship may be the crucial context for a child's understanding of "right and wrong."

Another major influence in the landscape of childhood is friendship. When do childhood friendships begin? Friends become increasingly important during the elementary school years. If forming strong, secure attachments with family members is an important task of early childhood, then one of the major psychological achievements of middle childhood is a move toward the peer group. Across the elementary school years, children spend ever-increasing time with peers in the neighborhood and at school. "Children without Friends" examines children's relationships with peers and describes different kinds of children—popular, rejected, neglected. This article helps us understand that friends are clearly a developmental and psychological advantage.

One interesting characteristic of children's peer relations in middle childhood is that boys and girls rarely play together. Most of the time, boys play with boys, girls play with girls. How might this gender segregation affect social and emotional development? Could gender segregation reinforce differences or create difficulties between boys and girls, and men and women? "Guns and Dolls" and "Girls and Boys Together . . . but Mostly Apart" discuss the central role of gender in social and emotional development.

Looking Ahead: Challenge Questions

What kinds of social and emotional skills do children learn from their parents versus their peers? What are some of the ways that friends can be beneficial or harmful to a child's self-concept and self-esteem? Why is it important for children to become members of a peer group? Can you think of popular books or movies that illustrate the values of friendship and peers?

When you were a child, did you experience gender segregation—boys playing with boys, girls with girls? Do you recall peers and teachers contributing to the separation between boys and girls? How might this have influenced your social and emotional development? How might gender segregation benefit boys' and girls' development? How might it hinder development? Can you think of specific things that a teacher or a parent might do to reduce gender segregation between the sexes?

Young Children's Understanding of Everyday Emotions

Janet Kuebli

Janet Kuebli, M.S., *is a doctoral student in the Department of Psychology at Emory University in Atlanta, Georgia, where she is studying parent–child narratives about children's emotional experiences.*

*This is one of a regular series of Research in Review columns. This column was edited by **Laura E. Berk,** Ph.D., professor of psychology at Illinois State University.*

What young children understand about emotion states and behaviors is of importance to early childhood educators who deal with children's feelings every day. Children, like adults, experience many emotions in the course of each day. Strong emotions arising from their own experiences may be very confusing for children. Children also have to make sense of other people's emotional reactions or feelings; therefore, we often try to help children talk about their own and others' feelings. We think of this especially when children encounter traumatic life events, such as when a child's parents divorce or someone in the family is very sick or dies.

Children may also need help in understanding everyday emotions. Teachers and parents may, for example, suggest ways that children can cope with feelings of distress, fear, or shyness on the first day of school or explain how it is possible to feel sad and happy at the same time about moving to a new school. Sometimes we urge children to talk about their anger or sadness as a way of handling minor daily conflicts and disappointments. By helping children to understand emotions, we hope to help them channel their feelings in self-enhancing ways and also prepare them to deal with similar experiences in the future.

As children mature, we also expect them to master their emotions to some extent. Learning to express some feelings and how to mask others are common everyday lessons in children's lives. Hochschild (1983) calls this learning how to do "emotion work." Getting along with others often means handling feelings in a socially acceptable fashion. Children who get mad because they have to wait their turn or who laugh at a crying child who has taken a fall and skinned a knee sometimes are encouraged to think about how others feel. A child who overexuberantly boasts about being a winner may be urged to remember how it also feels to be the loser. In some cases the ability to regulate and manage emotions tells us that a child is ready for new challenges.

Over the last decade, researchers have shown keen interest in the nature of children's understanding of emotion, especially as it relates to social–cognitive development. Much of this work has concerned school-age children. Results from these studies suggest, not sur-

> **At the heart of the studies with younger children are two related issues. The first concerns identifying links between early developments in emotion understanding and language.**

prisingly, that emotion understanding becomes more complex and sophisticated during elementary school. At these ages, for example, children begin to appreciate the fact that they can experience more than one emotion at a time (Carroll & Steward, 1984; Donaldson & Westerman, 1986; Harter & Buddin, 1987; Wintre, Polivy, & Murray, 1990). They also begin to take into greater account the situations that cause emotional reactions (Barden, Zelko, Duncan, & Masters, 1980; Strayer, 1986; Brody & Harrison, 1987; Camras & Allison, 1989). At this time children's skill in hiding their feelings also shows considerable improvement (Saarni, 1984, 1985; Davis, 1992), as does their understanding of emotions that involve self-evaluations, such as pride, guilt, and shame (Graham, Doubleday, & Guarino, 1984; Graham, 1988; Harter & Whitesell, 1989).

© Subjects & Predicates

while not exhaustive of the work in this area, provide a selective overview of what is known about emotion understanding in young children. Finally, I suggest ways that teachers can use these findings to facilitate children's understanding of their own and others' feelings.

Emotional experience

According to Lewis (Lewis & Michalson, 1983; Lewis, 1992), it's useful to think of emotional behavior as consisting of a variety of components. One of these components, *emotional experience,* refers to how individuals interpret and evaluate their emotions. Other components include (a) emotion states and (b) their expressions, which may be conveyed either verbally or through nonverbal changes in facial expressions, physical posture, or movement. The componential model of

---

One major conclusion derived from these studies is that conversations about feelings are an important context for learning about emotions and how to manage them.

Emotion-understanding studies with younger children are by comparison less common. New research, however, has begun to yield information both about what younger children know about emotions and how this understanding may develop. At the heart of the studies with younger children are two related issues. The first concerns identifying links between early developments in emotion understanding and language. The second issue centers on how children's emotion understanding is socialized in the course of children's interactions with others. One major conclusion derived from these studies is that conversations about feelings are an important context for learning about emotions and how to manage them.

This article considers the general nature of emotional experience first. The focus turns next to several studies

emotion proposes that our emotional experiences, states, and expressions do not always correspond to each other. On some occasions we may be unaware of our emotions or simply unable to name the particular feelings we are having. At other times we might intentionally express one emotion while experiencing a different feeling, or we might recognize our feelings but lack insight into the reasons for having them.

Among these various emotion components, emotional experience is considered the most cognitive (Lewis & Saarni, 1985) because it relies upon basic mental processes of attention, perception, and memory. We cannot begin, thus, to understand our feelings until we pay attention to them. Emotional experience further entails arriving at cognitive judgments and insights about our own emotion states and expressions. Emotional experience, in effect, depends upon being able to introspect or reflect upon ourselves (Lewis, 1992). Cognitive processes that underlie emotional experience essentially bring our emotions into consciousness and provide the basis for our having emotional experiences.

The developmental timetable for the emergence of various emotion states and expressions has already been well documented (e.g. Campos, Barrett, Lamb, Goldsmith, & Stenberg, 1983). Newborns, for example, display joy, interest, disgust, and distress; around eight months most babies show surprise, anger, fear, and sadness (Stenberg, Campos, & Emde, 1983; Izard & Malatesta, 1987). Embarrassment, empathy, pride, shame, and guilt only begin to appear at the end of infancy, usually after the age of 18 months. Much less is

---

The second issue centers on how children's emotion understanding is socialized in the course of children's interactions with others.

---

on children's early emotion vocabulary and concepts, followed by research on how emotions are discussed by young children with others. The studies described here,

Some Characteristics of Young Children's Emotion Language and Understanding

Approximate age of child	Description
Birth to 18 months	display emotions and respond to emotions in others at preverbal stage use emotion cues of others to guide own responses to new or ambiguous situations do not produce or comprehend emotion terms with a few exceptions
18 to 20 months	use first emotion words in vocabulary (e.g. cry, happy) begin to discuss emotions spontaneously in conversations with others
2 to 3 years	increase emotion vocabulary most rapidly correctly label simple emotions in self and others, and talk about past, present, and future emotions talk about the causes and consequences of some emotions and identify emotions associated with certain situations use emotion language in pretend play
4 to 5 years	show increased capacity to verbally reflect on emotions and to consider more complex relations between emotions and situations understand that the same event may call forth different feelings in different people and that feelings sometimes persist long after the events that caused them demonstrate growing awareness about controlling and managing emotions in accord with social standards
6 to 11 years	exhibit conceptual advances in their understanding of complex emotions (e.g. pride and shame) and of mixed or multiple emotions show marked improvements in the ability to suppress or conceal negative emotional reactions and in the use of self-initiated strategies for redirecting feelings take into fuller account the events leading to emotional reactions

known about the developmental course of emotional experience and understanding. The components model of emotion, however, suggests that it is not necessary for emotional states, expressions, and experience to develop in lock-step fashion all together. This model may explain why children have emotions and express them before they are able to reflect upon and understand their feelings (Michalson & Lewis, 1983; Lewis, 1992).

Researchers hypothesize that a fundamental prerequisite underlying emotional experience is having a *self-concept;* that is, children need a sense of an "I" who owns and knows her or his own emotion states and expressions in order to experience them. Even prior to forming a self-concept, however, children acquire several important cognitive skills related to self-understanding, which may also underlie their capacity for emotional experience. Collectively these skills are known as self-referential behaviors. They are first evident at ages between 15 and 24 months and include acquiring (a) an awareness of oneself as separate from others, (b) knowledge that objects independent of oneself have a permanent exist-

ence, (c) a sense of oneself as a causal agent, and (d) the ability to visually recognize oneself (Bertenthal & Fisher, 1978; Lewis & Brooks-Gunn, 1979; Sroufe, 1979; Kagan, 1981; Harter, 1983; Lewis, Sullivan, Stanger, & Weiss, 1989). Harter (1983) refers to these developments as contributing to the formation of an "existential self." Existential awareness of self forms the foundation for the child's initial self-concept. Together, these cognitive abilities enable children to make themselves objects of thought. Thereafter, emotional experience probably develops gradually, most likely in concert with changes in children's self-concepts. Emotions are, thus, integral to children's sense of who they are, helping them to form their own personal views of the world around them.

Learning words and concepts for emotions

Emotion theorists suspect that learning to talk is another critical factor in the development of emotional experience; acquiring word labels for emotions is re-

We cannot begin to understand our feelings until we pay attention to them.

garded as particularly important for developments in children's understandings of emotions. Certainly, parents refer to emotions in conversations with their children, almost from birth. Emotion communication enables others to draw attention to children's expressions of emotion. No doubt, this communication accelerates the development of emotional experience and understanding (Izard & Malatesta, 1987). Children's emotional self-understanding may start with being able to name emotion states and behaviors. From maternal reports, diary studies, and direct observations, we know that children begin to use emotion terms around the ages of 20 to 24 months (see Bretherton, Fritz, Zahn-Waxler, & Ridgeway, 1986 for a review of research on how children learn to talk about emotions). By 36 months children use emotion words to talk about both themselves and others, and in reference to events in the present, past, and future (Bretherton & Beeghly, 1982).

To learn about children's first emotion words, Bretherton and Beeghly (1982) gave mothers of 28-month-olds a list of terms for emotions as well as for mental states (e.g. knowing, remembering, dreaming), physiological states (e.g. hunger, fatigue), and perceptual states (e.g. seeing, hearing, tasting). Mothers indicated which words on the list their children used. At this age about 75% of the children had acquired the emotion words *mad* and *scared*, and well over half used *happy* and *sad*. Nearly all of the children used the emotion-behavior term *cry;* however, *surprise,* apparently a late acquisition, was reported for only 13% of the children. Additionally, children used emotion words to refer to both self and others, rather than only to self or only to others. This suggests that children's early emotional understanding of themselves and others may be closely related rather than developing separately. Finally, emotion terms were more common than mental-state words but less frequent than words for perceptual or physiological states. Notably, however, children talked about causes for emotions more often than causes for other kinds of states of being. This finding underscores the importance of emotional understanding as central to how children make sense of what happens to them.

In several experimental studies, researchers have looked at preschoolers' ability to label facial expressions. Michalson and Lewis (1985), for example, asked two- to five-year-olds "What kind of face" another child was making in a series of snapshots. They found that children knew the labels for *happiness* and *sadness* at earlier ages than they knew the terms for *anger, surprise, disgust,* or *fear*. In fact, children did not produce many verbal labels at all until after age three, and even by five years of age children had difficulty naming the surprise, disgust, and fear expressions. When asked to point to the face that matched the emotion label given by the experimenter, however, children as young as two demonstrated they knew something about the situations in which certain facial expressions were likely. Seventy percent of two-year-olds matched the happy face with a birthday-party drawing. These results tell us that children's early knowledge of some emotional situations may considerably outpace their ability to talk about those emotions. Less than half of the two- and

three-year-olds, however, matched the sad and disgust faces with the correct pictures; whereas, the majority of the four- and five-year-olds made the correct match. This more gradual development trend in understanding negative emotions has also been observed in several other studies (e.g. Borke, 1971; Glasberg & Aboud, 1982; Reichenbach & Masters, 1983).

Clearly, preschoolers become more adept at talking about their own and others' emotions. The largest and most rapid increase in the number of terms children have for emotions occurs between the ages of two and three (Ridgeway, Waters, & Kuczaj, 1985), but children continue to acquire new emotion words after this time. During the preschool period, caregivers also increasingly urge children to "use words" rather than act out their feelings. Research shows that young children are learning more than just an emotion vocabulary. Specifically, children learn more about the nature of emotional processes, including new insights about the causes and consequences of feelings.

Denham and Zoller (1993) were particularly interested in what preschoolers think causes various emotions. The two researchers showed children puppets with happy, sad, fearful, or angry faces and then asked them to think of what would make the puppets "feel that way." Results showed that the children more often associated

---

Emotional experience further entails arriving at cognitive judgments and insights about our own emotion states and expressions.

---

happiness with nonsocial causes (e.g. playing or going somewhere without reference to being with others) than with social ones. By contrast, the reasons children gave for sadness and anger were mostly social in nature. Children said that being hurt or left by others caused sadness, for example; their reasons for anger included being punished, fighting, or not liking someone else. Interestingly, neither social nor nonsocial reasons were given for feeling fearful; instead, children said fear was caused by make-believe creatures, such as monsters or ghosts. One notable gender difference in the responses was that girls gave more reasons for sadness than did boys. This outcome is intriguing in light of research with adults and adolescents in which females report thinking about sadness in relation to themselves and experiencing depression more often than do males (Brody, 1984; Conway, Giannopoulos, & Stiefenhofer, 1990).

Some preschoolers also have begun to recognize that a single event sometimes causes different feelings in different people. In one study (Gove & Keating, 1979) three- and five-year-olds heard a short story in which only one of two characters won a game. All of the older children, but only two thirds of the younger ones, judged that the victor would feel happy, while the loser would be sad in this social situation. This result is somewhat at odds

Emotional experience, in effect, depends upon being able to introspect or reflect upon ourselves.

with what Denham and Zoller found, but the differences may be products of the methods used in the two studies. In addition, although preschoolers demonstrate an increasing ability to reason about the causes and consequences of single emotions, few children prior to the age of five grasp the concept of mixed or conflicting feelings. That is, while preschoolers may say that one feeling can follow another one sequentially, they tend to deny that two different emotions can be experienced simultaneously (Harter & Buddin, 1987). Even after short training about mixed emotions, four- and five-year-olds have shown little improvement in their understanding of mixed emotions (Peng, Johnson, Pollock, Glasspool, & Harris, 1992). Younger children's greater difficulty with multiple feelings may be tied to their limitations in the cognitive skills necessary for integrating opposing emotions.

Socialization of emotion understanding

Studies on children's emotion concepts have sought to document at what ages children demonstrate higher levels of understanding about emotions. Other research has focused on identifying experiences in children's lives that influence the particular forms emotion understandings can take. A key assumption is that children's insights into their own emotions are socially shaped in important ways (e.g. Lutz, 1985; Gordon, 1989). Whereas research on the content of emotion concepts has concentrated on older children, studies examining how emotions are socialized have usually been conducted with younger children.

The goal of emotion socialization is usually to redirect or change the way children spontaneously express their emotions to conform more closely with social rules or conventions. Sometimes this means substituting one feeling for a different one, as when we smile after receiving a disappointing gift (Saarni, 1984) or look on the bright side of things that worry or sadden us. Saarni (1985; Saarni & Crowley, 1990) outlines three general classes of processes by which emotions may be socialized. First, *direct* socialization refers to occasions when others chide or praise children's immediately prior emotional behaviors. In this case an adult's behavior reinforces the child's expression of emotions. Reinforcement, either reward or punishment, gives children explicit information about the way certain emotions are valued by others. Didactic teaching is another direct form of socialization often used with children to convey social conventions for expressing emotions. A child may be told, for example, that "girls don't brag" about their successes or that "boys don't cry" about their failures.

Emotions are also socialized *indirectly*. A classic example is when a child imitates someone else's emotional reactions, such as one child's fearful reluctance to try

something new being copied by another child who only moments before was a willing and eager participant. We can view this situation, in part, as a case in which one person's emotional reactions are "catching." There are times when uncontrolled laughter seizes a group of children in this way or sadness sweeps through a classroom. Adults also provide ready models, of course, for children's emotional reactions. Research shows that children faced with a situation in which they do not know how to react will scan a caregiver's face in search of cues for the appropriate emotional response. This behavior, known as social referencing, has been studied extensively with infants. One study, for example, showed that eight-month-olds' reactions to a stranger were influenced by their mothers' immediately prior emotional reactions toward that person (Feinman & Lewis, 1983). Although fewer studies have considered this phenomena among preschoolers, the notion in all cases is that children learn about emotion states, expressions, and events by watching others and imitating their emotional behaviors.

A third channel for emotion socialization involves *expectancy communication*. For Saarni and Crowley (1990) emotion expectancies are beliefs about how emotions should be felt and expressed that are conveyed to children, verbally or nonverbally, in advance of particular events in which children's own emotional reactions are called forth. Saarni and Crowley liken the process to hypnosis, in which adults, first, plant "suggestions" in children's minds about how to respond in certain situations. If children subsequently encounter the same or similar situations, they may use this information to guide their own emotional responses. In this way children remember and act upon at later points in time the information previously acquired about emotions. So, when we tell young children, for example, about how we felt afraid (or excited) at their age, going on a ferris wheel ride or sleeping away from home the first time, these verbal suggestions may be internalized as expectancies upon which children subsequently rely. By such means, Saarni and Crowley (1990) contend, strategies for managing emotions initiated "outside" the child are imported into children's own private, emotional lives.

A general, theoretical framework for studies on emotion socialization is found in the works of Cooley (1902), Mead (1956), and Vygotsky (1978), who each discussed links between emotion, self, and cognition. These writers proposed that (a) we become conscious of ourselves through how others know us and (b) consciousness is forged, in large part, through social activity and discourse. Mead, for example argued that self-consciousness only arises when we take on the attitudes of others toward ourselves. He wrote

> the child can think about his conduct as good or bad only as he reacts to his own acts in the remembered words of his parents. (1913, p. 146)

The imagined judgments of others "drawn from the communicative life" (1902, p. 179) were also essential to Cooley's *looking-glass self*:

> in imagination we perceive in another's mind some thought of our appearance, manners, aims, deeds,

© Blendi Reynolds

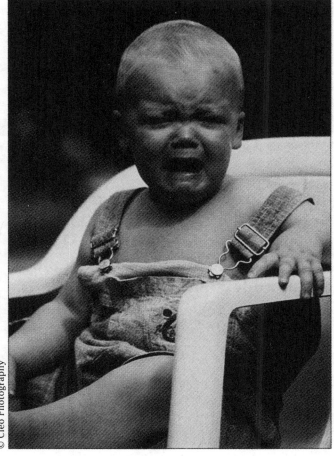

© Cleo Photography

character . . . and are variously affected by it. (1902, p. 184)

Although Vygotsky did not explicitly write about emotion development, he believed that children became self-conscious by using

the same forms of behavior in relation to themselves that others initially used in relation to them. (1981, p. 157)

In particular, Vygotsky stressed the role that everyday social speech plays in children's development.

Contemporary researchers speculate that asking about emotions provides children with "reflective distance" from feeling states themselves (Stern, 1985; Bretherton et al., 1986; Dunn, Brown, & Beardsall, 1991). Discussing emotions is thought to distance children from the rush and immediacy of affective responses. Distancing gives children space in which to interpret and evaluate their feelings and to reflect upon causes and consequences.

Emotion discourse may further allow adults and children to work out socially acceptable meanings of feeling states. Especially significant may be the way adults attribute meaning to children's own emotional behavior and development (Lutz, 1983). The way we talk about emotions with children, thus, has the potential to uniquely organize and transform their emotional lives.

Researchers also assume that preschoolers begin to formulate emotion concepts specific to their own culture or subculture (Lutz, 1983; Lutz & White, 1986; Miller & Sperry, 1987). From this perspective emotion concepts are viewed as embedded in broader cultural knowledge about situations and social relationships. How children come to understand emotions will presumably depend on the particular cultural vocabulary and meaning systems available to children for talking about emotions (Levy, 1984; Lutz & White, 1986; Gordon, 1989) and on existing social norms about ways emotions should be felt and expressed.

Cognitive processes that underlie emotional experience essentially bring our emotions into consciousness and provide the basis for our having emotional experiences.

Both psychologists and anthropologists have studied how emotions are variously viewed and talked about in different cultures. There is evidence that emotions downplayed or left undefined in some cultures are central to how other cultures make sense of experiences. Cross-cultural comparisons indicate that Americans and Chinese, for example, identify different types of causes for pride (Stipek, Weiner, & Li, 1989), and Japanese culture emphasizes shame more than other groups do (Lewis, 1992). Americans also report experiencing emotions longer and more intensely than do Japanese sub-

Children use emotion words to refer to both self and others, rather than only to self or only to others. This suggests that children's early emotional understanding of themselves and others may be closely related, rather than developing separately.

jects (Matsumoto, Kudoh, Scherer, & Wallbott, 1988). In contrast to the Western culture's sense of sadness as an emotion, Tahitians classify sadness as a physical illness or body state (Levy, 1984). How adults approach childrearing, moreover, is thought to be related to their knowledge and beliefs about emotions (Lutz & White, 1986; Miller & Sperry, 1987; Markus & Kitayama, 1991). Yet, until recently, few researchers have directly observed adult–child conversations about emotions. The few studies so far have, not surprisingly, focused mostly on how mothers talk with young children.

Miller and Sperry (1987), for example, interviewed three working-class mothers of two-and-one-half-year-old daughters and observed how they socialized anger and aggression. Notably, the mothers led lives in which violence and aggression were all too commonplace; they typically discussed these events in their daughters' presence but usually while talking to other family members or friends. It is striking that at least one child's own stories about anger and aggression were closely patterned after her mother's recollections. In this way what children overhear others relating about emotional events may be one context for learning about emotions. Miller and Sperry observed a second important context—episodes of anger between mothers and daughters. Mothers sometimes intentionally provoked their daughters' anger by teasing or trading insults with them as a way of teaching the girls how to stand up for themselves. Miller and Sperry also found that, rather than talking explicitly about the emotional state of anger itself, families referred to those emotion behaviors that only indirectly expressed anger (e.g. *fight, hit, punch*).

Children's interactions with their mothers and a sibling have been examined by Dunn and her associates. Their analyses of these three-way interactions included tracking how the amount and kind of emotion talk that

Some preschoolers have begun to recognize that a single event sometimes causes different feelings in different people.

occurs in the home changes as young children grow older. One study's home observations conducted when younger siblings were 18 and 24 months old revealed that family members' references to emotion states and to their causes and consequences increased over time (Dunn, Bretherton, & Munn, 1987). Mothers' comments during these interactions usually served to guide or explain children's feelings rather than simply to bring attention to children's emotions. This suggests that mothers, consciously or not, actively worked at shaping their children's emotional experiences, much like the mothers in the Miller and Sperry study. Moreover, the more frequently mothers and older siblings referred to feeling states at the 18-month visit, the more often the younger child talked about emotions at the 24-month visit. In other research Dunn and Kendrick (1982) found that two- and three-year-olds whose mothers commented more often about a new baby's feelings were more likely to have friendly interactions with that sibling one year later.

Dunn has also examined sibling conflicts as contexts for emotion socialization. Between the ages of 14 and 36 months, younger siblings' ability to tease and upset their older siblings appears to increase significantly (Dunn & Munn, 1985; Dunn, Brown, & Beardsall, 1991). This finding demonstrates how young children are learning to anticipate and influence others' feelings. Dunn et al. (1991) further found that mothers and children who

The way we talk about emotions with children has the potential to uniquely organize and transform their emotional lives.

engaged in more frequent emotion talk were more apt to also discuss the causes and consequences of siblings' disputes. Finally, three-year-olds from families with more emotion talk showed a better understanding of others' emotions three years later at age six. These results provide additional support for the contention that emotion talk provides an important context for learning about feelings.

Together, these studies indicate that exposure to different types and amounts of emotion talk may be related to individual differences in children's emotion understanding (Gordon, 1989). Especially intriguing in this regard are reports of differences in how mothers talk about emotions with daughters and sons. In the

Applications for Early Childhood Educators

For educators and parents, it is certainly not earthshaking to find that children learn about emotions from us; but, emotions are sometimes so "close to the skin" and fleeting that it is easy for feelings to slip out of one's conscious awareness. Becoming conscious of the roles we play in children's emotion socialization empowers us to provide children with better opportunities in their daily lives for understanding themselves and others. Teachers have some unique occasions for structuring children's activities in ways that can encourage children to talk about their own and others' emotions. Consider the following recommendations for meeting this objective.

1. Evaluate whether the emotional climate of the classroom itself is conducive to expressing emotions. In other words, caregivers need to legitimate children's feelings in order for children to feel it is acceptable to talk about and reflect upon their emotions. Leavitt and Power (1989) contend that we give meaning to children's emotions when we recognize and respond to their feelings. Essentially this means entering into authentic emotional relationships with children and regarding them as "emotional associates" (Leavitt & Power, 1989, p. 37) who are capable of interpreting and understanding their own and others' emotions.

2. Consider the physical environments in which children may learn about feelings. Play centers no doubt vary in the opportunities they afford for emotional engagement and reflection. Family-living or dramatic-play sections, for example, may encourage children to act out social interactions into which emotions figure. Well-stocked play centers can also provide sources of suggestions to children's imaginations for reworking earlier emotional altercations or experiences. Either from the sidelines or as players ourselves, adults can observe the way individual children play out emotion scripts dramatically. Introduce themes and ask questions that prompt children to vicariously explore the causes and consequences of emotions. Similarly, puppets and dolls are excellent vehicles for emotion play.

3. The arts center provides another valuable context for emotion conversation. Encourage children to make pictures that tell about personal events in their lives. This idea, borrowed from therapists who work with disturbed children, adapts well for children whose "troubles" are within the typical range of life experiences. Children might be encouraged to "draw about the time when . . ." they were upset with another child, afraid of something new, and so forth. Engaging children in conversations about their pictures, either as they are being created or afterwards, can give children chances to reflect upon their emotions. Children can also dictate the stories and feelings that go with their pictures. Older children may want to construct longer picture stories, several pages in length. Sometimes, children will enjoy "reading" back their picture stories to someone else, either during group times or on their own to other children and teachers.

4. Stories written for children are yet another readily available resource for talking about emotions. Books can be selected that show other children being emotional and dealing with their feelings (some titles well suited to this activity are suggested at the end of this article). Children and teachers can discuss the causes and consequences of story characters' emotions and then link them with children's own experiences. Certainly, other media (e.g. TV, movies, plays, children's magazines) provide similar options.

5. Tape recorders and video equipment can be used advantageously as well. Children might audiotape or videotape each other telling stories in which they recreate emotions. Subsequent viewing of these mini productions can serve as a springboard for later discussion about choices children have in responding to their own or others' emotions. Audiovisual projects can also be sources of collaborative production and pride. We show children that we value their emotions if we put the emotion work they do in projects of this sort on display for others to see and share. Invite parents or other classes for a film showing, or put on loan children's story tapes for other children's listening.

6. Dealing with children's quarrels and disputes offers a final classroom context in which children can develop their understanding of emotions. Fighting children learn more about anger and aggression if we do more than simply separate them. Ask each child to "tell what happened" from his or her perspective without interruption by the other participant(s). Teachers can convey back what the child says, asking for any corrections or clarifications before calling on the other child to tell her or his part in the altercation. All children should be urged to examine their personal contributions to the conflict. Teachers can also ask children to talk about how the events made them feel and how they think the other child feels, along with what they each could do differently next time. In this way teachers can help children to manage their feelings rather than simply to suppress or deny them; by doing so, Leavitt and Power (1989) claim that we enhance children's ability to develop authentic emotional understandings and relationships.

study by Dunn et al. (1987), for example, references to emotions were more frequent in mother–daughter, than mother–son, conversations at both 18 and 24 months; and by 24 months girls also talked about feeling states more often than boys did. Gender differences have also

---

How children come to understand emotions will presumably depend on the particular cultural vocabulary and meaning systems available to children for talking about emotions.

---

been reported by Fivush (1989; 1991). Reasoning that conversations about past emotions might provide even more reflective distance, Fivush asked mothers to talk with children about specific events in their child's past. In one study with 30- to 35-month-olds, Fivush (1989) found that mothers attributed more talk about sadness to daughters and more talk about anger to sons. Mother–daughter conversations also focused more on feelings, whereas mother–son pairs were more apt to discuss causes and consequences for emotions.

When fathers talk about the past with young children, they, too, seem to talk differently about emotions with daughters than with sons. Kuebli and Fivush (1992) found that both mothers and fathers of 40-month-olds talked about a greater number and variety of emotions with daughters than they did with sons; again, sadness was more often a topic in conversations with girls. At the age of 40 months, differences were not yet apparent in how boys and girls talked about emotions. Mother–child interviews conducted just before the children started kindergarten, however, revealed that the number of girls' references to emotions nearly quadrupled over this time, whereas boys' references had remained about the same (Kuebli & Fivush, 1993). These results suggest that girls' and boys' emotional lives may be socialized in somewhat different ways. In related research, moreover, adult women were found to be more likely than men to say they are emotional, to value the

expression of emotions, and to report experiencing a variety of emotions (Allen & Hamsher, 1974; Allen & Haccoun, 1976; Balswick & Avertt, 1977; Fitzpatrick & Indvik, 1982).

Conclusion

Research on young children's emotion understanding and socialization is still very new. Based on what we know so far, however, we can expect that children will show individual differences in the kinds of emotion understandings they possess. Differences will be apparent among children of different ages and even in the rate at which age-mates gain new insights into emotions; moreover, children's family backgrounds and histories are likely to translate into different ways of conceptualizing and using emotions. Cross-cultural evidence on emotion understanding should make teachers particularly sensitive to multicultural variation in the ways emotions figure in children's lives. Despite the differences, however, research also suggests that the basic processes by which children learn about emotions are similar, although much more needs to be learned about the nature of these mechanisms. What is, perhaps, fundamentally important is realizing that a great deal of what young children understand about feelings is apparently learned in the informal curriculum provided by their social interactions with others. Emotions frequently are at the heart of these interactions, and children may greatly benefit when we direct their attention to talking about these experiences.

Between the ages of 14 and 36 months, younger siblings' ability to tease and upset their older siblings appears to increase significantly. This finding demonstrates how young children are learning to anticipate and influence others' feelings.

Four processes by which emotions are socialized are
(1) chiding or praising children's immediately prior emotional behaviors;
(2) giving direct instruction regarding social conventions for expressing emotion ("girls don't brag about their successes");
(3) modeling emotion states, expressions, and events—children watch and imitate; and
(4) communicating expectancies, verbally or nonverbally, directly to the child or within his hearing ("when I was your age I was afraid the first time I slept away from home").

Books About Emotions for Young Children

Many books for young children afford opportunities for adults and children to talk about emotions. The following titles are good examples of books in which emotional themes are central to the story.

Carle, E. (1977). *The grouchy ladybug*. New York: Harper & Row.

Carlson, N. (1988). *I like me!* New York: Viking Kestrel.

Clarke, G. (1991). *. . . along came Eric*. New York: Lothrop, Lee, & Shepard.

Cole, J. (1990). *Don't call me names!* New York: Random House.

Engel, D. (1989). *Josephina hates her name*. New York: Morrow Junior.

Godwin, P. (1993). *I feel orange today*. New York: Firefly.

Gretz, S. (1981). *Teddy bears' moving day*. New York: Four Winds.

Havill, J. (1989). *Jamaica tag-along*. Boston: Houghton Mifflin.

Hazen, B.S. (1981). *Even if I did something awful*. New York: Atheneum.

Lakin, P. (1985). *Don't touch my room*. Boston: Little, Brown.

Macdonald, M. (1990). *Little hippo starts school*. New York: Dial.

Mayer, M. (1983). *I was so mad*. Racine, WI: Western Publishing.

Noll, S. (1991). *That bothered Kate*. New York: Puffin.

Sharmat, M.J. (1983). *Frizzy the fearful*. New York: Holiday House.

Stevenson, J. (1983). *What's under my bed?* New York: Greenwillow.

Viorst, J. (1972). *Alexander and the terrible, horrible, no good, very bad day*. New York: Atheneum.

Waber, B. (1972). *Ira sleeps over*. Boston: Houghton Mifflin.

Wells, R. (1988). *Shy Charles*. New York: Dial.

Wilhelm, H. (1990). *A cool kid—like me!* New York: Crown.

References

Allen, J.G., & Haccoun, D.M. (1976). Sex differences in emotionality: A multidimensional approach. *Human Relations, 29*(8), 711–722.

Allen, J.G., & Hamsher, J.H. (1974). The development and validation of a test of emotional styles. *Journal of Consulting and Clinical Psychology, 42*(5), 663–668.

Balswick, H., & Avertt, C.P. (1977). Differences in expressiveness: Gender, interpersonal orientation, and perceived parental expressiveness as contributing factors. *Journal of Marriage and the Family, 39*(1), 121–127.

Barden, R.C., Zelko, F., Duncan, S.W., & Masters, J.C. (1980). Children's consensual knowledge about the experiential determinants of emotion. *Journal of Personality and Social Psychology, 39*(5), 968–976.

Bertenthal, B.I., & Fisher, K.W. (1978). Development of self-recognition in the infant. *Developmental Psychology, 14*(1), 44–50.

Borke, H. (1971). Interpersonal perception of young children: Egocentrism or empathy. *Developmental Psychology, 5*(2), 263–269.

Bretherton, I., & Beeghly, M. (1982). Talking about internal states: The acquisition of an explicit theory of mind. *Developmental Psychology, 18*(6), 906–921.

Bretherton, I., Fritz, J., Zahn-Waxler, C., & Ridgeway, D. (1986). Learning to talk about emotions: A functionalist perspective. *Child Development, 57*(3), 529–548.

Brody, L.R. (1984). Sex and age variations in the quality and intensity of children's emotional attributions to hypothetical situations. *Sex Roles, 11*(1/2), 51–59.

Brody, L.R., & Harrison, R.H. (1987). Development changes in children's abilities to match and label emotionally laden situations. *Motivation and Emotion, 11*(4), 347–365.

Campos, J.J., Barrett, K.C., Lamb, M.E., Goldsmith, H.H., & Stenberg, C. (1983). Socioemotional development. In M. Haith & J.J. Campos (Eds.), *Handbook of child psychology: Vol. 2. Infancy and developmental psychobiology* (pp. 783–915). New York: Wiley.

Camras, L.A., & Allison, K. (1989). Children's and adults' beliefs about emotion elicitation. *Motivation and Emotion, 13*(1), 53–70.

Carroll, J.J., & Steward, M.S. (1984). The role of cognitive development in children's understanding of their own feelings. *Child Development, 55*(4), 1486–1492.

Conway, M., Giannopoulos, C., & Stiefenhofer, K. (1990). Response styles to sadness are related to sex and sex-role orientation. *Sex Roles, 22*(9/10), 579–587.

Cooley, C.H. (1902). *Human nature and the social order*. New York: Scribner's.

Davis, T.L. (1992, April). *Sex differences in the masking of children's negative emotions: Ability or motivation?* Paper presented at the Human Development Conference, Atlanta, GA.

Denham, S.A., & Zoller, D. (1993). *"When mommy's angry. I feel sad": Preschoolers' causal understanding of emotion and its socialization*. Manuscript submitted for publication.

Donaldson, S.K., & Westerman, M.A. (1986). Development of children's understanding of ambivalence and causal theories of emotions. *Developmental Psychology, 22*(5), 655–662.

Dunn, J., Bretherton, I., & Munn, P. (1987). Conversations about feeling states between mothers and their young children. *Developmental Psychology, 23*(1), 132–139.

Dunn, J., Brown, J., & Beardsall, L. (1991). Family talk about feeling states and children's later understanding of others' emotions. *Developmental Psychology, 27*(3), 448–455.

Dunn, J., & Kendrick, C. (1982). *Siblings: Love, envy and understanding*. Cambridge, MA: Harvard University Press.

Dunn, J., & Munn, P. (1985). Becoming a family member: Family conflict and the development of social understanding in the second year. *Child Development, 56*(2), 480–492.

Feinman, S., & Lewis, M. (1983). Social referencing at ten-months: A second-order effect on infants' responses to strangers. *Child Development, 54*(4), 878–887.

Fitzpatrick, M.A., & Indvik, J. (1982). The instrumental and expressive domains of marital communication. *Human Communications Research, 8*(3), 195–213.

Fivush, R. (1989). Exploring sex differences in the emotional content of mother–child conversations about the past. *Sex Roles, 20*(11/12), 675–691.

Fivush, R. (1991). Gender and emotion in mother–child conversations about the past. *Journal of Narrative and Life History, 1*(4), 325–341.

Glasberg, R., & Aboud, F. (1982). Keeping one's distance from sadness: Children's self-reports of emotional experience. *Developmental Psychology, 18*(2), 287–293.

Gordon, S.L. (1989). The socialization of children's emotions: Emotional competence, culture, and exposure. In C. Saarni & P.L. Harris (Eds.), *Children's understanding of emotion* (pp. 319–349). New York: Cambridge University Press.

Gove, F.L., & Keating, D.P. (1979). Empathic role-taking precursors. *Developmental Psychology, 15*(6), 594–600.

Graham, S. (1988). Children's developing understanding of the motivational role of affect: An attributional analysis. *Cognitive Development, 3*(2), 71–88.

Graham, S., Doubleday, C., & Guarino, P.A. (1984). The development of relations between perceived controllability and the emotions of pity, anger, and guilt. *Child Development, 55*(2), 561–565.

Harter, S. (1983). Developmental perspectives on the self-system. In E.M. Hetherington (Ed.), *Socialization, personality and social development, Vol IV, Handbook of Child Psychology* (pp. 275–385). New York: Wiley.

Harter, S., & Buddin, B.J. (1987). Children's understanding of the simultaneity of two emotions: A five-stage development acquisition sequence. *Developmental Psychology, 23*(3), 388–399.

Harter, S., & Whitesell, N.R. (1989). Developmental changes in children's understanding of single, multiple, and blended emotion concepts. In C. Saarni & P.L. Harris (Eds.), *Children's understanding of emotion* (pp. 81–116.). Cambridge, England: Cambridge University Press.

Hochschild, A.R. (1983). *The managed heart: Commercialization of human feelings.* Berkeley: University of California Press.

Izard, C.E., & Malatesta, C.A. (1987). Perspectives on emotional development I: Differential emotions theory of early emotional development. In J.D. Osofsky (Ed.), *Handbook of infant development* (2nd ed.), (pp. 494–554.) New York: Wiley.

Kagan, J. (1981). *The second year: The emergence of self-awareness.* Cambridge, MA: Harvard University Press.

Kuebli, J., & Fivush, R. (1992). Gender differences in parent–child conversations about past emotions. *Sex Roles, 27*(11/12), 683–698.

Kuebli, J., & Fivush, R. (1993, March). *Children's developing understanding of emotion and mind.* Paper presented at the biennial meetings of the Society for Research in Child Development, New Orleans, LA.

Leavitt, R.L., & Power, M.B. (1989). Emotional socialization in the postmodern era: Children in day care. *Social Psychology Quarterly, 52*(1), 35–43.

Levy, R.I. (1984). Emotion, knowing, and culture. In R.A. Shweder & R.A. LeVine (Eds.), *Culture theory: Essays on mind, self, and emotion* (pp. 214–237). Cambridge, England: Cambridge University Press.

Lewis, M. (1992). *Shame: The exposed self.* New York: The Free Press.

Lewis, M., & Brooks-Gunn, J. (1979). *Social cognition and acquisition of self.* New York: Plenum.

Lewis, M., & Michalson, L. (1983). *Children's emotions and moods.* New York: Plenum.

Lewis, M., & Saarni, C. (1985). Culture and emotions. In M. Lewis & C. Saarni (Eds.), *The socialization of emotions* (pp. 1–17). New York: Plenum.

Lewis, M., Sullivan, M.W., Stanger, C., & Weiss, M. (1989). Self-development and self-conscious emotions. *Child Development, 60*(1), 146–156.

Lutz, C. (1983). Parental goals, ethnopsychology, and the development of emotional meaning. *Ethos, 11*(4), 246–262.

Lutz, C. (1985). Cultural patterns and individual differences in the child's emotional meaning system. In M. Lewis & C. Saarni (Eds.), *The socialization of emotions* (pp. 37–53). New York: Plenum.

Lutz, C., & White, G.M. (1986). The anthropology of emotions. *Annual Review of Anthropology, 15,* 405–436.

Markus, H.R., & Kitayama, S. (1991). Culture and the self: Implications for cognition, emotion, and motivation. *Psychological Review, 98*(2), 224–253.

Matsumoto, D., Kudoh, T., Scherer, K., & Wallbott, H. (1988). Antecedents of and reactions to emotions in the United States and Japan. *Journal of Cross-Cultural Psychology, 19*(3), 267–286.

Mead, G.H. (1913). The social self. In A.J. Reck (Ed.), *Selected writings: George Herbert Mead* (pp. 142–149). Chicago: Chicago University Press.

Mead, G.H. (1956). *On social psychology: Selected papers.* Chicago: The University of Chicago Press.

Michalson, L., & Lewis, M. (1985). What do children know about emotions and when do they know it? In M. Lewis & C. Saarni (Eds.), *The socialization of emotions* (pp. 117–139). New York: Plenum.

Miller, P., & Sperry, L.L. (1987). The socialization of anger and aggression. *Merrill-Palmer Quarterly, 33*(1), 1–31.

Peng, M., Johnson, C., Pollock, J., Glasspool, R., & Harris, P. (1992). Training young children to acknowledge mixed emotions. *Cognition and Emotion, 6*(5), 387–401.

Reichenbach, L., & Masters, J.C. (1983). Children's use of expressive and contextual cues in judgments of emotion. *Child Development, 54*(4), 992–1004.

Ridgeway, D., Waters, E., & Kuczaj, S.A. (1985). Acquisition of emotion-descriptive language: Receptive and productive vocabulary norms for ages 18 months to 6 years. *Developmental Psychology, 21*(5), 901–908.

Saarni, C. (1984). An observational study of children's attempts to monitor their expressive behavior. *Child Development, 55*(4), 1504–1513.

Saarni, C. (1985). Indirect processes in affect socialization. In M. Lewis & C. Saarni (Eds.), *The socialization of emotions* (pp. 187–209). New York: Plenum.

Saarni, C., & Crowley, M. (1990). The development of emotion regulation: Effects on emotional state and expression. In E.A. Blechman (Ed.), *Emotions and the family: For better or for worse* (pp. 53–73). Hillsdale, NJ: Erlbaum.

Sroufe, L.A. (1979). Socioemotional development. In J.D. Osofsky (Ed.), *Handbook of infant development* (pp. 462–516). New York: Wiley.

Stenberg, C., Campos, J., & Emde, R. (1983). The facial expression of anger in seven-month-old infants. *Child Development, 54*(1), 178–184.

Stern, D. (1985). *The interpersonal world of the infant.* New York: Basic.

Stipek, D., Weiner, B., & Li, K. (1989). Testing some attribution-emotion relations in the People's Republic of China. *Journal of Personality and Social Psychology, 56*(1), 109–116.

Strayer, J. (1986). Children's attributions regarding the situational determinants of emotion in self and others. *Developmental Psychology, 22*(5), 649–654.

Vygotsky, L.S. (1978). *Mind in society: The development of higher psychological processes.* Cambridge, MA: Harvard University Press.

Vygotsky, L.S. (1981). The genesis of higher mental functions. In J.V. Wertsch (Ed.), *The concept of activity in Soviet psychology.* Armonk, NY: M.E. Sharpe.

Wintre, M.G., Polivy, J., & Murray, M.A. (1990). Self-predictions of emotional-response patterns: Age, sex, and situational determinants. *Child Development, 61*(4), 1124–1133.

For further reading

Berk, L.E. (1985). Research in review. Why children talk to themselves. *Young Children, 40*(5), 46–52.

Frieman, B.B. (1993). Separation and divorce: Children want their teachers to know—meeting the emotional needs of preschool and primary school children. *Young Children, 48*(6), 58–63.

Kemple, K.M. (1991). Research in review. Preschool children's peer acceptance and social interaction. *Young Children, 46*(5), 47–54.

Pellegrini, A.D., & Glickman, C.D. (1990). Measuring kindergartners' social competence. *Young Children, 45*(4), 40–44.

Rogers, D.L., & Ross, D.D. (1986). Encouraging positive social interaction among young children. *Young Children, 41*(3), 12–17.

Rousso, J. (1988). Talking with young children about their dreams: How to listen and what to listen for. *Young Children, 43*(5), 70–74.

Solter, A. (1992). Understanding tears and tantrums. *Young Children, 47*(4), 64–68.

Warren, R.M. (1977). *Caring: Supporting children's growth.* Washington, DC: NAEYC.

Zavitkovsky, D., Baker, K.R., Berlfein, J.R., & Almy, M. (1986). *Listen to the children.* Washington, DC: NAEYC.

Understanding and Accepting Separation Feelings

Sue Gottschall

Sue Gottschall, M.A., is an advisor and instructor of Head Start teachers and assistants in the CDA program at Chicago City-wide College. She received psychoanalytic training in understanding play from Bruno Bettelheim at the University of Chicago's Orthogenic School.

How often have teachers dreaded new children beginning school, wondering how long it will take them to settle into the classroom and stop wanting their parents?

How many parents feel that they have somehow failed if their child cries and clings instead of toddling happily into the classroom?

And doesn't every teacher want to be able to dry the child's tears quickly and move on with her plans for the entire group?

Wanting to "get over" the separation process quickly and efficiently is a natural reaction. But separation is a long and painful process for teachers and parents as well as for children. The complex process of separation begins not at school but at birth. In the child's first year the gradual realization of separateness from mother culminates around nine months. The recognition that she is able to leave the child provokes great anxiety over her leaving at the same time that it reinforces the child's dependence on and attachment to her. It is this attachment that makes changes to new people and places so difficult, the same attachment that has nurtured the child's readiness to venture out to school and to learn. It represents the good mothering that has prepared the child to expect good things from other people and settings. Teachers should, thus, take heart at the difficulties separation pain causes, knowing they are a strong indication the child will be ready to form additional attachments to teachers and school.

Teachers and parents might also observe that school separation appears to be easier for the young toddler if she or he has had some happy times while being separated, as in play groups, with babysitters at grandparents' houses, or on neighborhood visits. Children can, it seems, be "inoculated" against overwhelming anxiety. Research indicates, furthermore, that explaining what to expect to toddlers and preschoolers gives them a sense of predictability and control that eases separation stress. Before leaving, the parent can forecast the day with the child: "You're going to play awhile, then sing some songs, and go outside. When you've eaten lunch, I'll be back." This planning reduces fear (Powell, 1989).

All young children react to separation. Some cry; others hesitate to enter the room, want their mothers to stay, are very quiet, bring objects from home, act out symbolically, or feel very stressed.

Although most young children do not cry when they start attending a group program, every classroom has at least one—usually more than one—child who does. As distressing as this is, it expresses the feelings that all the children have. Many of those who do not cry will show their own anxieties in a variety of ways: hesitance to enter the room; wanting their mothers to stay; shy silence; use of transitional objects from home; symbolic play; conversations with teachers and other children; "acting up" or other kinds of problems *at home*. Recognizing and responding to these messages as expressions of anxiety enables the teachers to help the child deal with separation effectively.

PLAY OUT THE ANGER AND ANXIETY

If a child is embarked on sobbing over his mother's leaving him, however, verbal reassurance will seldom quiet him. The promise that his mother is coming back in a couple of hours is not enough for a child, and it does not address his anger at not having control over her coming and going. Play offers a natural, symbolic way for young children to begin to grapple with anxieties and anger over being left.

Caterpillars (i.e., mothers) come back

One little boy began crying angrily as his mother left with her new baby. Even though it was his second year of school, the arrival of a sibling had revived his separation difficulties. When comfort and reassurance didn't work, his teacher remembered that making things appear and disappear is probably the game best loved by young children. She covered a stuffed caterpillar with an old cloth, exclaiming, "Where is it? Where did it go?" A small group of children gathered around, concerned about the child's distress—distress that so graphically reflected their own anxieties. They watched as the teacher hid the caterpiller and then found him. They began asking the teacher to hide it again. They told the caterpillar how mad they were when it went away, and they showed joy and relief as the cloth was pulled away and the caterpillar reappeared. As the play continued, the boy's crying gradually stopped. His distress had turned to interest; each time the animal was hidden the boy's facial expression became curious and slightly anxious. Finally, when the animal reappeared, he burst into a wonderful grin. A simple game had assuaged his anger and distress by speaking directly to his fear on a playful level: Whatever goes away or disappears—whether a mother or a small animal—can be found and can reappear again.

This game can be played in all kinds of ways. Push a pull toy around a corner so that it can't be seen, then pull it back into view. Help children build a house or garage for small animals or cars to disappear into and then reappear at the other side. Engage toddlers in sending a ball or wheeled toy back and forth between you. Pick up and return to squeals of delight objects dropped over and over again from crib or highchair. Find the object under the cloth with young babies (9 months and older). Tape together tube after paper tube to build, as one child said, "a tunnel to my house." If a teacher is sensitive to the importance of this issue, many ways to play it out symbolically with children of all ages become basic to her curriculum.

AM I HERE BECAUSE I'M BAD?

A common theme appears in children's expressions of separation anxiety. Their experience of school starting is being sent away from home. Many children think they are being banished because of something they have done. A parent often reinforces this idea when saying, "You are going to school because you have gotten so big," or "You

are going to school to learn how to behave." Both confirm the child's thinking that she has done something to cause this change.

Erica was having difficulty entering the classroom each morning. One day Erica said to the teachers, "I can tell this story. My dog got too big last night and my Mama put him outdoors." Like many young children Erica identified with young animals. Here was her understanding of why she had been sent to school: She was "put out" of her house because she was too big.

Erica repeated her central concern throughout the day, asking her teacher later, "Does your little boy go to school? I don't know him. Can you bring him to see me one day? I have two sisters and a brother. I was mad this morning 'cause my mama put my dog out 'cause he got too big." Here she extended her concern to include separation from her siblings as well. In addition she asked directly, in referring to her teacher's boy, if a mommy and child could be together at school. It troubled this child, as it does many others, that school and learning mean being sent away from home.

DEALING WITH SEPARATION REACTIONS

Simply explaining to Erica and to other children that they are not being "kicked out" but sent to school to learn and to have fun would be expecting children to understand adult reasoning. Instead, we need to understand and accept what the children are feeling and expressing.

The child has two central concerns when entering school or child care: Is my parent coming back? And who will take care of me until she/he does? Games of disappearing and reappearing objects address the first concern; a teacher has many opportunities to speak to the second. She cares for the child not only physically, but also by understanding and encouraging his symbolic play.

Being a partner in symbolic play

Jeffrey's difficulties did not begin until January. His mother had had a second child and had taken three months off work to stay home. In the middle of the year, she returned to work and Jeffrey became desperate, turning his anger against other children in the classroom. His teacher engaged Jeffrey as soon as he entered the classroom each day. With the teacher following his lead in play, a ritual developed. Jeffrey would pretend that he was the jailer. He would take two chairs, making a jail, and lock up his teacher, the "bad" person. Then he would stand by the jail guarding her and listing all the bad things she had done (both real and imagined). After a few minutes, Jeffrey was able to join his class and manage the morning more easily. In this relatively short period of symbolic play, he became the person in charge who could control the adult caregiver. In addition, she became the person who was "bad" and "punished." Symbolically playing this out allowed Jeffrey to turn the tables and hold captive "a bad mom"—bad in his mind for having had another child, sending him away to school, and leaving him for work. This was a positive step in working out his feelings about separation. In pretend he could identify with the "good guy"—the jailer—and still vent his anger in an acceptable way. Most important, he stopped seeing himself as the "bad guy" who was constantly getting in trouble for his feelings and actions. He had found, instead, an appropriate way to express himself about desertion and powerlessness. The relief of the other children in the class was obvious as Jeffrey's feelings were directed toward the teacher in appropriate play rather than toward them.

Integrating home and school in play

Constructing buildings with Legos™ became Erica's medium for integrating home and school. One day as Erica and Bobby were building schools next to each other, the following conversation occurred:

Bobby: "I'm building a school for my teacher."
Erica: "This is my mama's school, but I'm going to let kids come in."
Bobby: "Your mama doesn't go to school. She's too old."
Erica: "Shut up, Bobby. Go play with your toys. You better play right."
Bobby: "My mama's not coming to pick me up."
Erica: "You listen to the teacher today, OK? Will you wash the table for me?"

They continued to play with Erica taking the teacher's role. Initially, in their play, Erica tried to bring her family and school life together by building a school that was her mama's school. When Bobby wouldn't accept this, she told him that he ought to play correctly. At this point

---

Teachers need to have the courage to stop a parent from sneaking out of the room when the child is not watching, knowing that separation cannot be solved by avoidance.

Bobby said that his mama was not coming to pick him up. Erica immediately switched to the role of teacher, taking care of Bobby. We know from this that Erica now saw the teacher as a comforting person—a major step each child must take in order to settle into school.

Sensory reassurance

While Erica and Jeffrey dealt with their mothers' absence symbolically, other children need to deal with it on a more concrete, sensory, and, often, nonverbal level. A particularly graphic example is a non-English-speaking Japanese boy, Haruo, who entered school shortly after arriving in the United States. His mother stayed quietly in the classroom, and Haruo would frequently run over to touch her and then return to continue his exploration of the room. With each transition in the school day he would make this physical or, later, visual contact with her. During this time, Haruo often played peek-a-boo games with his teacher—a variation of the hiding and finding game. Eventually his mother began to leave for gradually longer periods of time until he managed the morning well without her. Although his adjustment process was lengthened by the language and cultural differences, it nonetheless highlights the sensory contacts with the mother that some children need as they adjust to school and begin the separation process. Dependency needs and separation anxiety vary tremendously from one child and parent to another and must be met by the teacher with a great deal of flexibility rather than a preconceived idea of when all children should be ready to separate.

"Blankies" and other bits of home. Other children are able to separate from Mom when a transitional object (often a "blankie") is brought with them. The teacher must take seriously the child's need for this visual and tactile comfort that smells, feels, or looks like home. Her interest and concern that the object be kept in a safe place, for this child only, is usually all that is necessary to make things from home manageable in the classroom. One child brought a different toy each day. She deposited it faithfully in her cubby, and checked on it periodically throughout the morning. It was as if a small part of home needed to always accompany her. Her checking on it resembled Haruo's checks with his mother. As the year progressed, like Haruo, her checks became less frequent, until she no longer needed to bring something. The lessening of the young child's need for concrete, sensory reminders of home often parallels the growth of his feeling of security at school and his freedom to continue exploration there.

THE TEACHER'S EMPATHY IS KEY

What causes children to eventually move from their dependence on their mothers and reminders of home to being confident and happy explorers no longer in need of these supports? What makes the unfamiliar environment of the center or school become an extension of the security at home? It is the teacher's understanding and response. She establishes this security through the empathy she feels with the child, and through her ability to understand and communicate symbolically with the child about his concerns.

In addition to responding to the child's needs during the day, teachers can also plan for the group with separation issues in mind. Invite parents and children to visit the center before regular attendance begins. Schedule a small portion of the total group to start each day of the first week so staff has time to provide the support that most children *and parents* need. Encourage mothers to stay with their children at first; and reassure parents that distress in varying ways and degrees is a normal, healthy sign. Keep daily routines as simple and predictable as possible, changing them only when necessary and with careful thought as to how to prepare the children. Arrange the classroom so that children can participate in nonthreatening activities while observing the other children and the comings and goings at the classroom door: an easel in a corner where the child can have her back to the wall and a clear view of all that is happening; play dough, sand, and water in other areas that meet the same criteria. All of these activities involve the child's senses without demanding interpersonal play. They permit the child to observe classroom life carefully and to maintain visual contact with his mother or teacher whenever necessary.

Dependency needs and separation anxiety vary tremendously from one child and parent to another and must be met by the teacher with a great deal of flexibility rather than a preconceived idea of when all children should be ready to separate.

Another way a teacher can help a group of children with separation issues is through reading and acting out meaningful stories—fanciful stories in which a small person or animal ventures away from home and triumphs over adversity. These differ from books that deal realistically with separation issues in that they speak to the children in their own terms of pretend. *The Three Little Pigs* (Jacob, 1980) is probably the all-time favorite because it so pointedly responds to the children's needs in separating from parents and home. The Little Pigs, much like the children starting child care or school, have been sent out by their mother to "make their way." It is clearly not an easy job, but one that demands hard work and cleverness as well. The Big Bad Wolf (and other scary things like him) can be kept at bay and finally be gotten rid of through the industry and clever thinking of the Third Little Pig. These are achievements that guarantee him a happy life from then on. One year a young class of 3-year-olds asked again and again to have this story told. They soon began to act it out, taking different parts while keeping the most salient features of outwitting and doing away with the wolf. The importance of this play contin-

ued for them throughout the year, affording all children the opportunity to be the successful Third Little Pig. Other stories that embody this theme for very young children include *Mr. Gumpy's Motor Car* by Burningham (1976), *The Runaway Bunny* by Brown (1942), and *Swimmy* by Lionni (1963). For 4- and 5-year-olds, the following books pick up the same theme in a more elaborate story: *The Bremen Town Musicians* by the Grimms (1954), Steig's *The Amazing Bone* (1977) and *Sylvester and the Magic Pebble* (1969), and *The Tale of Peter Rabbit* by Potter (1902).

Keeping in mind that separation is a crucial issue that comes up periodically throughout the year, teachers can be receptive to what children and parents express about it and should know when and how to respond. A teacher can recognize and reassure an anxious child on a class trip that they will return to the center to meet his mother. A teacher can view a parent's dilemma compassionately, understanding the wish to have a child ready and eager to go to school, not angry at them for sending him. A teacher can have the courage to stop a parent from sneaking out of the room when the child is not watching, knowing that separation cannot be solved by avoidance, but only by facing its painfulness and "playing out" and expressing the feelings involved.

A teacher's sensitivity to and understanding of separation anxieties is the first step in helping children deal successfully with these feelings. Understanding the child's need for sensory and concrete reassurance helps teachers respond in ways that extend the child's safe environment from home into the classroom. Finally, recognizing that symbolic play is a primary way young children express their feelings guides teachers to facilitate this mode of expression, to understand what the child is saying, and to respond to it on a symbolic level that is immediately accessible to the child. If a child is able to express, accept, and respond to separation anxieties at an early age, there is good reason to expect that she or he will continue to deal successfully with them throughout life.

FOR FURTHER READING

Balaban, N. (1985). *Starting school: From separation to independence.* New York: Teachers College Press, Columbia University.

Bettelheim, B. (1987). *A good enough parent.* New York: Random House.

Bloom-Feshbach, S., Bloom-Feshbach, J., & Gaughran, J. (1980). Child's tie to both parents: Separation patterns and nursery school adjustment. *American Journal of Orthopsychiatry, 50,* 505–521.

Bowlby, J. (1973). *Attachment and loss: Vol. 2. Separation.* New York: Basic.

Erikson, E. H. (1950). *Childhood and society.* New York: Norton.

Fraiberg, S. (1959). *The magic years.* New York: Scribner's.

Gross, D. W. (1970). On separation and school entrance. *Childhood Education, 46*, 250–253.

Jalango, M. R. (1987). Do security blankets belong in preschool? *Young Children, 42*(3), 3–8.

Kleckner, K. A., & Engel, R. E. (1988). A child begins school: Relieving anxiety with books. *Young Children, 43*(5), 14–18.

Stone, J. G. (1987). *Teacher-parent relationships.* Washington, DC: NAEYC.

Viorst, J. (1987). *Necessary losses.* New York: Random House.

Winnecott, D. W. (1953). Transitional objects and transitional phenomena. *International Journal of Psychoanalysis, 34*, 89–97.

REFERENCES

Brown, M. W. (1942). *The runaway bunny.* New York: Harper & Row.

Bumingham, J. (1976). *Mr. Gumpy's motor car.* New York: Crowell.

Grimm, J. L. K., & Grimm, W. K. (1954). *Grimms' fairy tales.* New York: Doubleday.

Jacob, J. (1980). *The story of the three little pigs.* New York: Putnam.

Lionni, L. (1963). *Swimmy.* New York: Pantheon.

Potter, B. (1902). *The tale of Peter Rabbit.* London: Warne.

Powell, D. R. (1989). *Families and early childhood programs,* Washington, Dc: NAEYC.

Steig, W. (1969). *Sylvester and the magic pebble.* New York: Simon & Schuster.

Steig, W. (1977). *The amazing bone.* New York: Pulfin.

The Development of Self-Concept

Janie says "I can't" a lot, often before she even tries an activity. She seems to need constant encouragement from the teacher just to try.

Timmy speaks so softly that he is rarely heard. Even the teacher sometimes does not respond to his initiatives.

Maria describes all the things she can draw as she completes her picture. She tells the teacher about waiting for her mother in the doctor's waiting room by herself and not being afraid.

Hermine H. Marshall

Hermine H. Marshall, Ph.D., is Associate Professor, Department of Elementary Education, San Francisco State University. For the past 15 years, she has been involved in research concerning self-concept and self-evaluation.

This is one of a regular series of Research in Review columns. The column was edited by Celia Genishi, Ph.D., Associate Professor of Educational Theory and Practice at The Ohio State University.

Picture Gold

Positive self-image correlates with good mental health, good academic achievement, and good behavior.

W hy is it that some children try new things with enthusiasm and approach peers and adults with confidence, whereas other children seem to believe that they are incapable of succeeding in many situations? Children (and adults) behave consistently with the way they see themselves. Young children's beliefs about whether they can or cannot do things, therefore, influence how they approach new situations. In turn, their success in new situations affects the way they see themselves—in a seemingly circular process (Marsh, 1984).

Our concern with children like Janie and Timmy is justified by research that shows that low self-concept is related to poor mental health, poor academic achievement, and delinquency (e.g., Harter, 1983). But what can we learn from research that will allow us to help children approach new situations and other people with confidence?

To understand the factors that may influence the development of self-concept, we need first to be aware of the difference between such terms as *self-concept, self-image, self-esteem,* and *self-confidence.* We also need to recognize the relationships among self-concept, perceived competence, and locus of control. Based on our knowledge of factors that influence the development of positive self-concept, we can then take steps that will benefit young children.

Definitions and differentiation

We generally think of *self-concept* as the perceptions, feelings, and attitudes that a person has about himself or herself. The terms *self-concept* and *self-image* are often used interchangeably to designate a global conception of self. This global self-concept is made up of many dimensions.

One dimension is *self-esteem* (or self-

From *Young Children,* Vol. 44, No. 5, July 1989, pp. 44-51. © 1989 by the National Association for the Education of Young Children, 1834 Connecticut Avenue, NW, Washington, DC. Reprinted by permission.

worth). Self-esteem refers specifically to our self-evaluations—that is, our judgments about our own worth—whereas self-concept refers to other aspects as well—physical characteristics, psychological traits, and gender and ethnic identity. Our self-esteem may be affected by possessing culturally valued traits, such as helpfulness and honesty. It is also influenced by seeing that others perceive us as significant and worthy or possessing culturally valued traits.

Self-esteem develops in part from being able to perceive ourselves as competent. *Perceived competence* reflects our beliefs about our ability to succeed at particular tasks. According to White (1959), feelings of competence result from being able to act effectively and master one's environment. When our capacities are stretched to new heights, we feel competent.

Self-esteem and feelings of competence are related to acquiring a sense of *personal control* (Harter, 1983)—particularly in mainstream American culture. (In other cultures personal control may not be important for self-esteem.) As children perceive themselves gaining competence in a gradually widening sphere, they begin to see themselves as causal agents and are able to feel that they have greater ability to control more of their environment. This sense of personal control is often referred to as an *internal locus of control.* In contrast, external locus of control means decisions are in the hands of others or of fate.

As children develop, self-concept becomes increasingly differentiated into multiple domains. Perceptions of competence in the social skills domain become differentiated from perceptions of competence in cognitive and physical domains (Harter & Pike, 1984). Self-perceptions about interactions with peers become separated from those about interactions with parents and teachers. Cognitive or academic self-concept gradually further differentiates into math and verbal areas (Marsh, 1984).

Furthermore, the importance of each of these domains differs for individuals and families, and among cultures. A low self-evaluation in one domain, such as athletic ability, may have little effect on the individual if it is not considered important in a particular family or culture. On the other hand, in families or cultures where athletic skills are important or where skills that underpin academic ability are highly valued, low self-esteem in these culturally relevant areas may have increasingly devastating effects as children move through school (Harter, 1986).

Self-concept measurement

Unfortunately, many problems have hampered progress in understanding the development of self-concept. First, different investigators sometimes use different definitions and examine different dimensions of self-concept. This makes it difficult to compare and synthesize results from different studies (Shavelson, Hubner, & Stanton, 1976).

At the early childhood level, problems in measuring self-concept have further hindered progress. Few formal instruments are suitable for children younger than age 8, in part because of the difficulties young children have in understanding and verbalizing abstract ideas and internal processes like self-concept. In addition, the influence of momentary events on young children's self-concepts, such as a temporarily frustrating experience, often causes indicators of self-concept to vary over time and appear "unstable." Children's ability to see characteristics as stable over time develops gradually.

Furthermore, many instruments to measure self-concept have not considered developmental differences in children's levels of understanding and in how children think about themselves (Damon & Hart, 1982). Items appropriate for older elementary school children, such as "I'm not doing as well in school as I'd like to" may be meaningless for preschoolers. Other items, for example

"I'm pretty sure of myself," may be difficult for preschoolers to understand.

Rather than attempt to adapt for preschoolers instruments designed for older children, one investigation used several types of open-ended questions, asking 3- to 5-year-olds what the experimenter could "write about" each child (Keller, Ford, & Meacham, 1978). Others have used pictures of children succeeding or having difficulty with tasks (Harter & Pike, 1984).

To supplement knowledge based on research conducted with young children, we can also look at studies using older elementary children. At these age levels, self-concept is easier to measure. Although we do not know how early the relationships between self-concept and other variables such as the environment or childrearing practices begin, reviewing studies of preschool and elementary age children can give us clues about what we need to provide for young children so that they can develop a positive self-concept.

One note of caution: Much of the research on self-esteem in children has been conducted within mainstream Anglo culture. Items on self-esteem scales reflect the values of this culture. The childrearing and educational factors that have been found to be correlated with these indexes of self-esteem are, consequently, relative to this culture. Many of today's classrooms include children from diverse cultures with differing values. Therefore, we need to be sensitive to others' values and find ways of minimizing conflicts based on cultural differences.

Cognitive development and self-concept development

Preschool

The level of children's cognitive development influences self-concept development. Preschool children can often use multiple categories to describe themselves, but these categories are not yet very stable or consistent. For example, we may hear a preschooler say, "I am a boy," but "I will be a mommy when I grow up." Preschoolers' self-descriptions are also constrained by the particular events they are experiencing. A girl may say, "I'm strong. I can lift this rock." But she is not bothered if she cannot lift a chair.

Parents who use an "authoritative"—as opposed to an authoritarian or permissive —childrearing pattern are more likely to have children with high self-esteem.

Implications and applications

Ways to explore self-concept in young children

The level of self-esteem in some children, such as those cited at the beginning of this article, is more apparent than in others. It is easy to overlook some quiet children. Nevertheless, observing a child's willingness to explore the environment and assume control of events may be a way of assessing self-esteem in preschool children. For example, watch children's responses as they approach or are presented with a new task. Do they hang back or eagerly jump in? Do they say they can't before they try?

Another way to attend to young children's self-concepts is to listen deliberately to spontaneous statements of "I can" and "I am" or "I can't." You might also try open-minded questioning techniques, such as "I would like to write about you. What can I write? . . . What else can I say about you?" Other questions that teachers of young children have found revealing are

- "What can you tell me about yourself? . . . Why is that important?"
- "What can you tell me that is best about you?"
- "What are you good at doing?"

Remember that recent but temporary events influence young children's self-concepts; therefore, judgments about self-concept or self-esteem should not be based on only one or two statements.

Ways to influence self-concept

Because most of the studies reported in this review use correlational methods that do not indicate cause and effect, we need to be cautious in making interpretations. Nevertheless, many of the findings do suggest steps likely to enhance self-concept.

Help children feel they are of value

Listen attentively to what children say. Ask for their suggestions. Soliciting and respecting children's ideas and suggestions helps children feel that they are of value.

Help children identify their own positive and prosocial behavior. When children display cooperation, helpfulness, and other prosocial behavior, give children the words to describe themselves with these terms. For example, "You are being very helpful." They may then come to see themselves in a positive manner and act accordingly. This is a positive use of the self-fulfilling prophecy.

Highlight the value of different ethnic groups. Find ways of demonstrating the value of the cultures of your group's children. Read books that include children of different cultures. Find people of various ethnic groups to share their expertise with the children. Display pictures of women, men, and children of different ethnic groups succeeding in a variety of tasks.

Help children feel they are competent

Provide experiences for children where they can succeed. For some children, we need to provide a series of tasks that can be accomplished initially with little effort but that gradually increase in difficulty. Try to relate the task to something that children already recognize they can do.

Provide new challenges and comment on positive attempts. Some children appear to need a lot of encouragement and verbal reinforcement. Encouragement and statements of confidence in the child's ability to succeed may be necessary at first. However, the effects of verbal praise and persuasion may be short-lived (Hitz & Driscoll, 1988). Children will be more likely to benefit by seeing for themselves that they can, in fact, succeed.

Teach strategies to accomplish tasks. "I can't" sometimes means "I don't know how." Rather than encouragement, children sometimes need specific instruction in particular strategies to carry out a task. Break down these strategies into smaller steps.

Allow children to carry out and complete tasks by themselves. Because self-concept reflects perceived competence, allowing children to do for themselves whatever they can is important—even when some struggle to accomplish the task is necessary. Avoid the temptation to finish a task or button coats to save time. Help them do it themselves. Doing it for them may convey to children the message that they are not competent.

Help children feel they have some control

Provide opportunities for choice, initiative, and autonomy. Provide opportunities for children to accomplish a variety of tasks at a variety of levels. Give young children simple choices: for example, which task to do first or which of two colors to use. Let children choose which song to sing or game to play next.

Avoid comparison between children. Avoid competition. The self-concept of many children suffers when comparisons between children are made. Comparison and competition point not only to winners, but also to those who have not come out on top. Support each child's accomplishments independently.

Help children learn to evaluate their own accomplishments. Children need to learn to evaluate their own performance so that they will not become dependent on adults for feelings of self-worth. Ask them what their favorite part of their picture or story is, or ask them to look at how their letters compare with those they did last month.

Help children learn interpersonal skills

Help children learn skills to enter interactions with others. Give children the words they need to express their desires and feelings. Help them learn how to enter play and how to resolve conflicts. Knowledge of how to interact appropriately with peers is likely to enhance peer acceptance and liking. This in turn, is related to children's social self-concept.

Become aware of your own expectations for children

Be open to perceiving new information about children and looking at them in new ways. Young children can surprise us. All of a sudden they seem to show new skills. Reappraise your expectations frequently. Let them know you have confidence in their ability to learn new skills.

Be aware of whether your expectations differ for girls and boys. Different expectations for girls and boys may convey cues to children about areas where it is appropriate to become competent. If we expect boys rather than girls to play with the blocks, for example, we may deprive girls of developing positive attitudes and becoming competent in skills needed for success in mathematics and certain types of problem-solving. Initiate activities in all areas that both boys and girls may explore.

In making judgments that may appear to reflect self-esteem, preschoolers' attention is often focused on the value of a specific act. A child who says, "I am a good boy" may mean "I did something good," such as share his candy. Preschoolers also appear to view themselves, as well as others, as either all good or all bad. They do not believe they can be both at the same time. The evaluation may shift to the opposite pole as the child shifts attention to

Self-esteem develops when children possess culturally valued traits and feel competent.

other actions or events (Selman, 1980).

Preschoolers see the self in both physical and action terms (Damon & Hart, 1982). When asked what an observer could "write about you," 3- to 5-year-old children most frequently described themselves in terms of physical actions, such as "I can ride a bike" or "I can help set the table" (Keller et al., 1978). Kindergartners, too, describe themselves largely in terms of activities such as play (Damon & Hart, 1982). Young children seem to see themselves as "good at doing things" or not—without making the distinction between physical and academic competence that older children do (Harter & Pike, 1984). Nevertheless,

about 5% of the responses of the youngest children in the Keller study referred to psychological aspects, such as likes and dislikes.

Primary grades

Primary grade children begin to acquire more mature thinking skills, such as the ability to organize logically and classify hierarchically, and can extend these abilities to their thinking about the self. By age 7 or 8, they are also able to make comparisons between themselves and their peers concerning their abilities (Ruble, Boggiano, Feldman, & Loebl, 1980). By third grade, children still frequently describe themselves in terms of activities, but add comparison with their peers in their self-descriptive statements, such as "I can ride a bike better than my little brother" (Damon & Hart, 1982). They are also able to think inductively and may conclude that "I'm not very smart because I'm in the low group in reading and math."

Primary grade children also acquire new perspective-taking skills that allow them to imagine what other people are thinking, especially what others think of them. Children of this age begin to be more influenced by their perceptions of what significant adults think of them. With further development, what peers think becomes increasingly important.

External factors related to the development of self-concept

Responsiveness of caregivers

Self-concept develops largely within a social context. The interpersonal envi-

Research shows that low self-concept is related to poor mental health, poor academic achievement, and delinquency. But what can we learn from research that will allow us to help children approach new situations and other people with confidence?

ronment that caregivers provide has important influences on the development of self-concept. The quality, consistency, and timing of adults' responses to infants may carry messages about trust, caring, and the value of the infant. Caregiver responsiveness may also convey information about the developing child's capacity to become competent and to control her or his environment (see Honig, 1984). When caregivers respond positively and consistently to infants' cues, infants may come to learn that they are of value and that they can influence their social environment (Harter, 1983). This may contribute to beginning feelings of self-worth, personal control, and competence.

Physical environment

A number of aspects of the physical environment may influence the development of self-concept. For example, if we make developmentally appropriate materials (those that provide both challenge and success) easily accessible to young children for exploration in an encouraging environment, these children are likely to acquire feelings of competence and confidence in approaching new materials (see Bredekamp, 1987).

Other aspects of the environment may influence the development of infants' and toddlers' conceptions of their physical self and of themselves as separate and different from others. Mirrors and similar light-reflecting surfaces, for example, provide opportunities for very young children to learn not only about their physical characteristics but also about themselves as independent agents who can make things happen. When infants can see both themselves and their image moving at the same time, they can learn about the effects of their own actions and their ability to control their world (Lewis & Brooks-Gunn, 1979).

Parental attitudes and childrearing practices

Sears (1970) found that parents who were warm and accepting when their children were young (age 5) had children with high self-esteem measured at age 12. Parents who use an "authoritative"—as opposed to an authoritarian or permissive childrearing pattern (see Honig, 1984)—are also more likely to have children with high self-esteem. These parents make rea-

sonable demands that are accepted by children, but they do not impose unreasonable restrictions and they allow their children some choice and control (Maccoby & Martin, 1983).

Training in effective parenting, where parents learn to be more accepting of their children's feelings and behavior, has led to an increase in kindergarten and second grade children's self-concepts (Summerlin & Ward, 1978). Studies such as these point to the importance of efforts to help parents understand and implement practices that enhance self-esteem.

Feeling in control also helps children develop positive self-esteem.

Expectations

Teachers' and parents' expectations may influence children's self-esteem, both (a) directly through opportunities adults provide for children to learn and become competent and (b) indirectly through more subtle cues that children eventually come to perceive. If adults believe that certain children can learn or do more than others, they may furnish additional materials for these children. In this way, they provide opportunities to become competent in more areas and thus directly influence the children's perceived competence.

In addition, teachers' and parents' expectations influence self-concept in more subtle ways as children gradually become more adept at "reading" environmental cues. Young children are not very accurate in judging adults' expectations for them. They generally hold higher expectations for themselves than their teachers hold for them (Weinstein, Marshall, Sharp, & Botkin, 1987). The discrepancy between young children's expectations and those of their teachers may be due to their relatively undeveloped ability to take the perspective of others. Young children may also have less need to focus on what their teachers expect of them because most preschool and kindergarten classrooms do not emphasize evaluation. However, even at the kindergarten level, if teach-

ers make their evaluations of children salient—such as pointing out the children's best work—children's self-evaluations can show some consistency with those of the teacher (Stipek & Daniels, 1988). Consequently kindergarten and primary teachers need to be aware of subtle ways that their expectations may be conveyed to children and thus influence their self-esteem.

Classroom environments

Classroom structure and teachers' control orientations may influence children's self-concepts as well (Marshall & Weinstein, 1984). This is exemplified in studies comparing the effects of "unidimensional" with those of "multidimensional" classrooms (Rosenholtz & Rosenholtz, 1981). In unidimensional classrooms, teachers emphasize a narrow range of students' abilities (e.g., they value reading ability to the neglect of artistic ability), group students according to ability, assign similar tasks, and publicly evaluate performance. In multidimensional classrooms, in contrast, teachers emphasize multiple dimensions of ability (e.g., artistic and problem-solving skills as well as reading skills), have students work on a variety of different tasks using different materials at the same time, and evaluate students more privately. Although preschools are more often similar to multidimensional classrooms, some kindergarten and "academic" preschools are under pressure to become more unidimensional. In classrooms that emphasized academics, with characteristics similar to unidimensional classrooms, kindergartners' perceptions of their ability were lower than those of kindergartners in more multidimensional classrooms—although the two groups were learning the same skills (Stipek & Daniels, 1988). Teachers need to be aware, therefore, that pressures to prepare children for academics and to include and evaluate more school-like tasks may have detrimental effects on children's self-concepts of ability.

Whether teachers support children's autonomy or tend to control children through external means also affects children's perceptions of competence and self-esteem. Children in classrooms that supported autonomy had higher perceptions of their own cognitive competence, self-worth, and mastery motivation than those in classrooms

> # Sensitive parents and teachers may be better able to assess a child's self-concept than researchers are. Differences in definitions and dimensions make it difficult to compare and synthesize studies, but a child with good self-concept radiates it.

where teachers retained control (Ryan, Connell, & Deci, 1985). Because this study was conducted with older children, we do not know at what age this effect may begin. We should be aware, nevertheless, that providing opportunities for children to strive toward independence and to develop a sense of personal control is likely to have a positive effect on children's perceptions of competence and self-esteem.

Peers

Some research suggests that peer interactions may have an influence on self-esteem and social self-concept earlier than previously believed. In an attempt to explore sources of esteem, preschoolers were asked the question "Who likes you?" More than 50% of the children mentioned peers and 49% mentioned siblings (Kirchner & Vondraek, 1975).

Older children (third through eighth graders) who have a high self-concept in the social domain have higher status with their peers—as might be predicted (Kurdek & Krile, 1982). Again, we do not know how early this finding may hold, nor do we know the direction of causality. That is, (a) social self-concept may influence peer relationships, or (b) peer relationships may influence social self-concept, or (c) knowledge of interpersonal skills may affect peer relationships and/or social self-concept. Taken together, these results suggest that helping children learn the skills needed to interact successfully with their peers may ultimately affect their social self-concept.

References

Bredekamp, S. (Ed.). (1987). *Developmentally appropriate practice in early childhood programs serving children from birth through age 8.* Washington, DC: NAEYC.

Damon, W., & Hart, D. (1982). The development of self-understanding from infancy through adolescence. *Child Development, 53,* 841–864.

Harter, S. (1983). Developmental perspectives on the self-system. In E.M. Hetherington (Ed.), *Handbook of child psychology: Vol. 4. Socialization, personality and social development* (4th ed., pp. 275–386). New York: Wiley.

Harter, S. (1986). Processes underlying the construction, maintenance, and enhancement of the self-concept in children. In J. Suls & A. Greenwald (Eds.), *Psychological perspectives of the self* (Vol. 3, pp. 137–181). Hillsdale, NJ: Erlbaum.

Harter, S., & Pike, R. (1984). The pictorial scale of perceived competence and social acceptance for young children. *Child Development, 55,* 1969–1982.

Hitz, R., & Driscoll, A. (1988). Praise or encouragement? New insights into praise: Implications for early childhood teachers. *Young Children, 43*(5), 6–13.

Honig, A. (1984). Research in review: Risk factors in infants and young children. *Young Children, 39*(4), 60–73.

Keller, A., Ford, L., & Meacham, J. (1978). Dimensions of self-concept in preschool children. *Developmental Psychology, 14,* 483–489.

Kirchner, P., & Vondraek, S. (1975). Perceived sources of esteem in early childhood. *Journal of Genetic Psychology, 132,* 169–176.

Kurdek, L., & Krile, D. (1982). A developmental analysis of the relation between peer acceptance and both interpersonal understanding and perceived social self-competence. *Child Development, 53,* 1485–1491.

Lewis, M., & Brooks-Gunn, J. (1979). *Social cognition and the acquisition of self.* New York: Plenum.

Maccoby, E., & Martin, J. (1983). Socialization in the context of the family: Parent-child interaction. In E.M. Hetherington (Ed.), *Handbook of child psychology: Vol. 4. Socialization, personality, and social development* (4th ed., pp. 1–102). New York: Wiley.

Marsh, H. (1984). Relations among dimensions of self-attributions, dimensions of self-concept and academic achievement. *Journal of Educational Psychology, 76,* 1291–1308

Marshall, H., & Weinstein, R. (1984). Classroom factors affecting students' self-evaluations. *Review of Educational Research, 54,* 301–325.

Rosenholtz, S.J., & Rosenholtz, S.H. (1981). Classroom organization and the perception of ability. *Sociology of Education, 54,* 132–140.

Ruble, D., Boggiano, A., Feldman, N., & Loebl, J. (1980). Developmental analysis of the role of social comparison in self-evaluation. *Developmental Psychology, 16,* 105–115.

Ryan, R., Connell, J., & Deci, E. (1985). A motivational analysis of self-determination and self-regulation in education. In C. Ames & R. Ames (Eds.), *Research on motivation in education: Vol. 2. The classroom milieu* (pp. 13–52). New York: Academic.

Sears, R. (1970). Relation of early socialization experiences to self-concepts and gender role in middle childhood. *Child Development, 41,* 267–289.

Selman, R. (1980). *The growth of interpersonal understanding.* New York: Academic.

Shavelson, R., Hubner, J., & Stanton, G. (1976). Self-concept: Validation of construct interpretations. *Review of Educational Research, 46,* 407–442.

Stipek, D., & Daniels, D. (1988). Declining perceptions of competence: A consequence of changes in the child or in the educational environment. *Journal of Educational Psychology, 80,* 352–356.

Summerlin, M.L., & Ward, G.R. (1978). The effect of parental participation in a parent group on a child's self-concept. *Psychological Reports, 100,* 227–232.

Weinstein, R., Marshall, H., Sharp, L., & Botkin, M. (1987). Pygmalion and the student: Age and classroom differences in children's awareness of teacher expectations. *Child Development, 58,* 1079–1093.

White, R. (1959). Motivation reconsidered: The concept of competence. *Psychological Review, 66,* 297–333.

For further reading

Young Children has had a continuing series of Ideas That Work With Young Children by Polly Greenberg emphasizing encouraging self-esteem in infants and children. If you missed them, you may want to read:

"Positive Self-Image: More Than Mirrors" (May 1988)

"Avoiding 'Me Against You' Discipline" (November 1988)

"Learning Self-Esteem and Self-Discipline Through Play" (January 1989)

"Parents as Partners in Young Children's Development and Education: A New American Fad? Why Does It Matter?" (May 1989)

ALL ABOUT ME

Are We Developing Our Children's Self-Esteem or Their Narcissism?

LILIAN G. KATZ

Lilian G. Katz is professor of early childhood education at the University of Illinois, director of the ERIC Clearinghouse on Elementary and Early Childhood Education, and president of the National Association for the Education of Young Children.

DEVELOPING AND strengthening young children's self-esteem typically is listed as a major goal in state and school district kindergarten curriculum guides. Early childhood education has long been blessed with a variety of curriculum approaches that emphasize and advocate diverse goals and methods. In spite of this diversity, the one goal all the approaches agree is important is that of helping children to "feel good about themselves." The terms applied to this goal include: self-esteem, self-regard, self-concept, feelings of self-worth, self-confidence, and often, "feeling good about oneself."

For example, in a 1990 document titled "Early Childhood Education and the Elementary School Principal," the National Association of Elementary School Principals issued "Standards for Quality Programs for Young Children." The first of twelve characteristics given for "quality early childhood programs" is that they "develop a positive self-image."[1]

Many other books, kits, packets, and newsletters urge teachers to help children gain positive self-concepts. Here's a typical example of this view:

> . . . the basis for *everything we do* is self-esteem. Therefore, if we can do something to give children a stronger sense of themselves, starting in preschool, they'll be [a lot wiser] in the choices they make.[2]

Along similar lines, the prestigious Corporation for Public Broadcasting issued a twenty-page pamphlet, directed to teenagers, entitled "Celebrate Yourself. Six Steps to Building Your Self-Esteem."[3] The first main section, "Learn to Love Yourself Again," asserts that, as babies, we all loved ourselves, but as we grew up, "we found that not everyone liked everything we did," so we "started picking on ourselves." The pamphlet lists six steps toward self-celebration: The first is "Spot Your Self-Attacks"; The second step, "See What Makes You Special," includes a recommended "Celebration List," suggesting that the reader compile a 22-item list of all the "good things about me." The twenty-two items recommended under the heading "My Talents" include: thinking fast, playing trivia, and babysitting. The twelve items under "My Body" include physical attributes such as smile, hair, strength, legs, etc. Among eight items under "My Achievements" are: something special I made; a grade I got; a compliment I got; an award I won; and so forth. The third step of the celebration is "Attack your Self-Attacks." The fourth, "Make Loving Yourself a Habit," is illustrated by a cartoon character admiring itself in a mirror. The final two steps are "Go for the Goal" and "Lend a Hand to Others." This last step is subtitled "Love Grows When You Give It Away."

It is perhaps just this kind of literature that accounts for a large poster I came across in the entrance hall of a suburban school: Pictures of clapping hands surround the title, "We Applaud Ourselves." While the sign's probable purpose is to help children "feel good about themselves," it does so by directing their attention inward. The poster urges self-congratulation; it makes no reference to other possible ways of earning applause—by consider-

From *American Educator,* Summer 1993, pp. 18-23. Reprinted with permission from *American Educator,* the quarterly journal of the American Federation of Teachers.

ing the feelings or needs of others, for example. Many schools display posters that list the Citizen of the Week, Person of the Week, Super Spellers, Handwriting Awards, and other such honors that seem to encourage showing off.

I also noted a sign over an urban elementary school principal's office that says: "Watch your behavior, you are on display!" Although its purpose may be to encourage appropriate conduct, it does so by directing children's attention to how they *appear* to others rather than to any possible functions of appropriate behavior. What I am suggesting by these examples is, that as commendable as it is for children to have high self-esteem, many of the practices advocated in pursuit of this goal may instead inadvertently develop narcissism in the form of excessive preoccupation with oneself.

It was while observing a first-grade class in an affluent suburb of a large midwestern city that I first became aware of the ways in which self-esteem and narcissism can be confused. Working from dittoed pages prepared by the teacher, each student had produced a booklet called "All about Me." The first page asked for basic information about the child's home and family. The second page was titled "What I like to eat"; the third was called "What I like to watch on TV"; the next was "What I want for a present," and another was "Where I want to go on vacation," and so forth.

On each page, attention was directed toward the child's own inner gratifications. Each topic put the child in the role of consumer—of food, entertainment, gifts, and recreation. Not once was the child asked to assume the role of producer, investigator, initiator, explorer, experimenter, wonderer, or problem-solver.

These booklets, like many others I have encountered around the country, never had pages with titles such as "What I want to know more about," or "What I am curious about," or ". . . want to explore, . . . to find out, . . . to solve, . . . to figure out" or even "to make." Instead of encouraging children to reach out in order to investigate or understand phenomena around them worthy of their attention, the headings of the pages turned their attention inward.

Since first encountering these booklets, I have learned from teachers that the "All about Me" exercise is intended to make children "feel good about themselves" and to motivate them by beginning "where they are." The same intentions, however, could be satisfied in other, better ways. Starting "where children are" can be accomplished by providing topics that (1) encourage children to be curious about others *and* themselves, and, (2) reduce the emphasis on consummatory activities, and (3) at the same time, strengthen the intellectual ethos of the classroom.

Indeed, starting "where the children are" can just as easily be satisfied by pooling class data in a project entitled "All about *Us*." The individual data can be collected, summarized, graphed, compared, and analyzed in a variety of ways that minimize focusing the children's attention exclusively on themselves.

Several years ago, I saw this kind of project put into practice in a rural British infant school. The title of a large display on the bulletin board was: "We Are a Class Full of

Why should children's attention so insistently be turned inward?

Bodies"; just below the main heading was "Here Are the Details." The display space was filled with bar graphs showing birth dates, current weight and height, eye color, number of lost teeth, shoe sizes, etc., in which data from the entire class were pooled. The data started "where the children were." As the children worked in small groups to take measurements, prepare graphs, help one another to post displays of their analyses of the students' individual characteristics, the teacher was able to create an ethos of a community of researchers looking for averages, trends, and ranges.

I observed another example of practices intended to foster self-esteem that may instead contribute to self-preoccupation in a suburban kindergarten in which the comments made by the children about their visit to a dairy farm were displayed on a bulletin board. Each of the forty-seven children's sentences listed on the bulletin board began with the words "I liked. . . ." For example, "I liked the cows," ". . . the milking machine," ". . . the chicks," etc. There were no sentences that began "What surprised me was. . .," "What I want to know more about is. . .," or "What I am curious about. . . ."

The children's sentences can be analyzed on many levels. For the purposes of this article, their salient characteristic is the exclusive focus on gratification and the missed opportunity to encourage the natural inclination of children to examine worthwhile phenomena in the world around them. Surely there were features of the farm visit that might have aroused some children's curiosity and sparked further investigations of the real world. Such responses were not solicited and were therefore unlikely to have been appreciated and strengthened.

Another common example of a practice intended to enhance self-esteem but unlikely to do so, was a display of kindergartners' work that consisted of nine large identical paper-doll figures, each having a balloon containing a sentence stem that began "I am special because. . . ." The children completed the sentence with the phrases: ". . . I can color," ". . . I can ride a bike," ". . . I like to play with my friends," ". . . I know how to play," ". . . I am beautiful," ". . . I am learning to read," ". . . I can cut," ". . . everybody makes me happy." These children surely are not likely to believe for very long that they are special because they can color, ride a bike, or like to play. What might these children think when they discover just how trivial these criteria for being special are? The examples described above are not unusual; similar work can be found in schools all over the country.

WHY SHOULD children's attention so insistently be turned inward? Can such superficial flattery really boost self-esteem; and are young children's minds being intellectually engaged by such exercises? Can a child's propensity to explore and investigate worthwhile topics be strengthened by such activities? Is it possible the cumulative effect of such practices, when used frequently, undermines children's perceptions of their teachers as being thoughtful adults, worthy of respect?

Many books and kits for teachers recommend similar exercises that help children "feel good about themselves." One typical example is a booklet with tear-out worksheets called *Building Self-Esteem with Koala-Roo.*[4] One page is bordered by the phrase "YOU ARE SPECIAL!", which appears fourteen times, in capital letters. In the page's upper left-hand corner is a drawing of a smiling koala bear waving one paw, while holding a heart that says "I love you" in the other. The heading on the page is "You Are Special." Below the heading is a line for a child's name following the phrase "You are Special!" again. This is followed by "I am very glad that I have been your X grade teacher." No space is provided for the teacher's own name. This line is followed by text that reads "There's no one else quite like you," "You're one of a kind," "unique," and so forth.

I doubt whether the complete text of the page just described meets the readability index for kindergartners, first graders, or any children young enough to be taken in by such excessive pandering. It would be surprising (and disappointing) if children old enough to read these pages are inspired by their content.

Another example of the genre can be found advertised in a popular teachers' magazine. Titled "Excellence in Early Childhood," the ad promotes a unit of activities called "I Am Special" for 3-, 4- and 5- year-olds. The kit being offered includes a student activity book filled with colorful hands-on projects and illustrated stories, and a teacher guide for twenty-nine lesson plans, stories, and finger plays designed to promote "feeling good abut oneself." In answer to the question of what children will learn from the "I Am Special" kit, the advertisement claims that children "become aware that they are created in a very special and unique way," and "see themselves as good and worthwhile individuals." These illustrations are just two examples from among many similar teaching aids I have seen in early childhood classrooms all over the U.S.

The concept of specialness expressed in these activities seems, by definition, contradictory: If everybody is special, nobody is special. Furthermore, frequent feedback about how special a child is might even raise some doubt along the lines of "Methinks thou dost protest too much"!

In similar fashion, it is not clear whether the traditional "show-and-tell" (or "bring and brag") activity used in traditional early childhood programs does as much to enhance self-esteem as it does to encourage children to be unduly concerned about the impressions they make on others or to learn the techniques of one-upmanship. Many early childhood specialists justify the practice on the grounds that if gives children a chance to practice an early form of public speaking and thereby to strengthen their verbal expressive skills. Some teachers also hope children will sharpen their listening skills as they watch their peers show and tell. However, it is not clear what happens to children who feel that what they have to show and tell cannot compete with their peers' contributions. Furthermore, my observations of such group sessions suggest that more than a few children seem to be tuning out their peers rather than learning to listen to them.

I believe there are other more meaningful and intellectually defensible ways for children to speak to groups of their peers. For example, children can report discoveries and experiences derived from their own efforts, ideas, and real accomplishments.[5]

THE TREND toward overemphasizing self-esteem and self-congratulation may be due to a general desire to correct earlier traditions of eschewing compliments for fear of making children conceited. However, the current practices described above seem to me to be over-corrections of such traditions.

Although there is little doubt that many children arrive at preschool and school with less than optimum self-esteem, telling them otherwise is not likely to have much effect. Feelings cannot be learned from direct instruction. Furthermore, constant messages about how wonderful one is may raise doubts about the credibility of the message and the messenger.

Self-esteem is most likely to be fostered when children have challenging opportunities to build self-confidence and esteem through effort, persistence, and the gradual accrual of skills, knowledge, and appropriate behavior. In addition, adults can show their esteem for children in more significant ways than the awarding of gold stars and happy faces. Esteem is conveyed to children when adults and peers treat them with respect, ask them for their views and preferences (even if they are not acceded to), and provide opportunities for real decisions and choices about those things that matter to the children. Young children's opinions, suggestions, and preferences should be solicited respectfully and considered seriously. To be sure, some children come up with wild or silly notions, and their peers will quickly tell them so. In the course of discussion, however, teachers can gain insight into how children understand the matters at hand and can make sound decisions about which children need their help.

Cheap success in a succession of trivial tasks most likely will not foster self-esteem. Young children are more apt to benefit from real challenge and hard work than from frivolous one-shot activities.

For example, in many early childhood programs, the amount of time and effort given to activities related to holidays seems excessive. Although festive occasions alleviate the routine of daily life, like anything else, they can be overdone. Early childhood educators traditionally have emphasized that play is children's natural way of learning.[6] Indeed, a large body of research and years of practical experience attest to the powerful role of play in all facets of learning in the early years.

It is just as natural, however, for young children to learn through investigation. Children are born natural- and social scientists. Like anthropologists, they devote much time and energy to investigating and making sense of their environments. During the preschool and early school years, teachers can capitalize on this in-born disposition by engaging children in investigations through project work. In-depth investigations of real topics, real environments, events, and objects are worthy of children's attention and understanding.

In the course of such undertakings, children negotiate with their teachers to determine the questions to be answered, the studies to be undertaken, and ways to represent their findings in media such as paintings, drawings, and dramatic play. Project work provides children with ample opportunity for real discussion, decision making, cooperation, initiative, negotiation, compromise, and evaluation of the outcomes of their efforts. In this way, children learn the criteria of self-esteem. This self-esteem can be related to their contribution to the work of the group, to the quality of the effort, and its results.

Most of the tasks offered to young children in early childhood classes allow for individual effort and achievement. However, the interpersonal processes that foster healthy self-esteem require the amount of individual work to be balanced with group work in which each child can contribute to the total group effort through cooperation with other students.

EARLY CHILDHOOD practitioners are right to be diligent in encouraging children through the use of frequent positive feedback. The distinction between praise and flattery is often blurred however. Gushing over a child's fingerpainting may be accepted by the child with pleasure. But, it is difficult to know when frequent praise begins to lose its value and is dismissed by children as empty teacher talk. If children become accustomed to frequent praise, some of them will think its inevitable occasional absence is a rebuke—even when this is not intended. It is difficult for adults to maintain a constant flow of meaningful praise. And, if a child's sense of self-worth can be raised by simple flattery from one person, it just as easily can be deflated by another.

A large body of evidence indicates that children benefit from positive feedback. But, praise and rewards are not the only methods of reinforcement. Another kind of positive feedback is *appreciation*. By appreciation I mean positive reinforcement related explicitly and directly to the *content* of the child's interest and effort. If a child poses a thoughtful question, a teacher might, for example, come to class the next day with a new reference book. Or, she might share with the children ideas generated from reflecting on problems they had raised concerning procedures to try. In these ways, the teacher treats children's concerns with respect, thereby deepening interest in the issues they have raised and providing positive feedback without deflecting children from the content. The important point here is that the teacher shows in a positive way that she appreciates their concerns *without taking their minds off the subjects at hand or directing their attention inwards*. When children see that their concerns and interests are being taken seriously, they are more likely to raise them in the next discussion, and to take their own ideas seriously. Teachers can strengthen children's disposition to wonder, reflect, raise questions, and generate alternative solutions to practical and intellectual problems. Certificates, gold stars, stickers, and trophies also provide children with positive feedback, but the salience of such devices

Cheap success in a succession of trivial tasks most likely will not foster self-esteem.

is likely to deflect the children's and teacher's attention from the content of the work at hand.

Another form of frequent praise stems from teachers' eagerness to reinforce cooperative behavior among young children. Teachers often praise children's efforts by saying such things as "I was really glad when you used your words to get your turn. . . ." or "It made me happy to see you share your wagon with Sally." Such strategies may be helpful when first teaching children how to use verbal strategies for conflict resolution. But, like all strategies, they can be overdone, especially as children reach the preschool years. At issue here is the hypothesis that frequent praise can be taken by children to mean that the praised behavior is not expected—as though the unspoken end of these kinds of elliptical sentences is ". . . because I never expected you to." It may be that children sense our unspoken expectations, and will, indeed, frequently live up to them. Such teacher responses also may imply that the rationale for the desirable behavior is to please the teacher.

It would seem more appropriate for teachers to exercise a quiet and calm authority by stating clearly and respectfully precisely what behavior is expected as occasions arise. Because young children are in the early stages of acquiring interactive and conflict-resolution skills, teachers will have to exercise patience in using this strategy.

ANOTHER APPROACH that teachers might use to make children less dependent upon praise from others is to help them develop and apply their own evaluation criteria.

For example, rather than have children take their work home every day, encourage them to collect it in a special folder or portfolio for a week or so. Then at some point, encourage children to select an item they want to take home and discuss with them the criteria for selection they might apply. The emphasis should not be on whether a child likes a piece of work, or whether it is good or bad. Instead, guide children to think about whether a piece of work includes all they want it to, or whether it is sufficiently clear or accurate, or whether it shows progress compared to the last item they took home, and so forth. At first, parents might be disappointed when the flow of paintings, collages, and worksheets is interrupted; but teachers can help parents to engage their children in fruitful discussion about the criteria of selection used, thus encouraging children to take seriously their own evaluations of their work.

Similarly, when children are engaged with others in project work, they can evaluate the extent to which they have answered the questions they began with, and assess the work accomplished on criteria developed with their teacher concerning the accuracy, completeness, and interest value of their final products.[7] The children should be encouraged to discuss what they might do the next time they undertake an investigation, thus strengthening the propensity to vary their strategies and use their own experience as a source from which to improve their next undertakings. Applying such criteria to their own efforts helps children to become engaged in their work. It also helps them to gain understanding and competence rather than drawing their attention toward themselves or to the image they project to others.

When children are engaged in challenging and significant activities, they are bound to experience some failures, reverses, and rebuffs. Parents and teachers have an important role to play—not in avoiding such events—but in helping children cope constructively when they fail to get what they want—whether it's a turn with a toy or success at a task. In such incidents, the teacher can say something like "I know you're disappointed, but there's tomorrow, and you can try again." As long as the teacher accepts a child's feelings and responds respectfully, the child is more likely to learn from the incident than to be harmed by it. Children are able to cope with rebuffs, disappointments, and failures when adults acknowledge and accept their feelings of discouragement and at the same time tell children they can try again another time.

Another approach is to teach children how to use what they have learned from their own experiences as a source of encouragement. A teacher might, for example, help a child recall an earlier incident when he or she struggled with a task or situation and eventually mastered it.

Learning to deal with setbacks, and maintaining the persistence and optimism necessary for childhood's long and gradual road to mastery: These are the real foundations of lasting self-esteem. Children who are helped to develop these qualities will surely respect themselves—though they probably will have better things to think about.

REFERENCES

1 National Association of Elementary School Principals. 1990. *Early Childhood Education and the Elementary School Principal. Standards for Quality Programs for Young Children.* Arlington, Va.: NAESP.

2 Sandy McDaniel quoted in "Political Priority #1: Teaching Kids to Like Themselves," *New Options,* issue no. 27, April 28, 1986.

3 Corporation for Public Broadcasting. 1991. *Celebrate Yourself: Six Steps to Building Your Self-Esteem.* Washington, D.C.: Corporation for Public Broadcasting.

4 Femdel, L. and B. Ecker. 1989. *Building Self-Esteem with Koala-Roo.* Glencoe, Ill.: Scott, Foresman and Co.

5 Katz, L.G. and S.C. Chard. 1989. *Engaging Children's Minds: The Project Approach.* Norwood, N.J.: Ablex Publishing Corp.

6 Isenberg, J. and N.L. Quisenberry. 1988. *Play: A Necessity for All Children.* A position paper of the Association for Childhood Education International. Wheaton, Md.: Association for Childhood Education International.

7 Katz and Chard, op. cit.

Children Without Friends

Who Are They and How Can Teachers Help?

This article highlights an area that should be of great concern to educators—children without friends. The author notes the serious implications of growing up friendless: "The uniqueness of peer relationships contributes to a child's normal development." Now, proven techniques of identification allow teachers and other professionals to help such children.—R.J.S.

Janis R. Bullock

Janis R. Bullock is Assistant Professor, Human Development and Counseling, Montana State University, Bozeman.

Children who have difficulty forming friendships and gaining acceptance among peers have received a tremendous amount of interest over the past decade. Research indicates that approximately 6 to 11 percent of elementary school-age children have no friends or receive no friendship nominations from peers (Hymel & Asher, 1977). This figure varies depending upon the assessment procedure used and it may be even higher in some subgroups. For example, children who have learning disabilities (Gresham, 1988) or are mildly retarded (Taylor, Asher & Williams, 1987) may experience even more difficulties forming so-

cial relationships. Nonetheless, many average and above-average children are without friends. Consequently, research and intervention focusing on children with peer relationship problems are becoming more extensive.

Researchers continue to seek information that may contribute to the understanding and awareness of these children. Many children who experience poor peer relations are at risk and need support. Research on the consequences of peer rejection can provide teachers with the foundation and rationale for effective intervention. Teachers working closely with children who lack friends understand the frustration such students experience during attempts to interact with peers.

The uniqueness of peer relationships contributes to a child's normal development. Unlike adult-child relationships, child-child relations are more egalitarian and involve more reciprocal interactions. These interactions help

children achieve competency in many areas. Therefore, children who lack friends do not enjoy many important benefits of interaction. Peer relations should be viewed as necessary for a child's healthy development.

Identifying Children Without Friends

In order to determine a child's status within the peer group, researchers often use two variations of sociometric measurement techniques. These measurements rely on children's perceptions of others and can identify those children who are rejected or neglected by their peer group. A widely used sociometric technique is the peer nomination method (Hymel & Rubin, 1985). In this technique, children are asked to pick from a list the names of three children with whom they like to play and three children with whom they do not like to play. In general, this procedure provides a useful means of assessing children's impact on their peers. Rejected children receive few positive nominations and many negative nominations, while neglected children receive few positive *or* negative nominations.

The rating scale measure (Singleton & Asher, 1977), a slightly different approach, is used to assess social acceptance or preference within the peer group. Children are asked to rate each classmate on a 1-5 Likert-type scale, in response to questions about how much they like to play or work with that classmate. Rejected children receive very low overall ratings, whereas ratings of neglected children do not differ from those of average children. Although neglected children are generally liked, they very often lack friends.

Sociometric Status and Behaviors in Children

Once researchers were able to identify rejected and neglected children, they became interested in determining the behaviors associated with each status. Information is typically gathered on child behavior in three ways: peer reports, teacher reports and direct observation. The behaviors of the children are then correlated with sociometric status.

Peers can provide an important perspective on the behavior norms within a peer group, providing insight on areas often unavailable or unknown to adults. A common technique requires children to characterize the behavior of peers (e.g., aggressive, helpful, cooperative, shy). A variety of behaviors attributed to children by their peers are related to their sociometric status (Carlson, Lahey & Neeper, 1984; Coie, Dodge & Coppotelli, 1982; Wasik, 1987). Across age groups, peers accept children who are considered helpful, friendly, cooperative, cheerful and prosocial. Peer rejection is generally associated with aggression, disruption and fighting. Shy, quiet children lacking social involvement are often neglected.

Because of their considerable contact with children, teachers can provide a valuable perspective on children's behavior. French and Waas (1988) obtained teacher ratings on popular, rejected and neglected 2nd- and 5th-grade children. Rejected children were characterized as aggressive, hostile and task avoidant, while neglected children were described as having more school behavior problems

than popular children. Coie and Dodge (1988) asked teachers to rank 1st- and 2nd-grade boys of different sociometric statuses on a variety of peer aggression items. Well-accepted and neglected children were described as the least aggressive, whereas rejected children were described as the most aggressive. Rejected children also scored low in conformity to rules and interpersonal sensitivity. In general, teacher assessments coincided with children's perceptions.

Direct observational methods also contribute to research on the assessment of peer group behavior. Trained observers unacquainted with children can provide unbiased information on discrete behaviors of children. Various studies on school-age children (Dodge, Coie & Brakke, 1982; Gottman, Gonso & Rasmussen, 1975; Ladd, 1983) show a high degree of consistency in outcomes. Both popular and average-status children engage in more cooperative play and social conversation than do rejected children. Rejected children show many more inappropriate behaviors than any of the other status groups. Often alone, they wander around the room and are off-task during the work period. They are also more aggressive, argumentative and likely to engage in disruptive peer interactions.

Less observational information is available on neglected children. In general, they spend more time alone and make fewer social contacts. When they do attempt to make a social contact, they are often ignored. They are characterized as being neither aggressive nor disruptive and have difficulty integrating with peers. They engage in more solitary activities than other children (Dodge, Coie & Brakke, 1982). In general, research suggests that children who are rejected and neglected display certain behaviors that may contribute to their failure to interact with peers.

Children's Status and Dropping Out of School

Children who continually experience rejection are considered to be at risk for dropping out of school. Approximately 20 percent of children who enter school do not graduate for various reasons (Weiner, 1980). A small percentage leave reluctantly, generally due to family emergencies or crises. Others do so because of frustrations related to poor social adjustment. Yet, the majority of these students are considered at least average in intelligence with the ability to graduate.

Several studies provide support for the hypothesis that peer assessments of low acceptance can predict future dropouts. Gronlund and Holmlund (1958) reported that 54 percent of low-accepted boys dropped out of school, compared to 19 percent of high-accepted boys. Among girls, the dropout figure was 35 percent for low acceptance, compared to 4 percent for high acceptance. Barclay (1966) reported that low-accepted boys and girls were two to three times more likely to drop out of school.

These early studies did not distinguish between rejected and neglected children, a more recent concern. Kupersmidt's (1983) study does address the subclassification issue. In a 6-year longitudinal study of 5th-graders, she reports the dropout rate included 30 percent of the rejected, 10 percent of the neglected, 21 percent of the average and 4 percent of the popular sample. Although differences were only marginally significant, the rejected group did show a greater dropout rate. Kupersmidt suggests that perhaps only the rejected children are at risk.

In sum, evidence suggests that many adolescents who drop out of school experience poor peer adjustments in their earlier years of school. They are more likely to drop out of school than their more accepted peers. The effects appear to be stronger for boys than girls, yet patterns are consistent regardless of gender. Evidence suggests that peer rejection may be such an adverse experience that adolescents decide to leave school (Kupersmidt, Coie & Dodge, 1990). The relationship between neglected children and dropout rates is not so clear and needs further examination.

Considerations for Teachers

Children who are rejected by their peers often report feelings of loneliness and lower levels of self-esteem. A sensitive and supportive teacher will be aware of these feelings and will attempt to assess each child's situation. Teachers can begin by careful observation of the child. While observing the child who appears to be having difficulty interacting with peers, the teacher can ask:

- Do the children in the class seem to avoid, ignore and reject the child?
- Does the child lack certain social skills necessary for successful interaction with others?
- Does the child have difficulty interpreting other peoples' cues or requests?
- Does the child have difficulty communicating with others about his/her needs and desires?
- Does the child act aggressively while interacting with others?
- Is the child disruptive in the class?

Although there are no plans that work with every child, teachers can choose from several approaches found to be successful. Teachers will need to choose strategies that best fit the child's needs, are adaptable to the classroom and support their philosophy.

Some children are disliked by peers because they lack the skills necessary to get along with others.

Researchers (Oden & Asher, 1977) have developed techniques for coaching children in social skills. Coaching involves identifying the child's problem and providing some form of direct instruction regarding strategies for use when interacting with peers.

Children can be coached on specific concepts that will contribute to more positive interactions. Concepts that were used by Oden and Asher (1977) included participation (e.g., how to get started and the importance of paying attention), cooperation (e.g., the importance of

> *Evidence suggests that peer rejection may be such an adverse experience that adolescents decide to leave school.*

taking turns and sharing materials), communication (e.g., the importance of talking with others and listening) and being friendly and nice (e.g., the importance of smiling, helping and encouraging others). Coaches can assist children by:

- telling them why each concept is important to peer interaction
- asking for examples to assess children's understanding of the concept
- reinforcing the examples or providing suggestions when children have trouble finding their own examples
- discussing both positive and negative behavioral examples that are important to interactions

- trying out some of the ideas in a play situation
- assessing the situation afterward.

Some children may benefit from practice with younger age-mates. Coaching children has contributed to long-term changes in their behavior and sociometric status.

Children who have difficulty reading other children's cues may benefit by watching others who interact successfully. Low-status children can watch a variety of successful interactions on videotape or acted out by adults, other children or puppets. Studies (Gresham & Nagle, 1980; Jakibchuk & Smeraglio, 1976) indicate that low-status children exhibit an increase in positive interaction after viewing models, and the effects are maintained over time. Factors contributing to these positive outcomes seem to be:

- similarity of the model to the target child
- explicitly identifying the model's behavior to the target child
- using simple step-by-step narration to describe the purposes of the behavior (Asher, Renshaw & Hymel, 1982).

Children who act aggressively toward others are often the least liked in the classroom. Self-control training, also referred to as cognitive behavior modification, focuses on the maintenance of positive behaviors through internal cognitive control (Meichenbaum, 1985). In some cases, teaching aggressive children to self-regulate their behavior has proven more effective in reducing inappropriate behaviors than external reinforcers from teachers (Bolstad & Johnson, 1972). Researchers (Camp, Blom, Herbert & Van Doornick, 1977) have taught children to reinforce themselves directly by following a thinking-out-loud strategy that was found to reduce disruptive behaviors and increase prosocial behaviors. When using the thinking-out-loud strategy, children are trained to say to themselves, first out loud and then silently, "What is my problem? What is my plan? Am I using my plan? How did I do?" This process helps children interrupt their impulsive behavior, keeps them on task and reminds them of the necessary steps to take when carrying out their task. This training often includes social problem-solving skills, whereby children are encouraged to suggest and evaluate solutions to problems (Spivak, Platt & Shure, 1976).

Disruptiveness is another behavior often related to peer rejection. Disruptive children are often off-task and engage in inappropriate classroom behavior. The percentage of rejected children described as disruptive by peers ranges from 36 percent to 38 percent (Coie & Koeppl, 1990). Two techniques for reducing disruptive behavior in the classroom are use of reinforcement and token incentives.

Positive reinforcement, often used in connection with modeling, has produced some immediate positive outcomes (Asher, Renshaw & Hymel, 1982). The behavior of a child or group of children can be subjected to direct reinforcement. Teachers can make a point of praising socially cooperative interactions, while ignoring any undesirable interactions deemed tolerable. Specific praise of a child immediately after a desirable behavior provides the strongest results. Other studies (e.g., Gresham, 1979) used reinforcement procedures to reduce the frequency of negative social behaviors, and these effects were found to maintain over time.

The use of tokens as a reward for desirable behavior, in conjunction with positive reinforcement, tends to reduce disruptiveness and increase on-task behavior (Kazdin, 1977). In a token economy, teachers identify those behaviors deemed desirable and undesirable. When students act in a desirable manner, they are rewarded with a token of the teacher's choice. Tokens can range from a point system, plastic disks or plastic cards that can be exchanged for toys, food or other privileges. Several variations of token economies exist in schools and institutions. Descriptions of procedures, rules and additional considerations of this system can be found in Kazdin (1977).

Not having friends contributes to loneliness, low self-esteem and inability to develop social skills.

Although token economies have shown success, they are not without their critics. This procedure focuses on the symptoms rather than the causes, and the effects of the program do not always generalize to other settings—such as home or play settings (Kazdin, 1977). In some cases, the system may not work at all. For example, Coie and Koeppl (1990) point out that children who lack basic skills or are unable to perform classroom tasks may need specific coaching in academic skills.

Communicating with parents will be especially important for teachers working with children who have difficulty interacting with peers. The increasing number of single-parent families or families with both parents working outside the home means that teachers will need to utilize a variety of approaches to maintain contact.

Options may include telephone calls, notes, letters and parent conferences. In order for children to benefit, parents need to have an understanding of their child's development and progress. Teachers can discuss their observations of the child and share what they are doing in the classroom that might also be reinforced at home. In addition, teachers can ask for parental input and suggestions. Teachers can also share information with parents on child guidance or parent discussion groups that might be available in the community.

In some cases, teachers may find that some children will need more assistance than is possible within the classroom. Not all children will respond to the techniques suggested. At some point, teachers must acknowledge the need for additional help. Teachers will need to work with the family and suggest other resources. A professional teacher will understand the importance of compiling resources and referrals that can be useful for families. This information might include services such as the school psychologist; community mental health clinics; child, family and marriage counselors; and developmental screening clinics.

Summary

A significant percentage of children are rejected or neglected during childhood. A lack of friends can put children at risk for later problems. More immediately, not having friends contributes to loneliness, low self-esteem and inability to develop social skills. Rejection or neglect by peers is a traumatic experience for some children. Research indicates that identification and intervention may help modify the negative experiences that some children encounter.

References

Asher, S., Renshaw, R., & Hymel, S. (1982). Peer relations and the development of social skills. In S. G. Moore & C. R. Cooper (Eds.), *The young child: Reviews of research*, Vol. 3, pp. 137-158. Washington, DC: NAEYC.

Barclay, J. (1966). Sociometric choices and teacher ratings as predictors of school dropout. *Journal of Social Psychology, 4*, 40-45.

Bolstad, O., & Johnson, S. (1972). Self-regulation in the modification of disruptive classroom behavior. *Journal of Applied Behavioral Analysis, 5*, 443-454.

Camp, B., Blom, G., Herbert, F., & Van Doornick, W. (1977). Think aloud: A program for developed self-control in young aggressive boys. *Journal of Abnormal Child Psychology, 5*, 157-169.

Carlson, C., Lahey, B., & Neeper, R. (1984). Peer assessment of the social behavior of accepted, rejected, and neglected children. *Journal of Abnormal Child Psychology, 12*, 189-198.

Coie, J., & Dodge, K. (1988). Multiple sources of data on social behavior and social status in the school: A cross-age comparison. *Child Development, 59*, 815-829.

Coie, J., Dodge, K, & Coppotelli, H. (1982). Continuities and changes in children's social status: A five-year longitudinal study. *Developmental Psychology, 18*, 557-570.

Coie, J., & Koeppl, G. (1990). Adapting intervention to the problems of aggressive and disruptive rejected children. In S. R. Asher & J. D. Coie (Eds.), *Peer rejection in childhood*, pp. 309-337. New York: Cambridge University Press.

Dodge, K., Coie, J., & Brakke, N. (1982). Behavior patterns of socially rejected and neglected preadolescents: The roles of social approach and aggression. *Journal of Abnormal Child Psychology, 10*, 389-410.

French, D., & Waas, G. (1985). Behavior problems of peer-neglected and peer-rejected elementary-age children: Parent and teacher perspectives. *Child Development, 56*, 246-252.

Gottman, J., Gonso, J., & Rasmussen, B. (1975). Social interaction, social competence, and friendship in children. *Child Development, 46*, 709-718.

Gresham, F. (1979). Comparison of response cost and time out in a special education setting. *Journal of Special Education, 13*, 199-208.

Gresham, F. (1988). Social competence and motivational characteristics of learning disabled students. In M. C. Luang, M. C. Reynolds & H. J. Walberg (Eds.), *Handbook of special education: Research and practice*, Vol. 2, pp. 283-302. Oxford: Pergamon.

Gresham, F., & Nagle, R. (1980). Social skills training with children: Responsiveness to modeling and coaching as a function of peer orientation. *Journal of Consulting and Clinical Psychology, 48*, 718-729.

Gronlund, N., & Holmlund, W. (1958). The value of elementary school sociometric status scores for predicting pupils' adjustment in high school. *Educational Administration and Supervision, 44*, 225-260.

Hymel, S., & Asher, S. (1977, March). *Assessment and training of isolated children's social skills*. Paper presented at the biennial meeting of the Society for Research in Child Development, New Orleans. (Eric Document Reproduction Service No. ED 136 930).

Hymel, S., & Rubin, K. (1985). Children with peer relationships and social skills problems: Conceptual, methodological, and developmental issues. In G. J. Whitehurst (Ed.), *Annals of child development*, Vol. 2, pp. 251-297. Greenwich, CT: JAI Press.

Jakibchuk, Z., & Smeraglio, V. (1976). The influence of symbolic modeling on the social behavior of preschool children with low levels of social responsiveness. *Child Development, 47*, 838-841.

Kazdin, A. (1977). *The token economy: A review and evaluation*. New York: Plenum.

Kupersmidt, J. (1983, April). Predicting delinquency and academic problems from childhood peer status. In J. D. Coie (Chair), *Strategies for identifying children at social risk: Longitudinal correlates and consequences*. Symposium conducted at the biennial meeting of the Society for Research in Child Development, Detroit, MI.

Kupersmidt, J., Coie, J., & Dodge, K. (1990). The role of poor peer relationships in the development of disorder. In S. R. Asher & J. D. Coie (Eds.), *Peer rejection in childhood*, pp. 253-273. New York: Cambridge University Press.

Ladd, G. (1983). Social networks of popular, average, and rejected children in school settings. *Merrill-Palmer Quarterly, 29*, 283-308.

Meichenbaum, D. H. (1985). *Stress innoculation training*. New York: Pergamon Press.

Oden, S., & Asher, S. (1977). Coaching children in social skills for friendship making. *Child Development, 48*, 495-506.

Singleton, L., & Asher, S. (1977). Peer preferences and social interaction among third-grade children in an integrated school district. *Journal of Educational Psychology, 69*, 330-336.

Spivak, G., Platt, J., & Shure, M. (1976). *The problem-solving approach to adjustment*. San Francisco: Jossey-Bass.

Taylor, A., Asher, S., & Williams, G. (1987). The social adaptation of mainstreamed, mildly retarded children. *Child Development, 58*, 1321-1334.

Wasik, B. (1987). Sociometric measures and peer descriptions of kindergarten children: A study of reliability and validity. *Journal of Clinical Child Psychology, 16*, 218-224.

Weiner, I. P. (1980). Psychopathology in adolescence. In J. Adelson (Ed.), *Handbook of adolescent psychology*, pp. 447-471. New York: Wiley.

Guns and Dolls

Alas, our children don't exemplify equality any more than we did. Is biology to blame? Scientists say maybe—but parents can do better, too.

LAURA SHAPIRO

Meet Rebecca. She's 3 years old, and both her parents have full-time jobs. Every evening Rebecca's father makes dinner for the family—Rebecca's mother rarely cooks. But when it's dinner time in Rebecca's dollhouse, she invariably chooses the Mommy doll and puts her to work in the kitchen.

Now meet George. He's 4, and his parents are still loyal to the values of the '60s. He was never taught the word "gun," much less given a war toy of any sort. On his own, however, he picked up the word "shoot." Thereafter he would grab a stick from the park, brandish it about and call it his "shooter."

Are boys and girls *born* different? Does every infant really come into the world programmed for caretaking or war making? Or does culture get to work on our children earlier and more inexorably than even parents are aware? Today these questions have new urgency for a generation that once made sexual equality its cause and now finds itself shopping for Barbie clothes and G.I. Joe paraphernalia. Parents may wonder if gender roles are immutable after all, give or take a Supreme Court justice. But burgeoning research indicates otherwise. No matter how stubborn the stereotype, individuals can challenge it; and they will if they're encouraged to try. Fathers and mothers should be relieved to hear that they do make a difference.

Biologists, psychologists, anthropologists and sociologists have been seeking the origin of gender differences for more than a century, debating the possibilities with increasing rancor ever since researchers were forced to question their favorite theory back in 1902. At that time many scientists believed that intelligence was a function of brain size and that males uniformly had larger brains than women—a fact that would nicely explain men's pre-eminence in art, science and letters. This treasured hypothesis began to disintegrate when a woman graduate student compared the cranial capacities of a group of male scientists with those of female college students; several women came out ahead of the men,

Girls' cribs have pink tags and boys' cribs have blue tags; mothers and . . .

GIRLS

NEWBORNS

BOYS

. . . fathers should be on the alert, for the gender-role juggernaut has begun

and one of the smallest skulls belonged to a famous male anthropologist.

Gender research has become a lot more sophisticated in the ensuing decades, and a lot more controversial. The touchiest question concerns sex hormones, especially testosterone, which circulates in both sexes but is more abundant in males and is a likely, though unproven, source of aggression. To postulate a biological determinant for behavior in an ostensibly egalitarian society like ours requires a thick skin. "For a while I didn't dare talk about hormones, because women would get up and leave the room," says Beatrice Whiting, professor emeritus of education and anthropology at Harvard. "Now they seem to have more self-confidence. But they're skeptical. The data's not in yet."

Some feminist social scientists are staying away from gender research entirely—"They're saying the results will be used against women," says Jean Berko Gleason, a professor of psychology at Boston University who works on gender differences in the acquisition of language. Others see no reason to shy away from the subject. "Let's say it were proven that there were biological foundations for the division of labor," says Cynthia Fuchs Epstein, professor of sociology at the City University of New York, who doesn't, in fact, believe in such a likelihood. "It doesn't mean we couldn't do anything about it. People can make from scientific findings whatever they want." But a glance at the way society treats those gender differences already on record is not very encouraging. Boys learn to read more slowly than girls, for instance, and suffer more reading disabilities such as dyslexia, while girls fall behind in math when they get to high school. "Society can amplify differences like these or cover them up," says Gleason. "We rush in reading teachers to do remedial reading, and their classes are almost all boys. We don't talk about it, we just scurry around getting them to catch up to the girls. But where are the remedial math teachers? Girls are *supposed* to be less good at math, so that difference is incorporated into the way we live."

No matter where they stand on the question of biology versus culture, social scientists agree that the sexes are much more alike than they are different, and that variations within each sex are far greater than variations between the sexes. Even differences long taken for granted have begun to disappear. Janet Shibley Hyde, a professor of psychology at the University of Wisconsin, analyzed hundreds of studies on verbal and math ability and found boys and girls alike in verbal ability. In math, boys have a moderate edge; but only among highly precocious math students is the disparity large. Most important, Hyde found that verbal and math studies dating from the '60s and '70s showed greater differences than more recent research. "Parents may be making more efforts to tone down the stereotypes," she says. There's also what academics call "the file-drawer effect." "If you do a study that shows no differences, you assume it won't be published," says Claire Etaugh, professor of psychology at Bradley University in Peoria, Ill. "And until recently, you'd be right. So you just file it away."

The most famous gender differences in academics show up in the annual SAT results,

which do continue to favor boys. Traditionally they have excelled on the math portion, and since 1972 they have slightly outperformed girls on the verbal side as well. Possible explanations range from bias to biology, but the socioeconomic profile of those taking the test may also play a role. "The SAT gets a lot of publicity every year, but nobody points out that there are more women taking it than men, and the women come from less advantaged backgrounds," says Hyde. "The men are a more highly selected sample: they're better off in terms of parental income, father's education and attendance at private school."

Girls are encouraged to think about how their actions affect others . . .

2–3 YEARS

. . . boys often misbehave, get punished and then misbehave again

Another longstanding assumption does hold true: boys tend to be somewhat more active, according to a recent study, and the difference may even start prenatally. But the most vivid distinctions between the sexes don't surface until well into the preschool years. "If I showed you a hundred kids aged 2, and you couldn't tell the sex by the haircuts, you couldn't tell if they were boys or girls," says Harvard professor of psychology Jerome Kagan. Staff members at the Children's Museum in Boston say that the boys and girls racing through the exhibits are similarly active, similarly rambunctious and similarly interested in model cars and model kitchens, until they reach first grade or so. And at New York's Bank Street preschool, most of the 3-year-olds clustered around the cooking table to make banana bread one recent morning were boys. (It was a girl who gathered up three briefcases from the costume box and announced, "Let's go to work.")

By the age of 4 or 5, however, children start to embrace gender stereotypes with a determination that makes liberal-minded parents groan in despair. No matter how careful they may have been to correct the disparities in "Pat the Bunny" ("Paul isn't the *only* one who can play peekaboo, *Judy* can play peekaboo"), their children will delight in the traditional male/female distinctions preserved everywhere else: on television, in books, at day care and preschool, in the park and with friends. "One of the

things that is very helpful to children is to learn what their identity is," says Kyle Pruett, a psychiatrist at the Yale Child Study Center. "There are rules about being feminine and there are rules about being masculine. You can argue until the cows come home about whether those are good or bad societal influences, but when you look at the children, they love to know the differences. It solidifies who they are."

Water pistols: So girls play dolls, boys play Ghostbusters. Girls take turns at hopscotch, boys compete at football. Girls help Mommy, boys aim their water pistols at guests and shout, "You're dead!" For boys, notes Pruett, guns are an inevitable part of this developmental process, at least in a television-driven culture like our own. "It can be a cardboard paper towelholder, it doesn't have to be a miniature Uzi, but it serves as the focus for fantasies about the way he is going to make himself powerful in the world," he says. "Little girls have their aggressive side, too, but by the time they're socialized it takes a different form. The kinds of things boys work out with guns, girls work out in terms of relationships—with put-downs and social cruelty." As if to underscore his point, a 4-year-old at a recent Manhattan party turned to her young hostess as a small stranger toddled up to them. "Tell her we don't want to play with her," she commanded. "Tell her we don't like her."

No matter what their parents do, girls and boys will enthusiastically . . .

4–5 YEARS

. . . embrace the male/female stereotypes they find all around them

Once the girls know they're female and the boys know they're male, the powerful stereotypes that guided them don't just disappear. Whether they're bred into our chromosomes or ingested with our cornflakes, images of the aggressive male and the nurturant female are with us for the rest of our lives. "When we see a man with a child, we say, 'They're playing'," says Epstein. "We never say, 'He's nurturant'."

The case for biologically based gender differences is building up slowly, amid a great deal of academic dispute. The theory is that male and female brains, as well as bodies, develop differently according to the amount of testosterone circulating around the time of birth. Much of the evidence rests on animal studies showing, for instance, that brain cells from newborn mice change their shape when treated with testosterone. The male sex hormone may also account for the different reactions of male and female rhesus monkeys, raised in isolation, when an infant monkey is placed in the cage. The males are more likely to strike at the infant, the females to nurture it. Scientists disagree—vehemently—on whether animal behavior has human parallels. The most convincing human evidence comes from anthropology, where cross-cultural studies consistently find that while societies differ in their predilection toward violence, the males in any given society will act more aggressively than the females. "But it's very important to emphasize that by aggression we mean only physical violence," says Melvin Konner, a physician and anthropologist at Emory University in Atlanta. "With competitive, verbal or any other form of aggression, the evidence for gender differences doesn't hold." Empirical findings (i.e., look around you) indicate that women in positions of corporate, academic or political power can learn to wield it as aggressively as any man.

Apart from the fact that women everywhere give birth and care for children, there is surprisingly little evidence to support the notion that their biology makes women kinder, gentler people or even equips them specifically for motherhood. Philosophers—and mothers, too—have taken for granted the existence of a maternal "instinct" that research in female hormones has not conclusively proven. At most there may be a temporary hormonal response associated with childbirth that prompts females to nurture their young, but that doesn't explain women's near monopoly on changing diapers. Nor is it likely that a similar hormonal surge is responsible for women's tendency to organize the family's social life or take up the traditionally underpaid "helping" professions—nursing, teaching, social work.

Studies have shown that female newborns cry more readily than males in response to the cry of another infant, and that small girls try more often than boys to comfort or help their mothers when they appear distressed. But in general the results of most research into such traits as empathy and altruism do not consistently favor one sex or the other. There is one major exception: females of all ages seem better able to "read" people, to discern their emotions, without the help of verbal cues. (Typically researchers will display a picture of someone expressing a strong reaction and ask test-takers to identify the emotion.) Perhaps this skill—which in evolutionary terms would have helped females survive and protect their young—is

the sole biological foundation for our unshakable faith in female selflessness.

Infant ties: Those who explore the unconscious have had more success than other researchers in trying to account for male aggression and female nurturance, perhaps because their theories cannot be tested in a laboratory but are deemed "true" if they suit our intuitions. According to Nancy J. Chodorow, professor of sociology at Berkeley and the author of the influential book "The Reproduction of Mothering," the fact that both boys and girls are primarily raised by women has crucial effects on gender roles. Girls, who start out as infants identifying with their mothers and continue to do so, grow up defining themselves in relation to other people. Maintaining human connections remains vital to them. Boys eventually turn to their fathers for self-definition, but in order to do so must repress those powerful infant ties to mother and womanhood. Human connections thus become more problematic for them than for women. Chodorow's book, published in 1978, received national attention despite a dense, academic prose style; clearly, her perspective rang true to many.

Harvard's Kagan, who has been studying young children for 35 years, sees a different constellation of influences at work. He speculates that women's propensity for caretaking can be traced back to an early awareness of their role in nature. "Every girl knows, somewhere between the ages of 5 and 10, that she is different from boys and that she will have a child—something that everyone, including children, understands as quintessentially natural," he says. "If, in our society, nature stands for the giving of life, nurturance, help, affection, then the girl will conclude unconsciously that those are the qualities she should strive to attain. And the boy won't. And that's exactly what happens."

Kagan calls such gender differences "inevitable but not genetic," and he emphasizes—as does Chodorow—that they need have no implications for women's status, legally or occupationally. In the real world, of course, they have enormous implications. Even feminists who see gender differences as cultural artifacts agree that, if not inevitable, they're hard to shake. "The most emancipated families, who really feel they want to engage in gender-free behavior toward their kids, will still encourage boys to be boys and girls to be girls," says Epstein of CUNY. "Cultural constraints are acting on you all the time. If I go to buy a toy for a friend's little girl, I think to myself, why don't I buy her a truck? Well, I'm afraid the parents wouldn't like it. A makeup set would really go against my ideology, but maybe I'll buy some blocks. It's very hard. You have to be on the alert every second."

In fact, emancipated parents have to be on

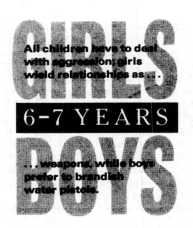

the alert from the moment their child is born. Beginning with the pink and blue name tags for newborns in the hospital nursery—I'M A GIRL/I'M A BOY—the gender-role juggernaut is overwhelming. Carol Z. Malatesta, associate professor of psychology at Long Island University in New York, notes that baby girls' eyebrows are higher above their eyes and that girls raise their eyebrows more than boys do, giving the girls "a more appealing, socially responsive look." Malatesta and her colleagues, who videotaped and coded the facial expressions on mothers and infants as they played, found that mothers displayed a wider range of emotional responses to girls than to boys. When the baby girls displayed anger, however, they met what seemed to be greater disapproval from their mothers than the boys did. These patterns, Malatesta suggests, may be among the reasons why baby girls grow up to smile more, to seem more sociable than males, and to possess the skill noted earlier in "reading" emotions.

The way parents discipline their toddlers also has an effect on social behavior later on. Judith G. Smetana, associate professor of education, psychology and pediatrics at the University of Rochester, found that mothers were more likely to deal differently with similar kinds of misbehavior depending on the sex of the child. If a little girl bit her friend and snatched a toy, for instance, the mother would explain why biting and snatching were unacceptable. If a boy did the same thing, his mother would be more likely to stop him, punish him and leave it at that. Misbehavior such as hitting in both sexes peaks around the age of 2; after that, little boys go on to misbehave more than girls.

Psychologists have known for years that boys are punished more than girls. Some have conjectured that boys simply drive their parents to distraction more quickly; but as Carolyn Zahn-Waxler, a psychologist at the National Institute of Mental Health, points out, the difference in parental treatment starts even before the difference in behavior shows up. "Girls receive very different messages than boys," she says. "Girls are encouraged to care about the problems of others, beginning very early. By elementary school, they're showing more caregiver behavior, and they have a wider social network."

Children also pick up gender cues in the process of learning to talk. "We compared fathers and mothers reading books to children," says Boston University's Gleason. "Both parents used more inner-state words, words about feelings and emotions, to girls than to boys. And by the age of 2, girls are using more emotion words than boys." According to Gleason, fathers tend to use more directives ("Bring that over here") and more threatening language with their sons than their daughters, while mothers' directives take more polite forms ("Could you bring that to me, please?"). The 4-year-old boys and girls in one study were duly imitating their fathers and mothers in that very conversational pattern. Studies of slightly older children found that boys talking among themselves use more threatening, commanding, dominating language than girls, while girls emphasize agreement and mutuality. Polite or not, however, girls get interrupted by their parents more often than boys, according to language studies—and women get interrupted more often than men.

Despite the ever-increasing complexity and detail of research on gender differences, the not-so-secret agenda governing the discussion hasn't changed in a century: how to understand women. Whether the question is brain size, activity levels or modes of punishing children, the traditional implication is that the standard of life is male, while the entity that needs explaining is female. (Or as an editor put it, suggesting possible titles for this article: "Why Girls Are Different.") Perhaps the time has finally come for a new agenda. Women, after all, are not a big problem. Our society does not suffer from burdensome amounts of empathy and altruism, or a plague of nurturance. The problem is men—or more accurately, maleness.

"There's one set of sex differences that's ineluctable, and that's the death statis-

tics," says Gleason. "Men are killing themselves doing all the things that our society wants them to do. At every age they're dying in accidents, they're being shot, they drive cars badly, they ride the tops of elevators, they're two-fisted hard drinkers. And violence against women is incredibly pervasive. Maybe it's men's raging hormones, but I think it's because they're trying to be a *man*. If I were the mother of a boy, I would be very concerned about societal pressures that idolize behaviors like that."

Studies of other cultures show that male behavior, while characteristically aggressive, need not be characteristically deadly. Harvard's Whiting, who has been analyzing children cross-culturally for half a century, found that in societies where boys as well as girls take care of younger siblings, boys as well as girls show nurturant, sociable behavior. "I'm convinced that infants elicit positive behavior from people," says Whiting. "If you have to take care of somebody who can't talk, you have to learn empathy. Of course there can be all kinds of experiences that make you extinguish that eliciting power, so that you no longer respond positively. But on the basis of our data, boys make very good baby tenders."

In our own society, evidence is emerging that fathers who actively participate in raising their children will be steering both sons and daughters toward healthier gender roles. For the last eight years Yale's Pruett has been conducting a groundbreaking longitudinal study of 16 families, representing a range of socioeconomic circumstances, in which the fathers take primary responsibility for child care while the mothers work full time. The children are now between 8 and 10 years old, and Pruett has watched subtle but important differences develop between them and their peers. "It's not that they have conflicts about their gender identity—the boys are masculine and the girls are feminine, they're all interested in the same things their friends are," he says. "But when they were 4 or 5, for instance, the stage at preschool when the boys leave the doll corner and the girls leave the block corner, these children didn't give up one or the other. The boys spent time playing with the girls in the doll corner, and the girls were building things with blocks, taking pride in their accomplishments."

Little footballs: Traditionally, Pruett notes, fathers have enforced sex stereotypes more strongly than mothers, engaging the boys in active play and complimenting the girls on their pretty dresses. "Not these fathers," says Pruett. "That went by the boards. They weren't interested in bringing home little

footballs for their sons or little tutus for the girls. They dealt with the kids according to the individual. I even saw a couple of the mothers begin to take over those issues—one of them brought home a Dallas Cowboys sleeper for her 18-month-old. Her husband said, 'Honey, I thought we weren't going to do this, remember?' She said, 'Do what?' So that may be more a function of being in the second tier of parenting rather than the first."

As a result of this loosening up of stereotypes, the children are more relaxed about gender roles. "I saw the boys really enjoy their nurturing skills," says Pruett. "They knew what to do with a baby, they didn't see that as a girl's job, they saw it as a human job. I saw the girls have very active images of the outside world and what their mothers were doing in the workplace—things that become interesting to most girls when they're 8 or 10, but these girls were interested when they were 4 or 5."

Pruett doesn't argue that fathers are better at mothering than mothers, simply that two involved parents are better than "one and a lump." And it's hardly necessary for fathers to quit their jobs in order to become more involved. A 1965-66 study showed that working mothers spent 50 minutes a day engaged primarily with their children, while the fathers spent 12 minutes. Later studies have found fathers in two-career households spending only about a third as much time with their children as mothers. What's more, Pruett predicts that fathers would benefit as much as children from the increased responsibility. "The more involved father tends to feel differently about his own life," he says. "A lot of men, if they're on the fast track, know a lot about competitive relationships, but they don't know much about intimate relationships. Children are experts in intimacy. After a while the wives in my study would say, 'He's just a nicer guy'."

Pruett's study is too small in scope to support major claims for personality development; he emphasizes that his findings are chiefly theoretical until more research can be undertaken. But right now he's watching a motif that fascinates him. "Every single one of these kids is growing something," he says. "They don't just plant a watermelon seed and let it die. They're really propagating things, they're doing salad-bowl starts in the backyard, they're breeding guinea pigs. That says worlds about what they think matters. Generativity is valued a great deal, when both your mother and your father say it's OK." Scientists may never agree on what divides the sexes; but someday, perhaps, our children will learn to relish what unites them.

GIRLS

When girls talk among themselves, they tend to emphasize mutuality . . .

9-10 YEARS

BOYS

. . . and agreement, while boys often try to command and dominate

Girls and Boys Together... But Mostly Apart: Gender Arrangements in Elementary Schools

Barrie Thorne

Michigan State University

Throughout the years of elementary school, children's friendships and casual encounters are strongly separated by sex. Sex segregation among children, which starts in preschool and is well established by middle childhood, has been amply documented in studies of children's groups and friendships (e.g., Eder & Hallinan, 1978; Schofield, 1981) and is immediately visible in elementary school settings. When children choose seats in classrooms or the cafeteria, or get into line, they frequently arrange themselves in same-sex clusters. At lunchtime, they talk matter-of-factly about "girls' tables" and "boys' tables." Playgrounds have gendered turfs, with some areas and activities, such as large playing fields and basketball courts, controlled mainly by boys, and others—smaller enclaves like jungle-gym areas and concrete spaces for hopscotch or jumprope—more often controlled by girls. Sex segregation is so common in elementary schools that it is meaningful to speak of separate girls' and boys' worlds.

Studies of gender and children's social relations have mostly followed this "two worlds" model, separately describing and comparing the subcultures of girls and of boys (e.g., Lever, 1976; Maltz & Borker, 1983). In brief summary: Boys tend to interact in larger, more age-heterogeneous groups (Lever, 1976; Waldrop & Halverson, 1975; Eder & Hallinan, 1978). They engage in more rough and tumble play and physical fighting (Maccoby & Jacklin, 1974). Organized sports are both a central activity and a major metaphor in boys' subcultures; they use the language of "teams" even when not engaged in sports, and they often construct interaction in the form of contests. The shifting hierarchies of boys' groups (Savin-Williams, 1976) are evident in their more frequent use of direct commands, insults, and challenges (Goodwin, 1980).

Fewer studies have been done of girls' groups (Foot, Chapman, & Smith, 1980; McRobbie & Garber, 1975), and—perhaps because categories for description and analysis have come more from male than female experience—researchers have had difficulty seeing and analyzing girls' social relations. Recent work has begun to correct this skew. In middle childhood, girls' worlds are less public than those of boys; girls more often interact in private places and in smaller groups or friendship pairs (Eder & Hallinan, 1978; Waldrop & Halverson, 1975). Their play is more cooperative and turn-taking (Lever, 1976). Girls have more intense and exclusive friendships, which take shape around keeping and telling secrets, shifting alliances, and indirect ways of expressing disagreement (Goodwin, 1980; Lever, 1976; Maltz & Borker, 1983). Instead of direct commands, girls more often use directives which merge speaker and hearer, e.g., "let's" or "we gotta" (Goodwin, 1980).

Although much can be learned by comparing the social organization and subcultures of boys' and of girls' groups, the separate worlds approach has eclipsed full, contextual understanding of gender and social relations among children. The separate worlds model essentially involves a search for group sex differences, and shares the limitations of individual sex difference research. Differences tend to be exaggerated and similarities ignored, with little theoretical attention to the integration of similarity and difference (Unger, 1979). Statistical findings of difference are often portrayed as dichotomous, neglecting the considerable individual variation that exists; for example, not all boys fight, and some have intense and exclusive friendships. The sex difference approach tends to abstract gender from its social context, to assume that males and females are qualitatively and permanently different (with differences perhaps unfolding through separate developmental lines). These assumptions mask the possibility that gender arrangements and patterns of similarity and difference may vary by situation, race, social class, region, or subculture.

Sex segregation is far from total, and is a more complex and dynamic process than the portrayal of separate worlds reveals. Erving Goffman (1977) has observed that sex segregation has a "with-then-apart" structure; the sexes segregate periodically, with separate spaces, rituals, groups, but they also come together and are, in crucial ways, part of the same world. This is certainly true in the social environment of elementary schools. Although girls and boys do interact as boundaried collectivities—an image suggested by the separate worlds approach—there are other occasions when they work or play in relaxed and integrated ways. Gender is less central to the organization and meaning of some situations than others. In short, sex segregation is not static, but is a variable and complicated process.

To gain an understanding of gender which can encompass both the "with" and the "apart" of sex segregation, analysis should start not with the individual, nor with a search for sex differences, but with social relationships. Gender should be conceptualized as a system of relationships rather than as an immutable and dichotomous given. Taking this approach, I have organized my research on gender and children's social relations around questions like the following: How and when does gender enter into group formation? In a given situation, how is gender made more or less salient or infused with particular meanings? By what rituals, processes, and forms of social organization and conflict do "with-then-apart" rhythms get enacted? How are these processes affected by the organization of institutions (e.g., different types of schools, neighborhoods, or summer camps), varied settings (e.g., the constraints and possibilities governing interaction on playgrounds vs. classrooms), and particular encounters?

METHODS AND SOURCES OF DATA

This study is based on two periods of participant observation. In 1976–1977 I observed for 8 months in a largely working-class elementary school in California, a school with 8% Black and 12% Chicano students. In 1980 I did fieldwork for 3 months in a Michigan elementary school of similar size (around 400 students), social class, and racial composition. I observed in several classrooms—a kindergarten, a second grade, and a combined fourth-fifth grade—and in school hallways, cafeterias, and playgrounds. I set out to follow the round of the school day as children experience it, recording their interactions with one another, and with adults, in varied settings.

Participant observation involves gaining access to everyday, "naturalistic" settings and taking systematic notes over an extended period of time. Rather than starting with preset categories for recording, or with fixed hypotheses for testing, participant-observers record detail in ways which maximize opportunities for discovery. Through continuous interaction between observation and analysis, "grounded theory" is developed (Glaser & Strauss, 1967).

The distinctive logic and discipline of this mode of inquiry emerges from: (1) theoretical sampling—being relatively systematic in the choice of where and whom to observe in order to maximize knowledge relevant to categories and analysis which are being developed; and (2) comparing all relevant data on a given point in order to modify emerging propositions to take account of discrepant cases (Katz, 1983). Participant observation is a flexible, open-ended and inductive method, designed to understand behavior within, rather than stripped from, social context. It provides richly detailed information which is anchored in everyday meanings and experience.

DAILY PROCESSES OF SEX SEGREGATION

Sex segregation should be understood not as a given, but as the result of deliberate activity. The outcome is dramatically visible when there are separate girls' and boys' tables in school lunchrooms, or sex-separated groups on playgrounds. But in the same lunchroom one can also find tables where girls and boys eat and talk together, and in some playground activities the sexes mix. By what processes do girls and boys separate into gender-defined and relatively boundaried collectivities? And in what contexts, and through what processes, do boys and girls interact in less gender-divided ways?

In the school settings I observed, much segregation happened with no mention of gender. Gender was implicit in the contours of friendship, shared interest, and perceived risk which came into play when children chose companions—in their prior planning, invitations, seeking-of-access, saving-of-places, denials of entry, and allowing or protesting of "cuts" by those who violated the rules for lining up. Sometimes children formed mixed-sex groups for play, eating, talking, working on a classroom project, or moving through space. When adults or children explicitly invoked gender—and this was nearly always in ways which separated girls and boys—boundaries were heightened and mixed-sex interaction became an explicit arena of risk.

In the schools I studied, the physical space and curricula were not formally divided by sex, as they have been in the history of elementary schooling (a history evident in separate entrances to old school buildings, where the words "Boys" and "Girls" are permanently etched in concrete). Nevertheless, gender was a visible marker in the adult-organized school day. In both schools, when the public address system sounded, the principal inevitably opened with: "Boys and girls...," and in addressing clusters of children, teachers and aides regularly used gender terms ("Heads down, girls"; "The girls are ready and the boys aren't"). These forms of address made gender visible and salient, conveying an assumption that the sexes are separate social groups.

Teachers and aides sometimes drew upon gender as a basis for sorting children and organizing activities. Gender is an embodied and visual social category which roughly divides the population in half, and the separation of girls and boys permeates the history and lore of schools and playgrounds. In both schools—although through awareness of Title IX, many teachers had changed this practice—one could see separate girls' and boys' lines moving, like caterpillars, through the school halls. In the 4th-5th grade classroom the teacher frequently pitted girls against boys for spelling and math contests. On the playground in the Michigan school, aides regarded the space close to the building as girls' territory, and the playing fields "out there" as boys' territory. They sometimes shooed children of the other sex away from those spaces, especially boys who ventured near the girls' area and seemed to have teasing in mind.

In organizing their activities, both within and apart from the surveillance of adults, children also explicitly invoked gender. During my fieldwork in the Michigan school, I kept daily records of who sat where in the lunchroom. The amount of sex segregation varied: It was least at the first grade tables and almost total among sixth graders. There was also variation from classroom to classroom within a given age, and from day to day. Actions like the following heightened the gender divide:

> In the lunchroom, when the two second grade tables were filling, a high-status boy walked by the inside table, which had a scattering of both boys and girls, and said loudly, "Oooo, too many girls," as he headed for a seat at the far table. The boys at the inside table picked up their trays and moved, and no other boys sat at the inside table, which the pronouncement had effectively made taboo.

In the end, that day (which was not the case every day), girls and boys ate at separate tables.

Eating and walking are not sex-typed activities, yet in forming groups in lunchrooms and hallways children often separated by sex. Sex segregation assumed added dimensions on the playground, where spaces, equipment, and activities were infused with gender meanings. My inventories of activities and groupings on the playground showed similar patterns in both schools: Boys controlled the large fixed spaces designated for team sports (baseball diamonds, grassy fields used for football or soccer); girls more often played

closer to the building, doing tricks on the monkey bars (which, for 6th graders, became an area for sitting and talking) and using cement areas for jumprope, hopscotch, and group games like four-square. (Lever, 1976, provides a good analysis of sex-divided play.) Girls and boys most often played together in kickball, and in group (rather than team) games like four-square, dodgeball, and handball. When children used gender to exclude others from play, they often drew upon beliefs connecting boys to some activities and girls to others:

> A first grade boy avidly watched an all-female game of jump rope. When the girls began to shift positions, he recognized a means of access to the play and he offered, "I'll swing it." A girl responded, "No way, you don't know how to do it, to swing it. You gotta be a girl." He left without protest.

Although children sometimes ignored pronouncements about what each sex could or could not do, I never heard them directly challenge such claims.

When children had explicitly defined an activity or a group as gendered, those who crossed the boundary—especially boys who moved into female-marked space—risked being teased. ("Look! Mike's in the girls' line!"; "'That's a girl over there,' a girl said loudly, pointing to a boy sitting at an otherwise all-female table in the lunchroom.") Children, and occasionally adults, used teasing—especially the tease of "liking" someone of the other sex, or of "being" that sex by virtue of being in their midst—to police gender boundaries. Much of the teasing drew upon heterosexual romantic definitions, making cross-sex interaction risky, and increasing social distance between boys and girls.

RELATIONSHIPS BETWEEN THE SEXES

Because I have emphasized the "apart" and ignored the occasions of "with," this analysis of sex segregation falsely implies that there is little contact between girls and boys in daily school life. In fact, relationships between girls and boys—which should be studied as fully as, and in connection with, same-sex relationships—are of several kinds:

1. "Borderwork," or forms of cross-sex interaction which are based upon and reaffirm boundaries and asymmetries between girls' and boys' groups;
2. Interactions which are infused with heterosexual meanings;
3. Occasions where individuals cross gender boundaries to participate in the world of the other sex; and
4. Situations where gender is muted in salience, with girls and boys interacting in more relaxed ways.

Borderwork

In elementary school settings boys' and girls' groups are sometimes spatially set apart. Same-sex groups sometimes claim fixed territories such as the basketball court, the bars, or specific lunchroom tables. However, in the crowded, multi-focused, and adult-controlled environment of the school, groups form and disperse at a rapid rate and can never stay totally apart. Contact between girls and boys sometimes lessens sex segregation, but gender-defined groups also come together in ways which emphasize their boundaries.

"Borderwork" refers to interaction across, yet based upon and even strengthening gender boundaries. I have drawn this notion from Fredrik Barth's (1969) analysis of social relations which are maintained across ethnic boundaries with-out diminishing dichotomized ethnic status.[1] His focus is on more macro, ecological arrangements; mine is on face-to-face behavior. But the insight is similar: Groups may interact in ways which strengthen their borders, and the maintenance of ethnic (or gender) groups can best be understood by examining the boundary that defines the group, "not the cultural stuff that it encloses" (Barth, 1969, p. 15). In elementary schools there are several types of borderwork: contests or games where gender-defined teams compete; cross-sex rituals of chasing and pollution; and group invasions. These interactions are asymmetrical, challenging the separate-but-parallel model of "two worlds."

Contests

Boys and girls are sometimes pitted against each other in classroom competitions and playground games. The 4th-5th grade classroom had a boys' side and a girls' side, an arrangement that re-emerged each time the teacher asked children to choose their own desks. Although there was some within-sex shuffling, the result was always a spatial moiety system—boys on the left, girls on the right—with the exception of one girl (the "tomboy" whom I'll describe later), who twice chose a desk with the boys and once with the girls. Drawing upon and reinforcing the children's self-segregation, the teacher often pitted the boys against the girls in spelling and math competitions, events marked by cross-sex antagonism and within-sex solidarity:

> The teacher introduced a math game; she would write addition and subtraction problems on the board, and a member of each team would race to be the first to write the correct answer. She wrote two score-keeping columns on the board: 'Beastly Boys' . . . 'Gossipy Girls.' The boys yelled out, as several girls laughed, 'Noisy girls! Gruesome girls!' The girls sat in a row on top of their desks; sometimes they moved collectively, pushing their hips or whispering 'pass it on.' The boys stood along the wall, some reclining against desks. When members of either group came back victorious from the front of the room, they would do the 'giving five' hand-slapping ritual with their team members.

On the playground a team of girls occasionally played against a team of boys, usually in kickball or team two-square. Sometimes these games proceeded matter-of-factly, but if gender became the explicit basis

of team solidarity, the interaction changed, becoming more antagonistic and unstable:

> Two fifth-grade girls played against two fifth-grade boys in a team game of two-square. The game proceeded at an even pace until an argument ensued about whether the ball was out or on the line. Karen, who had hit the ball, became annoyed, flashed her middle finger at the other team, and called to a passing girl to join their side. The boys then called out to other boys, and cheered as several arrived to play. 'We got five and you got three!' Jack yelled. The game continued, with the girls yelling, 'Bratty boys! Sissy boys!' and the boys making noises— 'weee haw' 'ha-ha-ha'-as they played.

Chasing

Cross-sex chasing dramatically affirms boundaries between girls and boys. The basic elements of chase and elude, capture and rescue (Sutton-Smith, 1971) are found in various kinds of tag with formal rules, and in informal episodes of chasing which punctuate life on playgrounds. These episodes begin with a provocation (taunts like "You can't get me!" or "Slobber monster!"; bodily pokes or the grabbing of possessions). A provocation may be ignored, or responded to by chasing. Chaser and chased may then alternate roles. In an ethnographic study of chase sequences on a school playground, Christine Finnan (1982) observes that chases vary in number of chasers to chased (e.g., one chasing one, or five chasing two); form of provocation (a taunt or a poke); outcome (an episode may end when the chased outdistances the chaser, or with a brief touch, being wrestled to the ground, or the recapturing of a hat or a ball); and in use of space (there may or may not be safety zones).

Like Finnan (1982), and Sluckin (1981), who studied a playground in England, I found that chasing has a gendered structure. Boys frequently chase one another, an activity which often ends in wrestling and mock fights. When girls chase girls, they are usually less physically aggressive; they less often, for example, wrestle one another to the ground.

Cross-sex chasing is set apart by special names— "girls chase the boys"; "boys chase the girls"; "the chase"; "chasers"; "chase and kiss"; "kiss chase"; "kissers and chasers"; "kiss or kill"—and by children's animated talk about the activity. The names vary by region and school, but contain both gender and sexual meanings (this form of play is mentioned, but only briefly analzyed, in Finnan, 1981; Sluckin, 1981; Parrott, 1972; and Borman, 1979).

In "boys chase the girls" and "girls chase the boys" (the names most frequently used in both the California and Michigan schools) boys and girls become, by definition, separate teams. Gender terms override individual identities, especially for the other team ("Help, a girl's chasin' me!"; "C'mon Sarah, let's get that boy"; "Tony, help save me from the girls"). Individuals may call for help from, or offer help to, others of their sex. They may also grab someone of their sex and turn them over to the opposing team: "Ryan grabbed Billy from behind, wrestling him to the ground 'Hey girls, get 'im,' Ryan called."

Boys more often mix episodes of cross-sex with same-sex chasing. Girls more often have safety zones, places like the girls' restroom or an area by the school wall, where they retreat to rest and talk (sometimes in animated postmortems) before new episodes of cross-sex chasing begin.

Early in the fall in the Michigan school, where chasing was especially prevalent, I watched a second grade boy teach a kindergarten girl how to chase. He slowly ran backwards, beckoning her to pursue him, as he called, "Help, a girl's after me." In the early grades chasing mixes with fantasy play, e.g., a first-grade boy who played "sea monster," his arms outflung and his voice growling, as he chased a group of girls. By third grade, stylized gestures—exaggerated stalking motions, screams (which only girls do), and karate kicks—accompany scenes of chasing.

Names like "chase and kiss" mark the sexual meanings of cross-sex chasing, a theme I return to later. The threat of kissing—most often girls threatening to kiss boys—is a ritualized form of provocation. Cross-sex chasing among sixth graders involves elaborate patterns of touch and touch avoidance, which adults see as sexual. The principal told the sixth graders in the Michigan school that they were not to play "pom-pom," a complicated chasing game, because it entailed "inappropriate touch."

Rituals of Pollution

Cross-sex chasing is sometimes entwined with rituals of pollution, as in "cooties," where specific individuals or groups are treated as contaminating or carrying "germs." Children have rituals for transfering cooties (usually touching someone else and shouting "You've got cooties!"), for immunization (e.g., writing "CV" for "cootie vaccination" on their arms), and for eliminating cooties (e.g., saying "no gives" or using "cootie catchers" made of folded paper) (described in Knapp & Knapp, 1976). While girls may give cooties to girls, boys do not generally give cooties to one another (Samuelson, 1980).

In cross-sex play, either girls or boys may be defined as having cooties, which they transfer through chasing and touching. Girls give cooties to boys more often than vice versa. In Michigan, one version of cooties is called "girl stain"; the fourth-graders whom Karkau, 1973, describes, used the phrase "girl touch." "Cootie queens," or "cootie girls" (there are no "kings" or "boys") are female pariahs, the ultimate school untouchables, seen as contaminating not only by virtue of gender, but also through some added stigma such as being overweight or poor.[2] That girls are seen as more polluting than boys is a significant asymmetry, which echoes cross-cultural patterns, although in other cultures female pollution is generally connected to menstruation, and not applied to prepubertal girls.

Invasions

Playground invasions are another asymmetric form of borderwork. On a few occasions I saw girls invade and disrupt an all-male game, most memorably a group of tall sixth-grade girls who ran onto the playing field and grabbed a football which was in play. The boys were surprised and frustrated, and, unusual for boys this old, finally tattled to the aide. But in the majority of cases, boys disrupt girls' activities rather than vice versa. Boys grab the ball from girls playing four-square, stick feet into a jumprope and stop an ongoing game, and dash through the area of the bars, where girls are taking turns performing, sending the rings flying. Sometimes boys ask to join a girls' game and then, after a short period of seemingly earnest play, disrupt the game:

> Two second-grade boys begged to "twirl" the jumprope for a group of second-grade girls who had been jumping for some time. The girls agreed, and the boys began to twirl. Soon, without announcement, the boys changed from "seashells, cockle bells'" to "hot peppers" (spinning the rope very fast), and tangled the jumper in the rope. The boys ran away laughing.

Boys disrupt girls' play so often that girls have developed almost ritualized responses: They guard their ongoing play, chase boys away, and tattle to the aides. In a playground cycle which enhances sex segregation, aides who try to spot potential trouble before it occurs sometimes shoo boys away from areas where girls are playing. Aides do not anticipate trouble from girls who seek to join groups of boys, with the exception of girls intent on provoking a chase sequence. And indeed, if they seek access to a boys' game, girls usually play with boys in earnest rather than breaking up the game.

A close look at the organization of borderwork—or boundaried interactions between the sexes—shows that the worlds of boys and girls may be separate, but they are not parallel, nor are they equal. The worlds of girls and boys articulate in several asymmetric ways:

1. On the playground, boys control as much as ten times more space than girls, when one adds up the area of large playing fields and compares it with the much smaller areas where girls predominate. Girls, who play closer to the building, are more often watched over and protected by the adult aides.

2. Boys invade all-female games and scenes of play much more than girls invade boys. This, and boys' greater control of space, correspond with other findings about the organization of gender, and inequality, in our society: compared with men and boys, women and girls take up less space, and their space, and talk, are more often violated and interrupted (Greif, 1982; Henley, 1977; West & Zimmerman, 1983).

3. Although individual boys are occasionally treated as contaminating (e.g., a third grade boy who both boys and girls said was "stinky" and "smelled like pee"), girls are more often defined as polluting. This pattern ties to themes that I discuss later: It is more taboo for a boy to play with (as opposed to invade) girls, and girls are more sexually defined than boys.

A look at the boundaries between the separated worlds of girls and boys illuminates within-sex hierarchies of status and control. For example, in the sex-divided seating in the 4th-5th grade classroom, several boys recurringly sat near "female space": their desks were at the gender divide in the classroom, and they were more likely than other boys to sit at a predominantly female table in the lunchroom. These boys—two nonbilingual Chicanos and an overweight "loner" boy who was afraid of sports—were at the bottom of the male hierarchy. Gender is sometimes used as a metaphor for male hierarchies; the inferior status of boys at the bottom is conveyed by calling them "girls":

> Seven boys and one girl were playing basketball. Two younger boys came over and asked to play. While the girl silently stood, fully accepted in the company of players, one of the older boys disparagingly said to the younger boys, 'You girls can't play.'[3]

In contrast, the girls who more often travel in the boys' world, sitting with groups of boys in the lunchroom or playing basketball, soccer, and baseball with them, are not stigmatized. Some have fairly high status with other girls. The worlds of girls and boys are assymetrically arranged, and spatial patterns map out interacting forms of inequality.

Heterosexual Meanings

The organization and meanings of gender (the social categories "woman/man," "girl/boy") and of sexuality vary cross-culturally (Ortner & Whitehead, 1981)—and, in our society, across the life course. Harriet Whitehead (1981) observed that in our (Western) gender system, and that of many traditional North American Indian cultures, one's choice of a sexual object, occupation, and one's dress and demeanor are closely associated with gender. However, the "center of gravity" differs in the two gender systems. For Indians, occupational pursuits provide the primary imagery of gender; dress and demeanor are secondary, and sexuality is least important. In our system, at least for adults, the order is reversed: heterosexuality is central to our definitions of "man" and "woman" ("masculinity"/"femininity"), and the relationships that obtain between them, whereas occupation and dress/demeanor are secondary.

Whereas erotic orientation and gender are closely linked in our definitions of adults, we define children as relatively asexual. Activities and dress/demeanor are more important than sexuality in the cultural meanings of "girl" and "boy." Children are less heterosexually defined than adults, and we have nonsexual imagery for relations between girls and boys. However, both children and adults sometimes use heterosexual language—"crushes," "like," "goin' with," "girlfriends," and "boyfriends"—to define cross-sex relationships. This language increases through the years of elementary school; the shift to adolescence consolidates a gender system organized around the institution of heterosexuality.

In everyday life in the schools, heterosexual and romantic meanings infuse some ritualized forms of interaction between groups of boys and girls (e.g., "chase and kiss") and help maintain sex segregation. "Jimmy likes Beth" or "Beth likes Jimmy" is a major form of teasing, which a child risks in choosing to sit by or walk with someone of the other sex. The structure of teasing, and children's sparse vocabulary for relationships between girls and boys, are evident in the following conversation which I had with a group of third-grade girls in the lunchroom:

> Susan asked me what I was doing, and I said I was observing the things children do and play. Nicole volunteered, 'I like running, boys chase all the girls. See Tim over there? Judy chases him all around the school. She likes him.' Judy, sitting across the table, quickly responded, 'I hate him. I like him for a friend.' 'Tim loves Judy,' Nicole said in a loud, sing-song voice.

In the younger grades, the culture and lore of girls contains more heterosexual romantic themes than that of boys. In Michigan, the first-grade girls often jumped rope to a rhyme which began: "Down in the valley where the green grass grows, there sat Cindy (name of jumper), as sweet as a rose. She sat, she sat, she sat so sweet. Along came Jason, and kissed her on the cheek . . . first comes love, then comes marriage, then along comes Cindy with a baby carriage. . . . Before a girl took her turn at jumping, the chanters asked her "Who do you want to be your boyfriend?" The jumper always preferred a name, which was accepted matter-of-factly. In chasing, a girl's kiss carried greater threat than a boy's kiss; "girl touch," when defined as contaminating, had sexual connotations. In short, starting at an early age, girls are more sexually defined than boys.

Through the years of elementary school, and increasing with age, the idiom of heterosexuality helps maintain the gender divide. Cross-sex interactions, especially when children initiate them, are fraught with the risk of being teased about "liking" someone of the other sex. I learned of several close cross-sex friendships, formed and maintained in neighborhoods and church, which went underground during the school day.

By the fifth grade a few children began to affirm, rather than avoid, the charge of having a girlfriend or a boyfriend; they introduced the heterosexual courtship rituals of adolescence:

In the lunchroom in the Michigan school, as the tables were forming, a high-status fifth-grade boy called out from his seat at the table: 'I want Trish to sit by me.' Trish came over, and almost like a king and queen, they sat at the gender divide—a row of girls down the table on her side, a row of boys on his.

In this situation, which inverted earlier forms, it was not a loss, but a gain in status to publically choose a companion of the other sex. By affirming his choice, the boy became unteasable (note the familiar asymmetry of heterosexual courtship rituals: the male initiated). This incident signals a temporal shift in arrangements of sex and gender.

Traveling in the World of the Other Sex

Contests, invasions, chasing, and heterosexually-defined encounters are based upon and reaffirm boundaries between girls and boys. In another type of cross-sex interaction, individuals (or sometimes pairs) cross gender boundaries, seeking acceptance in a group of the other sex. Nearly all the cases I saw of this were tomboys—girls who played organized sports and frequently sat with boys in the cafeteria or classroom. If these girls were skilled at activities central in the boys' world, especially games like soccer, baseball, and basketball, they were pretty much accepted as participants.

Being a tomboy is a matter of degree. Some girls seek access to boys' groups but are excluded; other girls limit their "crossing" to specific sports. Only a few—such as the tomboy I mentioned earlier, who chose a seat with the boys in the sex-divided fourth-fifth grade—participate fully in the boys' world. That particular girl was skilled at the various organized sports which boys played in different seasons of the year. She was also adept at physical fighting and at using the forms of arguing, insult, teasing, naming, and sports-talk of the boys' subculture. She was the only Black child in her classroom, in a school with only 8% Black students; overall that token status, along with unusual athletic and verbal skills, may have contributed to her ability to move back and forth across the gender divide. Her unique position in the children's world was widely recognized in the school. Several times, the teacher said to me, "She thinks she's a boy."

I observed only one boy in the upper grades (a fourth grader) who regularly played with all-female groups, as opposed to "playing at" girls' games and seeking to disrupt them. He frequently played jumprope and took turns with girls doing tricks on the bars, using the small gestures—for example, a helpful push on the heel of a girl who needed momentum to turn her body around the bar—which mark skillful and earnest participation. Although I never saw him play in other than an earnest spirit, the girls often chased him away from their games, and both girls and boys teased him. The fact that girls seek, and have more access to boys'

worlds than vice versa, and the fact that girls who travel with the other sex are less stigmatized for it, are obvious asymmetries, tied to the asymmetries previously discussed.

Relaxed Cross-Sex Interactions

Relationships between boys and girls are not always marked by strong boundaries, heterosexual definitions, or by interacting on the terms and turfs of the other sex. On some occasions girls and boys interact in relatively comfortable ways. Gender is not strongly salient nor explicitly invoked, and girls and boys are not organized into boundaried collectivities. These "with" occasions have been neglected by those studying gender and children's relationships, who have emphasized either the model of separate worlds (with little attention to their articulation) or heterosexual forms of contact.

Occasions where boys and girls interact without strain, where gender wanes, rather than waxes in importance, frequently have one or more of the following characteristics:

1. The situations are organized around an absorbing task, such as a group art project or creating a radio show, which encourages cooperation and lessens attention to gender. This pattern accords with other studies finding that cooperative activities reduce group antagonism (e.g., Sherif & Sherif, 1953, who studied divisions between boys in a summer camp; and Aronson et al., 1978, who used cooperative activities to lessen racial divisions in a classroom).

2. Gender is less prominent when children are not responsible for the formation of the group. Mixed-sex play is less frequent in games like football, which require the choosing of teams, and more frequent in games like handball or dodgeball which individuals can join simply by getting into a line or a circle. When adults organize mixed-sex encounters—which they frequently do in the classroom and in physical education periods on the playground—they legitimize cross-sex contact. This removes the risk of being teased for choosing to be with the other sex.

3. There is more extensive and relaxed cross-sex interaction when principles of grouping other than gender are explicitly invoked—for example, counting off to form teams for spelling or kickball, dividing lines by hot lunch or cold lunch, or organizing a work group on the basis of interests or reading ability.

4. Girls and boys may interact more readily in less public and crowded settings. Neighborhood play, depending on demography, is more often sex and age integrated than play at school, partly because with fewer numbers, one may have to resort to an array of social categories to find play partners or to constitute a game. And in less crowded environments there are fewer potential witnesses to "make something of it" if girls and boys play together.

Relaxed interactions between girls and boys often depend on adults to set up and legitimize the contact.[4] Perhaps because of this contingency—and the other, distancing patterns which permeate relations between girls and boys—the easeful moments of interaction rarely build to close friendship. Schofield (1981) makes a similar observation about gender and racial barriers to friendship in a junior high school.

IMPLICATIONS FOR DEVELOPMENT

I have located social relations within an essentially spatial framework, emphasizing the organization of children's play, work, and other activities within specific settings, and in one type of institution, the school. In contrast, frameworks of child development rely upon temporal metaphors, using images of growth and transformation over time. Taken alone, both spatial and temporal frameworks have shortcomings; fitted together, they may be mutually correcting.

Those interested in gender and development have relied upon conceptualizations of "sex role socialization" and "sex differences." Sexuality and gender, I have argued, are more situated and fluid than these individualist and intrinsic models imply. Sex and gender are differently organized and defined across situations, even within the same institution. This situational variation (e.g., in the extent to which an encounter heightens or lessens gender boundaries, or is infused with sexual meanings) shapes and constrains individual behavior. Features which a developmental perspective might attribute to individuals, and understand as relatively internal attributes unfolding over time, may, in fact, be highly dependent on context. For example, children's avoidance of cross-sex friendship may be attributed to individual gender development in middle-childhood. But attention to varied situations may show that this avoidance is contingent on group size, activity, adult behavior, collective meanings, and the risk of being teased.

A focus on social organization and situation draws attention to children's experiences in the present. This helps correct a model like "sex role socialization" which casts the present under the shadow of the future, or presumed "endpoints" (Speier, 1976). A situated analysis of arrangements of sex and gender among those of different ages may point to crucial disjunctions in the life course. In the fourth and fifth grades, culturally defined heterosexual rituals ("goin' with") begin to suppress the presence and visibility of other types of interaction between girls and boys, such as nonsexualized and comfortable interaction, and traveling in the world of the other sex. As "boyfriend/girlfriend" definitions spread, the fifth-grade tomboy I described had to work to sustain "buddy" relationships with boys. Adult women who were tomboys often speak of early adolescence as a painful time when they were pushed away from participation in boys' activities. Other adult women speak of the loss of intense, even erotic ties with other girls when they entered puberty and the rituals of dating, that is, when they became absorbed into the institution of heterosexuality (Rich, 1980). When Lever (1976) describes best-friend relationships among fifth-grade girls as preparation for dating, she imposes heterosexual ideologies onto a present which should be understood on its own terms.

As heterosexual encounters assume more importance, they may alter relations in same-sex groups. For example, Schofield (1981) reports that for sixth- and seventh-grade children in a middle school, the popularity of girls with other girls was affected by their popularity with boys, while boys' status with other boys did not depend on their relations with girls. This is an asymmetry familiar from the adult world; men's relationships with one another are defined through varied activities (occupations, sports), while relationships among women—and their public status—are more influenced by their connections to individual men.

A full understanding of gender and social relations should encompass cross-sex as well as within-sex interactions. "Borderwork" helps maintain separate, gender-linked subcultures, which, as those interested in development have begun to suggest, may result in different milieux for learning. Daniel Maltz and Ruth Borker (1983) for example, argue that because of different interactions within girls' and boys' groups, the sexes learn different rules for creating and interpreting friendly conversation, rules which carry into adulthood and help account for miscommunication between men and women. Carol Gilligan (1982) fits research on the different worlds of girls and boys into a theory of sex differences in moral development. Girls develop a style of reasoning, she argues, which is more personal and relational; boys develop a style which is more positional, based on separateness. Eleanor Maccoby (1982), also following the insight that because of sex segregation, girls and boys grow up in different environments, suggests implications for gender differentiated prosocial and antisocial behavior.

This separate worlds approach, as I have illustrated, also has limitations. The occasions when the sexes are together should also be studied, and understood as contexts for experience and learning. For example, assymetries in cross-sex relationships convey a series of messages: that boys are more entitled to space and to the nonreciprocal right of interrupting or invading the activities of the other sex; that girls are more in need of adult protection, and are lower in status, more defined by sexuality, and may even be polluting. Different types of cross-sex interaction—relaxed, boundaried, sexualized, or taking place on the terms of the other sex—provide different contexts for development.

By mapping the array of relationships between and within the sexes, one adds complexity to the overly static and dichotomous imagery of separate worlds. Individual experiences vary, with implications for development. Some children prefer same-sex groupings; some are more likely to cross the gender boundary and participate in the world of the other sex; some children (e.g., girls and boys who frequently play "chase and kiss") invoke heterosexual meanings, while others avoid them.

Finally, after charting the terrain of relationships, one can trace their development over time. For example, age variation in the content and form of borderwork, or of cross- and same-sex touch, may be related to differing cognitive, social, emotional, or physical capacities, as well as to age-associated cultural forms. I earlier mentioned temporal shifts in the organization of cross-sex chasing, from mixing with fantasy play in the early grades to more elaborately ritualized and sexualized forms by the sixth grade. There also appear to be temporal changes in same and cross-sex touch. In kindergarten, girls and boys touch one another more freely than in fourth grade, when children avoid relaxed cross-sex touch and instead use pokes, pushes, and other forms of mock violence, even when the touch clearly couches affection. This touch taboo is obviously related to the risk of seeming to *like* someone of the other sex. In fourth grade, same-sex touch begins to signal sexual meanings among boys, as well as between boys and girls. Younger boys touch one another freely in cuddling (arm around shoulder) as well as mock violence ways. By fourth grade, when homophobic taunts like "fag" become more common among boys, cuddling touch begins to disappear for boys, but less so for girls.

Overall, I am calling for more complexity in our conceptualizations of gender and of children's social relationships. Our challenge is to retain the temporal sweep, looking at individual and group lives as they unfold over time, while also attending to social structure and context, and to the full variety of experiences in the present.

ACKNOWLEDGMENT

I would like to thank Jane Atkinson, Nancy Chodorow, Arlene Daniels, Peter Lyman, Zick Rubin, Malcolm Spector, Avril Thorne, and Margery Wolf for comments on an earlier version of this paper. Conversations with Zella Luria enriched this work.

NOTES

1. I am grateful to Frederick Erickson for suggesting the relevance of Barth's analysis.

2. Sue Samuelson (1980) reports that in a racially mixed playground in Fresno, California, Mexican-American, but not Anglo children gave cooties. Racial, as well as sexual inequality, may be expressed through these forms.

3. This incident was recorded by Margaret Blume, who, for an undergraduate research project in 1982, observed in the California school where I earlier did fieldwork. Her observations and insights enhanced my own, and I would like to thank her for letting me cite this excerpt.

4. Note that in daily school life, depending on the individual and the situation, teachers and aides sometimes lessened, and at other times heightened, sex segregation.

REFERENCES

Aronson, E. et al. (1978). *The jigsaw classroom.* Beverly Hills, CA: Sage.

Barth, F. (Ed.). (1969). *Ethnic groups and boundaries.* Boston: Little, Brown.

Borman, K. M. (1979). Children's interactions in playgrounds. *Theory into Practice, 18,* 251–257.

Eder, D., & Hallinan, M. T. (1978). Sex differences in children's friendships. *American Sociological Review, 43,* 237–250.

Finnan, C. R. (1982). The ethnography of children's spontaneous play. In G. Spindler (Ed.), *Doing the ethnography of schooling* (pp. 358–380). New York: Holt, Rinehart & Winston.

Foot, H. C., Chapman, A. J., & Smith, J. R. (1980). Introduction. *Friendship and social relations in children* (pp. 1–14). New York: Wiley.

Gilligan, C. (1982). *In a different voice: Psychological theory and women's development.* Cambridge, MA: Harvard University Press.

Glaser, B. G., & Strauss, A. L. (1967). *The discovery of grounded theory.* Chicago: Aldine.

Goffman, E. (1977). The arrangement between the sexes. *Theory and Society, 4,* 301–336.

Goodwin, M. H. (1980). Directive-response speech sequences in girls' and boys' task activities. In S. McConnell-Ginet, R. Borker, & N. Furman (Eds.), *Women and language in literature and society* (pp. 157–173). New York: Praeger.

Greif, E. B. (1980). Sex differences in parent-child conversations. *Women's Studies International Quarterly, 3,* 253–258.

Henley. N. (1977). *Body politics: Power, sex, and nonverbal communication.* Englewood Cliffs, NJ: Prentice-Hall.

Karkau, K. (1973). *Sexism in the fourth grade.* Pittsburgh: KNOW, Inc. (pamphlet)

Katz, J. (1983). A theory of qualitative methodology: The social system of analytic fieldwork. In R. M. Emerson (Ed.), *Contemporary field research* (pp. 127–148). Boston: Little, Brown.

Knapp, M., & Knapp. H. (1976). *One potato, two potato: The secret education of American children.* New York: W. W. Norton.

Lever, J. (1976). Sex differences in the games children play. *Social Problems, 23,* 478–487.

Maccoby, E. (1982). *Social groupings in childhood: Their relationship to prosocial and antisocial behavior in boys and girls.* Paper presented at conference on The Development of Prosocial and Antisocial Behavior. Voss, Norway.

Maccoby, E., & Jacklin, C. (1974). *The psychology of sex differences.* CA: Stanford University Press.

Maltz, D. N., & Borker, R. A. (1983). A cultural approach to male-female miscommunication. In J. J. Gumperz (Ed.), *Language and social identity* (pp. 195–216). New York: Cambridge University Press.

McRobbie, A., & Garber, J. (1975). Girls and subcultures. In S. Hall and T. Jefferson (Eds.), *Resistance through rituals* (pp. 209–223). London: Hutchinson.

Ortner, S. B., & Whitehead, H. (1981). *Sexual meanings.* New York: Cambridge University Press.

Parrott, S. (1972). Games children play: Ethnography of a second-grade recess. In J. P. Spradley & D. W. McCurdy (Eds.), *The cultural experience* (pp. 206–219). Chicago: Science Research Associates.

Rich, A. (1980). Compulsory heterosexuality and lesbian existence. *Signs, 5,* 631–660.

Samuelson, S. (1980). The cooties complex. *Western Folklore, 39,* 198–210.

Savin-Williams, R. C. (1976). An ethologicai study of dominance formation and maintenance in a group of human adolescents. *Child Development, 47,* 972–979.

Schofield, J. W. (1981). Complementary and conflicting identities: Images and interaction in an interracial school. In S. R. Asher & J. M. Gottman (Eds.), *The development of children's friendships* (pp. 53–90). New York: Cambridge University Press.

Sherif, M., & Sherif, C. (1953). *Groups in harmony and tension.* New York: Harper.

Sluckin, A. (1981). *Growing up in the playground.* London: Routledge & Kegan Paul.

Speier, M. (1976). The adult ideological viewpoint in studies of childhood. In A. Skolnick (Ed.), *Rethinking childhood* (pp. 168–186). Boston: Little, Brown.

Sutton-Smith, B. (1971). A syntax for play and games. In R. E. Herron and B. Sutton-Smith (Eds.), *Child's Play* (pp. 298–307). New York: Wiley.

Unger, R. K. (1979). Toward a redefinition of sex and gender. *American Psychologist, 34,* 1085–1094.

Waldrop, M. F., & Halverson, C. F. (1975). Intensive and extensive peer behavior: Longitudinal and cross-sectional analysis. *Child Development, 46,* 19–26.

West, C., & Zimmerman, D. H. (1983). Small insults: A study of interruptions in cross-sex conversations between unacquainted persons. In B. Thorne, C. Kramarae, & N. Henley (Eds.), *Language, gender and society.* Rowley, MA: Newbury House.

Whitehead, H. (1981). The bow and the burden strap: A new look at institutionalized homosexuality in Native America. In S. B. Ortner & H. Whitehead (Eds.), *Sexual meanings* (pp. 80–115). New York: Cambridge University Press.

The Good, The Bad And The
DIFFERENCE

BARBARA KANTROWITZ

Like many children, Sara Newland loves animals. But unlike most youngsters, she has turned that love into activism. Five years ago, during a trip to the zoo, the New York City girl learned about the plight of endangered species, and decided to help. With the aid of her mother, Sara—then about 4 years old—baked cakes and cookies and sold them on the sidewalk near her apartment building. She felt triumphant when she raised $35, which she promptly sent in to the World Wildlife Fund.

A few weeks later, triumph turned into tears when the fund wrote Sara asking for more money. "She was devastated because she thought she had taken care of that problem," says Polly Newland, who then patiently told her daughter that there are lots of big problems that require continual help from lots of people. That explanation worked. Sara, now 9, has expanded her causes. Through her school, she helps out at an inner-city child-care center; she also regularly brings meals to homeless people in her neighborhood.

A sensitive parent can make all the difference in encouraging—or discouraging—a child's developing sense of morality and values. Psychologists say that not only are parents important as role models, they also have to be aware of a child's perception of the world at different ages and respond appropriately to children's concerns. "I think the capacity for goodness is there from the start," says Thomas Lickona, a professor of education at the State University of New York at Cortland and author of "Raising Good Children." But, he says, parents must nurture those instincts just as they help their children become good readers or athletes or musicians.

That's not an easy task these days. In the past, schools and churches played a key role in fostering moral development. Now, with religious influence in decline and schools wavering over

> **A sensitive parent is crucial in encouraging a child's sense of morality and values**
> ___

the way to teach values, parents are pretty much on their own. Other recent social trends have complicated the transmission of values. "We're raising a generation that is still groping for a good future direction," says psychologist William Damon, head of Brown University's education department. Many of today's parents were raised in the '60s, the age of permissiveness. Their children were born in the age of affluence, the '80s, when materialism was rampant. "It's an unholy combination," says Damon.

These problems may make parents feel they have no effect on how their children turn out. But many studies show that parents are still the single most important influence on their children. Lickona says that the adolescents most likely to follow their consciences rather than give in to peer pressure are those who grew up in "authoritative" homes, where rules are firm but clearly explained and justified—as opposed to "authoritarian" homes (where rules are laid down without explanation) or "permissive" homes.

The way a parent explains rules depends, of course, on the age of the child. Many adults assume that kids see right and wrong in grown-up terms. But what may be seen as "bad" behavior by an adult may not be bad in the child's eyes. For example, a young child may not know the difference between a fanciful tale and a lie, while older kids—past the age of 5—do know.

Many psychologists think that in children, the seeds of moral values are emotional, not intellectual. Such traits as empathy and guilt—observable in the very young—represent the beginning of what will later be a conscience. Even newborns respond to signs of distress in others. In a hospital nursery, for example, a bout of crying by one infant will trigger wailing all around. Research on children's attachment to their mothers shows that babies who are most secure (and those whose mothers are most responsive to their needs) later turn out to be leaders in

From *Newsweek*, Special Edition, Summer 1991, pp. 48-50. © 1991 by Newsweek, Inc. All rights reserved. Reprinted by permission.

school: self-directed and eager to learn. They are also most likely to absorb parental values.

The first modern researcher to describe the stages of a child's moral development was Swiss psychologist Jean Piaget. In his groundbreaking 1932 book, "The Moral Judgment of the Child," he described three overlapping phases of childhood, from 5 to 12. The first is the "morality of constraint" stage: children accept adult rules as absolutes. Then comes the "morality of cooperation," in which youngsters think of morality as equal treatment. Parents of siblings will recognize this as the "If he got a new Ninja Turtle, I want one, too," stage. In the third, kids can see complexity in moral situations. They can understand extenuating circumstances in which strict equality might not necessarily mean fairness ("He got a new Ninja Turtle, but I got to go to the ball game, so it's OK.")

Although Piaget's conclusions have been expanded by subsequent researchers, his work forms the basis for most current theories of moral development. In a study begun in the 1950s, Lawrence Kohlberg, a Harvard professor, used "moral dilemmas" to define six phases. He began with 50 boys who were 10, 13 and 16. Over the next 20 years, he asked them their reactions to carefully constructed dilemmas. The most famous concerns a man named Heinz, whose wife was dying of cancer. The boys were told, in part, that a drug that might save her was a form of radium discovered by the town pharmacist. But the pharmacist was charging 10 times the cost of manufacture for the drug and Heinz could not afford it—although he tried to borrow money from everyone he knew. Heinz begged the pharmacist to sell it more cheaply, but he refused. So Heinz, in desperation, broke into the store and stole the drug. Kohlberg asked his subjects: Did Heinz do the right thing? Why?

Kohlberg and others found that at the first stage, children base their answers simply on the likelihood of getting caught. As they get older, their reasons for doing the right thing become more complex. For example, Lickona says typical 5-year-olds want to stay out of trouble. Kids from 6 to 9 characteristically act out of self-interest; most 10- to 13-year-olds crave social approval. Many 15- to 19-year-olds have moved on to thinking about maintaining the social system and being responsible.

Over the years, educators have used these theories to establish new curricula at schools around the country that emphasize moral development. The Lab School, a private preschool in Houston, was designed by Rheta DeVries, a student of Kohlberg's. The teacher is a "companion/guide," not an absolute authority figure. The object of the curriculum is to get kids to think about why they take certain actions and to think about consequences. For example, if two children are playing a game and one wants to change the rules, the teacher would ask the other child if that was all right. "Moral development occurs best when children live in an environment where fairness and justice is a way of life," says DeVries.

Not everyone agrees with the concept of moral development as a series of definable stages. Other researchers say that the stage theories downplay the role of emotion, empathy and faith. In "The Moral Life of Children," Harvard child psychiatrist Robert Coles tells the story of a 6-year-old black girl named Ruby, who braved vicious racist crowds to integrate her New Orleans school—and then prayed for her tormentors each night before she went to bed. Clearly, Coles says, she did not easily fall into any of Kohlberg's or Piaget's stages. Another criticism of stage theorists comes from feminist psychologists, including Carol Gilligan, author of "In a Different Voice." Gilligan says that the stages represent only *male* development with the emphasis on the concepts of justice and rights, not female development, which, she says, is more concerned with responsibility and caring.

But many psychologists say parents can use the stage theories to gain insight into their children's development. At each phase, parents should help their children make the right decisions about their behavior. In his book, Lickona describes a typical situation involving a 5-year-old who has hit a friend over the head with a toy while playing at the friend's house. Lickona suggests that the parents, instead of simply punishing their son, talk to him about why he hit his friend (the boy played with a toy instead of with him) and about what he could do next time instead of hitting. The parents, Lickona says, should also discuss how the friend might have felt about being hit. By the end of the discussion, the child should realize that there are consequences to his behavior. In Lickona's example, the child decides to call his friend and apologize—a positive ending.

For older children, Lickona suggests family "fairness meetings" to alleviate tension. If, for example, a brother and sister are constantly fighting, the parents could talk to both of them about what seem to be persistent sources of irritation. Then, youngsters can think of ways to bring about a truce—or at least a cease-fire.

Children who learn these lessons can become role models for other youngsters—and for adults as well. Sara Newland tells her friends not to be scared of homeless people (most of them rush by without even a quick glance, she says). "Some people think, 'Why should I give to them?'" she says. "But I feel that you should give. If everyone gave food, they would all have decent meals." One recent evening, she and her mother fixed up three plates of beef stew to give out. They handed the first to the homeless man who's always on their corner. Then, Sara says, they noticed two "rough-looking guys" down the block. Sara's mother, a little scared, walked quickly past them. Then, she changed her mind and asked them if they'd like some dinner. "They said, 'Yes, God bless you'," Sara recalls. "At that moment, they weren't the same people who were looking through a garbage can for beer bottles a little while before. It brought out a part of them that they didn't know they had."

With TESSA NAMUTH *in New York and* KAREN SPRINGEN *in Chicago*

Parenting and Family Issues

Few people today realize that the potential freedom to *choose* parenthood—deciding whether to become a parent, deciding when to have children, or even deciding how many children to have in a family—is a development due to the advent of reliable methods of contraception and to other recent sociocultural changes. Moreover, unlike any other significant job we may aspire to, few, if any, of us will receive any formal training or information about the lifelong responsibility of parenting. For most of us, our behavior is generally based on our own conscious and subconscious recollections of how we were parented, as well as on our observations of the parenting practices of others around us. In fact, our society often behaves as if the mere act of producing a baby automatically confers upon the parents an innate parenting ability, and that a family's parenting practices should remain in the private domain of that family and not be subjected to scrutiny or criticism by outsiders.

Given this climate, it is not surprising that misconceptions about many parenting practices continue to persist today. Only within the last 30 years or so have researchers turned their lenses on the scientific study of the family. Social, historical, cultural, and economic forces also have changed dramatically the face of the American family today. For example, the articles "Little Big People" and "Putting Children First" discuss some of these potentially negative changes for the American family and allude to societal changes that may also be troubling for American children.

Picture the "typical" family of the 1950s, and images of the "Cleaver family" or "Father Knows Best" may spring to mind—families where father was the sole wage earner, surrounded by his adoring housewife and their smiling children. No longer does this Hollywood version of the family hold true. In fact, in 1990, fewer than 7 percent of all American families now fit this model of husband as breadwinner and wife as homemaker! Indeed, over 68 percent of women with school-age children are in the workforce today (compared to roughly 33 percent of women in 1975), and this percentage is projected to continue to increase, nearing 80 or 90 percent by the turn of the century. How does this rise in employed mothers affect children? As "Working Mothers and Their Families" reports, though dual-career families face complex challenges, maternal employment is nevertheless associated with multiple benefits for children and families. Thus, improvements in our current support system (e.g., availability of day care, parental leave policies, and societal support) will be required to ensure the success of future working families.

Another related shift in parenting involves the fact that significant numbers of children in our country will experience the divorce and/or remarriage of their parents at some point during their lifetime. "Marital Transitions: A Child's Perspective" reviews the data on this topic and concludes that children's responses to marital transitions vary as a function of many other factors including, for example, the child's temperament, its sex, and the available supports to its parents. These investigators also argue that rather than viewing single-parent or remarried families as inherently atypical or pathological, researchers today are shifting to examine more closely the specific factors that influence positive as well as negative outcomes for children experiencing changes in their family structure.

Parents are not the only influence on children in a family. In fact, about 90 percent of American children grow up with one or more siblings. However, much of the research on the family has neglected the role that siblings and birth order may play in development. The article "The Secret World of Siblings" discusses these issues and explains the paradox that, although from the "same" family, siblings are often more different from each other than alike.

Sooner or later every parent must face the question of how to discipline their children. When a young child fails to obey, should the parent reach for the paddle? "Why Spanking Takes the Spunk Out of Kids" presents evidence that short-term controls such as spanking are not only ineffective in the long run but may also cause lasting psychological and sometimes physical harm. Although spanking is a very common form of discipline (e.g., 90 percent of parents of 3- and 4-year-olds report having spanked their children), this article provides parents with more effective and less problematic forms of discipline.

Looking Ahead: Challenge Questions

Where did you get your ideas, values, and beliefs about how a parent behaves? If you were unsure about how to respond to a particular parenting situation, how would you or who would you consult in order to make your decision? How do you think your own history of parenting by your parents has affected your attitudes or possible parenting practices for your own future or current children?

The United States is the only Western industrialized nation that does not have an adequate national policy on parental leave (the 1993 Family and Medical Leave Act excludes the majority of workplaces) or on regulations governing day care. Why do you think this nation, with such prominent world status, seems unable to formulate a national policy on parental leave or day care? What could

you do to remediate this situation? In what ways do you think that the lack of national public policies has influenced the everyday lives of real families such as your own?

How have the growing numbers of women with children entering the workforce affected the roles of men and women in family life today?

Describe the different expectations that our society places upon working mothers versus working fathers. How do you react to the "Superwoman Myth"? Given that our societal expectations affect working mothers and fathers differently, what specific recommendations could you suggest to reduce the stress for all concerned?

Compared to past years, much of the stigma associated with being the child of divorce has been greatly reduced in our country. What factors might account for this shift in attitude? Though most children initially experience their parents' divorce and/or remarriage as stressful, can you think of any positive outcomes for children who experience these family transition? If you have a friend with several children who is contemplating divorce, what specific advice could you offer your friend regarding the children?

Try to imagine yourself occupying a different birth order (e.g., if you were a first-born, picture yourself the baby of the family). In what ways do you think you would be a different person today? Do you think that parents should try to treat all their children in exactly the same manner? Why, or why not?

Were you ever spanked by a parent or a teacher? If so, how did the experience make you feel? Now imagine being hit by your boss or spouse for disobeying or making a mistake—why is this situation between adults unacceptable while most find it acceptable for a parent to strike a child? How do you see yourself altering your future or current disciplinary style with children?

Little Big People

*A generation of affluent parents have raised the precocious,
worldly children they wanted to be—and are now confronted with
the results of their experiment.*

Lucinda Franks

*Lucinda Franks, a Pulitzer Prize-winning journalist, is
the author of the novel "Wild Apples."*

One day last may, my son's third-grade classroom
was left in the care of a substitute teacher. For
reasons still undetermined, a small riot broke
out, with children fighting, shrieking and shoving
chairs. Nine-year-olds going berserk in springtime is
not unprecedented, but consider what happened next:
The new principal lectured them with a sternness they
were unaccustomed to. Then she made them write
letters of apology and then they fell apart all over
again. Those who claimed they had not participated in
the brawl came down at dismissal time tearful and
incensed at the burden of collective guilt imposed upon
them. "Isn't it illegal for her to punish those of us who
did nothing?" one boy asked his mother. "Should we
sue her?" asked another. When told they should show
more respect for authority, one girl said, "Why should
we respect her when she showed no respect for us?"

In the office of a child therapist recently, a 10-year-
old girl leaned back and gazed at her mother with half-
lidded contempt. The child was there because her
divorced parents couldn't do anything with her. Her
father was bitter because he had brought her along to
buy his girlfriend an engagement gift and she had
sulked the whole time. Her mother complained that
she refused to make friends with the mother's boyfriend. "How do you expect me to have a relationship
with him," the girl said with the ennui of a 40-year-old,
"when he's always in your bedroom?"

The therapist shook her head when she recounted
the visit: "Sometimes I think I'm too old-fashioned to
practice in today's world. Half the time the children act
like adults and the adults behave like children."

For decades now, children have been growing up
faster and faster, each new generation emerging
more precocious than the last. But today's crop
of under-12's, particularly in middle- and upper-middle-
income families and particularly in urban America,
seems to have reinvented—or even bypassed—childhood as we knew it. They are proud, independent and
strong-willed; they are worldly-wise and morally serious. They are a generation that has been raised to
challenge and doubt authority, to take little at face
value—in short, to enter the world of maturity long
before they are mature.

This was no accident. The parents of many of these
children—those of us who began our families later in
life—came of age in the Vietnam War years. Our ideas
of child rearing were like our ideas about everything
else: radically different from our parents, who thought
a child was just a child, even when the child got old
enough to march against wars and otherwise protest-
the way the elder generation ran the world. Those of us
who were veterans of the 60's and 70's swore that we
would treat our children with respect. We vowed that
we would fold our own offspring into our daily lives,
treating them like "little people," empowering them
with the rights, the importance and the truth telling
we had been denied. We wanted to create the children
we always yearned to be. And now, many years later,
we are confronted with the results. Did it turn out the
way we meant it to? Will our independent children
thank us for making them the center of the universe,
or have we robbed them of a childhood they can never
regain?

The explosion in communications—with television
and movies thrusting sophisticated material on grade-
schoolers—as well as increasing competition for college
placement has intensified childhood burnout. The kids

of yesterday, who wandered into meadows of fantasy, whose tears were reserved for skinned knees and broken toys, has given way to the kid who is strapped to the competitive fast track before he is out of diapers. The urban, affluent child is crammed with gymnastics and tennis and French lessons and then is crowded with even more activities by working parents who try to make the most of the time they have with their children. The child who could once be seen playing cops and robbers in the park is no longer even in the park but at home simulating the same thing on his Nintendo screen. He is a computer whiz, a little philosopher, a tiny lawyer, bursting with opinions on the President, on the best museums, the best vacation spots and the college he thinks he will attend.

For childish comfort, he is taken into the capricious arms of television: the great cuddly dinosaur Barney leads him in singing "we're a happy family" and then the child switches the channel to see that the man who taught him tennis is a pedophile who has put a bullet through his brain. Language more appropriate to teenagers can be heard in elementary-school halls. One mother of a 7-year-old confided that a boy had told her daughter, "You're so yucky you must have sex with Nazis."

Economic hardship has long stolen childhood from the poor. The severity and the causes of their problems, which have only intensified, are far different from those of affluent children. Yet for the first time, these more privileged children are thrust unshielded into the middle of family crisis that would paralyze an adult: a parent is dying of AIDS or the child is a mediator in violent dramas of drug addiction or divorce.

Even in stable families, small children with two working parents learn to shift for themselves, cooking and caring for siblings and picking up the attitudes of their elders. Our generation—reared in an era in which sex was not discussed, conflict was suppressed and emotional distance was maintained—opened the gates for our children. But each day, the bleak river of honesty that runs through their lives grows dangerously higher.

"I was determined that there was going to be no more scary secrets, no more J. Edgar Hoover, when I got to be a parent; everything was going to be up front," says Marcia Roesch, a school admissions coordinator. "I talked and talked, but I wasn't listening and I wasn't keeping a sense of balance and appropriateness with my children. I hear parents all the time asking their kids 'Is that O.K.?' as though they need their kids to approve every decision."

Says Candace Stern, a New Jersey mother of an 8-year-old: "I used to express my insecurities and everything else to my daughter. One day, we were watching a takeoff of Little Red Riding Hood on Sesame Street and I thought it was hilarious. Then I looked at Caitlin and she was terrified. It was then that I realized that I didn't really know what was in her mind and that what she heard, what she held onto, was much different than what I, an adult, retained."

Contrary to our assumptions, we have found that children are much more than little people. They are the possessors of rather eccentric states of mind that some experts fear are being altered by the early use of computers and other technology.

"There is a period of childhood, until about age 9, when children should exist in a dreamlike state," says Kay J. Hoffman, an educator at a progressive school in Rockland County in New York. "Instead, they are being hardened too early, jarred into an awake adult consciousness that is preventing the natural development of their imaginations. The trend to intellectualize early education is a dangerous one. I see more children with high anxiety levels and learning problems caused by the enormous pressure that is being put on them to think and speak like adults before they are ready."

Highly verbal children will use words, without really understanding them, as coin of the adult realm. "They use them for protection, to push away their own experience as children," says one doctor who asked not to be identified to protect his patients. "One 4-year-old that I tested kept running out of the room saying he had to go get his 'concentration.' He couldn't just be a child and say, 'I don't want to do this test!' He had to parrot an adult concept that he hardly understood because he was afraid to disappoint me."

I think sometimes we cannot know how profound that fear runs in our children, especially since we have burdened them with such a sense of their own importance. At times, their officiousness seems to be bluff; they simply cannot afford to be wrong. In making them feel so trusted and believed, we have not only bridged the generation gap, we might have overlapped it. As we hover over their development as though we were tending orchids in a greenhouse, are we not also guilty of a kind of neglect? In integrating them into our daily lives, have we taken away their freedom to do childish things? Parents or nannies of old stayed at home and babbled and played games; we take them to department stores, to work, to lunch, to movies and plays. Parents push for intimacy so much that one child was overheard telling her mother, "If you say I can have my feelings one more time, I'm going to throw up."

Says Miriam Siffert, a grandmother in Manhattan: "We sent our children to the most progressive schools, but they knew their place. They knew their time. We didn't take them to dinner parties or on trips to Europe. But I see my grandchildren taking over the house, taking over adult conversation."

Peggy Rosenblatt, a mother of two, concurs: "There is so much familiarity and so little distance. We tell them where we are going, what we are doing. We ask their opinion as though they were our best buddies, and then we are surprised when we tell a 10-year-old to do something he doesn't want to do and he says, 'You can't make me.'"

So uncomfortable are we with being in authority that we have made a crusade of elevating our children at the expense of ourselves. Consider the way we portray ourselves in children's movies; no Mary Poppins or Clark Kent these days; instead, enter Hook, so realistically evil that he breaks the bounds of old-time fantasy, or an all-too-believable Mom and Dad who keep leaving their son home alone.

"Sometimes it seems like there is no bottom line anymore," says Sara Adler, a grade-school teacher for 20 years. "I have some kids who yell 'child abuse' if you discipline them. They know tag lines, but they don't know the lines they cannot and should not cross. The parents think, 'What are the teachers doing!' And the teachers wonder what is going on inside the homes."

We have abrogated the moral authority our parents wore as easily as gloves. In Westchester County in New York, for instance, where kids in their early teens come into the city to party until the early hours of the morning, some parents are afraid to give their children curfews for fear they will move out and live with a friend.

Even children themselves think that things sometimes go too far. "Trust me, I know some kids who are guilty of parent abuse," Jonathan Stein, 10, says. "They feel like they own their parents and that they could just take all their parents' money out of their bank account and run away if they wanted."

Michelle Denburg, a high-school senior, adds: "Some of my teachers were afraid to be authority figures. They couldn't control their class and partly it was the fault of the parents because they would say negative stuff about a teacher and then expect their kids to respect those teachers."

In spite of the confusion these children experience, few would disagree that they are, in many ways, a splendid generation. My son, Joshua, 9, and his friends are amazing in their generosity, sensitivity, ability to stretch across an intellectual canyon and meet adults on their own terms. They have highly developed senses of justice and fairness, rejecting stereotypes and embracing oddities in their peers, whether a hair style or a disability. They are disdainful of smoking and drug use, can sniff out hypocrisy and have social consciences that are poignant. They are so worried about the few trees on their block that last year they formed an earth club to keep them free of litter. At times, the child in our children pokes endearingly through the veneer of sophistication. "Mom, please don't buy Ivory soap anymore" as his most recent environmental request. "Why?" I asked. "Be-

cause they shoot elephants to get the ivory, don't they?" he replied.

Paul Shechtman, a New York lawyer, reports that when he argued with his daughter, 6, about going to school with a rip in the knee of her jeans, she asked him for one good reason why she shouldn't wear them. "Because my father never would have let me," he said, exasperated. "Just because your father made a mistake," she replied, "why should you?"

"At that moment," Shechtman said, "I knew that I had succeeded as a parent. Now, of course, I do have to live with my success."

Helene Stein, mother of three children 14 and under, including Jonathan, says she gets "a kind of wicked pleasure when I compare my children's childhood with my own." She and her sister had to be bathed, with hair brushed and bathrobes on, before they came to the table. "My parents were the ones who spoke," she says. "We listened. With my kids, I drop everything if they seem to want to talk."

Since the end of the Victorian era, when children emerged as entities that would be heard as well as occasionally seen, childhood has been considered increasingly precious. Members of my generation, however, gave new definition to the cult of child worship. When I was pregnant, one friend teased me for turning my apartment upside down and buying a king-size bed (big enough for three): "You'd think you were preparing for the arrival of Caesar." After Josh was born, I filled notebooks recording his every wiggle. And my husband insisted on carrying him in a sling on his hip virtually everywhere, including to cocktail parties, where, to everyone's horror, he let him sip beer. Not being able to recall one of my pictures ever gracing my mother's refrigerator door, I later hung his drawings of little people manning complicated machines up and down the hallway. One day, when 4, he smiled indulgently and said, "Mom, you'd think our house was the Metropolitan Museum of Joshua!"

Some parents applaud both the acceleration and involvement of today's children in the real world. A librarian expressed disbelief when a third-grader asked for books on the Holocaust. "We read those books together," his mother, Carol Saper, explains, "and we talk about them. I think it has made my son a more sensitive, caring person."

Nearly all parents, however, feel their best efforts are continually subverted by television. Much of the time, exhausted, overextended parents are caught unawares. "I'm a working mother and I move mountains to organize everything just right—we even manage to eat dinner together, but there's always some crack for the kids to fall through," says Susan Mascitelli, a hospital administrator who has a son, 9, and a daughter, 3. "The kids leave the table early and my husband

and I finally have 10 minutes of peace and then suddenly I hear the kids howling with laughter at "Married with Children," about a couple that hates each other and a child who acts like a hooker. The fact that they even understand this disgusting program stuns me."

Last year, one school on the Upper West Side of Manhattan held parent meetings to discuss a fourth grade whose girls were so sexually precocious that they were hotly pursuing certain boys and refusing to speak to others. "The last straw was when one child invited kids to his home for a dating party when his parents were out," says Ann Beaton, who has children aged 10, 7 and 1. "The kids' parents just delivered them with no questions asked. The girls wore halter tops and tiny bicycle shorts. It's hard to know whether they just wanted to look like Julia Roberts in "Pretty Woman" or whether they knew what they were up to."

Some parents complain that the culture has sexualized children long before they desired it. One third-grader, asked to list questions she had during a sex education course, replied, "Why do we have to know about stuff like this?"

Dr Richard A. Gardner, a child psychiatrist and author who has recently been outspoken in his defense of adults he thinks have been falsely accused of sex abuse, believes that although these crimes do exist, the country is undergoing a wave of sex abuse hysteria: "When I was a child, I had a book about having a fun day with Uncle Ralph. Now, Uncle Ralph is depicted as the kind of guy who, as soon as Mom goes into the kitchen, has his hand in your pants." Gardner says that data show the proliferation of early childhood sex abuse prevention programs are creating confusion and anxiety in youngsters and he predicts those programs will also result in sexual inhibition, mistrust and even long-term sexual dysfunction.

Schools and parents alike have begun taking steps to address these problems. Stephen M. Clement, the headmaster of a boys school in Manhattan, for instance, imposes strict order on the older boys who set standards of behavior for the younger ones: "One of our boys walked in bleeding—he had been mugged for his baseball cap. A school must try to provide a safe haven and some better models."

At Kay Hoffman's school in Rockland, teachers make unilateral decisions for young children so that they will have a good inventory of adult choices on which to base their own decisions later on. "We try to slow children down," Hoffman says. "We don't barrage them all at once. Learning evolves out of their own experience." The school also advises parents to ban television and not to talk about current events. "As soon as I did that, my child began to relax and act like a little girl again," says Candace Stern, whose daughter attends the school. "Her uncle was in Desert Storm and we didn't even tell her he had gone to Jidda until after it was all over. When we finally told her that he had been in a war, she asked, 'What side was he on?'"

Some worry about the repercussions of this generation's having lost its fleeting chance to be a child. "A person who does not have the opportunity to move through the stages of childhood at his own pace ends up with something missing," Jill Comins, a family therapist, says. "As an adult, he will search endlessly for it. He will experience powerful and regressive tugs backward."

Others, however, predict success. "I've been watching these kids grow up, grade by grade," says Gardner P. Dunnan, headmaster of a co-educational school on the Upper East Side. "They have had so much openness, so many opportunities, such a great arena to learn and grow, by the time they are adults they will be wonderful individuals and citizens."

Perhaps our children are simply rebelling against their parents much earlier than we did. And perhaps that means that they won't have to do it later. Perhaps our children will grow up to be the kind of people who wouldn't dream of inventing the motto "Never Trust Anybody Over 30."

"I feel they are in transition," says Sara Lebar, who lives in Greenwich Village. "We changed the rules and we have to expect them to react. I think that the next stage will be that our kids will be our friends, in a way we never were to our parents. Allison may not give me the respect I gave my mother, but I never aspired to be like my parents. And already Allison wants to be an environmentalist just like me.

For those of us who love our wonderful strong-willed children just the way they are—or almost just the way they are—there is a move afoot to readjust certain things ever so slightly. One day not long ago, having asked my own son several times to straighten out his room—which could not be penetrated because of a string that crisscrossed from wall to wall in some obscure scientific experiment—and having received no reply to this apparently trivial request, my voice became significantly louder. He finally looked up. "I'm not comfortable with cleaning out my room right now," he said.

"Get comfortable," I replied.

"Why?" he gazed at me.

"Because," I said, startled, as out of my mouth tumbled words that could have been taken out of a balloon in a comic strip of the 60's, "you are a child and I am the mother. You do not have the right to tell me what to do. On the other hand, I have the right to tell you what to do as long as you live under my roof."

First he gave me a withering look. Then he thought about it for a minute. And then he said "O.K." and headed for his room.

Working Mothers and Their Families

Sandra Scarr   *University of Virginia*
Deborah Phillips   *University of Virginia*
Kathleen McCartney   *University of New Hampshire*

ABSTRACT: The topic of maternal employment and its effects on the family is receiving considerable attention as more and more mothers enter the work force when their children are very young. This article reviews the effects of mothers' employment on marital relations, on the development of their children, and on mothers themselves. Research shows that maternal employment per se is not the major issue in either marital relations or child development. Rather, the circumstances of the family, the attitudes and expectations of fathers and mothers, and the distribution of time available have important effects. The needs of working mothers for social supports, such as parental leave, spouse support, child care, and better wages are considered.

"A woman's work is never done," or so goes the old adage about women's responsibilities to the home. Women who are mothers of babies and young children spend even more hours on their family roles than do non-mothers or mothers with older children. If one adds to home care and motherhood full-time employment in the labor force, a mother's job requires 50% more hours than that of working fathers and single people without children (Nock & Kingston, in press; Rexroat & Shehan, 1987).

Women all over the world work longer hours than men (Tavris & Wade, 1984). Mothers work longer hours than anyone else because their family responsibilities to household and children are not equally shared by fathers—anywhere. In industrialized countries, whether in the Western or Eastern worlds, mothers do the majority of the shopping, house cleaning, cooking, laundry, and child care, in addition to their paid employment. Whereas fathers in these societies work an average of 50 hours per week in combined employment and household work, mothers work an average of 80 hours per week at the same tasks (Cowan, 1983).

The degree to which most fathers do not share the family work with their wives is vividly demonstrated by Rexroat and Shehan (1987) in a study of 1,618 White couples from the 1976 wave of the Panel Study of Income Dynamics. Whereas in the case of childless working couples and empty nesters, wives worked an average of 5 to 9 hours more per week than their husbands in combined employment and housework, in families with infants and preschool children, mothers worked 16 to 24 hours more per week than did fathers. The actual total hours per week

worked by employed mothers of children under age three was 90!

Despite the enormous number of hours worked by most mothers in the world, the self-reports of mothers who are also employees demonstrate that their multiple roles are often not experienced as more stressful than the lives experienced by women with fewer roles and obligations (Crosby, 1987). These seemingly contradictory observations of actual workload and self-perceptions of well-being need to be resolved (Coleman, Antonucci, & Adelmann, 1987; Gove & Zeiss, 1987). Either the Puritans were right that hard work is good for the soul, or there is some self-selection of healthy women into complicated and demanding roles (Epstein, 1987; Reppetti, Matthews & Waldron, this issue, pp. 1394–1401).

In this article, we consider the implications of parental, particularly maternal, employment for family relationships and family well-being. Other articles in this Public Forum section take up the effects of women's employment on the physical and mental health of both mothers and non-mothers.

Why Do Mothers Work?

Most women in the labor force work primarily because the family needs the money and secondarily for their own personal self-actualization. Because of the decline in real family income from 1973 to 1988 (Congressional Budget Office, 1988), most families find it essential for both parents to work to support them at a level that used to be achieved by one wage-earner, and in many families two earners are required to keep the family out of poverty. Most divorced, single, and widowed mothers must work to avoid poverty.

However, most would not leave their paid employment, even if the family did not need the money (De-Chick, 1988). Indeed, 56% of full-time homemakers say that they would choose to have a career if they had it to do all over again, and only 21% of working mothers would leave their current jobs to stay at home with the children (DeChick, 1988). Professional career women are a small but vocal minority of women who value the social and political equality of women's employment, and their endorsement of mothers' employment is consistent with their position. Surveys of working class mothers, with jobs as waitresses, factory workers, and domestics, show that these women are quite committed to their jobs (Hiller & Dyehouse, 1987), satisfied with their diverse roles, and

From *American Psychologist*, Vol. 44, No. 11, November 1989, pp. 1402-1409. © 1989 by the American Psychological Association. Reprinted by permission.

would not leave the labor force even if they did not need the money. The social psychology of the workplace, with its social support, adult companionship, and contacts with the larger world, may explain the phenomenon (Repetti, Matthews, & Waldron, this issue). Like most men, most women want to participate in the larger society.

Several recent studies of mothers of newborns and infants show that returning to work soon after a birth is primarily a function of previously high involvement in the labor force and positive attitudes about mothers' employment, even among families who are economically marginal (Avioli, 1985; Greenstein, 1986; Pistrang, 1984). Mothers who are not employed during their child's infancy are less likely to have been employed prior to the birth and are more likely to have negative attitudes about maternal employment, regardless of the economic situation of the family. For more affluent mothers, attitudes carried more weight than any other factor (Greenstein, 1986). Thus, economic necessity may propel most women into the labor force, but other factors entice them to reenter after having a baby and to stay employed.

Regardless of the reasons, working mothers are here to stay. The Department of Labor projects that by 1995 roughly two thirds of all new labor force entrants will be women (Johnston, 1987), and 80% of those in their childbearing years are expected to have children during their work life. Yet, we as a nation are still ambivalent about mothers who work and whose children's care is delegated to others, and about their diminished time for responsibilities to husbands whose careers are generally presumed to be preeminent.

The major issues discussed in this article are the impact of mothers' employment on their marital relationships and on their children.

Working Mothers' Marital Relationships

Like other adults, mothers vary in their career ambitions, their sex-role expectations, and the degree to which they receive spousal support for their employment. Many reviews of research on mothers' employment show that such mediating factors are crucial to interpreting any effects of maternal employment on family relationships (Anderson-Kulman & Paludi, 1986; Locksley, 1980; Simpson & England, 1982; Smith, 1985). For women, spousal support is a key to the success of dual-career families; it is not maternal employment per se that affects marital satisfaction, but "the law of husband cooperation" (Bernard, 1974, p. 162). Husband cooperation includes positive attitudes toward maternal employment and cooperation with household and child care tasks (Bernardo, Shehan, & Leslie, 1987; Gilbert, 1985, 1988). Mothers who receive little or no spouse support, in either attitudes toward their employment or in participation in child care and household tasks, are indeed stressed by their multiple roles (Anderson-Kulman & Paludi, 1986; Pleck, 1985). Mothers who receive a great deal of positive spouse support feel positive about their spouses and their lives. For mothers, the quality of their roles matters more than how many or how seemingly stressful they are (Baruch & Barnett, 1987).

Husbands' appreciation for and enjoyment of their wives' employment depended both on their degree of participation in family affairs and on their own perceptions of work and family life (Pleck, 1985; Simpson & England, 1982). Gilbert (1985) found that men with children in dual-career families can be classified as traditional, participant, and role-sharing, depending on the degree to which they share household and child-care responsibilities.[1] Men who participate more in the family claim to be content with, even proud of, their wives employment (Wortman, 1987), but outside pressures also affect their support of their wives' careers.

The responses from men in the study indicate that for men who do experience role conflict, the tension often centers around wanting to support their spouses' career aspirations and to be involved in parenting and household roles while at the same time wanting to have their own career aspirations put first. Being highly competitive, experiencing high work demands, and working in an environment hostile to men's involvement in family roles ... all contribute to the tension. (Gilbert, 1985, p. 104)

For dual-career parents, their satisfactions as couples often depend on their socialization experiences and current attitudes about male and female roles (Aldous, 1982; Pepitone-Rockwell, 1980). Role-sharing and participatory men are more likely to see maternal employment as opportunities for the wife to have greater independent identity, more social interaction, and greater intellectual companionship, opportunities that are less often cited by traditional men. Because of their more egalitarian beliefs about gender roles and women's rights, such fathers appreciate and applaud their wives' careers, even though they also perceive family costs.

Costs of maternal employment more often cited by nontraditional men include decreased leisure time, increased time spent on household tasks, and decreased sexual activity due to fatigue and lack of time (Gilbert, 1985; Voyandoff & Kelly, 1984). Traditional arrangements in which the father is less involved with child care and household responsibilities have some perceived advantages for fathers, but even traditional men acknowledge the contribution of maternal employment to increased family income. That they do not share family responsibilities has a negative effect on wives' perceptions of the marital relationship, but not evidently on theirs (Bernardo et al., 1987; Gilbert, 1988; Pleck, 1985).

The costs and benefits of maternal employment have a positive balance for both husbands and wives in most working families (see Crosby, 1987; Gilbert, 1985; Wortman, 1987). Satisfactions and dissatisfactions of marital partners depend on attitudes toward gender roles and the degree to which they can manage time and effort (Voyandoff & Kelly, 1984). For mothers, satisfactions also depend on spouse support for their household and maternal roles and on their work commitment prior to becoming mothers; mothers with previously high work commitments who stay home for five or more months after a birth report greater irritability, greater depression, decreased marital intimacy, and lower self-esteem than mothers with previously low work commitments (Pistrang, 1984). For men, satisfactions depend primarily on the degree to which they are inconvenienced by maternal employment in exchange for larger family income (Gilbert, 1985, 1988).

Maternal Employment and Child Development

National concerns about the possible plight of children of working mothers prompted a large review of research in 1982 by the National Academy of Sciences (Kamerman & Hayes, 1982). A distinguished panel of social scientists reviewed all of the evidence and concluded that there were no consistent effects of maternal employment on child development. Rather, they said, maternal employment cannot have a single set of consistent effects on children because mothers work for various reasons and begin or interrupt work when their children are at various ages; furthermore, their employment is in contexts of various families and communities that support or do not support mothers' multiple roles.

Lois Hoffman (1984) reviewed 50 years of research on maternal employment, most of it predicated on the assumption that maternal employment should have negative effects on child development. Indeed, some of the investigators found that young sons were slightly disadvantaged by the loss of maternal attention in the early years. Of course, they were presumably in some form of day care, which may not have been of high quality.

Her reexamination of the data showed that daughters of employed mothers were often reported to be more self-confident, to achieve better grades in school, and to more frequently pursue careers themselves than were the daughters of nonemployed mothers. Whereas most sons had role models of competent, employed fathers, daughters of employed mothers also had such a model of achievement. Hoffman also noted that few investigators asked how maternal employment could benefit children by higher family income, higher self-esteem for mothers, a less sharp distinction between male and female roles, and a more positive role model for both sons and daughters for later in their own lives (Gottfried & Gottfried, 1987; Weinraub, Jaeger, & Hoffman, 1988).

When both parents in families with preschool children are employed, the fathers *do not* spend significantly more time on child care or household chores than do fathers in single-earner families (Bernardo et al., 1987; Nock & Kingston, in press). In fact, employed mothers also reduce their household work hours, primarily in categories of homemaking chores, rather than in child care activities (Nock & Kingston, in press). Thus, when both parents of preschool children are employed, both fathers and mothers spend about the same total amount of time in direct interaction with their children as do parents in families in which only fathers are employed. The biggest differences between the two-earner and one-earner families with preschool children are the distribution of time spent with children on weekdays versus weekends and in time spent on non-child care chores (Nock & Kingston, in press). Both parents in one-earner families have more leisure time for themselves.

Differences between one-earner and two-earner families with school-age children and adolescents are less pronounced but also involve a decrease in the amount of time spent on homemaking chores, for both employed fathers and mothers (Nock & Kingston, in press).

All in all, the question of what effects (if any) maternal employment has on children is not a productive one because it ignores the many contextual features of family life that moderate the effects of maternal employment (Grossman, Pollack, & Golding, 1988). We do know that

> the straightforward results of bad emotional, social, and intellectual outcomes for children of working mothers were not found, but no research can rule out yet unstudied subtleties. All we know is that the school achievement, IQ test scores, and emotional and social development of working mothers' children are every bit as good as that of children whose mothers do not work. (Scarr, 1984, p. 25)

Working Families and Child Care

Child care is *not* a women's issue; it is a family issue. However, the lack of high-quality, affordable child care has more impact on working mothers than on any others. Not only is there a critical shortage of high-quality child care in this country, but there also is such ambivalence about providing child care that we have a shameful national dilemma: More than 50% of American mothers of infants and preschool children are now in the labor force and require child care services, but there is no coherent national policy on parental leaves or on child care services for working parents.

With the exception of federal child care provided during the Great Depression and World War II, public provision of child care has been reserved for nonmainstream, generally poor families (Phillips & Zigler, 1987; Steinfels, 1973). Day care began in settlement houses in the 1850s for poor mothers who had to work because their husbands were inadequate providers or because they were not married. Early education, on the other hand, was begun by middle and upper class mothers who sponsored nursery schools and kindergartens to give their advantaged children good social and intellectual experiences (Scarr & Weinberg, 1986).

Today, the historical split between early education and day care is no longer tenable. Middle and upper class women have the same needs for work-related, full-day child care as do minority, poor, and single mothers. As of 1986, 51% of married mothers and 49% of single mothers were working (Kahn & Kamerman, 1987). Similarly, by 1985, 62% of both Black and White young children had working mothers. As a consequence, high rates of employment are now common to mothers of all races and marital statuses.

In sum, working mothers have become an everyday part of children's lives, of family life, and of our economic structure (Scarr, Phillips, & McCartney, 1988). Prior distinctions in the degree of child care use by children of different ages and in patterns of use by women with different demographic characteristics have merged into a universal pattern of extensive use. However, even this extensive, mainstream reliance on child care has not ensured that the child care needs of working families are adequately addressed (Hewlett, 1986; McCartney & Phillips, 1989). Kahn and Kamerman (1987) estimated that direct federal funding for child care programs actually decreased by 18% in real dollars between 1980 and 1986.

How Does the United States Compare?

The U.S. policies on child care and maternal leaves are an anomaly among industrialized countries. The United

States, among 100 countries, is the sole exception to the rule of providing paid, job-protected maternal leaves as national policy (Kamerman, 1986, 1989). Only five states require employers to provide temporary disability insurance, and federal law requires that pregnant women be eligible for these disability benefits. Even among private businesses that provide maternity benefits, this generally means an unpaid leave with no guarantee of reinstatement.

All other industrialized countries have some maternal leave policy. Sweden has one of the most extensive policies: Mothers and fathers have the right to a leave following childbirth that is paid at 90% of one parent's wages for 9 months, followed by a fixed minimum benefit for 3 additional months. Swedish parents may also take an unpaid, but job-protected, leave until their child is 18 months old and may work a six-hour day until their child is eight years old. In Italy, women are entitled to a 6-month job-protected leave, paid at a flat rate equal to the average wage for women workers. At the conclusion of this period, an unpaid, job-protected leave is also available for one year. In France, a job-protected maternity leave of 6 weeks before childbirth and 10 weeks after is provided.

Other countries also have much more systematic child care policies in conjunction with parental leave policies. As of 1986, Sweden had placed 38% of preschoolers with working mothers in subsidized child care programs (Leijon, 1986). France, Italy, Spain, and all of the Eastern European countries have more than half of their infants, toddlers, and preschool children in subsidized child care because their mothers are in the labor force. France, for example, maintains a system of preschools, open to all children two to six years old, and partially subsidized care is available for children under age two. Comparable figures concerning children in subsidized child care in the United States are not available, itself a sign of inattention.

Why the Policy Gap?

Cherished beliefs about maternal care have led us historically as a nation to favor marginal support for mothers to stay home with their babies, through paternal employment and through Aid to Families with Dependent Children (AFDC), rather than support for women's attainment of economic independence. Until the last few years, when employment and training opportunities for women on AFDC were begun as an experiment in several states, poor women with young children had no option but to accept the degradation of poverty-on-the-dole. Now poor mothers are captives of a system that is moving from AFDC to Workfare, which, even in the best of circumstances, does not sustain support for child care for more than one year after these mothers achieve the minimum-wage jobs for which they are being trained.

Working parents need options. One option currently under congressional consideration is an *unpaid* parental (read that as 95% maternal)[2] leave. Many mothers cannot afford to take months off from their jobs, especially without pay; unpaid leaves for divorced and single mothers and for women married to men who earn the minimum wage are not very useful.

Even among mothers who can afford the unpaid leaves, not all *want* to be away from their careers for more than a few months after the birth of a child. Upon serious and honest reflection, they consider themselves to be better parents when they work and mother, rather than attempt only one role, or their careers are such that there are professional costs for taking four to six months out of the office. These women do not want extended maternal leaves; they want high-quality child care, and some want fulfilling, well-compensated, part-time work opportunities.

Policies that create strong incentives for mothers to stay at home for extended periods or that require them to go to work soon after a birth are based on conflicting assumptions about the nature of women's participation in the society and assumptions about infants' needs. There are many reasons that most women would prefer to remain in close contact with their newborns. For one, many women need a rest period after a birth, especially if the pregnancy or the birth was difficult. For another, many new mothers need two or more months to establish reliable breastfeeding and to allow their babies to settle into a reasonably predictable routine. How long should a maternal leave be for either the mother's or the infant's benefit? Neither a mandatory child care nor a mandatory maternal leave policy suits all families. What we need are equally attractive options so that families can choose how best either to take advantage of quality child care while parents work or to arrange an extended leave for parents, usually the mother, to care for the baby. Still, many families (and policymakers) suffer great guilt and anxiety about mothers' return to work and placing infants and toddlers in child care. Psychological research has addressed their fears.

Effects of Child Care on Children

In psychological research, child care is often treated as a uniform arrangement that can be objectively characterized as "nonmaternal care" by investigators who in fact rarely study child care settings. By the same illogic, "home care" is treated uniformly as though all families were alike and is assumed to be preferred to other child care arrangements. Child care settings vary from babysitters in one's own home, to family day care in another's home, to centers that care for more than 100 infants and young children. The quality of these settings varies enormously in terms of their abilities to promote children's development and to provide support for working parents. Families also vary from abusive and neglectful of children's needs to supportive and loving systems that promote optimal development. So it is with other child care settings.

Recent reviews of the child care literature by psychologists of different theoretical persuasions agree that high-quality child care has no detrimental effects on intellectual or language development (Belsky, 1986; Clarke-Stewart, 1989; Scarr et al., 1988). In fact, high-quality day care settings have been shown to compensate for poor family environments (Ramey, Bryant, & Suarez, 1985) and to promote better intellectual and social development than children would have experienced in their own homes.

The media and parents are most concerned about the possible effects of child care on attachments of infants to their mothers and on children's possible social deviance. The earliest research questioned whether child caregivers replaced mothers as children's primary attachment figure. Concerns that daily separations from mother might weaken the mother– child bond were a direct heritage of the work on children in orphanages (e.g, Spitz, 1945). Early evidence provided no suggestion that nonmaternal child care constitutes a milder form of full-time institutionalization. Attachment was not adversely affected by enrollment in the university-based child care centers that provided the early child care samples. Bonds formed between children and their caregivers did not replace the mother–child attachment relationship (Belsky & Steinberg, 1978; Etaugh, 1980; Kagan, Kearsley, & Zelazo, 1978).

Now that infant day care is the modal middle-class experience, a new debate about infant day care and attachment has arisen. The critics question whether full-time nonmaternal care in the first year of life increases the probability of insecure attachments between mothers and infants (Belsky & Rovine, 1988). Although the new literature has many limitations (Clarke-Stewart, 1989; Clarke-Stewart & Fein, 1983; McCartney & Galanopoulos, 1988; Phillips, McCartney, Scarr, & Howes, 1987; Scarr et al., 1988), there is near consensus among developmental psychologists and early childhood experts that child care per se does not constitute a risk factor in children's lives; rather poor quality care and poor family environments can conspire to produce poor developmental outcomes (Alliance for Better Child Care, 1988; Howes, Rodning, Galluzzo, & Myers, 1988).

Research on the effects of child care on children's social development has yielded contradictory findings. Although some studies report no differences in social behavior between children with and without child care experience (Golden et al., 1978; Kagan et al., 1978), others show that children who had nonmaternal child care are more socially competent (Clarke-Stewart, 1984; Gunnarsson, 1978; Howes & Olenick, 1986; Howes & Stewart, 1987; Phillips, McCartney, & Scarr, 1987; Ruopp, Travers, Glantz, & Coelen, 1979), and others suggest lower levels of social competence (Haskins, 1985; Rubenstein, Howes, & Boyle, 1981). Positive outcomes include teacher and parent ratings of considerateness and sociability (Phillips et al., 1987), observations of compliance and self-regulation (Howes & Olenick, 1986), and observations of involvement and positive interactions with teachers (McCartney, 1984; Ruopp et al., 1979; Vandell & Powers, 1983). Haskins's (1985) study of a high-quality child care program for disadvantaged infants and preschool children found that, at kindergarten, teachers rated these children higher on scales of aggression than children with community-based child care or no nonmaternal care experience. (Behavior management training of caregivers in the day care center decreased aggression by 80% for later cohorts of children in this program; Finkelstein, 1982). However, children who spent comparable amounts of time in community-based child care programs were the least aggressive children in the study, so that the relationship of aggression to day care experience was not established.

What Is Quality Child Care?

Working parents are necessarily concerned about "what is quality?" in child care. Researchers have found that child care quality, operationalized by a number of policy-relevant variables, is important to young children's development. The most important of these factors are small child-caregiver ratio, small group size, caregiver training in child development, and stability of the child's care experience (see Bruner, 1980; Phillips, 1987; Ruopp et al., 1979; Scarr et al., 1988). These variables, in turn, appear to exert their influence by facilitating constructive and sensitive interactions among caregivers and children, which, in turn, promote positive social and cognitive development.

Concluding Comments

In our opinion, many of the fears about child care are not based on scientifically demonstrated facts but socially determined theories about mothers' roles and obligations to their families (Scarr et al., 1988). Of course, it is important for parents to arrange competent care for their children while they work, but it is not clear that mothers have to provide this care on a continuous basis during the entire first year, either for infants' well-being or for their own.

Critics of child care sometimes write as though working parents do not function as parents at all. For example, the term, "maternal absence," was used to describe employed mothers in the title of a recent article in the prestigious journal, *Child Development* (Barglow, Vaughn, & Molitor, 1987). The terms "maternal absence" and "maternal deprivation" seem uncomfortably close to and conjure up the specter of neglected, institutionalized infants.[3] Some seem to forget that employed mothers are typically with their babies in the mornings, evenings, weekends, and holidays, which for most fully employed workers constitutes about half of the child's waking time.[4] Furthermore, when the child is ill, mothers are more likely than other family members to stay at home with the child (Hughes & Galinsky, in press).

The quality of maternal care, just like other child care arrangements, depends on many aspects of the home situation and mothers' mental health. The fantasy that mothers at home with young children provide the best possible care neglects the observation that some women at home full time are lonely, depressed, and not functioning well (see Crosby, 1987; Pistrang, 1984). Home care does not promise quality child care.

Working Families of the Future

For the children of working families, the most pressing issue for the future is quality of care—care that will encourage and support all aspects of child development. In most cases, families will provide quality care themselves and try to buy it for their children while they work. Unfortunately, quality care costs more than inadequate care, and many parents today cannot afford good care without employer or public support.

For working parents, the most pressing family issues are shared family responsibilities, spousal support, and the affordability and availability of consistent, dependable child care. Working parents, especially mothers on whom most of the household and child care burdens fall, are constantly threatened psychologically by makeshift child care arrangements that fail unexpectedly and by the high cost of quality child care. Reluctance, even among high-income families, to hire household help means that mothers work more hours than they would need to if some income was invested in household help, rather than in consumer goods (Cowan, 1983; Scarr, 1984).

For policymakers at federal and state levels, the most pressing issues are how to fund a system of quality child care, regulate those aspects of quality that can be legislated and enforced, and coordinate efforts with the private sector and at all levels of government. If one could point to one "magic bullet" to improve the child care system in the United States, it would have to be money—more funding for every aspect of the child care system. Until the United States recognizes the rights of women to participate fully in the life of the society, through motherhood, employment, and political life, we will continue to fail to make appropriate provisions for the care of children of working families.

If statistical projections are correct, nearly 70% of mothers with infants and young children will be employed, most full-time, by the mid-1990s (Hofferth & Phillips, 1987). Such women will be devoted to their families, as they are now, but they will continue to be overworked and harassed by inadequate family supports, especially child care. One hopes that through concerted advocacy for women's rights and child care, there will be some improvements in their lives and in those of their families. Here are our suggestions:

1. Fathers should assume more personal responsibility for planning and implementing family life. At present, many fathers are willing to "fill in" or "help out" with family chores that they and the society consider the mother's responsibility. Indeed, such men are often heard to congratulate themselves on their efforts to aid their wife in her chores (Gilbert, 1985; Wortman, 1987). Fathers today "babysit" their children. Have you ever heard a mother say that she is "babysitting" her children? Even the U.S. Bureau of Census counts father-care as a form of child care alongside nonrelative care and child care centers. Attitudes must change to make the lives of working mothers more tolerable. One would not be likely to see an article on the effects of paternal employment on marital relations and child development, unless the father were unemployed.

2. Children have traditionally been the individual responsibility of families in this society, regardless of inequities in their life chances. Children's fates have been tied exclusively to the fates of their parents, unless there were legal infractions of neglect and abuse statutes, in which case society has stepped in tentatively and temporarily. Can we not as a society recognize that children are also a community responsibility? They are the next generation for all of us, regardless of who their parents are. Many countries have family allowances that compensate parents for the extraordinary financial costs of rearing children. Child care costs can be subsidized by the society, just as public educational costs are shared by all. Few citizens today object to public support of education for children from ages 5 to 18. Why should they object to child care and early education for children from age 1 to 5?

3. We must recognize changes in American families that make sole support for children more difficult than it has been in the past. Changes in the earning capacity of service workers, who cannot support a family on a full-time job, means that most families will require more than one worker. Increasing diversity in family composition means that children will be cared for in a variety of settings that may or may not include their biological parents. Single parents, mostly mothers who have been divorced or never married, are poor and cannot pay the full costs of child care while they work. They must be subsidized for child care, or they will have to live on welfare.

4. We can encourage employers to take more responsibility for the necessary balance of family and work life of their employees. Recently, in both Britain and the United States, some companies have recognized the shrinking labor pool projected for the 1990s and proposed measures to assist working families, and thereby they have become more attractive employers (Gardner, 1988a, 1988b). Proposals include now-familiar assistance with finding child care, provision of subsidies or on-site child care, and novel approaches (for these countries) such as paid and job-guaranteed maternal leaves for extended periods. Given the opposition of the National Chamber of Commerce to even an unpaid maternal leave for only 12 weeks, these changes may not come in the foreseeable future. Federal legislation will be required for paid, extended parental or maternal leaves to become a reality for most workers.

5. In Europe, North America, and most other parts of the world, mothers are economically disadvantaged compared with men and with non-mothers, especially if they are single parents. In the United States, more than 50% of single mothers and their young children are poor; in Australia, 65% of single mothers and their children are poor. These figures compare to poverty rates for single mothers of 35% to 39% for most of Europe and only 8.6% in Sweden (Smeedling & Torrey, 1988). Poverty rates for all families with children vary from a low of 5.1% in Sweden to a high of 17.1% in the United States (with Australia next to the bottom at 16.9%).

Employed women in the United States earn about 70% of men's wages. Even in Sweden, where women's earnings per hour are more than 90% of men's earnings, women work an average of 10 hours less per week than men and fill virtually all the part-time jobs (Leijon, 1986). Moreover, Swedish women are found in a much narrower band of occupations than are men, primarily concerned with "nursing, care, and services" (Leijon, 1986). It appears that, even when helpful options of parental leaves and subsidized child care are available, many mothers are economically disadvantaged, unless supported by a male worker. Rather than pursuing demanding, well-paid careers, they have part-time, lower status jobs. The combined responsibilities of motherhood and paid employment are an enormous burden that needs to be shared more equitably by fathers and by society as a whole.

---

[1] Traditional husbands do little to support their wives' employment by participating in family affairs. Participatory fathers take some responsibility for child care but do not do household chores. Role-sharing

husbands take more responsibility for both children and home, but few (even in the university community studied) were found to share equally with the wife.

[2] Sweden pays parents 90% of their salaries for one parent to take off nine months with a new infant. In practice, 95% of the leave is taken by mothers, even though there is an additional incentive for the parents to share the leave time with the baby.

[3] Research on maternal deprivation reached an emotional climax in the 1950s, when Spitz (1945), Bowlby (1951), and others claimed that institutionalized infants wasted away for want of maternal care. Reanalyses of the evidence (Ernst, 1988; Yarrow, 1961) found that lack of sensory and affective stimulation in typical institutions of the day caused infants to languish both intellectually and emotionally. Longitudinal studies of institutionalized children showed that their later adjustment problems owed more to their continued deprivation throughout childhood than to deprived infant care (Ernst, 1988).

[4] Consider five working days/week for 49 weeks of the year: 1.5 hours in the morning and 3 hours of the child's waking time in the late afternoon and evening, for a sum of 4.5 of the approximately 14 hours of the child's daily waking time. The caregiver accounts for approximately 9 hours, 2 hours of which the child typically spends in a nap. (A half hour is allocated for transportation.) The sum of work week hours of parents employed full time is 1,102; for caregivers, 1,715.

To the parental sum, add weekends (2 days/work week) for 49 weeks, a sum of 1,274. To that, add three weeks of vacation time and 10 days of personal and sick leave (for self and child) during the work weeks, a sum of 455.

By these calculations, the typical, fully employed parents spend 2,831 hours with the child; caregivers spend approximately 1,715.

REFERENCES

Aldous, J. (1982). *Two paychecks: Life in dual-earner families.* Beverly Hills, CA: Sage.

Alliance for Better Child Care. (1988, March). *Statement in support of the ABC Child Care Bill.* Washington, DC: Author.

Anderson-Kulman, R.E., & Paludi, M.A. (1986). Working mothers and the family context: Predicting positive coping. *Journal of Vocational Behavior, 28,* 241–253.

Avioli, P. S. (1985). The labor-force participation of married mothers of infants. *Journal of Marriage and the Family, 47,* 739–745.

Barglow, P., Vaughn, B.E., & Molitor, N. (1987). Effects of maternal absence due to employment on the quality of infant–mother attachment in a low-risk sample. *Child Development, 58,* 945–954.

Baruch, G.K., & Barnett, R.C. (1987). Role quality and psychological well-being. In F.J. Crosby (Ed.), *Spouse, parent, worker: On gender and multiple roles* (pp. 91–108). New Haven, CT: Yale University Press.

Belsky, J. (1986). Infant day care: A cause for concern? *Zero to Three, 6*(5), 1–9.

Belsky, J., & Rovine, M.J. (1988). Nonmaternal care in the first year of life and the security of infant–parent attachment. *Child Development, 59,* 157–176.

Belsky, J., & Steinberg, L.D. (1978). The effects of daycare: A critical review. *Child Development, 49,* 929–949.

Bernard, J. (1974). *The future of motherhood.* New York: Dial Press.

Bernardo, D.H., Shehan, C.L., & Leslie, G.R. (1987). A residue of tradition: Jobs, careers, and spouses' time in housework. *Journal of Marriage and the Family, 49,* 381–390.

Bowlby, J. (1951). *Maternal care and mental health.* Geneva, Switzerland: World Health Organization.

Bruner, J. (1980). *Under five in Britain.* London: Oxford University Press.

Clarke-Stewart, A. (1984). Day care: A new context for research and development. In M. Perlmutter (Ed.), *The Minnesota Symposia on Child Psychology: Vol. 17. Parent–child interaction and parent–child relations in child development* (pp. 61–100). Hillsdale, NJ: Erlbaum.

Clarke-Stewart, A. (1989). Infant day care: Malignant or maligned? *American Psychologist, 44,* 266–273.

Clarke-Stewart, A., & Fein, G. (1983). Early childhood programs. In M. Haith & J. Campos (Eds.), *Handbook of child psychology: Vol. 2. Infancy and developmental psychobiology* (pp. 917–1000). New York: Wiley.

Coleman, L.M., Antonucci, T.C., & Adelmann, P.K. (1987). Role involvement, gender, and well-being. In F.J. Crosby (Ed.), *Spouse, parent,*

worker: On gender and multiple roles (pp. 138–153). New Haven, CT: Yale University Press.

Congressional Budget Office. (March, 1988). *New report on family income.* Washington, DC: Author.

Cowan, R.S. (1983). *More work for mother: The ironies of household technology from the open hearth to the microwave.* New York: Basic Books.

Crosby, F.J. (Ed.). (1987). *Spouse, parent, worker: On gender and multiple roles.* New Haven, CT: Yale University Press.

DeChick, J. (1988, July 19). Most mothers want a job, too. *USA Today,* p. D1.

Epstein, C.F. (1987). Multiple demands and multiple roles: The conditions of successful management. In F.J. Crosby (Ed.), *Spouse, worker, parent: On gender and multiple roles* (pp. 23–25). New Haven, CT: Yale University Press.

Ernst, C. (1988). Are early childhood experiences overrated? A reassessment of maternal deprivation. *European Archives of Psychiatry and Neurological Sciences, 237,* 80–90.

Etaugh, C. (1980). Effects of nonmaternal care on children: Research evidence and popular views. *American Psychologist, 35,* 309–319.

Finkelstein, N. (1982). Aggression: Is it stimulated by daycare? *Young Children, 37,* 3–9.

Gardner, M. (1988a, June 9). Home with the kids—job break without penalty. *Christian Science Monitor,* p. 23.

Gardner, M. (1988b, June 30). Family-friendly corporations. *Christian Science Monitor,* p. 32.

Gilbert, L.A. (1985). *Men in dual-career families: Current realities and future prospects.* Hillsdale, NJ: Erlbaum.

Gilbert, L.A. (1988). *Sharing it all: The rewards and struggles of two-career families.* New York: Plenum Press.

Golden, M., Rosenbluth, L., Grossi, M.T., Policare, H.J., Freeman, H., Jr., & Brownlee, E.M. (1978). *The New York City Infant Day Care Study.* New York: Medical and Health Research Association of New York City.

Gottfried, A., & Gottfried, A. (Eds.). (1987). *Maternal employment and children's development: Longitudinal research.* New York: Plenum.

Gove, W.R., & Zeiss, C. (1987). Multiple roles and happiness. In F.J. Crosby (Ed.), *Spouse, parent, worker: On gender and multiple roles* (pp. 125–137). New Haven, CT: Yale University Press.

Greenstein, T. N. (1986). Social–psychological factors in perinatal labor force participation. *Journal of Marriage and the Family, 48,* 565–571.

Grossman, F.K., Pollack, W.S., & Golding, E. (1988). Fathers and children: Predicting the quality and quantity of fathering. *Developmental Psychology, 24,* 82–91.

Gunnarsson, L. (1978). *Children in day care and family care in Sweden* (Research Bulletin No. 21). Gothenburg, Sweden: University of Gothenburg.

Haskins, R. (1985). Public aggression among children with varying day care experience. *Child Development, 57,* 689–703.

Hewlett, S. (1986). *A lesser life.* New York: Morrow.

Hiller, D.V., & Dyehouse, J. (1987). A case for banishing "dual-career marriages" from the research literature. *Journal of Marriage and the Family, 49,* 787–795.

Hofferth, S.L., & Phillips, D.A. (1987). Child care in the United States, 1970 to 1995. *Journal of Marriage and the Family, 49,* 559–571.

Hoffman, L.W. (1984). Work, family, and the socialization of the child. In R. D. Parke (Ed.), *Review of child development research* (Vol. 7, pp. 223–281). Chicago: University of Chicago Press.

Howes, C., & Olenick, M. (1986). Family and child care influences on toddlers' compliance. *Child Development, 57,* 202–216.

Howes, C., Rodning, C., Galluzzo, D., & Myers, L. (1988). Attachment and child care: Relationships with mother and caregiver. *Early Childhood Research Quarterly, 3,* 403–416.

Howes, C., & Stewart, P. (1987). Child's play with adults, toys, and peers: An examination of family and child-care influences. *Developmental Psychology, 23,* 423–430.

Hughes, D., & Galinsky, E. (in press). Relationships between job characteristics, work/family interference, and marital outcomes. *Early Childhood Research Quarterly.*

Johnston, W.B. (1987). *Workforce 2000: Work and workers for the 21st century.* Indianapolis, IN: Hudson Institute.

Kagan, J., Kearsley, R.B., & Zelazo, P.R. (1978). *Infancy: Its place in human development.* Cambridge, MA: Harvard University Press.

Kahn, A.J., & Kamerman, S.B. (1987). *Child care: Facing the hard choices.* Dover, MA: Auburn House.

Kamerman, S. (1986). Maternity, paternity, and parenting policies: How does the United States compare. In S.A. Hewlett, A.S. Ilchman, & J.J. Sweeney (Eds.), *Family and work: Bridging the gap* (pp. 53–66). Cambridge, MA: Ballinger.

Kamerman, S. (1989). Child care, women, work and the family: An international overview of child care services and related policies. In J. Lande, S. Scarr, & N. Gunzenhauser (Eds.), *The future of child care in the United States* (pp. 93–110). Hillsdale, NJ: Erlbaum.

Kamerman, S., & Hayes, C.D. (Eds.). (1982). *Families that work: Children in a changing world.* Washington, DC: National Academy Press.

Leijon, A. (1986). The origins, progress, and future of Swedish family policy. In S.A. Hewlett, A.S. Ilchman, & J.J. Sweeney (Eds.), *Family and work: Bridging the gap* (pp. 31–38). Cambridge, MA: Ballinger.

Locksley, A. (1980). On the effects of wives' employment on marital adjustment and companionship. *Journal of Marriage and the Family, 42,* 337–346.

McCartney, K. (1984). The effects of quality of day care environment upon children's language development. *Developmental Psychology, 20,* 244–260.

McCartney, K., & Galanopoulos, A. (1988). Child care and attachment: A new frontier the second time around. *American Journal of Orthopsychiatry, 58,* 16–24.

McCartney, K., & Phillips, D. (1989). Motherhood and child care. In B. Birns & D. Haye (Eds.), *Different faces of motherhood* (pp. 157–183). New York: Plenum.

Nock, S.L., & Kingston, P.W. (in press). Time with children: The impact of couples' work-time commitments. *Social Forces.*

Pepitone-Rockwell, F. (1980). *Dual-career couples.* Beverly Hills, CA: Sage.

Phillips, D. (Ed.). (1987). *Quality in child care: What does research tell us?* Washington, DC: National Association for the Education of Young Children.

Phillips, D., McCartney, K., & Scarr, S. (1987). Child care quality and children's social development. *Developmental Psychology, 23,* 537–543.

Phillips, D., McCartney, K., Scarr, S., & Howes, C. (1987). Selective review of infant day care research: A cause for concern! *Zero to Three,7*(1), 18–21.

Phillips, D., & Zigler, E. (1987). The checkered history of federal child care regulations. In E. Rothkops (Ed.), *Review of research in education* (pp. 3–41). Washington, DC: American Educational Research Association.

Pistrang, N. (1984). Women's work involvement and experience of new motherhood. *Journal of Marriage and the Family, 46,* 433–447.

Pleck, J.H. (1985). *Working wives/working husbands.* Beverly Hills, CA: Sage.

Ramey, C.T., Bryant, D.M., & Suarez, T.M. (1985). Preschool compensatory education and the modifiability of intelligence: A critical review. In D. Detterman (Ed.), *Current topics in human intelligence (pp. 247–296).* Norwood, NJ: Ablex.

Repetti, R.L., Matthews, K.A., & Waldron, I. (1989). Effects of paid employment on women's mental and physical health. *American Psychologist, 44,* 1394–1401.

Rexroat, C, & Shehan, C. (1987) The family life cycle and spouses' time in housework. *Journal of Marriage and the Family, 49,* 737–750.

Rubenstein, J., Howes, C., & Boyle, P. (1981). A two year follow-up of infants in community based day care. *Journal of Child Psychology and Psychiatry, 22,* 209–218.

Ruopp, R., Travers, J., Glantz, F., & Coelen, C. (1979). *Children at the center: Final results of the National Day Care Study.* Boston, MA: Abt Associates.

Scarr, S. (1984). *Mother care/other care.* New York: Basic Books.

Scarr, S., Phillips, D., & McCartney, K. (1988). *Facts, fantasies and the future of child care in America.* Unpublished manuscript.

Scarr, S., & Weinberg, R.A. (1986). The early childhood enterprise: Care and education of the young. *American Psychologist, 41,* 1140–1146.

Simpson, I.H., & England, P. (1982). Conjugal work roles and marital solidarity. In J. Aldous (Ed.), *Two paychecks: Life in dual-earner families.* Beverly Hills, CA: Sage.

Smeedling, T. M., & Torrey, B. B. (1988). Poor children in rich countries. *Science, 242,* 873–877.

Smith, D.S. (1985). Wife employment and marital adjustment: A cumulation of results. *Family Relations, 34,* 483–490.

Spitz, R. (1945). Hospitalism: An inquiry into the genesis of psychiatric conditions in early childhood. *Psychoanalytic Studies of the Child, 1,* 53–74.

Steinfels, M. (1973). *Who's minding the children: The history and politics of day care in America.* New York: Simon & Schuster.

Tavris, C., & Wade, C. (1984). *The longest war: Sex differences in perspective.* New York: Harcourt Brace Jovanovich.

Vandell, D.L., & Powers, C.P. (1983). Day care quality and children's free play activities. *American Journal of Orthopsychiatry, 53,* 493–500.

Voyandoff, P. & Kelly, R. F. (1984). *Journal of Marriage and the Family, 46,* 881–892.

Weinraub, M., Jaeger, E., & Hoffman, L. (1988). Predicting infant outcome in families of employed and non-employed mothers. *Early Childhood Research Quarterly, 3,* 361–378.

Wortman, C. (1987, October). Coping with role overload among professionals with young children. In K. P. Matthews (Chair), *Workshop on Women, Work and Health.* Workshop conducted at the meeting of the MacArthur Foundation, Hilton Head, SC.

Yarrow, L. (1961). Maternal deprivation: Toward an empirical and conceptual evaluation. *Psychological Bulletin, 58,* 459–490.

PUTTING CHILDREN FIRST

WILLIAM A. GALSTON

William A. Galston, the author most recently of Liberal Purposes: Goods, Virtues, and Diversity in the Liberal State *(Cambridge University Press), teaches at the University of Maryland, College Park. He is an advisor to the Washington, D.C.–based Progressive Policy Institute and a co-editor of* The Responsive Community, *a new journal that seeks a better balance between rights and responsibilities. This article is an expanded version of an essay that appeared in the December 2, 1991, issue of* The New Republic, *with material drawn from* Putting Children First: A Progressive Family Policy for the 1990s *by Elaine Ciulla Kamarck and William A. Galston, published by the Progressive Policy Institute.*

THE AMERICAN family has changed dramatically in the past generation, and it is children who have paid the price. From Ozzie and Harriet to the Simpsons, from one breadwinner to two, from child-centered nuclear families that stayed together for the sake of the children to the struggling one-parent families of today; the revolution in the American family has affected us all. Divorce rates have surged, and child poverty has risen alarmingly. The signs are everywhere around us that America's children are suffering—economically, educationally, and emotionally. Although this fact is obvious, indeed increasingly obtrusive, it has hardly been discussed by intellectuals and policy elites until quite recently. Several broad forces—racial conflict, feminism, the culture of individual rights—help explain this odd silence.

The story begins in 1965, with the publication of Daniel Patrick Moynihan's *The Negro Family: The Case for National Action,* which identified the breakdown of the black family as a growing obstacle to racial progress. Although intended as the analytical backdrop to major federal initiatives, it was received as a call for quietism, even as a subtle relegitimation of racism. Black civil rights leaders and white liberal scholars argued that the emphasis on family structure would inevitably divert attention from economic inequalities and would justify "blaming the victims" for the consequences of discrimination. As William Julius Wilson has argued, this enraged response had the consequence of suppressing public debate over, and serious scholarly inquiry into, the relation between black family structure and the problems of the ghetto poor—suppressing it for an entire generation.

Feminism also contributed to the silence. The postwar American women's movement began as a criticism of the 1950s family. "Liberation" meant leaving the domestic sphere for the world of work outside the home. It also meant denying traditional theories of gender difference that seemed to legitimate inequalities of resources, power, and self-respect. To be equal was to be the same: to compete on the same terms as men, with the same focus on individual separateness and independence. As Sylvia Ann Hewlett argues, the unquestionable moral force of the feminist movement muted the voices of those who, though dubious about its denial of gender differences and deeply concerned about its consequences for the well-being of children, did not wish to be accused of a disguised effort to ratify the patriarchal or chauvinist status quo.

Then there was the cultural upheaval of the 1960s, which yielded an ethic of self-realization through incessant personal experimentation, the triumph of what has been termed "expressive individualism." An increasingly influential therapeutic vocabulary emphasized the constraints that relations could impose on personal growth and encouraged adults to turn inward toward the self's struggles for sovereignty, to view commitments as temporary or endlessly renegotiable—to behave, in effect, like adolescents. This vocabulary was anything but hospitable to the discourse of parental continuity, commitment, and self-sacrifice.

A related legacy of the generation just past has been an impoverishment of moral vocabulary. What some regard as a descent into relativism is more accurately

From *American Educator,* Summer 1992, pp. 8-13, 44-46. Reprinted with permission from *American Educator,* the quarterly journal of the American Federation of Teachers.

characterized as the relentless expansion of morality understood as the articulation of the rights of individuals. This development is not alien to the American experience, and it is not wholly to be deplored. Rights, after all, do support self-respect and offer protection against evils. Still, we now know that there is a difficulty: Although systems of rights can guide some spheres of life tolerably well, they can obscure and distort others. In particular, the effort to understand family relations as the mutual exercise of rights led to a legal and emotional cul-de-sac.

I N RECENT years, however, the climate has changed. Debates within the black community, and among social democrats as well as conservatives, have helped to relegitimate the discussion of the links between family structure and a range of social ills. To acknowledge such links, it is not necessary to sever the causal connections between structural inequalities at the political and economic level and disintegration at the family level, or to focus exclusively on the "culture of poverty." The point is, rather, that the cultural effects of past discrimination can take on a life of their own, that they can persist even in the face of changing opportunity structures.

The women's movement is changing, too. In place of equality understood as sameness, feminists such as Sara Ruddick, Carol Gilligan, and Jean Bethke Elshtain have embraced categories of difference, nurturance, and care. Martha Albertson Fineman insists that public policy "recognize and accommodate the positive and lasting nature of mothers' ties to their children." Surely this style of feminist argument will prove far more compatible with traditional understandings of the family than anyone could have predicted a decade ago.

And even broader cultural changes are under way, provoked by demographic shifts. Baby boomers who delayed marriage until their thirties have discovered that the moral universe of their young adulthood is not a suitable place for parents with young children. Others have discovered that the casting off of binding relationships is not necessarily the path to liberation and happiness. A generation that once devoted itself to the proliferation of rights and the expression of individuality has begun haltingly to explore counterbalancing notions of responsibility and community; several polls have documented rapid shifts during the past two years in public attitudes toward a range of family issues.

The most important shift is a welcome expansion of concern beyond narrow bounds of race and class. For too long, worries about children and families focused on such issues as teenage pregnancy, dire deprivation, and collapsing marriage rates. These are serious problems, but they are disproportionately characteristic of the ghetto poor. Such measurements, in other words, enabled the American middle class, scholars as well as citizens, to believe that families and children were someone else's problem. But with increased attention to the clash between work and family, to parental time deficits, and to the impact of divorce, the middle class can no longer sustain such an illusion. The decay of the family is its problem, too. The children of the middle class are also at risk; and its choices can be just as shortsighted, self-

There is growing recognition that we must place the family at the center of our thinking about social issues and children at the center of our thinking about the family.

indulgent, and harmful to the young as any ever contemplated in the culture of poverty.

T HESE RECENT trends are at last producing important changes at the level of national politics. For decades, the revolution in the American family evoked a polarized reaction: Liberals talked about structural economic pressures facing families and avoided issues of personal conduct, and conservatives did just the reverse. Liberals habitually reached for bureaucratic responses, even when they were counter-productive, and conservatives reflexively rejected government programs even when they would work.

Both are wrong. Traditional conservatives' support for families is largely rhetorical; their disregard for new economic realities engenders a policy of unresponsive neglect—expressed for example, in President Bush's misguided veto of the Family Leave Act. Conversely, traditional liberals' unwillingness to acknowledge that intact two-parent families are the most effective units for raising children has led them into a series of policy cul-de-sacs.

Recently, however, this clash of conflicting worldviews has begun to give way to a new spirit of accommodation. As E.J. Dionne Jr. has observed, recent proposals for pro-family tax reform reflect the realization that both values and dollars count. Many younger conservatives are addressing social problems long neglected by their movement. Many younger Democrats, meanwhile, are looking for new forms of nonbureaucratic, choice-based public activism as a supplement to the frequently cumbersome and intrusive institutions of the welfare state. There is growing recognition that we must place the family at the center of our thinking about social issues and children at the center of our thinking about the family. We need policies that support and compensate families as they carry out their critical social role—providing for the economic and moral well-being of children. As we will see, a large body of evidence supports the conclusion that in the aggregate, the intact two-parent family is best suited to this task. Making this premise our point of departure takes us toward policies that *reinforce* families and away from bureaucratic approaches that seek to *replace* family functions.

To avoid misunderstanding, I want to make it clear that a general preference for the intact two-parent family does not mean that this is the best option in every case. Nor does it mean that all single-parent families are somehow dysfunctional; that proposition would diminish the achievements of millions of single parents who are struggling successfully against the odds to provide good homes for their children. Rather, the point is that at the level of statistical aggregates and society-wide phenomena, significant differences do emerge between one-parent and two-parent families, differences that can and should shape our understanding of social policy.

I DO NOT mean to suggest that the renewed emphasis on the family is solely the product of cultural and ideological change. Equally important is a broad process of social learning—a growing (and increasingly painful) awareness of the consequences of the choices that we already have made, individually and collectively, over the past generation.

The economic facts are distressing. As Hewlett summarizes the data: Among all children eighteen years and under, one in five is poor, nearly twice the poverty rate for the elderly; among children younger than six, the rate is almost one in four; among children in families headed by adults younger than thirty, one in three; among black children, almost one in two. And noneconomic trends are no less stark. In the past quarter-century, the amount of time that parents spend with their children has dropped by 40 percent, from thirty hours a week to just seventeen; and there is no evidence that these remaining shreds of parental availability represent "quality time." On the contrary: As social historian Barbara Whitehead reports, "Increasingly, family schedules are intricate applications of time-motion principles."

These stress-filled lives reflect changes in the economy that have prompted momentous shifts in the labor force in this country. Since 1973, under the pressure of declining productivity and mounting international competition, family incomes have stagnated while the relative costs of a middle-class existence—in particular, of homeownership, health care, and higher education—have soared. Wage prospects have grown increasingly dismal, especially for young people with no more than a high school education. The surge of women into the work force may have begun three decades ago as a cultural revolt against household roles experienced as stifling, but it has been sustained by increasingly urgent economic necessity. Today two-thirds of all mothers with children younger than eighteen do at least some work outside the home, as do more than one-half of all mothers with children under five.

For tens of millions of American families, the second income means the difference between keeping and losing a tenuously maintained middle-class way of life. To be sure, some adjustments at the margin are possible: Young families can live in smaller houses and stop eating at restaurants. Still, the hope of many moral traditionalists that the 1950s family can somehow be restored flies in the face of contemporary market forces. The tension between remunerative work and family time will not be overcome in the foreseeable future—unless increased income from nonmarket sources allows parents with young children to do less work outside the home. Many thoughtful conservatives are coming to the realization that they must choose between their vision of a well-ordered family and their desire for smaller, less costly government.

THESE TENSIONS and others have clearly taken their toll. Test scores are down, and not just the much-discussed SATs. At BellSouth in Atlanta, for example, only about 10 percent of job applicants can pass exams that test basic learning ability, versus 20 percent a decade ago. Theft, violence, and the use of illicit drugs are far more prevalent among teenagers than they were thirty years ago; and the rate of suicide among teenagers has tripled.

It is tempting to dismiss these data as one sided, or to interpret them as mere cyclical variations within longer-term stability. After all, virtually every generation in every culture has complained of a decline of the family. But this is an alibi. We must face the fact that the conditions we take for granted are the product of a social revolution that has rapidly unfolded over just the past three decades. And at the heart of this revolution lie changes in family structure.

In thirty years, the percentage of children born outside of marriage has quintupled, and now stands at 18 percent for whites and 63 percent for blacks. In this same period, the divorce rate has tripled, as has the percentage of children living with only one parent. Of white children born in the early 1950s, 81 percent lived continuously until the age of seventeen with their two biological parents; the projected rate for children born in the early 1980s is 30 percent. The corresponding rate for black children has fallen from 52 percent in the 1950s to only 6 percent today.

These structural shifts are responsible for a substantial portion of child poverty. As David Ellwood has observed, "[t]he vast majority of children who are raised entirely in a two-parent home will never be poor during childhood. By contrast, the vast majority of children who spend time in a single-parent home will experience poverty." As Ellwood showed in *Poor Support,* in any given year, fully 50 percent of children in one-parent families will experience poverty, versus 15 percent for those in two-parent families; 73 percent of children from one-parent families will experience poverty at some point during their childhood, versus 20 percent for children from two-parent families; 22 percent of children from one-parent families will experience persistent poverty (seven years or more), versus only 2 percent from two-parent families.

These data suggest that the best anti-poverty program for children is a stable, intact family. And this conclusion holds even for families headed by younger parents with very modest levels of educational attainment. For married high school graduates with children, the 1987 poverty rate was 9 percent, versus more than 47 percent for families headed by female high school graduates. Even for married high school dropouts with children, the poverty rate was 25 percent, versus more than 81 percent for families headed by female high school dropouts. Overall, Frank Furstenberg Jr. and Andrew Cherlin conclude, the differences in family structure go "a long way toward accounting for the enormous racial disparity in poverty rates. Within family types, black families are still poorer than white families; but the racial gap in poverty shrinks considerably when the marital status of the household head is taken into account."

> *'The vast majority of children who are raised entirely in a two-parent home will never be poor during childhood. By contrast, the vast majority of children who spend time in a single-parent home will experience poverty.'*

TO BE SURE, the causal arrow could point in the opposite direction: differences in family structure might be thought to reflect differences in economic status. Wilson offered an influential statement of this counterthesis in *The Truly Disadvantaged:* Reduced black marriage rates reflect dramatically higher rates of black male unemployment, which reduces the "male marriageable pool"—under the assumption that "to be marriageable a man needs to be employed." But the most recent research offers only modest support for this hypothesis. Robert Mare and Christopher Winship find that changes in employment rates among young black males account for only 20 percent of the decline in their marriage rates since 1960; they speculate that the various family disruptions of the past three decades may be self-reinforcing.[1] Though Wilson continues to defend the validity of his thesis for the hard-hit central cities of the Northeast and Midwest, he is now willing to say that "the decline in marriage among inner-city blacks is not simply a function of the proportion of jobless men . . . it is reasonable to consider the effects of weaker social structures against out-of-wedlock births."

Along with family non-formation, family breakup is a potent source of poverty, especially among children. According to a recently released Census Bureau study by Susan Bianchi, who identified and tracked twenty thousand households, it turns out that after their parents separate or divorce, children are almost twice as likely to be living in poverty as they were before the split. The gross income of the children and their custodial parent (usually the mother) dropped by 37 percent immediately after the family breakup (26 percent after adjustment for the decline in family size) and recovered only slightly after sixteen months. These findings support the arguments of scholars who have long contended that divorce under current law spells economic hardship for most custodial parents and their minor children.

As Furstenberg and Cherlin show in their admirably balanced survey of current research, there are at least three sets of reasons for this outcome: Many women bargain away support payments in return for sole custody of their children or to eliminate the need to deal with their former spouses; when awarded, child support payments are on average pitifully inadequate; and many fathers cough up only a portion (at best) of their required payments. A Census Bureau report from the mid-1980s showed that of mothers with court-ordered support payments, only half received all of what they were owed, a

quarter received partial payments, and the remaining quarter got nothing at all.

IF THE economic effects of family breakdown are clear, the psychological effects are just now coming into focus. As Karl Zinsmeister summarizes an emerging consensus, "There is a mountain of scientific evidence showing that when families disintegrate children often end up with intellectual, physical, and emotional scars that persist for life. . . . We talk about the drug crisis, the education crisis, and the problems of teen pregnancy and juvenile crime. But all these ills trace back predominantly to one source: broken families."

As more and more children are reared in one-parent families, it becomes clear that the economic consequences of a parent's absence (usually the father) may pale beside the psychological consequences—which include higher than average levels of youth suicide, low intellectual and educational performance, and higher than average rates of mental illness, violence, and drug use.

Nowhere is this more evident than in the longstanding and strong relationship between crime and one-parent families. In a recent study, Douglas Smith and G. Roger Jarjoura found that "neighborhoods with larger percentages of youth (those aged 12 to 20) and areas with higher percentages of single-parent households also have higher rates of violent crime."[2] The relationship is so strong that controlling for family configuration erases the relationship between race and crime and between low income and crime. This conclusion shows up time and time again in the literature; poverty is far from the sole determinant of crime.

While the scarcity of intact families in the ghetto is largely a function of the failure of families to form in the first place, in the larger society the central problem is family disintegration, caused primarily by divorce. This pervasive phenomenon has effects that are independent of economics. It is to these studies that we now turn.

In 1981, John Guidubaldi, then president of the National Association of School Psychologists, picked a team of 144 psychologists in thirty-eight states, who gathered long-term data on seven hundred children, half from intact families, the other half children of divorce. Preliminary results published in 1986 showed that the effects of divorce on children persisted over time and that the psychological consequences were significant even after correcting for income differences.[3]

The problems engendered by divorce extend well beyond vanishing role models. Children need authoritative rules and stable schedules, which harried single parents often have a hard time supplying. As Guidubaldi puts it, "One of the things we found is that children who had regular bedtimes, less TV, hobbies and after-school activities—children who are in households that are orderly and predictable—do better than children who [did] not. I don't think we can escape the conclusion that children need structure, and oftentimes the divorce household is a chaotic scene."

The results of the Guidubaldi study have been confirmed and deepened by Judith Wallerstein's ten-year study of sixty middle-class divorced families. Among her key findings:

• Divorce is almost always more devastating for children than for their parents.

• The effects of divorce are often long lasting. Children are especially affected because divorce occurs during their formative years. What they see and experience becomes a part of their inner world, their view of themselves, and their view of society.

• Almost half the children entered adulthood as worried, underachieving, self-deprecating, and sometimes angry young men and women.

• Adolescence is a period of grave risk for children in divorced families; those who entered adolescence in the immediate wake of their parents' divorces had a particularly bad time. The young people told us time and again how much they needed a family structure, how much they wanted to be protected, and how much they yearned for clear guidelines for moral behavior.[4]

Furstenberg and Cherlin offer a nuanced, but ultimately troubling, account of the noneconomic consequences of divorce. For most children, it comes as an "unwelcome shock," even when the parents are openly quarreling. In the short-term, boys seem to have a harder time coping than girls, in part because of an "escalating cycle of misbehavior and harsh response between mothers and sons." Girls more typically respond with internalized disruption rather than external behavior—with heightened levels of anxiety, withdrawal, and depression that may become apparent only years later. These differences reflect the fact that divorce almost always means disrupted relations with the father. It is difficult to overstate the extent of the disruption that typically occurs. Even in the period relatively soon after divorce, only one-sixth of all children will see their fathers as often as once a week, and close to one-half will not see them at all. After ten years, almost two-thirds will have no contact.

These findings are less than self-interpreting, Furstenberg and Cherlin point out, because they must be compared with the effects on children of intact but troubled families. On the one hand, various studies indicate that the children of divorce do no worse than children in families in which parents fight continuously. On the other hand, a relatively small percentage of divorces result from, and terminate, such clearly pathological situations. There are many more cases in which there is little open conflict, but one or both partners feels unfulfilled, bored, or constrained. Indeed, the onset of divorce in these families can intensify conflict, particularly as experienced by children. As Nicholas Zill observes, "Divorces tend to generate their own problems."

Given the profound psychological effects of divorce, it is hardly surprising to discover what teachers and administrators have known for some time: One of the major reasons for America's declining educational achievement is the disintegrating American family. And if we continue to neglect the crisis of the American family, we will have undercut current efforts at educational reform.

Untangling just what it is about family structure that makes for high or low educational achievement is a dif-

ficult task. Clearly the economics of the family have a great deal to do with achievement; children from poor families consistently do less well than do children from non-poor or well-to-do families. Nevertheless, income is clearly not the whole story. When studies control for income, significant differences in educational achievement appear between children from single-parent families and children from intact families.

For example, a study conducted under the auspices of the National Association of Elementary School Principals and the Institute for Development of Educational Activities shows that family background has an important effect on educational achievement above and beyond income level—especially for boys. Lower-income girls with two parents, for instance, score higher on achievement tests than do higher-income boys with one parent. At the very bottom of the achievement scale are lower-income boys with one parent.[5]

WHAT SHOULD be our response to these developments? The recent literature suggests three broad possibilities. First, we may applaud, with Judith Stacey, the demise of the traditional (rigid, patriarchal) family and the rise of "postmodern" (flexible, variegated, female-centered) arrangements, which are allegedly far more consistent with egalitarian democracy. Second, we may accept Jan Dizard and Howard Gadlin's suggestion that moral change (in the direction of autonomy) and economic change (in the direction of a two-earner, postindustrial economy) have rendered obsolete the older model of the private family; in its place, they advocate a dramatically expanded public sphere on the Swedish model that assumes many of the private family's functions. And third, there is the response, neither postmodern nor socialist, that might be called neotraditional.

It goes something like this. A primary purpose of the family is to raise children well, and for this purpose stably married parents are best. Sharply rising rates of divorce, unwed mothers, and runaway fathers do not represent "alternative lifestyles." They are, instead, most truly characterized as patterns of adult behavior with profoundly negative consequences for children. Families have primary responsibility for instilling traits such as discipline, ambition, respect for the law, and regard for others; and it is a responsibility that cannot be discharged as effectively by auxiliary social institutions such as public schools. This responsibility entails a sphere of legitimate parental authority that should be bolstered—not undermined—by society. It requires personal sacrifice and the delay of certain forms of gratification on the part of parents. It means that government should devote substantial resources to stabilizing families and to enhancing their child-rearing capacity. But at the same time it must minimize bureaucratic cost, complexity, and intrusiveness, working instead to broaden family choice, opportunity, and responsibility.

The willingness to join the languages of economics and morals, and to consider new approaches to old goals, is increasingly characteristic of public discussion of the family. As Barbara Whitehead notes, this approach suffuses the recent report of the National Commission on Children. The volume edited by David Blankenhorn, Steven Bayme, and Jean Bethke Elshtain is particularly strong along the moral dimension. To be sure, it is easy for this stance to give the appearance of ineffectual exhortation. The editors of *The New York Times* assert that the commission's final report "swims in platitudes." Still, there are eminently practical ways of embedding moral concerns in policies and institutions. Richard Louv argues for moral change focused on the community as much as the individual. He urges us to reweave the tattered "web" of social relationships—parent-school ties, neighborhoods, communal child care arrangements, and the like—that provide a supportive environment for families and help nurture children. Although Louv emphasizes the importance of civil society, he does not imagine that the web can be adequately repaired without major changes in public policy.

Here Louv joins an emerging consensus that differs over details but not over essentials. The point is not to be driven to make a false choice between moral and economic concerns, but rather to combine them in a relation of mutual support. It might well be argued, for example, that the government has a responsibility not to tax away the money that families need to raise children. Four decades ago, the United States had a disguised family allowance: In 1948 the personal exemption was $600 (42 percent of per-capita personal income), while today's personal exemption is only 11 percent of per-capita income. This meant that a married couple at the median income with two minor dependents paid only 0.3 percent of their 1948 income in federal income taxes, compared to today's 9.1 percent. The 1948 couple's total tax bill (federal, state, and Social Security) was 2 percent of personal income. Today that total comes to about 30 percent.

Thus, one proposal now gaining support is to raise the personal exemption from the current $2,050 to at least $4,000, and perhaps eventually to $7,500. To make this more affordable, the bulk of the increase could be targeted to young children, and the increase could be phased out for upper-income taxpayers. Another approach, endorsed by the National Commission on Children, would create a $1,000 tax credit for each child; low-income families that owe no taxes would receive a cash payment for the amount of the credit. (To avoid potentially perverse incentives, this proposal should be coupled with a broader program of welfare reform.)

Reducing the tension between work and family will take changes in the private as well as the public sector. Hewlett, Louv, and many others argue for a "family-oriented workplace" with far more adaptable schedules: more flexible hours, greater opportunities for working at home and communicating by computer, for part-time employment, and for job sharing. Resistance to these changes reflects primarily the ignorance or the obduracy of middle-aged male managers, not negative impact on corporate balance sheets. Much the same is true of unpaid leave for parents following the birth of a child. Studies at the state level indicate that the costs and disruptive effects of such leaves, even when legally mandatory, are minimal. President Bush's opposition to federal family leave legislation is increasingly indefensible.

Adequate reward for labor force participation represents another important link between morals and public policy. If we believe that the presence of a parent who works outside the home furnishes a crucial moral example for his or her children, then surely the community has a responsibility to ensure that full-time work by a parent provides a nonpoverty family income. As Robert Shapiro of the Progressive Policy Institute has argued, the most efficient way to accomplish this goal would be to expand the Earned Income Tax Credit and tie it to family size.

This emphasis on the use of the tax code to promote family opportunity and responsibility is characteristic of a political outlook that has been called "neoprogressive." This is not to suggest that traditional liberal approaches are in every case misguided. Some of them—prenatal care, WIC (the nutrition program for poor women, infants, and children), childhood immunization, and Head Start—efficiently promote the well-being of children and families, and the political consensus supporting their expansion now stretches from KidsPac (a liberal, children-oriented political action committee) and the Children's Defense Fund to the Bush administration and the corporate-based Committee for Economic Development. And yet the neoprogressives are more willing than the traditional liberals to re-examine the programs of the past and to distinguish between what works and what doesn't.

IF THE PRIVATE and public sectors must assume greater responsibility for the well-being of families with children, so must parents. In particular, the moral obligation to help support one's biological children persists regardless of one's legal relationship to them, and the law is fully justified in enforcing this obligation. The 1988 Family Support Act requires states to collect the Social Security numbers of both parents (married or unmarried) at birth, to increase efforts to establish contested paternity, to use (as at least rebuttable presumptions) their guidelines concerning appropriate levels of child support, and to move toward collecting all new support awards through automatic payroll deductions.

These are steps in the right direction, but they don't go far enough. Mary Ann Glendon has argued powerfully that a "children first" principle should govern our spousal support and marital property law:

> The judges' main task would be to piece together, from property and income and inkind personal care, the best possible package to meet the needs of children and their physical guardian. Until the welfare of the children had been adequately secured in this way, there would be no question of, or debate about, "marital property." All assets, no matter when or how acquired, would be subject to the duty to provide for the children.[6]

Moreover, the state-level reforms mentioned above do nothing to address what is in many cases the chief impediment to support collection: fathers moving from state to state to slow or avoid apprehension. Conflicting state laws and a morass of administrative complexity discourage mothers from pursuing their claims across jurisdictions. Ellwood and others have called for the federalization of the system, with payroll deductions remitted to, and support payments drawn from, a centralized national fund. The U.S. Commission on Interstate Child Support, created by Congress to develop a blueprint for reform, is considering this idea.

Even when child support is collected regularly from absent parents who can afford to provide it, payments are typically set too low to avoid tremendous disruption in the lives of custodial mothers and their children. Writing from very different perspectives, Lenore Weitzman, Martha Albertson Fineman, and Furstenberg and Cherlin converge on the conclusion that the laws and the practices of many states leave men in a far more favorable situation after divorce. Furstenberg and Cherlin cite approvingly a proposal to require noncustodial fathers to pay a fixed proportion of their income, 17 percent to 34 percent, depending on the number of minor children; the adoption of this standard nationwide would raise total child support due by roughly two-thirds. Fineman advocates a need-based approach that would (she argues) yield better results for women and children than would ostensibly egalitarian standards.

During the past generation, the presumption in favor of awarding mothers custody of their children has been replaced in many cases by the presumption of equal claims. This development has generated a rising number of joint custody arrangements that do not, on average, work out very well. It has also worsened the post-divorce economic status of custodial mothers and their children: Because women tend to view custody as a paramount issue, they often compromise on economic matters to avoid the custody battle made possible by the new, supposedly more egalitarian, legal framework. And here, too, scholars from various points on the ideological spectrum are converging on the conclusion that the traditional arrangement had much to recommend it. They propose a "primary caretaker" standard: judges should be instructed to award custody of young children to the parent who has (in the words of a leading advocate) "performed a substantial majority of the [direct] caregiving tasks for the child."

THESE AND similar proposals will help custodial mothers and their children pick up the pieces after divorce, but they will do little to reduce the incidence of divorce. For Furstenberg and Cherlin, this is all that can be done: "We are inclined to accept the irreversibility of high levels of divorce as our starting point for thinking about changes in public policy." Hewlett is more disposed to grasp the nettle. While rejecting a return to the fault-based system of the past, she believes that the current system makes divorce too easy and too automatic.

Government should send a clearer moral signal that families with children are worth preserving. In this spirit, she suggests that parents of minor children seeking divorce undergo an eighteen-month waiting period, during which they would be obliged to seek counseling and to reach a binding agreement that truly safeguards their children's future.

The generation that installed the extremes of self-expression and self-indulgence at the heart of American culture must now learn some hard old lessons about commitment, self-sacrifice, the deferral of gratification, and simple endurance. It will not be easy. But other sorts of gratifications may be their reward. Perhaps the old morality was not wrong to suggest that a deeper kind of satisfaction awaits those who accept and fulfill their essential human responsibilities.

REFERENCES

[1] Mare, Robert D. and Winship, Christopher, "Socio-economic Change and the Decline of Marriage for Blacks and Whites." In *The Urban Underclass,* edited by Christopher Jencks and Paul Peterson. Washington, D.C.: The Brookings Institute, 1991.

[2] Smith, Douglas A., Jarjoura, G. Roger, "Social Structure and Criminal Victimization." In *Journal of Research in Crime and Delinquency,* Vol. 25, No. 1, February 1988.

[3] Guidubaldi, J., Cleminshaw, H.K., Perry, J.D., Nastasi, B.K., and Lightel, J., "The Role of Selected Family Environment Factors in Children's Post-Divorce Adjustment." In *Family Relations,* Vol. 35, 1986.

[4] Wallerstein, Judith S., and Blakeslee, Sandra, *Second Chances: Men, Women, and Children a Decade after Divorce.* New York: Ticknor and Fields, 1989.

[5] Sally Banks Zakariya, "Another Look at the Children of Divorce," *Principal Magazine,* September 1982, p. 35. See also, R.B. Zajonc, "Family Configuration and Intelligence," *Science,* Vol. 192, April 16, 1976, pp. 227-236. In a later and more methodologically sophisticated study, the authors try to define more completely what it is about two-parent families that make them better at preparing students for educational success. Income clearly stands out as the most important variable; but the close relationship between one-parent status, lower income, and lack of time for things like homework help and attendance at parent teacher conferences—to name a few of the variables considered—led the authors to say that "the negative effects of living in a one-parent family work primarily through other variables in our model." Ann M. Milne, David E. Myers, Alvin S. Rosenthal, and Alan Ginsburg, "Single Parents, Working Mothers, and the Educational Achievement of School Children," *Sociology of Education,* 1986, Vol. 59 (July), p. 132.

[6] Glendon, Mary Ann, *Abortion and Divorce in Western Law.* Cambridge, MA: Harvard University Press, 1987 (pp. 93-95).

Marital Transitions

A Child's Perspective

E. Mavis Hetherington, Margaret Stanley-Hagan, and Edward R. Anderson
University of Virginia

ABSTRACT: *Despite a recent leveling off of the divorce rate, almost half of the children born in the last decade will experience the divorce of their parents, and most of these children will also experience the remarriage of their parents. Most children initially experience their parents' marital rearrangements as stressful; however, children's responses to their parents marital transitions are diverse. Whereas some exhibit remarkable resiliency and in the long term may actually be enhanced by coping with these transitions, others suffer sustained developmental delays or disruptions. Others appear to adapt well in the early stages of family reorganizations but show delayed effects that emerge at a later time, especially in adolescence. The long-term effects are related more to the child's developmental status, sex, and temperament; the qualities of the home and parenting environments; and to the resources and support systems available to the parents and child than they are to divorce or remarriage per se. In recent years, researchers have begun to move away from the view that single-parent and remarried families are atypical or pathogenic families and are focusing on the diversity of children's responses and to the factors that facilitate or disrupt the development and adjustment of children experiencing their parents' marital transitions.*

The rate of divorce, particularly divorce involving families with children, rose dramatically between 1965 and 1979. Since 1979, however, the rate has begun to fall, declining 6% between 1979 and 1984 (Hernandez, 1988). Despite this leveling off, it is estimated that between 40% and 50% of the children born in the late 1970s and early 1980s will experience their parents' divorce and will spend an average of five years in a single-parent home before their custodial parents' remarriage (Glick & Lin, 1986). Because 75% of divorced mothers and 80% of divorced fathers remarry and the divorce rate in remarriages is higher

than that in first marriages, many children are exposed to a series of marital transitions and household reorganizations following their parents' initial separation and divorce. Thus divorce and remarriage should not be viewed as single static events but as part of a series of transitions modifying the lives and development of children. Children encounter widely varying sequences of family reorganizations and family experiences following divorce, and the patterning and timing of these experiences may be critical in their long-term adjustment.

In this article the changed experiences and responses of children to their parents' marital rearrangements are discussed, and divorce and remarriage from the perspective of the child is examined. Although the adjustment of children is related to the adaptation and behavior of parents, what may be a positive life situation or coping strategy for one family member is not necessarily salutary for other family members. The decision to divorce or remarry may be made on the basis of the possibility for improved well-being of the parent, in many instances with little or no consideration for the concerns of the child. Few children wish for their parents' divorce, and many children resent their parents' remarriages (Clingempeel, Brand, & Sevoli, 1984; Garbarino, Sebes, & Schellenbach, 1984; Hetherington, in press-a; Hetherington & Anderson, 1987; Hetherington, Cox, & Cox, 1985; Wallerstein & Kelly, 1980).

In spite of this, after a period of initial distress following divorce, most children and parents adapt to their situation in a single-parent household within two to three years if their new situation is not compounded by continued or additional adversity. The new family structure and equilibrium is usually disrupted, however by the custodial parent's remarriage within three to five years. The period of adjustment to remarriage seems to be longer than that for divorce, especially for older children (Hetherington, in press-a; Hetherington & Clingempeel, 1988). Moreover, because divorces tend to occur more rapidly in remarriages, in some families the child is already confronting a second divorce before adaptation to the remarriage may have occurred.

Correspondence concerning this article should be addressed to E. Mavis Hetherington, Department of Psychology, Gilman Hall, University of Virginia, Charlottesville, VA 22903.

The transition following divorce or remarriage both involve the restructuring of the household and changes in family roles and relationships; however, they differ in several important ways. Divorce usually involves high levels of family conflict and decrease or loss of contact with a parent, whereas remarriage involves the addition of a family member. Furthermore, a child whose parent remarries has already experienced life in his or her family of origin, divorce, and a period of time in a single-parent household before the remarriage occurs. Children's experiences in earlier family situations will modify responses to new situations. It has been argued that behavior problems exhibited by children in remarried families are attributable not to difficulties in adapting to remarriage, but to stresses associated with divorce and life in a single-parent household (Furstenberg, 1988; Zill, 1988).

Diversity in Children's Responses to Divorce and Remarriage

There is great diversity in children's responses to their parents' marital transitions. Many children manifest some behavioral disruptions and emotional upheaval immediately following their parents' divorce or remarriage. Anger, resentment, anxiety, depression, and even guilt are commonly experienced by children at this time. In the period immediately following divorce, children may grieve for the absent parent, may respond with noncompliance and aggression to parental conflict and family disorganization, and may become confused by and apprehensive of changing relationships with parents (Furstenberg & Allison, 1985; Hetherington, Cox, & Cox, 1982, 1985; Peterson & Zill, 1986; Wallerstein & Kelly, 1980). In the period following remarriage, the child must give up fantasies of parental reconciliation, may resent the new step-parent's attempts to control or discipline, and may perceive the new marital relationship as a threat to the restabilized parent–child relationship (Bray, 1988; Brand, Clingempeel, & Bowen-Woodward, 1988; Clingempeel et al., 1984; Hetherington, in press-a, in press-b; Hetherington & Clingempeel, 1988; Hetherington et al., 1982).

Following the initial responses to the crisis period in their parents' divorce and remarriage, some children exhibit remarkable resiliency and in the long term may actually be enhanced by coping with these transitions; others suffer sustained developmental delays or disruptions; still others appear to adapt well in the early stages of family reorganization but show delayed effects that emerge at a later time, especially adolescence (Hetherington, in press-a). The most commonly reported problem behaviors found in children from divorced and remarried families are aggressive, noncompliant, and acting-out behaviors; decrements in prosocial behavior; problems in academic achievement and school adjustment; and disruptions in peer and heterosexual relations (Bray, 1987, 1988; Camara & Resnick, 1988; Hetherington et al., 1982, 1985; Hetherington & Clingempeel, 1988; Stolberg & Anker, 1984; Stolberg, Camplair, Currier, & Wells, 1987; Zill, 1988). Although there are some reports of greater depression or internalizing disorders in these children when they reach adolescence (Hetherington & Clingem-

peel, 1988; Wallerstein, Corbin, & Lewis, 1988), these findings are less well substantiated and less consistently found than those citing externalizing problems. Researchers consistently find that children adapt better in a well-functioning single-parent or step-parent family than in a conflict-ridden family of origin (Block, Block, & Gjerde, in press; Hess & Camara, 1979; Hetherington et al., 1982; Lamb, 1977; Long & Forehand, 1987; Stolberg et al., 1987). Again it should be noted that being removed from a conflictual family situation through divorce or the introduction of a supportive step-parent may also have positive effects on the adjustment of children. Long-term effects of marital transitions are related more to new stresses encountered by the child, the individual attributes of the child, the qualities of the single-parent or stepfamily home environment, and resources and support systems available to the child than to divorce or remarriage per se (Forgatch, Patterson, & Skinner, 1988; Hetherington, 1987, in press-a, in press-b; Hetherington et al., 1985; Stolberg et al., 1987; Zill, 1988).

Cumulative Stress

Rutter (1980) reported that a single stress typically carries no appreciable psychiatric risk for children. When children are exposed to multiple stressors, however, the adverse effects increase multiplicatively. When parents divorce, children are frequently exposed to parental conflict and must adjust not only to the absence of the noncustodial parent but also to depressed economic resources, changes in the custodial parent's availability and overall parenting style, and more chaotic household routines. When the custodial parent remarries, the child again experiences changes in family structure and relationships. Moreover, it has been suggested that when roles and relationships in stepfamilies become increasingly complex, adjustment of family members becomes increasingly difficult (Cherlin, 1981). Support for this idea is found in evidence that children in stepfamilies have more difficulty in adjusting in stepfamilies with larger numbers of children, in blended families in which there are children from the custodial parent and the step-parent's previous marriages, and in families in which a new child is born to the biological parent and step-parent (Hetherington et al., 1982; Santrock & Sitterle, 1987; Zill, 1988).

Child Temperament and Personality

Temperamentally difficult children have been found to be less adaptable to change and more vulnerable to adversity than are temperamentally easy children (Hetherington, in press-a; Rutter, 1980). The more difficult child is more likely to be the elicitor and the target of aversive responses by the parents and step-parents, whereas the temperamentally easy child not only is less likely to be the recipient of criticism, displaced anger, and anxiety but also is more able to cope with these responses. If temperamentally easy children have support systems available to them, going through moderate levels of stress in a divorce or remarriage may actually enhance their ability to cope with later adaptive challenges. In contrast, for temperamentally difficult children, increasing stress leads to decrements in later coping skills and an increase in behavior problems (Hetherington, in press-a). Other individual attributes such as intelligence, independence, internal locus of control, and self-esteem also are related to children's adaptability in the face of stressful life experiences (Garmezy, 1983; Hetherington, in press-a; Hetherington et al., 1982; Masten, 1986; Rutter, 1983, 1987; Werner, 1987). Furthermore, a recent provocative paper by Block et al. (in press) suggests that children with personality and behavior problems may be not only more vulnerable to the effects of their parents' divorce but also more likely to have parents who later divorce. Behavior problems in children may exacerbate marital problems and contribute to divorce.

Developmental Status

The adaptation of children to family transitions also varies with their developmental status. Although some studies show that children who are younger at the time of their parents' marital disruption exhibit more problems (Kalter & Rembar, 1981; Santrock & Wohlford, 1979), others do not (Stolberg et al., 1987; Wallerstein et al., 1988). It might be more accurate to say that the type of behavior problems and coping mechanisms differ for children of different ages. Although nothing is known about the effects of divorce on infants, young children's responses are mediated by their limited cognitive and social competencies, their dependency on their parents, and their restriction to the home. During the interval immediately following divorce, preschool children are less able to appraise accurately the divorce situation, the motives and feelings of their parents, their own role in the divorce, and possible outcomes. Thus young children may blame themselves for the divorce, may fear abandonment by both parents, may misperceive parents' emotions, needs, and behaviors, and may harbor fantasies of reconciliation (Wallerstein et al., 1988).

The cognitive immaturity that creates profound anxieties for the child who is young at the time of their parent's divorce may prove beneficial over time. Ten years after divorce these children have fewer memories of either parental conflict or their own earlier fears and suffering (Wallerstein et al., 1988), and they typically have developed a close relationship with the custodial parent. Although approximately one-third of these children continue to experience anger at the unavailability of the noncustodial parent and may experience depression five and ten years after divorce, most are adapting reasonably well if they are not encountering new personal or family stressors. In contrast, those who had been adolescents and who retain memories of the conflict and stress associated with the divorce may be more consciously troubled (Wallerstein et al., 1988).

Like their younger counterparts, older children and adolescents experience considerable initial pain and anger when their parents divorce; however, they are better able to accurately assign responsibility for the divorce, to resolve loyalty conflicts, and to assess and cope with additional stresses such as economic changes and new family role definitions. The older child also is able to take advantage of extrafamilial support systems. Adolescents may show remarkable maturity as they assume greater responsibilities—in the words of Weiss (1979) they may "grow up faster," but many experience premature detachment from their families. It is estimated that one-

third of older children and adolescents become disengaged from their families. If this disengagement leads to greater involvement in a prosocial peer group, school attainment, or nurturant, constructive relationships outside of the family this can be an adaptive, positive coping mechanism. If, however, it is associated with involvement in antisocial groups and activities with little adult concern or monitoring, the outcomes can be disastrous (Hetherington, 1987).

Following remarriage, many children evidence a resurgence of problem behaviors (Bray, 1988; Hetherington, in press-a; Hetherington & Clingempeel, 1988; Hetherington et al., 1985). The younger child appears able to eventually form an attachment with a competent step-parent and to accept the step-parent in a parenting role. Developmental tasks facing early adolescents, however, may make them especially vulnerable and unable to adapt to the transition of remarriage (Brand et al., 1988; Hetherington, 1987, in press-a; Hetherington & Anderson, 1987; Hetherington & Clingempeel, 1988; Hetherington et al., 1985). In addition, because older children have more self-confidence and resources for fighting back, they may confront or question some aspects of family roles and functioning that younger children would not (Brown & Hobart, in press). Children entering adolescence are confronted with changing perceptions of their parents; a decreased dependence on parental control and establishing self-monitoring; balancing parental, individual, and peer expectations; and establishing autonomy and gaining power in decision making (Steinberg, 1985).

Moreover, the awareness and preoccupation with sexuality that emerges at adolescence may not only heighten stepfamily members' concerns about what appropriate affection might be, but also may cause children to resent closeness in the new marital relationship (Hetherington, in press-a, in press-b). Children in remarried families often misinterpret normal displays of affection between newly remarried spouses (Hetherington, in press-a, in press-b). These concerns may be less of an issue, however, when the parent's remarriage occurs prior to the child's adolescence, as opposed to when the remarriage occurs at adolescence. Parker and Parker (1986), for instance, report fewer cases of sexual abuse between stepfathers and stepdaughters if the remarriage occurred when the children were young. Furthermore, for older adolescents the entry of a step-parent may not be as aversive, because late adolescents are anticipating their departure from the home and new young adult roles and relationships. The introduction of a step-parent may relieve responsibilities for emotional and economic support of their divorced parents (Hetherington & Anderson, 1987).

Sex Differences

Following divorce, approximately 90% of children reside with a custodial mother. The deleterious effects of marital discord, divorce, and life in a single-parent family in which the mother has custody are more pervasive for boys than for girls (Hetherington et al., 1982, 1985; Porter & O'Leary, 1980; Rutter, 1980, 1987). In contrast to girls who live with single mothers and to children who live with nondivorced parents, boys living with single mothers show a higher rate of behavior disorders and problems in interpersonal relations both in the home and in the school with teachers and peers. Boys also are more likely to show more sustained noncompliant, aggressive behavior even two to three years after divorce (Hetherington et al., 1982, 1985). Disturbances in social and emotional adjustment in girls living with their mothers have largely disappeared by two years after divorce; however, problems may re-emerge at adolescence in the form of precocious sexual behavior and disruptions in heterosexual relations (Hetherington, 1972; Newcomer & Udry, 1987; Wallerstein et al., 1988).

There is some evidence that school-aged children adapt better in the custody of a parent of the same sex (Camara & Resnick, 1988; Zill, 1988). Boys in the custody of their fathers are more mature, social, and independent; are less demanding; and have higher self-esteem than do girls in their fathers' custody. Sons in the custody of their fathers, however, are also less communicative and less overtly affectionate, perhaps as a result of less exposure to women's expressiveness. Girls in the custody of their fathers show higher levels of aggression and behavioral problems and fewer incidences of prosocial behavior than do girls in the custody of their mothers (Furstenberg, 1988).

It should be noted, however, that research on children's adjustment in homes where the father has custody is scant. Moreover, there is evidence that the quality of the relationship of custodial fathers and their children is related to whether or not the father actively sought custody or was awarded custody because of his ex-wife's incompetence or inability to take custody (Hetherington & Stanley-Hagan, 1986). Boys in the custody of either mothers or fathers show more acting-out behaviors than do girls (Furstenberg & Allison, 1985; Hetherington & Camara, 1984; Hetherington et al., 1982; Zeiss, Zeiss, & Johnson, 1980). This may be attributed in part to the fact that boys are more likely than girls to be exposed to parental conflict. Parents fight more and their fights are longer in the presence of sons (Hetherington et al., 1982). Moreover, a recent study (Morgan, Lye, & Condron, in press) reports that families with sons are 9% less likely to divorce than are those with daughters. This may be because of the greater involvement and attachment of fathers to sons or to the reluctance of mothers to attempt raising sons alone. Whatever the reason, it seems likely that parents of sons may remain together longer even in an acrimonious marriage. Thus sons may be exposed to more conflict both before and after divorce. In addition, boys interpret family disagreements less positively than do girls (Epstein, Finnegan, & Gythell, 1979). Furthermore, since boys are more likely than girls to respond to stress with externalizing, noncompliant, antisocial behaviors, firm consistent authoritative control may be more essential in the parenting of boys. During and following divorce, however, the discipline of custodial mothers often becomes erratic, inconsistent, peremptory, and punitive. Finally, in times of family stress boys are less able than girls to disclose their feelings and to solicit and obtain support from parents, other adults, and peers (Hetherington, in press-a).

There are some reports that marital discord is associated with anxiety and depression in girls (Emery, 1982; Emery & O'Leary, 1982; Rutter, 1971; Wallerstein et al., 1988). Internalizing behaviors are sometimes found in girls following divorce, but girls demonstrate such behaviors less frequently than they do conduct disorders (Furstenberg & Seltzer, 1983; Garbarino et al., 1984; Hetherington & Clingempeel, 1988; Hetherington et al., 1985; Jacobson, 1984; Zill & Peterson, 1983).

Little is known about the effects of joint custody on the adjustment of children. In most cases, joint legal custody still involves residential custody by the mother (Maccoby, Depner, & Mnookin, 1988). It seems unlikely that the findings of early studies of voluntary joint custody (Steinman, 1981), before the legal preference for joint custody was established, are relevant to the current situation in which joint custody is now preferred in more than 30 states. These early studies usually involved friendly divorces in which the parents were willing to make sacrifices in order to maintain parental responsibilities. Children benefit from contact with both parents following divorce if there is cooperation and low conflict between parents. Encouraging joint custody by parents with acrimonious relationships may only prolong the child's involvement in conflict and make adaptation to the divorce even more difficult. Further research is needed in this area.

Following the remarriage of the custodial parent, there often is a reemergence of emotional and behavioral problems in girls and an intensification of problems in boys (Bray, 1987, 1988; Hetherington et al., 1985; Zill & Peterson, 1983). Whereas boys experience more pervasive problems in post-divorce adjustment, some studies report that girls have more problems adjusting to remarriage (Brand et al., 1988). Over time, preadolescent boys in families with stepfathers are more likely than girls to show improvement on measures of adjustment (Hetherington et al., 1985). Sex differences in response to remarriage are less consistently reported in adolescents (Hetherington & Clingempeel, 1988; Wallerstein et al., 1988). Sons who are often involved in conflictual, coercive relations with their custodial mothers may have little to lose and much to gain by the introduction of a warm, involved stepfather. In contrast, daughters who often have close relationships with their custodial mothers and considerable independence may find a stepfather disruptive and constraining.

The Child's Life Experiences Following Family Transitions

Children encounter many changes in their life situation and family roles and relationships following divorce and remarriage. Some of these changes have direct impact on the child, but many are mediated through the behavior of other family members.

The Economics of Divorce and Remarriage

Poor parents and those with unstable incomes are more likely to divorce (Hernandez, 1988). Divorce is associated with a marked drop in income for households in which mothers retain custody. Forty-three percent of divorced custodial mothers have annual incomes less than $10,000 (Hernandez, 1988). This may be attributed in part to the fact that a large proportion of ex-husbands fail to pay child support (Haskins, Schwartz, Akin, & Dobetstein, 1985) and to a tendency for divorced women to lack the education, skills, or experience to obtain well-paying jobs. Reduced economic resources are often accompanied by dependence on welfare; changes in maternal employment; poorer quality in housing, neighborhoods, schools and child care; and geographic mobility and a consequent loss of social networks and support for the child from familiar friends, neighbors, and teachers.

If a mother is forced to return to work around the time of the divorce, the preschool child may feel he or she has been abandoned by both parents (Hetherington et al., 1982). Moreover, if a mother resents or feels unhappy working or manages only to obtain part-time or temporary jobs requiring frequent job changes, the child may be negatively affected by interactions with an anxious, dissatisfied mother. There is some accumulating evidence that although the mother's employment often enhances the adjustment and independence of daughters, it may have deleterious effects on sons, particularly under stressful life situations such as those involved in poverty or divorce (Hetherington, in press-a; Werner, 1987). If the timing of the mother's entry into the work force is appropriate, however, and if the mother wishes to work, is satisfied with her job, and obtains adequate child care, her employment may improve the family finances, contribute to her social and psychological well-being, and have no adverse effects on the child.

Contrary to the experiences of custodial mothers, both noncustodial and custodial fathers typically maintain or improve their standard of living following divorce (Chase-Lansdale & Hetherington, in press; Hetherington & Stanley-Hagan, 1986). For noncustodial fathers, the improved financial status may be attributed to the fact that they cease to be the primary source of support for their ex-spouse and children. Even when paid, child support payments tend to represent a small percentage of the divorced fathers' usable income. Thus, children who reside with their fathers following divorce seldom encounter the stresses associated with limited financial resources that are experienced by children who reside with their mothers.

For families with single mothers, the financial picture improves significantly following remarriage. In fact, the financial status of step-families tends to parallel that found in families in which parents have never divorced (Hernandez, 1988). The improved financial resources are clearly beneficial to both parents and children (Arnett, 1986; Santrock & Sitterle, 1987), although problems are not necessarily absent. Newly remarried couples must face decisions regarding the division of resources among residential family members and nonresidential ex-spouses and children. Such decisions are reported frequently to be sources of conflict, jealousy, and resentment.

Interparental Relationships

Although divorce marks the legal end of the marital relationship, the parenting relationship continues to be a critical factor in the child's adjustment to family transitions. A high degree of discord frequently characterizes family relations in the period surrounding divorce, and conflict may even accelerate following divorce. This in-

tense, often irrational acrimony may be a way for divorced spouses to maintain an emotional relationship following divorce. Many spouses, especially men, have lingering bonds of attachment following divorce and may find conflict preferable to indifference or disengagement. The result is that children often are exposed to quarreling, denigration, and recrimination between their parents and may feel conflicting loyalties. As has been noted, researchers have documented that children, particularly boys, so exposed often exhibit disturbed behavior, (Block, Block, & Morrison, 1981; Hetherington et al., 1982; Patterson, 1982; Porter & O'Leary, 1980; Rutter, 1980, 1987). Moreover, it has been shown that high rates of continued aggression and conflict between the divorced parents is associated with the gradual loss of contact of the noncustodial parent, especially after the noncustodial parent remarries (Hetherington, in press-b). Continued contact with children is significantly higher by noncustodial mothers than noncustodial fathers.

The balance between conflict and cooperation and the conflict resolution strategies used by divorced parents seem to play an especially important role in the adjustment of children (Camara & Resnick, 1988; Forehand, Long, & Brody, 1988; Hetherington, in press-b; Hetherington et al., 1982). Although parents may feel angry or resentful, if they are able to control their anger, cooperate in parenting, negotiate differences, and not directly expose their children to quarrels or violence, children show fewer emotional and social problems. Most children wish to maintain relations with both parents, and continued positive relations with both parents has been shown to be an important factor in children's successful adjustment to family transitions. As Santrock and Sitterle (1987) stated, "When divorced parents continue to argue about the terms of their relationship, life is unpleasant for everyone with the children losing most of all" (p. 287). Even after the custodial parent's remarriage, continued contact with noncustodial fathers has salutary effects on children, especially boys (Hetherington et al., 1982, 1985; Zill, 1988). There is some recent evidence, however, that if a child has frequent contact with a noncustodial mother, he or she may have more difficulty accepting a stepmother (Santrock & Sitterle, 1987).

Changes in Family Relationships

In single-parent families, the well-being of the custodial parent and the quality of the parent–child relationship become central to the adjustment of the child. Yet the stress of separation and divorce places both men and women at risk for psychological and physical dysfunction (Chase-Lansdale & Hetherington, in press). Alcoholism, drug abuse, depression, psychosomatic problems, and accidents are more common among divorced than nondivorced adults. Recent research (Kiecolt-Glaser et al., 1987) suggests that marital disruption hampers the immunologic system, making divorced persons more vulnerable to disease, infection, chronic and acute medical problems, and even death.

In addition, parents undergoing divorce often exhibit marked emotional lability characterized by euphoria and optimism alternating with anxiety, loneliness and depression, and associated changes in self-concept and self-esteem. The significance of these psychological, emotional, and physical changes is that children are encountering an altered parent at a time when they need stability in a rapidly changing life situation. Furthermore, parents and children may exacerbate each other's problems. A physically ill, emotionally disturbed, or preoccupied parent and a distressed, demanding, noncompliant child may have difficulty giving each other support or solace.

A period of diminished parenting is often found following divorce (Hetherington et al., 1982; Wallerstein & Kelly, 1980). It is not uncommon for custodial mothers to become self-involved, erratic, uncommunicative, non-supportive, and inconsistently punitive in dealing with their children (Hetherington et al., 1982). A decline in effective control and monitoring of children's behavior is most notable, however, in both divorced and remarried mothers. Divorced mothers and their sons are particularly likely to engage in escalating, mutually coercive interchanges. Girls also exhibit increased noncompliance, anger, demandingness, and dependency in the year following divorce, but by two years after divorce their problem behaviors have largely vanished, and mothers and daughters have reestablished a positive or exceptionally close relationship.

Fathers who receive custody of their children also experience early problems. Most report feeling resentment, confusion, and apprehension about their abilities to parent (Hetherington & Stanley-Hagan, 1986)—emotions that are exacerbated by the fathers' perceived isolation. They report feeling ostracized by the community because of their unique status. Although parenting skills improve for both parents over time, by two years after divorce custodial fathers report better family adjustment and fewer problems with their children than do custodial mothers (Furstenberg, 1988). This may be because, unlike custodial mothers, custodial fathers have fewer financial worries, more available supports, and are more likely to be awarded custody of school-aged children and adolescents.

When either mothers or fathers have custody, different aspects of parenting are related to the adjustment of younger than older children going through stressful experiences and multiple changes. Structured, stable, supportive environments, however, are important to children of all ages. A predictable, controlled, responsive environment may be especially important to young children who are less able to select and shape their environments and to exert self-control. Thus, the young child adjusts more easily when the custodial parent can provide the child with a stable, well-organized household, and when the parent is nurturant, uses authoritative control, and makes reasonable maturity demands. In most single-parent households, particularly where the father has custody, parents expect older children and adolescents to assume greater household and child-care responsibilities more than do parents in two parent households. Moreover, parents may make inappropriate emotional demands and elevate the older child to the level of a confidant. For many children, the increased practical and emotional responsibilities accelerate the development of self-sufficiency and maturity. If, however, the parent makes excessive maturity demands, the child is likely to experience feelings of incompetence and resentment (Hetherington et al., 1982).

In the early months of remarriage, custodial mothers report being less effective and more authoritarian in their child rearing than nondivorced mothers (Bray, 1988). Compared to nondivorced mothers and like newly divorced mothers, newly remarried mothers report poorer family communication, less effective problem resolution, less consistency in setting rules, less effective disciplining, and less emotional responsiveness. Both remarried mothers and stepfathers report less family cohesion and more poorly defined family roles and relationships in the early months of remarriage (Bray, 1988). Control and monitoring of children's behavior by mothers is low initially, but begins to improve over time for children who are not yet adolescent at the time of the remarriage (Hetherington, 1987, in press-a, in press-b). With older children, however, control and monitoring remain low and are related to externalizing disorders in adolescence (Hetherington & Clingempeel, 1988).

Both stepmothers and stepfathers take a considerably less active role in parenting than do custodial parents (Bray, 1988; Hetherington, 1987, in press-a, in press-b; Santrock & Sitterle, 1987). Even after two years, disengagement by the step-parent is the most common parenting style (Hetherington, 1987, in press-a, in press-b; Hetherington & Clingempeel, 1988). Stepfathers who initially spend time establishing relations with their stepchildren by being warm and involved, but do not assert parental authority, may eventually be accepted by boys (Hetherington, 1987, in press-a, in press-b). This appears to occur in spite of the fact that stepfathers initially appear less supportive to boys than to girls (Hetherington, 1987). Acceptance of the stepfather by the stepdaughter, however, is uncorrelated with his behavior toward her and is more difficult to obtain (Hetherington, 1987).

There is some evidence that residential stepmothers are more involved and take a more active role in discipline than do stepfathers (Santrock & Sitterle, 1987), which may in part explain the finding that the response of children to remarriage appears to be mediated by the form of the stepfamily. In general, families in which the custodial father remarries and a stepmother enters the family experience more resistance and poorer adjustment for children than do families in which the custodial mother remarries and a stepfather enters the family (Brand et al., 1988; Clingempeel et al., 1984; Furstenberg, 1988; Hobart, 1987; Santrock & Sitterle, 1987; Zaslow & Hayes, 1987). Moreover, families in which both parents bring children from a previous marriage are associated with the highest levels of behavior problems (Hobart, 1987; Santrock & Sitterle, 1987). In evaluating the efficacy of parents over the course of adjustment to remarriage, it must be kept in mind that newly remarried parents report experiencing levels of both positive and negative stress twice that of nondivorced parents (Bray, 1987, 1988).

The quality of the new marriage can also affect the parenting role; however, this appears to vary with the sex of the child. More positive marital relations in families with either stepfathers or stepmothers are associated with more negative parent–child relations and poorer child adjustment for girls (Brand et al., 1988; Hetherington, in press-a, in press-b). For boys, however, after the first two years of remarriage positive marital adjustment is related to more positive outcomes as it is in nondivorced families (Hetherington, 1987).

Relationships With the Noncustodial Parent

Neither the quality nor the frequency of contact between the noncustodial parent and child can be predicted from the pre-divorce relationship (Hetherington et al., 1982; Hetherington & Stanley-Hagan, 1986). On the one hand, some intensely attached noncustodial fathers find intermittent parenting painful and withdraw from their children. On the other hand, a substantial number of noncustodial fathers report that their relationships with their children improve after divorce, and many such fathers, who were previously relatively uninvolved, become competent and concerned parents.

There is some evidence that noncustodial mothers are more likely to maintain contact with their children than are noncustodial fathers (Furstenberg, 1988; Zill, 1988). In the early months following divorce, fathers have as much or more contact with children as they did preceding the divorce, but most noncustodial fathers rapidly become less available to their children. Also, fathers are more likely to maintain frequent contact with their sons than with their daughters (Furstenberg, 1988).

The introduction of a step-parent forces a renegotiation of the noncustodial parent's role and may strain the parent–child relationship. It is interesting to note that the remarriage of the custodial parent is not related to changes in involvement of the noncustodial parent, although remarriage of the noncustodial parent typically means withdrawal of parenting by the noncustodial parent (Furstenberg, 1988). A few researchers have found that children in families with stepmothers report a higher level of involvement of the noncustodial mother than is found with the noncustodial fathers in families with stepfathers (Brand et al., 1988; Furstenberg, 1988; Santrock & Sitterle, 1987), yet some evidence suggests otherwise (Camara & Resnick, 1988). Increased involvement of the noncustodial father, however, appears to play a positive or neutral role in families with stepfathers (Brand et al., 1988; Furstenberg, 1988), whereas increased involvement of the noncustodial mother plays a negative role in families with stepmothers, especially for girls (Brand et al., 1988). Frequent visits by the biological mother have been associated with negative relations between the child and the stepmother (Brand et al., 1988).

In summary, although the meager research findings on the role of noncustodial parents in the development of the child are not entirely consistent, they suggest that under conditions of low interparental conflict, continued involvement of a competent, supportive, reasonably well-adjusted noncustodial father can have positive effects on the adjustment of children, especially boys (Hetherington et al., 1982). Moreover, such an involvement between the noncustodial father and child has not been found to interfere with the development of close family relations in a new stepfamily (Furstenberg, 1988; Hetherington, in press-b). In contrast, continued involvement of the noncustodial mother seems to precipitate loyalty conflicts that are manifested in greater acrimony between children and their stepmothers (Brand et al., 1988; Camara & Resnick, 1988). More research is needed before firm conclusions can be drawn about the effects on children of sustained contact with the noncustodial parent. It is important to note that these effects are likely to be modified by the quality of the relation between the divorced parents and the attributes and behavior of the noncustodial parent.

Support Systems

Support systems can serve as sources of practical and emotional support for both parents and children experiencing family transitions. Just as authoritative parents can offer support to children going through their parents' marital transitions, authoritative schools can offer support to children undergoing stressful experiences (Hetherington et al., 1982; Rutter, 1979). Day care centers and schools that provide warm, structured, and predictable environments can offer stability to children experiencing a rapidly changing family environment, chaotic household routines, an altered parent, and inconsistent parenting. Moreover, responsive peers and school personnel can validate the self-worth, competence, and personal control of the older child and adolescent who has access to these extrafamilial supports (Hetherington & Clingempeel, 1988; Hetherington et al., 1982, 1985; Rutter, 1987).

Supports offered by friends and family also can increase divorced parents' positive attitudes toward themselves and their life situation and facilitate the parenting role (Hetherington, in press-a). Following divorce, often for economic reasons, between 25% and 33% of newly divorced custodial mothers reside with a relative, usually their mothers (Hernandez, 1988). The grandmother often provides economic resources and shares in child care and household responsibilities, thus partially relieving the mother's financial concerns and sense of task overload, and providing the child with another source of needed emotional support. Researchers have found that in Black families children who live with both mother and grandmother adjust better than do children who reside with a divorced mother alone (Kellam, Ensminges, & Turner, 1977). Furthermore, sons in the custody of mothers show fewer behavior problems when they have an involved supportive grandfather than when none is available (Hetherington, in press-a). When they have the economic resources to do so, however, most custodial mothers prefer to establish their own households, thus avoiding feelings of dependency and conflict over childrearing issues that may arise when they share their residences with their own parents. Such conflicts between custodial mothers and their parents occur less often with grandfathers than with grandmothers (Hetherington, in press-a).

Grandparents also increase the complexity of the stepfamily household. Involvement with step-grandparents is highest when there are no biological grandchildren, when grandparents live nearby, and when the children in the stepfamily are young at the time of remarriage. Children appear to make little distinction between biological grandparents and step-grandparents (Furstenberg, 1988). It appears that most of the influence of grandparents is mediated by the relationships with parents (Hetherington, in press-a).

Children experiencing their parents' marital transitions also may receive support from sibling relationships. There is evidence that some siblings, especially female siblings of divorced parents, may act as buffers and fill emotional voids left by unresponsive parents (Hetherington, in press-b; Hetherington & Clingempeel, 1988; Wallerstein et al., 1988). In contrast, relations among male siblings of divorced mothers with custody are more antagonistic than among those with nondivorced parents (Hetherington, in press-b). Generally, however, rivalrous, aggressive, coercive sibling and step-sibling relationships are more common in stepfamilies than positive relationships, and these negative relationships may act as additional stressors, at least in the first two years following remarriage (Hetherington, in press-b; Hetherington & Clingempeel, 1988). Sibling relationships in stepfamilies improve somewhat over time, but they are still more troubled than those of siblings with nondivorced parents (Hetherington, in press-a, in press-b; Hetherington & Clingempeel, 1988). Although overt aggression may decrease with the duration of the remarriage and age of the child, this is often associated with disengagement and lack of involvement and empathy. Siblings who live with custodial mothers who are single parents or with remarried parents appear to have particularly troubled relationships, especially if one of the siblings is a boy. The quality of the sibling relationship during the time in a single-parent household may mediate the relationship in stepfamilies, but this has not been investigated.

Conclusion

Many children encounter their parents' divorce and life in a one-parent family. Moreover, since most parents remarry, it may be appropriate to think of the time a child spends in a single-parent household as a transitional period between life with nondivorced, often conflict-ridden, parents and life in a stepfamily. Most children initially experience their parents' marital rearrangements as stressful. Divorce and remarriage are often associated with experiences that place children at increased risk for developing social, psychological, behavioral, and academic problems. Yet divorce and remarriage also can remove children from stressful or acrimonious family relationships and provide additional resources for children. Many children eventually emerge from the divorce or remarriage of their parents as competent or even enhanced individuals.

In recent years, researchers have begun to move away from the view that single-parent and stepfamilies are atypical or pathogenic. More studies are focusing on the diversity of children' responses to their parents' marital transitions and on the factors that facilitate or disrupt the development and adjustment of children in these family situations.

REFERENCES

Arnett, J. (1986, April). Effects of husband's support for the mother on maternal functioning and children's behavior problems. In E. M. Hetherington (Chair), *Coping and remarriage.* Symposium conducted at the Conference on Human Development, Nashville, TN.

Block, J. H., Block, J., & Gjerde, P. F. (In press). Parental functioning and the home environment in families of divorce: Prospective and concurrent analysis. *Journal of the American Academy of Child Psychiatry.*

Block, J. H., Block, J., & Morrison, A. (1981). Parental agreement-disagreement on child-rearing orientations and gender-related personality correlates in children. *Child Development, 52,* 965–974.

Brand, E., Clingempeel, W. E., & Bowen-Woodward, K. (1988). Family relationships and children's psychological adjustment in stepmother and stepfather families: Findings and conclusions from the Philadelphia Stepfamily Research Project. In E. M. Hetherington & J. D. Arasteh (Eds.), *Impact of divorce, single-parenting, and stepparenting on children* (pp. 299–324). Hillsdale, NJ: Erlbaum.

Bray, J. H. (1987, August). *Becoming a stepfamily.* Symposium presented at the meeting of the American Psychological Association, New York, NY.

Bray, J. H. (1988). Children's development during early remarriage. In E. M. Hetherington & J. D. Arasteh (Eds.), *Impact of divorce, single-parenting, and stepparenting on children* (pp. 279–298). Hillsdale, NJ: Erlbaum.

Brown, D. & Hobart, C. (in press). Effects of prior marriage children on adjustment in remarriages. *Journal of Comparative Family Studies.*

Camara, K. A., & Resnick, G. (1988). Interparental conflict and cooperation: Factors moderating children's post-divorce adjustment. In E. M. Hetherington & J. D. Arasteh (Eds.), *Impact of divorce, single-parenting, and stepparenting on children* (pp. 169–195). Hillsdale, NJ: Erlbaum.

Cherlin, A. (1981). *Marriage, divorce, remarriage: Changing patterns in the postwar United States.* Cambridge, MA: Harvard University Press.

Clingempeel, W. G., Brand, C., & Sevoli, R. (1984). Stepparent-stepchild relationships in stepmother and stepfather families: A multimethod study. *Family Relations, 33,* 465–473.

Emery, R. E. (1982). Interparental conflict and the children of discord and divorce. *Psychological Bulletin, 92,* 310–330.

Emery, R., & O'Leary, K. (1982). Children's perceptions of marital discord and behavior problems of boys and girls. *Journal of Abnormal Child Psychology, 10,* 11–24.

Epstein, N., Finnegan, D., & Gythell, D. (1979). Irrational beliefs and perceptions of marital conflict. *Journal of Consulting and Clinical Psychology, 67,* 608–609.

Forehand, R., Long, N., & Brody, G. (1988). Divorce and marital conflict: Relationship to adolescent competence and adjustment in early adolescence. In E. M. Hetherington & J. Arasteh (Eds.), *Impact of divorce, single-parenting, and stepparenting on children* (pp. 155–167). Hillsdale, NJ: Erlbaum.

Forgatch, M. S., Patterson, G. R., & Skinner, M. L. (1988). A mediational model for the effect of divorce on antisocial behavior in boys. In E. M. Hetherington & J. D. Arasteh (Eds.), *Impact of divorce, single-parenting, and stepparenting on children* (pp 135–154). Hillsdale, NJ: Erlbaum.

Furstenberg, F. F. (1988). Child care after divorce and remarriage. In E. M. Hetherington & J. Arasteh (Eds.), *Impact of divorce, single-parenting, and stepparenting on children* (pp. 245–261). Hillsdale, NJ: Erlbaum.

Furstenberg, F. F., Jr., & Allison, P. D. (1985). *How marital dissolution affects children: Variations by age and sex.* Unpublished manuscript.

Furstenberg, F. F., & Seltzer, J. A. (1983, August). *Encountering divorce: Children's responses to family dissolution and reconstitution.* Paper presented at the meeting of the American Psychological Association, Detroit, MI.

Garbarino, J., Sebes, L., & Schellenbach, C. (1984). Families at risk for destructive parent–child relations in adolescence. *Child Development, 55*(1), 174–183.

Garmezy, N. (1983). Stressors of childhood. In N. Garmezy & M. Rutter (Eds.), *Stress, coping, and development in children* (pp. 43–84). New York: McGraw-Hill.

Glick, P. C., & Lin, S. (1986). Recent changes in divorce and remarriage. *Journal of Marriage and the Family, 48,* 737–747.

Haskins, R., Schwartz, J. B., Akin, J. S., & Dobelstein, A. W. (1985). How much support can absent fathers pay? *Policy Studies Journal, 14,* 201–222.

Hernandez, D. J. (1988). Demographic trends and the living arrangements of children. In E. M. Hetherington & J. D. Arasteh (Eds.), *Impact of divorce, single-parenting, and stepparenting on children* (pp. 3–22). Hillsdale, NJ: Erlbaum.

Hess, R. D., & Camara, K. A. (1979). Post-divorce family relationships as mediating factors in the consequence of divorce for children. *Journal of Social Issues, 25,* 79–96.

Hetherington, E. M. (1972). Effects of fathers' absence on personality development in adolescent daughters. *Developmental Psychology, 7*(3), 313–326.

Hetherington, E. M. (1987). Family relations six years after divorce. In K. Pasley & M. Ihinger-Tollman (Eds.), *Remarriage and stepparenting today: Current research and theory* (pp. 185–205). New York: Guilford Press.

Hetherington, E. M. (in press-a). Coping with family transitions: Winners, losers, and survivors. *Child Development.*

Hetherington, E. M. (in press-b). Parents, children and siblings six years after divorce. In R. Hinde & J. Stevenson-Hinde (Eds.), *Relationships within families.* Cambridge, England: Cambridge University Press.

Hetherington, E. M., & Anderson, E. R. (1987). The effects of divorce and remarriage on early adolescents and their families. In M. D. Levine & E. R. McAnarney (Eds.), *Early adolescent transitions* (pp. 49–67). Lexington, MA: D. C. Heath.

Hetherington, E. M., & Camara, K. A. (1984). Families in transition: The process of dissolution and reconstitution. In R. Parke (Ed.), *Review of child development research* (Vol. 3, pp. 398–439). Chicago: University of Chicago Press.

Hetherington, E. M., & Clingempeel, W. G. (1988, March). *Coping with remarriage: The first two years.* Symposium presented at the Southeastern Conference on Human Development, Charleston, SC.

Hetherington, E. M., Cox, M., & Cox, R. (1982). Effects of divorce on parents and children. In M. Lamb (Ed.), *Nontraditional families* (pp. 233–288). Hillsdale, NJ: Erlbaum.

Hetherington, E. M., Cox, M., & Cox, R. (1985). Long-term effects of divorce and remarriage on the adjustment of children. *Journal of American Academy of Psychiatry, 24*(5), 518–830.

Hetherington, E. M., & Stanley-Hagan, M. (1986). Divorced fathers: Stress, coping, and adjustment. In M. Lamb (Ed.), *The father's role: Applied perspectives* (pp. 103–134). New York: Wiley.

Hobart, C. (1987). Parent–child relations in remarried families. *Journal of Family Issues, 8,* 259–277.

Jacobson, D. S. (1984). *Factors associated with healthy family functioning in stepfathers.* Paper presented at the meeting of the Society for Research in Child Development, Lexington, KY.

Kalter, N., & Rembar, J. (1981). The significance of a child's age at the time of parental divorce. *American Journal of Orthopsychiatry, 51,* 85–100.

Kellam, S. G., Ensminges, M. E., & Turner, R. J. (1977). Family structure and the mental health of children: Concurrent and longitudinal community-wide studies. *Archives of General Psychiatry, 34*(9), 1012–1022.

Kiecolt-Glaser, J. K., Fisher, L. D., Ogrocki, P., Stout, J. C., Speicher, B. S., & Glaser, R. (1987). Marital quality, marital disruption, and immune function. *Psychosomatic Medicine, 40,* 13–34.

Lamb, M. (1977). The effects of divorce on children's personality development. *Journal of Divorce, 1,* 163–174.

Long, N., & Forehand, R. (1987). The effects of parental divorce and marital conflict on children: An overview. *Journal of Developmental and Behavioral Pediatrics, 8,* 292–296.

Maccoby, E. E., Depner, C. E., & Mnookin, R. H. (1988). Custody of children following divorce. In E. M. Hetherington & J. Arasteh (Eds.), *Impact of divorce, single-parenting and stepparenting on children* (pp. 91–114). Hillsdale, NJ: Erlbaum.

Masten, A. S. (1986, August). The patterns of adaptation to stress in middle childhood. Paper presented at the meeting of the American Psychological Association, Washington, DC.

Morgan, P. S., Lye, D. N., & Condron, G. A. (in press). Sons, daughters, and divorce: Does the sex of children affect the risk of marital disruption? *American Journal of Psychology.*

Newcomer, S., & Udry, J. R. (1987). Parental marital status effects on adolescent sexual behavior. *Journal of Marriage and the Family, 49,* 235–240.

Parker, H., & Parker, S. (1986). Father–daughter sexual abuse: An emerging perspective. *American Journal of Orthopsychiatry, 56*(4), 531–549.

Patterson, G. R. (1982). *Coercive family processes: A social learning approach.* (Vol. 3). Eugene, OR: Castalia.

Peterson, J. L., & Zill, N. (1986). Marital disruption, parent–child relationship, and behavior problems in children. *Journal of Marriage and the Family, 48,* 295–307.

Porter, B., & O'Leary, K. D. (1980). Marital discord and childhood behavior problems. *Journal of Abnormal Psychology, 8,* 287–295.

Rutter, M. (1971). Parent–child separation: Psychological effects on the children. *Journal of Child Psychiatry and Applied Disciplines, 12,* 233–260.

Rutter, M. (1980). Protective factors in children's responses to stress and disadvantage. In M. W. Kent & J. E. Rolf (Eds.), *Primary prevention of psychopathology: III. Promoting social competence and coping in children* (pp. 49–74). Hanover, NH: University Press of New England.

Rutter, M. (1983). Stress, coping, and development: Some issues and some questions. In N. Garmezy & M. Rutter (Eds.), *Stress, coping, and development in children* (pp. 1–42). New York: McGraw-Hill.

Rutter, M. (1979). Children's responses to stress and disadvantage. In M. W. Kent & J. E. Rolf (Eds.), *Primary prevention of psychopathology* (Vol. 3). Hanover, NH: University Press of New England.

Rutter, M. (1987). Psychosocial resilience and protective mechanisms. *American Journal of Orthopsychiatry, 57*(3), 316–331.

Santrock, J. W., & Sitterle, K. A. (1987). Parent–child relationships in stepmother families. In K. Pasley & M. Ihinger-Tallman (Eds.), *Remarriage and stepparenting: Current research and theory* (pp. 135–154). New York: Guilford Press.

Santrock, J. W., & Wohlford, P. (1979). Effects of father absence: Influence of reason for and onset of absence. *Proceedings of the 78th Annual Convention of the American Psychological Association* (Vol. 78). Washington, DC: American Psychological Association.

Steinberg, L. D. (1985, March). *The ABCs of transformations in the family at adolescence: Changes in affect, behavior, and cognition.* Paper presented at the Third Biennial Conference on Adolescence Research, Tucson, AZ.

Steinman, S. (1981). The experience of children in a joint-custody arrangement. *American Journal of Orthopsychiatry, 51,* 403–414.

Stolberg, A. L., & Anker, J. M. (1984). Cognitive and behavioral changes in children resulting from parental divorce and consequent environmental changes. *Journal of Divorce, 8,* 184–197.

Stolberg, A. L., Camplair, C., Currier, K., & Wells, M. J. (1987). Individual, familial and environmental determinants of childrens' post-divorce adjustment and maladjustment. *Journal of Divorce, 11,* 51–70.

Wallerstein, J., Corbin, S. B., & Lewis, J. M. (1988). Children of divorce: A ten-year study. In E. M. Hetherington & J. Arasteh (Eds.), *Impact of divorce, single-parenting and stepparenting on children.* (pp. 198–214). Hillsdale, NJ: Erlbaum.

Wallerstein, J. S., & Kelly, J. B. (1980). *Surviving the breakup.* New York: Basic Books.

Weiss, R. S. (1979). Growing up a little faster: The experience of growing up in a single-parent household. *Journal of Social Issues, 35,* 97–111.

Werner, E. E. (1987). Vulnerability and resiliency in children at risk for delinquency: A longitudinal study from birth to young adulthood. In J. D. Burchard & S. M. Burchard (Eds.), *Prevention of delinquent behavior* (pp. 68–84). Beverly Hills, CA: Sage.

Zaslow, M. J., & Hayes, C. D. (1987, September). Sex differences in children's responses to psychosocial stress. In W. A. Morrill (Chair), Symposium conducted at the meeting of the National Academy of Sciences Summer Study Center, Woods Hole, MA.

Zeiss, A., Zeiss, R. A., & Johnson, S. W. (1980). Sex differences in initiation of and adjustment to divorce. *Journal of Divorce, 4,* 21–33.

Zill, N. (1988). Behavior, achievement, and health problems among children in stepfamilies: Findings from a national survey of child health. In E. M. Hetherington & J. D. Arasteh (Eds.), *Impact of divorce, single-parenting and stepparenting on children* (pp. 325–368). Hillsdale, NJ: Erlbaum.

Zill, N., & Peterson, J. L. (1983, April). Marital disruption, parent–child relationships, and behavior problems in children. Paper presented at the meeting of the Society for Research in Child Development, Detroit, MI.

The
Secret World
of Siblings

Emotional ambivalence often marks the most enduring relationship in life

They have not been together like this for years, the three of them standing on the close-cropped grass, New England lawns and steeples spread out below the golf course. He is glad to see his older brothers, has always been glad to have "someone to look up to, to do things with." Yet he also knows the silences between them, the places he dares not step, even though they are all grown men now. They move across the greens, trading small talk, joking. But at the 13th hole, he swings at the ball, duffs it and his brothers begin to needle him. "I should be better than this," he thinks. Impatiently, he swings again, misses, then angrily grabs the club and breaks it in half across his knee. Recalling this outburst later, he explains, simply: "They were beating me again."

As an old man, Leo Tolstoy once opined that the simplest relationships in life are those between brother and sister. He must have been delirious at the time. Even lesser mortals, lacking Tolstoy's acute eye and literary skill, recognize the power of the word *sibling* to reduce normally competent, rational human beings to raw bundles of anger, love, hurt, longing and disappointment—often in a matter of minutes. Perhaps they have heard two elderly sisters dig at each other's sore spots with astounding accuracy, much as they did in junior high. Or have seen a woman corner her older brother at a family reunion, finally venting 30 years of pent-up resentment. Or watched remorse and yearning play across a man's face as he speaks of the older brother whose friendship was chased away long ago, amid dinner table taunts of "Porky Pig, Porky Pig, oink, oink, oink!"

Sibling relationships—and 80 percent of Americans have at least one—outlast marriages, survive the death of parents, resurface after quarrels that would sink any friendship. They flourish in a thousand incarnations of closeness and distance, warmth, loyalty and distrust. Asked to describe them, more than a few people stammer and hesitate, tripped up by memory and sudden bursts of unexpected emotion.

Traditionally, experts have viewed siblings as "very minor actors on the stage of human development," says Stephen Bank, Wesleyan University psychologist and co-author of *The Sibling Bond*. But a rapidly expanding body of research is showing that what goes on in the playroom or in the kitchen while dinner is being cooked exerts a profound influence on how children grow, a contribution that approaches, if it may not quite equal, that of parenting. Sibling relationships shape how people feel about themselves, how they understand and feel about others, even how much they achieve. And more often than not, such ties represent the lingering thumbprint of childhood upon adult life, affecting the way people interact with those closest to them, with friends and coworkers, neighbors and spouses—a topic explored by an increasing number of popular books, including *Mom Loved You Best*, the most recent offering by Dr. William and Mada Hapworth and Joan Heilman.

Shifting landscape. In a 1990s world of shifting social realities, of working couples, disintegrating marriages, "blended" households, disappearing grandparents and families spread across a continent, this belated validation of the importance of sibling influences probably comes none too soon. More and more children are stepping in to change diapers, cook meals and help with younger siblings' homework in the hours when parents are still at the office. Baby boomers, edging into middle age, find themselves squaring off once again with brothers and sisters over the care of dying parents or the division of inheritance. And in a generation where late marriages and fewer children are the norm, old age may become for many a time when siblings—not devoted sons and daughters—sit by the bedside.

It is something that happened so long ago, so silly and unimportant now that she is 26 and a researcher at a large, downtown office and her younger brother is her best friend, really, so close that she talks to him at least once a week. Yet as she begins to speak she is suddenly a 5-year-old again on

Christmas morning, running into the living room in her red flannel pajamas, her straight blond hair in a ponytail. He hasn't even wrapped it, the little, yellow-flowered plastic purse. Racing to the tree, he brings it to her, thrusts it at her—"Here's your present, Jenny!"—smiling that stupid, adoring, little brother smile. She takes the purse and hurls it across the room. "I don't want your stupid present," she yells. A small crime, long ago forgiven. Yet she says: "I still feel tremendously guilty about it."

Sigmund Freud, perhaps guided by his own childhood feelings of rivalry, conceived of siblingship as a story of unremitting jealousy and competition. Yet, observational studies of young children, many of them the ground-breaking work of Pennsylvania State University psychologist Judy Dunn and her colleagues, suggest that while rivalry between brothers and sisters is common, to see only hostility in sibling relations is to miss the main show. The arrival of a younger sibling may cause distress to an older child accustomed to parents' exclusive attention, but it also stirs enormous interest, presenting both children with the opportunity to learn crucial social and cognitive skills: how to comfort and empathize with another person, how to make jokes, resolve arguments, even how to irritate.

The lessons in this life tutorial take as many forms as there are children and parents. In some families, a natural attachment seems to form early between older and younger children. Toddlers as young as 14 months miss older siblings when they are absent, and babies separated briefly from their mothers will often accept comfort from an older sibling and go back to playing happily. As the younger child grows, becoming a potential playmate, confidant and sparring partner, older children begin to pay more attention. But even young children monitor their siblings' behavior closely, showing a surprisingly sophisticated grasp of their actions and emotional states.

Parental signals. To some extent, parents set the emotional tone of early sibling interactions. Dunn's work indicates, for example, that children whose mothers encourage them to view a newborn brother or sister as a human being, with needs, wants and feelings, are friendlier to the new arrival over the next year, an affection that is later reciprocated by the younger child. The quality of parents' established relationships with older siblings can also influence how a new younger brother or sister is received. In another of Dunn's studies, first-born daughters who enjoyed a playful, intense relationship with their mothers treated newborn siblings with more hostility, and a year later the younger children were more hostile in return. In contrast, older daughters with more contentious relationships with their mothers greeted the newcomer enthusiastically—perhaps relieved to have an ally. Fourteen months later, these older sisters were more likely to imitate and play with their younger siblings and less apt to hit them or steal their toys.

In troubled homes, where a parent is seriously ill, depressed or emotionally unavailable, siblings often grow closer than they might in a happier environment, offering each other solace and protection. This is not always the case, however. When parents are on the brink of separation or have already divorced and remarried, says University of Virginia psychologist E. Mavis Hetherington, rivalry between brothers and sisters frequently increases, as they struggle to hold on to their parents' affection in the face of the breakup. If anything, it is sisters who are likely to draw together in a divorcing family, while brothers resist forming tighter bonds. Says Hetherington: "Males tend to go it alone and not to use support very well."

Pretend play is never wasted. Toddlers who engage regularly in make-believe activity with older siblings later show a precocious grasp of others' behavior.

Much of what transpires between brothers and sisters, of course, takes place when parents are not around. "Very often the parent doesn't see the subtlety or the full cycle of siblings' interactions," says University of Hartford psychologist Michael Kahn. Left to their own devices, children tease, wrestle and play make-believe. They are the ones eager to help pilot the pirate ship or play storekeeper to their sibling's impatient customer. And none of this pretend play, researchers find, is wasted. Toddlers who engage regularly in make-believe with older siblings later show a precocious grasp of others' behavior. Says Dunn: "They turn out to be the real stars at understanding people."

Obviously, some degree of rivalry and squabbling between siblings is natural. Yet in extreme cases, verbal or physical abuse at the hands of an older brother or sister can leave scars that last well into adulthood. Experts like Wesleyan University's Bank distinguish between hostility that takes the form of humiliation or betrayal and more benign forms of conflict. From the child's perspective, the impact of even normal sibling antagonism may depend in part on who's coming out ahead. In one study, for example, children showed higher self-esteem when they "delivered" more teasing, insults and other negative behaviors to their siblings than they received. Nor is even intense rivalry necessarily destructive. Says University of Texas psychologist Duane Buhrmester: "You may not be happy about a brother or sister who is kind of pushing you along, but you may also get somewhere in life."

They are two sides of an equation written 30 years ago: Michèle, with her raven-black hair, precisely made-up lips, restrained smile; Arin, two years older, her easy laugh filling the restaurant, the sleeves of her gray turtleneck pulled over her hands.

This is what Arin thinks about Michèle: "I have always resented her, and she has always looked up to me. When we were younger, she used to copy me, which would drive me crazy. We have nothing in common except our family history—isn't that terrible? I like her spirit of generosity, her direction and ambition. I dislike her vapid conversation and her idiotic friends. But the reality is that we are very close, and we always will be."

This is what Michèle sees: "Arin was my ideal. I wanted to be like her, to look like her. I think I drove her crazy. Once, I gave her a necklace I thought was very beautiful. I never saw her wear it. I think it wasn't good enough, precious enough. We are so different—I wish that we could be more like friends. But as we get older, we accept each other more."

It is something every brother or sister eventually marvels at, a conundrum that novelists have played upon in a thousand different ways: There are two children. They grow up in the same house, share the same parents, experience many of the same events. Yet they are stubbornly, astonishingly different.

Two children grow up in the same house, share the same parents, experience many of the same events. Yet they are stubbornly, astonishingly different.

A growing number of studies in the relatively new field of behavioral genetics are finding confirmation for this popular observation. Children raised in the same family, such studies find, are only very slightly more similar to each other on a variety of personality dimensions than they are, say, to Bill Clinton or to the neighbor's son. In cognitive abilities, too, siblings appear more different than alike. And the extent to which siblings *do* resemble one another in these traits is largely the result of the genes they share—a conclusion drawn from twin studies, comparisons of biological siblings raised apart and biological children and adopted siblings raised together.

Contrasts. Heredity also contributes to the *differences* between siblings. About 30 percent of the dissimilarity between brothers and sisters on many personality dimensions can be accounted for by differing genetic endowments from parents. But that still leaves 70 percent that *cannot* be attributed to genetic causes, and it is this unexplained portion of contrasting traits that scientists find so intriguing. If two children who grow up in the same family are vastly different, and genetics accounts for only a minor part of these differences, what else is going on?

The answer may be that brothers and sisters don't really share the same family at all. Rather, each child grows up in a unique family, one shaped by the way he perceives other people and events, by the chance happenings he alone experiences, and by how other people—parents, siblings and teachers—perceive and act toward him. And while for decades experts in child development have focused on the things that children in the same family share—social class, child-rearing attitudes and parents' marital satisfaction, for example—what really seem to matter are those things that are not shared. As Judy Dunn and Pennsylvania State behavioral geneticist Robert Plomin write in *Separate Lives: Why Siblings Are So Different*, "Environmental factors important to development are those that two children in the same family experience differently."

Asked to account for children's disparate experiences, most people invoke the age-old logic of birth order. "I'm the middle child, so I'm cooler headed," they will say, or "Firstborns are high achievers." Scientists, too, beginning with Sir Francis Galton in the 19th century, have sought in birth order a way to characterize how children diverge in personality, IQ or life success. But in recent years, many researchers have backed away from this notion, asserting that when family size, number of siblings and social class are taken into account, the explanatory power of birth ranking becomes negligible. Says one psychologist: "You wouldn't want to make a decision about your child based on it."

At least one researcher, however, argues that birth order does exert a strong influence on development, particularly on attitudes toward authority. Massachusetts Institute of Technology historian Frank Sulloway, who has just completed a 20-year analysis of 4,000 scientists from Copernicus through the 20th century, finds that those with older siblings were significantly more likely to have contributed to or supported radical scientific revolutions, such as Darwin's theory of evolution. Firstborn scientists, in contrast, were more apt to champion conservative scientific ideas. "Later-borns are consistently more open-minded, more intellectually flexible and therefore more radical," says Sulloway, adding that later-borns also tend to be more agreeable and less competitive.

Many people believe in the logic of birth order. "I'm the middle child, so I'm cooler headed," they will say, or "Firstborns are high achievers."

Hearthside inequities. Perhaps most compelling for scientists who study sibling relationships are the ways in which parents treat their children differently and the inequalities children perceive in their parents' behavior. Research suggests that disparate treatment by parents can have a lasting effect, even into adulthood. Children who receive more affection from fathers than their siblings do, for example, appear to aim their sights higher in terms of education and professional goals, according to a study by University of Southern California psychologist

SIMIAN SIBLINGS
Mixed feelings in the treetops

Humans are not alone in having to deal with the ambivalence of sibling relationships. According to a growing body of scientific research simian siblings, too, carry on the subtle dances of cooperation and competition, generosity and animosity well known to any human brother or sister.

Conflict is actually more common—though less intense—among primate siblings than among non-kin, according to Lynn Fairbanks, a University of California at Los Angeles research psychologist and co-editor of the recent book *Juvenile Primates*. "It doesn't get to the Cain and Abel stage," she notes, but juvenile and adolescent brothers and sisters do battle regularly for their mother's attention and then for their own place in society, biting and kicking, interrupting grooming sessions, even pushing a suckling infant off the mother's nipple.

Brother's keeper. In the midst of this conflict, however, primate siblings do cooperate—grooming, sharing food and playing together. In the face of external threats, siblings often protect one another with a direct attack or an alarm call. Becky, a brave Barbary macaque,

even threatened a larger male to rescue her 2-month-old brother from danger. Some monkeys have even been known to "adopt" an infant sibling when the mother dies.

Both cooperation and conflict have roots in evolution, say scientists. In the Darwinian jungle, primates (like other animals) struggle ultimately to pass on their genes, about half of which they share with their siblings. With limited resources and constant external threats, they first try to secure their own survival, compromising siblings when necessary. But it also pays to aid brothers and sisters, since a rescuer is indirectly protecting and passing on a shared heredity. "Genes are thicker than water," notes Cornell University anthropologist Meredith Small.

Much like their human counterparts, simian sibs cycle in and out of affection and animosity. Whether on the jungle gym or the jungle floor, says UCLA's Fairbanks, "siblings have the most positive and the most negative relationships."

BY BETSY WAGNER

Laura Baker. Seven year-olds treated by their mothers in a less affectionate, more controlling way than their brothers or sisters are apt to be more anxious and depressed. And adolescents who say their parents favor a sibling over themselves are more likely to report angry and depressed feelings.

Parental favoritism spills into sibling relationships, too, sometimes breeding the hostility made famous by the Smothers Brothers in their classic 1960s routine, "Mom always loved you best." In families where parents are more punitive and restrictive toward one child, for instance that child is more likely to act in an aggressive, rivalrous and unfriendly manner toward a brother or sister, according to work by Hetherington. Surprisingly, it may not matter who is favored. Children in one study were more antagonistic toward siblings even when *they* were the ones receiving preferential treatment.

Many parents, of course, go to great lengths to distribute their love and attention equally. Yet even the most consciously egalitarian parenting may be seen as unequal by children of different ages. A mother may treat her 4-year-old boy with the same care and attention she lavished on her older son when he was 4. But from the 7-year-old's perspective, it may look like his younger brother is getting a better deal. Nor is there much agreement among family members on how evenhandedly love is apportioned: Adolescents report favoritism when their

mothers and fathers insist that none exists. Some parents express surprise that their children feel unequally treated, while at the same time they describe how one child is more demanding, another needs more discipline. And siblings almost never agree in their assessments of who, exactly, Mom loves best.

Strong friendships between siblings become less intense after adolescence, diluted by geography, marriage, child-rearing concerns and careers.

Nature vs. nurture. Further complicating the equation is the contribution of heredity to temperament, each child presenting a different challenge from the moment of birth. Plomin, part of a research team led by George Washington University psychiatrist David Reiss that is studying sibling pairs in 700 families nationwide, views the differences between siblings as emerging from a complex interaction of nature and nurture. In this scheme, a more aggressive and active child, for example, might engage in more conflict with parents and later

ONLY CHILDREN
Cracking the myth of the pampered, lonely misfit

Child-rearing experts may have neglected the psychology of sibling ties, but they have never been hesitant to warn parents about the perils of siring a single child. Children unlucky enough to grow up without brothers or sisters, the professional wisdom held, were bound to be self-centered, unhappy, anxious, demanding, pampered and generally maladjusted to the larger social world. "Being an only child is a disease in itself," psychologist G. Stanley Hall concluded at the turn of the century.

Recent research paints a kinder picture of the only child—a welcome revision at a time when single-child families are increasing. The absence of siblings, psychologists find, does not doom children to a life of neurosis or social handicap. Day care, preschool and other modern child-care solutions go far in combatting an only child's isolation and in mitigating the willfulness and self-absorption that might come from being the sole focus of parental attention. And while only children may miss out on some positive aspects of growing up around brothers and sisters, they also escape potentially negative experiences, such as unequal parenting or severe aggression by an older sibling. Says University of Texas at Austin social psychologist Toni Falbo: "The view of only children as selfish and lonely is a gross exaggeration of reality."

Indeed, Falbo goes so far as to argue that only children are often better off—at least in some respects—than those with brothers and sisters. Reviewing over 200 studies conducted since 1925, she and her colleague Denise Polit conclude that only children equal firstborns in intelligence and achievement, and score higher than both firstborns and later-borns with siblings on measures of maturity and leadership. Other researchers dispute these findings, however. Comparing only children with firstborns over their life span, for example, University of California at Berkeley psychologist B. G. Rosenberg found that only children—particularly females—scored lower on intelligence tests than did firstborns with a sibling.

Rosenberg distinguishes between three types of only children. "Normal, well-adjusted" onlies, he says, are assertive, poised and gregarious. "Impulsive, acting out" only children adhere more to the old stereotype, their scores on personality tests indicating they are thin-skinned, self-indulgent and self-dramatizing. The third group resembles the firstborn children of larger families, scoring as dependable, productive and fastidious.

Perhaps the only real disadvantage to being an only child comes not in childhood but much later in life. Faced with the emotional and financial burdens of caring for aging parents, those without siblings have no one to help out. But as Falbo points out, even in large families such burdens are rarely distributed equally.

become a problem child at school. A quieter, more timid child might receive gentler parenting and later be deemed an easy student.

In China, long ago, it was just the two of them, making dolls out of straw together in the internment camp, putting on their Sunday clothes to go to church with their mother. She mostly ignored her younger sister, or goaded her relentlessly for being so quiet. By the time they were separated—her sister sailing alone at 13 for the United States—there was already a wall between them, a prelude to the stiff Christmas cards they exchange, the rebuffed phone calls, the impersonal gifts that arrive in the mail.

Now, when the phone rings, she is wishing hard for a guardian angel, for someone to take away the pain that throbs beneath the surgical bandage on her chest, keeping her curled under the blue and white cotton coverlet. She picks up the receiver, recognizes her sister's voice instantly, is surprised, grateful, cautious all at once. How could it be otherwise after so many years? It is the longest they have spoken in 50 years. And across the telephone wire, something is shifting, melting in the small talk about children, the wishes for speedy recovery. "I

think we both realized that life can be very short," she says. Her pain, too, is dulling now, moving away as she listens to her sister's voice. She begins to say a small prayer of thanks.

For a period that seems to stretch forever in the timelessness of childhood, there is only the family, only the others who are unchosen partners, their affection, confidences, attacks and betrayals defining the circumference of a limited world. But eventually, the boundaries expand, friends and schoolmates taking the place of brothers and sisters, highways and airports leading to other lives, to office parties and neighborhood meetings, to other, newer families.

Adult bonds. Rivalry between siblings wanes after adolescence, or at least adults are less apt to admit competitive feelings. Strong friendships also become less intense, diluted by geography, by marriage, by the concerns of raising children and pursuing independent careers. In national polls, 65 percent of Americans say they would like to see their siblings more often than the typical "two or three times a year." And University of Indianapolis psychologist Victoria Bedford finds, in her work, that men and women of child-rearing age often show longing toward siblings, especially those close in age and of the same sex. Yet for some people, the detachment of adulthood brings relief, an escape from bonds that are largely unwanted but never entirely go away. Says one woman about her brothers and sisters: "Our values are different, our politics diametrically opposed. I don't feel very connected, but there's still a pressure to keep up the tie, a kind of guilt that I don't have a deeper sense of kinship."

How closely sibling ties are maintained and nurtured varies with cultural and ethnic expectations. In one survey, for example, 54 percent of low-income blacks reported receiving help from a brother or sister, in comparison with 44 percent of low-income Hispanics and 36 percent of low-income whites. Siblings in large families are also more likely to give and receive support, as are those who live in close geographical proximity to one another. Sex differences are also substantial. In middle and later life, sisters are much more likely than brothers to keep up close relationships.

So important, in fact, is the role that sisters play in cementing family ties that some families all but fall apart without them. They are the ones who often play the major role in caring for aging parents and who make sure family members stay in touch after parents die. And in later life, says Purdue University psychologist Victor Cicirelli, sisters can provide a crucial source of reassurance and emotional security for their male counterparts. In one study, elderly men with sisters reported greater feelings of happiness and less worry about their life circumstances.

Warmth or tolerance? Given the mixed emotions many adults express about sibling ties, it is striking that in national surveys the vast majority—more than 80 percent—deem their relationships with siblings to be "warm and affectionate." Yet this statistic may simply reflect the fact that ambivalence is tolerated more easily at a distance, warmth and affection less difficult to muster for a few days a year than on a daily basis. Nor are drastic breaches between siblings—months or years of silence, with no attempt at rapprochement—unheard of. One man, asked by a researcher about his brother, shouted, "Don't mention that son of a bitch to me!" and slammed the door in the psychologist's face.

Sibling feuds often echo much earlier squabbles and are sparked by similar collisions over shared responsibility or resources—who is doing more for an ailing parent, how inheritance should be divided. Few are long lasting, and those that are probably reflect more severe emotional disturbance. Yet harmonious or antagonistic patterns established in childhood make themselves felt in many adults' lives. Says psychologist Kahn: "This is not just kid stuff that people outgrow." One woman, for example, competes bitterly with a slightly older co-worker, just as she did with an older brother growing up. Another suspects that her sister married a particular man in part to impress her. A scientist realizes that he argues with his wife in exactly the same way he used to spar with an older brother.

For most people, a time comes when it makes sense to rework and reshape such "frozen images" of childhood—to borrow psychologist Bank's term—into designs more accommodating to adult reality, letting go of ancient injuries, repairing damaged fences. In a world of increasingly tenuous family connections, such renegotiation may be well worth the effort. Says author Judith Viorst, who has written of sibling ties: "There is no one else on Earth with whom you share so much personal history."

ERICA E. GOODE

Sibling connections

That most vital but overlooked of relationships

Laura M. Markowitz

The Family Therapy Networker

We agonize over ups and downs with our parents, spouses, and children, but mostly ignore one of our first and most primal bonds—our relationships with our brothers and sisters.

Whether as adults we find those relationships harmonious, acrimonious, or somewhere in between, we discount them at our peril. For the sibling bond is powerful, providing us with connection, validation, and belonging like no other.

Brothers and sisters push buttons you'd forgotten you had, never forget old humiliations and painful nicknames, never let you grow up. They share your obscure, ancient memories of car trips and long-dead pets, know just what you mean about Mom and Dad, and can make you laugh so hard you cry.

To understand the potent cocktail of anger, love, competitiveness, and protectiveness that is the sibling bond is ultimately to come closer to understanding ourselves. Not that understanding always leads to trouble-free friendship. Indeed, achieving tension-free kinship with a sibling is probably impossible, since ambivalence seems to be the most natural state of the relationship. But coming to know why no one else can make you feel more empathy, anger, or delight than those earliest companions provides a useful insight. May it also lead to a closer bond.

At first, the case appeared to have nothing at all to do with siblings. Alice, a 40-year-old journalist and single mother, came in with her only child, 18-year-old Becky, who had threatened to run away form home because "my mom is like a prison warden." Becky told the therapist, Syracuse University doctoral student Tracy Laszloffy, that she would go live with her Aunt Tess, who had told her she was always welcome. This was her trump card, and it had the desired effect: Her mother's eyes narrowed in anger. "I always knew she'd do something like this to get even with me," said Alice.

"Why do you think Becky wants to get even with you?" the therapist asked.

"Not Becky," explained Alice. "Tess! My older sister always hated me and has never let me forget that when I was born, she had to take care of me.

For there is
no friend like a
sister
In calm or
stormy weather;
To cheer one on
the tedious way,
To fetch one if
one goes astray,
To lift one if one
totters down,
To strengthen
whilst one
stands.
—Christina
Rossetti

She's always making me pay for that. Now she wants to steal my daughter away!"

Laszloffy helped Alice and Becky find a compromise for their most pressing problems—Becky's demand to be allowed to go to unsupervised parties and Alice's insistence that Becky get better grades. Despite Becky's description of her mother as harsh, it became evident that Alice vacillated between the conflicting roles of parent and peer. Laszloffy felt that the real work for this family needed to happen elsewhere. She decided that including Tess in a session might be the key, and her hunch was confirmed when Alice flinched at the suggestion. "Why her? She already knows I'm a screwup." She agreed, however, for Becky's sake.

From the first moment the sisters walked in—Tess a matronly 50-year-old woman in sensible shoes, and Alice looking fashionable in a miniskirt—it was clear their relationship organized the way they thought about themselves. The sisters immediately began to compare themselves to each other: "She was always the creative one," said Tess. "I never had any real talent, except for making pot roast."

"Yeah, but you were also the good daughter, the one everyone approved of," countered Alice. Tess bristled. Was Alice mocking her for being a stay-at-home mom and housewife?

"I feel judged by Alice constantly," Tess said. "I have arguments with her in my head while I'm vacuuming about who has it better, me or her." She admitted that she did sometimes have regrets about her life, but said she never felt comfortable letting down her guard with her sister.

"I guess I feel threatened when Tess isn't her usual confident and bossy self," Alice said. "It's like a balance we have. One of us is the caretaker, one of us is the. . . . Well, I'm used to being the one who needs taking care of. I'm not sure I'd know what to do if she needed my advice, or help."

The next session began with the sisters reporting on a lunch that week that had ended with a big fight over their memories of their mother. Tess had recalled her as a cold, disengaged woman wrapped up in her own problems; Alice remembered her as being affectionate to the point of being stifling. Laszloffy explained that no siblings grow up in the same family—the emotional, economic, and even physical circumstances of the family are distinct for each child, and the parents often respond differently to each. Tess looked irritated, unused to relinquishing her right, as eldest, to define the way things were. Alice said she felt guilty that she had gotten the "nice" mother while Tess had gotten the "mean" one.

"So why did you run away from home, if Mom was so loving and caring?" Tess asked her sister, referring to the year when 18-year-old Alice dropped out of high school three weeks before graduation and moved to California.

"To get away from her! She was *too* loving; it was suffocating me!" Alice said, frustrated that her sister needed to be told the obvious.

Tess's mouth dropped open. "I thought you ran away because you were mad at me for leaving you at home with Mom when I got married and had kids of my own."

"No! In fact, I was trying to get out of your hair so you wouldn't have to keep taking care of me, because I knew you hated that—and hated me because of it," Alice choked on the last words, tears welling up.

"I never hated you," Tess said softly. "What ever gave you that idea?"

Alice blew her nose. "I'll never forget the time when I was 5, you were 15, and you were supposed to take me to the playground. You

The parent-child bond has been under the microscope, yet sibling connections have been largely ignored.

yelled at Mom that you hated me and wanted to go out with your friends. Then you left." Alice, with her tear-streaked face and forlorn expression, looked like the abandoned little girl she was describing.

Tess had no memory of the incident Alice was talking about. Of course there had been moments she resented having to take care of her baby sister, but most of the time she loved and cherished Alice. "Why do you think I rushed ahead to have babies of my own?" Tess asked her. "Because you had been the best thing in my life, and I wanted to have kids just like you." For the first time in 35 years, Alice could hear the love in her sister's voice.

"I've wanted to be close to you for a long time, but you kept pushing me away," said Tess. "I could never figure out what I had done to make you hate me—hate me so much that you don't even want Becky to visit me." Now Tess was crying too.

"Why didn't we ever talk about this stuff before?" Alice wondered. "We've wasted so much time being mad at things that never really happened the way we thought they did."

4. PARENTING AND FAMILY ISSUES

They also had spent a lot of time frozen in roles that no longer fit them as adults. In therapy, Alice learned that she could be more of an adult with and parent to Becky without turning into her sister. Tess began to accept that she wasn't as stuck in her life as she imagined. As if they were unfolding a map and seeing a multitude of possible roads to take, each of the sisters could now see herself as more than simply the other's road not taken.

Clearly, the sibling relationship was the pivotal factor in this case, yet there was little in her training to lead Laszloffy—or most family therapists—to consider siblings as a point of leverage. Mental health practitioners have spent a century putting the parent-child bond and marital relationship under the microscope, yet sibling connections have been largely ignored. "My pet peeve with the field is that when we say 'family of origin,' most of us really mean parent-child relationships, which is a very limited and linear view of family that derives from our rigidly hierarchical way of seeing the world," says Ken Hardy, professor of family therapy at Syracuse University.

Laszloffy's case is striking because the intensity between the siblings lay close to the surface. Most of us respond to our brothers and sisters with subtler rumblings, having long ago learned to bury powerful emotions in order to survive years of living with them—resentment at having been an easy target of a sibling's anger; longing for closeness masked by habitual guardedness; hidden desires for attention, approval, vindication. As adults, we still may wish our siblings would apologize for past hurts, abandonments, humiliations; we still may feel responsible for them, afraid for them, stuck with them.

Normally articulate and insightful people grow tongue-tied when it comes to describing their relationships with their siblings. Writers of books about siblings struggle to manufacture encompass-

Only children

Is it really so bad to grow up without sibs?

AT 14 I LEARNED A LESSON THAT MOST KIDS master well before their age hits double digits. When a boy who'd taunted me all through junior high asked me to sign his yearbook, I thought it was a trick—I knew he hated me; he'd been my tormentor for years. So of course I refused. To my surprise, his genuinely quizzical look told me that the request had been sincere.

It was an understandable mistake on my part, though. Most of the kids I knew had learned how to tease and be teased much earlier in life than I finally did. That's because they all had something I lacked: siblings.

As the only child in my family, I grew up with no one to make faces at me, slam me against the wall, steal my hair ribbon, or frighten me with rubber bugs. My parents may have had a bad day now and then, but hey, they never hid my math book or called me "bunnyface." How was I to know that most kids deal with such treatment every day of their lives?

This lack of sibling savvy made me more sensitive than most of my peers, and maybe I didn't roll with the punches as easily as they did. But those appear to be about the worst effects the absence of brothers and sisters had on me. Otherwise, I grew up happy, made friends, did well in college, and married a great guy (who also happens to be an only child).

So what about the pervasive idea that all children without siblings are selfish, lonely, and spoiled? Well, according to nearly everyone who studies these things, the stereotypical attention-grabbing, foot-stamping, tantrum-throwing only child resides mainly in our collective imagination.

"Being an only child accounts for no more than about 2 percent of the variants affecting personality and behavior," says Toni Falbo, a professor of sociology and educational psychology at the University of Texas at Austin. "The other 98 percent are determined by a host of more important factors: social class, gender, education, quality of parenting, and family members' physical and psychological health."

After reviewing almost 150 published studies and conducting her own research on the subject, Falbo—who's the country's leading authority on only children—has concluded that onlies are generally just as happy and well-adjusted as kids with siblings. What's more, the differences that do exist are frequently to the onlies' advantage. Only children tend to get slightly better grades, be more ambitious, earn more advanced acing theories about our connection to these people after we no longer have to wear their hand-me-downs, share a bedroom, or put up with their teasing. But there are no givens for what kind of relationships emerge between adult siblings. Some grow up to be one another's closest friends; others become like distant acquaintances, sharing nothing of their adult lives. Some continue to use their siblings as a compass point for measuring who they have become. Some consider each other ancient enemies to avoid, while others casually drift apart without concern. For every "truth" about siblings, the exact opposite also may be correct. Most of us are still trying to figure out who these familiar strangers are to us.

In the beginning we orbit our parents like planets vying for the position closest to the sun. They are the primary source of light, warmth, and love, but we have to compete with omnipresent siblings who at times eclipse us, collide with us, and even, at odd moments,

awkwardly love us. In myth and literature, the bond between siblings is portrayed as far more ambivalent than the attachment between parents and children, dramatized in extremes of enmity and loyalty. In the Bible, the relationship between the first brothers, Cain and Abel, ended in fratricide. Joseph's brothers sold him into slavery in Egypt. In *King Lear,* Cordelia's older sisters outmaneuvered her to get their father's kingdom and delighted in her banishment. Still, Hansel took hold of Gretel's hand in the forest and promised to protect her; Joseph forgave his brothers and saved them during a deadly famine.

The seeds of enmity between siblings may be planted early: The introduction of a new child into the family is often experienced as an irretrievable loss by the older child. The trauma of being displaced by a younger sibling can turn into rage, envy, even hatred of the usurper. The earliest impulses to commit murder are felt in the young child who has been dethroned as centerpiece of the family. Therapists report cases in which older siblings tried to drown their younger

---

ademic degrees, and display greater self-esteem.

Then why the negative stereotype? Perhaps it's because most people don't have much firsthand experience with only children, who have traditionally been in short supply. A decade ago, just 10 percent of American women had had a single child by the end of their childbearing years. These days, however, that number has jumped to an all-time high of 17 percent—which means that one in six women will be the mother of an only child.

Despite their increasing numbers, Falbo notes that typecasting of only children persists. "The truth," she says, laughing, "is that last-born kids often act more spoiled than onlies do."

Perhaps the sharpest concern many one-child parents feel is that their kids will be lonely. "I did worry at first," admits Anita Daucunas of

Boulder, Colorado, who has a 5-year-old daugher. "But Jennifer is in school all day with other kids, and when she gets home she goes right out to play with the neighborhood children."

At the same time, onlies are often more comfortable playing by themselves. Sandra Lee Steadham of Dallas says that her daughter, 9-year-old Zoe, is outgoing but also enjoys spending time on her own. "For Zoe," she explains, "being alone isn't the same as being lonely."

Like any other type of family, single-child households do have trouble spots. For one thing, the parents of an only child have a tendency to be overly attentive, says Murray Kappelman, a professor of pediatrics and psychiatry at the University of Maryland. Too much concern about the child's health, for example, can encourage hypochondria. Performance

expectations that are too rigorous can create a heightened need for approval, and an overabundance of material rewards can give the child a bad case of the I wants.

"But those tendencies exist with most firstborns," Kappelman emphasizes, "not just with onlies." The fact is that *any* family size creates its own set of problems. There is no perfect number of children.

—Katy Koontz
Special Report

Excerpted with permission from Special Report *(March/April 1993). Subscriptions: $15/yr. (6 issues) from Special Report, Box 2191, Knoxville, TN 37901.*

brothers and sisters, or "helped" them have accidents near sharp objects or open windows.

Freud codified the notion of sibling rivalry, which was already widely accepted, saying it was natural that the introduction of a new sibling into a family would stir up envy, aggression, and competitiveness in the other siblings. But normalizing sibling rivalry created an expectation that brothers and sisters were destined to feel lifelong antagonism, resent one another's accomplishments, and envy one another's talents and privileges. Until recently, the phenomenon was believed to be so self-evident that no one bothered to challenge it. But are aggression and envy really the overarching emotions siblings have for one another? Recent feminist theorists suggest that Freud's theory was tainted by male bias. Siblings may not always be locked in mortal combat; interdependence and companionship are as much a part of siblinghood as competition and antagonism, says Laura Roberto, family therapy professor at Eastern Virginia Medical School. "Until we began to see how female development is also forged in affiliation and relationship, we tended to ignore these facets of the sibling bond." Feminists point to the lifelong friendship between many sisters who, increasingly outliving their male relations, may spend the last years of their lives together. This feminist challenge has given us a new lens for regarding both female and male sibling relationships, suggests family therapist Michael Kahn, co-author of *The Sibling Bond*. "Women are more interested in horizontal ties," says Kahn, "and are asking new kinds of questions like, 'What is lost when one sibling wins at another's expense?' "

Other critics point out that sibling rivalry isn't a primary force among siblings in other cultures; in some African societies, for example, one's greatest support, both material and emotional, comes not from one's parents but from one's siblings. Not all families in our society operate exclusively from Eurocentric values of individualism, points out Ken Hardy. For example, as a response to racism, African-American parents, brothers, and sisters often pour all their resources and energy into one child, who carries the family torch like a bright beacon into the institutions of mainstream success. "It is not uncommon to see an African-American family in which one brother is a surgeon or lawyer while the other siblings are locked into menial jobs or struggling with unemployment," he says. "The one who made it sends back money and helps the others, repays the debt."

To look only at the negative feelings of siblinghood is to forget how important we are to one another, how in a sense our siblings are as responsible for creating us as our parents are. All planets, though drawn to the sun, exert a pull on one another, shaping one another's course. "I

was the coddled one; he the witness of coddling," wrote novelist Vladimir Nabokov about his older brother, describing the natural complementarity that exists among siblings.

Our siblings are peers who share not only the same family, but also the same history and culture, not to mention a sizable chunk of our genetic material. Even among those with a significant age difference, siblings' personal histories intertwine so that there is no escaping a mutual influence. During a family therapy session, two adult sisters and their brother talk about how they were influenced by one another. "I learned to be the family entertainer because you and Mom were always fighting," says the brother to his older sister. "I hated the yelling, so I would try to make you both laugh. I still do that whenever I'm around conflict—try to defuse it."

"I think I wouldn't have been such a rebel if you two hadn't been such goody-goodies," says the younger sister. "You still compete with each other, like who's more successful or whose kids are the smartest. Since I was never in the running, I tried to do things neither of you did. Using a lot of drugs was a way to feel like I had something over both of you, like I was more mature or cool."

"I always felt so responsible for you two," says the older sister. "Mom would yell at me if you guys made a mess or got in a fight. I grew up believing that everyone else's problems come first, because other people are younger, smaller, more needy, or whatever. In my marriage, I kept on doing the same thing, putting his needs first because it was what I knew. And having kids just replicated what it was like to be the oldest sister. Since the divorce, I've been trying to figure out who takes care of me."

What exactly does it mean to be the product not only of one's parents, but also of one's siblings? How does it happen? The most elaborate theory of siblinghood concerns birth order. Although Freud said that "a child's position in the sequence of brothers and sisters is of very great significance for the course of his later life," the main work in the area of birth order has been done by Austrian-born family therapist Walter Toman, author of *Family Constellation: Its Effects on Personality and Social Behaviour*. Toman's basic assertion is that the order of one's birth determines certain personality characteristics that shape the choices we make and the likelihood of our success and even how we think about ourselves. Toman developed profiles of sibling positions, including only children, saying, for example, that older siblings tend to take on more responsibility and to be somewhat overcontrolling while only children are inclined to be loners, and women who are not fond of children tend to be youngest siblings.

> I was the older brother. And when I was growing up I didn't like all those brothers and sisters. No kid likes to be the oldest.... But when they turn to you for help—what can you do? They kept me so busy caring for them that I had no time to become a junkie or an alcoholic.
> —James Baldwin

> The younger brother hath the more wit.
> —English proverb

> All happy families resemble one another, but each unhappy family is unhappy in its own way.
> —Leo Tolstoy

But even without a highly schematized birth order theory about siblings, practitioners have described siblinghood as the first social laboratory, where we learn how to be a peer. Even when the fights make us cry, we are growing a thicker skin, which we need later on as adults; we learn that life doesn't always seem fair; we learn how to forgive. "After listening to my brother and sister hurl insults at each other one day, I was surprised to see them playing together the next morning as if nothing had happened," says a 40-year-old man. "It was a revelation to me that you could hate someone one day and forget about it the next."

It is possible that in siblinghood we experience more intensity of emotion than in any other relationship that follows. Our worlds are shoulder to shoulder, and our vulnerabilities are laid bare. "I've never loved or hated as intensely as I love and hate my brothers," says a 36-year-old youngest brother of six boys. With our siblings, we test the limits of tolerance and forgiveness more than we do in any other relationship. As long as the family provides an appropriate container for the intensity, siblings can benefit from the lessons.

Unless something goes dramatically wrong, as in sibling incest or sibling illness or death, our relationships with our brothers and sisters rarely take center stage in the therapy room. But increasingly, family therapists are discovering what a gold mine of information and support siblings can be. As inheritors of the same multigenerational legacy, albeit with different views of the family stories, they can often make a unique contribution to therapy. One family therapist was having a hard time with an 8-year-old boy who had set himself on fire twice because he believed his father hated him. The father was a large, impassive man who never looked at his son and spoke to him only when he had to. Hoping for some clue about why the father was so inaccessible, the therapist invited the father's younger brother to a session.

After the therapist outlined the situation, the younger brother turned to his nephew and asked him to wait in the next room. Then he said to his brother, the boy's father, "I remember right before Mom left him, Dad used to tell everyone you were someone else's bastard." The older brother looked numb, but the therapist sighed with relief. He finally understood what was going on under the surface of this family. His own father's rejection of him had left this father feeling confused about what fathers were supposed to say to sons. "He loved his child, but regarded his own silence as a way of protecting his son from the possibly abusive things that might come out of his mouth in anger," says the therapist. What the man was only dimly aware

of himself, his brother had been able to put his finger on immediately.

Family therapy also can help people get out of constraining roles with their siblings. Family-of-origin specialist Murray Bowen years ago described how he dramatically disentangled himself from a lifetime of emotional triangles with his siblings. He believed the family's ongoing emotional process was responsible for the legacy that Walter Toman attributed to birth order. Accordingly, Bowen reasoned that one ought to be able to go back and change the family's emotional process, which created and sustained sibling roles.

One Bowen-trained therapist treated a couple who were fighting about the husband's intrusive family. Lisa was fed up with hearing about her in-laws' problems and wanted Henry to separate himself from their incessant dramas. She was upset that he had loaned his irresponsible younger sister money and had become caught up in the ongoing fight between his older brother and their father. The constant phone calls from Henry's family were driving her crazy. When she drew their family diagram, the therapist says, "a million things seemed to jump out at me," particularly the multigenerational patterns of enmeshment in Henry's family and cutoffs in Lisa's, but the overwhelming fact was the contrast in the couple's birth positions: Henry was a middle child, Lisa an only child.

As an only child, Lisa was used to being the center of attention and didn't like competing with her brother- and sister-in-law. As a middle child, Henry was the family caretaker and peacekeeper, but he wasn't sure he wanted to keep the role. "If I wasn't in the middle of their lives, maybe I'd have more of a life of my own," he said.

The therapist coached Henry on how to develop more independence from his family. "The next time my brother called to complain about Dad, I told him I was sure he could work it out and changed the subject to football," says Henry. His sister called to cry over her latest investment flop, hinting that she needed another loan. "I told her she had a lot of experience pulling herself out of holes, and I was sure she would find a way to do it again," Henry recalls.

The therapist suggested that Lisa could help Henry remember that he was entitled to be the center of attention sometimes, too. During the next family gathering, Henry and Lisa both deliberately steered the conversation to Henry's latest project at work. "It was a surprise to realize that no one in my family knew much about me," says Henry. Changing his behavior shifted his relationship with his siblings, who became "much more respectful of my boundaries," almost timidly asking if it was all right to call, spending more time listening to Henry instead of talking at him.

> Our word *cad* originally meant a younger brother.
> —Bergen Evans

> A brother is born for adversity.
> —*Proverbs 17:17*

> Some uninformed newspapers printed: "Mrs. C.L. Lane, Sister of the Famous Comedian Will Rogers." They were greatly misinformed. It's the other way around. I am the brother of Mrs. C.L. Lane, the friend of humanity.... It was the proudest moment of my life that I was her brother.
> —Will Rogers, after the funeral of his sister Maud

4. PARENTING AND FAMILY ISSUES

One of the most wrenching issues that brings siblings to family therapy occurs at midlife, when they face the failing health of parents and need to make long-term decisions about their

In siblinghood we may experience more intense emotions than in any other relationship that follows.

care. It's extremely difficult for a family to have to acknowledge the demise of its elders, evoking buried fears of death and abandonment. Often, the grown children don't feel ready for the changing of the guard. "I look in the mirror and see an older, white-haired man, but inside I still feel 25 and way too young to become the older generation," says one therapist, whose elderly father recently came to live with him. "I look at his shrunken body and I can't help feeling repulsed. He used to be a strapping, handsome guy. Now the chronic pain from arthritis doesn't let him sleep. I have to feed him by hand as if he were a baby. It's very sad, and very surreal." Is this what will happen to us, siblings wonder?

Not only does the individual's relationship with the parent change dramatically as the older generation loses its authority, but the need to collaborate closely with a sibling, sometimes after 40 years of mutual alienation, can revive feelings of insecurity, competitiveness, and resentment. In the face of huge existential issues like death, some adult siblings find it is easier to fall back on picking on one another, feeding the illusion that they will be children forever instead of accepting terminal adulthood.

Boston family therapist David Treadway worked with three siblings in their 60s—an eminent jurist, a history professor, and a successful businesswoman. They were not interested in talking about the past, but needed a facilitator to help them come to an agreement about their aging mother.

"They didn't acknowledge that their struggle had anything to do with their childhood roles, but the roots of the conflict surfaced within the first 10 minutes," says Treadway. They found that they could not come to any agreement without first understanding the curse of each one's sibling position. After this exercise, they could begin the hard work of real negotiation and compromise.

In some families, a parent's death removes the force that holds siblings in their habitual

orbits. The question then becomes, Will the brothers and sisters drift apart, finally dissolving the tenuous threads of connection? Most of the time siblings find the pull among them is strong enough to draw them into a new configuration. In a family of two brothers and two sisters, after the parents died no one came forward at first to organize family gatherings during the holidays. After spending the first Thanksgiving of their lives apart, they set up a rotation so they would each plan one holiday a year.

When adult siblings maintain their connection in later life, the relationship takes on a special importance because, as veterans of multiple losses—deaths, divorce, children moving away—they realize that no one else alive can remember the way it was when they were children. The parents' deaths may even open up a space for siblings to know each other for the first time without competitive friction. "I never really thought, 'Would I like this person if he were not my brother?'" says a 56-year-old therapist. "After our parents were gone, I found myself calling him up, and he'd call me. We enjoy each other's company now. It's comfortable in a way I don't feel with anyone else because we've known each other forever." It can be a sweet and unexpected discovery to realize that the people with whom one feels the most affinity and closeness after a lifetime of struggle or emotional distance are our own siblings.

Many of us take our siblings for granted. They simply are, as unavoidable as gravity. Even as adults, we may not have devoted much thought to figuring out how they fit into our lives and how they shaped us. There's something in us that resists giving our sibling relationships the credence and attention they deserve. Cherishing our adult autonomy and freedom, we strive to bury our childish vulnerabilities and reinvent ourselves, but our sibs get in the way.

The boy who was teased by the neighborhood kids and grows up to be a confident, successful businessman doesn't want to remember those days of hot tears and humiliation. He may feel uneasy in the presence of the older sister who remembers all too clearly a time he'd rather forget. In a sense, our siblings don't let us put the past behind us. "Every time I see you, I try to be open to the idea that you are a different person than the one I used to know," one brother told his sister. "But it's hard, because I know you so well."

In this knowledge is, perhaps, the paradox of the sibling relationship. Siblings are the living remnant of our past, a buffer against the loss of our own history, the deepest, oldest memories of us. But in these memories lies a terrible power:

I worry about people who get born nowadays because they get born into such tiny families—sometimes into no family at all. When you're the only pea in the pod, your parents are likely to get you confused with the Hope Diamond.
—Russell Baker

Relations are simply a tedious pack of people, who haven't got the remotest knowledge of how to live, nor the smallest instinct about when to die.
—Oscar Wilde

Our siblings hold up a mirror before us, forcing us to look at an image of ourselves that may be either comforting or devastating, perhaps evoking self-acceptance and pride, perhaps shame and humiliation.

There is a fateful perpetuity about sibling relationships: Our brothers and sisters will always be our contemporaries; we can't ever quite leave them. However convenient it would be, we can't consign them to irrelevancy. No wonder that when sibling relationships are bad, they leave deep, irreparable scars of bitterness, betrayal, and rage. No wonder that when they are good, they are a source of profound satisfaction, one of the best and most fulfilling of human ties. Whether our siblings are thorns in our side or balm for our wounds, they are fellow travelers who have witnessed our journey, living bridges between who we once were and who we have become.

Why *Spanking* Takes the Spunk Out of Kids

Nick Gallo

Nick Gallo is a writer in Seattle.

There was an old woman, who lived in a shoe.

She had so many children she didn't know what to do.

She gave them some broth without any bread,

Then whipped them all soundly and sent them to bed.

"Why did she do that?" my 3-year-old son, Alex, asks, as I turn the page to another nursery rhyme.

"Why?" I repeat. "Well, I guess she. . . ." I pause, fumbling around for a good answer. "She must have, ummm, something must have happened—"

"She's mean," he announces, eyeing me evenly.

"Oh, I don't know, maybe she. . . ." I stop again. "Maybe," I admit, "she *is* mean."

I sit back in the chair and grimace as I remember that last time I "lost it" with my son. Upset for being scolded at a restaurant, he sailed his grilled cheese sandwich at my head. Then, before I had a chance to stop the action, he flung his booster seat across the room. As he howled and howled, I grabbed him and fled. Retreating quickly to the parking lot, I jammed him in his car seat about as gently as Patrick Ewing slamdunks a basketball. I didn't smack him—and I

HOW TO KEEP YOUR COOL WHEN YOUR KID BREAKS THE RULES

Count to 10. It works. Close your eyes. Take a deep breath. Unclench your fists. Go in another room and close the door, if necessary. Resist your first impulse.

Recognize cues. An angry reaction often involves an escalating cycle of frustration, exasperation, and then finally random hitting. Think about what your child does to push your buttons. Try to interrupt the cycle before you are caught up.

Express your hurt. Parents often aren't just mad, but disappointed and hurt when their children displease them. Explaining to your child why a behavior upsets you may help defuse the situation. Experts advise parents to use "I-messages" to relay feelings, yet to avoid recrimination and blame. For example, instead of screaming at a child about a messy room, try something like, "I'm unhappy when the house is messy."

---

haven't yet—but it was obvious I'd shaken him hard enough to hurt him. As we drove home, he was enraged, hysterical, and finally exhausted. I was all of that—and frightened.

Spanking children, of course, is an age-old tradition. It goes back at least 6,000 years according to prescriptions found on clay tablets from southern Babylonia—which recommended a whack on the behind for disobedient youths.

Still, I suspect spanking scares most parents, stirring a dark fear that we may injure our children—psychologically, physically. According to a recent national survey, only 7 percent of parents think spanking is the most effective form of discipline, though that doesn't mean they haven't resorted to it at times.

"Spanking often is a parent's admission of failure," says Lawrence Hartmann, M.D., child psychiatrist at Harvard Medical School, in Cambridge, Massachusetts. "It means you can't stop bad behavior by any other means."

Yet, discipline is essential. Children need structure, a basic framework that provides for rules and limits and order. The child who doesn't learn the world operates by such regulations is more likely to grow up frustrated, insecure, and incapable of self-discipline, at risk for problems with school, drugs, and the law.

As a result of the over-permissive attitudes toward child-rearing popular several years ago, the pendulum may be swinging back. Many parents today have said they want to return to the good old days, with its emphasis on traditional values, basic skills, and strict discipline. But most child experts caution against embracing a return to spanking.

"There is no research that demonstrates spanking is highly effective at changing long-term behavior," says Martin Drell, M.D., chief of child psychiatry at LSU School of Medicine, in New Orleans, Louisiana.

Perhaps there are instances where a swat on the butt has its uses. It shows a child who's boss. It may clear the air sometimes and allow a parent and child to start over. It may even be a beneficial way to improve a child's behavior, provided it doesn't inflict physical harm and is part of a consistent, reliable, and predictable system.

Often, however, it's not so measured or logical. It's the back of the hand when the kid whines once too often. Or it's a slap to the head for playing near the street. Or, as Ralph Welsh, Ph.D., clinical psychologist in private practice, found in his research, it can cross the line into child abuse, involving excessive use of force. In the words of my 3-year-old, it's mean.

Because so many factors are usually intertwined with spanking, its effects are difficult to determine. Certainly, a case can be made against it. Some studies show physical punishment can increase a child's hostility and cause him or her to act, *more*, not less, aggressively. Spanking sends a message to children that "might makes right," that the way to settle disputes is to use physical force and inflict pain, rather than strive for cooperation. Ultimately, it is self-defeating because a child learns that the way to avoid punishment is simply to be increasingly devious.

"At best, corporal punishment is ineffective; at worst, it can cause long-term coping problems," says Temple University psychology professor Irwin Hyman, Ed.D., director of the National Center for Study of Corporal Punishment and Alternatives in Schools in Philadelphia.

Lost in the research and statistical analyses is perhaps a sadder consequence. As my son and I lapsed into a lull following our clash, I saw a wariness in his eyes that hadn't been there before. I was left with a basic, visceral feeling that hitting isn't something a loving father does to his young son. Trust seems too fragile a thing to risk smothering it with fear.

A BETTER WAY TO DISCIPLINE

Bennett Leventhal, M.D., director of child and adolescent psychiatry at the University of Chicago, reminds us that "punishment" and "discipline" are not synonymous. Punishment, whether it's spanking or what you might call verbal spanking—yelling and name-calling—is pure reaction. Discipline, says Dr. Leventhal, is something you teach. Designed to help children gain self-control and motivation, it often produces conflicts, especially when children are exploring feelings of power and autonomy, but ultimately it should teach a child to respect the rights of others, to act responsibly, and to enjoy freedom within limits. In fact, discipline is derived from the word "disciple," meaning a follower or a learner.

"That's the whole purpose of discipline—to develop *self-discipline*," says Dr. Hartmann. "The policeman is not always around."

Time-outs can be very effective, but they often are misused. They shouldn't be a form of punishment, but rather a chance for the child to calm down.

Okay, but how does this help an angry parent, say an Italian father with a short fuse who has just caught a grilled cheese sandwich in the face?

Develop alternatives to spanking, answers Dr. Drell, acknowledging that parents need an entire repertoire of options if they wish to avoid resorting to spanking. "If parents have only one arrow, that's what they'll use," he says. "If they have five arrows in their quiver, then they may not have to use the one marked: 'spanking.' There's a saying: If all you have is a hammer, everything in the world is a nail."

But before you even get to the moment when you need to choose an alternative, there are important steps to take. Try to focus on *prevention*, says Dr. Hyman.

Gary Peterson, M.D., a child psychiatrist and associate professor of psychiatry at the University of North Carolina in Chapel Hill, points out that the real reason most children refrain from bad behavior is fear of disapproval, not spanking. "Generations ago, we didn't have all these behavior-shaping methods," he says. "We need to use them." Here are some of the best.

Set limits. Often it's the little things, such as conduct at the breakfast table, that precipitate discipline problems. If you don't provide specific guidelines on routine, everyday matters, your child will have a harder time knowing what is expected of them, warns Dr. Drell. Clear, firm limits give kids the blueprint for a pattern of behavior.

One note: Sometimes, it's parents, not kids, who don't want to play by the rules. If you're stressed-out and can't tolerate activity that you normally accept, warn your child beforehand.

Establish order. Children are great individualists. Some thrive on structured situations more than others, but, in general, regular schedules for such affairs as eating, sleeping, and brushing teeth reduce opportunities for fights and conflicts, notes Dr. Peterson. "Be consistent," he says. "That's the key."

Adapt your environment to your child. Child-proofing your home as much as possible reduces the number of no-no's you have to say.

Plan ahead. Anticipating difficult times and activities can avoid many problems and frustrations, believes Elizabeth Crary, M.S., author of *Without Spanking or Spoiling* (Parenting

Press, Seattle). If your child gets antsy when you stand in line, make sure to bring along some diversions. If your child gets grouchy because of hunger or tiredness at a certain time of the day, think about rearranging schedules. Be sure, she notes, to allow enough time for transitions, such as bed time, meal times, and departures.

Crary also recommends *foreshadowing*—preparing a child for experiences and events that are new or uncomfortable. Don't wait until you're at the zoo to tell your child what's expected. Explain ahead of time what will take place, what behavior is permitted.

Have the right expectations. Many parents aren't sure what normal behavior is, says Crary. Parents who punish an energetic 2-year-old for not sitting quietly in church may be setting an impossible standard. Be aware, she says, that children learn at different rates, so don't judge your child by another child's progress.

Try distraction. For young toddlers, diversion prevents power struggles. While youngsters at this age can be tremendously willful, their memory and attention span is limited. Steer the 1-year-old headed for a light socket. toward fun and games elsewhere.

Offer choices. Problem: It's 7 a.m. and your child won't wear her red shirt. You can insist that she does, accompanying your command with words like, "You have to learn to listen to me." Or you can allow her to choose between the red shirt and a blue one. Presenting alternatives often gets you off the hook. Just as importantly, say child development experts, choices boost children's self-esteem, giving them confidence to make decisions. But don't confuse questions with commands and offer choices when you don't mean to. You probably aren't really soliciting an opinion when you ask, "Isn't it time to brush you teeth?"

Praise your child. Sometimes, children misbehave because it's the only way they can get attention, notes Cliff Siegel, M.D., director of child psychiatry at Denver Children's Hospital. Verbal praise and attention feed a child's self-esteem, enhancing mastery and control over the world. The likely result: a more confident kid who is less frustrated and less likely to misbehave.

Reward good behavior. The carrot often works better than the stick, remarks Dr. Siegel. Kids respond to positive reinforcement, he says, recalling a mother who spanked her rambunctious 20-month-old with few results. "She never noticed when the boy did anything good," he says. "He'd bring her a toy and she wouldn't acknowledge it. After she changed that, the entire nature of their relationship changed. She didn't have to spank him after that. All she did was say, "Stop that,' and the boy listened."

Sooner or later your child will test you. And that's when it's important to have your options available. One of the most popular methods of discipline today is the use of "time-outs." It involves briefly isolating a child who has misbehaved from the scene of a conflict. The child, removed to an area such as a bedroom, is told to wait five or ten minutes before returning to the scene. Time-outs can be very effective, but they often are misused, says Crary. Properly used, they are a calming device, not punishment; therefore, they're best reserved for children who can understand the concepts of quiet and waiting—age 2½ to 3½ and up—and who can substitute acceptable behavior when calmed down.

As children get older, a disciplinary system can include grounding them or restricting television-watching. Dr. Hyman, who counsels parents in Philadelphia, believes your system will have a better change of working if you allow your child to help establish rules—and the consequences for breaking those rules. Include restitution, not just punishment, in your system so that a child who breaks a window after being told not to play ball in the house can work to "pay" for the damage.

Try at all times to avoid humiliating or demeaning your child. Last year in California, a mother was fined for punishing her 7-year-old son by forcing him to sit on a public bench and wear a pig's snout and a sign saying he was a liar and a thief. While the case was extreme, many parents scream, yell, and inflict psychological abuse that can be as harmful as or more so than spanking to a child's self-image.

Parents are fallible, of course, and given to mistakes. Forgive yourself when you lose your patience and temper and vow to do better. An old-fashioned "I'm sorry" might help. Says E. Gerald Dabbs, M.D., a New York City psychiatrist, "There's nothing wrong with a parent saying to a small child, 'I made a mistake, I lost control, let's start over.' "

"There are two ways to parent," Dr. Leventhal remarks. There's the *authoritarian*, who teaches for fear. Children follow because they're physically intimidated. And there's the *authoritative* parent, who teaches from a position of knowledge. Children follow because they want to learn.

Tarnished trophies

Rewards don't work. They can even sabotage desire and stifle creativity

The desire for achievement is one of life's great mysteries. Social scientists have devoted lifetimes to studying the drives that spur us out of bed in the morning, compel us to work or study hard and spark all manner of human endeavor. Indeed, a 1992 textbook actually documents 32 distinct theories of human motivation.

Given this diversity of thought, it's easy to forget that for a half century, American society has been dominated by the psychological school known as behaviorism, or Skinnerian psychology (after its leading American light, B. F. Skinner). Although behaviorism and its fundamental principle of "positive reinforcement" have long since lost their sway in academic circles, the Skinnerian legacy remains powerful in every realm of daily life, from the home and classroom to the workplace. Don't want to take the trash out? Do it, and you can go to the movies Friday night. Not in the mood for work? Keep plugging away, and you might get a bonus. Not interested in calculus? Strive for an A in the class, and you'll make the honor roll. The theory may be bankrupt, but incentives and rewards are so much a part of American culture that it's hard to imagine life without them.

Yet that's exactly what a growing group of researchers are advocating today. A steady stream of research has found that rather than bolstering motivation and productivity, rewards actually can undermine genuine interest and diminish performance. "Our society is caught in a whopping paradox," contends Alfie Kohn, author of the new book *Punished by Rewards* (Houghton Mifflin), which surveys recent research on the effectiveness of rewards. "We complain loudly about sagging productivity, the crisis of our schools and the

warped values of our children. But the very strategy we use to solve those problems—dangling rewards like incentive plans and grades and candy bars in front of people—is partly responsible for the fix we're in."

It's a tough argument to make in a culture that celebrates the spoils of success. Yet study after study shows that people tend to perform worse, to give up more easily and to lose interest more quickly when a reward is involved. Children who are given treats for doing artwork, for example, lose their initial love of art within weeks. Teenagers who are promised a reward for tutoring youngsters don't teach as enthusiastically as tutors offered nothing. And CEOs who have been awarded long-term incentive plans have often steered their companies toward lower returns.

Rewards, like punishments, are attempts to control behavior.

The quintessential problem is not with prizes themselves, researchers say, but rather with the underlying assumption that humans can be effectively conditioned, much like Pavlov's dog. "Early theories of motivation . . . assumed that if one could 'push' or 'pull' the right buttons, motivation would result," notes Stanford psychologist Martin E. Ford in his 1992 textbook, *Motivating Humans*. These outmoded theories, he says, constitute "a highly mechanistic view" of human motivation that fails to take into account important human factors like the drive for self-control; in practice, rewards rob individuals of control by forcing them either to comply with or defy

someone else's rules. "Do this and you'll get that," says Kohn, "is not much different from do this or else."

While rewards can bring about temporary compliance, studies show that over the long haul they almost always backfire. Stanford psychologist Mark Lepper offered preschoolers rewards for drawing with Magic Markers. At first the children thought they had struck the deal of the century; but within weeks, they had lost interest in the activity. Another study found that students offered rewards for reading did indeed read more—for a while. When the program ended, however, their reading dropped to lower levels than before the program started. One possible explanation is that an external incentive distracts people from the task itself, reducing it to a means to an end; when the reward is gone, so is any original interest in the task. A related explanation, favored by several motivation researchers, is that rewards convey the message that the task is not worth doing for its own sake.

Creativity takes a special beating in a reward-driven system. Place a reward in front of someone and he or she will tend to take the quickest and surest—but not necessarily the most imaginative—route to that reward. A 1992 study by Brandeis University psychologist Teresa Amabile found that professional artists produce less creative works (as judged by other artists) when they have signed a contract to sell the art upon completion. When other study subjects were rewarded for remembering certain types of information from a piece of reading, not only did they have a tough time recalling what they were asked to, but their recollection of other facts in the piece—what researchers call incidental learning"—dropped to almost nothing. Cognitive psychologists consider incidental learn-

PERILS OF PRAISE

When words are rewards

Ah, praise. So powerful are simple words of approval and admiration that the late psychologist B. F. Skinner once called praise giving "the greatest tool in behavior modification."

Yet precisely because praise is such heady stuff, motivation researchers warn of its psychological perils. Although the researchers agree that encouragement is essential for everyone, studies have found that poorly chosen words of praise can be as manipulative as any other reward—and just as destructive to creativity, perseverance and performance. Even behaviorists who advocate heavy use of praise for positive reinforcement in the classroom warn that its power can easily be misused.

Such condemnation of simple good words is difficult even for those who can clearly see the destructive potential of gold stars and other glittery enticements. But in fact, Kohn argues, praise should not always be considered synonymous with human kindness. Children, he contends, can become completely dependent on praise and in that emotional process lose any love of doing things for their own sake. Experiments show, for example, that children who are praised for being generous with others actually end up being less generous than those who received no strokes.

Fear of failure. Praise has also been shown to have very disruptive effects on confidence, concentration and performance. People who receive praise often become so self-conscious of their tentative good standing that they cannot focus on the task at hand, or alternatively they simply avoid challenging themselves in order to prevent the possibility of failure. Case Western Reserve University researcher Roy F. Baumeister found that compliments are an effective way to increase pressure, making a person more likely to "choke." Subjects who were praised just before a test of video skills consistently performed worse than did those who were not. And students who were heavily praised became more tentative in their answers and gave up more quickly on ideas teachers disagreed with. "I worry about children whose eyes light up every time they are praised," says Kohn. "Many of them will grow to be adults desperate for others' approval, unable to formulate their own standards."

Although words of praise may be more subtle than other rewards, the basic psychological issue is one of power and manipulation. "Often, the most striking thing about a positive judgment is that it's a judgment," says Kohn. "It implies, 'I have power over you.' " What's more, he adds, praise carries with it the possibility of criticism, which can make the loftiest paean threatening. Today's "you're perfect" can become tomorrow's "you're worthless."

So what's a loving parent to do? Kohn isn't advocating stony-faced silence, and in fact recommends plenty of warmth and encouragement. But there can't be any real or implied strings attached. "Praise that is contingent—'only if you do this will you get my praise'—is the opposite of the unconditional support children need." Parents need to make sure, he cautions, that they are praising for the right reasons—to encourage a child rather than to urge him or her to behave a certain way.

---

ing essential to creativity because it gives the learner a wide base of knowledge with which to form new associations and ideas. "In children as young as 3 as well as working adults, rewards, competition and performance evaluations consistently reduce creativity," says Amabile, who has conducted two dozen such studies.

Rewards discourage risk taking and encourage shortcuts.

"And it does so in areas ranging from art to writing to complex problem-solving."

One of the reasons rewards are so ubiquitous, researchers find, is that they actually destroy intrinsic motivation and create a dependence on external rewards. This vicious cycle can be seen throughout society, researchers say, from the home to the school to the workplace.

"Rewards motivate people very well," says Kohn. "They motivate people to get more rewards. The more rewards are used, the more they are needed."

Of special concern to motivation researchers is the growing prevalence of rewards used with children, especially in education. Schools nationwide are offering certificates, plaques and other treats for everything from studying to finishing homework to making a certain grade. Local stores have gotten in on the act as well. Pizza Hut sponsors a program to induce kids to read by offering them free pizza, a practice University of Illinois education Prof. John Nicholls jokingly predicts will lead to "a lot of fat kids who don't like to read."

The grading process itself is an external reward (and punishment) that makes kids like learning less, argues Kohn, and leads to a "Do we have to know this for the test?" attitude toward knowledge. He advocates de-emphasizing grades and other rankings, to help children get rid of anxiety about how well they are doing, and giving students more control over how they learn.

Not all educators agree that rewards are harmful to learning. Psychologist and teacher Paul Chance argues that students actually learn better when given appropriate reinforcements, such as rewards clearly signaling that they are making progress. Although Chance acknowledges that some rewards can be harmful—if standards are set too high, for example—he contends that intrinsic motivation is not always enough to guarantee efficient learning and that rewards can act as a valuable supplement. "If students show little or no interest in an activity, it is silly to refuse to provide rewards for fear of undermining their interest," writes Chance in the June 1993 issue of the education journal *Phi Delta Kappan*. Kohn disagrees: "Offering incentives to someone who's not intrinsically motivated is like offering salt water to someone who's thirsty."

CREATIVE LIVES

The anatomy of genius

Few things inspire more wonder than the power of genius. While scores of psychological studies have illuminated the ordinary mind at work, history's most creative minds clearly operate on a different plane.

So it is perhaps not surprising that when cognitive psychologist Howard Gardner set out to explore what he calls "an anatomy of creativity," he focused on the lives of a handful of thinkers who transformed 20th-century science, culture and society. In his book *Creating Minds* (Basic Books), Gardner argues that there are common themes in the lives of creative geniuses as diverse in their interests as Sigmund Freud, Albert Einstein, Pablo Picasso, Igor Stravinsky, T. S. Eliot, Martha Graham and Mahatma Gandhi.

A professor at Harvard University and himself a recipient of the MacArthur "genius" award, Gardner derives his view of genius from his earlier, groundbreaking research on the specialized nature of intelligence. Freud, Gardner notes, was adept at linguistic and personal skills but had weaknesses in spatial and musical abilities. Picasso was a poor scholar, despite his obvious spatial "intelligence."

Gardner's study of the six lives results in a profile of what he whimsically calls the "exemplary creator," or E.C., whose attributes include:

■ **Marginality.** The E.C. typically grows up in a place removed from cultural or scientific centers and struggles to remain at the intellectual margins by disdaining mainstream thought. Freud, for instance, became suspicious when his ideas were accepted too readily, and Einstein harbored a lifelong resistance to the theoretical formulations of quantum mechanics.

■ **Bourgeois roots.** The E.C.'s upbringing is typically middle class, with an emphasis on hard work, achievement and moral training.

■ **Social distancing.** The E.C. is consummately absorbed in his work, opting for "the perfection of art over the perfection of life." As a result, social relationships with others are secondary and often strained, from Eliot and Einstein's aloofness to Picasso's undiluted cruelty to others.

■ **The 10-year rule.** The E.C. typically has two great bursts of creativity, the first a radical breakthrough and the second, roughly 10 years later, a comprehensive synthesis and cultural benchmark. Thus Eliot's *The Love Song of J. Alfred Prufrock* was followed a decade later by *The Waste Land.*

■ **Childlike vision.** Creative geniuses draw their inspiration from their ability to perceive their field with an intellectual innocence. Einstein's theories of relativity, for instance, came from his playful questioning of the very notions of space and time.

Gardner believes that creativity must be more than mere novelty; a genius must also change other, less creative people's lives. From this perspective, he questions whether creative minds of the caliber of Freud's or Einstein's will ever come to dominate the 21st century. These earlier geniuses made their mark by challenging the well-established thinking of the day. But today, Gardner says, there is really no such thing as establishment thought. "Instead of one truth challenging another, the whole notion of truth is abandoned," he writes. "Mannerism, spectacle, effects become all."

BY WILLIAM F. ALLMAN

Kohn's thesis is causing consternation in the business world, where the vast majority of American companies offer some form of incentive or merit-pay plan to inspire workers. Kohn rejects these programs as both insulting and destruc-

Rewards can pit students or workers against one another.

tive to high-quality work; they betray a belief that workers need to be controlled and coerced. Instead, Kohn insists that workers should be well compensated but not led to compete for bonuses or raises.

Kohn's thinking is echoed by proponents of the trendy concept of Total Quality Management, who point out that performance-appraisal systems discourage employee cooperation. The typical incentive plan is "dumb, it's unfair and it doesn't work," agrees Bob Filipczak, staff editor of the trade journal *Training* and an expert on workplace incentives. But the idea of scrapping such plans altogether, he is quick to add, leaves both managers and workers flabbergasted.

Indeed, Kohn and others who study rewards know that incentives are not about to disappear anytime soon. Nor do they advocate a completely reward-free society. "It's not that all rewards are bad," says Amabile, "but rewards which are used in a manipulative way sap the intrinsic motivation that leads to excel-

lence." Intrinsic motivation can be fostered or rekindled, say researchers, by allowing students and workers more control over their daily lives—by putting away the carrot-and-stick style of leadership in favor of a more democratic style of decision making.

Is it a utopian vision? Definitely. Motivation researchers know society won't transform itself overnight and might never cease to be reward-driven. But Kohn argues that it is no more utopian to believe Americans can give up their addiction to rewards than it is to think that the top-down control exercised by managers and teachers can ever produce committed workers or dedicated learners.

JOANNIE M. SCHROF

Cultural and Societal Influences

- Social Issues (Articles 33–37)
- Special Challenges (Articles 38–40)

Social scientists and developmental psychologists have come to realize that children are influenced by a multitude of social forces that surround them. In this unit we present articles to illuminate how American children are influenced by broad factors such as economics, culture, politics, and media. These influences also affect the family, which is a major context of child development, and many children are now faced with more family challenges than ever. In addition, analysis of exceptional or atypical children gives the reader a more comprehensive account of child development. Thus, articles are presented on special challenges of development, such as sexual abuse, AIDS, and attention deficit disorders.

Children's development is also influenced by economic factors. In the United States, roughly one in five children live in poverty, which is likely to impair development in many ways. What can be done to help America's poor children? "America's Children: Economic Perspectives and Policy Options" presents public policy options that address this distressing social problem.

A growing subclass of poor children are those who are homeless. In the past, the homeless were mostly men. Today, 30 percent of the homeless are families comprised of women with children under the age of five years. These families and children are often driven to live on the streets because of inadequate financial resources to cover housing, food, clothing, and medical bills. "Homeless Families: Stark Reality of the '90s" discusses this new class of homeless—mothers with young children in America.

However, having a home is no guarantee of optimal, safe development for children. In 1993 there were one million confirmed cases of child neglect and abuse in the United States (there were likely many more that went unreported). "Why Leave Children with Bad Parents?" raises difficult and provocative issues about how America cares for its children at risk. For example, the child welfare system in many states tries to keep families intact rather than remove at-risk children and place them with foster parents. Another controversial family issue to emerge in the 1990s, perhaps the most controversial, is recovered memory of child abuse—adults recalling, often while in therapy, being abused as a child. "Memories Lost and Found" presents some personal and scientific perspectives on this complex issue.

Another influence on children is television, the "electronic family member." Nearly all American homes have a television set, and two-thirds of homes have at least two. In fact, more families in the United States have a television set than a telephone. Given that by the time children graduate from high school, they will have spent more time watching television than attending school, children's exposure to television is likely to affect many aspects of development. "Screen Violence and America's Children" discusses many of the potentially negative and indeed dangerous effects of television on children's development in our society today.

Some children are faced with challenges such as attention deficit disorder, sexual abuse, and even AIDS. These children are often misunderstood and mistreated and pose special challenges to parents, teachers, and society. Are schools and families prepared to deal with such children? Teachers and parents need information to be better able to identify and deal with these children. These issues are discussed in "How to Recognize and Prevent Child Sexual Abuse," "Young Children with Attention Deficits," and "Children with AIDS."

Looking Ahead: Challenge Questions

Due to changes in family structure, increasing poverty rates, child abuse, and so on, many American children are at risk. What should our nation do to help children?

If family breakdown is related to numerous problems for children, should public policy be designed to help families stay intact?

How can the enormous number of children living in poverty in our country be reduced?

What do you believe should be done for children in high-risk families, such as those discussed in "Why Leave Children with Bad Parents?" In light of the fact that many states have a policy of striving to keep problematic families intact, what additional measures or safeguards would you recommend to improve the chances for children from these at-risk families?

What is the role of television in child development? How might television contribute to many of children's and society's problems? What advantages does television have for children's development?

What can parents and schools do to help children become more "media literate" to protect them from influences on television and advertising?

How do you balance our First Amendment rights to free speech with the data showing a correlation between media violence and murder rates in this country? Is censorship warranted or necessary?

Schools must devise ways for educating and responding to the needs of children who have suffered sexual abuse or have attention deficit disorders. As an educator or policymaker, what would you propose schools do to effectively identify and teach these children?

After reading "Memories Lost and Found," do you think it is possible to determine if childhood abuse actually occurred through recovered memories in adulthood? This divisive issue leads many to take sides, as some argue that therapists can "implant" false memories—events that never happened—into people's minds, whereas others argue that the personal, subjective memories of abuse should be respected. Where do you stand on this issue?

America's Children: Economic Perspectives and Policy Options

VICTOR R. FUCHS AND DIANE M. REKLIS

V. R. Fuchs is the Henry J. Kaiser, Jr., Professor at Stanford University, Stanford, CA 94305–8715, and also research associate at the National Bureau of Economic Research. Diane Reklis is a research assistant at the National Bureau of Economic Research, Stanford, CA 94305–8715.

American children are worse off than those in the previous generation in several important dimensions of mental, physical, and emotional well-being. During the 1960s cultural changes adversely affected children while their material condition improved substantially. By contrast, material conditions deteriorated in the 1980s, especially among children at the lower end of the income distribution. Public policies to improve the material condition of children require a transfer of resources from households that do not have children to those that do. Government programs such as tax credits and child allowances are more efficient and equitable than employer-mandated programs.

AMERICAN CHILDREN ARE IN TROUBLE. NOT ALL CHILdren, to be sure, but many observers consider today's children to be worse off than their parents' generation in several important dimensions of physical, mental, and emotional well-being. Has the status of children really worsened over the past three decades? If so, why? And what policy options are available that might help children?

Most explanations can be classified as cultural or material. In the cultural realm observers point to the waning influence of religion on the daily lives of most Americans, the fragmentation of the family through divorce and unwed motherhood, and the harmful influence of television on intellectual development and physical activity (1). In this vein, some observers relate the problems of children to a permissive society in which adults fail to set high standards or provide sufficient attention and discipline. In *Childhood's Future*, Louv argues that children today experience a freedom that is closer to abandonment (2).

The other set of explanations emphasizes changes in the material realm. Has government failed to provide the goods and services needed by children? Have changes in the distribution of household income (both earned and transfers from government) adversely affected the ability of parents to provide for their children? What has happened to the production of goods and services for children within the household (meals at home, childcare, and help with homework)?

In this article, we focus primarily on the material side, but also consider important interactions between the two sets of explanations. Cultural changes, such as the growing incidence of divorce and unwed motherhood, reduce the income available to children. Material changes, such as a decrease in household income—either absolute or relative to expectations—may induce both parents to seek paid jobs, with possible negative implications for families and neighborhoods.

One frequently mentioned explanation that can be dismissed at the outset is that children are increasingly born to women of low education. There is a significant gap between the schooling of women with children and those who are childless, but the relative gap was not appreciably greater in 1988 than in 1960. In absolute terms, today's parents have much more schooling than those of the previous generation. The proportion of children living in households with a woman who had not completed high school was 50% in 1960 but only 21% in 1988; the proportion where the woman had 4 years of college or more jumped from five to 15%.

The Status of Children

Between 1960 and 1990 the number of children in the United States remained roughly constant at about 64 million. During that same period the number of adults ages 18 to 64 increased from 100 million to 152 million, and the number of Americans 65 and older jumped from 17 to 31 million. With many more adults available to provide and care for children, a substantial increase in the well-being of children might have been expected. Instead, the reverse seems to have occurred. A national household survey of parents in 1988 reported that nearly 20% of children ages 3 to 17 had one or more developmental, learning, or behavioral disorders (3). By the time they reached ages 12 to 17, one in four adolescents had suffered at least one of these disorders. Comparable data for the previous generation are not available, but several other indicators suggest deteriorating conditions for children both absolutely and relative to adults (Table 1) (4).

Declining performance on standardized tests between 1960 and 1980 has been well documented and is only partially accounted for by the characteristics of those taking the tests. Between 1980 and 1988 test scores rose slightly, but then fell again between 1988 and 1991, with results on the verbal portion reaching an all-time low (5). The tripling of the teenage suicide rate occurred during a period when the age-adjusted suicide rate for adults 25 and older remained approximately constant. Homicide rates have increased at all ages, but more rapidly for teenagers than for adults. The sharp increase in obesity in children is of concern because it raises the risk of hypertension, psychosocial problems, respiratory disease, diabetes, and orthopedic problems (6). Poverty rates for children and adults dropped sharply between 1960 and 1970, but since then the incidence of poverty among children has increased while remaining roughly constant among adults (7).

Not all trends have been adverse. In particular, infant and child mortality has fallen by more than 50% since 1960. Life expectancy tables for that year show 41 of every 1000 newborns dying before their 20th birthday; by 1988 the comparable figure was only 19. On the other hand, reported rates of child abuse tripled between 1976 and

Table 1. The status of children, selected years, 1960 to 1988. Children are under age 18 unless otherwise specified.

Variable	1960	1970	1980	1988
SAT scores				
Verbal	477	466	424	428
Math	498	488	466	476
Suicide rate, ages 15 to 19*	3.6	5.9	8.5	11.3
Homicide rate, ages 15 to 19*	4.0	8.1	10.6	11.7
Obese (%)				
Ages 6 to 11	18†		27§	
Ages 12 to 17		16‡	22§	
Children in poverty (%)	26.9	15.1	18.3	19.5
Children whose parents divorced during the year (%)	0.72	1.25	1.73	1.68¶
Births to unwed mothers (%)	5.3	10.7	18.4	25.7
Children in households with only one adult (%)	5.5	9.2	12.1	14.2
Married women in the labor force with children under age 6 (%)	18.6	30.3	45.1	57.1

*Rate per 100,000.   †About 1964.   ‡About 1968.   §About 1978.   ¶1986.

1986 (8); whether this reflects only better reporting is not known. A recent assessment of proficiency in mathematics revealed that only one in seven eighth graders could perform at the level that educators expect for that grade (9). Even at age 17, one-half of all high school students cannot "compute with decimals, fractions, and percentages; recognize geometric figures; and solve simple equations" (10). To what extent are these problems of children correlated with trends in government spending and household income and behavior?

Government Purchases of Goods and Services

In 1988 purchases of goods and services by government (federal, state, and local) amounted to $962 billion (Table 2). Some of these purchases were clearly intended for children—for example, public spending for elementary and secondary schools. Others were clearly intended for adults—for example, Medicare and higher education. We allocated to children or to adults all clearly identifiable purchases; some items (amounting to 57% of the total in 1988) such as national defense or general administration could not be allocated by age. Similar estimates for 1960, 1970, and 1980 were adjusted to 1988 dollars by a price index of goods and services purchased by government (11). Government transfers of money to households through programs such as Social Security retirement or Aid to Families with Dependent Children are not part of government purchases; they are included in the estimates of household income to be discussed below.

The data in Table 2 show that government purchases of goods and services for children (in real dollars) have risen throughout the period both in the aggregate and on a per child basis. Although the allocation of purchases by age is not precise, separate analyses of the most important components of government spending for children reveal the same upward trend. For instance, expenditures per pupil in public elementary and secondary schools adjusted by the input price index for education rose by 2% per annum between 1975 and 1987 (12). Government spending for personal health care per child, adjusted by the medical care component of the consumer price index, also rose by 2% per annum between 1977 and 1987 (13).

Although Table 2 gives no support to the notion that government purchases of goods and services for children have declined, it does show that purchases for adults have increased at a much faster pace, primarily as a result of the introduction of Medicare and Medicaid in 1965 and the subsequent rapid growth of those programs. Moreover, those who argue that children's problems result from insufficient government spending argue that the increase in purchases has not been sufficient to allow the schools and other publicly supported institutions to cope with the greater problems they now face. These problems are attributed to an increase in the percentage of children coming from non-English speaking homes, from one-parent homes, or from homes where both parents are in paid employment. Also, more resources are needed to "mainstream" children who were previously neglected by public institutions because of physical, mental, or emotional disabilities.

Money Income

Most goods and services consumed by children (and adults) depend on the money income received by households (Table 3) (14). Using public use samples of the 1960, 1970, and 1980 Censuses of Population, and the March 1988 Current Population Survey (15), we calculated the money income of each household, including wages and salaries, self-employment income, dividends, interest, and other nonwage income, transfers from government such as retirement income or welfare payments, and private transfer income received in the form of alimony or child support payments. Within each household, we allocated the money income equally on a per person basis to the adults and the children, if any, in the household (16). The children are then arrayed from the lowest to the highest income, and the income per child at various points in the array, such as the first quartile, the median, and the third quartile, is determined. Similar calculations are performed for adults as a whole and for adults divided into two age groups, those between 18 and 64, and those 65 and older. Income estimates in current prices for 1960, 1970, and 1980 are converted to 1988 dollars by a price index of goods and services purchased by households (17).

The first row of Table 3 shows a substantial increase in the median money income per child from $4133 in 1960 to $6917 in 1988. The rate of increase over the entire period in real dollars was 1.84% per annum. Although this was slightly lower than the 2.04% per annum increase experienced by adults, these data provide little support for the view that a fall in household income available to children is the cause of their declining well-being. This conclusion, however, needs to be qualified in three important ways.

First, the growth of median income per child was much more rapid between 1960 and 1970 (2.80% per annum) than between 1970 and 1988 (1.30% per annum).

Second, our calculations reveal that inequality in income among children increased appreciably, especially between 1980 and 1988. Thus, looking at income per child at the lower end of the distribution (first quartile) (B of Table 3), we see that the rate of growth was appreciably slower than at the median; between 1980 and 1988 there was no growth at all. By contrast, the rate of growth for children at the third quartile (not shown in the table) was 1.94% per annum between 1960 and 1988. Adults do not show any increase in inequality between 1960 and 1988; the rates of growth at the first quartile, median, and third quartile were all between 2.01% and 2.06% per annum.

The third important qualification concerns the source of income for children. Since 1960 there has been a huge increase in the proportion of mothers in paid jobs (Table 1) (*18*). The importance of their earnings in sustaining income for children can be seen in parts C and D of Table 3, where the calculations are identical to those in parts A and B, except that the earnings of women in households with children have been subtracted from total income (*19*). That adjustment reduces the rate of growth of the median income per child to only 0.95% per annum, while the rate for adults remains at a sizeable 1.92% per annum. The earnings of women in households with children became most important at the first quartile; without them, the gains of the 1960s were completely offset by losses between 1970 and 1988 (*20*).

An important trend adversely affecting children's income is the increase in households without an adult male. In 1960 only 7% of children lived in such households; by 1988 that proportion had jumped to 19%. The median income per child in 1988 was $7640 with an adult male, but only $2397 without an adult male. As a rough approximation, if the proportion of children without an adult male had stayed at 7%, average income per child in all households would have been about 9% higher than it was in 1988 (*21*).

Figure 1 shows that income trends have varied by type of household and type of measure. With an adult male present, median and first quartile income rose in all three decades. These households, however, became increasingly dependent on women's earnings over time as evidenced by the widening gap between the curves that do not include women's earnings (dashed lines) from those that do (solid lines). This effect is particularly strong for children at the lower end of the income distribution: without women's earnings real income in 1988 was no higher than in 1970. In households without an adult male, median and first quartile income rose in the 1960s and 1970s, but declined between 1980 and 1988. No trend is shown for the first quartile in households without an adult male when women's earnings are subtracted because the value was zero in all 4 years (*22*).

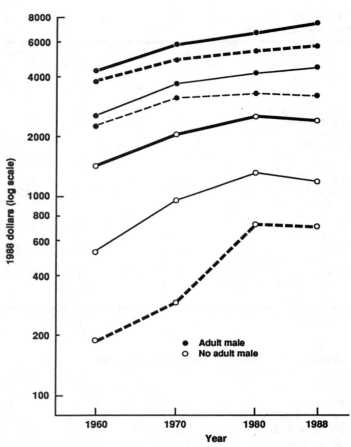

Fig. 1. Income per child in households with and without an adult male. Thick lines represent the median; thin lines, the first quartile; solid lines, all income; and dashed lines, minus women's earnings.

Nonmarket Production

Children's material well-being depends primarily on three sources: the goods and services provided by government, the goods and services purchased for them by their parents with household income, and the goods and services provided by adults to children within the household through so-called nonmarket production. Data on non-

market production comparable to the government and money income time trends are not available. However, data on the proportion of children in one-adult households and the labor force participation rates of married mothers suggest a downward trend in nonmarket production.

We see in Table 1 that the percentage of children living in households with only one adult almost tripled between 1960 and

Table 2. Federal, state, and local government purchases of goods and services for children (<18) and adults (≥18), selected years, 1960 to 1988.

Variable	1960	1970	1980	1988	Rate of change 1960 to 1988 (percent per year)
Aggregate purchases (billions of dollars, 1988)*					
Children	83.1	141.6	154.3	188.1	2.92
Adults	34.0	102.8	160.2	228.7	6.81
Not allocated by age†	381.0	461.7	450.3	545.7	1.28
Number of persons (millions)					
Children	64.5	69.7	63.8	63.8	−0.04
Adults	116.1	133.5	162.8	182.0	1.60
All ages	180.7	203.2	226.5	245.8	1.10
Purchases per person (dollars 1988)*					
Children	1289	2032	2420	2946	2.95
Adults	292	770	984	1257	5.21
Not allocated by age†	2109	2272	1988	2220	0.18

*Adjusted by the GNP implicit deflator for government purchases of goods and services.   †For example, national defense, general administration, and public safety.

1988. Even more striking is the jump in the proportion of married women with one child or more under age six who are in the labor force. Such striking changes in the number of adults and in their employment status probably resulted in some decrease in home-cooked meals, help with homework, and other nonmarket goods and services since 1960. By 1986, in white households with children, there were about 10 hours less per week of potential parental time (total time minus time in paid work); the decrease for black households with children was approximately 12 hours per week (23). The principal reason for the decline was an increase in the proportion of mothers holding paid jobs, but the increase in one-parent households was also important, especially for black children.

Consideration of women's earnings, nonmarket production, and the presence of an adult male shows that the cultural and material explanations are not completely distinct. Divorce or birth to an unwed mother usually has an adverse effect on the material well-being of children quite apart from any psychological or social implications. The slow growth of the real earnings of young fathers since 1970 (especially for those at the first quartile of the income distribution) induced more mothers to take paid employment, with repercussions for the cultural realm. Interactions between the two realms need to be considered in any discussion of policy options to help children.

Policy Options

The menu of policy options to help children tends to divide into two categories similar to the cultural and the material explanations. There are those who argue that only a return to more traditional family structures and values can provide the combination of care and discipline that children need. Some advocate changes in public policy such as more stringent divorce laws or holding parents responsible for the antisocial acts of their children in order to reverse the cultural changes of recent decades.

Most advocates for children tend to emphasize the necessity to improve their material condition through new or expanded programs of education, health, childcare, and the like. Because society's resources are fixed at any given time, such programs must involve a reallocation of resources from adults to children, either within households that have children or between households that do not have children and those that do. The mechanisms for reallocation may involve business firms or the government, but ultimately all resources flow from and to households.

One possibility is for adults in households that have children to devote more money and time to the children and less to themselves. In practice it is difficult for public policy to compel such redistributions; except for extreme abuse, parents are free to treat their children as they wish. However, to the extent that parents care about their children's well-being, a well-chosen combination of taxes on adult consumption and subsidies of children's goods and services might induce some reallocation of household income toward children.

The most likely source of additional revenues for children is from households that do not have children. Such households have grown in relative importance from 49% of the total in 1960 to 62% in 1988. In households headed by someone between 25 and 44 (the prime ages for having children) the proportion without children has almost doubled—from 20% in 1960 to 37% in 1988. Given the present distribution of income in the United States, revenue transfers to households with children would be "progressive," from higher to lower income persons. Among all households without children, median income per person is 67% higher than among households with two children (1988). Holding the age of the householder constant, the differential is substantially larger.

Comparisons of income per person tend to exaggerate household differences in living standards for two reasons: first, a child may not require as much income as an adult; second, large households may not require as much income per person as small households in order to achieve the same level of material well-being. The official poverty rate calculations adjust for these factors; for example, a household

Table 3. Household income per child and per adult, selected years 1960 to 1988.

Variable	Household income (1988 dollars)*				Rate of change 1960 to 1988 (percent per year)
	1960	1970	1980	1988	
Total income					
A. Median					
Child	4,133	5,470	6,220	6,917	1.84
Adult	6,201	8,145	9,342	10,992	2.04
18 to 64	6,375	8,513	9,665	11,281	2.04
≥65	4,924	6,232	7,687	9,831	2.47
B. First quartile					
Child	2,390	3,284	3,568	3,555	1.42
Adult	3,598	4,812	5,579	6,310	2.01
18 to 64	3,788	5,107	5,750	6,313	1.82
≥65	2,841	3,623	4,978	6,152	2.76
Income minus earnings of women in households with children					
C. Median					
Child	3,726	4,603	4,839	4,866	0.95
Adult	5,568	7,273	8,249	9,539	1.92
18 to 64	5,708	7,383	8,416	9,511	1.82
≥65	4,719	6,031	7,554	9,679	2.57
D. First quartile					
Child	2,005	2,501	2,312	2,015	0.02
Adult	3,175	4,154	4,664	5,081	1.68
18 to 64	3,254	4,343	4,611	4,854	1.43
≥65	2,782	3,619	4,876	6,017	2.76

*Adjusted by GNP implicit deflator for personal consumption expenditures.

Table 4. Characteristics of households with one or more children under 6 years of age, by presence and employment status of adults, 1988. Employment is defined as paid employment for at least 1000 hours in year.

Adults in household	Children <6 (%)	Poor children <6 (%)	Median income per person (dollars)	Schooling of women (years)
One woman and one man				
Both employed	27.1	3.2	9956	13.5
Man employed	37.7	21.0	7028	12.8
Woman employed	2.5	2.1	5361	12.9
Neither employed	6.1	16.2	2535	11.9
One woman				
Employed	3.9	5.1	5233	12.7
Not employed	8.0	33.8	1388	11.0
Other*	14.7	18.7	5702	11.1

*Includes two or more women, three or more adults (with at least one man), and one or more men (with no women). Totals may not equal 100 because of rounding.

with two adults and two children is assumed to require only twice as much income as a one-adult household in order to exceed the poverty level of living. Nevertheless, poverty is more likely in households with children, and the incidence rises sharply for households with three or more children. Regardless of the method of comparison, it is indisputable that a redistribution of income from households without children to those with children would result in greater equality. A corollary is that a general redistribution from higher to lower income (without regard to the presence of children) would tend to benefit children.

One way of achieving redistribution to children is to require employers to offer benefits such as paid parental leave or subsidized child care with the costs of such benefits spread among all workers (in the form of lower wages or foregone other benefits) or among consumers (in the form of higher prices). The employer-mandate mechanism appeals to many in government because it avoids difficult budgetary choices, but it will usually be less efficient and less equitable than direct government programs supported by general taxation.

Mandated child-benefit programs reduce economic efficiency because the costs fall disproportionately on the consumers of particular products and on workers in particular industries and firms—those that employ relatively more women of childbearing age (24). These distortions in relative prices and wages cause consumers and workers to change their behavior and reduce the overall efficiency of the economy much as if the government put a special tax on commodities that were produced by women with small children. Moreover, firms would be less likely to hire women of child-bearing age or to promote them to higher level positions.

The distributional consequences of employment-based child benefit programs are particularly regressive, as may be seen in Table 4. Most poor children do not live in households that would be the chief beneficiaries of employer-mandated programs. Indeed, the households that would receive the bulk of the benefits (where both the woman and the man are employed) have the highest income and the smallest poverty rate. Paid parental leave would provide the greatest dollar benefits for children with the best paid parents; many of the poorest children would receive no benefit at all because their mothers are not employed and have poor job prospects. Those women who are raising children alone and are not currently employed have, on average, only 11 years of schooling.

An alternative way to help children is for government to provide

tax credits, subsidies, or child allowances with the costs met by raising taxes or cutting spending for other programs. These benefits could be means tested (available only to children below a certain income level), or they could be available to all children. Even the latter approach, if financed by general revenue, would have a progressive distributional impact because so many children are in households with low income. A major challenge for government is to devise tax credits or allowances for children without exacerbating cultural changes (such as more divorce or more births to unwed mothers) that would increase the number of children in poverty.

Conclusion

Both cultural and material changes have probably contributed to the problems of America's children; the relative importance of the different explanations, however, varies over time. Between 1960 and 1970 the fall in test scores, the doubling of teenage suicide and homicide rates, and the doubling share of births to unwed mothers cannot be attributed to economic adversity. During that decade purchases of goods and services for children by government rose very rapidly, as did real household income per child, and the poverty rate of children plummeted. Thus, we must seek explanations for the rising problems of that period in the cultural realm.

By contrast, material conditions did deteriorate in the 1980s, especially among children in households at the lower end of the income distribution. Between 1980 and 1988 real income per child at the first quartile declined slightly, and even the gain of 1.0% per annum at the median was almost entirely accounted for by mothers taking on paid employment. At the first quartile, income per child fell at the rate of 1.4% per annum if women's earnings are excluded. Moreover, the sharp increase in the proportion of children living in households in which all adults are employed implies a decrease in time available for nonmarket production of goods and services.

What of the future? Expressions of concern about the well-being of children span the political spectrum (25), but no consensus has been reached regarding the causes of children's problems or the policies that would alleviate them. Some analysts seek to reverse the cultural changes of the past several decades by making divorce more difficult or holding parents responsible for their children's antisocial acts. Even those who emphasize cultural changes, however, experience difficulty devising public policies that would reverse them. How can government change the public's values and lifestyles without intruding on what many claim are fundamental individual rights?

Most policy discussions focus on improving the material well-being of children through government mandates on employers or direct government programs such as tax credits or child allowances. Implicit in many of the proposals is the hope that higher income for households with children will lead to more parental inputs at home and less time spent in paid employment. Alternatively, credits and allowances could facilitate the purchase of more services for children.

In order to formulate an efficient and equitable set of policies about children, society must reach some agreement concerning the objectives of such policies, the means to reach those objectives, and the distribution of the costs. There seems to be some truth to both conservative critiques of the cultural changes that were launched in the 1960s as well as liberal complaints about the uneven prosperity of the 1980s. But mutual recrimination does little to help children. All adults need to recognize that the nation's future depends critically on our willingness and ability to help America's children today (26).

REFERENCES AND NOTES

1. See, for instance, many of the papers in *Rebuilding the Nest*, D. Blankenhorn, S. Bayme, J. B. Elshtain, Eds. (Family Service America, Milwaukee, 1990).
2. R. Louv, *Childhood's Future* (Houghton Mifflin, Boston, 1990).
3. N. Zill and C. A. Schoenborn, "Developmental, learning, and emotional problems: Health of our nation's children, United States, 1988," in *Advance Data* (U.S. Department of Health and Human Services, no. 190, 1990).
4. Details on sources and methods for all tables available on request.
5. "College Board verbal scores decline to an all-time low," *New York Times*, 27 August 1991, p. 16.
6. "Health implications of obesity," National Institutes of Health, Consensus Development Conference Statement (U.S. Department of Health and Human Services, PHS, February 1985), vol. 5, no. 9.
7. M. J. Bane and D. T. Ellwood, *Science* **245**, 1047 (1989).
8. Bureau of the Census, *Statistical Abstract of the United States* (U.S. Government Printing Office, Washington, DC, 1990), p. 176.
9. K. DeWitt, "Eighth graders' math survey shows no state is 'cutting it'," *New York Times*, 7 June 1991, p. 1.
10. A. N. Applebee, J. A. Langer, I. V. S. Mullis, "Crossroads in American education," (Educational Testing Service, Princeton, NJ, February 1989), p. 21.
11. That is, the GNP implicit deflator for government purchases; see *Economic Report of the President* (U.S. Government Printing Office, Washington, DC, January 1991), p. 291.
12. U.S. Department of Commerce, *Statistical Abstract* (U.S. Government Printing Office, Washington, DC, 1989), p. 172.
13. D. R. Waldo *et al.*, *Health Care Financing Rev.* **10**, 114 (1989), tables 2 and 3.
14. Reported money income is a good but not perfect measure of command over goods and services because it does not include fringe benefits, such as health insurance, or income from the underground economy, nor does it exclude personal income taxes. Estimation of the effects of these variables on the true net income available to households is very difficult, and even more difficult if separate estimates for children and adults are required.
15. Because the data gathered by the Bureau of the Census through the Current Population Surveys differs slightly from that gathered in the decennial censuses, the 1988 figures were adjusted to census levels by linking changes in the Current Population Survey results between 1980 and 1988 to the 1980 census levels. The number of persons in the samples are: 175,123 in 1960, 197,345 in 1970, 220,916 in 1980, and 155,654 in 1988.
16. Alternative calculations in which each child is weighted as some fraction of an adult, for example, 0.75 or 0.50, show that the trends over time that are discussed here are not sensitive to assumptions about the "adult equivalence" of children unless the assumption is changed appreciably from one year to another. We have no basis for making such changes.
17. That is, the GNP implicit deflator for personal consumption expenditures [*Economic Report of the President* (U.S. Government Printing Office, Washington DC, January 1991), p. 290].
18. The rapid growth in the female labor force participation rate since 1960 is accounted for primarily by women in households with children. Participation rates among childless women have always been high and show little change. Participation rates of older women whose children no longer live with them have shown only modest increases since 1960.
19. The purpose of this calculation is to show the contribution of women's earnings to the income available to children, not to suggest that women should not have paid jobs.
20. This statistical adjustment does not capture all the labor market and income effects of the increase in mothers taking paid jobs; to do so would require a complex model beyond the scope of this paper.
21. The weighted average of $7640 and $2397 is $7273 when the weights are 93% and 7%, but only $6644 when the weights are 81% and 19%.
22. That is, in more than 25% of the households without an adult male, women's earnings were the only source of income.
23. V. R. Fuchs, *Women's Quest for Economic Equality* (Harvard Univ. Press, Cambridge, 1988), p. 111.
24. Even if the mandate legislation is gender-neutral, the Swedish experience indicates that many more women than men will use the benefits ["A land where father (sometimes) is left holding the baby," *Sweden Now* 6, 27 (1986)].
25. *Beyond Rhetoric: A New American Agenda for Children and Families*, Final Report of the National Commission on Children (U.S. Government Printing Office, Washington, DC, 1991).
26. Financial support for this work was provided by the Andrew W. Mellon Foundation. Helpful comments from V. Foster, A. Garber, E. King, E. Lewit, R. Olshen, and M. Shuchman are also gratefully acknowledged.

Homeless families: stark reality of the '90s

Researchers look into one of America's most disturbing problems: homeless families.

Tori DeAngelis

Monitor staff

The landscape of homelessness has changed since the early 1980s, when nearly all homeless people were men. Today, families—typically women with two children under age 5—make up about 30 percent of the homeless population.

Psychologists are starting to look more closely at the basic characteristics of homeless families: how they become homeless, how homeless mothers' mental health and substance abuse compares to that of other groups and how homeless children compare in behavioral and mental health problems, school functioning and other characteristics to poor youngsters who have housing.

Several factors have conspired to increase the numbers of homeless families since the mid-1980s, said John C. Buckner, PhD, associate director of research at the Better Homes Foundation and lecturer in the department of psychiatry at Harvard Medical School. Demographically, the "baby boom" led to larger numbers of people competing for the same number of affordable living spaces, he noted. On top of that, for the poor, children "are a vulnerability factor" who "make your living expenses higher and make it harder for you to hold down a full-time job," he said. "Plus, if you're doubled up" with other families, "children may become a liability" who can "strain the good will" of those poor families [they] are living with, he said.

The rise in the number of homeless people has led to a growing amount of research in the area, Buckner said. While researchers have looked at the "skid row" homeless for some 100 years, only since the late 1970s have they started examining the general homeless population in earnest, he said. Their work on homeless families is even more recent, beginning in the mid-1980s.

"Basically, researchers see families as another at-risk group for homelessness," he said.

HOMELESS WOMEN

In the last several years, some research consensus has emerged on homeless families: In general, "homeless families look very different from homeless individuals," said Marybeth Shinn, PhD, psychology professor in the Community Psychology Project at New York University. A range of studies has shown, for instance, that these families "have much lower levels of substance-abuse and mental health problems" than homeless individuals, she said. Homeless families are also younger on average than poor-housed families, studies have found.

And compared to other kinds of homeless women—those without children and those who have children but whose children live elsewhere—homeless women with children fare better in several ways, studies show. In a study she conducted last year and is now analyzing, for instance, Marjorie Robertson, PhD, senior scientist at the California Pacific Medical Center's Institute of Epidemiology and Behavioral Medicine in Berkeley, and colleagues are finding that homeless women whose children are with them are the most likely to have finished high school and to have the lowest average number of adult arrests of the three groups. In addition, homeless women with children are homeless for the lowest average total days, and are more likely to receive welfare payments and food supplies, the team is finding.

Homeless women with children also attempt suicide less often than single homeless women, other studies have found. And while homeless women with children have lower rates of mental illness than homeless single women, they show greater psychological distress, studies show.

About half of all homeless women are ethnic minorities, and many of those are mothers, according to a policy paper being prepared by a task force of the American Psychological Association's Div. 27 (Community). Robertson's study shows that approximately 28 percent of homeless women have some of their children on the street with them, while another 43 percent have children who aren't with them.

Research has also found "a higher level of recent and past domestic violence in the lives of homeless women," than among the housed poor, Robertson said. "These women are already vulnerable economically." Domestic violence "is just one more element in a living situation they have little control over."

The Div. 27 task force report—and many researchers in the field—conclude that poverty is the root of the increase in homeless families, not individual factors like mental illness or domestic violence.

According to the report, the poorest 20 percent of families became even poorer during the 1980s. That decline was greatest among the poorest single mothers and the poorest young families with children, it states.

Although psychological researchers have accumulated some basic knowledge on homeless families, "we are just now beginning to study them in a way that gives us some insight into their lives," Robertson said.

RECENT STUDIES

In New York, Shinn and colleagues at New York University have been trying to determine what differentiates poor homeless families from other poor families in an attempt to find the precursors to homelessness. Hers is one of the major ongoing studies to date on homeless families.

The team interviewed mostly women in the study, which has two phases. In the first, conducted in 1988, Shinn and James Knickman, PhD, and Beth Weitzman, PhD, of the university's Wagner School of Public Service, collected data on 700 families that requested shelter and 524 housed families on public assistance to detect "early warning signs for homelessness among people on a public-assistance caseload," Shinn said.

Interviewing women directly before they entered shelters let the team examine causes versus consequences of homelessness—something researchers have not previously done because they usually begin their studies after people have been homeless for a while, Shinn noted.

In the second phase, which Shinn and Weitzman are now completing, the two are reinterviewing and examining public records of 915 people from the original group. The purpose is to look at "predictors of mental health and the long-term consequences of homelessness for mothers and children, and to determine what helps people establish stable residences in the community," Shinn said.

SOME PREDICTORS

In analyzing the first set of data, the team found that 44 percent of shelter requesters had never been primary tenants in a residence, compared to 12 percent of the housed poor. More than 80 percent of shelter requesters had dou-

bled up with another family, compared to 38 percent of the housed poor. About 45 percent of shelter requesters had lived with three or more people per bedroom, compared to 26 percent of the housed poor. And 47 percent of shelter requesters experienced two or more serious building problems, such as rats or lack of heat in the winter, compared to 38 percent of the housed poor.

Shelter requesters were also pregnant in greater numbers than their housed counterparts: 34 percent compared to 6 percent. However, family sizes were smaller among shelter requesters, probably a reflection of the fact they were younger on average, Shinn said.

In keeping with other studies, the team found that family factors such as childhood victimization and early separation from the family of origin occurred more often for those requesting shelter than for the public-assistance group, Shinn said.

So far, the study suggests that "our most vulnerable folks are the ones who are becoming homeless," Shinn said.

HOMELESS CHILDREN

Researchers at the Better Homes Foundation—a nonprofit organization established by *Better Homes* magazine in 1988 to study and help the homeless—are comparing homeless women and children to poor housed women and their children, Buckner said. The team plans to collect data on 250 people in each group. Results should be out this fall, he said.

Only a quarter of homeless children were with their mothers. About 10 percent were in foster care; the rest were living with other family members.

As in Shinn's study, the team will try to isolate risk factors for homelessness by looking at differences between the two groups, and will also examine "the immediate consequences of homelessness on women and children," he said.

Like the New York team, the Better Homes researchers hope to untangle which factors cause and which are a

result of homelessness, Buckner said. For instance, past research has "identified group differences between homeless and housed children in developmental delays and behavioral and disciplinary problems," with homeless children exhibiting higher levels of those difficulties than their poor housed peers, he said. "But it's not clear how much those differences are attributable to the experience of homelessness or to coexisting factors such as parental substance abuse, mental health problems and family violence."

As part of a larger study on homeless adults, Robertson, Alex Westerfelt, PhD, and Cheryl Zlotnick, DrPH, interviewed 179 homeless families in Alameda County, Calif. Zlotnik is with the Center for the Vulnerable Child at Children's Hospital in Oakland, Calif.; Westerfelt is with the University of Kansas School of Social Welfare.

To the researchers' surprise, only a quarter of the children of homeless mothers were with their mothers, Robertson said. About 10 percent were in foster care; the rest were living with other family members, she said.

The findings suggest "that [homeless] women with children are having a very hard time keeping their families together," Robertson said. Although she doesn't have hard data on why, "I'm imagining it as a choice the mom is making for her children," she said.

Interviews with some of the women partly confirmed that hypothesis. One woman, for instance, told Robertson that three of her five children were living with the woman's mother, because she thought they would be better off.

In a study of stress levels in homeless and poor housed children, Pamela Reid, PhD, and doctoral students at the City University of New York confirmed other psychologists' findings that there are more similarities than differences between very poor and homeless children, including their feelings about their top stressors.

The team conducted in-depth interviews from 1990 to 1992 with 45 homeless and poor housed second- and fifth-graders. The two groups reported having the same two major concerns that were constant realities in their lives, Reid said: violence and the death and loss of parents, relatives and friends. "A lot of kids were handling death on their own," and reported a high rate of it in their circles, Reid said.

One difference Reid found is that the homeless youngsters reported less peer support than the housed poor children, as one might expect given their living conditions, she said.

Besides their research program, the team set up an after-school program where older homeless and poor housed children tutored the younger ones and the doctoral students tutored the older children, Reid said.

While the programs weren't formally evaluated, the teachers said they "could see changes in the kids who attended," Reid said. The school kept the programs for two years, but cut them this year because of budget problems, she said. Their success underscores the need for "simple, direct interventions that can make a difference," Reid believes.

The Div. 27 report notes that homeless children share a number of common physical and emotional problems, including malnutrition, poor physical development, severe stomach disorders, delayed social and emotional development, ag-gressive and demanding behaviors, sleep disorders, abnormal social fears and speech difficulties. For children older than age 5, more than half need psychiatric help, and their "school performance is consistently below average," the report states.

THE FATHER'S ROLE

While many questions remain about homeless families, homeless fathers remain a research black hole, Shinn commented. "I don't think we have a handle on the men who are involved" with homeless mothers, she said.

One reason so little is known about homeless fathers is that the fathers often are not part of homeless families. For another, "many shelters are not eager to have men around," because of concerns about privacy and heightened levels of aggression and violence, and researchers tend to gather a lot of their data from shelters, she said.

A third reason is methodological, Shinn said. In her New York study, 22 percent of shelter requesters and 6.5 percent of the housed group reported having male partners, she said. "If you believe our data, it says having men around is a big risk factor for homelessness—but I don't believe our data," she said.

Shinn explained that homeless and housed women may not respond truthfully to surveys because those on public assistance stand to lose their benefits if they report they have husbands. Homeless men can't enter some shelters with families unless they can prove they are a woman's legal spouse or a child's biological father, she said.

Shinn hopes to get around those problems by "asking a more sensitive set of questions about women's relationship status" in the second round of her study, she said.

Why Leave Children With Bad Parents?

Family: Last year, 1,300 abused kids died—though authorities knew that almost half were in danger. Is it time to stop patching up dead-end families?

MICHELE INGRASSIA AND JOHN McCORMICK

THE REPORT OF DRUG PEDdling was already stale, but the four Chicago police officers decided to follow up anyway. As they knocked on the door at 219 North Keystone Avenue near midnight on Feb. 1, it was snowing, and they held out little hope of finding the pusher they were after. They didn't. What they discovered, instead, were 19 children living in horrifying squalor. Overnight, the Dickensian images of life inside the apartment filled front pages and clogged network airwaves.

For the cops that night, it seemed like a scavenger hunt gone mad, each discovery yielding a new, more stunning, find. In the dining room, police said, a half-dozen children lay asleep on a bed, their tiny bodies intertwined like kittens. On the floor beside them, two toddlers tussled with a mutt over a bone they had grabbed from the dog's dish. In the living room, four others huddled on a hardwood floor, crowded beneath a single blanket. "We've got eight or nine kids here," Officer John Labiak announced.

Officer Patricia Warner corrected him: "I count 12." The cops found the last of 19 asleep under a mound of dirty clothes; one 4-year-old, gnarled by cerebral palsy, bore welts and bruises.

As the police awaited reinforcements, they could take full measure of the filth that engulfed this brigade of 1- to 14-year-olds. Above, ceiling plaster crumbled. Beneath their feet, roaches scurried around clumps of rat droppings. But nothing was more emblematic than the kitchen. The stove was inoperable, its oven door yawning wide. The sink held fetid dishes that one cop said "were not from that day, not from that week, maybe not from this year." And though the six mothers living there collected a total of $4,500 a month in welfare and food stamps, there was barely any food in the house. Twice last year, a caseworker from the Illinois Department of Children and Family Services (DCFS) had come to the apartment to follow up reports of serious child neglect, but when no one would let her in, the worker left. Now, it took hours to sort through the mess. Finally, the

police scooped up the children and set out for a state-run shelter. As they left, one little girl looked up at Warner and pleaded, "Will you be my mommy?"

Don't bet on it. Next month the children's mothers—Diane Melton, 31; Maxine Melton, 27; May Fay Melton, 25; Denise Melton, 24; Casandra Melton, 21, and Denise Turner, 20—will appear in Cook County juvenile court for a hearing to determine if temporary custody of the children should remain with the state or be returned to the parents. Yet, for all the public furor, confidential files show that the DCFS is privately viewing the 19 children in the same way it does most others—"Goal: Return Home."

Why won't we take kids from bad parents? For more than a decade, the idea that parents should lose neglected or abused kids has been blindsided by a national policy to keep families together at almost any cost. As a result, even in the worst cases, states regularly opt for reunification. Even in last year's budget-cutting frenzy, Congress earmarked nearly $1 billion for family-preservation programs over the next five years. Yet there is mounting evidence that such efforts make little difference—and may make things worse. "We've oversold the fact that all families can be saved," says Marcia Robinson Lowry, head of the Children's Rights Project of the American Civil Liberties Union. "All families *can't* be saved."

Last year there were 1 million confirmed

cases of abuse and neglect. And, according to the American Public Welfare Association, an estimated 462,000 children were in substitute care, nearly twice as many as a decade ago. The majority of families can be repaired if parents clean up their acts, but experts are troubled by what happens when they don't: 42 percent of the 1,300 kids who died as a result of abuse last year had previously been reported to child-protection agencies. "The child-welfare system stands over the bodies, shows you pictures of the caskets and still does things to keep kids at risk," says Richard Gelles, director of the University of Rhode Island's Family Violence Research Program.

Nowhere has the debate over when to break up families been more sharply focused than in Illinois, which, in the last two years, has had some of the most horrific cases in the nation. Of course, it's not alone. But unlike many states, Illinois hasn't been able to hide its failures behind the cloak of confidentiality laws, largely because of Patrick Murphy, Cook County's outspoken public guardian, who regularly butts heads with the state over its aggressive reunification plans. The cases have turned Illinois into a sounding board for what to do about troubled families.

The Chicago 19 lived in what most people would consider a troubled home. But to veterans of the city's juvenile courts, it's just another "dirty house" case. In fact, Martin Shapiro, the court-appointed attorney for Diane Melton, plans to say that conditions could have been worse. He can argue that Melton's children weren't malnourished, weren't physically or sexually abused and weren't left without adult supervision. He's blunt: "Returning children to a parent who used cocaine—as horrific as that might seem—isn't all that unusual in this building." If only all the cases were so benign.

What Went Wrong?

ON THE LAST NIGHT OF JOSEPH Wallace's life, no one could calm his mother's demons. Police say that Amanda Wallace was visiting relatives on April 18, 1993, with 3-year-old Joseph and his 1-year-old brother, Joshua, when she began raving that Joseph was nothing but trouble. "I'm gonna kill this bitch with a knife tonight," Bonnie Wallace later told police her daughter threatened. Bonnie offered to keep the boy overnight, but Amanda refused, so Bonnie drove them to their apartment on Chicago's impoverished West Side. It's unclear what forced Amanda's hand, but authorities tell a harrowing tale: at about 1:30 a.m., she stuffed a sock into Joseph's mouth and secured it with medical tape. Then she went to the kitchen, retrieved a brown extension cord and wrapped it around Joseph's neck several times. She carried her

son to the living room, stood him on a chair, then looped the cord around the metal crank arm over the door. In the last act of his life, Joseph waved goodbye.

Amanda Wallace, 28, has pleaded not guilty to charges of first-degree murder. No one ever doubted that Amanda was deeply troubled. When Joseph was born, she was a resident at the Elgin Mental Health Center in suburban Chicago, and a psychiatrist there warned that Amanda "should never have custody of this or any other baby." Three times, the DCFS removed Joseph from his mother. Yet three times, judges returned him to Amanda's dark world. Six months after the murder—which led to the firing of three DCFS employees—a blue-ribbon report blasted the Illinois child-welfare system, concluding that it had "surely consigned Joseph to his death."

Even in the most egregious instances of abuse, children go back to their parents time and again. In Cook County, the public guardian now represents 31,000 children. Only 963 kids were freed for adoption last year. But William Maddux, the new supervising judge of the county's abuse and neglect section, believes the number should have been as high as 6,000. Nationwide, experts say, perhaps a quarter of the children in substitute care should be taken permanently from their parents.

But it's not simply social custom that keeps families together, it's the law. The Adoption Assistance and Child Welfare Act of 1980 is a federal law with a simple goal—to keep families intact. The leverage: parents who don't make a "reasonable effort" to get their lives on track within 18 months risk losing their kids forever. The law itself was a reaction to the excesses of the '60s and '70s, when children were often taken away simply because their parents were poor or black. But the act was also one of those rare measures that conservatives and liberals embraced with equal passion— conservatives because it was cheap, liberals because it took blame away from the poor.

By the mid-'80s, though, the system began to collapse. A system built for a simpler time couldn't handle an exploding underclass populated by crack addicts, the homeless and the chronically unemployed. At the same time, orphanages began shutting their doors and foster families began quitting in droves. The system begged to know where to put so many kids. It opted for what was then a radical solution: keeping them in their own homes while offering their parents intensive, short-term support— child rearing, housekeeping and budgeting. But as family-preservation programs took off, the threat of severing the rights of abusive parents all but disappeared. What emerged, Gelles argues, was the naive philosophy that a mother who'd hurt her child is not much different from one who can't keep house—and that with enough supervi-

sion, both can be turned into good parents.

In hindsight, everyone in Chicago agrees that Joseph Wallace's death was preventable, that he died because the system placed a parent's rights above a child's. Amanda could never have been a "normal" parent. She had been a ward of the state since the age of 8, the victim of physical and sexual abuse. Between 1976 and Joseph's birth in 1989, her psychiatrist told the DCFS, she swallowed broken glass and batteries; she disemboweled herself, and when she was pregnant with Joseph, she repeatedly stuck soda bottles into her vagina, denying the baby was hers. Yet 11 months after Joseph was born, a DCFS caseworker and an assistant public defender persuaded a Cook County juvenile-court judge to give him back to Amanda, returning him from the one of the six foster homes he would live in. The judge dispatched Amanda with a blessing: "Good luck to you, Mother."

Over the next two years, caseworkers twice removed Joseph after Amanda attempted suicide. But a DCFS report, dated Oct. 31, 1992, said she had gotten an apartment in Chicago, entered counseling and worked as a volunteer for a community organization. And though the report noted her turbulent history, it recommended she and Joseph be reunited. Joseph Wallace was sent home for the last time 62 days before his death, by a judge who had no measure of Amanda's past. "Would somebody simply summarize what this case is about for me and give me an idea why you're all agreeing?" the judge asked. Amanda's lawyer sidestepped her mental history. Nevertheless, the DCFS and the public guardian's office signed on. When Amanda thanked the judge, he said, "It sounds like you're doing OK. Good luck."

Murphy says that deciding when to sever parents' rights should be obvious: "You remove kids if they're in a dangerous situation. No one should be taken from a cold house. But it's another thing when there are drugs to the ceiling and someone's screwing the kids." Ambiguous cases? "There haven't been gray cases in years."

No one knows that better than Faye and Michael Callahan, one of the foster families who cared for Joseph. When Joseph first came to them he was a happy, husky baby. When he returned after his first stretch with Amanda, "he had bald spots because he was pulling his hair out," Faye says. By the third time, she says, Joseph was "a zombie. He rocked for hours, groaning, 'Uh, uh, uh, uh'." The fact that he was repeatedly sent home still infuriates them. Says Michael: "I'd scream at those caseworkers, 'You're making a martyr of this little boy!'"

See No Evil, Hear No Evil

EARLY LAST THANKSGIVING, ARETHA McKinney brought her young son to the emergency room. Clifford Triplett was semiconscious, and his body was pocked with burns, bruises and other signs of abuse, police say. The severely malnourished boy weighed 17 pounds—15 percent less than the average 1-year-old. Except Clifford was 5.

This wasn't a secret. In a confidential DCFS file obtained by NEWSWEEK, a state caseworker who visited the family last June gave a graphic account of Clifford's life: "Child's room (porch) clothing piled in corner, slanted floor. Child appears isolated from family—every one else has a well furnished room. Child very small for age appears to be 2 years old. Many old scars on back and buttocks have many recent scratches." In April, another caseworker had confronted McKinney's live-in boyfriend, Eddie Robinson Sr., who claimed that Cliff was a "dwarf" and was suicidal—neither of which doctors later found to be true. Robinson added that Cliff got "whipped" because he got into mischief. "I told him that he shouldn't be beat on his back," the caseworker wrote. "Robinson promised to go easy on the discipline."

It's one thing to blame an anonymous "system" for ignoring abuse and neglect. But the real question is a human one: how can caseworkers walk into homes like Clifford's, document physical injury or psychological harm and still walk away? A Cook County juvenile-court judge ruled last month that both McKinney and Robinson had tortured Clifford (all but erasing the possibility that he'll ever be returned to his mother). But caseworkers are rarely so bold. In Clifford's case, the April worker concluded that abuse apparently had occurred, but nine days later another found the home "satisfactory." Says Gelles: "Caseworkers are programmed by everything around them to be deaf, dumb and blind because the system tells them, 'Your job is to work to reunification'."

Murphy charges that for the past two

SAONNIA BOLDEN

"The amount of stress and frustration has been reduced. Sadie appears to have a lot more patience with her children and she continues to improve her disciplinary techniques." The same day the worker wrote this, Sadie's daughter Saonnia died after boiling water was poured on her. An autopsy uncovered 62 injuries, many recent.

FROM CASEWORKER REPORT ON SAONNIA BOLDEN

---

years, Illinois has made it policy to keep new kids out of an already-clogged system. "The message went out that you don't aggressively investigate," he says. "Nobody said, 'Keep the ----ing cases out of the system'." But that, he says, is the net effect. "That's just not true," says Sterling Mac Ryder, who took over the DCFS late in 1992. But he doesn't dispute that the state and its caseworkers may have put too much emphasis on reunification—in part because of strong messages from Washington.

The problems may be even more basic. By all accounts, caseworkers and supervisors are less prepared today than they were 20 years ago, and only a fraction are actually social workers. Few on the front lines are willing, or able, to make tough calls or buck the party line. In the end, says Deborah Daro, research director of the National Committee to Prevent Child Abuse, "the worker may say, 'Yeah, it's bad, but what's the alternative? I'll let this one go and pray to God they don't kill him'."

In most cases, they don't. Nevertheless, children who grow up in violent homes beyond the age of 8 or 10 risk becoming so emotionally and psychologically damaged that they can never be repaired. "The danger," says Robert Halpern, a professor of child development at the Erikson Institute in Chicago, "is not just the enormous dam-

---

age to the kid himself, but producing the next generation of monsters."

Clifford Triplett is an all-too-pointed reminder of how severe the injuries can be. He has gained eight pounds, and his physical prognosis is good. But there are many other concerns. "When he came, he didn't know the difference between a car and a truck, the difference between pizza and a hot dog," says his hospital social worker, Kathleen Egan. "People were not introducing these things to him." Robinson and McKinney are awaiting trial on charges of aggravated battery and felony cruelty. McKinney's attorney blames Robinson for the alleged abuse; Robinson's attorney declined to comment. Clifford is waiting for a foster home. A few weeks ago he had his first conversation with his mother in months. His first words: "Are you sorry for whipping me?"

Band–Aids Don't Work

ACCORDING TO THE CASEWORKER'S report, 2½-year-old Saonnia Bolden's family was the model of success. Over 100 days, a homemaker from an Illinois family-preservation program called Family First worked with Sadie Williams and her boyfriend Clifford Baker. A second helper—a caseworker—shopped with Sadie for shoes and some furniture for her apartment; she evaluated Sadie's cooking, housekeeping and budgeting. She even took her to dinner to celebrate her progress. On March 17, 1992, the caseworker wrote a report recommending that Sadie's case be closed: "Due to the presence of homemaker, the amount of stress and frustration has been reduced. Sadie appears to have a lot more patience with her children and she continues to improve her disciplinary techniques."

What the Family First caseworker evidently didn't know was that, just hours before she filed her report, Saonnia had been beaten and scalded to death. Prosecutors claim that Williams, angered because her young daughter had wet herself, laid the child in the bathtub and poured scalding water over her genitals and her buttocks. Williams and Baker were charged with first-degree murder; lawyers for Baker and Williams blame each other's client. Regardless of who was responsible, this wasn't

---

Race of Foster Children

Contrary to public opinion, foster care is not dominated by minorities. Nearly half the kids there are white.

white	47.2%
hispanic	13.7%
black	30.8%
others	4.6%
unknown	3.7%

SOURCE: AMERICAN PUBLIC WELFARE ASSOCIATION

Where Do Children Go?

Two thirds of children who leave foster care are reunited with their parents; only a fraction are adopted.

reunited	66.6%
adopted	7.7%
adulthood	6.5%
other	15.7%
unknown	3.5%

SOURCE: AMERICAN PUBLIC WELFARE ASSOCIATION

A One-Man Children's Crusade

Twenty years ago, an angry young lawyer named Patrick Murphy wrote a book that exposed an injustice: state social workers too often seized children from parents whose worst crime was poverty. Today Murphy is the scourge of a child-welfare system that too often leaves kids with their abusive, drugged-out parents. He has not made the about-face quietly. In many cities, confidentiality laws protect caseworkers and judges from public outcries when their bad decisions lead to a parent's murder of a child. In Chicago, Murphy calls blistering press conferences to parcel out the blame. To those who say he picks on parents who are poor, black and victimized, he hotly retorts: "So are their kids."

Murphy is the Cook County (Ill.) public guardian, the court-appointed lawyer for 31,000 abused and neglected children. He's also a self-righteous crusader. last year, campaigning to rein in one "family preservation" program, Murphy sent every Illinois legislator color autopsy photos of a little girl scalded and beaten to death after caseworkers taught her family new disciplinary skills. It's a loner's life, poring over murder files and railing at fellow liberals who think the poor can do no wrong. "A lot of people hate my guts," Murphy shrugs. "I can't blame them."

His views on family reunification changed because child abuse changed. Drugs now suffuse 80 percent of the caseload; sexual and physical assaults that once taxed the imagination are now common. Murphy believes that most families should be reunited—but the child-welfare agencies waste years trying to patch up dead-end families when they should be hurrying to free children for early adoption. Murphy, 55, blames such folly on bleeding hearts like himself, who once lobbied for generous social programs without working to curb welfare dependency and other ills.

Now children of troubled families must pay the price—sometimes with their lives. "We inadvertently pushed a theory of irresponsibility," he says. "And we created a monster—kids having kids."

To Murphy's critics, that smacks of scorn for the less fortunate. "He's a classic bully," says Diane Redleaf of the Legal Assistance Foundation of Chicago, who represents parents trying to win back their kids. "Thousands of poor families are *not* torturing their children." Redleaf has drafted legislation that would force Murphy to get a judge's order each time he wants to speak about a case. That would protect children's privacy—and give the system a convenient hiding place. Murphy will fight to keep things as they are. His is the only job, he says, in which a lawyer knows that his clients are truly innocents.

J.M.

---

the first assault. The autopsy on Saonnia's visibly malnourished body found 62 cuts, bruises, burns, abrasions and wrist scars, among other injuries. Eleven were still healing—meaning they probably happened during the time the homemaker was working with the family.

Since Illinois's Family First program began in 1988, at least six children have died violently during or after their families received help. In many other instances, children were injured, or simply kept in questionable conditions. Such numbers may look small compared with the 17,000 children in Illinois who've been in the program. But to critics, the deaths and injuries underscore the danger of using reunification efforts for deeply troubled families. Gelles, once an ardent supporter of family preservation, is adamant about its failures. "We've learned in health psychology that you don't waste intervention on those with no intention of changing," he argues.

A University of Chicago report card issued last year gave the Illinois Family First program barely passing grades. Among the findings: Family First led to a slight *increase* in the overall number of children later placed outside their homes; it had no effect on subsequent reports of maltreatment; it had only mixed results in such areas as improving housing, economics and parenting, and it had no effect on getting families out of the DCFS system. John R. Schuerman, who helped write the report, says it's too simplistic to call Family First a

failure. Still, he concedes that the assumption that large numbers of households can be saved with intensive services "just may not be the case."

Nevertheless, in the last decade, family-preservation programs have become so entrenched there's little chance they'll be junked. Health and Human Services Secretary Donna Shalala carefully sidesteps the question of whether it's possible to carry the reunification philosophy too far. Asked where she would draw the line in defining families beyond repair, she diplomatically suggests that the answers be left to child-welfare experts. "Nobody wants to leave children in dangerous situations," says Shalala. "The goal is to shrewdly pick cases in which the right efforts might help keep a family together." So far, not even the experts have come up with a sure way to do that.

Where Do We Go From Here?

POLICYMAKERS BELIEVE THAT IF THEY could just remove the stresses from a family, they wouldn't have to remove the child. But critics argue that the entire child-welfare network must approach the idea of severing parents' rights as aggressively as it now approaches family reunification. That means moving kids through the system and into permanent homes quickly—before they're so damaged that they won't fit in anywhere. In theory, the Adoption Assistance Act already requires that, but no state enforces that part of the law. Illinois is typical: even in the most straightforward cases, a petition to terminate parental rights is usually the start of a two-year judicial process—*after* the 18-month clean-up-your-act phase.

Why does it take so long? Once a child is in foster care, the system breathes a sigh of relief and effectively forgets about him. If the child is removed from an abusive home, the assumption is that he's safe. "There's always another reason to give the parent the benefit of the doubt," says Daro. "They lose their job, the house burns down, the aunt is murdered. Then they get another six-month extension, and it happens all over again. Meanwhile, you can't put a child in a Deepfreeze and suspend his life until the parent gets her life together."

In the most blatant abuse and neglect cases, parents' rights should be terminated immediately, reformers say. In less-severe cases, parents should be given no more than six to 12 months to shape up. "You have social workers saying, 'She doesn't visit her child because she has no money for carfare'," says Murphy. "But what parent wouldn't walk over mountains of glass to see their kids? You know it's a crock. You have to tell people we *demand* responsibility."

And if parents can't take care of them, where are all these children supposed to go? With just 100,000 foster parents in the system, finding even temporary homes is difficult. For starters, reformers suggest professionalizing foster care, paying parents decent salaries to stay home and care for several children at a time. Long range, many believe that society will have to confront its ambivalence toward interracial adoptions. Perhaps the most controversial alternative is the move to revive orphan-

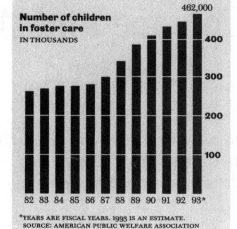

Number of Foster Children

The dramatic rise in the number of children needing foster care began in 1986, coinciding with the start of the nation's crack epidemic.

Number of children in foster care
IN THOUSANDS

462,000

*YEARS ARE FISCAL YEARS. 1993 IS AN ESTIMATE.
SOURCE: AMERICAN PUBLIC WELFARE ASSOCIATION

ages, at least for teenagers, who are the least likely to be adopted. One of the fiercest supporters is Maddux, the new supervising judge of Cook County's abuse section. Maddux, 59, says that his own family was so desperately poor they once lived in a shanty with two rooms—one of which was an old car. When the family broke up, he and his younger brother went to live at Boys Town, Neb. He believes that many foster children today could benefit from the nurturing-yet-demanding atmosphere of group living. "I wasn't raised in a family after the age of 12," Maddux says. "I didn't miss it. Thousands of kids at Boys Town knew that being in a destitute, nonfunctioning family was a lot worse than not

being in a family." In Illinois, some are taking the idea seriously—among the proposals is turning closed military bases into campuses for kids.

Ironically, Illinois could wind up with one of the best child-welfare systems in the nation. Pressed by public outrage over Joseph Wallace's death, state legislators last year passed a law that puts the best interest of children ahead of their parents'. Foster parents will be given a voice in abuse and neglect cases. And the DCFS is beefing up caseworker training, so that those in the field will learn how to spot dangerous situations more quickly.

Some of the toughest changes are already underway in Cook County. The much-criticized Family First program has been replaced with a smaller, more intensely scrutinized family-preservation project known as Homebuilders. And the county's juvenile-court system has been expanded so that there are now 14 judges, not eight, hearing abuse and neglect cases; that cuts each judge's caseload from about 3,500 to about 2,000 children per year. But reform doesn't come cheap. The DCFS budget has tripled since 1988, to $900 million, and it could top $1 billion in the next fiscal year.

Whether any of this can save lives, it's too soon to tell. In its report on Joseph Wallace's death, the blue-ribbon committee was pessimistic. "It would be comforting to believe that the facts of this case are so exceptional that such cases are not likely to happen again," the panel wrote with a dose of bitterness. "That hope is unfounded." The temptation, of course, is to blame some faceless system. But the fate of children really lies with everyone—caseworkers, supervisors, prosecutors, judges—doing their jobs.

Screen Violence and America's Children

Studies show that murder rates have risen in response to televised violence, not only in the United States, but elsewhere. Despite this correlation, the broadcast industry continues to saturate children's programming with violence.

David S. Barry

David S. Barry is a television and script writer and a member of the editorial board of The Journal of the Writers Guild of America, West.

If you were a teen-ager in the 1950s, you remember the shock effect of news headlines about the new specter of juvenile delinquency. The book *The Amboy Dukes* and the movies *Blackboard Jungle* and *Rebel Without a Cause* were deeply alarming in their portrayal of teen-agers willing to defy their school teachers and beat up other students. The violence portrayed in those stories, terrifying as it was, consisted almost entirely of assaults with fists and weapons that left victims injured, but alive. It was nonlethal violence. The notion of American teen-agers as killers was beyond the threshold of credibility.

Since the 1950s, America has changed so far as to be almost unrecognizable in terms of the level of criminal violence reported in everyday news stories. In looking for a root cause, one of the most obvious differences in the social and cultural fabric between postwar and prewar America is the massive and pervasive exposure of American youth to television. Behavioral scientists and medical researchers have been examining screen violence as a causative element in America's crime rate since the 1950s. Study after study has been published showing clear evidence of a link. And researchers say that the evidence continues to be ignored as the violence steadily worsens.

The statistics about children and screen violence—particularly that shown on TV—are grim. You've probably seen figures that show an average of 28 hours of weekly TV watching by children from 2 to 11. For prime time programming, which contains an average of five violent acts per hour, that works out to 100 acts of violence seen each week, 5,000 a year. But children also watch cartoons, which contain far more violence than adult programming. For Saturday morning car-toon shows, the violence rate spikes up to 25 acts per hour, the highest rate on TV. With children's programming added to the mix, the average child is likely to have watched 8,000 screen murders and more than 100,000 acts of violence by the end of elementary school. By the end of the teenage years, that figure will double.

Those numbers are not mere statistics. They do not occur in a social vacuum, but in a culture and society with a murder rate increasing six times faster than the population. Whether we like to acknowledge it or not, America is in the grip of an epidemic of violence so severe that homicide has become the second leading cause of death of all persons 15 to 24 years old (auto crashes are the first)—and the leading cause among African-American youth. In 1992, the U.S. Surgeon General cited violence as the leading cause of injury to women ages 15 to 44, and the U.S. Center for Disease control considers violence a leading public health issue, to be treated as an epidemic.

America now loses more adolescents to death by violence—especially gun violence—than to illness.

If you read the newspaper, particularly in Los Angeles, you know that there has been a drastic shift in crime patterns over the past four decades. From the 1950s, when I was a teen-ager, to now, America has gone from being one of the safest to one of the most violent countries on earth. Here are some numbers: In 1951, with a population of 150 million, federal crime reports showed a national total of 6,820 homicides, 16,800 rapes, and 52,090 robberies. For 1980, with a population of 220 million (a 47 percent increase) the numbers were 23,000 murders, 78,920 rapes and 548,220 robberies.

From *Spectrum*, Vol. 66, No. 3, Summer 1993, pp. 37-42. © 1993 by *The Journal of the Writers Guild of America, West.* Reprinted by permission.

In big cities, changes were more drastic. In Detroit, for instance, the 1953 murder total was 130, with 321 in New York and 82 in Los Angeles. Thirty years later, the Detroit murder tally was up to 726, the New York toll 1,665—and the Los Angeles murder total was 1,126. The fastest climbing sector of the rising crime rate is youth, with the past 10 years showing a 55 percent increase in the number of children under 18 arrested for murder. America now loses more adolescents to death by violence—especially gun violence—than to illness.

The reason these numbers belong in this discussion is that the medical community seeks a direct link between screen violence and criminal behavior by viewers. In panel discussions on this subject, we usually hear claims from TV and movie industry spokespersons that opinion is divided in the medical community. Different conclusions can be drawn from different studies, so the arguments go, and no clear consensus exists. Yet, the American medical establishment is clear—in print—on the subject of just such a consensus. The American Medical Association, the National Institute of Mental Health, the U.S. Surgeon General's Office, the U.S. Center for Disease Control and the American Psychological Association have concluded that study after study shows a direct link between screen violence and violent criminal behavior.

The research goes back decades. The 1968 National Commission on the Causes and Prevention of Violence cited screen violence as a major component of the problem. The 1972 *Surgeon General's Report on TV and Behavior* cited clear evidence of a link between televised violence and aggressive behavior of viewers. A 10-year follow-up to the *Surgeon General's Report* by the National Institute of Mental Health added far more data in support of the link. The NIMH report, a massive study covering an additional 10 years of research, was clear and unequivocal in stating: "The consensus among most of the research community is that violence on television does lead to aggressive behavior by children and teen-agers who watch the programs."

Research data confirms that childhood watching of TV violence is directly related to criminally violent behavior later on.

A 1985 task force for the America Psychological Association Commission on Youth and Violence came to the same conclusion. A 1992 study for the APA Commission on Youth and Violence took the issue further, examining research evidence in light of its effect or implementation. The finding was that the research evidence is widely ignored. The APA report was authored by Edward Donnerstein, Ph.D., chair of the Department of Communications, UC Santa Barbara, by Leonard Eron, Ph.D., University of Chicago, and Ron Slaby of the Education Development Center, Harvard University. Their report states definitively that, contrary to arguments of people in the TV and Motion Picture Industry, there is consistency and agreement in the conclusions drawn by the major medical organizations' studies of media violence.

After discussing a massive number of studies and an extensive body of research material, Donnerstein's study quotes from the 1982 NIMH report. "In magnitude, television violence is as strongly correlated with aggressive behavior as any other behavioral variable that has been measured."

Specifically, the report noted the agreement by the NIMH, the APA, and the Center for Disease Control that research data confirms that childhood watching of TV violence is directly related to criminally violent behavior later on.

Adding scope to the APA report is a study recently conducted for the nonprofit Center for Media and Public Affairs in Washington, D.C. The CMPA tabulated all the violence encountered during an 18-hour broadcasting day (a Thursday) in Washington, including cable TV. The tally showed an overall average of 100 acts of violence per hour for a total of nearly 2,000 acts of violence in the 18-hour period. Most of the violence involved a gun, with murder making up one-tenth of the violent acts recorded. A breakdown by channel, of network, showed cable to be far more violent than network broadcasting. WTBS was clocked at 19 violent acts per hour, HBO at 15 per hour, USA at 14 and MTV, the youth-oriented music video channel, at 13 violent acts per hour.

The networks (except for CBS, whose violence content was skewed by the reality show *Top Cops*) were as low in violence content as PBS, which showed two violent acts per hour. ABC showed three violent acts per hour, and NBC tallied at 11 violent acts per hour. But only one-eighth of the violence occurred in adult-oriented TV entertainment. The bulk of the violence occurred in children's TV programming, with cartoons registering 25 violent incidents per hour—six times the rate of episodic drama. Toy commercials ranked with cartoons in violence content. Next were promos for TV shows and movies, which were four times as violent as episodic drama.

The most violent period of daily TV programming was mornings from 6 to 9 a.m., where 497 scenes of violence were recorded for an hourly rate of 165.7. Next was the 2 p.m. to 5 p.m. afternoon slot with 609 violent scenes, or 203 per hour. The morning and afternoon slots compared to 320 violent scenes in prime time, from 8 p.m. to 11 p.m., or 106 per hour, and a late-night rate (from 11 p.m. to 12 a.m.) of 114.

In addition to recording totals, the CMPA examined the context in which the screen violence occurred. The finding was that most TV violence was shown with no visible consequences, nor any critical judgment. A significant amount of the violence occurred in movie promos, where it was shown out of context. Music videos, another source, generally present violence without comment or judgment. Similarly, violence in cartoons and toy commercials usually occurs without consequence or comment. More than 75 percent of the violence tallied in the study (1,640 of the nearly 2,000 violent acts) was presented with no judgment as to its acceptability as behavior. Violence was judged criminal in fewer than one-tenth of the incidents. And, ironically, while violence in episodic TV drama and TV movies for adult viewers is subject to close scrutiny for context and suitability, the bulk of the screen violence viewed by children is not.

The studies mentioned above make a compelling argument, particularly when looked at as a group. But a new study, by Dr. Brandon Centerwall of the University of Washington Department of Epidemiology and Psychiatry, takes the discussion much farther. In a study published in the June 1992 *Journal of the American Medical Association,* Centerwall looked for statistical connections between the change in violent crime rates following the introduction of TV in the United States. To correct for possible inaccuracies in crime reporting, he focused on homicides, which consistently get the most faithful reporting. Centerwall tracked the rise in homicide rates following the introduction of TV in three countries: the United States and Canada, which got TV in 1945, and South Africa, where television was banned until 1975.

Centerwall found this: murder rates in Canada and the United States increased almost 100 percent (92 percent in Canada, 93 percent in the U.S., corrected for population increase), between 1945 and 1970. In both countries, the ownership of TV sets increased in almost the same proportion as the homicide rate. Because the racial and political mix of South Africa is so volatile and so different from that of Canada or the U.S., Centerwall used only the white homicide rate in his study. What he found was a gradual decline in the South African homicide rate between 1945 and 1970. After 1975, when the government allowed TV, the homicide rate (again—white only) exploded, increasing 130 percent by 1983, after decades of decline.

There are controls in Centerwall's study that rule out firearms, political upheaval, alcohol and drug abuse and urban population shifts as causative factors. For instance, the civil rights and anti-Vietnam war strife could easily be seen as an element in the U.S. homicide rate increase, save for the fact that Canada, which experienced none of this upheaval, showed an identical increase. Similarly, limiting the study to white homicide rates excludes the anti-apartheid struggle of the late 1980s as a factor in the South African homicide rate. Centerwall's stark and unmistakable conclusion is this: White homicide rates in Canada, the U.S. and South Africa were stable or declining until the advent of television. Then, in the course of a generation, the murder rates doubled.

"Given that homicide is primarily an adult activity, if television exerts its behavior—modifying effects primarily on children, the initial 'television generation' would have had to age 10 to 15 years before they would have been old enough to affect the homicide rate. If this were so, it would be expected that, as the initial television generation grew up, rates of serious violence would first begin to rise among children, then several years later it would begin to rise among adolescents, then still later among young adults, and so on. And that is what is observed," says Centerwall.

Centerwall describes the U.S., Canada and South Africa as multiparty, representative federal democracies with strong Christian religious influences. Although television broadcasting was prohibited prior to 1973, white South Africa had well developed book, newspaper, radio and cinema industries. "Therefore, the effect of television could be isolated from that of other media influences," he states.

In summing up, Centerwall echoes that APA report in saying that irrefutable evidence, like his, continues to be ignored. He makes the parallel between the tobacco industry and the lung cancer issue, saying that "in that conflict, the tobacco industry was the last place to go for help on the health problem." He notes further that a 1989 federal law allowed TV networks to confer on the issue of TV violence without running afoul of antitrust laws. As Centerwall states, the networks announced before the bill was passed that they had no intention of using the antitrust exemption, and they did not.

The APA study by Donnerstein, Slaby and Eron also makes the point that research evidence of TV violence effects has "for decades been actively ignored, denied, attacked and even misrepresented in presentations to the American public, and popular myths regarding the effects have been perpetuated." Consequently, Donnerstein says, a major education gap exists regarding television's contribution to the problem of violence in America.

The discouraging point made in both studies is that, despite the massive research evidence of screen violence as a direct contributing factor to America's homicide rate, the screen violence level continues to rise.

As a writer deeply committed to the constitutional guarantees against censorship, I don't like to hear the suggestion of government regulation of movies or TV. But it's time we at least face the evidence of what screen violence is doing to our children, and come to some sober conclusions about our responsibilities to the common good.

What kind of study is this?

MEMORIES LOST AND FOUND

One man's account of his painful past raises complex questions about child abuse, human psychology, ethics and American law

For Ross Cheit, it began with a phone call in the spring of 1992. "I have happy news," his sister promised, speaking from her California home. "Your nephew is joining a boys' chorus. Aren't you pleased he wants to follow in the footsteps of his Uncle Ross?"

Though he could not yet name the reason, Cheit felt sickened by the news—and gradually began sinking into a bewildering depression. He didn't link it to the phone call; indeed, he blamed anything and everything else for what his wife Kathy Odean now calls "the months Ross lost his mind." It must be professional pressures that had thrown his life into such turmoil, thought the 38-year-old Brown University ethics professor. Or perhaps it was his marriage, which had been happy for 10 years but now seemed dried up, built of sand. He told his wife he thought their marriage was failing. He entered therapy. Then on August 23 while on vacation, he had something like a dream.

He woke with the baffling sense that a man he had not seen or thought of in 25 years was powerfully present in the room. William Farmer had been the administrator of the San Francisco Boys Chorus summer camp, which Cheit had attended in the late '60s between the ages of 10 and 13. Cheit could picture him clearly—the big stomach and bent shoulders, the round head, wispy hair. Over the course of the day, he recalled still more. How Farmer would enter his cabin night after night, just as the boys were

going to sleep. How he would sit on Cheit's bed, stroking the boy's chest and stomach while he urged him in a whisper to relax, relax. "I was frozen," says Cheit. "My stomach clenched against his touch. And then he would slowly bring his hand into my pants."

For Cheit, the memory was embarrassing and disgusting. There was no spectacular epiphany.

Fifteen months later, Cheit is engaged in a lawsuit that may have far-reaching implications for one of the most divisive questions ever to emerge in human psychology: whether it is possible for an adult to recover a lost memory of childhood sexual abuse. The charge two weeks ago by 34-year-old Steven Cook that 17 years earlier he had been sodomized by Roman Catholic Cardinal Joseph Bernardin—an event Cook claims he remembered in therapy—heightens an already bitter controversy whose stakes are inordinately high. In 1990, George Franklin became the first person in history convicted on the basis of a recovered memory—his daughter Eileen's recollection of witnessing, 20 years earlier, his rape and murder of her 8-year-old friend. Nineteen states have recently revised their statutes of limitations, making it possible for adults to bring civil suits against sexual abusers, even if decades have passed; several hundred such cases are now in the courts. Juries have made awards as high as $5 million to adult victims of childhood incest. No institution has been more affected than the Catholic church, which since 1982

has paid close to $500 million in legal fees and compensation to men and women molested as children by priests.

Equally dramatic countersuits are being filed. Adult children now recanting their "memories" of sexual abuse and parents who say they have been wrongly accused are suing therapists for inducing false memories through methods they charge are akin to brainwashing. In a trial set to begin in March, a California man is suing a medical center and two therapists who, he claims, helped his bulimic adult daughter manufacture memories of his sexually abusing her as a child; on the basis of the charges against him, his wife has divorced him and sought custody of their two minor daughters. Two years ago in Ohio, an appeals court upheld a malpractice award to a woman whose psychiatrist injected her with "truth serum" more than 140 times to help her uncover buried memories of alleged childhood sexual abuse by her mother. The backlash has even spawned its own organization. Since 1992, when the False Memory Syndrome Foundation was founded in Philadelphia to assist those claiming to be wrongly charged with abuse, the organization has received more than 6,500 calls.

While the debate grows increasingly virulent, most psychologists and psychiatrists are convinced that memories of external trauma can be placed out of reach of consciousness and later retrieved—though many now avoid the Freudian term "repression" (see box) in favor of a more purely descriptive vocabulary. Judith Herman, a clinical professor of psychiatry at Harvard Medical School and author of *Trauma and Recovery,* refers simply to "amnesia and delayed recall," which, she says, are beyond dispute." Others refer to dissociation, which describes the mind's protective detachment from a

From *U.S. News & World Report,* November 29, 1993, pp. 52-56, 60, 62-63. © 1993 by U.S. News & World Report. Reprinted by permission.

traumatic experience as it is happening, effectively fragmenting consciousness. Researchers who study dissociative disorders maintain that memories of traumatic events formed while a person is in the altered state of mind induced by terror are frequently inaccessible to ordinary consciousness.

Although unconscious, experts say, dissociated memories remain indelible and can be triggered decades later by a related sensation or event. Eileen Franklin's memory returned, she told the court, when an innocuous gesture by her 5-year-old daughter brought back a similar gesture by Eileen's childhood friend as she tried to ward off George Franklin's murderous blows. Frank Fitzpatrick, a 38-year-old insurance adjuster in Rhode Island, was lying in bed, trapped in an anguish he could not explain, when he remembered being molested as a child. "I began to remember the sound of heavy breathing," he said, "and realized I had been sexually abused by someone I loved." When Fitzpatrick went public with his suit against Father James Porter, several of the nearly 100 Porter victims who came forward said they remembered only when they heard about the case on the news.

The physiology of such memory loss and recovery is only beginning to be understood. Memories are stored, scientists believe, as electrical patterns in neurons deep in the brain's hippocampal region. Over time, these patterns are translated into new neural circuitry in different brain areas, creating a permanent record of the events. Intensely traumatic events, says Yale University psychiatry Prof. Michael Davis, "produce unusually strong nerve connections that serve as long-lasting memories." Years later the right stimulus can set those nerve circuits firing and trigger the fear, with no immediate understanding of its source.

"My God, that's me."
For Cheit, there was no spectacular epiphany. The memory of Farmer was embarrassing and disgusting but hardly momentous. It was not until October, when at his therapist's suggestion Cheit went to a bookstore to buy Mic Hunter's *Abused Boys,* that he felt the full impact of what he had remembered. "As soon as I pulled the book off the shelf, I began to shake all over. I thought I was going to collapse. I looked at the title and thought, 'My God, that's me.' "

Compelled now to know more, Cheit began to dredge his past. From his parents, he recovered the letters he had written from camp, and reading them brought the most painful revelation yet. "He broke down and cried with his whole body, as if he would never stop," says his wife. "He came into the bedroom where I was half asleep, saying over and over, 'But he was such a great guy.' He was so hurt that someone he loved did this to him." It was only then, says Cheit, that he fully understood the damage that had been done. "These were not just perverse sexual acts," he says, "but the most profound betrayal possible for a kid."

While many scientists accept the idea that a memory can be lost for years and then accurately recovered, a growing number do not. "Sixty years of experiments have failed to produce any empirical evidence that repression exists," says University of California at Berkeley sociologist Richard Ofshe. "People forget things, of course, or intentionally avoid painful subjects. They may even have selective traumatic amnesia, if the terror of an experience is so great that the normal biological process underlying information storage is disrupted—as in an alcohol-induced blackout. But no one has ever shown that the memory of repeated abuses can be uncontrollably and completely stripped from a person's consciousness." In fact, says psychiatry Prof. Paul McHugh of Johns Hopkins University, "most severe traumas are not blocked out by children but remembered all too well." In one study of children ages 5 to 10 who saw a parent's murder, not one repressed the memory.

COURTESY OF ROSS CHEIT

Ross Cheit (in front with glasses), shown here with other campers in 1968, spent four summers at the choral camp in the Sierras.

Psychologists also dispute the possibility of any kind of reliable retrieval. "What's being claimed," says Elizabeth Loftus, a memory researcher at the University of Washington, "is that traumatic memory is driven into a corner of the unconscious where it sits like Rip van Winkle and doesn't age and wakes up 20 years later. But memory is not a computer or videotape recording. We don't just pop in a tape or call it up in perfect condition. Memory is not objective fact but subjective, suggestible and malleable." In experimental situations, Loftus has firmly implanted in adults false memories of unhappy childhood incidents simply by having the event recounted by an authoritative older sibling.

The possibility of retrieving pristine memories is made all the more unlikely, say skeptics, by the use of such methods of "memory retrieval" as age regression, hypnosis and injections of sodium amytal ("truth serum"), all of which are known to promote confabulation of extraordinarily vivid memories and to cement in the patient's mind the certainty of their truth. The American Medical Association has twice warned against the use of such techniques.

The current "tabloid and talk show" culture of abuse, experts believe, is an equally effective creator of false memories. The bestselling self-help book *The Courage to Heal* advises that even if you are unable to remember any specific instances but still have a feeling that something happened to you, it probably did." E. Sue Blume's *Secret Survivors* offers an all-embracing list of symptoms of unremembered abuse, ranging from eating disorders and intestinal problems to substance abuse and suicidal tendencies. Group therapy and survivor support groups add to the pressures. New members may feel the need to match the drama of the other members' stories and may even internalize them as their own. Troubled patients, debunkers believe, may embrace a "discovery" of past abuse because it offers a single, unambiguous explanation for complex problems and a special identity as "survivors."

Therapists may be eager to dig up evidence of abuse, says University of Minnesota law Prof. Christopher Barden, "to turn a $2,000 eating-disorder patient into a $200,000 multiple-personality disorder." Or they may be politically motivated; since most charges are brought by women against male relatives, some critics perceive a radical feminist agenda, another avenue for women to voice rage against sexual violence. Due process is sometimes thrown to the wind: For $10 and the name of an alleged perpetrator, one organization will inform neighbors, the police and local employers without the accuser having ever to be named.

When the charges become most extreme—involving alleged "satanic cults" engaged in baby breeding for human sacrifice and cannibalism—critics see a misguided form of fundamentalism at work. In the most notorious case, in 1988 in Olympia, Wash., allegations of sexual abuse against Paul Ingram by his two daughters—based on memories "recovered" at a Pentecostal retreat, assisted by the visions of a charismatic Christian who claimed to be filled with the Holy Spirit—quickly spun into accounts of witch covens and ceremonial weddings to Satan. Under pressure of zealous investigators, Ingram confessed to crimes more horrible than those charged; his wife, her eyes rolling, described a book spilling blood. "We now have hundreds of victims alleging that thousands of offenders are abusing and even murdering tens of thousands of people as part of organized satanic cults," says Kenneth Lanning of the FBI's Behavioral Science Unit, "and there is little or no corroborative evidence." The epidemic of allegations, contends Ofshe, who testified for the Ingram defense, is a "way of reasserting the authority of fundamentalist perspectives on society."

In the discussion of recovered memory, the distinction between satanic rituals and sexual abuse is often obscured. But if the prosecution of the former is indeed a "witch hunt," the latter is all too real. More than 200,000 cases of sexual abuse are documented annually, according to the National Committee to Prevent Child Abuse, and evidence suggests that the majority of cases go unreported.

Of all traumas, many researchers say, sexual abuse may be the most likely to result in memory disturbances, surrounded as it is by secrecy and treachery. To fix a childhood memory so that it lasts into adulthood requires shaping those events into a story, says Emory psychologist Ulric Neisser, and then rehearsing the narrative, telling the tale. Yet in cases of child sexual abuse, the events are rarely confronted, shared, ratified, even adequately described. Psychologist John Daignault, who teaches at Harvard Med-

The San Francisco Boys Chorus is one of the city's most revered cultural institutions. The "Singing Angels" have performed for U.S. presidents, the queen of England and the pope.

ical School and evaluated more than 40 of Father Porter's victims, says children "lack the perspective to place the trauma in the overall course of life's events." When the abuser is in a position of power or veneration, the child's ability to make sense of the event is more compromised still.

It is perhaps not surprising, then, that studies show that from 18 to 59 percent of sexual-abuse victims repress memories for a period of time. In one follow-up study of 200 children who had been treated for sexual abuse, Linda Williams of the Family Violence Research Laboratory at the University of New Hampshire found that 1 in 3 did not recall the experiences that had been documented in

---

Intent on finding Farmer, Cheit hired private investigator Frank Leontieff.

---

their hospital records 20 years before. A study by Judith Herman of women in group therapy found a majority reporting delayed recall of abuse; approximately 75 percent of those were able to obtain corroborating evidence. "False claims of childhood sexual abuse are demonstrably rare," says Herman (in the range of 2 to 8 percent of reported cases), "and false memories of childhood trauma are no doubt equally so. To fasten upon false memory as the main event is far-fetched and bizarre."

The debate over the credibility of some memories, researchers worry, is

being used to discredit people making legitimate assertions. Some question the motives of the False Memory Syndrome Foundation, which gathers data on denials of abuse charges but concedes it has no way of knowing the truth or falsity of any report it receives. "Denial signifies little," says Herman. "Research with known pedophiles has illustrated that they often exhibit a cognitive distortion, minimizing or rationalizing their behavior." In fact, the FMSF recently asked one of its board members, Ralph Underwager, to resign after he gave an interview to a Dutch journal in which he seemed permissive and sympathetic toward pedophilia.

"The strongest compulsion in my life"
Intent on finding William Farmer, Cheit hired private investigator Frank Leontieff—a man he had known from his own previous career as a lawyer—and in January went to visit the 87-year-old founder of the chorus, Madi Bacon, in Berkeley. It was under Bacon's guidance in the '60s that the chorus became one of San Francisco's most revered arts institutions. Nicknamed "the Singing Angels," it regularly performed with the San Francisco Opera and sang for U.S. presidents, the pope and the queen of England. Much to his surprise, says Cheit, at the mention of Farmer's name, Bacon launched into how she'd once almost had to fire the man for what she called "hobnobbing" with one of the boys. When Cheit told her he had been one of those boys, he says, Bacon said that if he'd been a strong kid he would have shaken it off. And why didn't he tell his friends,

she wanted to know. Didn't he want to protect them? (Asked about the conversation, Bacon told *U.S. News* she "may well have said those things, but I don't remember." Elsewhere, Bacon said that had she known of the abuse, she would have done something.)

Until that moment, Cheit had been embarked on a private search for private solace.

Until that moment, Cheit had been on a private search for private solace. Now, he had not only his first external evidence of the authenticity of his memory but a recognition that there might be more at stake. He was not, it seemed, the only one. Worse, it appeared chorus officials had known. It was at that moment, says Cheit, that the investigation became "the strongest compulsion in my life."

The history of responses by organizations confronted with accusations of child sexual abuse has not been particularly noble. A recent report by the Boy Scouts of America revealed that between 1971 and 1991, 1,800 scoutmasters suspected of molesting boys were removed from their positions—but "quietly," so that many simply went elsewhere and continued to abuse scouts. The Catholic Church, concerned to protect its reputation, has similarly relied on what child advocates call "the geographic cure." In the course of the Father Porter trial, church officials admitted that they had witnessed the priest's assaults or were told of them but permitted him to continue supervising altar boys and youth activities. When parents complained, documents uncovered in the lawsuits revealed, Porter was simply transferred from parish to parish. Porter's was not an isolated case. In *Lead Us Not into Temptation*, Jason Berry chronicles the decade-long nationwide effort by the Catholic Church to protect itself from its flock. Kids who made accusations were asked what the state of their soul was that they could cast such judgment and were forced to face the accused; defamation suits were often filed in the secular courts. At one point, Milwaukee Archbishop Rembert Weakland went so

FREUDIAN ORIGINS
Is it abuse or fantasy?

The battle over the nature of memory has its origins in Freud, who was the first to propose that painful or dangerous memories are "repressed"—buried beyond reach in the unconscious. The goal of psychoanalysis, as Freud conceived it, was to bring repressed material into consciousness where it could be disarmed.

Over the course of the 1890s, Freud's beliefs shifted, an evolution critical to the present battle. In 1893, he believed that many of his adult patients had been sexually abused as children by adults, and that it was the repressed memory of those "seductions" that caused their "hysteria." Four years later, he was insisting that most such memories were actually the child's repressed incestuous fantasies and desires. Freud critic Jeffrey Masson deems that shift a cowardly and destructive lie, an attempt to avoid professional ostracism. But others dismiss Masson as politically fashionable, contending that Freud feared his patients' stories were being suggested or distorted by his own analytic probings and deemed them fantasies in order to dodge that conclusion.

Freud's focus on childhood fantasies as opposed to real trauma has dominated psychotherapeutic thought for most of the century. Only in the '70s did the return of damaged Vietnam vets rekindle interest in post-traumatic stress reactions. Today, that interest has once again expanded to include the effects of childhood trauma.

far as to suggest that "not all adolescent victims are so innocent."

To conceal the criminal behavior of child molesters is exceedingly dangerous. Most experts consider pedophilia an incurable disease, and studies of known sex offenders have found that men who target male children will, over a career, assault on average more than 100 boys. Still, in conversations with *U.S. News,*

Madi Bacon expressed dismay that Cheit had broken the code of silence. "I don't see what good it's going to do for a young man with a family to be known publicly as having been abused. I mean it's such bad taste. And for Ross to involve other boys is serious. The boys would say that's snitching, wouldn't they?"

He managed to track down dozens of the 118 boys who had been at camp with him 25 years earlier.

"This is your one chance, Bill"
After his visit to Bacon, Cheit accelerated the investigation. Using chorus records from the time, he tracked down dozens of the 118 boys who had been at camp with him in the Sierra foothills 25 years earlier. The conversations usually began with warm reminiscences of greased watermelon races and idyllic afternoons floating in inner tubes in the warm sun. Soon, however, the recollections turned dark. For a professor at a Michigan university, Cheit's phone call brought back his own lost memory of a time Farmer invited him to his cabin, unzipped the child's pants and began to fondle him. He began to cry, he now recalls, and ran away. A librarian in the Midwest told Cheit on the phone that Farmer had invited the boy into his sleeping bag, but that he had refused; he wrote in a troubled letter the next day that he had been deceiving himself for years and now realized he had in fact climbed in. "I remember feeling something warm and hard pressed up against my lower abdomen. My T-shirt must have been pushed up and it was sticky. . . . Then I saw his penis. . . . I'm glad you called me, but I've been feeling sick about it all day." The camp nurse from the time, Lidia Ahumada, told the investigator and *U.S. News* of an event at the end of the summer of 1968, when she walked into the infirmary and caught Farmer in bed with a sick boy. Bacon recalled for *U.S. News* the nurse's angry report, adding: "I think Farmer's somewhat sick. To me it's an illness. But the man apologized, said to the chairman of the board that he would never do it again.

What do you do when camp's over? The chairman certainly wanted to play a thing like that down from a public standpoint because he didn't want to embarrass anybody." The investigator subsequently tracked down the child identified by the nurse. He has spent the past 15 years in San Francisco flophouses and has no memory of a man named Bill Farmer.

In letters and phone calls, former campers alleged what Cheit's first conversation with Bacon had implied, that at least two other men on the staff had been molesting boys and that on at least four occasions both children and adult staff

---

Cheit began to dial Farmer's number. After 34 attempts, he answered.

---

had told the chorus director of the abuses, with no result. One alleged report came in 1967, when a whole cabin full of boys ran to Bacon to tell her of molestations by a staff member who is now dead. A second allegedly came at the beginning of the summer of 1968, when a counselor, 21 years old at the time, twice witnessed Farmer's molestations of a boy and went with the child to report it to the director. Bacon doesn't recall the incident. Farmer remained.

Cheit's investigator, meanwhile, had tracked Farmer's movements over the years. Farmer had been a student minister from 1966–68 at the Point Richmond, Calif., Methodist Church, the investigator learned from church historian Mildred Dornan (who confirmed the account for *U.S. News*), but had abruptly left after parents overheard children discussing the "massages" he had given them. Farmer then secured a ministerial position in Georgetown, near Sacramento, Calif. He hadn't been there three weeks, the church's district supervisor from the time told the investigator (and confirmed for *U.S. News*), when a former El Dorado County Municipal Court judge complained that Farmer had molested his son. If Farmer would leave the ministry and seek help, said the judge, he would not press charges. Farmer signed a statement withdrawing from his position and surrendered his ministerial credentials, according to the supervisor. He then moved to Oregon, where he held teaching credentials for several years and for a time ran a ministry out of his home.

COURTESY OF ROSS CHEIT

Bill Farmer was the administrator of the chorus's summer camp, which Cheit attended from age 10 to 13. Farmer is circled in this staff photograph from the summer of 1968.

Having located Farmer, now 55, in the tiny town of Scio, Ore., Cheit began to dial his phone. After 34 attempts, Farmer answered. "What can I do for you?" Farmer asked his former charge, whom he had quickly recalled. "You can tell me whether you have any remorse, responded Cheit, his breath rapid and fierce. "Give me your number so I can call you back at another time." "This is your chance, Bill. This is your one chance." For nearly an hour, Cheit held Farmer on the phone, a tape recorder running all the while. Farmer admitted molesting Cheit in his cabin at night, confessed he had lost jobs and fled California because of "it," acknowledged that Bacon knew what happened at the end of the summer but allowed him to remain camp administrator because "no act had been consummated." Though Farmer conceded knowing that the acts he committed were criminal, he balked at Cheit's suggestion that he register as a sex offender. "It's 25 years, Ross," he said, his voice weary. "It's nine months, Bill, [since I remembered]. And I have to live with it for the rest of my life."

The chorus's attempt to disconnect from its past, says Cheit, is a luxury I don't have.

Six months earlier, says Cheit, he had been terrified of anyone finding out what had happened; now, he says, "I realized that is the problem." On July 2, Cheit's lawyers sent a letter to the chorus offering to settle without litigation if the organization would publicly acknowledge what had happened, investigate evidence that the problem had persisted over many years, install safeguards to ensure it would never happen again and provide $450,000 to Cheit "for injuries beyond compensation." On August 6, the chorus responded. "The SFBC sees no purpose at this point in even attempting to challenge the charges," stated the letter from Pillsbury, Madison & Sutro, the esteemed law firm handling pro bono the chorus's defense. It went on to raise doubts as to the chorus's liability, pointed out its meager financial resources and concluded "it is hard to imagine how bankrupting or ruining the reputation of an organization that has done so much to serve the Bay Area community would serve any good purpose."

The response infuriated Cheit. "The chorus's attempt to disconnect from their past is a luxury I don't have. To claim their reputation is to cash in on their past, but selectively; they don't want those parts of their history that might be shameful. And if this is how they handle a corroborated claim from an adult, how would they respond if a 10-year-old came to them right now? Would they value their reputation over their moral responsibility to children?" On August 19, Cheit and his parents filed suit, charging that the chorus "negligently or intentionally" permitted molestation of boys in its care. The chorus denied all the allegations.

The entanglement of psychology and the law is not an entirely easy marriage. The clinic and the courtroom have different criteria for establishing truth. Those who dispute the possibility of recovering memories insist the courts should not be admitting what Barden calls "pseudoscience" into testimony. Ofshe questions the wisdom of extending statutes of limitations designed to protect the accused, who after decades may find it impossible to gather the necessary evidence and witnesses to mount an effective defense. Of the 19 states that have extended their civil statutes on child sexual abuse, 16 have done so on the basis of the "delayed discovery doctrine." Just as a patient can sue who discovers 20 years later that a doctor had left a surgical instrument in his abdomen, so too, the theory goes, should a victim of child abuse be permitted to sue when he or she discovers the injury through recovering a memory. "If that's the premise, then how you characterize the forgetting is critical," says Ofshe. "If the plaintiff just avoided thinking about it, or later forgot how as a young adult he'd agonized over it, that's different than if the memory was put wholly out of reach by some imagined trick of the mind." Three states have simply extended statutes for civil prosecution of sexual abuse a set number of years beyond the victim's age of majority; nine states have no statutes of limitations on criminal prosecution of such crimes. "That's a straightforward social choice," says Ofshe, "not predicated on some mythic mental mechanism."

"Let a jury decide"
Addressing the three demands made in the suit—for open accounting, protective procedures and financial compensation—chorus lawyer Kim Zeldin told *U.S. News* that efforts are being made to investigate the allegations, though "it is difficult because so many years have passed." She has not been able to evaluate the validity of the Farmer tape, she says, because she has not been provided with a copy. But Farmer has called her firm to deny Cheit's charges, she added, and to deny ever telling Cheit otherwise. (Farmer's lawyer, Carleton Briggs, con-

firms that his client, who now lives in Corpus Christi, Texas, says he has never admitted to any of the charges. Farmer himself would not talk to *U.S. News*.) As for protecting the boys in the chorus's charge, Zeldin listed unwritten procedures she says have been in place for 10 years, including careful screening of staff, involvement of parents in many camp activities and policies to ensure boys are never alone with any staff member. In response to Cheit's letter, she says, the chorus also retained over the summer an outside consultant to instruct the boys on how to avoid unwanted contact. As for money demands, she questioned Cheit's motivations, saying "he's trying to reach into a deep pocket that doesn't exist." Cheit responds that the demand for money was made to ensure that his suit be taken seriously, but remains his last priority. "If they offered me a million dollars tomorrow, with the condition that they admit no liability and that I keep silent, the answer would be no. We are now in a suit requesting unspecified damages. I'm perfectly content to let a jury decide." In one last odd twist to the suit—signifying just how important the cultural climate now surrounding memory has become to the resolution of these cases—Pillsbury Madison & Sutro submitted to the court a two-part *New Yorker* story on Ingram's apparently false recovered memories of satanic abuse.

If there is one area of consensus among warring psychologists, it is that the sexual abuse of children does enduring damage. A summary of major studies published this year in the bulletin of the American Psychological Association concluded that, while no one set of symptoms characterized all victims, abuse tends to produce an inappropriate conditioning of sexual responsiveness, the shattering of a child's trust and an enduring sense of stigmatization and powerlessness. The report further hypothesized that for some, traumatization may occur later. Studies of adults who were sexually abused in childhood have consistently found them to be more prone to depression, substance abuse, sexual problems and thoughts of suicide.

"Forever, my childhood"
The boy who was allegedly molested by Farmer at the beginning of that summer of 1968—now a professor in New York—

COURTESY OF ROSS CHEIT

Bill Farmer, now 55, was photographed earlier this year in Scio, Ore. He now lives in Corpus Christi, Texas.

lives with an injury of a different kind. When he and his counselor reported Farmer to Bacon, he says, she assured him that she would fire Farmer and tell the boy's parents the whole thing, but did neither. For 24 years, until Cheit's call, he was left believing that his parents knew about Farmer's actions but had left him to cope on his own. 'Even more than the molestation, it is the lie that changed my life."

The past remains a persistent presence for Cheit as well. In the past year, he has often wondered whether he could go on teaching ethics. "They're such moral relativists," he says of his students. "In the midst of this whole thing, one of my seniors asked, 'Aren't these moral taboos just cultural constructions? Isn't incest bad just because we think it is?' I wanted to shake her and say, "There is evil in the world. I just got off the phone with it.' "

The loss he suffered, Cheit says, can never be redeemed. "Forever, this is going to be my childhood." And he knows that more painful disclosures may yet come. "I think they thought all along I couldn't stomach the publicity. But if I have to divulge in a courtroom the most private consequences of this, I will. It's not me who should be ashamed of this, but them. And I can't be upset with people who did nothing then if I do nothing now, for the same reasons. I have so much support. If I don't do this, who ever will?"

MIRIAM HORN

How to Recognize and Prevent Child Sexual Abuse

Parents and others who work with children are deeply concerned about possible child sexual abuse. With this guide, you can help them prevent such abuse, recognize potential abusers, and know what to do if they suspect a particular child is being abused.

David L. Corwin, MD

David L. Corwin is Psychiatric Consultant, Multidisciplinary Team, Oakland Children's Hospital, Oakland, CA.

Exploding the myth that child sexual abuse is rare, numerous recent surveys have found that 20%–30% of the women and 10%–20% of the men questioned had been abused during childhood.[1] Most experts believe that sexual abuse of children has probably always been widespread but was usually kept secret and denied or disbelieved when discovered.

Child sexual abuse is the source of many emotional and behavioral problems in both children and adults. This is apparent among those who were sexually abused as children via a higher incidence of anxiety, depression, drug and alcohol addiction, dissociation, eating and sleeping difficulties, hostility, marital discord, mistrust, multiple personalities, sexual problems, and suicide.

The legal definition of child sexual abuse varies from state to state, but generally includes all sexual behaviors from fondling to intercourse. Exhibitionism in the presence of a minor, showing pornography to a child, or involving a child in the production of pornography are also forms of child sexual abuse. The legal penalties for these offenses vary from state to state, according to the seriousness of the act and the particular circumstances. Many first-time offenders are given probation with treatment, while repeat offenders and those who commit more serious forms of child sexual abuse face lengthy prison sentences if convicted.

Profile of child sex abusers

Unfortunately, it is not easy to identify adults who sexually abuse children, since they come from all social classes, races, and vocations. Some are successful or highly respected members of the community. Many child molesters are men or adolescent boys; some are pedophiles (child lovers) who seduce children with attention, rewards, and special privileges; others are child haters or sociopaths. Perhaps as many as one third of molesters are substance abusers. Some are interested in children for the financial profit to be gained from child pornography or child prostitution. Others sexually abuse children as part of bizarre rituals.[2] There are even some adults who believe adult-child sex is good for children.[3]

Most perpetrators are men ranging in age from adolescence to middle age. Among known child sexual abusers, men outnumber women about eight or nine to one. I have found adolescent male baby-sitters to be a high-risk group for molesting young children, but I have also seen cases of such abuse by adolescent girls and adult women who were caring for children.

Most of the perpetrators are known to the child victim; within

Help for parents who sexually abuse their children

In many communities special treatment programs are available for families in which parents have sexually abused one or more of their children. These programs try to help all family members, including the abusing parent, if the parent is willing to accept responsibility for past behavior. Parents United (which has chapters throughout the country) is a self-help organization for incestuous families. This organization helps these families overcome the stigma of incest and achieve greater self-esteem through self-help groups as well as professionally supervised treatment.

families, the most frequent molesters are fathers, stepfathers, uncles, grandfathers, cousins, and brothers. Girls are more likely than boys to be molested by a family member.

Many cases of father-child incest appear to be precipitated by stresses and losses that threaten the father's masculine pride, such as the loss of a job or a marital conflict or breakup. In some of these cases, the father regresses and turns to his daughter or son for affection and sexual gratification; in others, the father's sexual abuse of the child may be a way of expressing anger at the mother.

Profile of child sex abuse victims

Children are vulnerable to sexual abuse because they are smaller, weaker, and less knowledgeable than adolescents or adults. They are taught to obey adults and authority figures. By nature, children are curious, often eager to please, and easy to deceive and intimidate. In short, children are easy prey for those who want to exploit them sexually.

Among adults who report having been molested during childhood, women outnumber men five

to two. It is estimated that as many as one third of all sexually abused children are under 6 years of age. Infants and toddlers are also sexually victimized, but this abuse is difficult to detect unless there are eyewitnesses, photographs, videotapes, or definite medical evidence. Because many sexual practices such as fondling, simulated intercourse, oral copulation, and even anal intercourse seldom leave specific findings, medical evidence is present in only a minority of sexually abused young children.

What to look for

Parents and others who live and work with children need to recognize the behavioral as well as the physical signs of child sexual abuse. You can counsel worried parents who suspect sexual abuse to bring their child to your office for a physical examination. At that time, you can show them how to be alert for a wide array of emotional clues.

Behavioral and emotional indicators. You can explain to parents, teachers, and other concerned adults that although sexually abused children tend to exhibit certain emotional and behavioral

reactions, these reactions can also be due to other factors. Among the many less specific behavioral and emotional indicators of child sex abuse, for example, are such behaviors as increased anxiety, bed wetting, bodily complaints, depression, soiling, hyperactivity, impaired trust, lying, running away, self-destructive behavior, sleep and appetite disturbances, social withdrawal, substance abuse, unexplained guilt feelings, and school difficulties for which there are no apparent reasons.

Conversely, make those you counsel aware of the most suspicious findings: dramatic changes in sexual awareness or activity; unexplained avoidance or fear of certain people, places, or objects; severe nightmares accompanied by vocalizations or physical movements that might indicate sexual abuse experiences; and dissociative phenomena including (in extreme cases) multiple personalities.

Explain that changes in sexual awareness and behavior may include increased preoccupation with the genitals, excessive masturbation, or repeated attempts to engage others in sexual behavior. In contrast, some sexually abused children appear overly anxious or inhibited about sexual anatomy and behavior. You'll need to stress, however, that it is critically important not to confuse the normal modesty of school-aged children regarding nudity with the more dramatic inhibition and fearfulness of some sexually abused children.

Children who dissociate may demonstrate some of the following behavior: an apparent dream-like (or trance-like) state; unexplained abrupt changes in mood or manner; denial of clearly observed behavior; unexplained intense episodes of rage; use of different names; use of imaginary playmates beyond the age of 6 years.

Physical indicators. Certain physical signs, such as minor genital or anal redness or discomfort, and vaginal or urinary tract infections, may be due either to sexual abuse or other factors. Sexual abuse is more likely, however, if there are genital or anal injuries, if the child is pregnant, or if there is evidence of any sexually transmitted diseases (STDs) such as gonorrhea and syphillis. *Chlamydia trachomatis,* condylomata acuminata, *Gardnerella vaginalis,* herpes simplex virus, and *Trichomonas vaginalis* may also be associated with child sexual abuse.[4] A noted authority on STDs in children recommends that when testing children for *N gonorrhoeae,* the clinician insist on at least two of the three available tests—biochemical sugar, enzyme substrate, and serologic—and not rely on rapid diagnostic tests such as Gonozyme. The use of cultures to detect *C trachomatis* rather than direct fluorescein antibody tests is also recommended.[5]

Because examination of children for possible indicators of sexual abuse has potential legal as well as healthcare implications, some experts advise physicians to always have a nurse or other appropriate adult present during the physical examination. This additional person can help reassure the child and assist in documenting and witnessing the child's statements and behaviors.

The child's description. The most positive indication of molestation is the combination of definite physical findings and the child's clear description of his/her sexual abuse. Thus, it is essential to record the child's story accurately.

Although most experts on child sexual abuse agree that children seldom fabricate these accounts, it does happen occasionally. In some instances, children have been misled or indoctrinated by another person into making a false allegation of sexual abuse. Another infrequent but troubling situation occurs when a child has been sexually abused by one person and, at a later time, falsely accuses another of such an act.

"Before asking specific questions . . . reassure the child that he/she has nothing to fear in telling you the truth. . ."

Questioning the child about possible sex abuse

If you suspect that a child has been or is being sexually abused, or if a parent contacts you with this suspicion, you must decide whether you, the parent, or, if available, a specialized assessment team should ask the child about it. If you decide to question the child yourself, do so in a supportive, accepting, calm, straightforward manner. Be certain to maintain that demeanor no matter what the child reveals. In most cases, primary care physicians should leave detailed questioning to expert evaluators or investigators who may utilize a coordinated approach that avoids redundant interviewing and minimizes the stress on the child. Depending on the information available, you must decide whether a specialized assessment is needed and whether you should make a report to the local child protective service or law enforcement agency.

Provide reassurance. When speaking with young children about possible sexual abuse, choose a time when the child is calm, alert, and in no visible distress. Before asking specific questions about possible abuse, reassure the child that he/she has nothing to fear in telling you the truth about anything you may ask.

Adults need to be aware that many abusers instruct the children they molest not to tell anyone about it—under threat of dire consequences to the child or parents. Children are often told that if the parent discovers the abuse, the child will be punished. It is clear, therefore, that in order for the child to reveal sexual abuse, he/she needs support and reassurance.

Even if the child has not been threatened, a molested child may find it too upsetting or embarrassing to talk about the abuse when first asked. If you sense that the child is unduly upset by a question such as "Has anyone touched your private parts?" explain to the child that if anything like that has happened, it is important for him/her to tell a parent or some other trusted adult.

Speak at the child's level. In speaking to 2- and 3-year-old children, it is essential to use words they understand and to use open-ended questions. For example, "Has anyone touched you on the bottom? The front? Has anyone asked you to touch them?" If the child answers yes to any of these questions, ask the child to explain what happened, who did what, where did it happen, and how he/she felt. Older children can usually state when the abuse occurred, but younger children have difficulty placing events accurately in time.

After the child has said enough to confirm your suspicions of sexual abuse, do not press for more details. Leave further questioning and evaluation to qualified professionals with special training and experience in assessing possible victims of child sexual abuse. Care should be taken to ensure that the evaluating professional has such knowledge and experience, since basic training in child psychology or social work does not guarantee expertise in child sexual abuse evaluation.

When concluding your questioning, thank the child for answering your questions and reassure him/her that he/she is a good boy or girl. Tell the child that you will help keep him/her safe and that you are going to talk to someone else who can help deal with the situation.

Reporting child sex abuse

As soon as possible, write down the questions you asked as well as the child's answers as accurately as you can remember. If the child has revealed abuse by a parent or other family member (which means that the child cannot be protected without removing him/her from the home), you may need to contact your local child protective service or law enforcement agency immediately. As a physician, you must report the suspected abuse, according to your state's reporting requirements.

After your initial questioning of the child, do not rehearse or go over the information again with the child. Doing so could be construed as an attempt on your part to influence the child's account. If the child wants to tell you more about the experience, listen carefully and ask questions only in order to clarify what the child is saying; tell the child you are glad he/she can talk about it with you

and that it is also important for him/her to give this information to the evaluator or investigator. Write down the circumstances of the additional disclosure, the child's statements, and your questions so that you can provide an accurate account to the professional investigator.

If the child denies abuse but you still suspect present or past molestation, discuss your concerns with other qualified professionals; you may need to report your suspicions to the appropriate child protective authorities.

> **"If the child has revealed abuse by a family member ... you may need to contact your local child protective service immediately."**

Preventing child sexual abuse

Aside from educating children to resist and to report any attempts by older children or adults to engage them in sexual touching, there is little we can do to prevent some people from sexually abusing children. One possible warning sign, however, is an adult (other than the parent) who shows too much interest in or spends too much time alone with a child. While adults generally prefer adult companionship, many child molesters prefer to spend their time with children. Unfortunately, some people who want "socially acceptable" access to children in order to sexually abuse them

choose occupations or volunteer activities that entail working with children. Although most teachers, daycare workers, and healthcare personnel do not sexually abuse children, we must be aware of and on the lookout for those who do.

The parents' role. The most effective way in which parents can protect their children from sexual abuse is to make sure the youngsters can distinguish between appropriate and inappropriate touching. You can advise parents to review and expand their children's sex education every year or two beginning at about age 3 or 4; this provides an opportunity to reinforce previous lessons about sexual safety and touching. Children need to be taught that the private parts of the body should be touched only by the child himself, by the parents for the purpose of washing or taking care of them, and by the family doctor during a checkup.

All baby-sitters and child caretakers—especially men and adolescent boys—should be carefully screened. Unfortunately, most of the adults and adolescents I have seen who molested the children in their care appeared to be respectable and trustworthy. Those with the lowest risk for sexual abuse are women such as aunts or grandmothers. It is interesting to note that in years past, when large families were the norm, mothers, aunts, and grandmothers were the ones who traditionally cared for children.

Advise parents to arrange to drop in unexpectedly from time to time at their children's daycare center, preschool, or baby-sitter's home. If they are not allowed immediate access to their child, parents should find other institutions or sitters where they will have such access.

In the case of older children, perhaps the best thing parents can do to protect them from sexual abuse is to give them lots of time and attention. Pedophiles who regularly prey on children claim they can easily determine which ones are most likely to permit themselves to be abused; they are the isolated, lonely kids whose parents are emotionally distant and uninvolved.

Conclusion

If you begin to suspect that a child is being sexually abused, whether because of a parent's concerns or physical evidence you detect during the child's office visits, first decide who should speak to the child about your concerns. Don't jump to hasty conclusions with insufficient information. If your examination leaves you concerned about possible sexual abuse, seek assistance from a mental health professional who is experienced in evaluating cases of suspected child sexual abuse, and, if you have a reasonable suspicion, report your suspicions to the relevant child protective service or law enforcement agency.

Child sexual abuse is not an unsolvable problem. You can be part of the solution by educating yourself and the children around you. Tell parents to speak with their children, to know where they are and what they're doing, and to make time for them. Parents can help protect their sons and daughters from sexual abuse by demonstrating their love through the way they care for and guide them.

References

1. Peters SD, Wyatt GE, Finkelhor D: Prevalence, in Finkelhor D: *A Sourcebook on Child Sexual Abuse*. Newbury Park CA, Sage Publications, 1986, chap 1.
2. Kelly SJ: Ritualistic abuse of children: Dynamics and impact. *Cultic Studies J* 5(2):228, 1988.
3. Crewdson J: *By Silence Betrayed*. Boston, Little Brown and Company, 1988, chap 6, pp 96–98.
4. Hammerschlag MR: Pitfalls in the diagnosis of sexually transmitted diseases in children. *The Advisor* (newsletter of the American Professional Society on the Abuse of Children) 2(3):4, 1989.
5. Hammerschlag MR, Rettig PJ, Shields ME: False positive results in the use of chlamydial antigen detection tests in the evaluation of suspected sexual abuse in children. *Pediatr Infect Dis J* 7:11, 1988.

Bibliography

Conte JR: A look at child sexual abuse. National Committee for Prevention of Child Abuse, 1986. (332 South Michigan Ave, Suite 950, Chicago, IL 60604-4357; (312) 663-3520)

Corwin DL: Early diagnosis of child sexual abuse: Diminishing the lasting effects, in Wyatt GE, Powell GJ (eds): *The Lasting Effects of Child Sexual Abuse*. Newbury Park, CA, Sage Publications, 1988, chap 14.

Finkelhor D, Williams LM, Burns N: *Nursery Crimes: Sexual Abuse in Day Care*. Newbury Park, CA, Sage Publications, 1988.

Kluft RP (ed): Treatment of victims of child sexual abuse. *Psychiat Clin North Am* 12(2):237, 1989.

Levental JM, Bentovim A, Elton A et al: What to ask when sexual abuse is suspected. *Arch Dis Child* 62:1188, 1987.

Meyers EB: Role of physician in preserving verbal evidence of child abuse. *J Pediatr* 109:409, 1986.

Myers JEB, Bays J, Becker J, et al: Expert testimony in child sexual abuse litigation. *Nebraska Law Review* 68:401, 1989.

Renshaw DC: When you suspect child sex abuse: Take the child's sexual history. *Medical Aspects of Human Sexuality* 20(6):19, 1986.

Whittington WL, Rice RJ, Biddle JW, et al: Incorrect identification of *Neisseria gonorrhoeae* from infants and children. *Pediatr Infect Dis J* 7:3, 1988.

Young Children With Attention Deficits

Steven Landau and Cecile McAninch

Steven Landau, Ph.D., is a professor of psychology at Illinois State University. Previously a school psychologist, his research interests include ADHD and problems associated with peer rejection.
Cecile McAninch, M.A., is completing her doctorate in clinical psychology at the University of Kentucky. Her areas of interest include children's self-concept and social cognition.

Three-year-old Jamie was expelled from preschool after frequent fights with other children. If Jamie and the other boys were playing with trucks, Jamie was the first one to start crashes, which escalated into wild behavior. In the sandbox it was always Jamie who threw sand in someone's face or grabbed the shovel from another child. After a month of preschool, Jamie's teacher became worried that Jamie might seriously hurt another child, and she asked Jamie's mother to keep him home.

Jamie's parents were dismayed by this request. They knew that he was a difficult child. They found Jamie hard to manage because he seemed to have an excessive activity level and a short attention span and was prone to numerous temper outbursts. Indeed, he had been "difficult" since infancy; however, they wanted to believe that this was simply a phase he was going through—a difficult period of development—and that he would outgrow these problems sometime soon. They even considered the possibility that Jamie's preschool teacher didn't understand him—that she could intervene more before he became too excited and wound up. These problems were thus simply developmental (i.e., he is just "all boy"), or they were best understood as a function of an intolerant preschool teacher. Maybe a better preschool would be the answer.

Jamie, who was first described by Campbell (1988), is representative of many young children referred for attention-deficit hyperactivity disorder (ADHD). What is ADHD, and how does it differ from hyperactivity? ADHD is the current psychiatric term used to describe a set of symptoms reflecting excessive inattention, overactivity, and impulsive responding. It is important to note that the presence of these symptoms must be established in the context of what is developmentally appropriate for the child's age and gender group. ADHD is found in 3 to 5% of the childhood population (American Psychiatric Association, 1987) and is clearly a disorder that is far more prevalent in males; sex differences among children referred for treatment average about six males to one female. Because ADHD is the formal diagnostic label from the psychiatric classification scheme (i.e., the *Diagnostic and Statistical Manual of Mental Disorders* [DSM–III–R]; American Psychiatric Association, 1987), this is the term used by family physicians, pediatricians, psychiatrists, and other mental health clinicians. Indeed, all professionals who deal with children, *except* professionals in the public school system, employ the psychiatric classification scheme and, thus, the term ADHD.

The fact that children considered "in need of special services" by their school according to Public Law 94–142 are not required to have a formal DSM–III–R psychiatric diagnosis for placement creates confused communication among parents, school personnel, and community professionals. Confusion is further increased by the fact that the nomenclature pertaining to this disorder has changed several times over the years. The disorder has previously been known as "brain damage syndrome"; "minimal brain dysfunction"; "hyperkinetic reaction to childhood"; "attention deficit disorder (with and without hyperactivity)"; and, most recently, "attention-deficit hyperactivity disorder." Although frustrating for some, this trend of changing terminology clearly represents improved understanding of the disorder (Schaughency & Rothlind, 1991).

Primary symptoms

The preceding overview of evolving terminology makes it apparent that there has been a shift in emphasis regarding what is considered most central to the disor-

The column in this issue was edited by Laura E. Berk, Ph.D., professor of psychology at Illinois State University.

From *Young Children*, Vol. 48, No. 4, May 1993, pp. 49-58. © 1993 by the National Association for the Education of Young Children, 1834 Connecticut Avenue, NW, Washington, DC. Reprinted by permission.

der. Many researchers agree that a deficit in *sustained attention,* the inability to remain vigilant, represents the area of greatest difficulty for the child with ADHD (Douglas, 1983); thus, children with ADHD show significantly less persistence than their classmates. Even though many teachers use the term *distractible* to characterize their observations of school performance, distractibility implies that the child with ADHD seems unable to select relevant from irrelevant stimuli that compete for their attention (i.e., a *selective attention* deficit). The bulk of current research, however, suggests that their greatest difficulties stem from an inability to *sustain a response* long enough to accomplish assigned tasks, that is, they lack perseverance in their efforts. As a consequence, parents and teachers attribute to them characterizations such as "doesn't seem to listen," "fails to finish assigned tasks," "can't concentrate," "can't work independently of supervision," "requires more redirection," and "confused or seems to be in a fog"—all apparently the result of this inability to sustain attention (Barkley, 1990).

It is important to stress, however, that even though inattention may be the source of some difficulty in a less structured, free-play setting, highly structured academic settings create the greatest problem for these children (Milich, Loney, & Landau, 1982). The specific expectations within a setting and the degree of structure in that setting thus play important roles in determining the presence of the disorder. This may explain, in part, why parents and teachers do not tend to agree when rating the symptoms of these children (Achenbach, McConaughy, & Howell, 1987). Expectations in the home environment are simply different from those at school. This point was recently reinforced in a study by Landau, Lorch, and Milich (1992). These investigators were intrigued by the surprising but frequent parent report that their child with ADHD is able to attend to television (e.g., "What do you mean he can't pay attention in school? He sits glued to the TV for hours!"). In fact, a recent advice column in *Parents* magazine suggested that parents could rule out thoughts of ADHD if their child was able to pay attention to television. Results of the study by Landau and his colleagues indicated that boys diagnosed with ADHD who were extremely inattentive in the classroom were able to attend to educational television programming to a high degree, and their attention was indistinguishable from that of normal agemates under some circumstances. It seems evident that television may hold greater intrinsic appeal than schoolwork for the child with ADHD, plus TV does not represent the historical source of frustration and failure associated with classroom performance. Apparently the nature of the task seems crucial when determining if the child has significant difficulty paying attention.

Related to problems with inattention, children with ADHD are *impulsive;* they experience difficulty *inhibiting* their response in certain situations (Barkley, 1990). As with inattention, impulsivity is a multidimensional construct; it can be defined in several ways (Olson, 1989). Children with ADHD, for example, are impulsive when confronted with academic tasks. They are extremely quick to respond without considering all alternatives; thus they are known as fast but careless and inaccurate problem solvers. This type of response style can have a profound influence on the child's ability to perform in an academic setting. Besides affecting cognitive performance, impulsivity can also manifest itself as an inability to suppress inappropriate behavior. As such, children with ADHD are also known to be high-risk takers, as evidenced by their running out in traffic. In addition, they seem unable to delay gratification (Campbell, Szumowski, Ewing, Gluck, & Breaux, 1982). In school they experience difficulty waiting their turn in line, blurt out answers in class, constantly touch other children, and tend to be undesirable playmates because of their difficulty with turn taking, sharing, and cooperation, and their low tolerance for frustration while playing games (Landau & Moore, 1991).

The third primary symptom involves motor excess, or *overactivity.* Historically overactivity was considered the hallmark characteristic of the disorder and served as the source for the enduring "hyperactivity" label applied to these children. This is probably because overactivity remains the most salient symptom and possibly the symptom most annoying to others. In fact, parents of children with ADHD retrospectively report overactivity to be an early marker of the disorder (Campbell, 1988), even though it is also a common complaint from parents of normal children (Lapouse & Monk, 1958; Richman, Stevenson, & Graham, 1982). As with the other symptoms, overactivity can take many forms but is especially apparent as excessive body movements (both major and minor motor) and vocalizations; for example, these children are described as "always on the go" or "squirmy and fidgety," or as a child who "can't sit still," "hums and makes other odd noises," "talks incessantly," and "climbs excessively" (Barkley, 1990).

When children with ADHD engage in table activities or academic seatwork, they constantly get up and down from the desk (or do all seatwork while standing). Many show minor motor fidgeting, such as pencil tapping or leg shaking, and they seem unable to keep their hands off objects unrelated to the task at hand. During individual psychological testing, children with ADHD can be extremely challenging subjects because they attempt to manipulate the examiner's test materials throughout the evaluation. Finally, they are often overactive and incessantly talkative in the context of social play—behaviors that seem to have a negative effect on peer relations (Landau & Moore, 1991). Again, it is important to remember that setting demands—in particular, the degree of structure in the environment—affect the extent to which these children are problems to their teachers. The child with ADHD may be considered quite troublesome, for example, in a highly structured academic setting, with desks placed in rows and all work to be accomplished in one's seat. In contrast, in the open-classroom setting where cooperative learning is encouraged and children are expected to move about and collaborate with others, the child with ADHD may be less distinctive and disturbing to others (Jacob, O'Leary, & Rosenblad, 1978).

Secondary symptoms or associated characteristics

Children with ADHD experience numerous difficulties that go beyond inattention, impulsive responding, and overactivity. Although these problems are not related to the diagnosis of ADHD, the fact that children with ADHD present these added difficulties accounts for the extreme heterogeneity among ADHD cases.

First, children with ADHD are at elevated risk for problems related to conduct disorder. Although the rates of overlap vary with each study, most investigators agree that at least one half of all children with ADHD also meet diagnostic criteria for conduct disorder. In these children one finds extreme stubbornness, noncompliance, hostility, rule violations, stealing, lying, and aggressive acts (Hinshaw, 1987). Studies of children with ADHD indicate that those who show conduct disorder not only are more difficult to manage as children but also will have more serious adolescent and adult adjustment problems (Weiss & Hechtman, 1986).

Second, many children with ADHD are rejected by their peers (Landau & Moore, 1991). In fact, many boys with ADHD who are not aggressive seem to be more "disliked" than their classmates who are highly aggressive but do not have ADHD (Milich & Landau, 1989), and this negative reputation may be established after only brief contact with unfamiliar children (Pelham & Bender, 1982). This effect on others is not surprising, as children with ADHD tend to be bossy, intrusive, disruptive, and easily frustrated while in the play group. They have few, if any, friends. Peer rejection is a serious outcome of ADHD because children who are rejected early in life tend to be at high risk for many adult adjustment difficulties, including job terminations, bad-conduct discharge from the military, negative contact with police, and psychiatric hospitalization (Parker & Asher, 1987).

Third, children with ADHD are at high risk for achievement difficulties, and many meet special-education placement criteria as learning disabled (McGee & Share, 1988). Because children with ADHD in the academic setting are typically off task, noisy, disruptive, out-of-seat, and do not finish schoolwork or homework, parents and teachers complain of underachievement. These children's work tends to be highly inefficient and disorganized, and their performance often shows great fluctuations.

Finally, these children seem to experience problems dealing with the numerous transitions in school (such as going from recess back to class). They have difficulty adapting their behaviors as situational expectations change (Landau & Milich, 1988). Consequently, there may be a grave discrepancy between actual achievement in school and the child's estimated potential for learning. As children with ADHD accumulate a history of negative feedback from parents, teachers, and peers, it is little wonder that they are also at risk for low self-esteem and depression as they mature.

Effects on the classroom

Children with ADHD can be an extremely negative force in the classroom setting. They tend to evoke numerous negative interactions with their teachers and take teacher time away from other children. They are disruptive to learning activities; try to dominate social situations; and, to make matters worse, do not perform well academically. Indeed, the presence of a child with ADHD in the preschool setting serves as a catalyst for significantly more

negative teacher feedback to all children in the classroom (Campbell, Endman, & Bernfeld, 1977).

Causal hypotheses

Many causal explanations for ADHD have been proposed over the years. First, research indicates that the role of genetic transmission must be taken seriously. Parents and siblings of children diagnosed with ADHD are more likely to have the disorder, and studies of twins indicate that identical twins are much more likely to share the disorder than are fraternal twins. Second, researchers are currently working on identifying a neurobiological cause, such as a deficit in the neurotransmitters that control attention, although none has yet been isolated (Hynd, Hern, Voeller, & Marshall, 1991). Third, there is intriguing correlational evidence that maternal smoking and/or alcohol use during pregnancy may be linked to increased risk for ADHD. Fourth, in spite of widespread belief among lay persons and the popularity of the "Feingold Diet" (1975), sugar consumption does *not* seem to be related to the symptoms of ADHD (Wolraich, Milich, Stumbo, & Schultz, 1985). Finally, there is no evidence to suggest that parenting or childrearing is in any way related to the primary symptoms of the disorder; however, some of the secondary problems associated with ADHD (such as conduct disorder and self-esteem problems) may be the consequence of factors in the child's social environment.

Assessment of ADHD

Because symptoms of impulsivity, poor attention, and excessive activity may differ among children with ADHD and across various situations, a multidimensional approach to assessment is necessary. Parent, teacher, and possibly even peer reports, plus observation in the naturalistic setting, are considered in the evaluation of ADHD. This assessment is designed to go beyond offering an actual diagnosis. A comprehensive school-based evaluation should provide data to develop a thorough intervention plan for the child.

Parents

Parents are, of course, an important source of information about children's behavior because they observe the children daily and in a variety of settings. In addition, parents are in a position to notice fluctuations in behavior in response to different situations and varying responses to treatment. Parent reports are not sufficient in the evaluation of ADHD, however, for two reasons. First, parents do not have exposure to the full range of child behavior. They may be unaware of developmental norms and what constitutes age-appropriate behavior. Second, as stated earlier, the symptoms of ADHD may not be as troublesome in the home, a setting that typically is less structured than school. Although parent reports are necessary, information from other sources must be considered as well.

Teachers

Teachers serve as an essential source in the assessment of ADHD, and there are several rating scales by which teachers may easily communicate their knowledge and concerns regarding the child. These scales provide a normative comparison; teachers are asked to rate the degree to which the child's behavior differs from the behavior of other children in the class. Like parents, teachers have almost daily contact with these children. Unlike parents, teachers are also exposed to many other children of the same age and are able to use their *normative perspective* to determine if the referred child is behaving in age-inappropriate ways. In addition, teachers observe these children in unstructured play settings as well as highly structured academic settings, where symptoms of ADHD are more likely to emerge. Teacher input is thus integral in the assessment of ADHD (see Barkley, 1990, for a review of these rating scales).

Naturalistic observation data

An important source of information regarding the child with ADHD—one that has direct implications for treatment planning—involves systematic observation of the child in classroom and play settings. By using previously defined code categories that quantify the amount of time the child with ADHD spends engaged in on-task behavior and in various inappropriate off-task behaviors, it is possible to get *direct* information about how the child is functioning. In addition, it is helpful to collect these data on the same-sex classmates of the child. In this way it is possible to determine that Billy, who presents symptoms suggestive of ADHD, attends to math or storytime 22% of the time, while the other boys in his class attend an average of 84% during that same observation session. Because parent and teacher reports are based on previous contact with the child (i.e., numerous *retrospective* observations) and may be biased by the disruptive nature of the child's behavior, direct observation of the child with ADHD is the only way to provide data on *current* behavior, and these data will facilitate interpretation of the reports from parents and teachers.

Peers

One final area to be considered in the assessment process involves the child's peer interactions. Classroom sociometric assessment, which can provide information about peer popularity and rejection, in combination with measures of social loneliness and social anxiety offers valuable information about the child's social functioning and may highlight areas for intervention (see Landau & Milich, 1990, for a discussion of appropriate measures).

Preschool issues

Special issues arise in the assessment of preschool-age children. Most measures used to diagnose ADHD, for example, are not normed for preschoolers and may be developmentally inappropriate for this age group (Barkley, 1990). Furthermore, high activity level and noncompliance in very young children may either signify

Many children with ADHD are rejected by their peers. Children with ADHD tend to be bossy, intrusive, disruptive, and easily frustrated while in the play group. They have few, if any, friends. Peer rejection is a serious outcome of ADHD because children who are rejected early in life tend to be at high risk for many adult adjustment difficulties, including job terminations, bad-conduct discharge from the military, negative contact with police, and psychiatric hospitalization.

problems or simply represent normal development. In assessing preschoolers, therefore, special emphasis must be placed on the severity and frequency of a disruptive behavior rather than on its presence or absence (Campbell, 1990). Parents who are unaware of developmental norms tend to overreport problems with their children due to unrealistic expectations, thereby engendering additional conflict. On the other hand, some parents may be overly lenient and thus fail to notice potential problems.

Finally, teacher reports of behavior are obviously unavailable for those young children who do not attend preschool. Problems exist, however, even when teacher reports are obtainable (Barkley, 1990). As mentioned earlier, the public school classroom is an important arena in which to assess ADHD due to its structure; preschool settings are generally less structured and can therefore accommodate children with attentional deficits more easily. Preschool-based assessments thus may yield much less informative information than assessments conducted in grade school. Activities of daily living (e.g., eating, dressing) are more likely to be the source of conflict at this age. Even in this area, however, it is important to not confuse the child's normal attempts at autonomy with ADHD-related management difficulties.

Treatment of ADHD

Once assessment has indicated a possibility of ADHD, what can teachers and caregivers do? It is important to remember that children with ADHD benefit from the same environments that all children do; thus, designing classrooms appropriately for the child's development is an important step toward managing the behavior of a child with ADHD. For young children this means a loosely structured environment in which active involvement is an integral part of the learning process. In addition, tailoring work to fit the child's individual needs and encouraging collaboration and cooperation are practices recommended for children with ADHD, as they are for all children.

The two primary methods of intervention are stimulant medication and behavioral management; however, the most effective treatment involves a combination of the two (Pelham, in press).

Medication therapy

The most common treatment for ADHD is medications that stimulate the central nervous system (Barkley, 1990). Research suggests that children with ADHD may not be as sensitive to feedback from the social and physical environment as other children; stimulant medication appears to render these children more sensitive by lowering response thresholds in the nervous system (Barkley, 1989). Ritalin, or methylphenidate (the generic drug name), is the most common stimulant used. Approximately 70 to 75% of children responded positively to this medication, while about one fourth are unaffected (Pelham, 1987); thus, these medications will help many but not all children with ADHD.

Effects of medication. For those children who do respond positively, the effects are immediate and typically quite strong. Attention, impulse control, and short-term memory may all be improved (Barkley, 1990). Children talk less, are less disturbing, follow rules better, and exhibit less aggression (Pelham, 1987). These changes often lead to improved relations with parents, teachers, and peers. As these children become more cooperative, the need for close adult supervision should diminish; however, in spite of substantial reduction in disruptive behavior, the majority of children with ADHD will still show problem behaviors. Medication is thus often helpful, but not sufficient, in managing the disorder.

In addition to reducing disruptive behavior, stimulant medication has been found to help children attend better when involved in organized athletic play with other children (Pelham et al., 1990). Because these activities, such as soccer or T-ball, involve peer interactions, medication may indirectly improve the peer relations and self-esteem of children with ADHD. Even while on medication, however, it is difficult for most children with ADHD to gain peer acceptance (Pelham & Milich, 1984).

Children with ADHD who are on medication are also better able to concentrate on schoolwork. They complete more assignments and are more careful and accurate; thus, they show improved academic *performance* (Barkley, 1990). Medication is much less effective in improving children's scores on academic *achievement* tests, however. In other words, medication does not necessarily help children with ADHD master more difficult tasks and may not directly relate to enhanced learning; thus, academic achievement *per se* appears to be only minimally improved by medication, if at all.

Recently there has been growing interest in the effects of medication on the attitudes and motivation of children with ADHD. Some experts have suggested, for example, that medication may cause children to believe that they are responsible for their own misbehavior—that they must rely on some external agent (the drug) for control of their difficulties. Consequently, when children behave inappropriately or do not succeed at schoolwork, they might conclude that the medication must not be working that day—in other words, these problems are not their fault. In contrast, other researchers suggest that because medication leads to improved performance, children with ADHD may be able to personalize this newly discovered success and thus feel greater responsibility for their own behavior than if they had not been medicated—they have greater control than before. Although more study is necessary, current results support the second hypothesis: Medicated children with ADHD seem to credit themselves for good performances (i.e., they *internalize* and personalize their successes) while *externalizing* or blaming poor performance on factors beyond their control (Milich, 1993). The fact that these children attribute successes to their personal responsibility, and not to the medication, may contribute to their self-esteem. In summary, medication seems to improve behavior in a variety of ways and may also help children to feel better about themselves.

Despite the important effects of medication, several cautions should be kept in mind. First, as mentioned earlier, not all children with ADHD benefit from stimulant medication. Second, four- to five-year-old children do not experience improvement to the same extent as do older children (Barkley, 1989). In a review of medication studies with preschoolers, Campbell (1985) noted that few benefits were obtained and that side effects, such as increased solitary play and clinging, appeared serious enough to potentially disrupt social development. Third, all of the medication-induced benefits represent short-term effects only; that is, improvements are noticeable only while the child is taking the medication. In the evenings, weekends, and summers, when children are typically not medicated, their symptoms generally return to pretreatment levels; thus medication brings no lasting benefits.

Side effects. Many parents express concern about potential negative side effects of stimulant medication; for example, there is evidence that mild insomnia and lessened appetite, especially at lunchtime, can occur (Barkley, 1990). This latter effect has been thought to lead to suppressed weight and height gains. Research indicates, however, that effects on growth can be corrected by altering dosage and tend to occur only during the first year of medication therapy (Barkley, 1990). Height and weight tend to catch up to age norms in subsequent years even if medication is continued (Mattes & Gittleman, 1983). There is little research on this side effect in pre-school children, however, even though medication is sometimes given to children as young as age three (Campbell, 1990). As a consequence, medication is not recommended for children in this age group. Because medication effects tend to wear off within a four-hour period, most children with ADHD receive a noontime dose to cover their afternoon activities at school. One simple way to avoid the lunchtime appetite loss is to have the child eat lunch prior to taking the afternoon medication dose.

Mild headaches and stomachaches may also occur, but they tend to disappear within a few weeks (Barkley, 1990). These problems, along with mood changes, such as irritability, and individual reactions (e.g., lip licking, rashes) may be alleviated by a simple dosage adjustment. Research indicates that there are no known long-term side effects; for example, these children do not appear to be at increased risk for drug abuse later in life. Any side effects, therefore, tend to be mild, short term, and easily relieved.

One unfortunate consequence of drug treatment is that many parents and teachers tend to rely on medication exclusively and not invest in other, more lasting interventions. Within the past few years, the lay press has expressed alarm about overmedication of children. If parents seek medication for their child to manage home-based behavior problems, this concern may be valid; however, if medication is used to help the child attend to important classroom instruction and adjust well to school, this concern seems to be exaggerated. It is important to remember that medicated children with ADHD, although improved, are not made symptom free. For these reasons, medication is not adequate by itself as a treatment for children with ADHD. The "best practice," based on research, is to combine medication and behavioral treatments in the management of ADHD. This is done not only because medication is insufficient in the treatment of most cases but also because it permits the use of a lower dose of medication. There is strong evidence that a low dose of Ritalin, in combination with behavioral intervention, results in at least the same improvement—and sometimes greater improvement—in the child as does a high dose of Ritalin alone (Pelham, in press). In addition, when the low dose is used, most undesirable side effects can be avoided. In fact, it has been suggested that behavioral interventions be attempted in school *before* thought is given to the use of medication (National Association of School Psychologists, 1992).

Behavioral treatment

Because many children with ADHD demonstrate an inability to follow rules and govern their own behavior (Barkley, 1989), behavioral treatment is necessary for these self-regulatory difficulties. Aspects of successful behavioral intervention include rewarding appropriate behavior, giving effective directions and requests, and using consistent methods of discipline. If teachers can receive assistance from consultants (such as school psychologists) to implement these procedures, most children with ADHD can have their educational and social needs met in the regular education setting. In addition, collaboration with parents is essential because home-based support for school behavior and performance will enhance the success of programs at school.

Appropriate behavior. Many parents and teachers do not think that children should be rewarded simply for "doing what they ought to do," and most children do not need a heavy overlay of rewards to promote acceptable behavior; however, if a child with ADHD seldom engages in an important behavior (such as playing cooperatively), then rewards may be necessary to promote the behavior. As the child learns the behavior, rewards should be gradually removed. Research shows that the use of rewards is particularly helpful when dealing with children who have ADHD (Pelham, 1992). Their inappropriate behavior tends to be extremely compelling; adults cannot ignore it. As a consequence, much of the feedback these children receive from parents, teachers, and peers is expressed as a complaint or reprimand. It is little wonder that many children with ADHD develop self-concept difficulties and depression. Rewarding positive behaviors thus not only encourages the child to continue behaving well but also provides the child with desperately needed success, thereby building self-esteem.

Verbal praise is crucial for a child with ADHD and is especially powerful when the positive behavior is also clarified (e.g., "I like the way you are playing so nicely with the other boys"). Praise may not, however, provide adequate incentive initially due to the child's lower sensitivity to feedback from the social environment; thus, children with ADHD often require more frequent and powerful rewards for a time (Barkley, 1990). At first, parents and teachers may need to give material rewards, along with praise, to teach appropriate behavior; subsequently they may use praise alone to maintain the behavior—for example, smiley faces or gold stars may be given to the child every half hour for engaging in appropriate classroom behavior. A star chart on which different classroom activities (e.g., storytime) are separated as intervals can make implementation of such a reward system easier. To avoid a problem with classroom equity (other children wondering why they do not earn these rewards), the smiley faces could be granted discreetly, perhaps on a special card to be taken home at the end of each day. Even though some teachers may find these procedures intrusive and distracting, the fact remains that the use of behavioral intervention disrupts classroom routine less than does an untreated child with ADHD.

Directions. Unfortunately, the disruptive behavior of children with ADHD causes parents and teachers to often find themselves issuing numerous directives and commands to these youngsters throughout the day. To increase the likelihood that the child will cooperate with adult requests, directions should be specific and brief (Pelham, 1992). Those that are vague or issued in question format (e.g., "Let's get back to work, shall we?") or that involve several directives strung together are not likely to be obeyed. Instead, adults should obtain the child's attention, issue the direction (e.g., "Joey, finish picking up those blocks now"), and wait a few seconds. The child should then be praised for cooperating. Research shows that these techniques are effective. They prevent adult interactions from escalating into impatience and reduce the tendency of children with ADHD to ignore or resist adult direction.

In instances in which a child with ADHD does not respond to adult guidance, school psychologists can work with teachers to implement a variety of other behavioral interventions. Ignoring mildly negative behaviors may prove effective, but often increased adult monitoring and immediate consequences to reduce disruptive acts (e.g., asking the child to sit out an activity) are necessary. If the child engages in aggressive outbursts or is extremely uncooperative, a time-out procedure may also have to be implemented (Barkley, 1990). Consistency is essential for all of these methods to work well.

Daily report card. Parents can serve as an effective back-up to school-based interventions. An important behavior-management strategy involves sending home a brief daily report card reflecting the child's performance for each day (Barkley, 1990). Parents may thus praise the child for success in school, thereby supporting teachers'

Acknowledging teachers' need for effective consultation and collaboration in this area, the National Association of School Psychologists (NASP) recently issued the following position statement describing a "best-practice" approach for dealing with children with attention deficits.

NASP believes that effective intervention should be tailored to the unique learning strengths and needs of every student. For children with attention deficits, such interventions will include the following:

1) Classroom modifications to enhance attending, work production, and social adjustment;

2) Behavioral management systems to reduce problems in arenas most likely to be affected by attention deficits (e.g., large group instruction, transitions, etc.);

3) Direct instruction in study strategies and social skills, within the classroom setting whenever possible to increase generalization;

4) Consultation with families to assist in behavior management in the home setting and to facilitate home-school cooperation and collaboration;

5) Monitoring by a case manager to ensure effective implementation of interventions, to provide adequate support for those interventions, and to assess progress in meeting behavioral and academic goals;

6) Education of school staff in characteristics and management of attention deficits to enhance appropriate instructional modifications and behavior management;

7) Access to special education services when attention deficits significantly impact school performance;

8) Working collaboratively with community agencies providing medical and related services to students and their families.

NASP believes appropriate treatment may or may not include medical intervention. When medication *is* considered, NASP *strongly* recommends:

1) That instructional and behavioral interventions be implemented before medication trials are begun;

2) That behavioral data be collected before and during medication trials to assess baseline conditions and the efficacy of medication; and

3) That communication between school, home, and medical personnel emphasize mutual problem solving and cooperation. (National Association of School Psychologists, 1992)

efforts. In addition, parents should consider using small toys and special activities (e.g., going to a movie) as back-up rewards for positive school performance because these children need rewards of high salience. Parents should target small successes first (e.g., remaining seated throughout storytime) then gradually increase expectations as the child demonstrates mastery.

Preschool issues. Unfortunately, dealing with ADHD symptoms among preschool-age children can be quite a challenge because some of these problems simply represent individual differences in developmental rates. Excessive activity, impulsive responding, and an inability to pay attention—all symptoms of ADHD among school-age children—may not be particularly unusual behaviors for many preschool-age children. Even so, some preschool children receive a diagnosis of ADHD. In these cases—such as Jamie, who was described earlier in this article—parents may feel overwhelmed with the child's discipline problems at home and with aggressive conduct with playmates. The primary symptoms of ADHD *per se* thus do not represent the major source of difficulty, and a diagnosis of ADHD would be premature. Parent training, however, may be an appropriate intervention, in which Jamie's parents are given systematic guidance on how to manage his behavior at home. If Jamie continues to experience difficulties once he reaches school age, when classroom demands require a greater restraint on activity and more persistent attention, a diagnosis of ADHD may be given serious consideration.

Conclusion

ADHD is a problem that has many facets and affects the child in many areas of functioning, including academic performance, interpersonal relations, and emotional well-being. Because of ADHD's complexity, successful treatment requires a multidisciplinary approach reflecting the collaboration of many professionals. Teachers must have assistance in dealing with children with ADHD.

References

Achenbach, T.M., McConaughy, S.H., & Howell, C.T. (1987). Child/adolescent behavioral and emotional problems: Implications of cross-informant correlations for situational specificity. *Psychological Bulletin, 101*, 213–232.

American Psychiatric Association. (1987). *Diagnostic and statistical manual of mental disorders* (3rd ed., revised). Washington, DC: Author.

Barkley, R.A. (1989). Attention deficit-hyperactivity disorder. In E.J. Mash & R.A. Barkley (Eds.), *Treatment of childhood disorders* (pp. 39–72). New York: Guilford.

Barkley, R.A. (1990). *Attention-deficit hyperactivity disorder: A handbook for diagnosis and treatment.* New York: Guilford.

Campbell, S.B. (1985). Hyperactivity in preschoolers: Correlates and prognostic implications. *Clinical Psychology Review, 5*, 405–428.

Campbell, S. (1988, October). *Longitudinal studies of active and aggressive preschoolers: Individual differences in early behavior and in outcome.* Paper presented at the Second Rochester Symposium on Developmental Psychopathology, Rochester, NY.

Campbell, S.B. (1990). *Behavioral problems in preschool children: Clinical and developmental issues.* New York: Guilford.

Campbell, S.B., Endman, M.W., & Bernfeld, G. (1977). Three year follow-up of hyperactive preschoolers into elementary school. *Journal of Child Psychology and Psychiatry, 18*, 239–249.

Campbell, S.B., Szumowski, E.K., Ewing, L.J., Gluck, D.S., & Breaux, A.M. (1982). A multidimensional assessment of parent-identified behavior problem toddlers. *Journal of Abnormal Child Psychology, 10*(4), 569–592.

Douglas, V.I. (1983). Attentional and cognitive problems. In M. Rutter (Ed.), *Developmental Neuropsychiatry* (pp. 280–329). New York: Guilford.

Feingold, B. (1975). *Why your child is hyperactive.* New York: Random House.

Hinshaw, S.P. (1987). On the distinction between attentional deficits/hyperactivity and conduct problems/aggression in child psychopathology. *Psychological Bulletin, 101*, 443–463.

Hynd, G.W., Hern, K.L., Voeller, K.K., & Marshall, R.M. (1991). Neurobiological basis of attention-deficit hyperactivity disorder (ADHD). *School Psychology Review, 20*(2), 174–186.

Jacob, R.B., O'Leary, K.D., & Rosenblad, C. (1978). Formal and informal classroom settings: Effects on hyperactivity. *Journal of Abnormal Child Psychology, 6*(1), 47–59.

Landau, S., & Milich, R. (1988). Social communication patterns of attention-deficit-disordered boys. *Journal of Abnormal Child Psychology, 16*, 69–81.

Landau, S., & Milich, R. (1990). Assessment of children's social status and peer relations. In A.M. LaGreca (Ed.), *Through the eyes of the child* (pp. 259–291). Boston: Allyn & Bacon.

Landau, S., & Moore, L. (1991). Social skill deficits in children with attention-deficit hyperactivity disorder. *School Psychology Review, 20*(2), 235–251.

Landau, S., Lorch, E.P., & Milich, R. (1992). Visual attention to and comprehension of television in attention-deficit hyperactivity disordered and normal boys. *Child Development, 63*, 928–937.

Lapouse, R., & Monk, M. (1958). An epidemiological study of behavior characteristics in children. *American Journal of Public Health, 48*, 1134–1144.

Mattes, J.A., & Gittleman, R. (1983). Growth of hyperactive children on maintenance regimen of methylphenidate. *Archives of General Psychiatry, 40*, 317–321.

McGee, R., & Share, D.L. (1988). Attention deficit disorder-hyperactivity and academic failure: Which comes first and what should be treated? *Journal of the American Academy of Child and Adolescent Psychiatry, 27*, 318–325.

Milich, R. (1993). *Children's response to failure: If at first you don't succeed, do you try, try again?* Manuscript submitted for publication.

Milich, R., & Landau, S. (1989). The role of social status variables in differentiating subgroups of hyperactive children. In L.M. Bloomingdale & J. Swanson (Eds.), *Attention deficit disorder: Current concepts and emerging trends in attentional and behavioral disorders of childhood: Vol. 5* (pp. 1–16). Elmsford, NY: Pergamon.

Milich, R., Loney, J., & Landau, S. (1982). The independent dimensions of hyperactivity and aggression: A validation with playroom observation data. *Journal of Abnormal Psychology, 91*, 183–198.

National Association of School Psychologists. (1992, May). Position statement on students with attention deficits. *Communique, 20*, 5.

Olson, S.L. (1989). Assessment of impulsivity in preschoolers: Cross-measure convergence, longitudinal stability, and relevance to social competence. *Journal of Clinical Child Psychology, 8*(2), 176–183.

Parker, J.G., & Asher, S.R. (1987). Peer relations and later personal adjustment: Are low-accepted children "at risk"? *Psychological Bulletin, 102*, 357–389.

Pelham, W.E., Jr. (1987). What do we know about the use and effects of CNS stimulants in the treatment of ADD? In J. Loney (Ed.), *The young hyperactive child: Answers to questions about diagnosis, prognosis and treatment* (pp. 99–110). New York: Haworth.

Pelham, W.E. (1992). *Children's summer day treatment program: 1992 program manual.* Unpublished manuscript, University of Pittsburgh School of Medicine, Western Psychiatric Institute and Clinic, Pittsburgh, PA.

Pelham, W.E. (in press). Pharmacotherapy for children with attention deficit hyperactivity disorder. *School Psychology Review.*

Pelham, W.E., & Bender, M.E. (1982). Peer relationships in hyperactive children: Description and treatment. In D.C. Gadow & I. Bialer (Eds.), *Advances in learning and behavioral disabilities: A research annual: Vol. 1* (pp. 365–436). Greenwich, CT: JAI.

Pelham, W.E., & Milich, R. (1984). Peer relations in children with hyperactivity/attention deficit disorder. *Journal of Learning Disabilities, 17*, 560–567.

Pelham, W.E., Jr., McBurnett, K., Harper, G.W., Milich, R., Murphy, D.A., Clinton, J., & Thiele, C. (1990). Methylphenidate and baseball playing in children with ADHD: Who's on first? *Journal of Consulting and Clinical Psychology, 58*, 130–133.

Richman, N., Stevenson, J., & Graham, J.J. (1982). *Preschool to school: A behavioral study.* London: Academic.

Schaughency, E.A., & Rothlind, J. (1991). Assessment and classification of attention deficit hyperactive disorders. *School Psychology Review, 20*(2), 187–202.

Weiss, B., & Hechtman, L.T. (1986). *Hyperactive children grown up.* New York: Guilford.

Wolraich, M., Milich, R., Stumbo, P., & Schultz, F. (1985). The effects of sucrose ingestion on the behavior of hyperactive boys. *Pediatrics, 106*, 675–682.

Children with AIDS

**Peggy O. Jessee, M. Christine Nagy
and Deborah Poteet-Johnson**

Peggy O. Jessee is Assistant Professor, Department of Human Development and Family Studies; M. Christine Nagy is Director of Health Research, Department of Behavioral and Community Medicine; Deborah Poteet-Johnson is Assistant Professor, Department of Pediatrics, The University of Alabama, Tuscaloosa.

Teachers spend a lot of time discussing and dealing with "at-risk" children. In the Summer 1992 issue of *Childhood Education*, Selma Wassermann reminded us of the varied troubles that some children bring to school. We should ask ourselves what more can we do, as teachers, to help these child victims of poverty, physical and emotional abuse, drug abuse, disease and, most pertinent to this article, pediatric AIDS. The current and future realities of AIDS-infected children in the classroom are forcing teachers to evaluate and, perhaps, redefine their definition of "at-risk" in a very personal sense.

Etiological Background
What is the true scope of the problem? During the 1980s, acquired immunodeficiency syndrome (AIDS) became one of the most important public health problems in the United States. In the 1990s, health officials will record the 200,000th case of AIDS (Fennell, 1991). Even this figure is considered only the "tip of the iceberg," as an estimated 1 to 1.5 million people in the United States are infected with the human immunodeficiency virus (HIV), the retrovirus that causes AIDS (Fauci, 1988; Watkins, 1988).

The rate of AIDS infection in children under 13 is also increasing. The number of pediatric AIDS cases diagnosed in the last six years has leaped from a cumulative total of 232 in December 1984 to 4,249 in December 1992 (Moll, 1991; U. S. News & World Report, 1993). As in adult AIDS, the number of pedi-

For every child with AIDS, another 2 to 10 children are likely to be HIV-infected.

atric AIDS cases reported is a severe underestimate of the true scope of the problem. For every child with AIDS, another 2 to 10 children are likely to be HIV-infected. AIDS has become one of the top ten causes of death for children under 5. According to estimates, AIDS will rank in the top five by the year 2000 (U. S. News & World Report, 1993).

The most important factor in the increased incidence of pediatric AIDS is the rate of heterosexual transmission. Nationwide, heterosexual contact accounts for about 6 percent of diagnosed AIDS cases. In many states, such as New York, Florida and Alabama, that figure is more than doubled (Alabama Department of Public Health [ADPH], 1992). These statistics have definite implications for the health of children. As AIDS affects the female

population, more and more children are being born HIV-positive. Today, 1,800 HIV-infected infants are born each year in the United States. By the year 2000, there will be from 5 to 10 million infants born with HIV worldwide (U. S. News & World Report, 1993).

What do these projections really mean to teachers and administrators? It means that: 1) probably all teachers, at some point in their careers, will have an AIDS-infected child in their classroom; 2) minority children will bear more of the burden of this disease than others; 3) teachers will be among those leaders asked to deal with the fears and phobias of the public; and 4) knowledge of and attitudes toward the disease will need to be addressed in teacher training.

Quality of Life
The statistics clearly demonstrate that more and more children are becoming infected with the AIDS virus. Since the Federal Drug Administration (FDA) approved zidovudine and dideoxyinosine for use with pediatric patients, AIDS-infected children are remaining symptom-free and are functioning at more normal developmental levels for longer periods of time (Burroughs-Wellcome Co., 1991; Santelli, Birn & Linde, 1992). AIDS-infected children experiencing this increased quality of life must have opportunities to attend education programs appropriate for their age and developmental level. Since the largest number of AIDS-infected children are from low-income minority groups, their educational needs will have to be met by federally funded child care, Head Start and other government programs.

Minority Children

Although census figures identify Black and Hispanic children as minority populations, they are in the majority when it comes to AIDS infection. These subpopulations contract the disease at rates that are very disproportionate to their distribution in the general population. Seventy-five percent of pediatric AIDS cases are diagnosed among Black and Hispanic children, while only 26 percent of the pediatric population is Black or Hispanic (Moll, 1991).

Several factors account for the overrepresentation of minority children among HIV-infected patients. High-risk groups for pediatric AIDS include infants of infected mothers, children needing blood transfusions, sexually abused children, and infants of intravenous drug abusers and/or sexual partners of abusers. Many of these at-risk groups are often found in minority families living at or below the poverty level in inner-city environments (Cruz, 1988). Most of these families are faced with a day-to-day struggle for survival. The children's lives are tremendously complicated by poverty, poor education, unemployment, single-parent households, inadequate housing or homelessness, and drug use by family members (Nicholas, Sondheimer, Willoughby, Jaffe & Katz, 1989).

School and health care systems serving in low-income areas are already severely overburdened trying to provide education, social and intervention services to this population. Additional responsibilities brought on by the AIDS crises may stretch already slim resources to the breaking point.

Concerns Surrounding AIDS

The increased awareness of AIDS has raised the public's concern about AIDS-infected children attending public schools and child care centers. Fear and misinformation about all aspects of AIDS are widespread among the general

population. School boards have adopted restrictive policies, teachers have threatened work stoppages and parents have boycotted schools to block admission of AIDS-infected children (Black, 1986). Research literature documents fears concerning transmission of the virus and possible infection of healthy children and education professionals (Brucker, Martin & Shreeve, 1989; Jessee, Poteet-Johnson & Nagy, 1993; Morrow, Benton, Reves & Pickering, 1991; Rubinstein, 1986; Wetterau & Stegelin, 1991).

For example, Brucker and his colleagues found that well over half of the teachers surveyed in their study (N=500) were fearful about having either children or fellow teachers diagnosed with AIDS participate in day-to-day school activities. In a study of child care centers (N=151), more than half of the teachers (59.2 percent) felt that infected people should be banned from working in health care settings and hospitals, over one-third (37.2 percent) felt they should not be allowed to work in education and child care settings, and a few (16.5 percent) felt that infected individuals should be quarantined (Jessee et al., 1993). Sixty-eight percent reported they would feel uneasy if an AIDS-infected child were in their center.

Only 43 percent of the parents (N=219) in the study conducted by Morrow et al. (1991) were willing to allow their child to stay in the same room with an HIV-infected child. Forty-eight percent of child care providers were unwilling to care for a child with HIV. They believed that such a child was likely to infect others, was dangerous to others and that common child care center contacts could transmit HIV. Some of these fears are based on realistic concerns, whereas others are not. A majority of respondents, however, were interested in knowing more about modes of transmission and specific ways of

dealing with infected people and/or children.

When young children are in group environments, concerns arise about the frequency of biting and opportunity for casual contact with blood and other body fluids. An incidence of approximately three biting episodes per 100 child-days among toddlers in group care was reported by Garrard, Leland & Smith (1988). Although low, this incidence still presents a risk for disease transmission.

There have been reported cases in which bites from an HIV-infected child were suspected of having infected otherwise healthy persons (Anonymous, 1987; Shirley & Ross, 1989; Wahn, Kramer, Voit, Bruster, Scrampical & Scheid, 1986). Until the mechanisms of disease transmission vis-a-vis casual contact and typical child behaviors are resolved, parents and child care providers will continue to worry about the risk of contracting HIV from an infected young child, whether or not this fear is warranted.

As the HIV-infected child reaches school age, classmates, teachers and parents of other children are also concerned about disease transmission through casual contact. Special precautions in school, however, should focus on reducing the transmission of childhood diseases to the HIV-infected child. Because of their depressed immune system, HIV-children need to be protected from infection (Black, 1986; Santelli, Birn & Linde, 1992). Normal childhood diseases, as well as inoculations for certain diseases, can be fatal for a child with HIV or AIDS.

Current Knowledge

Are teachers being prepared to deal with the issues of pediatric AIDS on an intellectual and emotional level? Studies dealing with teachers' knowledge and attitudes suggest that they are not. Brucker and Hall (1991) have noted, however, a slight increase in knowledge among new teachers as compared to teachers who graduated five years ago. Results of a pediatric AIDS workshop held at the National Institutes of Health (NIH) in Bethesda, Maryland, determined that child-to-child transmission of HIV infection is one of the areas most urgently needing further research (Nicholas et al., 1989).

Such research efforts are particularly germane to issues of group care for young HIV-infected children. Within our current knowledge base, AIDS is not spread through the kinds of contact children in group situations have with each other, including touching, hugging or sharing meals and bathroom facilities. Studies show that

> ... AIDS is not spread through the kinds of contact children in group situations have with each other ...

family members who have cared for both adults and children with AIDS have not been infected (Black, 1986; Friedland et al., 1986; Kaplan et al., 1985). Furthermore, the transmission of HIV from an infected child to other children or caregivers has not been documented in a child care setting (Lifson, 1988; Rogers et al., 1990). Education personnel also can take some reassurance from research on health care workers whose occupational exposure has led to relatively few documented cases of disease transmission (Hirsch et al., 1985).

Institutional Responses

In response to some of the many medical, psychosocial and education needs of these children, national pediatric health institutions developed goals to increase public and professional awareness of the education needs of AIDS-infected children and their families by fostering collaborative, community-wide efforts to enhance their quality of life. Coordinated approaches to caregiving that are family-centered and community-based have been suggested by the American Academy of Pediatrics' Task Force on Pediatric AIDS.

The task force also recommended that existing school and child care services be open to AIDS-infected or HIV-seropositive children who are well enough to participate in group activities when special programs are not available (American Academy of Pediatrics' Task Force on Pediatric AIDS [AAP], 1989). The Centers for Disease Control issued guidelines that address the need for teaching caregivers about modes of possible virus transmission and procedures for handling blood, urine and other body fluids (Centers for Disease Control, 1988).

Because of the complex medical and social needs, a multidisciplinary team approach is necessary to provide care to HIV-infected children and their families. Effective programs provide special services for families, including affordable medical care, culturally appropriate advocacy, outreach translators, child care help and school involvement (Stein & Jessop, 1985). Programs that are the most effective are tailored to meet specific cultural and language needs of individual communities (AAP, 1989). Successful efforts, such as the Baltimore City experience, can be models for protecting families' confidentiality, providing access to education and promoting special care for HIV-infected students (Santelli, Birn & Linde, 1992).

As the number of AIDS cases continues to increase and our knowledge base continues to expand, additional ethical and legal issues emerge. Many of these issues will have a major effect upon the education system. In a review of HIV-related court cases through

> ... a multi-disciplinary team approach is necessary to provide care to HIV-infected children.

February 1990, 469 cases were decided, settled, pending or filed at the federal, state and local levels (Gostin, 1990). Sharp differences in perception of public health, ethics and civil liberties have resulted in the largest body of legal challenges based on a single disease in the history of jurisprudence. This new body of case law will fundamentally affect public health policy and expose conflicts in values that will possibly require resolution by legislatures and the courts.

What practical procedures should group caregivers or teachers follow when dealing with an AIDS-infected child? First, everyone should practice universal precautions. Universal precautions include washing hands after contact with any bodily fluids from a child, wearing gloves when contact with fluids is necessary and assuming every child in the class could be HIV-infected. Observing universal precautions also means understanding that, to date, no concrete evidence exists of horizontal transmission of HIV to or from people by contacts such as holding, touching, hugging or sharing meals and bathroom facilities.

Because a child with AIDS is very susceptible to normal childhood diseases that can be deadly in an immunosuppressed system, parents and teachers must make every attempt to prevent such infections. When outbreaks do occur or when children in the class are to receive immunizations, parents of the AIDS-infected child need to be informed immediately.

Second, if teachers and providers are fearful about having HIV-positive children or fellow teachers participate in school activities, then school administrators should accept the responsibility for developing education and support programs. Programs that are appropriate for teachers and parents should provide current information on AIDS and HIV transmission and clarify school policy on the placement of HIV-infected children in the classroom (AAP, 1989) (see appendix). Open and honest interactions should be encouraged among participants. Knowledgeable and supportive staff will then be able to facilitate positive interchanges.

Conclusion

Teachers have confronted the ethical issues of how and when to teach children about sex and drug abuse for a long time. Today, the issue is expanded to include the urgent question of how, when and who should teach children about HIV infection and its relationship to sex and drugs. Eighty-seven percent of Americans polled said they approved of teaching children about AIDS and other sexually transmitted diseases in the early grades (U.S. News & World Report, 1993). A study assessing opinions about who should have primary responsibility for conducting HIV education ranked teachers first (36 percent), parents second (27 percent) and school nurses third (26 percent) (Kerr, Allensworth & Gayle, 1989).

The researchers pointed out that improvement of knowledge alone is insufficient for changing attitudes and motivating people toward healthful behaviors. Other studies also yield data to suggest that attitudes and appropriate beliefs about the disease do not necessarily correlate with the level of knowledge (Basch, 1989; Fennell, 1990; Kerr, Allensworth & Gayle, 1989; Walker, 1992).

Schools are the optimal setting for reaching the vast majority of

Teachers . . . need to be prepared to deal with the multiple issues and concerns that surround AIDS.

young people. Teachers, however, need to be prepared to deal with the multiple issues and concerns that surround AIDS. One way to address these additional responsibilities is to include in the teacher training curriculum the kind of information that will lead to a broader understanding of the problems surrounding AIDS. Potential educators must have hands-on opportunities to develop skills in areas outside the traditional subject-focused curriculum, such as:

- having sensitivity to a variety of attitudes and cultural values
- being able to advise and counsel students regarding human sexuality
- being able to communicate effectively with students
- feeling comfortable dealing with a variety of human emotions, including hostility and fear
- being able to assume roles as group moderators and facilitators of learning.

Some education organizations are attempting to communicate AIDS information and needs assessment through their professional journals. Many, if not most, of the articles, however, are being published in journals concerned only with school health; i.e., *Journal of School Health, Journal of Health Education*. Unfortunately, these journals do not always reach the classroom teacher. Professional journals from

all education disciplines should consider AIDS education a top priority for their readers. For teachers in the field, inservice education that addresses the issue of AIDS and caring for children affected by AIDS should be available.

The resources and policies needed to provide medical care and social services for children with AIDS will come with teachers' education, knowledge and attitudinal changes. It has been stated that education is our "best weapon against HIV" (Cruz, 1988, p. 909). This is especially true for educators.

References

Alabama Department of Public Health. (1992). Special edition. *Alabama HIV/AIDS Update, 3*(2).

American Academy of Pediatrics' Task Force on Pediatric AIDS. (1989). Infants and children with acquired immunodeficiency syndrome: Placement in adoption and foster care. *Pediatrics, 83,* 609-612.

Anonymous. (1987). Transmission of HIV by human bite. *Lancet, 2,* 522.

Basch, C. E. (1989). Preventing AIDS through education: Concepts, strategies, and research priorities. *Journal of School Health, 59*(7), 296-300.

Black, J. L. (1986). AIDS: Preschool and school issues. *Journal of School Health, 56*(3), 93-95.

Brucker, B. W., & Hall, W. H. (1991). AIDS in the classroom: Are teacher attitudes changing? *Early Child Development and Care, 77,* 137-147.

Brucker, B. W., Martin, J. J., & Shreeve, W. C. (1989). AIDS in the classroom: A survey of teacher attitudes. *Early Child Development and Care, 43,* 61-64.

Burroughs-Wellcome Company. (1991, April). *Management of HIV infection treatment team workshop handbook.* Raleigh, NC: Author.

Centers for Disease Control. (1988). Education and foster care of children infected with human T-lymphotrophic virus III/lymphadenopathy-associated virus. *The Morbidity and Mortality Weekly Report, 34*(34).

Cruz, L. D. (1988). Children with AIDS: Diagnosis, symptoms, care. *AORN Journal, 48*(5), 893-910.

Fauci, A. S. (1988). The human immunodeficiency virus: Infectivity and mechanisms of pathogenesis. *Science, 239,* 617-622.

5. CULTURAL AND SOCIETAL INFLUENCES: Special Challenges

Fennell, R. (1990). Knowledge, attitudes and beliefs of students regarding AIDS: A review. *Health Education, 21*(4), 20-25.

Fennell, R. (1991). AIDS/HIV articles published in selected professional health journals: 1981-1990. *Journal of School Health, 61*(9), 385-387.

Friedland, G. H., Saltzman, B. R., Rogers, M. F., Kahl, P. A., Lesser, M. L., Mayers, M. M., & Klein, R. S. (1986). Lack of transmission of HTLV-III/LAV infection to household contacts of patients with AIDS or AIDS-related complex with oral candidiasis. *New England Journal of Medicine, 314,* 344-349.

Garrard, J., Leland, N., & Smith, D. K. (1988). Epidemiology of human

bites to children in a day care center. *American Journal of Diseases of Children, 142,* 643-650.

Gostin, L. O. (1990). The AIDS litigation project: A national review of court and human rights commission decisions. Part 1: The social impact of AIDS. *Journal of the American Medical Association, 263*(4), 1961-1970.

Hirsch, M. S., Wormser, G. P., Schooley, R. T., Ho, D. D., Filenstein, D., Hopkins, C. C., Joline, C., Duncanson, F., Sarngadharan, M. G., Saxinger, C., & Gallo, R. C. (1985). Risk of nosocomial infection with human T-cell lymphotrophic virus III (HTLV-III). *New England Journal of Medicine, 382,* 1-4.

Jessee, P. O., Poteet-Johnson, D., & Nagy, M. C. (1993). Fear of AIDS among day care administrators and teachers. *Early Child Development and Care, 89,* 19-30.

Kaplan, J. E., Oleske, J. M., Getchell, J. P., Kalyanaraman, V. S., Minnefor, A. B., Zabala-Ablan, J., Joshi, V., Denny, T., Cabradilla, C. D., Roger, M. F., Sarngadharan, M. G., Sliski, A., Gallo, R. C., & Grancis, D. P. (1985). Evidence against transmission of HIV-III/LAV in families of children with AIDS. *Pediatric Infectious Diseases, 4,* 468-471.

Kerr, D. L., Allensworth, D. D., & Gayle, J. A. (1989). The ASHA national HIV education needs assessment of health and education professionals. *Journal of School Health, 59*(7), 301-307.

Lifson, A. R. (1988). Do alternate modes of transmission of human immunodeficiency virus exist? A review. *Journal of the American Medical Association, 259,* 1353-1356.

Moll, L. (1991). Pediatric AIDS: Hitting closer to home. *Pediatric Management,* 38-41.

Morrow, A. L., Benton, M., Reves, R. R., & Pickering, L. K. (1991). Knowledge and attitudes of day care center parents and care providers regarding children infected with human immunodeficiency virus. *Pediatrics, 87*(6), 876-883.

Nicholas, S. W., Sondheimer, D. L., Willoughby, A. D., Jaffe, S., & Katz, S. L. (1989). Human immunodeficiency virus infection in childhood,

adolescence and pregnancy: A status report and national research agenda. *Pediatrics, 83*(2), 293-308.

Rogers, M. F., White, C. R., Sanders, R., Schable, C., Sell, T. E., Wasserman, R. L., Bellanti, J. A., Peter, S. M., & Wray, B. B. (1990). Lack of transmission of human immunodeficiency virus from infected children to their household contacts. *Pediatrics, 85,* 210-214.

Rubinstein, A. (1986). Schooling for children with acquired immune deficiency syndrome. *Journal of Pediatrics, 109,* 242-244.

Santelli, J. S., Birn, A., & Linde, J. (1992). School placement for human immunodeficiency virus-infected children: The Baltimore City experience. *Pediatrics, 89*(5), 843-848.

Shirley, L. R., & Ross, S. A. (1989). Risk of transmission of human immunodeficiency virus by bite of an infected toddler. *The Journal of Pediatrics, 114*(3), 425-427.

Stein, R. E., & Jessop, D. J. (1985). Delivery of care to inner-city children with chronic conditions. In N. Hobbs & J. M. Perrin (Eds.), *Issues in the Care of Children with Chronic Illness* (pp. 382-401). San Francisco: Jossey, Bass.

U. S. News & World Report. (1993, February 22). Outlook, p. 8.

Wahn, V., Kramer, H. H., Voit, T., Bruster, H. T., Scrampical, B., & Scheid, A. (1986). Horizontal transmission of HIV infection between two siblings. *Lancet, 2,* 694.

Walker, S. H. (1992). Teenagers' knowledge of the acquired immunodeficiency syndrome and associated risk. *Journal of Pediatric Nursing, 7*(4), 246-250.

Wassermann, S. (1992). Professional teachers deal with children "in trouble." *Childhood Education, 68,* 232-236.

Watkins, J. (1988). *Report of the Presidential Commission of the Human Immunodeficiency Virus Epidemic.* Washington, DC: U.S. Government Printing Office. Publication No. 0-214-701.

Wetterau, P. K., & Stegelin, D. A. (1991). Day care providers' knowledge and attitudes about AIDS: A needs assessment. *Children's Health Care, 20*(2), 108-113.

APPENDIX

Resources for Teachers

Association for the Care of Children's Health (ACCH), National Center for Family-Centered Care, Family-Centered HIV Project, 7910 Woodmont Ave., Suite 300, Bethesda MD 20814

American Red Cross, AIDS Education Office, 1730 D Street, NW, Washington, DC

Centers for Disease Control, U. S. Department of Health and Human Services, National AIDS Information and Exchange Program, Atlanta, GA 30333

Children's Hospital National Medical Center, 111 Michigan Ave., NW, Washington, DC. 20010

Division of Services to Children with Special Health Needs, Bureau of Maternal and Child Health and Resources Development, Department of Health and Human Services, Washington, DC 20202

New Parents Network Computer Bulletin Board System, P. O. Box 44226, Tucson, AZ 85733

Office of Public Affairs, U. S. Department of Education, AIDS and the Education of Our Children, 400 Maryland Ave., SW, Washington, DC 20202

State Departments of Education, AIDS Awareness and Education, capital cities of individual states

Credits/ Acknowledgments

Cover design by Charles Vitelli

1. Conception to Birth
Facing overview—UNICEF photo. 7—© 1994 by Bob Sacha. 10—Courtesy of Drs. E. Fuller Torrey and Daniel R. Weinberger, National Institute of Mental Health Neuroscience Center, Washingthon, D.C. 11—Nick Kelsh. 12—American Philosophical Society. 19—Century City Hospital.

2. Cognition, Language, and Learning
Facing overview—United Nations photo by John Isaac. 65—United Nations photo by Marta Pinter. 95—United Nations photo by John Isaac.

3. Social and Emotional Development
Facing overview—United Nations photo by Marcia Weistein.

4. Parenting and Family Issues
Facing overview—Photo by M. Marcuss Oslander.

5. Cultural and Societal Influences
Facing overview—United Nations photo by Y. Nagata.

PHOTOCOPY THIS PAGE!!!*

ANNUAL EDITIONS ARTICLE REVIEW FORM

■ NAME: _____ DATE: _____

■ TITLE AND NUMBER OF ARTICLE: _____

■ BRIEFLY STATE THE MAIN IDEA OF THIS ARTICLE: _____
_____
_____
_____
_____

■ LIST THREE IMPORTANT FACTS THAT THE AUTHOR USES TO SUPPORT THE MAIN IDEA:
_____
_____
_____
_____
_____
_____

■ WHAT INFORMATION OR IDEAS DISCUSSED IN THIS ARTICLE ARE ALSO DISCUSSED IN YOUR
TEXTBOOK OR OTHER READING YOU HAVE DONE? LIST THE TEXTBOOK CHAPTERS AND PAGE
NUMBERS:
_____
_____
_____
_____
_____
_____
_____
_____

■ LIST ANY EXAMPLES OF BIAS OR FAULTY REASONING THAT YOU FOUND IN THE ARTICLE:
_____
_____
_____
_____
_____

■ LIST ANY NEW TERMS/CONCEPTS THAT WERE DISCUSSED IN THE ARTICLE AND WRITE A
SHORT DEFINITION:
_____
_____
_____
_____
_____

*Your instructor may require you to use this Annual Editions Article Review Form in any number of ways:
for articles that are assigned, for extra credit, as a tool to assist in developing assigned papers, or simply
for your own reference. Even if it is not required, we encourage you to photocopy and use this page;
you'll find that reflecting on the articles will greatly enhance the information from your text.

ANNUAL EDITIONS:
CHILD GROWTH AND DEVELOPMENT 95/96
Article Rating Form

Here is an opportunity for you to have direct input into the next revision of this volume. We would like you to rate each of the 40 articles listed below, using the following scale:

1. **Excellent: should definitely be retained**
2. **Above average: should probably be retained**
3. **Below average: should probably be deleted**
4. **Poor: should definitely be deleted**

Your ratings will play a vital part in the next revision. So please mail this prepaid form to us just as soon as you complete it.
Thanks for your help!

Annual Editions revisions depend on two major opinion sources: one is our Advisory Board, listed in the front of this volume, which works with us in scanning the thousands of articles published in the public press each year; the other is you—the person actually using the book. Please help us and the users of the next edition by completing the prepaid article rating form on this page and returning it to us. Thank you.

Rating	Article
	1. Eugenics Revisited
	2. Nature or Nurture? Old Chestnut, New Thoughts
	3. Making Babies
	4. Do You Hear What I Hear?
	5. Prenatal Purgatory
	6. When a Pregnant Woman Drinks
	7. The Fantastic Voyage of Tanner Roberts
	8. The Amazing Minds of Infants
	9. Infants to Toddlers: Qualities of Effective Transitions
	10. Where Pelicans Kiss Seals
	11. The Civilizing of Genie
	12. Child Development and Differential School Performance: A Challenge for Teachers in School Development Program Schools
	13. Understanding Bilingual/Bicultural Young Children
	14. Equitable Treatment of Girls and Boys in the Classroom
	15. How Asian Teachers Polish Each Lesson to Perfection
	16. How Kids Learn
	17. Young Children's Understanding of Everyday Emotions
	18. Understanding and Accepting Separation Feelings

Rating	Article
	19. The Development of Self-Concept
	20. All about Me
	21. Children without Friends
	22. Guns and Dolls
	23. Girls and Boys Together . . . but Mostly Apart
	24. The Good, the Bad, and the Difference
	25. Little Big People
	26. Working Mothers and Their Families
	27. Putting Children First
	28. Marital Transitions: A Child's Perspective
	29. The Secret World of Siblings
	30. Sibling Connections
	31. Why Spanking Takes the Spunk Out of Kids
	32. Tarnished Trophies
	33. America's Children: Economic Perspectives and Policy Options
	34. Homeless Families: Stark Reality of the '90s
	35. Why Leave Children with Bad Parents?
	36. Screen Violence and America's Children
	37. Memories Lost and Found
	38. How to Recognize and Prevent Child Sexual Abuse
	39. Young Children with Attention Deficits
	40. Children with AIDS

(Continued on next page)

ABOUT YOU

Name_____ Date_____

Are you a teacher? ☐ Or student? ☐

Your School Name _____

Department _____

Address _____

City _____ State _____ Zip _____

School Telephone # _____

YOUR COMMENTS ARE IMPORTANT TO US!

Please fill in the following information:

For which course did you use this book? _____

Did you use a text with this Annual Edition? ☐ yes ☐ no

The title of the text? _____

What are your general reactions to the Annual Editions concept?

Have you read any particular articles recently that you think should be included in the next edition?

Are there any articles you feel should be replaced in the next edition? Why?

Are there other areas that you feel would utilize an Annual Edition?

May we contact you for editorial input?

May we quote you from above?